# Network Management

# Network Management

*William Stallings*

IEEE Computer Society Press
Los Alamitos, California

Washington • Brussels • Tokyo

Library of Congress Cataloging-in-Publication Data

Network Management / [edited by] William Stallings.
    p. cm.
  Includes bibliographical references (p.  ).
  ISBN 0-8186-4142-8. — ISBN 0-4141-X (microfiche)
  1. Computer networks — Management. I. Stallings, William.
TK5105.5.N46611 1993                                        93-23152
004.6 — dc20                                                            CIP

Published by the
IEEE Computer Society Press
10662 Los Vaqueros Circle
PO Box 3014
Los Alamitos, CA 90720-1264

© 1993 by the Institute of Electrical and Electronics Engineers, Inc. All rights reserved.

Copyright and Reprint Permissions: Abstracting is permitted with credit to the source. Libraries are permitted to photocopy beyond the limit of US copyright law, for private use of patrons, those articles in this volume that carry a code at the bottom of the first page, provided that the per-copy fee indicated in the code is paid through the Copyright Clearance Center, 27 Congress Street, Salem, MA 01970. For other copying, reprint, or republication permission, write to IEEE Copyrights Manager, IEEE Service Center, 445 Hoes Lane, PO Box 1331, Piscataway, NJ 08855-1331.

IEEE Computer Society Press Order Number 4142-01
Library of Congress Number 93-23152
IEEE Catalog Number EH0364-0
ISBN 0-8186-4141-X (microfiche)
ISBN 0-8186-4142-8 (case)

Additional copies can be ordered from

| IEEE Computer Society Press | IEEE Service Center | IEEE Computer Society | IEEE Computer Society |
|---|---|---|---|
| Customer Service Center | 445 Hoes Lane | 13, avenue de l'Aquilon | Ooshima Building |
| 10662 Los Vaqueros Circle | PO Box 1331 | B-1200 Brussels | 2-19-1 Minami-Aoyama |
| PO Box 3014 | Piscataway, NJ 08855-1331 | BELGIUM | Minato-ku, Tokyo 107 |
| Los Alamitos, CA 90720-1264 | | | JAPAN |

Technical Editor: A.R.K. Sastry
Production Editor: Lisa O'Conner
Copy Editor: Tom Culviner
Cover design: Joe Daigle
Printed in the United States of America by Braun-Brumfield, Inc.

 THE INSTITUTE OF ELECTRICAL AND ELECTRONICS ENGINEERS, INC.

# Preface

## Objective

Networks and distributed processing systems are of critical and growing importance in business, government, and other organizations. Within a given organization, the trend is toward larger, more complex networks supporting more applications and more users. As these networks grow in scale, two facts become painfully evident:

- The network and its associated resources and distributed applications become indispensable to the organization.
- More things can go wrong, disabling the network or a portion of the network or degrading performance to an unacceptable level.

A large network cannot be put together and managed by human effort alone. The complexity of such a system dictates the use of automated network management tools. The urgency of the need for such tools is increased, and the difficulty of supplying such tools is also increased, if the network includes equipment from multiple vendors. In response, standards have been developed both for TCP/IP-based networks and OSI-based networks. The purpose of this text is to provide an overview of network management technology and then explore these two sets of standards.

## Intended audience

This tutorial is intended for a broad range of readers interested in network management, including:

- *Students and professionals in data processing and data communications:* This tutorial provides a convenient means of reviewing some of the important papers in the field. Both the organization of the papers and the content of the new material will aid the reader in understanding this exciting area of data communications.
- *Network management designers and implementers:* This tutorial discusses critical design issues and explores approaches to meeting communication requirements.
- *Network management system customers and system managers:* This tutorial helps the reader understand what features and structures are needed in a network management facility, and provides information about current and evolving standards to enable the reader to assess a specific vendor's offering.

Much of the material can be comfortably read by those with no background in data communications. The original material and the glossary provide supporting information for the reprinted articles.

## Organization of the material

This tutorial is a combination of original material and reprinted articles, and is organized in the following chapters and supporting sections:

1. *Network Management Technology:* The original material in this chapter is a survey of the fundamentals of network management technology, including a discussion of functional requirements, organization of the network management function, and standards.

2. *Management Information:* This chapter focuses on the representation of information for network management. The original material in this chapter introduces two key supporting elements: Abstract Syntax Notation One (ASN.1) and object-oriented design principles. The reprinted

papers discuss general principles of management information system design and specific approaches.

3. *Simple Network Management Protocol (SNMP):* This chapter is devoted to SNMP and its enhancements. The original material in this chapter introduces the TCP/IP protocol suite, for which SNMP was designed; discusses the standards-making process; and provides an overview of SNMPv2.

4. *OSI Systems Management:* This chapter is devoted to OSI-based network management standards. The original material in this chapter introduces the OSI model and provides an overview of OSI systems management.

5. *Glossary:* The Glossary includes definitions for most of the key terms appearing in the text.

6. *List of Acronyms:* This list includes most of the acronyms appearing in the text.

7. *Annotated Bibliography:* The bibliography provides a guide to further reading, including periodicals and electronic mailing lists. All references in the text are found in the Annotated Bibliography.

**Related materials.** *SNMP, SNMPv2, and CMIP: The Practical Guide to Network Management Standards* (Addison-Wesley, 1993), by William Stallings, is a companion to this tutorial text. It is intended as a textbook as well as a reference book for professionals. The author has also prepared a videotape course on this subject, available from the Media Group, Boston University, 565 Commonwealth Avenue, Boston, MA 02215; telephone (617) 353-3217.

The reader may also be interested in a new book from IEEE Press: *Network Management into the 21st Century* (1993), edited by S. Aidarous and T. Plevyak. It is a collection of original papers that focuses on telecommunications network management, whereas this book focuses on data network management. Thus, the two books are complementary.

# Table of Contents

**PREFACE** ........................................................................................................................................... v

**CHAPTER 1: NETWORK MANAGEMENT TECHNOLOGY** ............................................................... 1

Network Management Functional Requirements .............................................................................. 12
    R. Aronoff et al (*NIST Special Publication 500-175, Management of Networks
    Based on Open Systems Interconnection (OSI): Functional Requirements and
    Analysis*, Nov. 1989, pp. 24-52)
Integrated Network Management Systems ........................................................................................ 41
    L. Feldkhun (*Proc. First Int'l Symp. Integrated Network Management*, 1989,
    pp. 279-301)
Distributed Network Management ..................................................................................................... 64
    J. Herman (*Data Communications*, June 1992, pp. 74-84)
Finding Fault ....................................................................................................................................... 72
    S.M. Dauber (*Byte*, March 1991, pp. 207-214)
Knowledge Technologies for Evolving Networks ............................................................................. 77
    S.K. Goyal (*Proc. Second Int'l Symp. Integrated Network Management*, 1991,
    pp. 439-461)

**CHAPTER 2: MANAGEMENT INFORMATION** ............................................................................ 101

Managing Communication Networks by Monitoring Databases .................................................... 116
    O. Wolfson, S. Sengupta, and Y. Yemini (*IEEE Trans. Software Engineering*,
    Sept. 1991, pp. 944-953)
Network Information Modeling for Network Management ............................................................. 126
    H. Yamaguchi, S. Isobe, T. Yamaki, and Y. Yamanaka (*Proc.
    IEEE 1992 Network Operations and Management Symp.*, 1992, pp. 57-67)
Development and Integration of a Management Information Base ................................................. 137
    B. Stewart (*Connexions*, June 1991, pp. 2-11)
Understanding Network Management with OOA ........................................................................... 147
    L. Olson and A. Blackwell (*IEEE Network Magazine*, July 1990, pp. 23-28)
System Management Information Modeling ................................................................................... 153
    S.M. Klerer (*IEEE Communications Magazine*, May 1993, pp. 38-44)
Distribution of Managed Object Fragments and Managed Object Replication:
The Data Distribution View of Management Information .............................................................. 160
    S.M. Klerer and R.S. Cohen (*Proc. Second Int'l Symp. Integrated Network Management*,
    1991, pp. 763-774)
OSI Management Information Base Implementation ..................................................................... 172
    S. Bapat (*Proc. Second Int'l Symp. Integrated Network Management*, 1991,
    pp. 817-832)

**CHAPTER 3: SIMPLE NETWORK MANAGEMENT PROTOCOL (SNMP)** ................................. 189

Network Management in the TCP/IP Protocol Suite ....................................................................... 206
    C. Partridge and K. McCloghrie (*Handbook of Computer-Communications Standards,
    Volume 3: The TCP/IP Protocol Suite*, 1990, pp. 198-222)
An Integrated Architecture for LAN/WAN Management ............................................................... 231
    S. Rabie and X.-N. Dam (*Proc. IEEE 1992 Network Operations and Management
    Symp.*, 1992, pp. 254-265)

MIB II Extends SNMP Interoperability .................................................................................................. 243
    C. Vandenberg (*Data Communications,* Oct. 1990, pp. 119-124)
SNMP Security ........................................................................................................................................ 247
    K. McCloghrie, J.R. Davin, and J.M. Galvin (*Connexions,* June 1991, pp. 12-16)
Coming Soon to a Network Near You .................................................................................................. 252
    M. Jander (*Data Communications,* Nov. 1992, pp. 66-76)

**CHAPTER 4: OSI SYSTEMS MANAGEMENT** .................................................................................. 261

Components of OSI: Systems Management ......................................................................................... 274
    P.J. Brusil (*Connexions*, April 1991, pp. 2-15)
An Implementation of an OSI Network Management System ............................................................ 288
    F. Halsall and N. Modiri (*IEEE Network Magazine,* July 1990, pp. 44-53)
The OSI Network Management Model ................................................................................................. 298
    Y. Yemini (*IEEE Communications Magazine,* May 1993, pp. 20-29)
Management By Exception: OSI Event Generation, Reporting, and Logging ................................... 308
    L. LaBarre (*Proc. Second Int'l Symp. Integrated Network Management,* 1991,
    pp. 227-242)
Optimizing OSI Management System Performance ............................................................................ 324
    S. Bapat (*Proc. IEEE 1992 Network Operations and Management Symp.,* 1992,
    pp. 149-159)
Network Management of TCP/IP Networks: Present and Future ...................................................... 335
    A. Ben-Artzi, A. Chandna, and U. Warrier (*IEEE Network Magazine,* July 1990, pp. 35-43)

**GLOSSARY** ........................................................................................................................................... 344

**LIST OF ACRONYMS** ........................................................................................................................ 347

**ANNOTATED BIBLIOGRAPHY** ...................................................................................................... 348

**ABOUT THE AUTHOR** ...................................................................................................................... 354

# List of Tables

1-1 OSI management functional areas ..................................................................................... 4

2-1 Universal class tag assignments ..................................................................................... 104
2-2 Applicability of subtype value sets ................................................................................. 106

3-1 SNMP-related RFCs ....................................................................................................... 190
3-2 SNMP version 2 (SNMPv2) documents ......................................................................... 191
3-3 Allowable data types in SNMPv2 ................................................................................... 194
3-4 The TCP/IP protocol suite .............................................................................................. 201

4-1 The OSI layers ................................................................................................................ 262
4-2 Application layer terms .................................................................................................. 265
4-3 Association control protocol data units and parameters ................................................. 266
4-4 ROSE operation classes .................................................................................................. 268
4-5 Remote operations service primitives and parameters .................................................... 270
4-6 OSI systems management standards ............................................................................... 271

# List of Figures

1-1 Important network management features ........................................................................ 3
1-2 Summary of responses from respondents to Network Management Forum survey ......... 5
1-3 Elements of a network management system .................................................................... 7
1-4 Distributed network management architecture ................................................................ 9

2-1 Example of use of ASN.1 ................................................................................................ 110
2-2 SNMPv2 PDU format definitions .................................................................................... 111
2-3 An inheritance hierarchy of object classes ....................................................................... 114
2-4 A containment hierarchy of object instances ................................................................... 115

3-1 SNMPv2-managed configuration .................................................................................... 193
3-2 An example of an SNMPv2 table ..................................................................................... 195
3-3 SNMPv2 message formats ............................................................................................... 196
3-4 SNMPv2 PDU formats ..................................................................................................... 197
3-5 A comparison of the OSI and TCP/IP communications architectures ............................. 202
3-6 Standards track diagram ................................................................................................... 204

4-1 The OSI environment ....................................................................................................... 263
4-2 Linked operations ............................................................................................................. 269
4-3 OSI network management architecture ............................................................................ 272

# Chapter 1: Network Management Technology

## The need for network management

The relentless growth in the information processing needs of organizations has been accompanied by rapid development in computer and data networking technology to support those needs, and an explosion in the variety of equipment and networks offered by vendors. Gone are the days when an organization would rely on a single vendor and a relatively straightforward architecture to support its needs. The world is no longer divided into the pure mainframe-based, IBM-compatible centralized environment and the PC-based, single-LAN-type, distributed environment. Today's typical organization has a large and growing but amorphous architecture, with a variety of local area networks (LANs) and wide area networks (WANs), supported by bridges and routers, and a variety of distributed computing services and devices, including PCs, workstations, and servers. And, of course, despite over two decades of premature eulogies, the mainframe lives on in countless distributed and a few centralized configurations.

To complicate matters for the system manager, even the basic communications software infrastructure is characterized by diverse and complex choices. The long-awaited open systems interconnection (OSI) set of standards has at last arrived, and is making slow but steady progress in the marketplace. But it enters a marketplace already dominated by a well-entrenched set of standards known as the TCP/IP protocol suite. In the face of these two competing approaches, complicated by proprietary schemes, the system manager must develop a strategy for managing what the organization has now and what it may acquire.

Once the scope of a computing environment extends beyond a single LAN and a few PCs, effective network management is possible only with a set of automated network management tools. To deal with the multivendor environment of the typical installation, a network management system is needed that is based on standardized network management protocols and applications. Unfortunately, here too we see two competing approaches evolving. The Simple Network Management Protocol (SNMP) was developed to provide a basic no-frills service for TCP/IP-based environments. Just as TCP/IP now dominates the interoperable communications software market, SNMP dominates the interoperable network management software market. The alternative approach is a set of standards being developed for use in OSI-based environments, known as OSI Systems Management. Just as OSI is gradually gaining market share, so too OSI Systems Management should increase in importance over the next few years.

## What is network management?

Network management is a term with many meanings. Consider the following definitions:

> Network management means deploying and coordinating resources in order to plan, operate, administer, analyze, evaluate, design, and expand communication networks to meet service-level objectives at all times, at a reasonable cost, and with optimum capacity [Terplan, 1992].

> Network management involves the planning, organizing, monitoring, accounting, and controlling of network activities and resources [Black, 1992].

> Network management is the process of using hardware and software by trained personnel to monitor the status of network components and line facilities, question end-users and carrier personnel, and implement or recommend actions to alleviate outages and/or improve communications performance as well as conduct administrative tasks associated with the operation of the network [Held, 1992].

> Systems management provides mechanisms for the monitoring, control, and coordination of resources within the OSI environment, and OSI protocol standards for communicating information pertinent to those resources [ISO 10040, Systems Management Overview, 1991].

While there is not widespread agreement on exactly what network management is, most would agree that (1) the increasing complexity of computer and telecommunications networks demands increasingly powerful and user-friendly network management tools, and (2) the evolution of network management technology and products has not kept up with needs.

There are a number of ways in which we might try to characterize network management, including:

- What is to be managed
- User requirements
- Functional areas
- Operational modes
- Organization of the network management facility
- Network management standards
- Applicable technologies

Let us briefly examine network management from each of these perspectives.

**What is to be managed.** Just as the communications and computer technologies have merged in recent years, there are two distinct traditions of network management that are coming together.

The older of these traditions is the management of telecommunications networks. Telecommunications network management has always been concerned with managing the network assets of basic telecommunications providers, such as the public telephone network of AT&T. Such management has included the switching centers, trunks, and subscriber lines of the network. As subscribers have been given greater flexibility and control over their use of these networks, and with the divestiture of the Bell Operating Companies from AT&T, the scope of telecommunications network management has broadened significantly. There is still a need to manage the internal assets of the network. In addition, customers are now provided with an array of options, including private networks using dedicated or leased lines, and software-defined or virtual networks. Network providers have enabled subscribers to manage the services that they receive and to incorporate those network management functions into their own network management systems.

The other tradition of network management is based on the management of a data network or collection of data networks supporting computers, terminals, and other digital devices. This type of network management is sometimes referred to as computer network management. The scope of objects to be managed in this case includes LANs, wide area networks, modems and other transmitting/receiving equipment, and the communications software in end systems. This type of network management also includes automated control devices typically found in manufacturing networks.

It is typical for a computer network complex to include some telecommunications services, either switched or private. It is also typical for even pure voice networks to include some computer capability in PBXs and other end systems. Finally, it is typical for the internal assets of a telecommunications network to include intelligent switches and other computer-based devices, and a sophisticated control signaling facility based on networked computers. Thus, the scope of network management has unified and broadened to include telecommunications equipment, data networks, computing systems, and related data transmission and data processing devices.

**User requirements.** With any design, it is best to begin with a definition of the users' requirements. This is certainly true of an area as complex as network management. At a basic level, a network management system should provide users with automated tools to do the following:

- *Configure:* Set up the components of the network, initialize subsystems, set parameters, and define relationships.
- *Operate:* Monitor utilization and perform accounting and charging functions.
- *Maintain:* React to failures and overloads.
- *Control access:* Define and enforce absolute and prioritized access controls.
- *Plan:* Assess requirements for future growth in capacity and services.

The above list details the major tasks or applications that a user requires. Another way to characterize a user's needs is to consider the features that are most important to the user. Figure 1-1 shows the results of a recent survey. Given the cost of network management and the magnitude of the task, it should be no surprise that ease of use is by far of most critical importance to users.

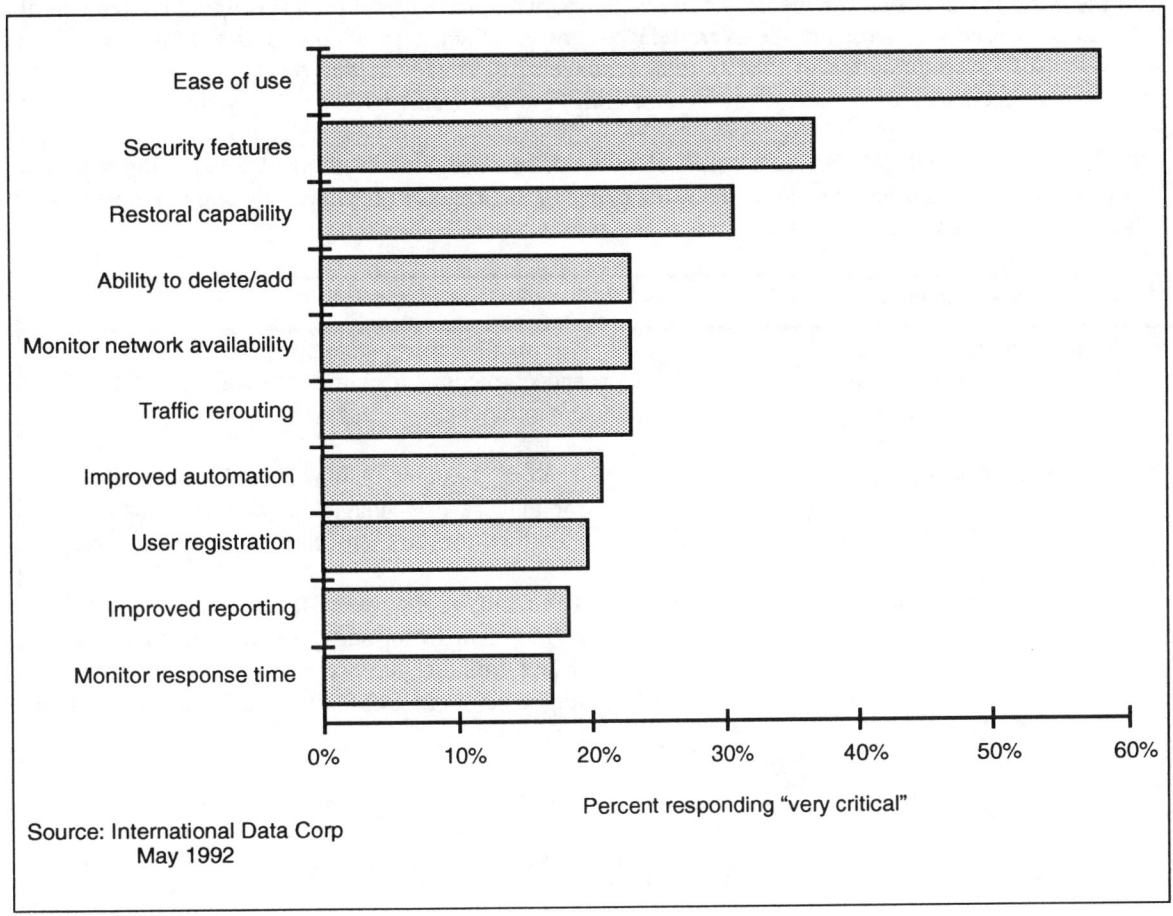

Figure 1-1: Important network management features

Terplan provides another breakdown of users' requirements [Terplan, 1992], which lists the following as the principal driving forces for justifying an investment in network management:

- *Controlling corporate strategic assets:* Networks and distributed computing resources are increasingly vital resources for most organizations. Without effective control, these resources do not provide the payback that corporate management requires.
- *Controlling complexity:* The continued growth in the number of network components, users, interfaces, protocols, and vendors threatens management with loss of control over what is connected to the network and how network resources are used.
- *Improving service:* Users expect the same or improved service as the information and computing resources of the organization grow and distribute.
- *Balancing various needs:* The information and computing resources of an organization must provide a spectrum of users with various applications at given levels of support, with specific requirements in the areas of performance, availability, and security. The network manager must assign and control resources to balance these various needs.
- *Reducing downtime:* As the network resources of an organization become more important, minimum availability requirements approach 100 percent. In addition to proper redundant design, network management has an indispensable role to play in ensuring high availability.

- *Controlling costs:* Resource utilization must be monitored and controlled to enable essential user needs to be satisfied with reasonable cost.

**Functional areas**. While surveys and qualitative statements of user requirements are useful, and can guide the designer in developing the details of a network management facility, a functional breakdown of applications is needed to structure the overall design process. Such a breakdown has been developed by ISO as part of its specification of OSI systems management. However, this functional breakdown has found broad acceptance as a useful way of describing the requirements for any network management system.

Table 1-1 lists the key functional areas of network management as defined by the International Organization for Standardization (ISO). The first paper in this chapter provides a detailed elaboration of each of these functional areas.

| Table 1-1. OSI management functional areas. | |
|---|---|
| Fault management | The facilities that enable the detection, isolation, and correction of abnormal operation of the OSI environment. |
| Accounting management | The facilities that enable charges to be established for the use of managed objects and costs to be identified for the use of those managed objects. |
| Configuration management | The facilities that exercise control over, identify, collect data from, and provide data to managed objects for the purpose of assisting in providing for continuous operation of interconnection services. |
| Performance management | The facilities needed to evaluate the behavior of managed objects and the effectiveness of communications activities |
| Security management | Addresses those aspects of OSI security essential to operate OSI network management correctly and to protect managed objects. |

Figure 1-2, based on a survey of network management users conducted by the Network Management Forum[1] [Adams, 1991], assesses the relative importance of these functional areas. Users were asked to rank the functional areas in terms of relative importance of multivendor interoperability to each function. Within each of the five areas, the users were also asked to assess the relative importance of key subfunctions. Some comments on each area:

- *Fault management:* The users indicated that fault management was by far the most critical need, specifically functions relating to alarms. Many users commented that until they could "stop the bleeding" they were unable to spend adequate time working on other important issues, like performance. Alarms alert managers to faults in a timely fashion. The ability to filter and correlate alarms is an important time-saving aid.
- *Configuration management:* This area was viewed as the next most important function, because it establishes the inventory of resources to be managed, without which alarm management is not

---

[1] The paper by Embry et al. in Chapter 4 introduces and describes the Network Management Forum.

possible. Others view configuration management as most important for the reconfiguration function, especially the ability to shift traffic to available resources when performance problems occur.
- *Performance management:* This is an essential function to ensure that the network continues to meet its design and, ultimately, the business purpose for which it is operated. Of particular importance is being able to monitor and manage response time. Another important area, particularly for LANs, is network utilization, which is used to assess current demand and plan for future growth. The key problem in meeting this objective is the lack of common metrics and common terms for critical performance parameters.
- *Security management:* This area is generally perceived as covering two requirements. Management of security is concerned with the protection of the network from unauthorized use. Security of management is concerned with protecting the network management system from unauthorized use. Although both requirements are considered important, this area was deemed less pressing than the three areas that ranked above it.
- *Accounting management:* This area was ranked least important. Users do need to be able to account for resource usage and, in many cases, generate billing. However, while other issues still require work, few users are yet able to turn their attention to these problems.

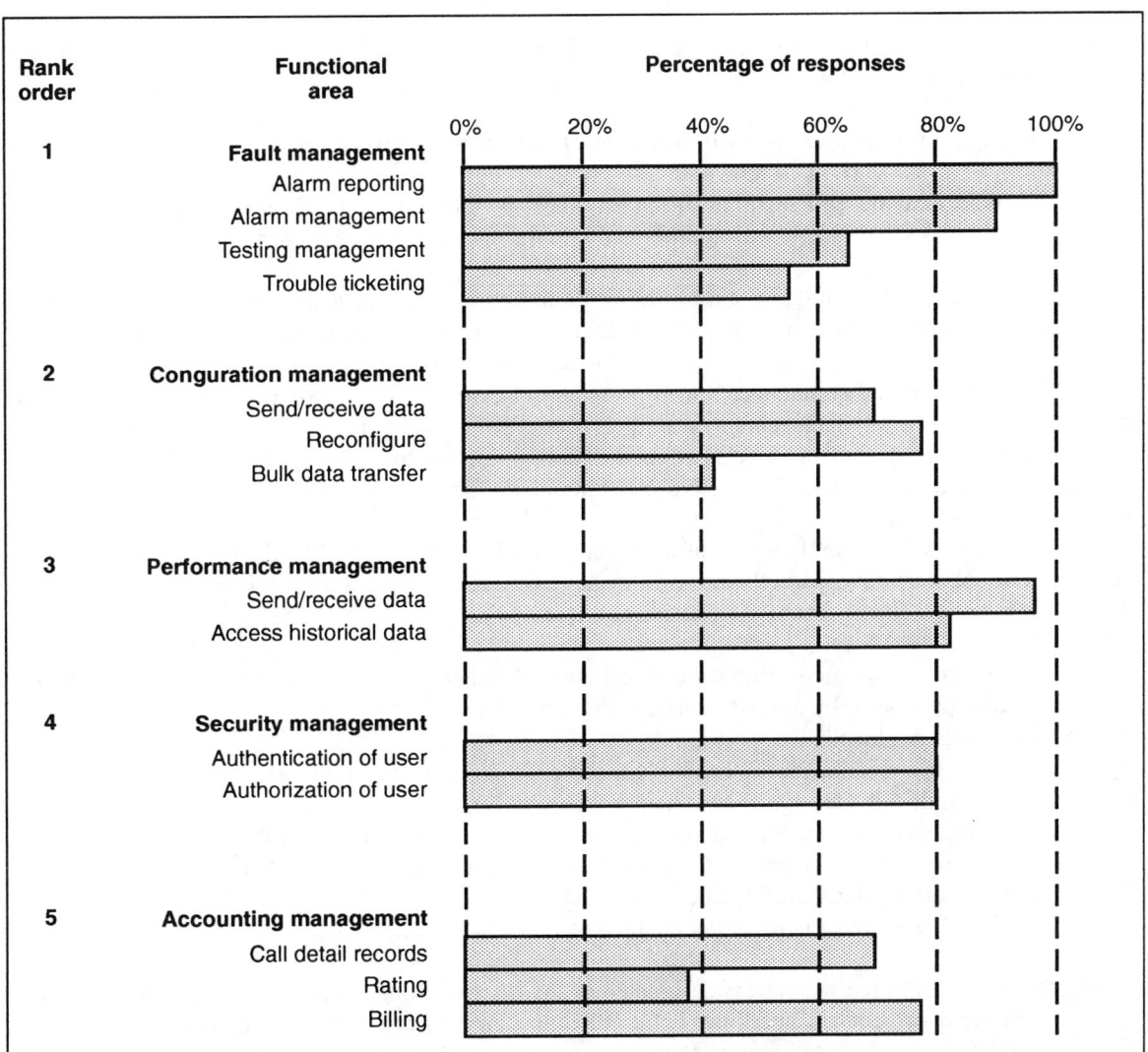

Figure 1-2: Summary of responses from respondents to Network Management Forum survey

**Operational modes.** Network management functions can be grouped into two categories, or operational modes: network monitoring and network control. Network monitoring is a "read function." It is concerned with observing and analyzing the status and behavior of the configuration and its components. Network monitoring is fundamental to network management and, indeed, many network management systems provide only a network monitoring capability. Network control is a "write function." It is concerned with altering parameters of various components of the configuration and causing predefined actions to be performed by various components of the configuration. Because of the obvious security and integrity concerns raised by network control, network control functions are less widely available.

**Organization of the network management facility.** Over the years, a diverse set of automated tools for network management has been developed. Each of these tools can aid the network manager in operating the network, maintaining high availability and low response time, and evaluating network behavior to plan for future network growth. The difficulty faced by the network manager is the very diversity of these tools. For example, in a medium to large network, it may be useful to have a network technical control system, a network monitoring system, and some software monitors. Each of these may be from a different vendor, requiring its own operator interface and training. As networks become more complex and more indispensable to business operations, some more powerful and flexible approach is needed.

From the user's point of view, the best approach would be a set of tools for control and monitoring that is integrated in the following senses:

- A single operator interface with a powerful but user-friendly set of commands for performing most or all network management tasks.
- A minimal amount of separate equipment. That is, most of the hardware and software required for network management are incorporated into the existing user equipment.

We will refer to a system that provides this integration as a *network management system*. A network management system consists of incremental hardware and software additions implemented among existing network components. The software used in accomplishing the network management tasks resides in the host computers and communications processors (for example, front-end processors, terminal cluster controllers). A network management system is designed to view the entire network as a unified architecture, with addresses and labels assigned to each point and the specific attributes of each element and link known to the system. The active elements of the network provide regular feedback of status information to the network control center.

Figure 1-3 suggests the architecture of a network management system. Each network node contains a collection of software devoted to the network management task, referred to in the diagram as a network management entity (NME). Each NME performs the following tasks:

- Collect statistics on communications and network-related activities. This is in principle the type of work performed by a stand-alone software monitor.
- Store statistics locally.
- Respond to commands from the network control center, including commands to:
  1. Transmit collected statistics to network control center
  2. Change a parameter (for example, a timer used in a transport protocol)
  3. Provide status information (for example, parameter values, active links)
  4. Generate artificial traffic to perform a test
  5. Generate an event notification under specified conditions

At least one host in the network is designated as the network control center. In addition to the NME software, the network control host includes a collection of software called the network control center (NCC). The NCC includes an operator interface to allow an authorized user to manage the network. The NCC responds to user commands by displaying information and/or by issuing commands to NMEs throughout the network. This communication is carried out using an application-level network management protocol that employs the communications architecture in the same fashion as any other distributed application.

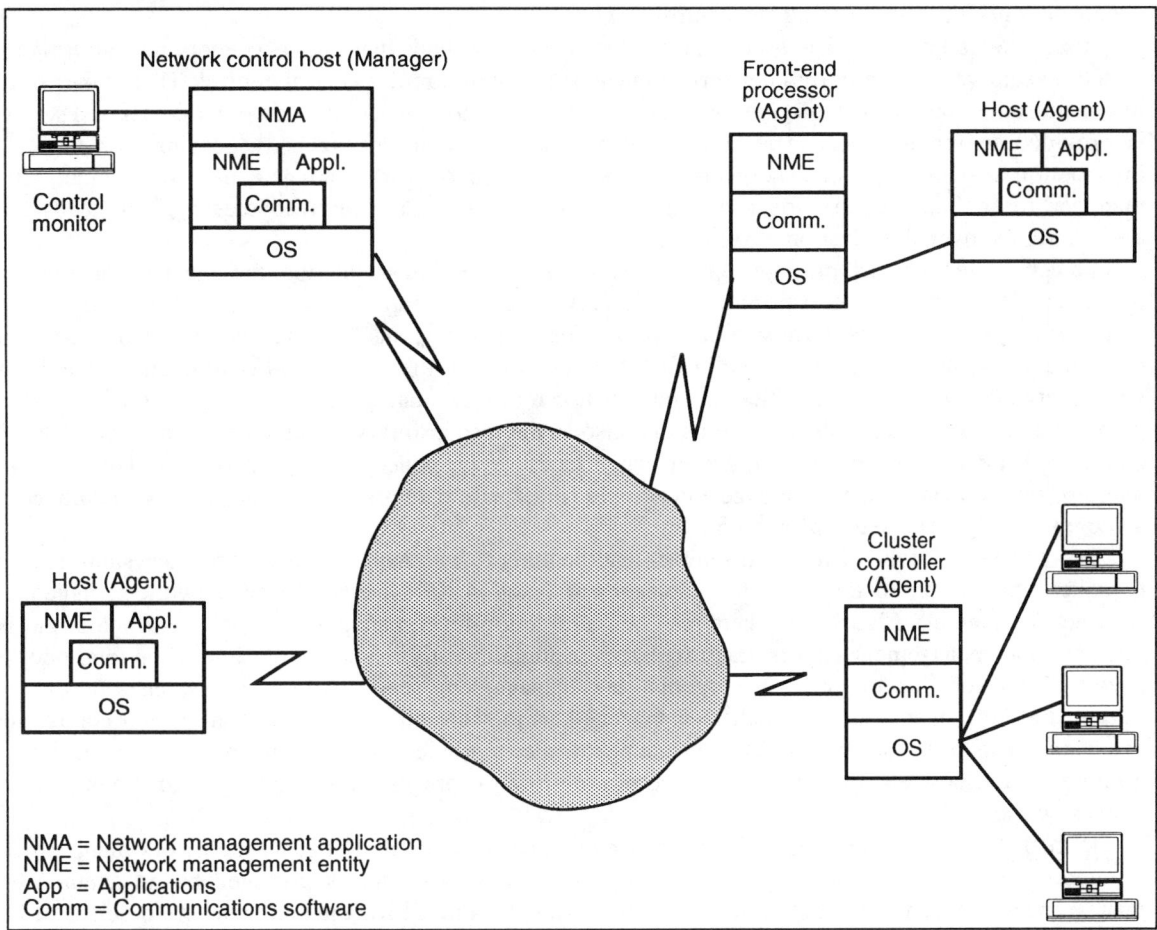

Figure 1-3: Elements of a network management system

Several observations are in order:

1. Since the network management software relies on the host operating system and on the communications architecture, most offerings to date are designed for use on a single vendor's equipment. In the case of a network of personal computers, there are a number of LAN network management packages that will tie together personal computers from a number of vendors. Standards in this area are still evolving. However, recent years have seen the emergence of standardized network management systems designed to manage a multiple-vendor network.

2. As depicted in Figure 1-3, the network control center communicates with and controls what are essentially software monitors in other systems. The architecture can be extended to include technical control hardware and specialized performance monitoring hardware as well.

3. For maintaining high availability of the network management function, two or more network control centers are used. In normal operation, one of the centers is idle or simply collecting statistics, while the other is used for control. If the primary network control center fails, the backup system can be used.

The configuration depicted in Figure 1-3 suggests a centralized network management strategy, with a single network control center and perhaps a standby center.

In such a configuration, the network control center may be considered the *manager*, with the other devices in the configuration acting as *agents*. With a centralized strategy, managers can delegate to agents only primitive monitoring and control tasks.

This is the strategy that has traditionally been favored by both mainframe vendors and information system executives. A centralized network management system implies central control. This makes sense in a mainframe-dominated configuration, where the key resources reside in a computer center and service is provided to remote users. The strategy also makes sense to managers responsible for the total information system assets of an organization. A centralized network management system enables the manager to maintain control over the entire configuration, balancing resources against needs and optimizing the overall utilization of resources.

In a centralized network management scheme, to perform a typical function, the manager must micromanage the agent in a series of primitive steps. This approach is both costly and ineffective. The central manager may become a performance bottleneck. The manager/agent dialogue may either impose great overhead on the network or be limited in such a way as to limit the manageability of complex and high-speed networks. But the difficulties inherent in a centralized management strategy relate not just to network overhead and reliability concerns, but also to the responsibility of the human operator. There is clearly a limit to how much information can effectively be concentrated and delivered to a single operator for the management of a huge and complex enterprise network with countless nodes deployed in a geographically dispersed configuration.

The very nature of the difficulty is the fact that the thing to be managed is a distributed system. Hence, it makes sense to try to distribute the management function. In a decentralized network management scheme (for example, Figure 1-4), there may be multiple top-level management stations, which might be referred to as management servers. Each such server might directly manage a portion of the total pool of agents. However, for many of the agents, the management server delegates responsibility to an intermediate manager. The intermediate manager plays the role of manager to monitor and control the agents under its responsibility. It also plays an agent role to provide information and accept control from a higher-level management server. This type of architecture spreads the processing burden and reduces total network traffic.

Figure 1-4 also illustrates a technique for managing devices that do not share a network management protocol with a manager, using a proxy approach. A proxied device is managed by an agent using management commands tailored to the device (for example, a modem), and can then act on behalf of the manager to monitor and control the proxied device. Proxy relationships can be used in both centralized and distributed network management schemes.

While maintaining the capacity for central control, the distributed approach offers a number of benefits:

1. Network management traffic overhead is minimized. Much of the traffic is confined to a local environment.

2. Distributed management offers greater scalability. Adding additional management capability is simply a matter of deploying another inexpensive workstation at the desired location.

3. The use of multiple, networked stations eliminates the single point of failure that exists with centralized schemes.

Traditionally, network management systems have followed the centralized model. With the increasing complexity and use of distributed systems, network management systems are becoming increasingly distributed.

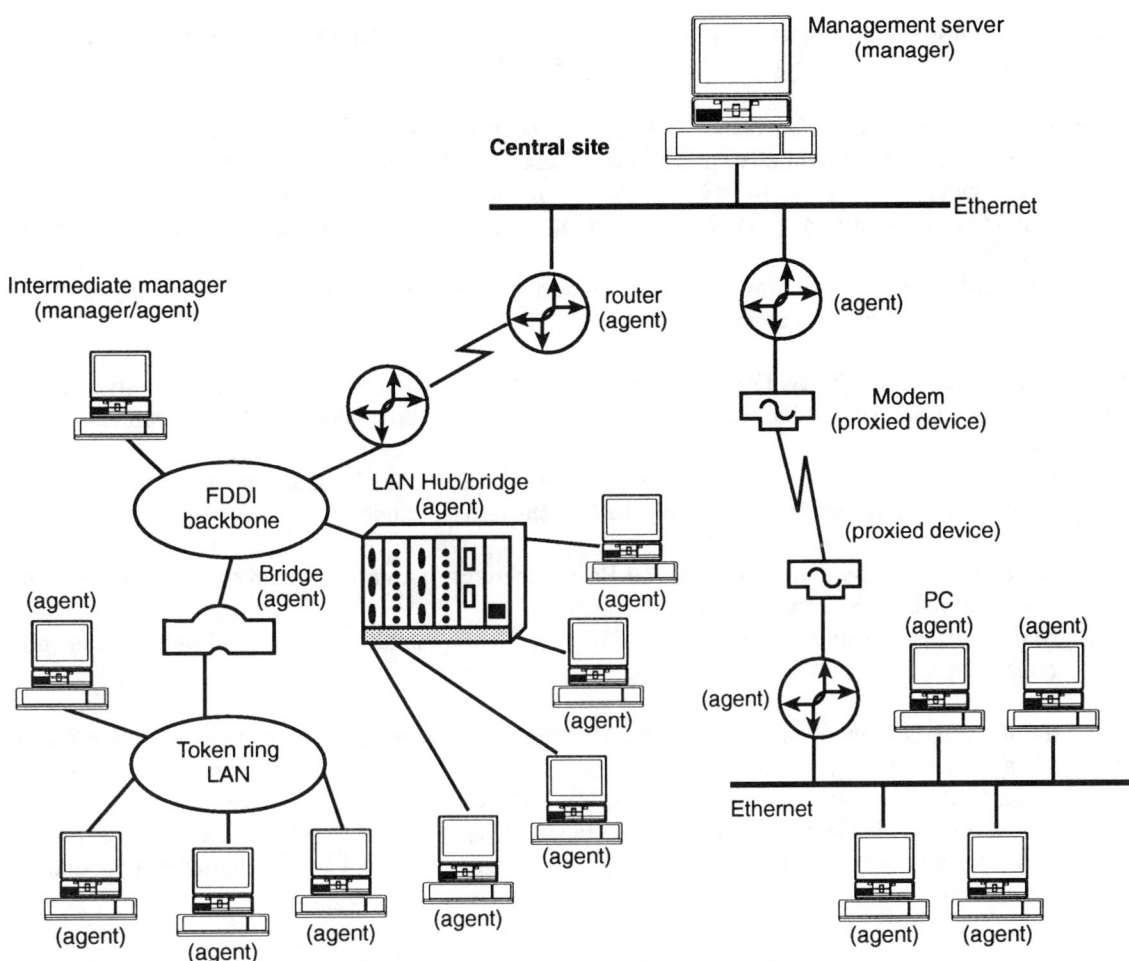

Figure 1-4: Distributed network management architecture

**Network management standards.** Virtually all distributed systems of any size involve equipment from multiple vendors. To control costs and to make integrated network management practical, standardized network management facilities are needed that can be used across a broad spectrum of product types, including end systems, bridges, routers, and telecommunications equipment, and that can be used in a mixed-vendor environment. In response to this need, two standardization efforts are under way:

- *SNMP family:* The simple network management protocol (SNMP) refers actually to a set of standards for network management, including a protocol, a database structure specification, and a set of data object definitions. SNMP was adopted as the standard for TCP/IP-based internets in 1989 and has enjoyed widespread popularity. In 1993, an upgrade known as SNMP Version 2 (SNMPv2) was adopted. The latter is intended to run on OSI-based networks as well as TCP/IP-based networks.
- *OSI systems management:* This term refers to a large and complex set of standards that define a set of general-purpose network management applications, a management service and protocol, a database structure specification, and a set of data objects. This set of international standards is still evolving; as of this writing some of the standards are final ISO standards, while others are still in a draft stage. Because of its complexity and the slow pace of standardization, OSI systems management is only gradually gaining acceptance.

It is important to emphasize that neither SNMP nor OSI systems management covers the entire range of network management requirements. In the case of SNMP, the following are provided:

- *Management information base:* The SNMP specifications include the definition of managed objects. These are essentially variables with data types that can be used to characterize resources to be managed. The creation of a standardized set of data elements to represent the elements to be managed is the first step in the creation of an integrated multivendor network management system.
- *Protocol:* The protocol allows managers to access (read) objects maintained by agents and to set (write) values in objects at agents.

This is a very basic capability. From the user's point of view, network management consists of a set of applications. What SNMP provides are the underlying, primitive tools upon which such applications can be developed.

OSI systems management is a much more ambitious undertaking. In addition to the definition of a management information base and a protocol, the OSI standards include:

- *Systems management functions (SMFs):* Basic functions that utilize the protocol and management information base, such as alarm management.
- *Systems management functional areas (SMFAs):* The five application areas defined earlier in this chapter.

The set of SMFs is growing, and individual SMFs are at various stages in the standardization process. The SMF specification indicates how the SMF makes use of the underlying management protocol and perhaps other SMFs to achieve certain basic functions. The orchestration of the various SMFs to support the SMFAs is an area that has not yet been developed. Thus, even OSI systems management provides primarily a structure on which network management applications can be built, rather than the applications themselves.

**Applicable technologies**. A number of technologies are assuming growing importance in the design and development of network management systems. Among the most promising:

- *Object-oriented technology:* Object-oriented techniques provide a powerful tool for modeling resources to be managed and for supporting interoperable network management. With the increasing incorporation of object-oriented capability in operating systems, this technology should enjoy increased use in network management. One indication of this trend is the reliance on object-oriented techniques in OSI systems management.
- *Artificial intelligence:* AI techniques, particularly expert system techniques, can ease the burden on the human network manager greatly.
- *Simulation and modeling:* In the area of performance monitoring, the manager is often overwhelmed with too much data. Effective simulation and modeling tools enable the manager to use this data to assess the overall present and likely future performance of the system.

## Paper summary

"Network Management Functional Requirements" provides a detailed look at requirements using the categories that form the basis for OSI network management. For each category, users' requirements are stated, followed by an analysis of functional requirements needed to support the user requirements. The result is an excellent overview of what functions and services should constitute a comprehensive network management system.

The next two papers discuss issues relating to the functions and organization of integrated network management systems. "Integrated Network Management Systems" provides a comprehensive and detailed description of the ingredients and architecture for integrated network management systems.

"Distributed Network Management" examines the distributed organization of network management that has become typical among vendor offerings.

"Finding Fault" examines the environment in which network faults occur and presents a discussion of network management techniques related to faults.

Finally, "Knowledge Technologies for Evolving Networks" looks at the application of AI technologies to network management.

## 3. NETWORK MANAGEMENT FUNCTIONAL REQUIREMENTS

A primary goal of network management (NM) users is to have a network management system (NMS) that allows the control and monitoring of a network composed of products from different vendors. An important prerequisite for such a management system is the development of interoperable NM products. However, interoperable NM products cannot be assured unless they are produced in accordance with an agreed upon set of standards.

Many NM standardization activities are currently underway to develop such a set of standards. As with any large undertaking of such complexity and broad scope, the authors of this study feel it is important to reexamine NM functional requirements, at this stage in the development of these standards, to insure that the emerging standards, in fact, meet user requirements.

This study has gathered and examined NM user requirements from a variety of sources. Based on an analysis of user requirements, we have prepared a set of functional requirements designating the functional elements which must be incorporated in NM in order to meet users' needs. The primary sources for the user requirements include IFIP WG 6.6 user requirements [IFIPUSR], WAN and LAN vendor NM products, MAP 3.0 Network Management requirements, private communication with a network services provider, and comments received from an earlier draft of this study.

NM user requirements may be viewed from two different perspectives; that of the end user of a network (i.e., not a network administrator), and that of the operator, administrator or manager of a network. End users expect reliable network services with consistently good performance. They may want to retrieve accounting and performance information and be notified of any configuration changes that affect them. The network operator, administrator, and manager require sophisticated network management tools that are both necessary and sufficient to perform all types of functions to support the network services expected by end users. In order to prepare a set of NM functional requirements that encompass both network end user and network manager's needs, requirements from both communities are considered. The term, "NMS users," used in this section indicate both the end users and the network administrators including operators and managers. For functions that are usually only required by the network administrators, the term "network administrator, NM manager or operator" is used.

The functional level requirements are grouped into seven categories that are similar to the functional areas defined within the ISO Management Framework [FRMWK]. The categories are architecture, configuration, fault, security, performance, accounting, and others. We have chosen to organize the functional requirements in this manner for ease of comparison with OSI NM standards, and subsequent analysis. Each functional requirement section follows a user requirements section that describes and justifies its needs. Some user requirements may lead to more than one functional requirement and, conversely, one functional requirement may satisfy all or part of more than one user requirement. Therefore, the correspondence between user requirements and functional requirements is not necessarily one-to-one.

## 3.1. Architecture

Due to the complexity and broad scope of areas and functions that are involved with a network management system (NMS), it is a logical approach to begin with a model for the management system when developing standards. The model should describe the architecture (structure) of the system, identify the purpose of each component within the system, and identify the relationships among all the components within the system so that it can provide a formal basis for developing the elements of the network management system in a systematic manner.

The NMS provides its users with the capability to control and monitor the communications in a system interconnection (networking) environment. Since the communications aspect of these interconnected systems already has a standard model (i.e., the OSI reference model), it is only natural that a system to manage implementations of this communications model employ an architecture that is compatible with the standard communications model. In this sense, the NMS model needs to be designed around the OSI reference model.

Most networks of any considerable size have a network control center where the network management functions are coordinated and controlled. The staff of a network control center typically includes: 1) technicians who are charged with resolving problems as they occur, 2) operators (administrators) who are responsible for management of the physical resources of the network, 3) consultants who run the user help desk that serves as the single point of contact for end users with problems or questions, and 4) the managers who are responsible for monitoring and controlling the operational network.

The network control center usually oversees configuration, fault, and security management functions, while most accounting management functions are performed in the billing/accounting department and most performance management functions are handled by the performance analysis and/or capacity planning organization. In some organizations the security management functions are administered by security group within the organization. Organizations such as network design/architecture, network engineering and development, software control and strategic planning, use diverse management information and functions for performing some of their jobs. Network management information is therefore widely needed and used. An effective network management system is one that enhances the productivity, effectiveness, and responsiveness of the network control center staff and, ultimately, the end users of the communications system.

The architectural requirements specify network management functions that are essential building elements for a NMS from an architectural point of view. They include the model, the directory services which are required by all the NMS components, the management protocols and services for transferring the network management information, layer management, and specific resources to be managed and for controlling them.

### 3.1.1. User Requirements

Most users of a network management system require a single integrated system that allows them to remotely monitor and control the operation of the network. To provide this integrated network management system, a network management model has to be in place to give an overview of the system, to indicate how the management information can be transferred and collected, and to identify the functions that need to be standardized for providing an interoperable and integrated network management system.

Many users of a NMS require network-wide distributed NM control for large networks. Such a NMS may contain many, possibly loosely coupled, network managers rather than a single centralized network manager. However, these distributed managers may themselves be centrally managed. This concept of distributed managers implies the need for manager-to-manager protocols and services. According to the IFIP user requirements document [IFIPUSR], the user requirements that support the distributed NM control are the following:

a) Distributed NM control better reflects the structure of a large network, with each network manager supporting some segment of a large network. However, it may be more logical to manage some segments centrally.

b) In instances where there is a strong geographic locality of reference, network management information can be put logically closer to the NM user, reducing communication time and cost.

c) Network-wide management dispersion reduces the likelihood that a disaster will affect more than one part of the network.

d) When one NM control node goes down for maintenance or updates, the NM functions within its domain can be redirected to another node.

e) Each network manager in a domain tailors its user interface to its own needs (e.g., German, English, Japanese). The only point common to all the network managers is that they all support the same standard when accessing each others' network management information.

A NMS needs to be capable of performing the required network management functions on any component of a multi-vendor network. Therefore, the network management system should support collection and distribution of management information from heterogeneous components.

NMS users need the flexibility to select any cost-justified technological alternative that best meets their business requirements. NMS users should not be unduly restricted (i.e., "locked-in") by the existing NMS.

NMS users expect the network management system to maximize the availability of network component resources, whether those resources are communications links, processing nodes, software or data. The network management system should be robust enough to continue network operation in spite of most common hardware and/or software failure.

### 3.1.2. Functional Requirements

#### 3.1.2.1. Model

The model of a network management system (NMS) describes the essential NMS components and the functions of each component. The model needs to clearly define the organization of the network management system including the relationships, interactions and interdependencies among its components. In addition, the model should allow for:

a)   hierarchical and distributed control of access to and manipulation of network management information and network resources;

b)   centralized management of distributed network managers;

c)   the flexibility to accommodate and support new technologies so that there is no need to build a new NMS in order to manage a network with new technology;

d)   additional proprietary network management solutions;

e)   additional proprietary network management security control;

f)   future network management system expansion;  For example, as new types of managed objects are identified, the NMS developed based on network management standards should be able to perform actions on these new objects with minimal detrimental effects by using the standard methods to specify and add new managed objects to the data bases or directories.

g)   redundant managers or out-of-band signaling to ensure maximum availability of the network management system;

h)   message distribution in a hierarchical distributed network management system.  This will be required for broadcasting status, caution, warning, bulletins and management directives (e.g., start all performance functions, stop all activity to prepare for network shutdown).

#### 3.1.2.2. Services and Protocols

The network management system requires manager-to-agent management information exchange services and a supporting protocol. These services and protocol are necessary (but not sufficient) for any network management system.

Manager-to-manager management information exchange services and protocol are required to support multiple managers within a network management system. Manager-to-agent protocols may be sufficient to support peer manager-to-manager operations. However, various types of manager-to-manager protocols may be required when hierarchical management structure is considered.

The services provided by these protocols must be sufficient to perform all the functions specified in the following five sections (i.e., configuration, fault, security, performance and accounting management.). The form of management information exchange must be able to support all the required services across various levels of hierarchical management and control of distributed management subsystems.

### 3.1.2.3. Resource Identification

The OSI and related non-OSI resources to be managed must be identified. Each resource can be viewed as a managed object with attributes. The definition includes the managed object, its attributes, the set of operations that can be performed on the attributes, and the semantics of these operations. These resources consist of layer, system, and network component level entities. A buffer is an example of a non-OSI resource while a Transport connection or a Transport Layer retransmission count are examples of OSI resources. The resources associated with manager-to-manager functions also need to be identified. These include all types of data base logs such as security events, failure events, and configuration changes.

### 3.1.2.4. Information Structure

The network management system needs a common structure for heterogeneous management information to facilitate exchanging information across various vendors' products. In other words, the difference in data formats, source, structure and semantics should be transparent to the NMS users. A standard method to describe the common structure for heterogeneous management information is therefore required.

### 3.1.2.5. Layer Management

Those resources identified as necessary and important for management need to be collected, stored and made available to remote management systems by local management systems. Each local layer entity must have sufficient functionality to support the local management system.

### 3.1.2.6. The Directory

To provide quick access to the desired management information, directories are needed to identify applications, users and resources in a network. Directories also should contain or at least be capable of determining the routing information for interconnected networks, perhaps by pointing to the appropriate OSI directory services. The Directory standard should specify:

      a) where directory information is stored,
      b) how information in the directory is created and updated,
      c) how access to the information is controlled,
      d) the structure of the information stored in the directory, and

e) how the information is used by local and remote management systems.

The directories require accurate and organized information from the network components. Before building useful directories, the four functional requirements described in sections 3.1.2.2 - 3.1.2.5 (i.e., the management protocols and services, the layer management, the common management information structure, and the identification and definition of network resources) must be in place.

### 3.1.2.7. Network Management Communications Overhead and Performance

Most users expect the NMS to impose minimal overhead on network operations, and dictate that the NMS functions should not interfere with routine, ongoing workloads. Many users require that the NMS perform to a user specified level and out-of-band signaling that transfers management commands and information to remote devices without affecting normal data channels is one way to meet these requirements.

### 3.1.2.8. Support for Efficient Information Transfer

Network management traffic can often be categorized into a large number of small exchanges or a few high volume exchanges. Information exchange may have other diverse data volume and data transfer frequencies. For example, software distribution and "up-line" retrieval of statistics blocks are examples of high volume transfers which require file transfer capability. Transaction processing, order entry, and DBMS updates may require low volume, reliable transaction services. Standard ways of transferring various amounts of management information from one node to another need to be provided by the network management system. The information transfer can be done either directly through a management protocol or through the use of other services such as FTAM or through transaction processing protocols.

### 3.1.2.9. Standardization of Terminology

To provide NMS users with an integrated view of network management capability, terminologies used across multi-vendor NM products should be defined in the standards. Examples of such terms are the definition of faults, the definition of security terms, the definition of performance measures, the definition of terms used in the model and the services and protocols, and the definition of configuration states and the relationships among configurable network components.

## 3.2. Configuration Management

Modern data communication systems are composed of individual components and logical subsystems (e.g., queue managers in an operating system) that can be configured to perform many different applications. The same device, for example, can be configured to act either as a gateway or as an end system node, or both. Once the manager decides how he intends to use the device, he can choose to establish values for the appropriate set of attributes associated with this device. The device can be considered a system resource, or managed object where "A managed object is the OSI Management view of a system resource that is subject to management, such as a layer entity, a connection or an item of physical communications equipment." [SMO] Furthermore, "Attributes are properties of managed objects. An attribute has an associated value, which may have a simple or complex structure." [SMO] The value of an attribute "... may determine or reflect the behaviour of the managed object." [MIM]

Configuration management (CM) is that aspect of network management which embodies the functionality to, among other things, assign that set of attributes to the device. Configuration management is concerned with initializing a network and gracefully shutting down part or all of the network. It is also concerned with maintaining, adding, and updating: 1) the relationships among components, 2) the status of the relationships among the components and 3) the status of the components themselves during network operation. By its nature, CM interacts with other aspects of network management, to a greater degree than other functional areas, to provide important monitoring and reconfiguration services.

During initialization, configuration management identifies and specifies the characteristics of the network components and resources (managed objects) which will constitute the network. The managed objects include both high level composite objects (e.g., an end system or gateway), and lower level atomic objects (e.g., a Transport Layer retransmission timer). The configuration manager provides the capability to set attribute values individually or collectively to predefined default values. This process causes these managed objects to commence operation in the proper states, possess the proper attribute values, and form the desired relationships with other network components.

While the network is in operation, configuration management functions monitor the network components and may reconfigure managed objects when desired or necessary. In this regard, configuration management functions may be allied with the functions of other management areas and used to support their operations. For example, if the performance management developed Workload Monitoring Function determines that network performance is degrading (e.g., increased response times are causing excess retransmissions), or the fault management developed Error Reporting and Information Retrieval Function detects a malfunctioning component, the services of a configuration management function (e.g., State Management Function) can be enlisted to modify the appropriate managed objects to remedy these situations. The actions taken in these cases might include increasing the appropriate retransmission timeout periods and reconfiguring the network to work around the malfunctioning component until it is repaired.

The OSI Management Framework document (ISO 7498-4), defines CM as follows:

"Configuration identifies, exercises control over, collects data from and provides data to open systems for the purpose of preparing for, initialising, starting, providing for the continuous operation of, and terminating interconnection services. Configuration management includes functions to:

a) set the parameters that control the routine operation of the open system;
b) associate names with managed objects and sets of managed objects;
c) initialise and close down managed objects;
d) collect information on demand about the current condition of the open system;
e) obtain announcements of significant changes in the condition of the open system;
f) change the configuration of the open system." [FRMWK]

The following two sections present a more in-depth view of Configuration Management, presenting first the users' view of this aspect of network management followed by the functional elements which are needed to provide such capabilities.

### 3.2.1. User Requirements

Startup and shutdown operations on a network are the specific responsibilities of configuration management. It is often desirable, and even necessary, for these operations on certain components to be performed unattended on distributed systems (e.g., starting or shutting down a remote line multiplexor).

Network operators or administrators need the capability to identify the components that comprise the network and to define the desired connectivity of these components. Users who regularly configure a network with the same or similar set of resource attribute values need ways to define and modify default attributes and to load these predefined sets of attribute values into the specified network components. This avoids specifying the same resource attributes and values every time.

Network managers or operators need the capability to change the connectivity of network components when users request such changes or when reconfiguration is mandated by performance, fault, or security requirements. Reconfiguration of a network is often desired in response to performance evaluation or in support of network upgrade, fault recovery, or security checks.

Network users often need to, or want to, be informed of the status of network resources and components. Therefore, when changes in configuration occur, users should be notified of these changes. Configuration reports can be generated either on some routine periodic basis or in response to a request for such a report. Before reconfiguration, the operator or the manager often wants to inquire about the status of resources and their attributes.

Company administrators and network managers usually want only authorized users and operators to manage and control network operations such as software distribution and updating.

Network capacity planning, network performance and usage trend analysis, and the management of the inventory of information system components (including software, hardware and microcode) are also network managers' NM requirements. These requirements, however, are beyond the scope of this study because they are not needed for interoperability. (See sec. 5.7 for further discussion.)

### 3.2.2. Functional Requirements

#### 3.2.2.1. Defining Resources and Attributes

Mechanisms are needed to allow the NMS users to specify resources and the attributes associated with a resource. Attributes can be, for example, name, address, identification number, states, operational characteristics, software version number, and release level. Network resources include network physical resources (e.g., modems, the communications media, or computers), and network logical resources (e.g., timers, counters, virtual circuits, and connections).

The NMS users should be allowed to specify the range and type of values to which the specified resource attribute can be set. The range can be a list of all possible states, or the allowed upper and lower limits for parameters and attributes. The type of value allowable for an attribute can also be specified.

#### 3.2.2.2. Setting and Modifying Attribute Values

Mechanisms are needed to allow the NMS users to set and modify values of resource attributes (e.g., activate and deactivate ports, set and trace a retransmission timer value, and monitor and adjust buffer allocation).

The NMS users require mechanisms to load predefined default attribute values such as default states, values and operational characteristics of resources on a system-wide, individual node, or individual layer basis.

The NMS must allow users to set clocks for network components.

#### 3.2.2.3. Defining and Modifying Relationships

The NMS users must have the ability to specify relationships among network resources. A relationship usually describes an association, connection or condition that exists between network resources or network components. These relationships can take the form of a topology, a hierarchy, a physical or logical connection or a management domain. What is meant here by a management domain is a set of resources that share a set of common attributes or a set of common resources that share the same management authority.

Mechanisms are needed to allow the NMS users to add, delete, and modify the relationships among network resources. The NMS must also allow its users to expand the network or change existing relationships among resources without taking all or part of the network down (i.e., the relationships may be modified on-line during network operation).

### 3.2.2.4. Examining Attribute Values and Relationships

Mechanisms are needed to allow the NMS users to examine resources. This requires the ability to locally or remotely examine the attributes associated with the resources and the current values of these attributes.

Mechanisms are needed to allow the NMS users to locally or remotely examine the existing relationships among network resources.

To provide the above two capabilities, the NMS must be able to keep track of configuration changes from which the existing network resources and attributes, their status, and relationships can be determined.

### 3.2.2.5. Distributing Software Throughout the Network

The ability to distribute software throughout the network is essential. This requires facilities to permit software loading requests, to transmit the specified versions of software, to notify the NMS user at the completion of software loading, and to update the configuration tracking systems.

The NMS user needs mechanisms (e.g., downline loading capability) to examine, update and manage different versions of software and routing information. For example, users can specify the loading of different versions of software or routing tables based on a specified condition, such as error rate.

### 3.2.2.6. Initializing and Terminating Network Operations

The NMS must provide mechanisms to allow its users to initialize and close down network, or subnetwork, operation. Initialization involves, among other things, verifying that all settable resource attributes and relationships have been properly set, notifying users of any resource attribute or relationship still needing to be set, and validating the users' initialization command. For termination, mechanisms are needed to allow the NMS users to request retrieval of specified statistics blocks or status information before the termination procedures have completed.

Mechanisms are needed to allow the NMS users to remotely reinitialize (reboot) a system.

### 3.2.2.7. Verifying NMS Users' Authorization

The most privileged NMS users have the ability to specify: 1) the hierarchy of authorization for performing various configuration functions and 2) the methods used for assigning and validating various levels of authorization.

Mechanisms are required to allow only authorized NMS users to perform various configuration functions. This is related to security issues, but it is required by configuration management to ensure that only authorized personnel can gain access to or change network configuration information as well as start or stop a network's operation.

### 3.2.2.8. Reporting Configuration Status

Notification of configuration changes in resources and in relationships among resources must be available to the NMS users. In order to accomplish this, managing systems (i.e., those that manage other systems) must be able to inform agent systems (i.e., those that are managed) under what conditions, and where, configuration change notification is to be sent by the agent system.

Mechanisms are needed to allow the NMS users to request and obtain configuration reports. The configuration reports focus on such things as network connectivity, network topology and node resources, attributes, and values. Furthermore, these configuration reports may display routine snapshots of the network configuration and the status of the components (e.g., a NMS can display a snapshot of network topology every 5 minutes alternating with performance snapshots).

The NMS users must have the ability to broadcast or multicast configuration news (information about network configuration) to other network managers. Such news can include notification of when certain components or facilities will become available or unavailable.

## 3.3. Fault Management

To maintain proper operation of a complex system such as a computer network, care must be taken that the system as a whole, and each essential component, individually, is in proper working order. Accomplishing this requires the ability to take corrective action and make repairs when needed. Where down-time cannot be tolerated, it is essential to anticipate problems so that preventive maintenance procedures can be invoked to avoid the actual occurrence of problems or faults.

Fault Management (FM) is that aspect of Network Management (NM) which attends to these concerns. It represents a logical division of labor within network management activities. FM seeks to maintain system operation as close as possible to a fault free level. The OSI Management Framework document [FRMWK] defines FM as follows:

> "Fault management encompasses fault detection, isolation and correction of abnormal operation of the OSI Environment. Faults cause open systems to fail to meet their operational objectives and they may be persistent or transient. Faults manifest themselves as particular events (e.g., errors) in the operation of an open system. Error event detection provides a capability to recognize faults. Fault management includes functions to:
>
> a) maintain and examine error logs;
> b) accept and act upon error detection notifications;

      c) trace and identify faults;
      d) carry out sequences of diagnostic tests;
      e) correct faults."

Central to the definition of fault management is the fundamental concept of a "fault." Faults are to be distinguished from errors. A fault is an abnormal condition which requires management attention (or action) to repair. A fault is usually indicated by failure to operate correctly, or by excessive errors. Certain errors, (e.g., CRC errors on communication lines), may occur occasionally and are not normally considered to be faults. Ordinarily, these errors are handled by an (N)-layer entity as part of (N)-layer operation.

The fault administrator (whether it be a person, a dedicated "expert" computer process, a particular facet of a general management process, or some combination of these) can be envisioned as an overseer of network activities who is continually seeking the answers to the following three questions: 1) Is there (or, perhaps, will there be) a fault? 2) If there is a fault, where is it and what are the offending components? and finally 3) If there is a fault and its cause has been identified, how can it be repaired? Thus, the fault administrator is charged with probing and/or monitoring the network for the purpose of: 1) detecting the existence or imminent occurrence of faults, 2) diagnosing the cause of the fault, and 3) setting in motion corrective measures to either repair or bypass the offending component in order to return the system to the highest level of operation as quickly as possible.

Detection of faulty behavior can be achieved in various ways. One way is to test components directly with loopback tests. Another approach is to send threshold information to subordinate fault management agents on the appropriate network nodes. When a threshold is exceeded, the agent notifies the manager that such an event has occurred. This remote servicing of the manager's request is possible because of the common understanding and identification of the resources of concern, and because both the manager and agent are speaking the same language (protocol). Faults may also be detected, in some cases, by functions designed for other aspects of NM (e.g., Performance or Configuration Management) which inform the FM administrator that there is a problem requiring attention.

These thresholds and critical events are used to indicate the actual existence of a fault, or the imminent occurrence of a fault which may still be avoidable. In addition, since not all faults can be detected on-line, out-of-band signaling or other off-line techniques, such as a remote user telephoning the network administrator to report his system malfunction, are still reasonable techniques for detecting network faults and notifying FM to take appropriate action.

The fault administrator can establish a set of a priori assumptions and decisions about which components in the system are subject to faults and, therefore, are of concern to him. He may use certain preprogrammed defaults in this process. He also determines the error levels and other parameters which serve as thresholds to signal fault conditions for each of these resources. In addition, he has the ability, possibly based upon his analysis of actual network operational data, to add new assumptions, change detection criteria, and even add components to his list of resources potentially subject to faults. The FM administrator is supported by the FM system in all these activities.

Once having detected a fault, the fault administrator must next ascertain the cause of that fault. Possibly enough information has been gleaned from the detection phase to diagnose the cause. If not, however, additional probing will be required to identify the cause of the fault and, if appropriate, the location of the offending component.

Finally, the FM system can attempt to correct the fault using the observational and analytical data derived from the detection and diagnosis stages. Often, FM may enlist the aid of functions developed and designed for other aspects of NM to effect the correction of the fault (e.g., The State Management Function developed for Configuration Management may be used to reconfigure the network around a faulty component). Sometimes problems can be corrected by on-line measures such as remotely rebooting a system. At other times, either the problem cannot be corrected on-line and service personnel must be dispatched for the repair, or the repair cannot be done quickly enough and the component must be bypassed by either on-line or off-line measures.

The following functional requirements address, in greater detail than this brief introduction, the issues involved in providing these types of fault management capabilities to the user.

### 3.3.1. User Requirements

Users expect fast and reliable problem resolution. While they expect very high quality network services delivered on a consistent basis, most end users understand that even the most advanced technology will at times suffer failure. Most end users, therefore, will tolerate an "occasional" outage. When these infrequent outages do occur, however, the end user, generally, expects the problem to be corrected immediately. To provide this level of fault resolution requires very reliable error detection and diagnostic management functions. Redundant paths between major nodes have been implemented in some networks to enhance the possibility of "fault-tolerant" operation and some users even demand redundant fault management to increase network reliability. Most users desire immediate notification when outages occur.

Users expect to be kept informed of the network status, including both scheduled and unscheduled maintenance. In the event of failure, users expect to be notified of the approximate time that the service will be resumed. Users expect reassurance of correct network operation through mechanisms that run confidence tests or analyze dumps, logs, event reports or statistics blocks.

When a fault occurs, a partial or complete resolution can be implemented (i.e., the correction may be temporary or permanent in nature). In a simple case, such as a printer failure, the system may bypass the reported offender by directing printer output to an alternate printer.

After correcting a fault and restoring the system to its operational state, the fault management system must ensure that the problem is truly resolved and that no new problems are introduced. This requirement is called "problem tracking and control."

If the fault management system restores system operation by substituting redundant components, the fault management system should ensure that any failed components be identified so that repairs can be made as quickly as possible to maintain redundancy.

Moreover, FM must provide status reporting of failed items. This should be done in a coordinated manner with CM developed functions since CM also will require status reporting of subsequently repaired resources. The correct current status of resources (operating or redundant) should be available to the administrator at all times. Fault recovery actions such as scheduling repair actions and determining the format of trouble tickets are user requirements not critical for interoperability and, therefore, beyond the scope of our study.

Failure of fault NM functions should not affect regular network operation.

### 3.3.2. Functional Requirements

### 3.3.2.1. Detecting and Reporting Faults

The NMS must provide mechanisms to allow its users to log events and errors. This includes the facilities to allow users to create and change logging filter settings (logging criteria), to initialize and stop the event/error logging on a routine or a demand basis, to specify what information is to be logged for what duration while the logging filters are satisfied and to specify where the logged information is to be sent. It may be sent either to a local information store or be sent remotely.

The NMS must be able to monitor the specified events or errors. This includes the facilities to allow the NMS users to specify the events or errors to be monitored, to specify the starting and stopping time for monitoring, to specify how frequently the monitored events or errors are to be polled and recorded, and to specify the threshold level or the count when a notification of abnormality should be given. For example, an event can be activities associated with: 1) a specific timer or counter, 2) a group of counters, 3) other parameters, or 4) a virtual circuit.

The ability to anticipate faults as a result of analyzing errors and/or events is needed. (The errors and events may be either monitored or logged.) For example, when a particular line shows an unusually high error rate then the situation must be investigated and appropriate action taken, if necessary, without causing problems for the network users. The method of analyzing monitored and/or logged information does not need to be standardized. However, analysis of errors and faults is a very important and necessary function.

Mechanisms are needed to generate event reports and to send them to the NMS users when a fault has occurred or when it is anticipated (e.g., a threshold level is reached).

A NMS must allow its users to broadcast or multicast notification of faults to network managers or to user specified network entities. This can be done either by a multicast/broadcast facility within the NM facilities, or, alternatively, by coordinated use of a separate facility to provide this messaging service.

### 3.3.2.2. Diagnosis of Faults

The NMS must allow its users to activate predefined diagnostic and testing procedures for the purpose of determining or verifying where the faults are and for the purpose of testing network components before they are put in use in a network. The diagnostic and testing procedures may be executed either on-line or off-line. At first, the NMS users have to be able to define diagnostic and testing procedures or to select test procedures from a set of already defined procedures. Then the users of NMS need the mechanisms to collect test data and to have access to other network information for analyzing test data in order to isolate faults and to identify the possible causes of it.

The NMS users, including NM expert systems, must be able to request fault related data, such as dumps, statistics blocks and status information for the purpose of diagnosing faults. The NMS must have ways of providing this requested information. In cases where expert systems are used in diagnosing and/or correcting faults, NM users need the ability to inquire as to the status of the diagnosis and/or correction.

NMS users need to analyze event reports of faults, error conditions, and other information they requested such as dumps and the results of testing and diagnosis. Although the method of analysis does not necessarily need to be standardized, NMS users do need standard mechanisms to exchange information for use in proprietary fault diagnostic and analysis programs. And they need standard definitions of the measures and metrics upon which the analysis is based. Fault testing and isolation may need to be standardized along with the measures and derived metrics from the analysis so that all parties involved have a common understanding of the nature and meaning of events.

### 3.3.2.3. Correction of Faults

The NMS must allow its users to change or reset resource attribute values, take components or lines down, or put components or lines back in service. As corrective actions in response to a fault, NMS users need the ability to request reconfiguration of all or part of the network. (Functions derived for Configuration Management may be invoked to satisfy this requirement).

NMS users require mechanisms to track network operations following fault correction attempts to ensure that the faulty situations are, in fact, corrected. With respect to this capability, NMS users must be able to specify what parameters are to be tracked and how long the tracking is to be maintained.

### 3.3.2.4. Robust Fault Management

The NMS users require sufficient robustness from fault management, perhaps in the form of redundant fault managers, to ensure that fault management functionality will be available even in the event of a major FM component failure or during maintenance.

## 3.4. Security Management

Security itself is concerned with more than secure communications. Applications using stand-alone and networked computer resources, and those requiring varying degrees of security control or protection, span all sectors of society. These sectors include, but are not restricted to, banking, business, insurance, credit bureau services, legal, national security, and military. Vast computer networks, for example, have evolved to handle transaction processing for banks and retail establishments. Smart cards, on-line sales-inventory control systems, computerized buying services, electronic mail, and electronic office memoranda are just some of the commercial applications which can no longer rely on such traditional security methods as physical control of access to facilities and paper audit trails in order to insure integrity of data and desired levels of privacy. The specific security requirements of government, security agencies, and the military also present significant needs for security which are often described as more stringent and somewhat different from commercial security needs.

With respect to communications interests, networks have the disadvantage of being highly distributed and of affording relatively easy access to network facilities and resources. An interesting problem which arises in this regard for the military, for example, relates to problems of secrecy on LANs. Since LANs operate in a broadcast mode requiring the destination station to recognize messages addressed to it, it is necessary for every station on that LAN to be capable of recognizing or deciphering at least the destination address field of the message to determine if the message is for it. Therefore, in this regard, LANs are susceptible to traffic analysis.

Security, generally, provides for the confidentiality and privacy, integrity, and appropriate availability of data and data processing capabilities (often referred to, appropriately enough, as "CIA," the principles of security). Security "refers to a complex of ... procedural, logical and physical measures aimed at prevention, detection and correction of certain kinds of misuse ... together with the tools to install, operate and maintain these measures ... [Security refers to the] characteristics of data processing systems that give resistance to attack and misuse, intentional or otherwise." [ECMASEC] Security elements perform such functions as that of limiting access to particular users and/or applications, and limiting access to and corruption of stored and transmitted data.

In order to provide this protective, secure environment, thereby supporting the "CIA" security principles, supportive security services are required. The following is a list of supportive services (usually referred to mnemonically as the "3A's" and the "5S's").

The 3A's are:

- Authentication,
- Authorization,
- Audit/accountability,

and the 5S's are:

- Secret,
- Sealed,
- Sequenced,
- Signed,
- Stamped.

Security between peers, as with any other communication related activity, requires certain understandings and agreements as to services, mechanisms, and information interpretation. Therefore, in order to perform the security function, a particular security policy must be agreed upon between interacting open systems. Agreement upon the security policy is essential because of the potential for different open systems to adopt policies which will not interoperate. A security policy generally specifies:

-- "how data transmissions between open systems will be protected from unauthorized reception or corruption;

-- how access to resources in one open system will be granted to entities on another open system;

-- how the identity of entities wishing to intercommunicate will be determined with certainty;

-- how and to whom significant events relating to security will be reported; and

-- how audit trail information will be collected, and how and to whom that information will be reported." [SECURE]

Additionally, the security policy should specify how communication services between open systems are reliably provided and maintained. Moreover, the concept of "security domain" depends upon this security policy concept in that a "security domain" comprises a "bounded group of security objects and security subjects to which a single security policy, executed by a single security administration," applies. [ECMASEC]

After a security policy has been selected to govern part or all of a particular communication session between open systems, the security policy is realized by properly configuring the security services, mechanisms and security related information which will control security during that session. These security service applications require functionality both to provide their particular security services (e.g., authentication), and to manage those security services (e.g., key or credential distribution). Security management (SM), then, is needed in this regard, to provide the means by which the security services, mechanisms and security related information are managed.

The issue of importance here is: What is the scope of security management? Security management is involved with such activities as generating, distributing, and storing encryption keys. Password and other authorization or access control lists must be maintained and distributed. Moreover, security management is concerned with monitoring and controlling access to computer networks, or access to all or part of the management information obtained from the network nodes. Logs are an important tool for security management and, therefore, security management is very much involved with the collection, storage, and examination of audit records and security logs, as well as with the enabling and disabling of these logging facilities. Security management oversees the facilities needed to secure communication on a network as well as those needed to secure the management operations themselves.

The OSI Management Framework document [FRMWK], defines SM as follows.

"The purpose of security management is to support the application of security policies by means of functions which include:
 a) the creation, deletion and control of security services and mechanisms;
 b) the distribution of security-relevant information;
 c) the reporting of security-relevant events."

More specifically, SM encompasses three categories of management: system security management, security service management, and security mechanism management [SECURE]. That is, security management deals with the management of "security aspects of the overall OSI environment[,] ... particular security services, such as peer entity authentication and access control," and the security support mechanisms used to provide the security services [SECURE].

Security management can be further characterized as "that aspect of systems management which defines management information exchanges for performing the task of administering systems security." [SECURE] Security management primarily differs from other systems management functional areas only in the class of objects it manages, not in the operations which it uses to manage them. A small sample list of the types of objects appropriate for security objects includes: keys, authentication information, access right information, and operating parameters of security services and mechanisms [SECURE].

Management activities required to support security functions are generally of three types (administration, detection, and recovery). The first of these types, security "administration," refers to both the gathering (reading) of system security management information and the addition, modification, or deletion (writing) of this system security management information.

The second type of management activity, security event "detection," deals with the auditing of system security operations. Auditing is normally considered to have four components: audit trail content specification, audit trail analysis, audit reporting, and audit trail archiving.

The final type of management activity, security "recovery," is concerned with recovering from an actual, or suspected security attack. This can entail such corrective measures as altering security procedures or modifying security information at appropriate nodes in the system.

The following two sections present a more in-depth view of security management, presenting first the users' view of this aspect of network management followed by the functional elements which are needed to provide such capabilities.

### 3.4.1. User Requirements

In the limited space available here to discuss security management requirements, it would be impossible, and, in fact, undesirable, to enumerate the scores of individual user requirements that have been documented in the references of this report as well as in numerous other documents and implementations not referenced here. However, it is appropriate to attempt to characterize the general nature of these user requirements so as to give guidance in generating and evaluating relevant functional requirements.

Since the function of security is to protect the integrity and confidentiality of "security objects" (i.e., entities "in a passive role to which a security policy applies" [ECMASEC] -- e.g., programs and data), it is essential that security management assure that the services providing this protection are fully functional and have all the support that they need to operate. In fact, security management must be very robust and, to that end, requires a high degree of fault tolerance, for example, to maintain its own "CIA."

Security management provides mechanisms for the protection of network resources and user information. Network security functions should be available for authorized users only. Appropriate validation procedures should be provided to ensure this obligation. In view of this, SM must provide support for security functions by assisting in transferring, monitoring, and controlling security related data; by providing for the recording of attacks and attempted attacks on systems as well as the capability of archiving and retrieving this information; and by providing the capability for notification of security related activity of interest.

The several concepts that follow, often referred to as constituting the major OSI security goals, comprise the set of security facilities that security management is intended to keep intact and properly functioning.

1. The need to prove the identity of security subjects (i.e., those attempting to access some security object). This is generally referred to as Authentication.

2. The need to verify authorization for access to some security object. This activity is generally termed Access Control.

3. The need to prevent disclosure of information. This is generally called Confidentiality.

4. The need to detect various activities such as modification, loss, insertion, replay, or reflection of information. This is referred to as Integrity.

5. And finally, it is often necessary to provide for third party registration of activity in order to be able to be certain that some activity has indeed occurred. Non-repudiation is the term applied to this activity.

Security of the physical location of the network control center in terms of access, data storage, fire, flood and power supply disruption, while all legitimate user concerns, are generally considered to be beyond the scope of OSI security and therefore are also beyond the scope of OSI security management as investigated by this study.

### 3.4.2. Functional Requirements

An analysis of security management yields the following categorization of management activity and requirements into three general areas. These are:

1. **The Ability to Control Access to Resources**

    The security manager must be able to grant or restrict access to the entire network or selected critical parts of the network. The following capabilities can be used to enable the security manager to fulfill this requirement:

    -Authorization control,
    -Authentication control,
    -Control access to security codes,
    -Control access to source routing and route
        recording,
    -Control access to directories and information bases,
    -Control of updates to directories (including addition,
        deletion, and modification of directory entries),
    -Control of the distribution of directory information
        and routing tables,
    -Control of the setting of threshold levels and
        accounting tables,
    -Prioritized access to requested network resources,

-Maintenance of general network user profiles, and usage
    profiles for specific resources, for the purpose of
    controlling access to security resources.

2. **The Ability to Archive and Retrieve Security Information**

   Security management requires the ability to gather appropriate information, store the information and access that information for analysis and control purposes. This requirement entails the following capabilities:

   -Event logging,
   -Monitoring security audit trails,
   -Monitoring usage and the users of security related
     resources,
   -Reporting security violation,
   -Receiving notification of security violation,
   -Maintaining and examining security logs,
   -Maintaining redundant or backup copies for all or part
     of the security related files.
   -Maintaining general network user profiles, and usage
     profiles for specific resources, to enable reference
     for conformance to designated security profiles.

3. **The Ability to Manage and Control the Encryption Process**

   The security manager must both be able to encrypt its communications, when desired, and facilitate the encryption process, in general. This requires the following functionality:

   -Encryption (e.g., encryption algorithm selection),
   -Key management.

## 3.5. Performance Management

Modern data communications network systems are composed of multiple complex components which must intercommunicate and share data and resources. In some cases, it is critical to the effectiveness of an application that the communication over the network be within certain performance limits. On the other hand, while it is usually desirable to perform at the highest level, performance characteristics may not always be critical, and, at times, less than optimal performance levels can be tolerated.

Performance management (PM) is that aspect of Network Management (NM) which attends to these concerns. It represents a logical division of labor within network management activities. The OSI Management Framework [FRMWK], defines PM as follows:

"Performance management enables the behavior of resources in the OSIE and the effectiveness of communication activities to be evaluated. Performance management includes functions to:

- a) gather statistical information;
- b) maintain and examine logs of system state histories;
- c) determine system performance under natural and artificial conditions;
- d) alter system modes of operation for the purpose of conducting performance management activities."

Whereas fault management is concerned with whether all or part of the network is working, performance management is concerned with how well the network or its parts are working. Performance management deals with the quality and effectiveness of network communications. It involves the processes of quantifying, measuring, and reporting error levels, the responsiveness, availability, and utilization of individual network components and the network as a whole. An airline reservations system, which normally provides reasonably fast response times to queries, will be performing at an unacceptable level if response times triple or quadruple, angering both ticket agents and customers. Are delays within acceptable limits for the transfer of data from one station to another? Are response times within reason for the virtual terminal or database application, or are these times so long that the productivity in the office environment is absolutely effected?

At least conceptually, performance management of computer networks includes two broad functional categories -- monitoring and tuning. Monitoring is the performance management function which tracks activities on the network. The tuning function enables performance management to make adjustments to improve network performance. Performance management enlists these mechanisms to provide an awareness of the degree to which the network is fulfilling the service expectations of the users and the degree to which the overall resources of the network are being used. What is the level of bandwidth utilization? Is there excessive traffic? Has throughput been reduced to unacceptable levels? Are there bottlenecks? Are response times increasing? Are performance levels within the limits that the user expects or was promised? These are just some of the issues of concern to a performance administrator.

To deal with these concerns, performance management must initially focus on some basic (default) set of resources to be monitored in order to assess performance levels. This includes associating appropriate metrics and their values with relevant network resources as indicators of different levels of performance. For example, how many retransmissions on a Transport connection should be considered a performance problem requiring attention? Performance management, therefore, must monitor many resources which provide information in determining the performance level of networks. By collecting this information, analyzing it, and then using the resultant analysis as feedback to the set of threshold values of the metrics, the performance administrator can become more and more adept at recognizing situations indicative of present or impending performance degradation.

It should be noted that the definition of PM quoted above from the framework document does not include performance control (needed for tuning) in PM. However, for discussion here it seems appropriate to follow through with the insight that once a problem has been recognized, it is appropriate to try to remedy the situation, regardless of who or what performs that function.

The first stage of PM, monitoring, entailing observation and probing of designated resources, serves to gather information which is stored for later analysis. Particularly in large network environments, the performance administrators (e.g., a human administrator of the performance management software), use this information to analyze the network operation, either manually or through automated methods, and determine areas of performance degradation. His analysis also yields appropriate threshold values which are indicative of various levels of performance. When problems are recognized, a managing system might employ functions developed for fault and/or configuration management to diagnose and rectify the situation. This is necessary to avoid duplication of functionality.

Systems management developed functions which can set and configure managed objects, can assist performance management developed functions to control a degrading performance situation. Often this is accomplished by setting the necessary parameters for management of the traffic on the network. Sometimes, however, additional network resources must be allocated or procured to solve the problem (e.g., more resources may need to be procured, as indicated by capacity planning analysis). If the problem is severe and unexpected, one natural place to turn for assistance is to functions developed for fault management. In fact, it is a natural symbiotic relationship for the monitoring and analytical functions developed for PM reasons to provide input to functions developed for fault management when a situation becomes or is approaching a pathological state.

In order to evaluate whether acceptable performance levels are being maintained, it is necessary to have a well-defined expectation of what they should be. Likewise, it is essential to be able to determine what it is that the performance parameters are indicating.

The following requirements address, in greater detail than this brief introduction, the issues involved in providing these types of performance management capabilities to the user.

### 3.5.1. User Requirements

The behavior of network resources and the effectiveness of interconnection activities need to be evaluated. Before using a network, potential users often want to know information such as the average and worst case network response times for their applications (e.g., VT or FTAM), variability in response, and the reliability and availability of network services. The NMS must also be able to monitor the usage of various resources and be able to focus monitoring efforts upon those resources that are most important.

Network managers need performance statistics to help them plan, manage, and maintain large networks. Performance statistics can be used to recognize potential bottlenecks before they cause problems for the end users. Appropriate corrective action can then be taken. This action can take the form of changing communications traffic routes to balance or redistribute traffic load during times of peak usage or when a bottleneck is identified by a quickly growing load in one area. Over the longer term, capacity planning based on performance information can indicate the proper decisions to make, for example, with regard to expansion of the number of communications lines in that area.

Performance tuning involves first recognizing and diagnosing the existence of performance deficiencies and the load associated with these performance deficiencies, then identifying where and how performance tuning should be done. The use of various performance testing algorithms can help diagnose problem areas and determine where and how to tune the network. Once modifications have been made, it is essential to track the results of these performance tuning efforts to assure the effectiveness of these interventions.

End users expect network resources to be managed in such a way as to consistently afford their applications minimal response time and minimal delays. The end user community will not accept excessive or unanticipated variations in network performance. As performance degrades, business processes within the organization may falter. Therefore, when performance degrades because of traffic levels, high priority messages required for profits or safety should not be affected.

The users want to know that the network has adequate capacity to handle their loads under normal and adverse (e.g., heavily loaded) conditions. Also, as the network grows in size and usage, they are concerned that performance levels can be maintained. They also want to be assured that the network is reliable (i.e., as immune as possible to component failures and transmission losses).

Even though managers of large networks often use analytical and/or simulation models to predict network performance and to help plan for network expansion, actual network traffic and performance measurement is generally still needed to verify modeling results and to provide real network activity profiles as input to these models. Performance statistics should allow analysts to trace the reasons for performance results and anticipate performance changes. In addition, these statistics should allow administrators to anticipate when capability margins are close to being exceeded.

### 3.5.2. Functional Requirements

#### 3.5.2.1. The Ability to Monitor Performance

The NMS needs to be able to monitor performance relevant events, measures and resources. This includes the facilities to allow NMS users to select the events, resources, or measures to be monitored, to specify the starting and stopping times for monitoring, to specify how frequently the monitored events, measures or resources are to be polled and recorded, to specify other related performance information to be collected during each polling, and to specify the threshold level when a notification of performance abnormality or degradation should be given. The NMS must ensure that statistical measures are based upon a minimally accepted number of samples. When time stamps associated with the reported information or activities or events are involved, either adjustment to the same time instance is required or synchronized clocks among devices are needed.

The collected performance information needs to be parsed and reduced for performance analysis. The NMS users need to be able to select the performance analysis criteria and algorithms for various performance measures.

### 3.5.2.2. The Ability to Tune and Control Performance

When an indication of a performance abnormality or degradation is reported, the NMS user needs mechanisms to execute predefined performance tests, and to collect test results for the purpose of diagnosing network performance anomalies and determining the appropriate performance tuning strategy. The same set of functions can be used to evaluate the results (i.e., the effectiveness) of performance tuning.

NMS users need to be able to change (potentially non-OSI) resource allocation (e.g., buffer allocation method, flow control allocation level), to modify resource (managed object) attributes and to set managed object attribute values in order to provide better performance or resolve performance problems that cause bottlenecks or prevent the flow of high priority data. Some of these capabilities are the same as those required for configuration management.

### 3.5.2.3. The Ability to Evaluate Performance Tuning

The NMS users need the ability to keep track of the performance tuning results in terms of user specified measures or criteria. The set of facilities required to satisfy this evaluation (tracking) function may duplicate some of those functions that are required for performance monitoring and tuning.

### 3.5.2.4. The Ability to Report on Performance Monitoring, Tuning, and Tracking

Notification of abnormal performance changes must be able to be spontaneously generated and sent to the NMS users who have previously requested such notification. Recognition of such abnormal performance changes may occur, for example, when performance measure thresholds are exceeded.

The network managers need to initially select a predefined domain (a set of systems to be managed) or subdomain as a base for generating performance trending reports. In addition, NMS users need to be able to create, delete and modify domains or subdomains within a network in order to view the performance characteristics of a portion of a network that is of particular interest to them.

Mechanisms are needed for NMS users to request and obtain performance reports based on user specified criteria (e.g., throughput of a specified domain in the past 24 hours, the past week, month or year). The performance trending reports that represent current (real-time) network performance or network performance histories can be saved for a specified period of time to be used as benchmarks. These reports can relate to an individual domain, subdomain or the network as a whole. Accumulation of daily performance reports into weekly, monthly and yearly reports should be possible.

The NMS should have the ability to display routine snapshots of network performance in terms of those user specified measures (e.g., network utilizations versus load, traffic or load distribution among subnetworks, ratio of overhead packets to data packets, detail of traffic profile and peak hour rates, and average network response time). The NMS should have the ability to compute and display statistics of standard metrics such as average, median, maximum, minimum, ratios and standard deviation.

### 3.5.2.5. The Ability to Test Capacity and Special Conditions

In order to assure that capacity margins for network components are sufficient, it may be necessary to run tests to determine the effects of additional network loading under natural or artificial conditions. By imposing test loads on the network, managers can perhaps more accurately predict when additional equipment must be brought on-line than they could using analytic or simulation models. Tests could also be designed to establish the effects of equipment failures to determine the reliability of the networks. It might be possible to run tests during normal operations to determine incremental effects, but often tests should be run during late evening or early morning off-peak hours under artificial conditions so as not to disturb real user traffic or to obtain test results under more controllable conditions that do not include "random" background traffic. Such tests can also be used to validate simulation or analytic models.

### 3.6. Accounting Management

"Accounting management enables charges to be established for the use of resources in the OSIE, and for costs to be identified for the use of those resources. Accounting management includes functions to:

a) inform users of costs incurred or resources consumed;
b) enable accounting limits to be set and tariff schedules to be associated with the use of resources;
c) enable costs to be combined where multiple resources are invoked to achieve a given communication objective." [FRMWK]

Accounting management provides information about the use of resources for cost analysis, tracing network usage, and user billing. The results of statistical analysis of accounting information will help plan network expansion or the types of network services and may further indicate the trend of the development of new network technology. Information gathered for accounting may also prove useful in the development of "expert systems" for automated network management. (See sec. 6.)

### 3.6.1. User Requirements

When a network or a system of interconnected networks are used by more than one organization or cost center within an organization, there is a need to apportion costs for network services in proportion to the amount of resources consumed by each chargeable user. Therefore, information on usage of resources needs to be recorded, collected and archived to provide the necessary information for proper distribution of resource costs.

NMS end users and administrators need to be able to specify the kinds of accounting information to be recorded at various nodes, the desired interval between sending the recorded information to higher level management nodes, and the algorithms to be used in calculating and reporting the accounting information. Accounting reports should be generated in user specified form and sent to user designated output devices.

In order to limit access to accounting information, the NMS must provide the capability to verify user's authorization to access and manipulate that information. As with other areas of network management, accounting management should have minimal effect on network performance.

The ability to adjust billing rates and accounting factors are legitimate administrative requirements, but they are outside of the scope of this study.

### 3.6.2. Functional Requirements

#### 3.6.2.1. The Ability to Record and Generate Accounting Information

The NMS must allow its users to specify the accounting information to be collected as well as the duration of the collection period, or the criteria to be used to determine the duration of the collection period. The definition of accounting information and units must be defined by related standards making groups. The format and options associated with this accounting information also need to be defined by NM standards. Examples of accounting information include network user network connection time, quantity of data transmitted, and class of service provided for each user or group of users.

Mechanisms are needed for the NMS, through layer management entities or the layer entities, to record and/or collect user distinguishable accounting information, and to generate accounting messages. The generated accounting messages are to be forwarded to the default or NMS user specified files or nodes.

#### 3.6.2.2. The Ability to Specify Accounting Information to Be Collected

The NMS must allow its users to specify what accounting information is to be collected (e.g., connection time or transmission time) and how it is stored (e.g., selecting predefined accounting units or even calculation algorithms for statistics about resource usage and individual or group user charges).

Daily raw accounting information or calculated statistics are saved in data bases for use in periodic weekly, monthly or quarterly accounting reports.

### 3.6.2.3. The Ability to Control the Storage of and Access to Accounting Information

The NMS must provide standard procedures to retrieve and store accounting information and standard ways to name archived accounting information files. Accounting information can be stored on disk, or output to the printer or screen.

Access to accounting information is limited to authorized personnel only. If current access authorization algorithms are not adequate, new algorithms must be developed. To make use of these algorithms, mechanisms must be provided to allow authorized NMS users to select or change authorization algorithms.

### 3.6.2.4. The Ability to Report Accounting Information

The NMS must be capable of reporting degree of resource usage and resource usage charges at an NMS user specified level. In other words, the NMS user can specify what information is to be reported, in what form to report it, and to which network user's accounting profile or to which output device to report it.

Mechanisms are needed to allow NMS users to create and transmit selectively or broadcast, as appropriate, accounting news such as network resource billing rate changes or accounting limit changes.

### 3.6.2.5. The Ability to Set and Modify Accounting Limits

The network manager must be able to read, set and change accounting limits for various groups of users. For example, to balance the usage of network transmission capacity among users, a user may be limited in his access to the network to various levels at different times depending on the overall network load or accounting (finance) policy changes.

Mechanisms are needed to allow the network manager to change the priorities assigned to the network users for access to network resources, including, for example, the priorities in using various classes of network services at various layers.

### 3.6.2.6. The Ability to Define Accounting Metrics

In order to obtain and use the accounting information, the standard metrics and the definition of accounting information unit need to be established. For example, the type of accountable units needs to be defined such as the call (connection) duration or the number of bits, characters, blocks or files transmitted. A standard method for defining these accounting metrics will allow expansion or changes of accounting metrics.

## 3.7. Other Requirements

The aspects of network management which are not critical for interoperability and therefore do not require standardization lie mainly in the areas of man-machine interface, analysis, and the management of large amounts of management data. These areas are important, however, since they may be keys that determine the popularity and usefulness of a network management system. They may be major factors in discriminating among implementations of NM standards.

The man-machine interface should offer the NMS user a standard management application interface. The interface should enable the NMS user to quickly and easily comprehend the network management system's capabilities, to use the NMS efficiently, and to allow flexibility in performing the desired operations.

The inclusion of "help text" to explain the use of and purpose of the network management commands can be quite useful. Easy and efficient input to the NMS can be provided by menu-driven management commands, programmable function keys, and mechanisms to permit users to build command files. The output generated may include 1) color graphics (e.g., different colors can be used to indicate the severity of faults or the degree of traffic load distributed over a single network or interconnected networks), 2) choices in formatting and presenting displays and reports, and 3) generation of real-time and/or historical displays or reports concerning areas of particular interest determined by user specified criteria.

Analysis of collected management information is very important for successful network management. Efficient analysis tools help, for example, to diagnose and isolate faults. The analysis results can be used to predict network performance, to forecast network expansion needs, to plan network upgrades, to balance network load among network users or groups of network users, to minimize the network management cost, and to optimize overall network performance.

Because of the size and complexity of data communications networks, expert systems may be required for the management of network management information. (See sec. 6.) Successful network management presupposes that the NMS can process information at a rate faster than the information is generated.

# INTEGRATED NETWORK MANAGEMENT SYSTEMS
(A Global Perspective on the Issue)

Lev Feldkhun

Technology Concepts Inc.
A Bell Atlantic Company
40 Tall Pine Drive
Sudbury, Massachusetts 01776
(508)443-7311

## ABSTRACT

The inherent problem of managing a multi-vendor network is that the management tools provided by each vendor are disparate and not integrated.

An enormous technical and intellectual effort is presently being committed by leading companies within the computer and telecommunications industry and by national and international standardization organizations to develop Integrated Network Management Systems (INMS). At the same time, the evolving INMS technology is still in its infant stage. An indication of this is the plurality of definitions and visions of Integrated Network Management. A stable reference base for INMS is needed, both by vendors to drive their R & D efforts, and by customers to help them strategize their product and services selection process.

This paper discusses the overall INMS problem/solution spaces from a global perspective. A model is presented to describe a typical non-integrated network management environment in terms of the real network objects managed, the functional scope achieved through diverse and incompatible management tools, and the user interfaces employed.

The main objectives of an Integrated Network Management System are then formulated and a generic model of an INM system is introduced. This model focuses on levels of integration (both from user and from internal system perspectives) and on segmentation of INMS systems into modular architectural components.

The approaches of emerging INM systems and standards are then contrasted in terms of the INMS model. Finally, certain open issues are identified as per the scope and the overall methodology of developing standards in the area of Integrated Network Management.

## 1. NETWORK ENVIRONMENT

Heterogeneous is becoming a common term for describing today's network environments. In most networks, there are products and services from multiple vendors, and these products incorporate multiple technologies. The evolution of a typical network starts with a relatively small set of homogeneous products, and grows to incorporate a wide variety of complex, interconnected technologies. This evolution is often beyond the control of the network planner. It occurs because the network growth is driven by the needs of corporate users who are often organizationally separated and have varying needs. Over time, a variety of network products and technologies are used to address these needs.

As these networks grow in size and complexity, they also grow in importance. The information carried by a network becomes vital to the corporation it serves, often to the point of being considered a strategic asset. Without effective management to ensure timely and reliable delivery of information, business operations (and therefore profitability) will suffer.

## 2. THE MANAGEMENT PROBLEM [1]

Management of a multi-vendor environment is complicated by the fact that each vendor provides a different management system, often for each of that vendor's product lines (see Figure 1). Each of these management systems will:
- Apply to a usually very limited and specific set of network components,
- Offer different levels of functionality even to network components of similar types (e.g., modems, transmission lines, packet switches, etc.),
- Employ vendor-specific management data in terms of syntax and semantics,
- Employ proprietary management procedures and management application-level communications protocols delivered by usually non-portable software,
- And, use a different interface to the network operator.

From the user point of view, this requires the operator to be trained on the operation of each management system. In addition, the operator must be trained on the unique characteristics of each product. This training is needed mainly due to unique categorization and terminology ("jargon") for describing network components, features, states and commands, although the underlying concepts and principles are often the same between vendors of similar equipment (e.g., multiplexors).

From the systems integrator point of view (be it either network user or vendor organization), the existing incompatibility of management data, procedures, communications protocols and delivery platforms makes the introduction of management systems for multi-vendor network environments a formidable technological task for the telecommunications industry.

In short, there is a critical need to effectively manage networks, but the disparity of management systems and the shortage of trained operators make this very difficult, if not impossible. The result is reduced availability and quality of service of the network which ultimately adversely affects corporate profits.

A recent poll of telecommunications managers [2] found, among other things, that:

(1) "Network management and control, meeting changing user needs and reducing or containing communications costs are the three most critical issues facing communications managers today." (Figure 2)
(2) "Network management and control are perceived by the majority of telecommunications managers as the top technological issue which will increase in importance by 1990." (Figure 3)

Despite the critical need, there are currently no solutions on the market that can effectively address this problem.

## 3. INTEGRATED NETWORK MANAGEMENT SYSTEMS - THE VISION

In response to growing customer needs to solve the management problem of heterogeneous network environments, leading companies within the computer and telecommunications industries, as well as national and international standardization organizations, are presently committing enormous technical/intellectual effort to develop Integrated Network Management Systems (INMS). At the same time, the evolving INMS technology is still in its infant stage. An indication of this is the plurality of definitions and visions of Integrated Network Management.

From a practical user perspective (and, in my opinion, this shall be the predominant targeted perspective), INMS can be viewed (See Figure 4) as a value-added network management system which will:

(1) Interoperate with the universe (or at least a critical subset of it) of existing Native Network Management Systems (i.e. vendor-specific NMS).
(2) Adapt to functional/performance growth of Native NMS's.
(3) Introduce a single image of a multi-technology/multi- vendor network environment by employing a unified user/NMS interface rich with generic (i.e. non-vendor-specific) semantics and graphic notations.
(4) Provide for smooth, non-disruptive on-the-job training of the operators and their transition from a "native" to "generic" mode of interaction with INMS, and for coexistence of these two modes of operation when necessary.

The power of an Integrated Network Management System can be defined in terms of its SCOPE and DEPTH of integration.

*Scope of network management integration includes:*
- The space of managed objects and the specific set of native network management systems with which INMS interoperates, and
- The network management functional capabilities. Space of managed objects can be viewed as being comprised of network domains, each of which in turn is formed of network objects specific to a given network domain as well as of network objects common to various network domains.

A network domain represents a class of networks distinguished in terms of the following major groups of attributes (see Figure 5) and their values:

- Types of network services provided (e.g., voice, data, image, integrated),
- Typical geographical coverage (e.g., local area networks, metropolitan area networks, wide area networks),
- Network technology employed [e.g., switching technology (packet, circuit, etc.), transmission technology (media, signaling, etc.), processing technology (call processing, adaptation to topological changes and load fluctuation), etc.].
- Level of ownership of network resources (e.g., private, public, hybrid, virtual).

It is useful to notice that in most cases the telecommunications professionals of the 1990's are brought up by studying specific types of network equipment and their functional and other properties in the context of conventional categories of networks. It is therefore important, when modeling the managed object space, to use classifications that can provide certain continuity in the overall development of understanding of components of the global telecommunications infrastructure.

*Network Management Functional Capabilities* represent the second main factor in categorizing the scope of Integrated Network Management Systems. To facilitate a market driven approach to the development of INMS technology, the telecommunications industry has to offer a vision of network management functional capabilities which can be understood by a broad user community in the practical context of their network management activities.

Although the necessity and the high methodological value of a stable classification of network management functions is generally understood by network management vendors, research and standardization organizations, a recent review of a sample of sources on network management standardization [3,4,5] and of vendor approaches [6,7,8] indicates that there is still a confusion in terminology, implied classification criteria and on the relation of network management functions to user network management practices.

The following is the author's contribution to the formation of a stable vision on network management functional capabilities:

From a telecommunications manager's point of view (who, in many cases is the ultimate decision-maker on acquisition of network management products and services), the network management environment can be viewed as consisting of people assigned specific network management taskand using network management tools (e.g., INMS capabilities) to perform their network activities (see Figure 6), [9].

INMS user activities within a network management organization can then be described in terms of the skill level of personnel and network management tasks (see Figure 7). According to their skills, users perform the roles of staff members, network planners, network designers, technicians/operators, help-desk operators, etc., just to mention a few.

Typical network management tasks may include:
- Long term network planning and provisioning of network service,
- Network design, installation, test and activation,
- Network operations (e.g., support of management of real network traffic),
- Network maintenance (both preventive and corrective), and
- Network administration.

By using further modeling of the life cycle of networks, telecommunications organizations will be able to establish a stable reference base for network management tasks and to better understand user activities, whose organization basically forms the problem space. This problem space can then be used in determining the level of sufficiency or deficiency of various functional capabilities offered by providers of INMS solutions.

Currently, the emerging taxonomy of network management functions appears to be the one developed by the ISO group on OSI management [3,4]. This taxonomy includes the following functional areas:
- Configuration management
- Fault (problem) management
- Performance management
- Security management
- Accounting management
- Directory management

Although this functional classification has been introduced for the OSI environment, it is getting broad acceptance by the vendors of real networks.

It is important to notice that specific network management tasks may require interaction (i.e. integration) of a number of discrete functional capabilities provided by an INMS. The degree to which INMS functional capabilities shall be integrated in INMS products versus integrated by users (by means of software-based function-integration tools) will depend on the stability of the models of network management tasks.

In summary, the range of INMS functional capabilities and the level of their integration depends on an adequate understanding of the user activities. This understanding can be effectively advanced by modeling the network management tasks based on network life cycle and on reflection of organizational structures.

*Depth of network management* integration is defined in terms of the various levels at which integration can be achieved; each level offering specific benefits to customers. From the user's perspective, three levels of integration can be identified: Physical terminal level, user interface level and user activity flow level.
- Physical terminal level: the functions of the Native NMSs are presented through the same screen (physical terminal), although the management function and user activity flows (see below) of the Native NMS may vary and overlap. No change is implied to NMSs being integrated. The benefit of this level of integration to the user is minimal in that the user can only access to and interact with various Native NMSs from a single focal point. The user will still be required to be "multi-lingual" and "multi-cultural" in terms of the specific notations and philosophies of managing various networks.

- User interface level: in addition to physical terminal integration, the user interface integration provides for consistent presentation technology (e.g., graphics, menus, multi-windowing), generic semantics of notation used, and a built-in methodology of examining various specific vendor networks of the same class in a systematic and consistent way. This level of integration will require substantial INMS value-added feature development and may require some modifications to the Native NMS as well.
  The benefit of this level of integration to the user is greater in that the user will be shielded from the discrepancies of the Native NMS to the highest degree possible, thereby accomplishing one of the key objectives of INMS - increased user productivity achieved with reduced technical skills required.
- User activity flow level: the user activity flow represents users' involvement in network management tasks as described in the previous subsections. It implies the need for the user to interact with various discrete functions defined in the network management functional areas (e.g., configuration, performance and security management) in order to accomplish a simple task (e.g., service provisioning). Integration of these functions is based on network management tasks and addresses the ultimate need of the user.

From the system design perspective, one can identify the following four major levels of integration: application procedure level, management data level, communications level, and delivery environment level.
- Application procedure level: procedure integration level could be used to integrate applications that overlap between Native NMS involved in integration. This form of integration requires a high degree of coordination and interdependency among Native NMSs. This interdependency can be achieved only through integration of management data and use of communications conventions.
  The difficulty of integration at the application "procedure" level is projected to be lesser for expert-system-based applications than for conventional applications.
  This projection is based on the benefits of the explicitness of management rules and their structural separation from procedural control in the case of expert system-based applications[10].
- Management data level: data integration implies the Native NMS will be able to access to, interpret and manipulate shared data in a consistent and synchronized way. The syntax of the data used and/or supplied by Native NMS may differ from one used/supplied by value-added INMS applications. In this case, data translation performed by a network management gateway function will be required.
- Communications level: this level of integration will introduce standard application level protocols enabling an exchange of management data and service requests between application procedures of Integrated NMS and Native NMS, as well as among distributed application components within the Integrated NMS. Standard network management application protocols are at the root of building distributed and open Integrated NMS and are currently in the focus of major international standardization bodies (e.g., CCITT, ISO, IFIP, ECMA, etc.).
- Delivery environment level: integration of computer environment for delivery of INMS data, functional and communications capabilities can be viewed as unification of applications interfaces to operating systems, data base management systems, information presentation systems and underlying communications systems. Although unified delivery environment is not a prerequisite for introduction of INMS, its benefits lie in the reduction of cost and time associated with expansion of INMS technology throughout the market.

Progress in each of the identified areas of integration (both from the user and network design perspective) will contribute to the total depth of integration and, consequently, to the overall power of an Integrated Network Management System.

## 4. AN ARCHITECTURE MODEL FOR INTEGRATED NETWORK MANAGEMENT SYSTEMS

Having formulated the vision of an Integrated NMS and having identified the types of reference points against which one can compare the effectiveness (i.e. power) of an INMS, we now proceed with an outline of an architectural model which will focus on the internal organization of an INMS.

The purpose of the proposed architectural model is to identify INMS's fundamental internal architectural components and their interaction, and thereby facilitate a practical introduction of INMS technology by the telecommunications industry in an evolutionary modular fashion. The model is based on the following architectural components (see Figure 8):
- Unified user/INMS interface,
- Conventions on presentation of network management information to users,
- Family of Integrated Network Management application elements,
- Management application level protocols,
- A set of communications protocols and shared services,
- Management data repository, and
- A range of Network Management Gateways for various Native Network Management Systems.

The *Unified User Interface* is the functional means through which interaction between INMS and its users takes place. We envision this interface possessing the following properties:
- Single focal point through which management of any of the underlying managed network domains and its objects can be achieved,
- Generic symbolic (i.e. graphic) and textual notations of managed objects and of management data and controls associated with the managed objects,
- Built-in zooming capability for examining network conditions in a systematic, hierarchical way,
- Multi-windowing capability for supporting a multi-tasking mode of users' activities,
- Built-in help/advisory (i.e. expert) function. Together, these properties constitute what can be referred to as user interface myth. It is of utmost importance that the user interface myth be consistent across various managed network domains and functional areas so that operator training is minimized and ease of use is maximized.

Through the UUI, the heterogeneous environment will be presented to and managed by the operator generically to the degree possible and practically justifiable

*Presentation Conventions:* In order to achieve the single-image capability of INMS, its integrated network management applications shall apply industry-wide adopted conventions on the semantics and syntax of the user-oriented network management information. This information will be exchanged between the User Interface function and the Integrated Network Management Application function so that generic visual (and potentially audio) constructs can be conveyed to and obtained from INMS users.

*Integrated Management Application Elements:* The integrated management applications provide the value-added management functions that may be accessed via the UUI. These management functions will behave similarly when used for various network domains, although there may be differences between classes of networks (e.g., between LAN and T1 multiplexor networks).

Integrated Network Management Applications (INMA) of INMS are contrasted with Native Network Management Applications (NNMA) of vendor-specific network management systems and/or managed objects. INMAs provide both network management functions directly, and provide access to NNMAs. For example, software loading of a device may be done directly by INMA, or by NNMA at the request of INMA.

Regardless of where a function is performed, the interface to the operator shall remain consistent and generic. Thus, the varying levels of functions provided by Native Network Management systems can be made consistent through INMS.

To develop and utilize INMS generic applications in a modular fashion, the functional space of INMS can be segmented into task-oriented Integrated Network Management Applications, based on classification of user activities. Integrated Network Management Applications may share a set of discrete INMA-Elements defined in the context of several major functional areas (e.g., based on OSI Management Standard).

Each INMA-Element represents the lowest level (i.e. indivisible) architectural application module and is defined in terms of management application services which it provides.

These services are not defined to be a set of services as seen by the INMS user. Rather, they are services provided within the INMS to support open cooperative processing environments by a number of INMA-elements, as well as to support interaction of INMA-elements into task-oriented management application. Thus, the functional area services are used internally among INMS integrated management application elements, while the INMS user sees only the results of these services as provided by the task oriented management applications.

In order to deal with highly complex dynamically changing and relatively uncertain behavior of modern network environments, the task-oriented INMAs are envisioned to include expert system components in addition to conventional procedure-based software nodules.

The expert system components (see fig. 9) will provide for the following features:
- Capture the knowledge of network management experts and represent it explicitly in the form of network management rules (i.e., domain knowledge base),
- Separate the network management information (i.e., facts about network behavior and anatomy from program control structure (represented by a shared logic commonly called Inference Engine),
- Account for qualitative network characteristics along with quantitative ones,
- Introduce limited learning capability through discovery of "new" facts and automatically creating new rules,

These features will produce two major benefits:
- Facilitate an iterative, incremental upgrading of the network management knowledge base both by the users and by the INMS itself. This will augment the INMS's intelligence and reduce the skill requirements to manage networks,
- Allow for modular architecture of the application space and its effective modification.


*Repository of Generic Management Data. Concept of a Generic Managed Object:* The Unified User Interface and Integrated Network Management Applications are based on providing a unified and generic view of heterogeneous networks.

The key to this approach is to define a broad set of generic management information items for describing managed objects and their relations.

Managed Objects (MO) are individual manageable components of a network. Management applications can access and act upon managed objects within a network. Applications can also represent managed objects within the application for the purpose of performing management functions (e.g., to prepare a configuration or record a fault). The offered INMS architectural model makes use of two distinguished concepts - Real Managed Object and Generic Managed Object.
A Real Managed Object (RMO) [11] is simply an actual managed object within a vendor-specific (native) network. Real managed objects are various software and hardware components of a network. Their actual manifestation in a network will be unique to the native network implementation.

An Example of a model of a Real Managed Object which supports OSI communication conventions is illustrated in Figure 10. This object can either represent a Real Open System or a component of a Real Open System and can be viewed as consisting of OSI resources (generic by definition) and of Vendor Specific Real Resources (VSRR) (e.g., CPU, memory blocks, I/O devices, ports, etc.). RMOs can be described for the purpose of management in terms of their vendor-specific anatomy (i.e. configuration), behavior (e.g., status, events, etc.) and controls. INMS integrated management applications ultimately can access and act upon real managed objects. However, because these applications deal only with generic management information items, they cannot access RMOs directly. These must be accessed via a Network Management Gateway (described below), and a generic representation must be used for the RMO.

*Generic Managed Objects (GMO):* are the generic representations of RMOs. Essentially, they are the information "view" an INMS integrated management application has of a real management object.

An example of a model of a Generic Managed Object which supports OSI communications conventions is illustrated in Figure 10. This object can be viewed as consisting of OSI resources (generic by definition) and of Generic Real Resources (GRR) (generic memory blocks, generic I/O devices, etc.).

Generic Managed Objects are specified in terms of Generic Management Information Items (GMII) describing their generic anatomy, behavior and controls.

The INMS Management Information Base then can be viewed as a conceptual repository of those Generic Management Information Items, subsets of which describe Generic Managed Objects plus those Generic Management Information Items which reflect the peculiar needs of the Integrated Network Management Applications themselves (e.g., attributes of a trouble ticket in a Fault Management Application). (See Figure 11).

In summary, GMOs are components of INMS's Management Information Base and will be used as the basis of the design for INMS applications, and will provide a consistent and unified approach to representing the real objects managed by INMS.

*Network Management Gateway - Relation of Generic to Real Objects:* As described above, the use of generic constructs by INMS integrated applications insulates them and the network operator from the unique aspects of each native network. However, a facility is needed to access each native network and to translate (mediate) between the generic INMS constructs and the native constructs of each network.

As shown in Figure 12, the proposed INMS model addresses this need by providing a Network Management Gateway for each native network.

INMS integrated management applications interact with the gateway using a stable set of generic services and protocols. The gateway in turn interacts with the native network objects and management system(s) using native (i.e. vendor-specific) physical and logical interfaces.

The "heart" of the Network Management Gateway is the mapping between Generic Management Information Items used by INMS applications and the equivalent ones of the native network. It is important to notice two basic types of mapping that are performed by the Network Management Gateway:
- Mapping between management data, in essence, establishing a relation (i.e. synchronizing) between a Real Managed Object and its generic information image (i.e. Generic Managed Object),
- Mapping between management applications (i.e. generic and native), in essence emulating Integrated Network Management Application Elements and then employing INMA applica-

tion-level protocols for interaction between INMA-elements of Integrated NMS and emulated INMA-elements of Native NMS.

*Management Application Level Protocols and Shared Communication Services:* One of the key architectural requirements to any practical INMS offering is the provision of a flexible and open distributed organization of the integrated management application.

Flexibility of a distributed organization of INMAs refers to:
- The ability of grouping integrated network management application elements and generic management information items into applications sets, called INMS Network Managers (or simply Integrated Network Managers) and management data sets, called MIB partitions, respectively.
- Non-restrictive assignment of Integrated Network Managers and/or INMS MIB partitions to different and often geographically dispersed computerized systems (e.g., Open End System), from which they can be delivered and, most importantly,
- Perform the integrated management functions in a cooperative processing mode through the use of management application-level protocols.

Openess of a distributed organization of INMAs refers to the interoperability of INMS (or INMS component) offerings from various vendors. This interoperability is being achieved through the use of industry-wide, standard network management protocols (at both the application level and at the supporting communications levels).

International standardization organizations (e.g., CCITT, ISO) and other groups of telecommunications vendors and users (e.g., FORUM) are currently intensively developing initial sets of such application-level protocols.

It is of utmost importance to notice that in order to achieve any meaningful level of commercially viable management-level protocols, a minimum set of generic managed objects shall be developed to represent the corresponding real managed objects. This shall be coupled with a critical set of management services.

In this respect the emerging OSI standards on Common Information Management Protocol [12,13] represent a first important and necessary step. At the same time, without available standards on generic management information items, even limited to OSI resources, the CMIP protocol by itself does not represent a sufficient foundation for building truly open integrated network management systems.

In addition to management application level protocols, the architectural model envisions a range of shared services and communications protocols in support of distributed open Integrated communications protocols in support of distributed open Integrated Network Management Systems (e.g., OSI communications protocols and services, security, directory, remote operation, file transfer accesses and modification, application level protocols and services, to mention some).

*Segmentation of an Integrated Network Management System:* The distributed capabilities of INMS outlined in the previous section will provide for flexible segmentation of INMS into various domains based on specific user needs. Each Integrated Network Manager will be responsible for an assigned subset of managed objects and functional capabilities. Where user network environment represents a strategic business or mission asset, special survivability requirements will dictate both standby INMS domain configurations and multiple alternative connectivity paths available for communication among numerous Integrated Network Managers, and between the managers and critical managed objects.

In summary, the proposed architectural model outlines the major INMS architectural components and their interactions. It offers a modular approach to building commercially viable Integrated Network Management Systems and their components by multiple vendors.

Indeed, the model exhibits the following features and benefits:
- Accommodates incremental expansion of the INMS scope by means of gradual introduction of new generic managed objects and integrated management function elements coupled with the growth of the number of network management gateways to native networks and management systems.
- Calls for integration of discrete network management application elements into user-task oriented management applications. This application level of integration can be significantly advanced by combining expert rules with the generic management information items reflecting the real network environment.
- It is based on standard network management application level protocols along with a range of standard communications support level services and protocols. This facilitates introduction of flexibly segmented and open distributed Integrated Network Management Systems.
- Introduces the concept of a Generic Managed Object as the methodological means for achieving integration at a data level and thereby facilitating integration at application procedure and application protocol levels.
- Identifies key properties of a Unified User Interface which will ultimately convey all benefits of network management integration to the user.

## 5. INTEGRATED NETWORK MANAGEMENT - TRENDS IN THE INDUSTRY

The critical need for integration of disparate network management systems and the emergence of network management integration capabilities as a key differentiator in market competition of various filecommunications products have not gone unnoticed by the industry.

World leading computer manufacturers and communications systems and service providers have articulated their approaches to INMS in architecture/product announcements in the last few years; among them:

IBM's     SNA/Management Services Architecture supported by introduction of a family of NetView and NetView/PC products,
DEC's     Enterprise Management Architecture(EMA)- (not publicly available as of this writing),
AT&T's     Unified Network Management Architecture (UNMA).

To the extent of publicly available information we will contrast these approaches in terms of the proposed INMS model.

*Scope of Integration (the managed object space)*

All three approaches pursue heterogeneous communication equipment environment. At the same time the entry areas of the INMS solution providers are indicative of their business priorities.
IBM's initial focus has been on integration of its own diverse base of customers premise based network components and network management applications.

DEC is expected to follow a similar path due to its installed base of customer premise computer and communication equipment.

AT&T's initial focus is on common carrier equipment (e.g., circuits) with the emphasis on End-to-End management capability, clearly reflecting its positioning in the telecommunications industry.

*Scope of Integration (the functional capabilities)*

The approaches differ in their segmentation and scope of the network management functions (table 1). The table shows that an explicit user task-orientation in functional integration is not present in the approaches. This suggests that targeted network management products may, in the worst case, be deficient in addressing practical user work flows and market needs or, in the best case, require significant customization.

In another observation, all three vendors clearly identify Configuration, Fault and Performance areas as the critical mass" of the functional capabilities in their respective offerings (i.e., products and/or architecture specifications).

*Depth of Integration*

Contrasting the approaches in terms of depth of integration is premature at this time due to the embryonic stage of the offerings.

Nevertheless, the UNMA architecture specifications indicate that AT&T has recognized the prerequisites for high level integration (i.e., at the MIB and procedural levels) and is positioning itself to achieve competitive advantage in the area of depth of integration by publishing an initial set of generic management information items for the critical management functions (i.e., Fault and Configuration management).

*Architectural Approaches*

In terms of the NIMS architectural model all three approaches explicitly identify the equivalents of:
- INMS Unified User Interface,
- Integrated Network Management, Applications
- The Management Application Level Protocols.

   Presently, IBM has introduced its proprietary management application-level protocol (i.e., Network Management Vector Transport) and, at the same time, has announced its plans for supporting OSI management protocols.
   On the other hand both DEC and AT&T have announced that their INMS architectures will be based on evolving OSI management standards.

*Network Management Gateway*
The Network Management Gateway is getting different treatment by the vendors. Although all of them recognize the necessity of interfacing with a variety of specific network management systems, only IBM has explicitly identified the Network Management Gateway as a key INMS architectural component and included a technological platform for its development in the first NetView product line announcement (i.e., NetView/PC).

Management Information Base
The critical role of the Management Information Base in network management integration is getting an increasing recognition by vendors. Both EMA and UNMA have chosen an object oriented approach to MIB structuring [14,15] along the lines of OSI management direction. The first steps are being taken to populate the MIB with generic management information items (e.g.,, NetView's generic alerts, UNMA's generic attributes of circuits, and configuration management messages).

Presentation Conventions
No visible progress has as of yet been achieved in the area of conventions on presentation of network management information to users. It is the author's belief that development of such presentation conventions will facilitate a better understanding of user task-oriented work flows and thereby affect creation of practical INMS-tools.

*Standardization activities in network management*

Standards are the key technological means for achieving cooperative integrated network management.

Numerous national and international forums are working on network management conventions, among them: ISO, CCITT, ECMA, IFIP, IEEE.

While complimentary to each other in effort, these organizations have their own missions and orientations. Specific areas of differentiation and overlaps in the activities of various standards bodies can be easily identified by applying the components of the INMS model.
- For example, based on the targeted space of managed objects IEEE is focused on management of Local and Metropolitan area networks, while CCITT is more oriented towards common exchange carrier networks and interfaces to them, and OSI is developing standards for managing OSI-resources (regardless of the classes of networks these resources are used in - i.e. LANs, ISDNs, Packet Switched Public Data Networks, etc.).
- Another area of different orientation is the segmentation of functional capabilities. While ISO employs the classification of generic functional areas (e.g., Configuration, Fault, Performance Management), CCITT's classification is oriented towards major network management tasks (e.g., Operations, Administration, Maintenance and Provisioning).
- In terms of the INMS architectural model the contributions of ISO focus mostly on the MIB and on application-level protocols, while CCITT includes Network Management Gateway (called Mediation Device) and interfaces to user workstations as part of its architecture of Telecommunications Management Network.

*Challenges.* Currently, standardization of management is developing a momentum and is getting wide attention in the user, vendor and service sectors of the telecommunications industry.

Application of the INMS model to the evaluation of standardization activities reveals a number of fundamental tasks yet to be accomplished by the industry. Among them:
- Reaching consensus in categorization and definition of network management functional capabilities,
- Defining MIB information components through comprehensive modelling of network management functional capabilities and real network objects (e.g., modems, multiplexors, switches, transmissions facilities, etc.)
  Note: The scope of OSI work is limited to management of OSI resources and represents a necessary but in itself insufficient effort to accommodate requirements for managing real network environment.
- Developing conventions on presentation of network management information to INMS users

## 6. Conclusion

Proliferation of heterogeneous networks and their growing strategic role in the functioning of business enterprises and social institutions is becoming one of the characteristics of a modern information intensive society.

This paper has explored the issue of Integrated Management of heterogeneous network environment from a global perspective.

It offered an overall problem statement, a vision for Integrated Network Management Systems and a reference base for evaluating the scope and depth of network management integration.

In addition an architectural model of INMS has been described and applied to contrast directions and offerings of world leading vendors and standards organizations in the area of integrated network management.

The introduced concept of INMS "power of integration" and its components in conjunction with INMS architectural model is intended to facilitate adoption by the industry of a stable INMS reference base. This will help both vendors to drive their R & D efforts, and customers to strategize their INMS product and services selection process.

Although the approach to network management formulated in the INMS model is ambitious and requires substantial research and cooperation between various sectors of the telecommunications industry, it is an approach whose time has come to optimally address the problem of managing heterogeneous networks.

## ACKNOWLEDGEMENTS

I would like to extend my thanks to my ex-colleagues John Erickson and Dr. David Eitelbach from U.S. West/Network Systems Inc. for many thought provoking discussions and for making extremely valuable suggestions on the draft of this paper.

## REFERENCES:

[1] Lev Feldkhun and John Erickson, "Towards an Integrated Management System for Heterogeneous Network Environments", MILCOM 88, San Diego, California

[2] Sandra L. Borthnic, "Take the Job of Communications Management ... Please", Business Communications Review, May-June 1988

[3] ISO DIS 7498/4: Information Processing Systems - Open System Interconnection - Basic Reference Model Part 4-OSI Management Framework, 1987

[4] ISO/IEC JTC1/SC21/WG4 N571: Information Processing Systems - Open Systems Interconnection - Systems Management: Overview (Modified Second Working Draft), 1988

[5] ANSI, T1 Telecommunications, Document Number:T1M1/88-041 Subject: Proposed Standard - Principles of Functions, Architectures, and Protocols for Interfaces Between Operations Systems and Network Elements, 1988

[6] D.B. Rose, J.E. Munn. "SNA Network Management Directions", IBM Systems Journal, Vol 27, No 1, 1988

[7] D. Kanyuh, "An Integrated Network Management Product", IBM System Journal, Vol 27, No 1, 1988

[8] AT&T, "AT&T Network Management Protocol Documentation Overview", Technical Reference TR54004A Addendum 1, 1988

[9] K. Klemba and T. Reusser, USA Expert paper on "Management scenarios as context for OSI Management Standards" ANSI X3T5.4, 87-136

[10] Robert N. Cronk, Paul H. Callahan, Lawrence Bernstein, "Rule-Based Expert Systems for Network Management and Operations: An Introduction", IEEE Network, Vol 2, No 5, September 1988

[11] Lev Feldkhun, USA Expert paper "Comments and Recommendations on the scope and the overall methodology of developing OSI management standards, ANSI X3T5.4, 88-09

[12] ISO DP 9595/1: Information Processing Systems - Open Systems Interconnection- Management Information on Services Part 2 - Common Management Information Services

[13] ISO DP 9596/1: Information Processing Systems - Open Systems Interconnection - Management Information Protocol Part 2 - Common Management Information Protocol

[14] Mark W. Sylor, "Managing Phase V DECnet Networks: The Entity Model", IEEE Network, Vol 2, No 2 March 1988

[15] AT&T, "AT&T Network Management Protocol, Data Modelling and Naming Framework, Issue 1" TR 54007, April 1988

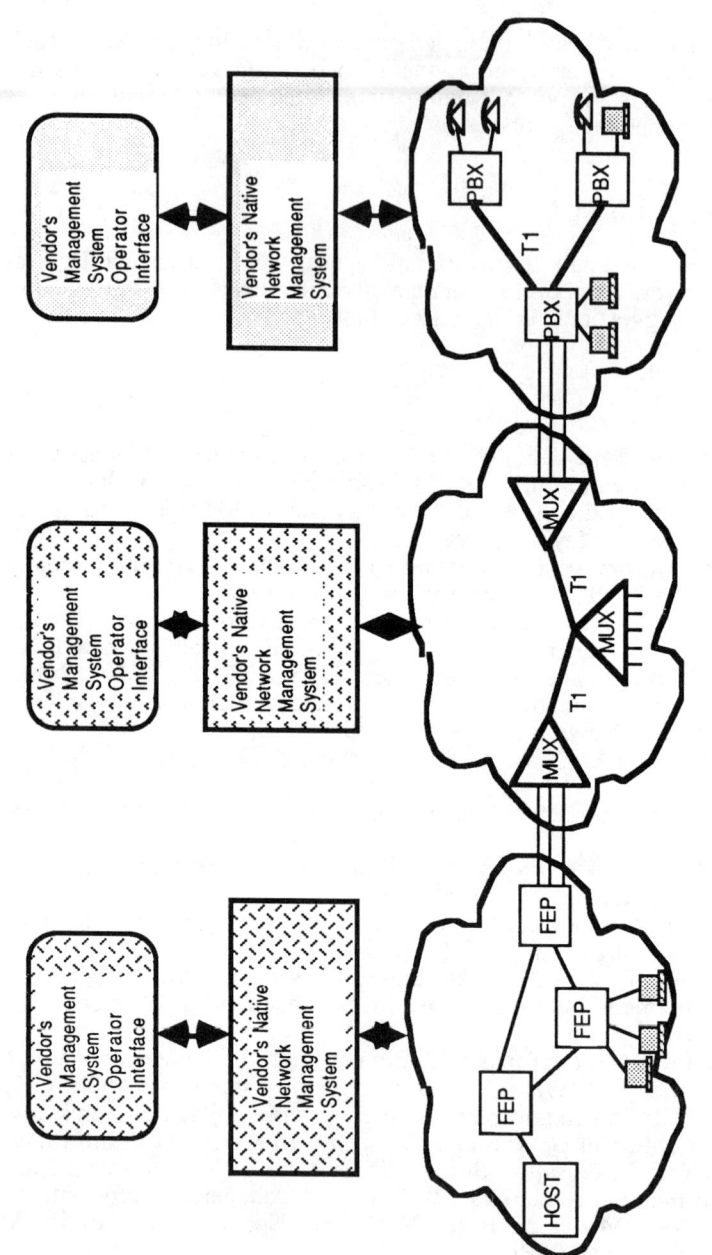

Figure 1. Problems of desparate management systems for a heterogeneous network.

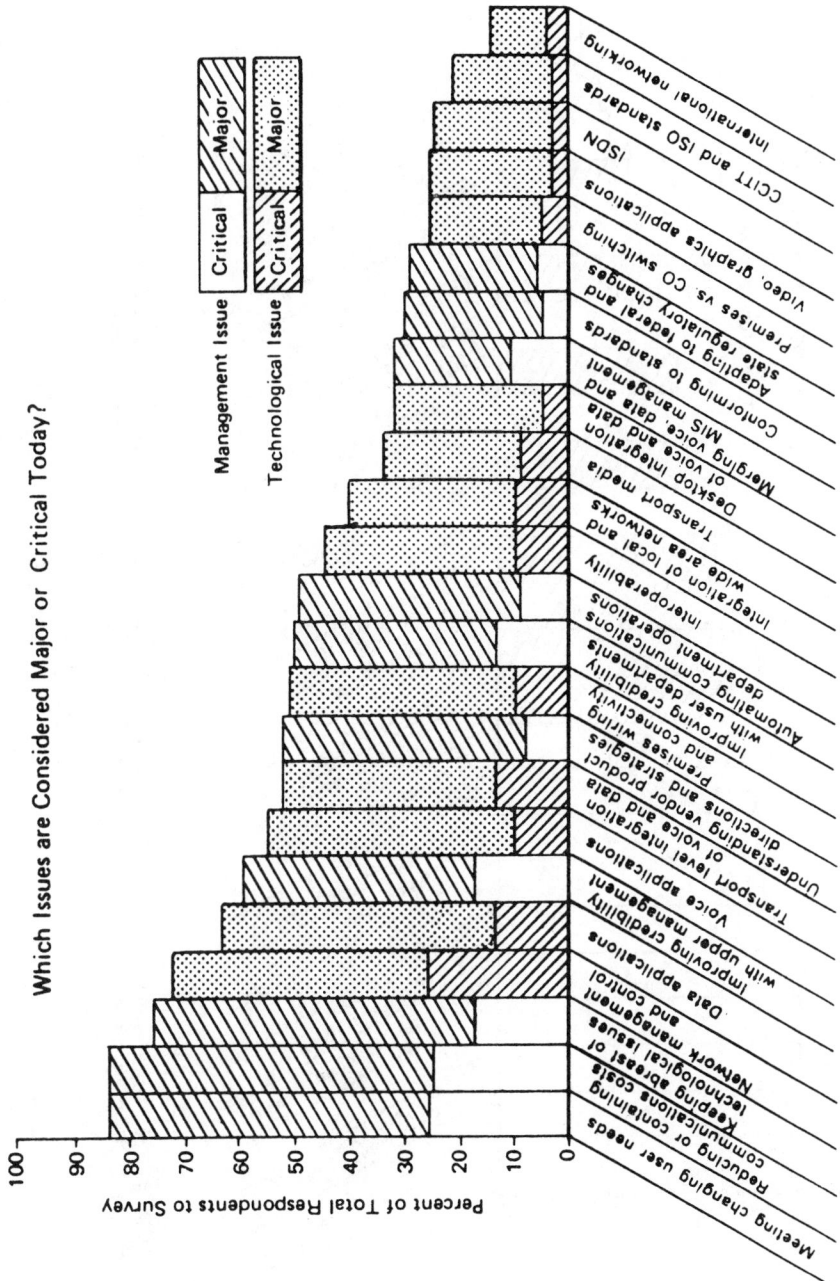

Fig. 2

Copied with permission from Business Communication Review. Results from BCR's Survey of major communications management issues. (May - June 1988)

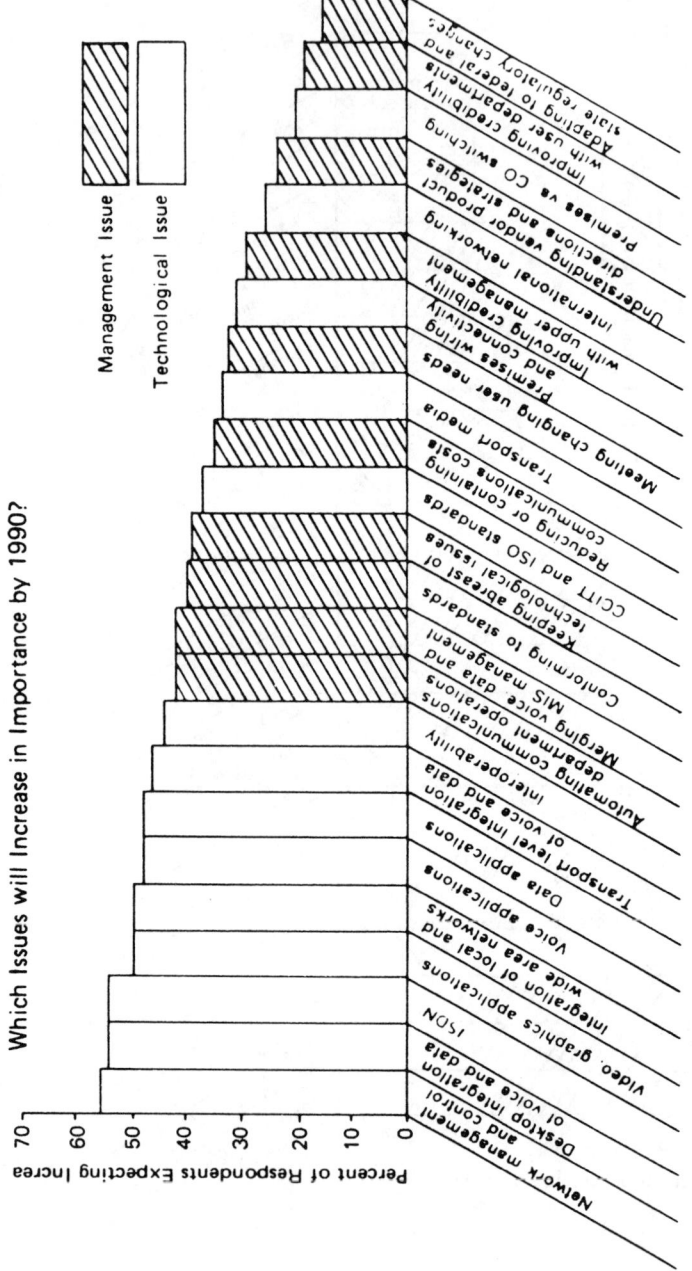

Fig. 3

Copied with permission from Business Communication Review. Results from BCR's survey of major communications management issues. (May - June 1988)

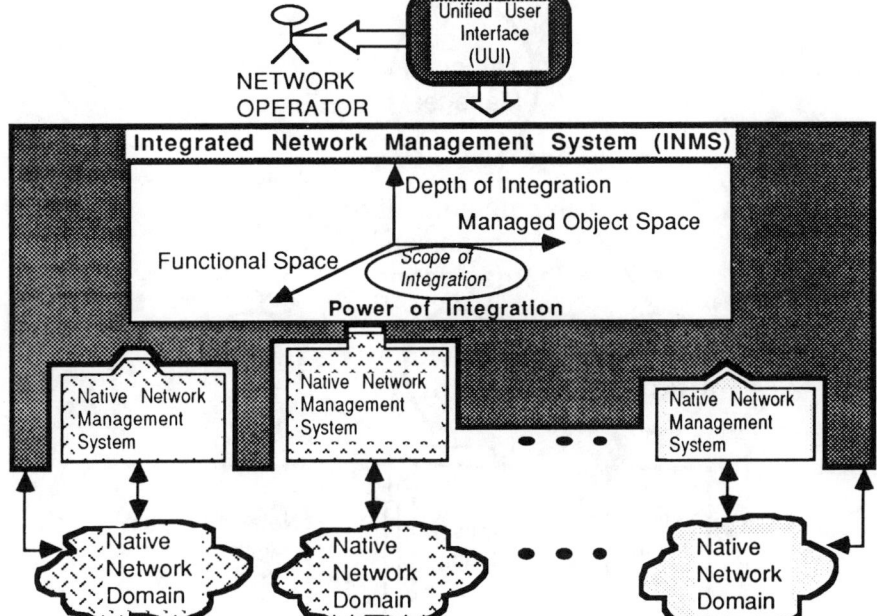

Figure 4. INMS approach to providing a generic network management system.

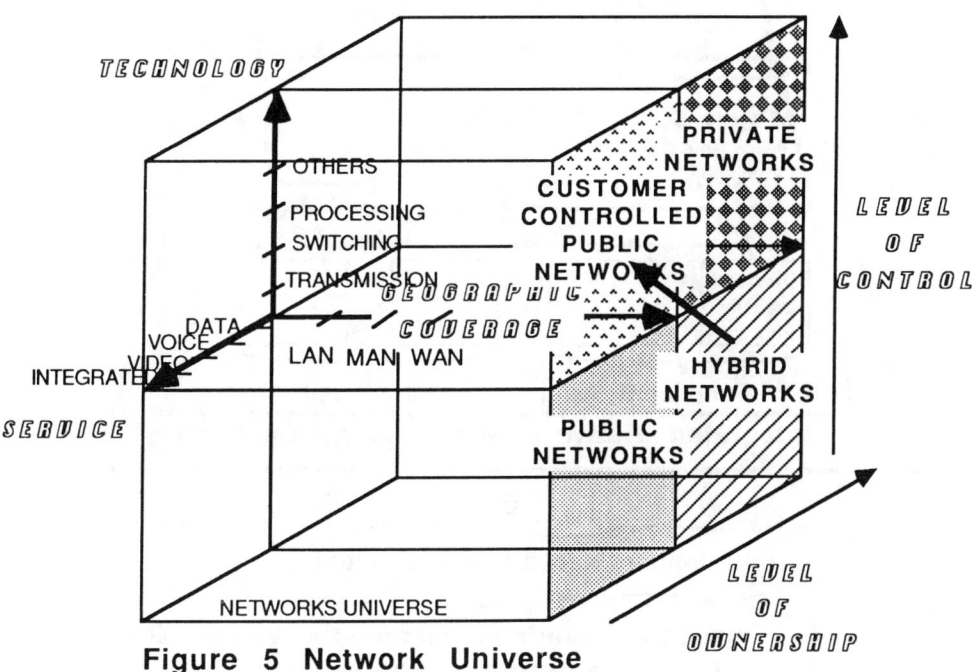

Figure 5 Network Universe

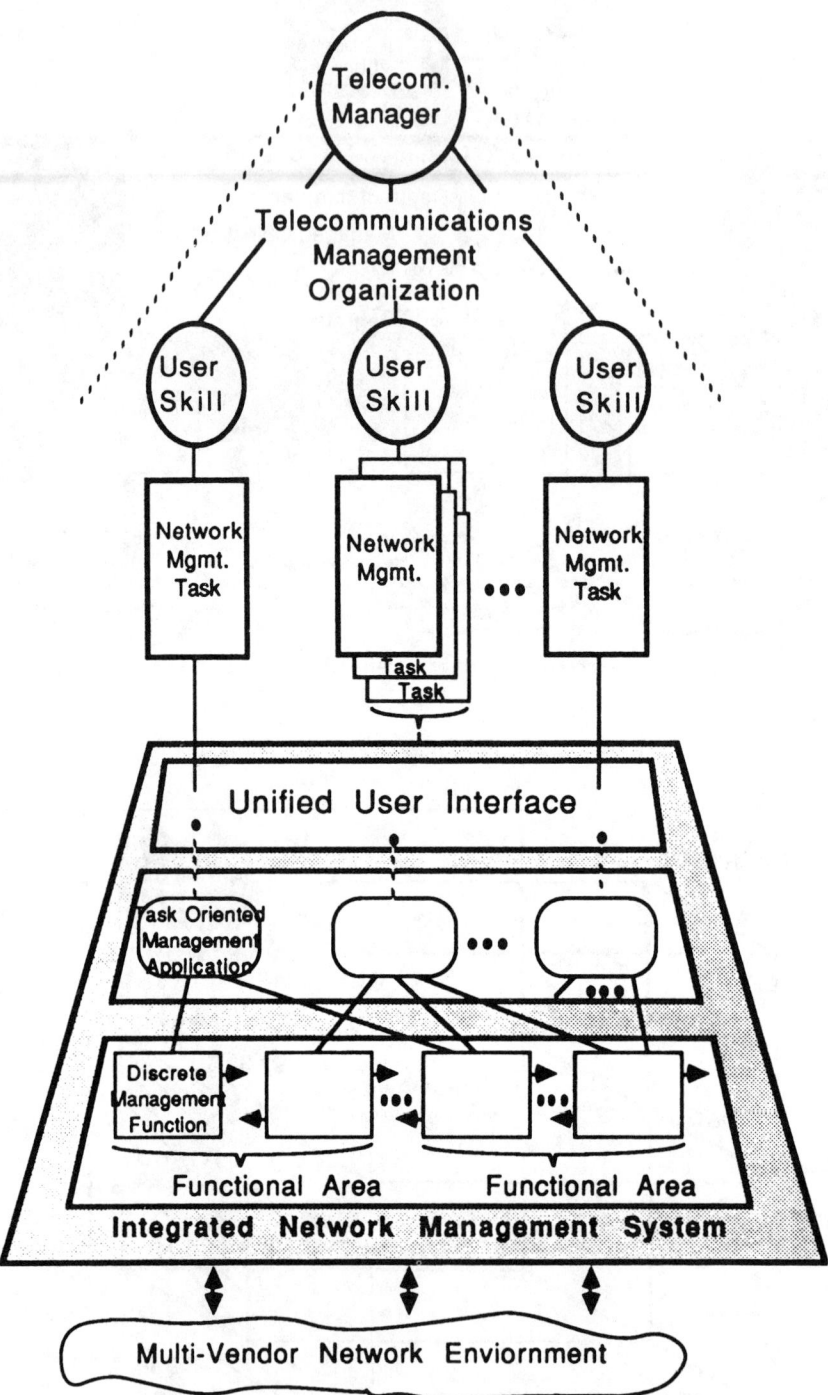

Fig. 6 Telecommunications Manager's Vision On Network Management Enviornment

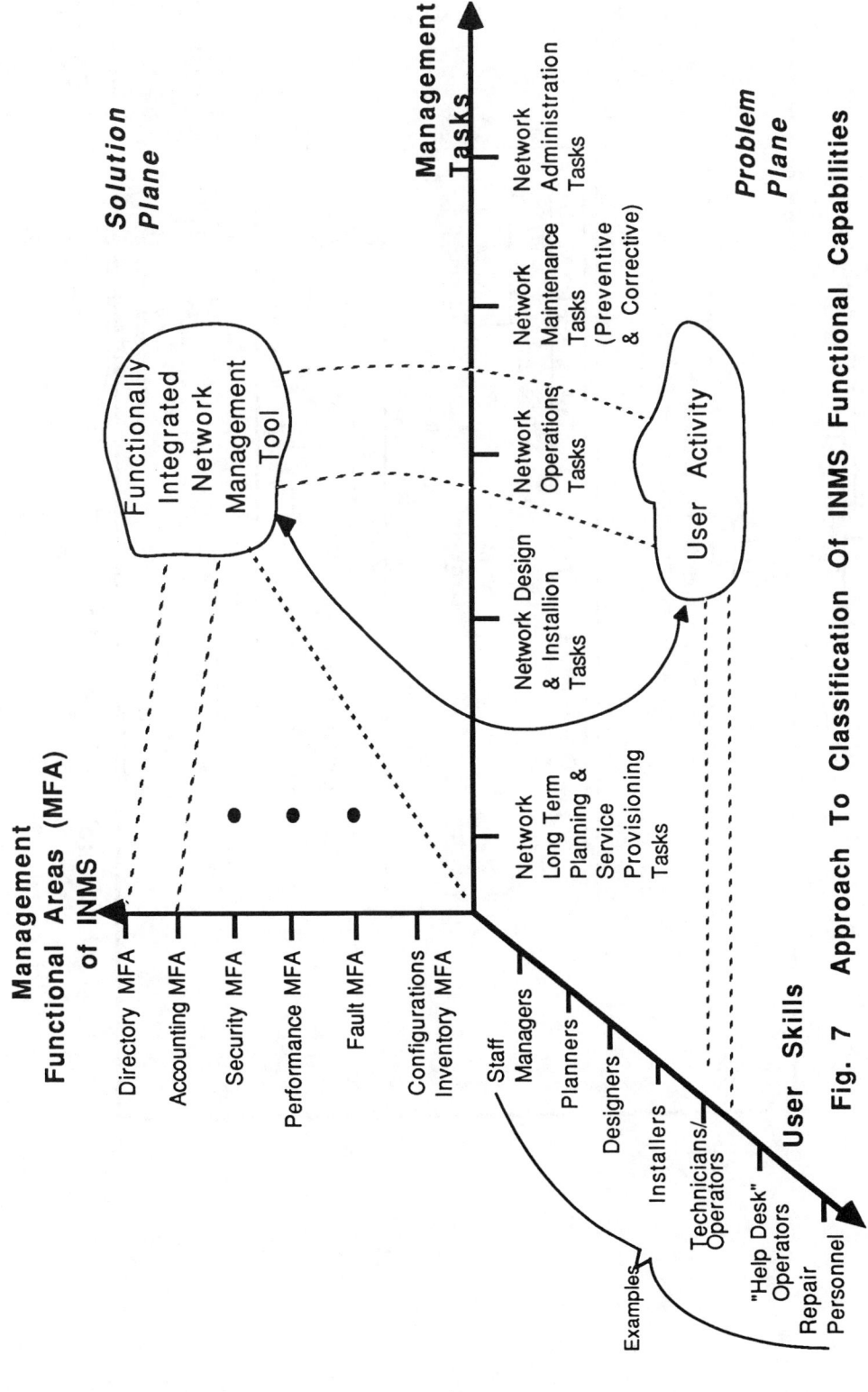

Fig. 7  Approach To Classification Of INMS Functional Capabilities

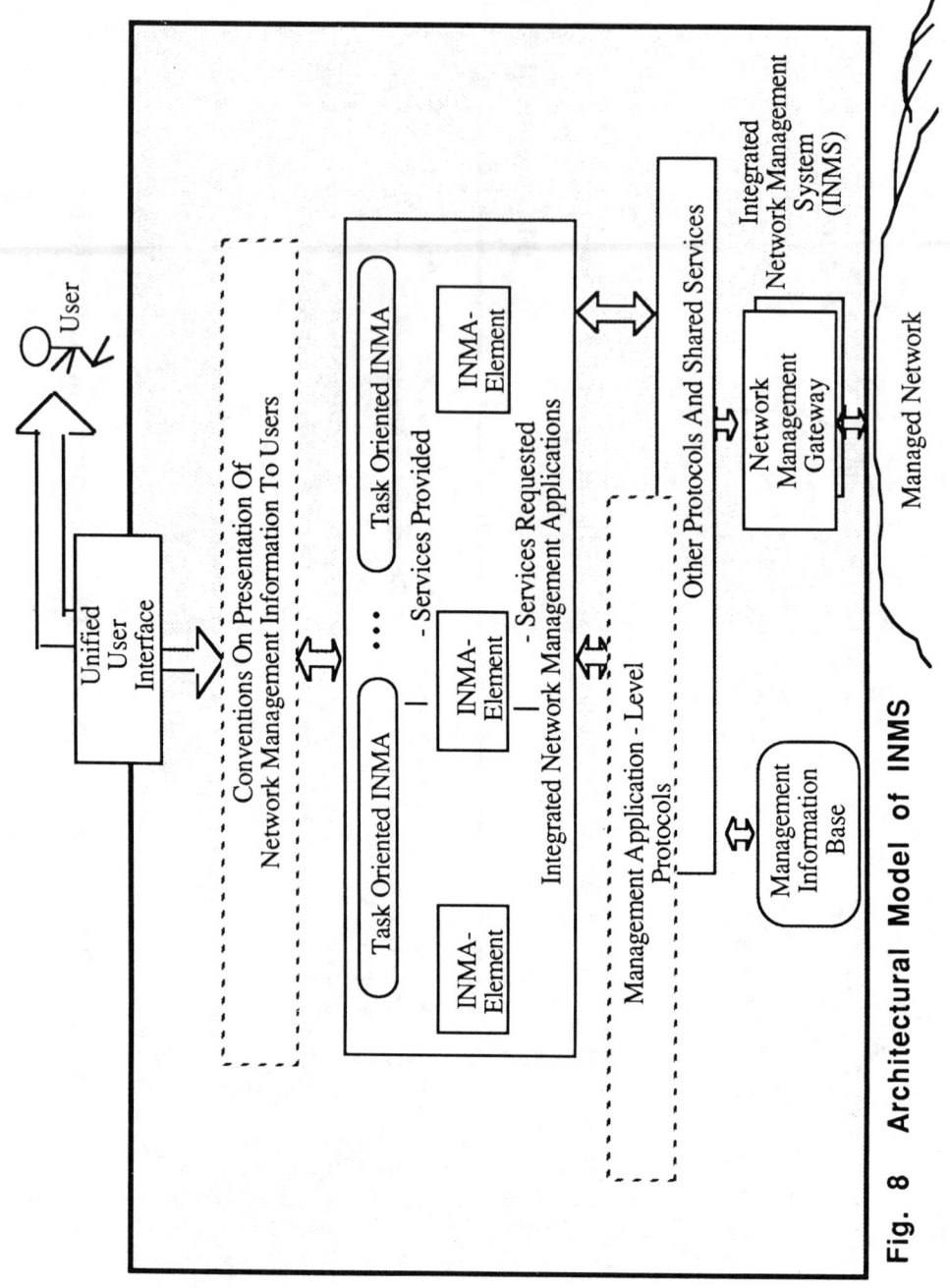

Fig. 8 Architectural Model of INMS

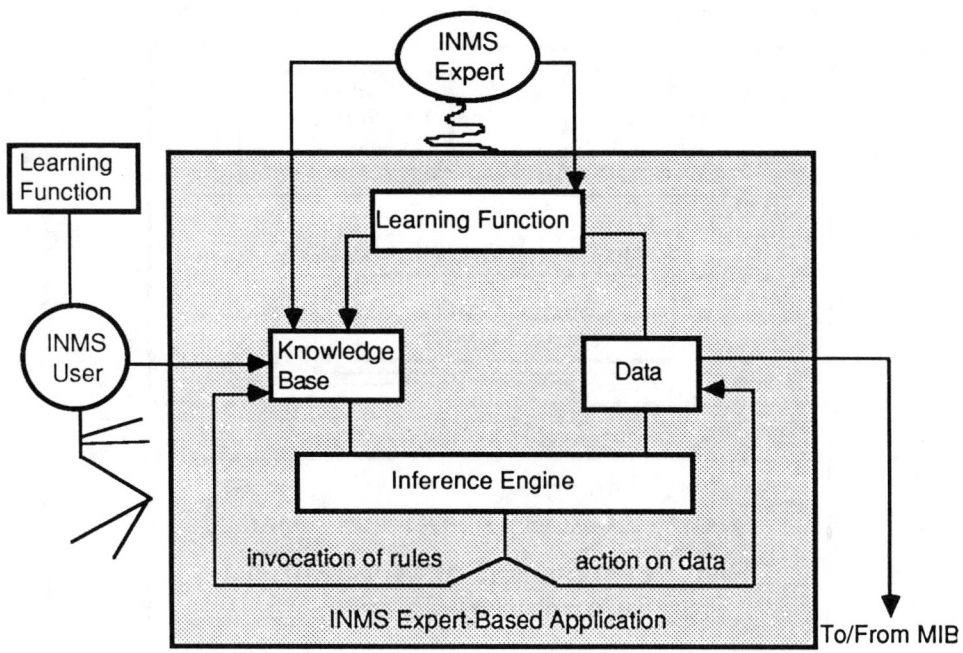

Fig. 9    Role of Expert-based Application in INMS

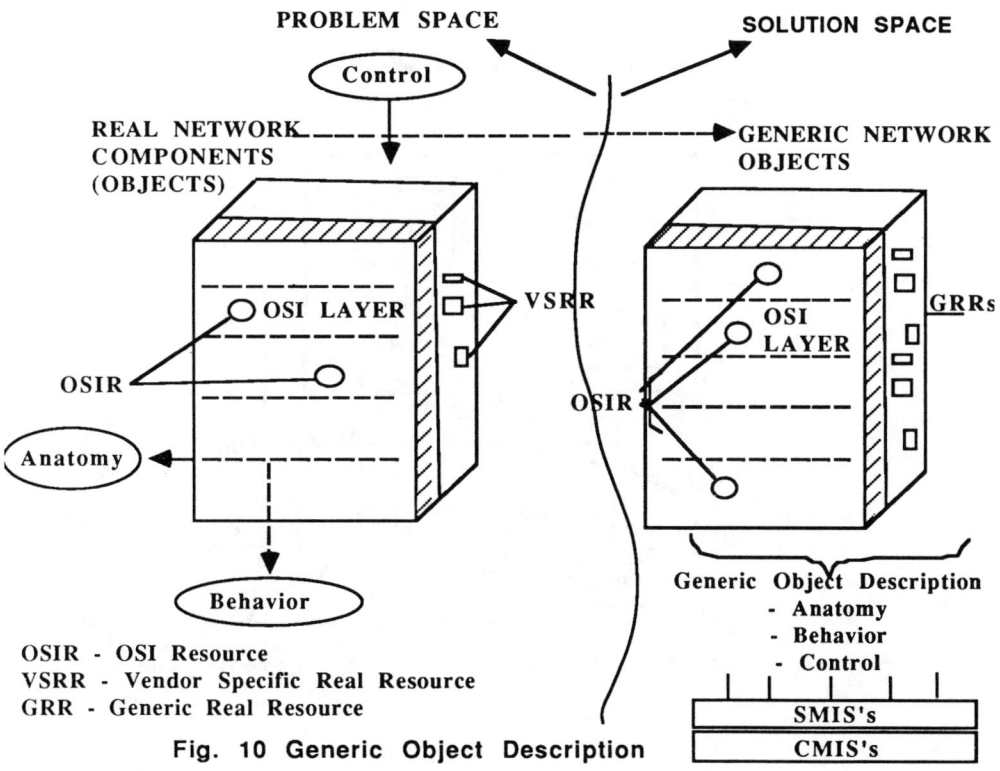

OSIR - OSI Resource
VSRR - Vendor Specific Real Resource
GRR - Generic Real Resource

Fig. 10  Generic Object Description

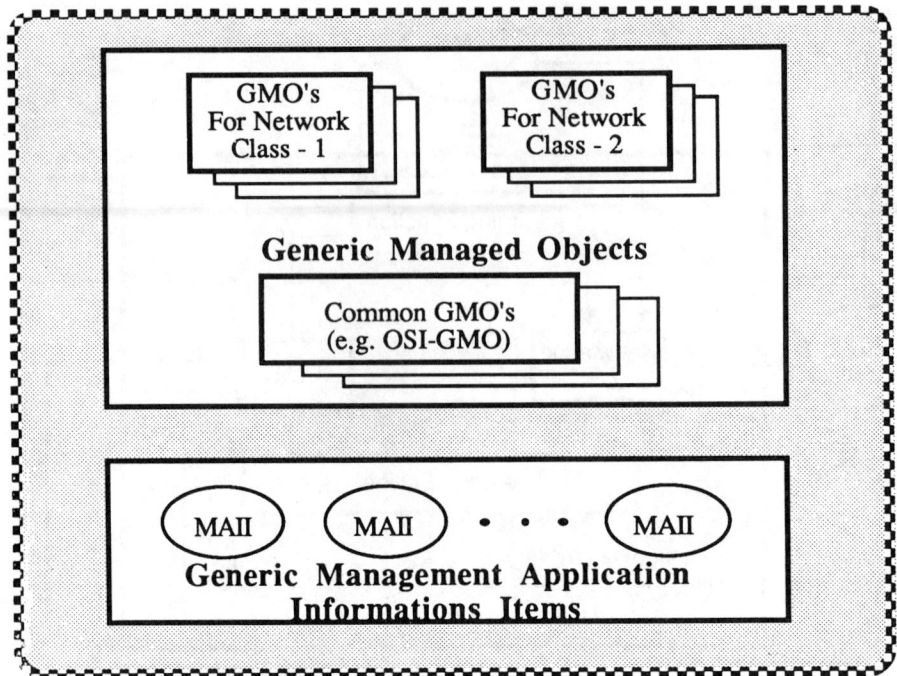

Fig. 11 INMS Management Data Repository

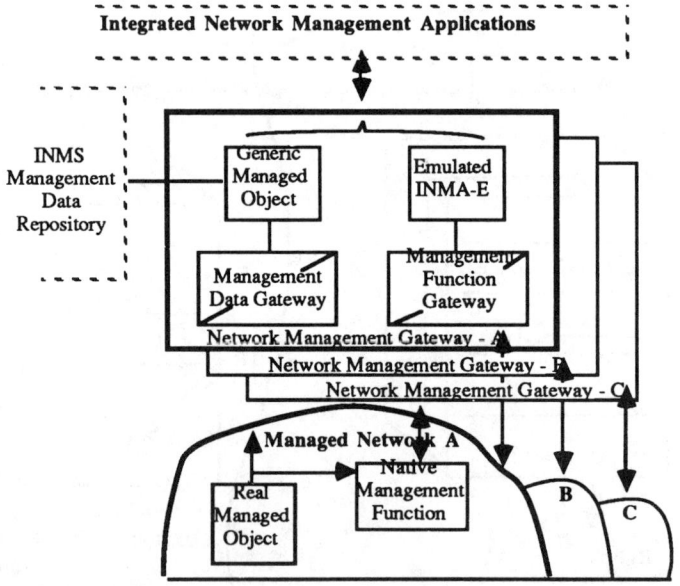

Fig. 12. Architectural Role OF Network Management Gateway

| IBM – SNA/MS | AT&T – UNMA | OSI | CCITT |
|---|---|---|---|
| Problem Management | Fault Management | Fault Management | Administration |
| Configuration Management | Configuration Management | Configuration Management | Maintenance |
| Performance Management | Performance Management | Performance Management | Operations |
| Operation Management | Security Management | Security Management | Provisioning |
|  | Accounting Management | Accounting Management |  |
|  | Network Planning Management | Directory Management |  |
|  | Operations Planning | Note: Information on DEC EMA functional decomposition is not publicly available. It is assumed EMA will follow OSI's functional catagories |  |
|  | Programmability |  |  |
|  | Integrated System Control |  |  |

TABLE 1  Network Management Functional Categories adopted by leading network management industry representatives.

## NETWORK MANAGEMENT

# Distributed Network Management

## Time runs out for mainframe-based systems

What will it take to resolve the network management problems that have plagued the industry since the beginning of distributed computing? Sometimes the most vexing questions have startlingly simple answers: Distributed applications need distributed management.

Two years ago the solution was nowhere near as apparent. In fact, the debate at that time revolved around which centralized management system—IBM's Netview or AT&T's Integrator—would first break free of its proprietary restrictions and move into widespread (multivendor) use (see "Enterprise Management Vendors Shoot It Out," November 1990).

It's not that distributed management schemes were unknown in 1990. Hewlett-Packard's Openview—the pioneering effort in this field—was introduced in 1988. DEC's EMA followed soon after, and Sunnet Manager from Sun Microsystems

---

**James Herman** is a principal with Northeast Consulting Resources Inc. (Boston), a consulting firm focused on strategic management and information technology. His involvement with network management goes back to the mid-1970s, when he worked on management systems for the Internet.

---

made its debut the next year. At best, though, these systems were viewed as promising precursors of a distant future.

But their day has come surprisingly soon. And that means time has run out for mainframe-based management. The Integrator is history. Netview's multivendor effort is stalled in development, though IBM can hardly be ignored when it comes to distributed management. It recently went public with two multivendor management systems: DSM, based on OS/2, and AIX/Netview 6000, based on Openview. The latter is for its recently released 6611 multiprotocol router.

The past two years have brought other changes: While DEC's Enterprise Management Architecture (EMA) helped show the way to distributed management software, users have balked at its proprietary approach. Openview, in contrast, is more closely modeled on emerging open standards and is now a leading distributed management system with broad third-party support. Sunnet Manager has been integrated into almost all of Sun's products, and many suppliers of network devices have based their management systems on it. But Sun, the foremost vendor of Unix workstations, refuses to back industry efforts at standardization, which could hurt it in the long term. Novell, meanwhile, is pushing third-party developers to use its open management platform and proprietary APIs (application program interfaces) to write management software for Netware—an interesting turn of events for the preeminent supplier of PC LANs. Although Novell's APIs are proprietary, it seems to be one of the few vendors that can still get away with setting a de facto standard.

Further, where industry standards were once set by the likes of IBM and based on OSI, they're now the work of such consortia as the Open Software Foundation (OSF, Cambridge, Mass.) and—to a lesser degree—Unix International (UI, Parsippany, N.J.). The former is close to specifying a standard set of services for a Distributed Management Environment (DME) that will bring management to everything from bridges, routers, hubs, and similar equipment through server-based operating systems and applications. Once OSF DME is released early next year it will likely become the blueprint for management systems from both system vendors and third parties. OSF's rival Unix International also is working on a specification for distributed management as part of UI-Atlas; it's expected to include many of the same features as DME. Whether Atlas will garner the same level of industry support is uncertain.

One thing is sure: The same distributed computing model that has shifted applications from data centers to far-flung departments is pushing manage-

By James Herman, Northeast Consulting Resources Inc.

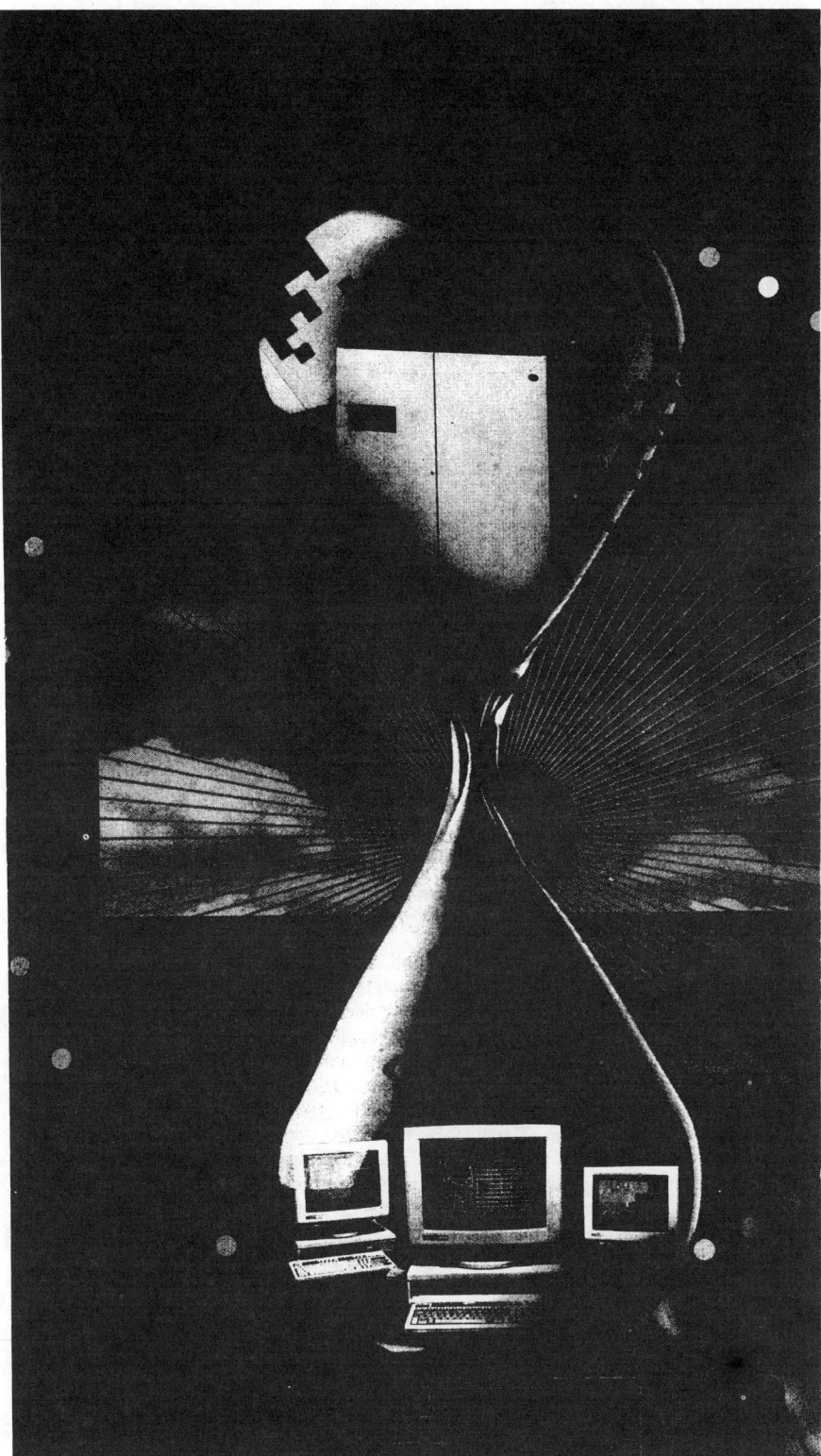

ment out of its glass house. But if centralized management consoles are a thing of the past, what will take their place? The answer—for now—is interoperable workstations located throughout the LANs that make up an enterprise. With a distributed architecture, managers who must watch over downsized applications and PC LANs have the tools they need to keep networks, systems, and applications humming along. And MIS diehards needn't worry that decentralization is tantamount to anarchy. One central workstation on a LAN, with global access rights and the ability to manage all network resources, can interact with less-enabled management stations while reserving the final say about what can and can't be done.

Or, to keep it simple, management systems are going where the applications are.

**BITS AND PIECES**

Distribution allows management software to be split up and run on separate computers linked over high-speed networks, with numerous benefits. First off, RISC workstations and PCs deliver more power at lower cost than mainframes. Distributed management also means greater scalability. Since the software in a distributed system doesn't know or care if it is on one computer or many, adding management is merely a question of deploying another inexpensive workstation at the desired location. And multiple, networked stations eliminate the single point of failure that exists with centralized schemes.

Distributed management on Unix platforms gives LAN administrators access to some of the best software development tools available, increasing programming productivity and yielding higher-quality programs. As a result, distributed systems can generally be counted on to improve more quickly than their older, centralized counterparts. And users at workstations get the benefit of graphical user interfaces rather than being faced with character-based dumb terminals.

In essence, distribution delivers management information and tools wherever they're needed in a network. In this it parallels distributed applications that give such diverse groups as engineering and marketing access to the wealth of information stored in a database. Information contained in configuration databases

## NETWORK MANAGEMENT

## Decentralized Control

might be equally valuable to management personnel at different levels of an enterprise. They also might want to monitor alarms and trouble tickets. A distributed management system makes it possible to forward alarms to all clients and servers that request such information, keeping everyone who may be affected up to date on a variety of network events. For example, a critical alarm might be passed from the alarm collection server to the trouble-ticket database servers, where a problem record would be automatically created. That record could then be propagated across the network.

Bear in mind that one of the great advantages of distributed management is that it allows clients and network resources from different vendors to be brought into one cohesive system and put under the watchful eye of one server-based management system. In the future, management servers from different suppliers will be mixed and matched across a network as well.

Most of the distributed management systems now being built follow the same basic structure (see Figure 1). At the top are management clients that give users access to management services and implement the graphical user interface. The interface between the client and the management service is usually based on X-Windows; the user interface typically implements the OSF's Motif or AT&T/Sun's Openlook. Most advanced management systems will eventually offer native support for a number of different clients, including one or more versions of Unix, OS/2, DOS and DOS with Windows from Microsoft Corp. (Redmond, Wash.), and Macintosh System X from Apple Computer Inc. (Cupertino, Calif.).

Clients can be linked to management servers in a variety of ways. Remote procedure calls (RPCs) are emerging as the preferred approach, since they allow the client to handle a larger share of the processing than any other communications scheme (see "Distributed Management: Pieces of the Puzzle," page 78).

The main components of a distributed management system are the management servers. These store management information and run most of the management software. They also store common management-data models and route management information to applications and clients. As mentioned, the key to distrib-

### Figure 1: Distributed Management at a Glance

Today's distributed management systems typically are built around multiple management servers that interact with clients, network resources, and one another. Clients and network gear need not be from one vendor.

uted management is dividing software and data among a number of servers, as the processing needs of the enterprise dictate. That is what makes distributed management both scalable and flexible.

Agents and element managers communicate directly with network resources. Agents—software modules that reside in the devices being managed—collect management information and forward it to the management servers. The dialogue between an agent and management server is usually based on a standard such as the simple network management protocol (SNMP) or the common management information protocol (CMIP). In some cases, management servers can only reach resources through a vendor-specific element manager. This shortcoming is the biggest obstacle to the effective use of distributed management.

Until all devices support standard management protocols, users will have to maintain separate element-management systems. Management agents are typically supplied by vendors of routers, bridges, hubs, file servers, operating systems, and applications. The management software that runs on the servers is furnished by systems vendors such as IBM, Digital Equipment Corp. (Maynard, Mass.), and Hewlett-Packard Co. (Palo Alto, Calif.).

Makers of general-purpose servers and software like Novell Inc. (Provo, Utah) also provide it, as do equipment vendors like Cabletron Systems Inc. (Rochester, N.H.). Management applications and database software is available from such third-party software developers as Concord Communications Inc. (Marlborough, Mass.), CACI Products

## NETWORK MANAGEMENT

## Decentralized Control

Co. (La Jolla, Calif.), Make Systems Inc. (Mountain View, Calif.), Protools Inc. (Beaverton, Ore.), and Remedy Corp. (Mountain View, Calif.).

**OSF ON TOP**

Almost all distributed management vendors have pledged to support the APIs and the protocols included in the OSF's DME. Given that the OSF's original charter was to develop an industry-standard version of Unix, its pivotal role in the creation of communications and management standards for distributed applications is nothing short of phenomenal.

The OSF's biggest success so far has been its Distributed Computing Environment (DCE), released earlier this year. DCE software, when installed on servers and clients, delivers a common set of communications services. IBM, DEC, HP, Groupe Bull S.A. (Paris), and Siemens AG (Munich) are among those that have given their blessing to DCE. UI has incorporated DCE services into UI-Atlas.

DCE uses RPCs for application-to-application communications; it also includes a distributed file system, security system, and distributed directory. If there is a downside to DCE, it's that its success will add a new layer of management problems (distributed servers, operating systems, applications) on top of the old (bridges, routers, hubs, modems, multiplexers).

The OSF realizes this. To promote effective management of open, distributed systems based on DCE, it has defined a distributed management environment. Although DME is specifically tailored to DCE, it already has earned strong industry backing. Indeed, the OSF standard will likely be adopted for a broad range of management applications.

The OSF has chosen to implement most of DME as object-oriented software, which it believes will make it easy to integrate management applications from many vendors. In essence, DME will exist chiefly as a large, distributed collection of objects that represent resources being managed. Object-oriented software is structured as small pieces (methods) that are attached to data structures (objects). Each method will perform a specific function in the context of a particular kind of managed resource. Thus, the "load" method attached to the object "router" will initiate a different action from the "load" method attached to the object "PC." Users work with the DME graphical user interface to invoke management functions (methods) and re-

### Distributed Management: Pieces of the Puzzle

Distributed management is making great strides. But true interoperability remains elusive. In order for multivendor management workstations to appear as one system to an operator, all the management products deployed on an enterprise must share a common set of communications technologies. These technologies include an interprocess communications (IPC) mechanism, distributed directory, database (unified management data model), and security system.

An IPC allows management clients to communicate with management servers, enables management servers to communicate with one another, and permits managed devices (such as application servers) to communicate with management servers.

At the moment, remote procedure calls (RPCs) have gained the greatest acceptance as the IPC for all kinds of distributed systems, not just network management. RPCs are a generalized version of the standard subroutine call used in most modular programming systems. In an RPC environment, one module (program) can call another, pass arguments to it, and receive values back—even though the modules reside on different computers. The same procedure call also works if the modules happen to be on the same platform, which means that resources can be relocated easily and without any recoding.

With RPCs, the management system itself is extended right into the system being managed. Conventional management protocols like CMIP are actually eliminated and replaced by subroutine calls between management agents and the rest of the system. The obvious simplicity of this approach is very appealing. Equally appealing is the fact that RPCs cut down on network traffic: Managed devices (say, servers) can perform a greater share of processing than they could using a low-level management protocol. SNMP, for instance, is not geared toward cooperative processing; its purpose is to ensure that agents are kept small and the operations they perform remain simple.

The problem with the RPC approach, in particular, and distributed management, in general, is that industry standards are lacking. Sun's RPC, which is part of its Open Network Computing (ONC) package, is the most widely used, but it's not available on all major workstations. The RPC specified in the Open Software Foundation's distributed computing environment (DCE) should fill this gap.

Communications can be further simplified by using message passing instead of or in conjunction with RPCs. Message passing lends itself to object-oriented software like the OSF's distributed management environment (DME). In essence, objects communicate by sending back and forth messages that invoke routines (methods).

The OSF agrees that message passing is the best long-term approach to communicating in an object-oriented environment like DME and has decided to layer a message-passing facility on top of its RPC facility.

Distributed management also needs distributed directories to keep track of its many components. In general, there's a growing need to integrate directory systems with management systems in all types of applications. DEC has done the best job so far in this regard. The DECmcc implementation of its Enterprise Management Architecture (EMA) is tightly coupled with its Distributed Name System (DNS), allowing any module on any system to access data about any object the system is managing. Other vendors use kludgey ASCII files that must be updated manually to keep track of network retrieve management data (objects).

If all goes according to the OSF's plan, DME will ultimately comprise a growing number of generic objects (say, a router or a software routine that generates a certain kind of report) and vendor-specific objects (for instance, a Cisco AGS+ router running Release 9 software). Both types of objects will be written by users, vendors, and independent software developers.

The two key components of the DME are the Management Request Broker (MRB) and Object Server (see Figure 2). The MRB implements the basic APIs that access the services furnished by the DME. Management agents or applications make calls to the MRB, which executes the requisite management function and returns information to the agent or application.

The MRB establishes a standardized programming interface to SNMP and CMIP, which is known as the Consolidated Management API (CM-API). This interface is the handiwork of Groupe Bull and has been adopted by industry consortium X/Open (London), which renamed it XMP (X/Open Management Protocol).

More important, the MRB provides a way for management applications to invoke one of the methods associated with a DME object. Methods are called by sending a message to the object indicating the method to be executed and including any arguments to be passed to it. The MRB sends the message to the particular object server associated with the target object. The MRB finds that object by using the DCE directory services. DME objects "live" in an object server. The object server also furnishes access to the data stored in the object and can create or delete instances of an object.

### DISTRIBUTION WITHOUT DELAY

Just a few years ago IBM was advising customers to take a mainframe-based approach not just to network management but for managing all network and system resources. These days, its OS/2 business group (Austin, Texas) is making an all-out effort to produce a fully open, distributed management system based on OS/2—OS/2 Distributed Systems Management (DSM). It expects to deliver late in 1992 or early in 1993.

Why the change of heart? IBM knows that users are relying more and more on PCs, workstations, and high-powered servers for most of their computing, and it wants OS/2 to play a big part in their futures. Making OS/2 serv-

---

sources. The OSF's DCE includes a directory system based on X.500 and a variant of DEC's DNS. Objects that are part of the DME are registered in the directory; the DME Management Request Broker (MRB) locates them by making calls to the directory.

The greatest challenge for distributed management is designing a database that can deliver configuration and inventory information to all management servers. Most distributed management systems use relational databases. DEC is the chief exception; it employs an object-oriented DBMS (database management system).

Few, if any, relational databases can be distributed efficiently. While it is possible to fully replicate an entire relational database on multiple servers, it's not yet possible for databases on different servers to update one another by sending only changes: The entire database must be sent each time, with obvious drawbacks. The most popular relational databases from Oracle Corp. (Redwood Shores, Calif.) and Sybase Inc. (Emeryville, Calif.) cannot partially replicate data. Thus, the database is potentially the Achilles' heel of distributed management because the entire relational database must be kept on one server. That server can quickly become a performance bottleneck when WANs are involved. For the time being, then, distributed management is limited to workstations linked over high-speed LANs in a building or on a campus.

This is not a severe restriction. Although network resources are often managed over WANs using remote clients, it's not often necessary for management servers to be connected over WANs. Those corporations that do have multiple, remote operation centers today can define multiple databases located at each site. One database might include information about the network at that site, while the database at a different site would contain similar information about the network there. This approach might prevent the corporation from preparing reports about its entire network, but it would not limit the effective management of the entire network.

Security also is a major issue for distributed management—in three specific regards. First, a way is needed to authenticate users on clients and control access to data. Simple password schemes are used in most systems, but they are insufficient. The Kerberos system developed as part of Project Athena at the Massachusetts Institute of Technology (Cambridge) is rapidly gaining acceptance as an encryption-based approach to authentication. OSF's DME will use Kerberos-style authentication.

Second, a way must be found to protect against computers masquerading as legitimate management servers. Hackers could easily spoof a management server and hence take control of critical enterprise resources. Once again, encryption-based authentication can offer the needed protection. The OSF's DCE authenticates any RPC request using a security service. Few distributed management systems deliver this level of protection, another reason that OSF DME will be an important step forward in industrial-strength management technology.

Third, a way is needed to secure the interactions between management servers and agents so that hackers cannot masquerade as management servers and extract sensitive management data from an agent, or worse, tell the agent to disrupt the operation of the device it is managing. An active program of development and testing is under way to add security mechanisms to SNMP. It seems that efforts to secure CMIP are still a few years off.  —*J.H.*

## Decentralized Control

ers extremely manageable and making OS/2 management applications easy to develop are two ways that IBM plans on realizing its goal.

OS/2 DSM conforms closely to the distributed model described earlier and typifies the approach taken by most vendors (see table). A DSM server implements the operating system, DSM system software, APIs, IBM and third-party applications, and a graphical interface (see Figure 3). More than one DSM server can be located on the same network.

DSM incorporates the CM-API offered with OSF DME, as well as SNMP, CMOT (CMIP over TCP/IP), and CMOL (CMIP over Logical Link Control), the new IEEE LAN management standard. By accommodating so many management protocols, IBM expects to be able to keep tabs on nearly all the clients, servers, bridges, routers, and so forth that can be found on a network. IBM also is developing a stripped-down version of DSM that will serve as an agent in OS/2 clients and servers running business applications. Here again, it will use the CM-API agent so that third-party developers can readily build DSM-compatible applications.

At first, CMIP will be used as the communications mechanism between OS/2 DSM servers, but as the object-oriented components of OSF DME stabilize, IBM will incorporate RPC or message-passing mechanisms into its management framework. Management servers can be accessed by clients running the IBM Common User Access (CUA) interface. Thus, a distributed, client-server approach is possible in which any number of intelligent clients running OS/2, DOS, DOS with Windows, or Unix can access the OS/2 DSM software running on the servers. DSM supports a standard SQL (structured query language) interface to access a relational database. The database can be from any vendor, although IBM recommends using OS/2 Extended Services database manager. OS/2 DSM can pass information to mainframe-based Netview, but a centralized host is not needed for a complete management solution.

IBM's second distributed management system is AIX Netview/6000. This product is based on HP's Openview, and for now is intended primarily to manage IBM's 6611 multiprotocol routers. It should be available this month. AIX Net-

### Figure 2: DME in Detail

The chief components of the OSF's DME are management request brokers (MRBs) and object servers. Together, the two fulfill requests for information from management applications and control the flow of information to and from agents and network resources.

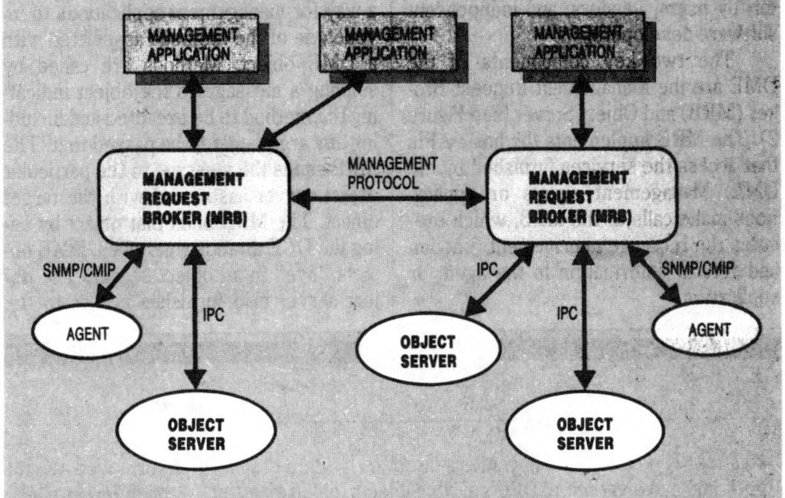

CMIP = Common management information protocol   IPC = Interprocess communication

view/6000 is being developed separately from DSM, although many of its APIs and functions are based on the same industry standards. Applications developed on one system should thus be able to run on the other, and the choice between DSM and Netview/6000 may well come down to whether a user wants OS/2 or Unix.

**TAKING IN THE VIEW**

Of all the network and system management vendors, HP has been pushing the open, distributed approach longest and hardest. Openview runs on HP workstations and minicomputers, as well as on Sun stations, and can manage almost the entire line of HP products, including hubs, bridges, routers, and servers.

Openview typifies the distributed management systems running under Unix that employ the X-Windows user interface and are being ported to many vendors' hardware. Its components include communications protocols, data storage services, user interface services, object managers, and management applications. All are linked with what HP calls its Distributed Communication Infrastructure, which at the moment uses a variant of CMIP.

Since Openview has been chosen as a core component of OSF DME, HP will have to adapt it to the OSF RPC.

Openview is enjoying increasing popularity among vendors; both IBM and Network Equipment Technologies Inc. (NET, Redwood City, Calif.) are using it as an underlying technology in management systems. HP also has a DOS version of Openview, but this is not really a distributed manager. The real thing is the Unix version, which HP will now be calling the Openview Distributed Manager. When the next release is available—in the third quarter of this year—it will support CM-API, as well as an enhanced Motif-based user interface and a full SQL database.

**ALL DECKED OUT**

DEC has been bringing out EMA software for its network products since 1988 and has been careful to build new products that support EMA. As a result, EMA now manages most DEC products. As part of EMA, DEC has defined the DECmcc open management platform, which uses a combination of RPCs and its own Distributed Name Service (DNS) to deliver the most

## NETWORK MANAGEMENT

### Decentralized Control

sophisticated distributed management architecture of any of the vendors.

DEC has defined APIs that allow three types of application modules to plug into a DECmcc management server: access modules, function modules, and presentation modules. Access modules control the link between the server and agents in managed resources. Function modules take care of processing the management information. Presentation modules establish user interfaces and handle report processing.

What sets DECmcc apart is the use of DNS to locate modules and dynamically establish connections between modules. All other vendors rely on more primitive tables and files to locate the different pieces of their systems. Such tables and files must be updated manually whenever a change is made to the network.

When the OSF DME is completely operational, it too will use a fully distributed directory service to establish RPC connections between different components. DEC's architectural specifications for DECmcc show a completely distributed platform. It's true that the APIs communicate via an RPC service, thus allowing modules to be located on separate systems. But at this point, all DECmcc management software has to be located on one server (multiple clients are possible). A truly distributed product should be available by the end of this year.

DECmcc has gotten only lukewarm support from third parties. A few U.S. vendors of network equipment have created access modules to make their equipment visible to EMA, but virtually no U.S. software developers have written function modules to deliver network management to those network devices. It's a different story in Europe, where Alcatel N.V. (Paris) and Ing. C. Olivetti & Co. SpA (Milan, Italy) have put DECmcc to work in a number of management software applications. In addition, DEC's Polycenter program has helped it work successfully with some third-party developers to produce management applications for large VAX minicomputers and mainframes from DEC, IBM, and Unisys Corp. (Blue Bell, Pa.).

## Distributed Management from Today's Leaders

| Vendor | IBM | DEC | HP | Novell | Sun |
|---|---|---|---|---|---|
| Product | OS/2 Distributed Systems Management (OS/2-DSM) Circle No. 412 | DECmcc Circle No. 413 | Openview Circle No. 414 | Network Management System (NMS) Circle No. 415 | Sunnet Manager Circle No. 416 |
| Status | Close to shipping | Shipping; manages all DEC products, some third-party interfaces and applications | Shipping; manages all HP products, many third-party interfaces and applications | Just shipping now; many third-party applications promised | Shipping; manages all Sun products, many third-party applications |
| Server operating system | OS/2 | VMS, Ultrix, OSF/1 | HP-UX | OS/2, Windows | SunOS |
| Clients | OS/2 | X-Windows | OSF Motif | OS/2, Windows | X-Windows |
| Management protocol | SNMP, CMOT, CMOL | SNMP, NICE, CMIP | SNMP, CMOT (CMIP 4Q92) | SNMP, Novell-specific protocols | SNMP, Sun RPC |
| Interprocess communications (IPC) | CMIP | DEC RPC | CMIP variant | None; no multiple management servers | Sun ONC |
| Database | Any SQL; comes with OS/2 ES Database Manager | Proprietary, object-oriented | Any SQL; comes with Ingres | Shipped with Novell Btrieve | None |
| API | CM-API | DEC proprietary, full OSF support promised, no timeframe announced | Third-quarter release will support CM-API; full OSF support promised, no timeframe announced | Published Novell-specific APIs including Novell Hub Management Interface; no OSF support announced | Sun-specific; no OSF support announced |
| Comments | Major thrust into distributed management from mainframe giant | Only system to use full-fledged directory service | First vendor likely to release DME-compatible system | Most sophisticated management architecture of any PC LAN vendor | Only management system to make full use of RPCs |
| Outlook | Good third-party management applications likely; overall success depends on success of OS/2 | Long-term outlook good with OSF APIs; having trouble gaining short-term acceptance | Most widely accepted distributed management system; more third-party applications likely | Excellent; Novell is one of the few vendors left that can unilaterally set de facto standards. NMS will become one of those | Good so far, but long-term support weakening due to refusal to back open interfaces |

CM-API = Consolidated Management Application Program Interface
Cmip = Common management interface protocol
CMOL = CMIP over Logical Link Control
CMOT = CMIP over TCP/IP
NICE = Network Information and Control Exchange
ONC = Open Network Computing
RPC = Remote procedure call
SQL = Structured query language

# NETWORK MANAGEMENT

## Decentralized Control

### SETTING SUN?

Sunconnect, the networking subsidiary of Sun Microsystems Inc. (Mountain View, Calif.) also has taken a distributed approach to network and systems management. Sunnet Manager is based primarily on the Sun Open Network Computing (ONC) services for distributed computing, which include an RPC. Sun has defined a fairly simple management architecture in which the ONC RPC is the main method for linking managers to agents, as well for linking the various management applications on different servers. Sunnet Manager also supports SNMP, which extends its reach to a large number of devices. The management protocol is implemented under Sunnet Manager via a remote proxy agent that talks to Sunnet Manager software using ONC RPC. Working with a remote proxy agent instead of a direct link between Sunnet Manager and network devices stops polled SNMP messages from traveling outside their immediate workgroup, reducing network overhead. Messages between the proxy agent and Sunnet Manager are only sent over the wide area when a change occurs that is worth reporting.

Many device vendors have built management systems based on Sunnet Manager, including Synoptics Communications Inc. (Santa Clara, Calif.), Cabletron, and Concord Communications. But Sun is hurting itself by refusing to support OSF's DME. Sun, which is the leading vendor of Unix workstations, sees the OSF as a threat because its proposed standards will enable Sun rivals like IBM, DEC, and HP to thrive in the Unix market. In fact, Sun has charged that OSF really stands for "Oppose Sun Forever." Sun's refusal to back DME, along with its relatively modest investment in enhancing Sunnet Manager to deliver more functions, has led numerous vendors to select other management workstations as the basis for future management products. If Sun does have a long-term plan to enhance Sunnet Manager with the functionality offered by DME, it hasn't told anybody.

### NOTICING NOVELL

Of all PC LAN vendors, Novell has the strongest network and system management strategy. It has defined an open management platform and APIs that enable third-party vendors to create applications for managing PC LANs using Netware. Among them are Compaq Computer Corp. (Houston), HP, Network General Corp. (Menlo Park, Calif.), and Remedy. Novell Network Management System (NMS) calls for a management platform that uses SNMP or a Novell-defined management protocol (or both) to access management agents. Novell will furnish agents for Netware and has published APIs so other vendors can write compatible agents for their PC LAN products.

As might be expected of a PC LAN vendor, Novell has chosen a client-server model for its management architecture. Both client and server can be implemented with either OS/2 or DOS with Windows. The server runs the management software and controls access to gateways to other management systems, such as Netview. The client establishes a graphical map as its user interface and furnishes access to collected management information. Novell has not yet embraced a more general distributed architecture that uses RPCs in place of SNMP or its own management protocol. Its management approach will probably work well for small companies or workgroups that are almost entirely based on Netware and third-party SNMP-compliant equipment. It may have difficulty scaling up to integrated management of larger enterprises. Novell seems to be willing to let other vendors solve these more difficult problems. The company recently joined the OSF but has not detailed its plans to support DME.

Not all PC vendors share Novell's enthusiasm. Microsoft may be the king when it comes to standalone PCs, but it is without a strategy or stated direction when it comes to network and system management. It appears to be focusing its efforts on client software and may leave networked servers and distributed architectures to DEC, with whom it has product development alliances. ∎

### Figure 3: OS/2 DSM Observed

IBM's OS/2 Distributed Systems Management (OS/2 DSM) exemplifies the general trend in distributed management products. An OS/2 DSM server sets up the graphical user interface and implements the base operating system, DMS system software, APIs, and IBM and third-party applications.

**OS/2 DSM SERVER**

**MANAGED OS/2 CLIENTS AND SERVERS**
- NETWORK
- LAN SERVER
- COMMUNICATIONS MANAGER
- DATABASE
- OS/2
- CM-API
- MANAGEMENT FRAMEWORK
- OS/2 2.0

**OTHER MANAGED SYSTEMS**
- DOS
- SNMP AGENT
- DOS WITH WINDOWS
- TCP/IP DEVICE

---

**REQUEST FOR COMMENT**
If you would like to see more articles on this subject please circle **408** on the Reader Service Card.

## STATE OF THE ART

# FINDING FAULT

As networks become more widespread and important,
fault management and performance monitoring become business necessities

**STEVEN M. DAUBER**

At Boeing in Seattle, a computer network helps operate the 747 aircraft assembly line. At Wells Fargo Bank, the entire nationwide system of automated teller machines communicates with central computers by way of computer networks. A computer network helps run Apple Computer's Macintosh automated production facility.

Networks are rapidly becoming the lifeline of businesses worldwide. Because networks provide distributed control, better scalability, resource sharing, and, ultimately, cost advantages over mainframes and minicomputers, companies are moving their mission-critical applications to multiplatform networks. With this movement, thorough network management becomes vital to a business's success.

**Paying the Price**
In recent studies, major corporations have reported capital losses of astounding magnitude when they have had problems with their networks. One study calculated the average lost productivity resulting from network problems to be in excess of $3 million per year. It also found that the average network is completely or partially disabled about twice a month, for an average period of more than half a business day.

Many other companies have since echoed the primary conclusion of these studies: Network downtime, the time that the network is either down or degraded, can cause extreme monetary loss, particularly when it affects mission-critical data. As companies recognize the increased importance of their networks,

ILLUSTRATION: DAVE ROTOLONI © 1991

Reprinted with permission, from the March 1991 issue of *BYTE Magazine.* © by McGraw-Hill, Inc., New York, NY. All rights reserved.

# FINDING FAULT

| ISO NETWORK MANAGEMENT | |
|---|---|
| **Area** | **Issues** |
| Fault management | Detects anomalous network behavior<br>Isolates network problems<br>Attempts to control network problems |
| Performance management | Analyzes network error rates<br>Analyzes network throughput<br>Attempts to create optimal network performance |
| Configuration management | Detects physical and logical configurations<br>Understands and manipulates network state |
| Accounting management | Collects resource utilization data<br>Processes resource utilization data |
| Security management | Controls network access |

**Figure 1:** *The ISO network management model divides management functions into five subsystems.*

pressure mounts to keep systems up and running. This, in turn, puts pressure on the vendors, fueling the demand for the network application of the 1990s: network management.

## Network Management Today
Network management's twin goals are to reduce the number of network problems and, once problems occur, to minimize inconvenience and contain the damage.

## BYTE ACTION SUMMARY

### Monitoring Networks

Network downtime can have a serious effect on your company's bottom line. This article details a four-step process that lets you correct network faults systematically. It also describes network problems and solutions and discusses the importance of both fault management and performance monitoring.

To achieve these goals, the ISO has identified five management subsystems: fault, configuration, performance, security, and accounting.

Fault management detects, isolates, and controls anomalous network behavior; configuration management attempts to understand and control the network's state; performance management analyzes and controls the network's throughput; security management controls access to network resources; and, finally, accounting management records and processes network resource-utilization data. Figure 1 lists the issues that these network management areas address.

Four important network management product categories deal with these issues: physical-layer tools, network monitors, network analyzers, and integrated network management systems. Each category has an essential role to play in today's large, heterogeneous networks.

### Tool Types
Physical-layer tools include time-domain reflectometers (TDRs), oscilloscopes, breakout boxes, power meters, and similar products that find problems such as cable opens and shorts, unterminated cables, and poorly functioning connection hardware. (See the text box "Let's Get Physical" on page 212 for details about network cable management.)

Perhaps the most popular physical-layer tool is the TDR, which sends signals along the physical medium at regular intervals. The returning signal reflections provide a representative waveform showing the placement of network devices and cable problems. TDRs provide a reasonably accurate estimate of the location of physical media problems. Since a large percentage of network faults occur at the physical layer, most companies with large networks own and use TDRs or similar products. TDRs are currently priced from about $1500 to more than $10,000.

Network monitors are computer devices that attach to a network and monitor all or a selected portion of the network traffic. By examining frame-level information in each packet, network monitors can compile statistics on network utilization, packet type, number of packets sent and received by each network node, packet errors, and other important variables.

Network monitors are relatively inexpensive, permitting you to use one per network segment. They are generally allowed to run unattended 24 hours per day, recording data and looking for anomalies. The monitors' primary advantages are relatively low cost, reasonable error-detection facilities, and the ability to participate in integrated network management schemes. Network monitors are priced from several hundred dollars (for software-only products) to about $10,000.

While network monitors can detect network problems, network analyzers can help you track down and fix those problems. Network analyzers contain sophisticated features for real-time traffic analysis, packet capture and decoding, and packet transmission. Some even include troubleshooting expertise, in the form of test suites. Network analyzers also incorporate a built-in TDR-like capability. The most sophisticated network analyzers use special-purpose hardware to detect problems not visible to standard network controllers.

Prices for network analyzers start at about $10,000, and they can cost well over $30,000 with support for multiple physical media and protocol decoding. They are sold as *kits* (a network interface card and software that you install on a PC) and as *packages* (the card and software preinstalled in a PC of the vendor's choice), with the latter being substantially more expensive.

The fourth and final type of product available for managing a network is the integrated network management system. Using the INMS, you can monitor and control your entire network from a central location. The INMS implements all

# FINDING FAULT

## TYPES OF NETWORK MANAGEMENT PRODUCTS

| Product type | Strength | Weakness |
|---|---|---|
| Physical-layer tools | Reasonably accurate | Some are complex and difficult to use<br>Limited to physical-layer problems |
| Network monitor | Continuous monitoring useful for long-term trend analysis<br>Low cost | Limited troubleshooting capability |
| Network analyzer | Advanced troubleshooting capability<br>Portable<br>Can stress-test new protocols, applications | Relatively expensive |
| Integrated Network Management System | Advanced monitoring capability<br>Supports all five ISO network management subsystems | High cost<br>Unavailable for some platforms |

**Figure 2:** *Network management tools can be classified into four types. Each type has its corresponding strengths and weaknesses.*

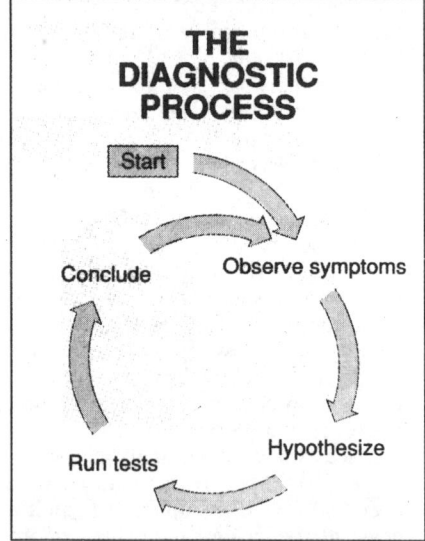

**Figure 3:** *The network diagnostic cycle resembles a blackboard system, where successive cycles contribute toward the solution to the problem.*

five ISO network management areas: fault, performance, configuration, security, and accounting. You use the INMS through a console device that provides a graphical user interface. The console device is integrated with a network management station that communicates with agents—software programs—on remote computer devices to determine the state of the network. Agents collect interesting information, such as the number of packets the device has received, and make it available to the INMS upon query. When a problem occurs, agents can also send alarms to the console to immediately alert the network manager.

INMSes hold tremendous promise but have to be implemented across a wide variety of platforms to be truly effective. Resolving differences between operating systems, hardware platforms, and networks makes this task difficult and time-consuming. As a result, INMSes are the most expensive network management products. In the coming years, you will see an increasing number of product introductions in this area. Figure 2 compares the various strengths and weaknesses of the four types of network management products.

## Using the Tools

If you've spent any time managing a network, you know that this often-difficult task is both a science and an art. As a science, troubleshooting demands that you understand network operation and the relationship between symptoms and underlying causes. As an art, it requires that you implement the proper diagnostic process, which consists of four critical steps repeated continuously until the problem is ultimately solved: observing symptoms, developing a hypothesis, testing the hypothesis, and forming conclusions (see figure 3).

The first step of the process is to observe problem symptoms. A common mistake here, made in the interest of saving time, is to begin experimentation before thoroughly examining the symptoms. Unfortunately, in many cases, the most obvious symptoms can lead you off on a costly tangent. Why are the most obvious symptoms not always the most important? To understand this, you must understand the essence of network protocols.

Have you ever wondered why a computer sometimes takes so long to respond to a network access request? The reason is that network protocols are designed to hide, not to expose, network problems. Most network protocols incorporate retry mechanisms and other techniques to recover from problems. As a result, most network problems display a single obvious symptom: long response times. Although retry mechanisms increase network reliability, they also make network troubleshooting more difficult by displaying a common symptom for many different problems.

Therefore, it is critical that you uncover as many clues as possible prior to the beginning of the next step in the diagnostic process. Since the first symptom that is encountered—longer response times—may not be very illuminating, you must push not only to identify the other symptoms, but also to discover the following:

- The range and scope of the symptoms. Does this problem affect everyone, everyone in a given area, random individuals?
- The percentage of time the problem manifests itself. Is the problem continuous or intermittent? Does it occur regularly?
- What has changed recently? Has a computer device been added to the network? Have any internetworking devices been reconfigured?
- All release variables in the environment experiencing the problem. What are the vendor and release numbers of the computer systems, network interface cards, hubs, routers, bridges, application software, and network software?

As soon as you have gathered all this information, you can then move to the

# FINDING FAULT

next step in the diagnostic process: the formation of a valid hypothesis that is consistent with the data.

## Signature Analysis

Before you can use the data gathered about problem symptoms and construct a valid hypothesis, you have to know whether what you're seeing is something unusual. Therefore, you first have to understand the "usual." Networks are like fingerprints—no two are exactly alike. Even if two networks are configured identically, usage patterns will almost certainly differ. The process of determining the characteristics of an in-

**Development of the troubleshooting library is one of the most effective ways of minimizing network downtime.**

dividual network signature is called *baselining*.

Baselining is not one of the four steps in the diagnostic process: It must be done prior to a problem occurring. (Needless to say, once the problem situation exists, observing typical network performance is impossible.) Having a proper baseline for the network means you can answer detailed questions about the following:

- *Network utilization.* What is the average network utilization? How does it vary during the business day?
- *Network applications.* What are the dominant network applications on the network? What version numbers is it running?
- *Network protocol software.* What protocols are running on your network? What are the performance characteristics of these protocols?
- *Network hardware.* Who manufactured the network interface controllers, media attachment units, hubs, and other network connection hardware? What versions are they? What are their performance characteristics?

- *Internetworking equipment.* Who manufactured the repeaters, bridges, routers, and gateways on the network? What versions of software and firmware are they running? What are their performance characteristics?

This list is by no means complete, but it provides an example of the necessary level of detail. In general, the better you know the network, the less frequently problems occur and the more quickly they are solved when they do occur. This will be increasingly true as networks become more complicated.

## Theory and Experimentation

Armed with the appropriate data about problem symptoms and a complete understanding of differences between the data and corresponding baselines, you are ready to form a first hypothesis of the problem. This is the stage where troubleshooting experience and expertise is most important.

You need to know which network problems are capable of causing the observed deviation from the baselines. This often requires a good understanding of the protocols and applications running on the network. For example, too many collisions on an Ethernet are often a result of excessive network traffic but can also result from overlong segments or malfunctioning transceivers.

You can gain troubleshooting expertise from experience or from several books on the subject. Recently, some network analyzers have incorporated on-line troubleshooting guides that give tips on probable causes of observed symptoms. Using all this information and expertise, you form a hypothesis.

The next step in the troubleshooting process is to test the hypothesis. A network analyzer is usually the best tool for this purpose, since it provides the most flexible set of capabilities. Some network analyzers offer important features that aid the test-development process, such as preprogrammed experiments. Each experiment is designed to test one or more hypotheses, thereby saving you the hassle of programming the test parameters.

Following the experiments necessary to test the hypothesis, you enter the final step in the diagnostic process: forming conclusions. If the other steps were executed correctly, this step may well be the most straightforward. Good network troubleshooters know what they will conclude for each possible outcome of the experiment. In the event that the test results are unfamiliar, you must expand or revise your view of the problem so that you can map the symptoms to the observed test results.

The diagnostic process is cyclical. Following the conclusions drawn from one test, you often need another hypothesis. Sometimes, you need to change the problem environment prior to reexamining the symptoms. For example, you might want to remove a node from the network and then observe the symptoms again. In any event, the process cycles until you can converge on the appropriate conclusion, or set of conclusions, and finally solve the problem.

The value of techniques that shorten the time taken to cycle through the diag-

**Incompatibilities among protocol software from different vendors are not unusual.**

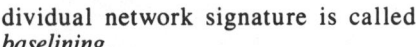

nostic process is obvious. Baselining and gathering of anomalous data is critical to differentiating the unusual from the usual. On-line troubleshooting guides and similar features can then shorten the hypothesizing process. Finally, preprogrammed tests often minimize the testing phase. The combination of these features can dramatically reduce the length of the diagnostic cycle, providing immediate returns in the form of increased network uptime.

As you employ these techniques, you form a library of information and tests for solving common problems. With such a library, observing symptoms, forming a hypothesis, and testing the hypothesis become an extremely rapid process. Each time you solve a new problem, you should document the problem and save the tests used to solve it. The next time the problem occurs, solving it will be a simple matter. An additional advantage of this library is that it embodies expertise that can be used by anyone, not just the person who originally solved the problem. Development of the troubleshooting library is one of the most effective methods of minimizing network downtime.

# FINDING FAULT

### Common Problems
A typical network administrator spends a great deal of time solving problems and trying to understand the network's performance. The better that understanding, the more infrequent faults are likely to be, since you avoid problems when performance is managed proactively.

Different parts of a network experience different kinds of problems. Understanding the problem sets that affect the different parts is critical to effective troubleshooting. A complete list of problems and solutions would fill volumes, but the general relationship between network components and fault types can be drawn here. For this purpose, network components will be divided into four categories: network hardware, internetworking equipment, network protocol software, and network applications.

Starting with the lowest layers of the Open Systems Interconnection model and working up, you first encounter the problems endemic to network hardware. Because hardware is subject to environmental stresses and is accessible, physical connectivity problems are the most common fault type. These include cable breaks (a cable is cut or not terminated properly), cable shorts (a cable is damaged), breaks elsewhere in the circuit (a vampire transceiver is jostled so that it no longer makes positive contact with the medium), and malfunctions in the actual network hardware circuitry (a bad network interface controller or a jabbering transceiver).

Cable problems can be discovered using a network analyzer or TDR. Problems with hardware circuitry can often be found by examining error traffic on the network using a network analyzer. Other times, these problems must be attacked by a process of elimination to isolate the problem.

As networks grow, internetworking products are increasingly common problem sources. Since these products sit at intersections within the network traffic pattern, they can quickly cause significant problems when they malfunction. Configuration errors are also common with complex products such as routers, brouters, and gateways. If nodes on only one side of an internetworking product are affected, start the search with that product. Check to see that processing queues have not grown unmanageably large. Ask yourself what has changed recently and what unplanned side effects that change might have had.

Although protocol software is just as error-prone as any other kind of software, you usually can't do more than identify these problems. For actual solutions or workarounds, consult with the vendor and obtain a new version of the software. Incompatibilities among protocol software from different vendors are not unusual. Network analyzers with built-in protocol decoders are helpful in detecting this variety of problem.

Finally, applications sometimes have bugs. There is little you can do to solve these problems directly unless your organization wrote the application. If not, use the network analyzer to find the problem and then contact the vendor with details.

### Performance Management
Unlike fault management, performance management should be almost entirely proactive. However, most people tend to ignore performance management until it actually results in an emergency. The first lesson of performance management is to be proactive.

Network monitors and analyzers are important tools for completing a comprehensive traffic analysis on your network. Using these devices, you can come to understand the daily network utilization patterns, the heaviest users, the various percentages of different protocol traffic, where network bottlenecks exist, why those bottlenecks exist, and other similar information.

You can also use the traffic-generation capabilities of a network analyzer to study how much additional traffic the network can support. A reactive benefit from this exercise is knowing where to look first when performance problems occur, but proactive benefits also accrue, including how to best spend money to improve network performance.

As a result of analyzing the network's traffic patterns, you can make critical decisions regarding where to partition the network for optimal throughput and response time and how to allocate resources. Despite the fact that these performance management techniques are sometimes merely the result of common sense, most organizations still do not believe they have the time to engage in the exercise. Unfortunately, this way of thinking often leads to emergencies that force you to spend the time later.

Network management technology and practice has advanced significantly in the last decade. Through the 1990s, look for many of these advances to have a positive impact on networks and the people who manage and use them. ■

---

*Steven M. Dauber is product marketing manager at Novell, Inc. (San Jose, CA). He can be reached on BIX c/o "editors."*

# Knowledge technologies for evolving networks

Shri K. Goyal

GTE Laboratories Incorporated
40 Sylvan Road
Waltham, MA 02254

## Abstract

Expert systems have moved out of the laboratory; a whole new style of automation system design and programming is being introduced in the world of telecommunication systems. The paradigm of rule-based knowledge representation and reasoning is the basic technology involved in this process, and it has been successfully applied to a wide range of "real world" problems: from basic equipment troubleshooting to global network management. Although this paradigm appears better suited to those automated reasoning tasks than any other software technology that came before it, there is some evidence that expert systems may be limited in their abilities to handle anticipated automation requirements of the intelligent network.

The academic and industrial AI communities have been pursuing advanced knowledge technologies, often dubbed second-generation expert systems. In this paper we take a look at some of the characteristics of the future network environment and attempt to evaluate how those knowledge technologies might penetrate even further in automating ever more complex control, problem-solving, and decision-making tasks. We present examples of laboratory technologies in each of three key areas of AI from the standpoint of telecommunication network operation and management: distributed AI, knowledge representation, and machine learning.

## 1. INTRODUCTION

During the last quarter of the century, and more so in the last decade, worldwide telecommunication network capabilities have rapidly advanced to meet the challenge of the information age. The pace has been further fueled by customer demand for a variety of innovative services that require the support of a high quality reliable voice/data network. Current day network technology enhancements have given rise to many sophisticated network surveillance, control, and decision-support systems [1]. Management and administration of a complex integrated network presents a new challenge for network operators, designers, and technology innovators.

The current telecommunication environment is dynamic and transitional. The US Public Switched Telephone Network (PSTN) is currently operating with a mostly digital switching and inter-office transmission plant. Fiber optics is now the prevalent transmission growth and replacement medium, and is also penetrating the outside plant of the Local Exchange Carriers (LECs). At a different level, SS7 out-of-band signalling is being rapidly introduced, and the hierarchical routing structure of conventional long-distance networks has been replaced by dynamic non-hierarchical routing, resulting in a marked improvement in network availability and robustness at reduced costs. Those major evolutionary steps have created the need for sophisticated Operations Support Systems (OSS) for surveillance, monitoring, testing, and control [2-3].

In this environment, expert systems have moved out of the laboratory and into the PSTN OSS arena. Along with them, a whole new style of automation system design and programming is being introduced in telecommunication systems. The paradigm of rule-based knowledge representation and reasoning has been the basic technology used, and it has been successfully applied to a wide range of "real world" problems, from basic equipment troubleshooting to global network management. Although this paradigm has been a powerful software technology, there is some evidence that expert systems may be limited in their abilities to handle anticipated automation requirements of what is most often referred to as the Advanced Intelligent Network (AIN).

At the most generic level, some of the driving factors in developing intelligent systems to manage the evolving telecommunication network are the following:

- Increasing rate of technology change (causing, among others, a knowledge acquisition and expertise development bottleneck).
- Increased levels of system complexity, causing the decision-making task to be very difficult.
- Inherent distribution of control at some levels and centralization at others.
- Real-time control in a dynamic environment.
- Need for knowledge technologies in the control loop rather than in advisory off-line functions.

The academic and industrial AI communities have been pursuing research in knowledge technologies, often dubbed second-generation expert systems. In this paper, we take a look at some of the factors listed above and attempt to evaluate how knowledge technologies might penetrate even further in automating ever more complex control, reasoning, and decision-making tasks. We also present examples of laboratory technologies in some of the key areas of AI from the standpoint of telecommunication network operation and management.

## 2. ARTIFICIAL INTELLIGENCE (AI) TECHNOLOGIES

Traditional algorithmic approaches have, in the past, proven satisfactory for managing networks. These approaches alone are not sufficient anymore for the management and control of complex networks [4]. These must be complemented with more powerful heuristic approaches, such as in Artificial Intelligence (AI) systems [5].

AI is, among other things, a set of programming methodologies that focus on the techniques used to solve problems by generating new strategies and plans, and even generate new domain knowledge. Expert systems, a sub-field of AI, provides a new, often successful, way of attacking problems that previously have been considered not solvable by machines. Utilizing human expertise and domain knowledge, the techniques focus on the use of declarative (factual) knowledge and relatively simple rules of inference for putting that knowledge to work on a specific problem.

Research has shown that the basic knowledge about the domain alone was not enough to get the performance exhibited by most experts. The people performing the tasks acquired another kind of knowledge, "experience," that allowed them to concentrate on the most likely causes of a problem and to adapt answers to the specific problems. The people who do this well are regarded as experts. The programs that capture their problem-solving strategies and selectively apply them under specific circumstances are called expert systems.

Most current expert systems utilize rule-based and other simple technologies. Several important technologies, which would potentially provide much-needed power to future AI systems, are under development in various laboratories. Three such key technologies are *Distributed AI* for sharing of expertise and better coordination in problem solving, *Knowledge Representation* for more robust and better utilization of domain experts' knowledge, and *Machine Learning* for providing the self-improving ability to the systems in a dynamic environment. These technologies and their ramifications are further discussed in Section 4.

## 2.1 Expert systems in support of network operations

A variety of expert systems have been employed in telecommunications as operation support systems (OSS) and for other functions. Many more systems are under development. A recent survey article [6] categorizes the existing systems in three main functional categories: maintenance, provisioning, and network administration. The maintenance systems provide monitoring, troubleshooting, and diagnosis support in keeping the networks operating. Provisioning and planning applications support development of network evolution plans by design, configuration, and execution of these plans. Network administration and management applications help manage the network traffic, and plan and execute a workable strategy when exceptions occur. This application also includes billing, facility assignment, and record keeping. In addition, a miscellaneous application area relates to sales and system configuration support.

Table 1 lists some expert systems that have been tested and/or are in use in telecommunications today [7–16]. Diagnostic expert systems are, by far, the most popular application in telecommunication, spanning public telephone to packet switched networks. Well over a dozen expert systems have been reported to provide monitoring, troubleshooting, and fault diagnosis. Switch maintenance, typically for the older technology switches, is a common application. Perhaps expertise on the older switches tends to disappear as the switch technicians move on and learn the new switches. Also, new switches are quite sophisticated, with much processing power and built-in self-diagnostics to identify and report their own hardware faults. Software faults or bugs are difficult to diagnose internally and by external systems. Therefore, no systems are currently available for the latest generation of switches, despite the clear need in this area.

Table 1
Examples of expert systems in the network management domain

| System | Task Performed | AI Method | Type, Status | Environment |
|---|---|---|---|---|
| Advanced Maintenance Facility (AMF) [7] (BRITISH TELECOM) | Finds faults in TXE4A telephone exchanges | Basically a production system | Diagnostic, field tested | 16-bit Micro; UNIX SAGE and LISP |
| Central Office Maintenance Printout Analysis and Suggestion System [8] (COMPASS) (GTE) | Finds Faults in GTE's No. 2 EAX telephone exchanges | Mix of frames, rules, LISP, and active values | Diagnostic, field tested | Xerox 11xx KEE and INTERLISP-D |
| Automated Cable Expertise (ACE) [9-10] (AT&T) | Troubleshoots telephone company local loop plant | Forward-chaining rules | Diagnostic, commercial product, over 40 systems deployed | AT&T 3B2; UNIX OPS4 and LISP C |
| Network Management Expert System (NEMESYS) [11] (AT&T) | Reviews traffic completion data and suggests traffic control changes | Mix of rules, procedures and active rules | Monitor, research prototype | Symbolics KEE |
| Network Trouble Shooting Ethernet Consultant [12] | Finds problems in DECnet and LANs | Forward-chaining rules with confidence factors | Diagnostic, field tested | VAX EXPERT |
| Net/Advisor [13] (BB&N) | Monitors real-time network status and suggests actions to take when problems are diagnosed | Back-chaining rules (PROLOG) with LISP interface code | Diagnostic, commercial | Symbolics PROLOG and LISP |
| DESIGNET [14] (BB&N) | Assists in building a data communications network | Object-oriented programming | Design, research prototype | Symbolics 36xx ZETALISP |
| MAX (NYNEX) | Analyzes local loop trouble reports and outputs dispatch recommendations | ART rules and mixed paradigm locations | Diagnostic, deployed in 42 NYNEX | SUN Inc. workstation |
| IAS [15] | Analyzes alarm for Italian packet network | C & OPS-83 | Monitoring/diagnostic prototype under evaluation | VAX workstation |
| ARACHNE (NYNEX) | Supports planning interoffice hierarchical network | | Planning/provisioning prototype | SUN communicating with IMS databases |
| NEC's Network Configurer | Planning for corporate communication and multiservice planning | OPS-83 | Planning/provisioning under evaluation | 32-bit workstation |
| NETREX [5] (CALTECH) | Diagnose and repair faults in BANCS network in real-time | Teknowledge S1 | Proof of concept prototype | SUN 3/160 and C tools |
| AT2 [16] (AT&T) | Isolates fault in Special Service Circuits using SARTS remote test system | Rule-based programming OPS-83 (and routines) | Diagnostic, deployed product | OPS-83 and C in UNIX on AT&T 3B2 |
| SSCFI (GTE) | Isolates faults in Special Service circuits using AT2, SARTS, and other test systems | ART-IM rules and schemes, C code, CrossTalk | Diagnostic, prototype under evaluation | ART-IM and C on IBM-PC,DOS |

Systems for diagnosing faults in telephone outside plants (ACE [9], MAX), Special Service Circuits (Autotest [16], SSCFI) and specific equipment other than the switches have also been built and several have been tested and deployed. Some of them have had a significant impact on day-to-day operations and company profitability. For example, over forty ACE systems are operational in six RBOCs. MAX is in use in over forty

NYNEX locations. Autotest2 is going through a deployment phase for use in diagnosis of faults in special service circuits by automating testing.

In the provisioning arena, the focus has been on design (e.g., DESIGNET [14]) and system configuration. Only recently is expert system technology being applied to network planning (e.g., ARACHNE).

The most common application in the network administration area is traffic routing or traffic management. In the public network, experts (and, thus, potentially expert systems) monitor traffic data and install switching controls to redirect traffic and relieve congestion in the network. NEMESYS [11] at AT&T Bell Labs is an attempt to automate some of the decision-making abilities of the traffic manager. The routine decisions NEMESYS makes are influenced by network topology and the possible cause of congestion. Several specialized billing applications, such as toll fraud detection systems, are also being developed and evaluated.

Over a period of time, it has been recognized that expert systems should act as background processes to support and complement decision-making activities. Expert systems were originally proposed as stand-alone systems not easily integrated due to their specialized hardware and software platforms and with little intercommunication ability with existing databases. This brought about a lot of resistance from the MIS and operator community. The situation is changing drastically as professional workstations, lately using a UNIX environment, are becoming an acceptable development and deployment environment (to the MIS community) as powerful tools are becoming available for these workstations. Most of these are general-purpose tools. Some efforts to build specialized development tools with knowledge representation suitable for the telecommunication domain have met only limited success, partly due to lack of a formal model of network entities and their interoperability. For a specialized network application tool to be useful, there should be a common structure between the problems to be solved, using a common and complete network knowledge base. Due to the lack of these facilities, network applications have been unable to use specialized, and potentially powerful, knowledge representation mechanisms (e.g., model-based [17], experience-based techniques). These common structures and models are slowly evolving as their need and value is being recognized. The pace of this formalization process is accelerating with the work of various worldwide standardization bodies.

Expert systems also exhibit brittleness in their behavior. Within the region of expertise, they perform at expert level and totally fail beyond these limits. Most systems today are off-line, advisory systems performing a well-defined and confined task. Expansion of the breadth of coverage and, thus, their power and usefulness will be achieved by using advanced technologies. Some of these are discussed in Section 4.

## 3. EXPERT SYSTEM LIMITATIONS AND THE NEED FOR ENABLING TECHNOLOGIES

It seems that telecommunications has been less successful than other industries in fielding expert systems and reaping benefits from their use. Without detracting from the successes of the systems, we can identify limitations of existing expert system technology, and speculate on why some of these limitations are especially critical for successful use of expert systems in the telecommunications industry.

One of the most significant impediments to fielding expert systems is not strictly technical, but rather reflects the typical organizational structure of the telecommunications industry. Telephone operation organizations tend to have relatively inflexible boundaries between functional groups; this is important for establishing responsibility and for evaluating performance, but it somewhat constrains opportunities for deployment of expert systems or, indeed, of automation systems in general. It is noteworthy that the "successful" expert systems listed above perform largely *within a single organizational* function. The perceived benefit of inter-organizational automation can be much more significant than the benefit accruing to any individual organizations. However, in the present organizational structure, the benefit is often neglected because it is distributed across several organizations.

Despite this organizational limitation, the bridging function is such a compelling opportunity for automation that the payoff to the larger enterprise can sometimes override internal struggles. Unfortunately, an expert system may create boundaries between itself and the rest of the world. All these aspects need some attention, particularly in view of the changing telecommunications environment, if the industry is to reap the benefits of AI.

- One such boundary exists between different expert systems. Significantly lacking from the technology is a standard "knowledge interface" language by which disparate expert systems can communicate. This is the topic of Distributed AI, a technology that is especially critical in telecommunications. Such technology is crucial for an inherently distributed industry where coordination across regions and functions is crucial for any acceptable network performance.
- Another boundary that critically affects the acceptance of any expert system is that which exists between it and the human being whose decisions it is to support. Recent advances in user interface technology (including natural language processing, as well as speech recognition and synthesis technologies) have improved the usability of expert systems for operational personnel. Many more significant developments are on the horizon.
- The boundary between computing environments, especially between AI systems and conventional OSSs, was a serious handicap in the early days of AI for telecommunications. This boundary has essentially vanished in recent years, as platform-independent AI environments have emerged, and as expert system techniques have been recognized as part of the standard embedded-systems toolkit.

The well-known "knowledge-acquisition bottleneck" is another kind of boundary, one that lies between the expert and the expert system. This limitation is experienced across industries, but is manifested in telecommunications in unique ways:

- Knowledge representation schemes developed for other industries are often inappropriate for telephony knowledge. A notable example is the kind of knowledge used by network traffic managers, which is largely experience-based, rather than derivable from precompiled heuristics or well-behaved domain models. Discussed in a later section is research on eliciting and representing this kind of "case-based" knowledge.

- The rate of technological change in telecommunications networks is remarkably high; the expertise needed to operate the network evolves with each introduction of new hardware, signalling systems, routing strategies, or service offerings. Expert systems, as currently fielded, capture only a snapshot of this changing knowledge, and "evolve" only to the extent that they are revised by their maintainers. Machine learning is therefore a clear requirement for future systems in order to keep pace with accelerating change in network technology.

Another feature of network operations, the time-constrained nature of decision-making, has two effects that are especially significant for AI technology:

- The need for real-time response is inherent in many network operations, such as traffic control, for which the timing of an intervention is crucial to its effect on network performance. Real-time expert systems are only beginning to be evaluated, and remain an active research area.
- Because human reaction times are too long for many network operations, especially those in support of future service offerings such as dynamic reallocation of bandwidth, the human role in such tasks must be only supervisory. As automated systems perform more "closed loop" functions, the performance of the network is increasingly dependent on their reliability. For expert system technology, this requires improved verification and validation techniques. These topics have only recently begun receiving attention.

The challenges for expert systems that are posed by network applications will determine the role of this technology in the future of telecommunications. The remainder of this paper will identify some critical technologies and focus on how three of the key technology challenges identified here are being met by emerging AI technology. We will also provide an overview of the research at GTE Laboratories that applies these advanced techniques to solve telecommunication-specific problems.

## 4. ENABLING KNOWLDGE TECHNOLOGY

### 4.1 Some critical technologies

The future siblings of the existing systems will be broader in scope, coverage, and more integrated with the control of the systems they monitor. Thus, rather than covering a subset of messages or alarms produced by some piece of equipment, they will cover a majority of meaningful messages from a variety of equipment. Similar systems will be built for pieces of equipment not covered today. Table 2 lists a set of future operations system functions and attempts to match them with a set of enabling technologies. Network managers implement appropriate control even when definite decisions cannot be made in the absence of hard data or under time constraints. Future systems should be able to suggest such controls by using fuzzy logic. The knowledge and accuracy of expert systems will be enhanced by incorporating the knowledge from several experts, leading to the creation of corporate knowledge repositories for each critical expertise area. This corporate resource will be updated and enhanced on a continuous basis through machine learning technologies. All this will free up the brightest staff members to learn newer systems, and this will allow the company to keep pace with changing network technology, while the networks will manage themselves effectively by using integrated automated intelligent systems.

Table 2
Enabling technologies in future operations support systems

| Function | Future Operation | Underlying Technology |
|---|---|---|
| Testing | Non-vendor-specific monitoring and data analysis systems with expert repair capability. | • Standard interfaces<br>• Data filtering, data correlation<br>• Expert system |
| DB Maintenance & Software Update | Automatic DB consistency check.<br>Non-interruptive SVR updates. | • Object-oriented programming<br>• Distributed DB's<br>• Advanced software technologies |
| Network Maintenance | Proactive maintenance of switches and outside plant. Mechanized trouble analysis and dispatch. | • Patterning<br>• Expert system<br>• Operations research |
| Operator Support | Automated directory/operator assisted functions. | • Speech recognition and synthesis |
| Provisioning of special and enhanced services. | Automatic provisioning of dynamically reconfigurable circuits through software control. Mechanized design and testing of special circuits. Customer-controlled network configuration for new services. | • Network operating system<br>• Expert system for design, analysis, and testing<br>• Service provisioning using scripts<br>• Enhanced transaction systems<br>• Network security<br>• Machine learning |
| Traffic Management | Dynamic network reconfiguration by generating alternate routing methods. | • Integration<br>• Operations research<br>• Expert system<br>• Machine learning |
| Data Collection and Billing | Intelligent billing systems to avoid toll fraud. | • Decision-support system |
| Planning and Design | Dynamic planning. | • Enhanced planning and database access systems |
| Performance measurement | Monitoring and support for performance enhancement and tuning. | • Distributed interoperable intelligent system |
| Network Management | AI-based dynamic network management. Intelligent customer and operator interfaces. Centralized customer contact systems. | • Real-time AI systems<br>• Fuzzy logic<br>• Distributed problem solving<br>• Man-machine interface<br>• System integration<br>• Machine learning |

The network domain is a difficult one to manage. It requires a combination of situation assessment, problem solving, planning, and control in near real time, almost on a continuous basis [4–5]. It is a domain for which a formal model does not exist, and expertise, at best, is "spotty" and often uncoordinated. What makes the situation much more difficult is that the domain has been very dynamic with changing architectures and functionality of various network elements as the new generation of innovative services is being integrated to meet the future requirements. Perhaps all these factors are contributing to the slow rate of introduction of expert systems in this domain. Broader and more powerful systems are needed to make a real difference. This requires significant technical developments in key technology areas. Some examples follow.

Networks require a wide variety of coordinated expertise. Activities and operations of a large number and variety of disparate components must be coordinated. This demands cooperation (and negotiations) among individual intelligent systems [18–19]. Issues such as these are being addressed under Distributed AI (DAI) research. At GTE, we are developing a framework for cooperative problem solving and building a Team-CPS testbed for Customer Network Control application [20]. This activity is discussed under Section 4.2.

The dynamic nature of today's evolving network demands utilization of changing expertise. Model-based reasoning and experience-based reasoning support decision making based on a formal problem model or instances of successful experiences, respectively. Such knowledge representation paradigms have proven to be powerful and useful in selected application domains. A testbed for traffic management, called NETTRAC, utilizing Case-Based Reasoning (CBR) is being developed at GTE for network traffic management [21]. This activity is discussed under Section 4.3.

Network configurations and functionality change on a regular basis, and so also does the needed expertise in managing the network. The ability of systems to learn from their successful experiences and mistakes will become an essential requirement as intelligent systems proliferate in the existing telecommunications environment. Major initiatives on machine learning research are being pursued at various universities and industrial organizations. Section 4.4 discusses GTE's activities in the machine learning area.

## 4.2 Distributed artificial intelligence

The current expert system technology supports developing systems in small, well-constrained domains. In order to tackle larger, more complex problems, several of these autonomous systems have to be integrated in a team and made to work cooperatively. This is the goal of DAI.

A central objective for DAI research lies in the hope of, some day, creating a "society" of expert systems in which a set of selected computer programs can cooperate and share their (local) expertise in much the same way as human experts do, for example, in a meeting room in an ad hoc consultative relationship. A metaphor for this form of cooperative problem solving can be described by a "chef and architect" interaction, each an expert in his domain and with specific viewpoints in designing a kitchen, making decisions and compromises through negotiations [22].

*A chef wants a kitchen. He knows all about cooking requirements, recipes, needed tools, and appliances. He can read floor plans and suggest changes to suit his preferences. He can design a convenient kitchen, but he does not know about building codes, architectural issues, and costs associated with a design choice.*

*An architect knows about the building design constraints, building codes, and architectural requirements for an "aesthetically pleasing" kitchen. He does not know the optimum and detail requirements that suit the cuisine style of the chef.*

The joint design process must proceed interactively. The architect proposes an initial layout. The chef fine-tunes the design to meet his specific requirements, and the architect considers and evaluates the proposed changes against his constraints. There may be a need for a negotiating dialogue, for example, to meet the cost requirements.

Among the requirements that stand out in the example are (1) a language for communication between the chef and the architect, (2) a negotiation strategy and (3) a framework to represent the domain expertise of the chef and the architect. It is expected that a better design, for both parties, evolves through a cooperative dialogue as their respective expertise is utilized.

The following section describes the work at GTE Laboratories on cooperative problem solving research. After examining several telecommunications-related application areas, Customer Network Control (CNC) was chosen for the initial experiments. Some key ideas motivated the selection, including the inherent distribution of network control, the occurrence of conflicts among controllers, and the tightly coupled interdependence of problem solvers during crisis management.

Customer networks can include a diverse range of elements: voice/data switches, multiplexers and digital cross-connect systems, the backbone transport network, etc. Some facilities may be customer-owned and some public-network-owned. Currently, the key attributes of CNC are multi-class traffic control, dynamic load balancing and network reconfiguration, and access control of external traffic inbound to the customer networks. A composite example of a private network with extensive customer network control would involve a corporate network that can reconfigure in real time to meet a demand for multipoint video sessions, temporarily offload voice traffic to the public network, reassign incoming 800 traffic to various call answering centers, and balance its use of virtual private network service and dedicated leased public facilities.

**Cooperative problem solving for customer network control**

TEAM-CPS (Testbed Environment for Autonomous Multiagent Cooperative Problem Solving) is a research testbed that explores the dynamics of cooperative problem solving among dissimilar agents [23]. Interagent cooperation in the testbed is currently demonstrated by having two agents with different views of the network, but with the common purpose of implementing a self-healing network, help each other improve their respective local solutions and jointly solve a facility failure problem.

Two agent types, the private or customer network manager and the public network manager, are defined. An agent in this context is a computer program with autonomous reasoning, problem solving (e.g., an expert system), and communication expertise that can participate in organized joint problem solving with other agents.

TEAM-CPS agents are based on a blackboard inference engine which encodes local expertise, agent control knowledge, and knowledge about the cooperative environment as knowledge sources activated by a common object store. Areas of AI research involved in the design of such agents include automated reasoning, planning, meta-level control of autonomous agents, hypothetical world reasoning, and interagent communications. To support a meaningful cooperative dialogue, agents need a common language, a dialogue control mechanism, knowledge, and goal sharing capabilities, including explicit models of other agents' goals and strategies. We have implemented an approach to interagent cooperation that models shared semantics of action and intent between agents as a goal tree planning, transfer, and integration mechanism. Customer and the public network manager agents cooperate in TEAM-CPS, as illustrated in Figure 1 and discussed in the following scenario.

> *In the face of a facility failure that affects both the public and the customer network, all the agents begin to plan for restoral. In this initial planning, the customer agents do not know of any resource restrictions in the public network, so they simply request that their lost capacity be restored. Each affected customer agent communicates its request, in the form of a goal tree plan, to the public agent. The public agent then combines these requests, and attempts to fairly distribute the available resources among the requesting agents, denying the remaining, infeasible parts of the customer plans. Again, these replies are communicated in the form of annotations and extensions to the respective customers' goal-tree proposals. Thus, goal trees provide the inter-agent language as well as the internal planning representation used by the agents.*

> *Just as the public agent was able to refine the customers' plans because of its knowledge of the physical limitations of the network, the customer agents can refine the public agent's counter-proposal to conform to their local knowledge of traffic loads and priorities. In addition, they may propose to exercise other control options, such as reconfiguration of existing leased trunks, rerouting of voice traffic to the public network, or re-targeting 800 traffic to bypass the failed facility. When the public agent receives these updated proposals, it makes one last stage of improvement by using both its knowledge of traffic demand on the public network (which could interfere with the customer's off-net or 800 rerouting) and of the physical implementation of existing leased trunks (to create more efficient reconfigurations than could be found by the customer alone).*

As this example demonstrates, inter-agent cooperation and negotiation yields a better overall solution, superior to any that could be obtained without the dialogue. This sharing of expertise and interactive exchange of partial solution spaces among the agents is crucial to maintaining coherent control of the customer and public networks, and is thus an essential supporting technology for future networks.

In general, it cannot be assumed that agents have the same reasoning mechanism and are able to communicate using the same representation as for planning and problem solving; e.g., exchanging goal trees like our current agent system. As part of our ongoing activities, we are developing a planner with the capability of planning for partial goal satisfaction and extending TEAM-CPS to handle dissimilar agents which will require more general and explicit inter-agent models and communication language. Some of the other issues relate to the scaling of TEAM-CPS to consider larger systems of agents and the associated problems; role of multiple modes of communication, such as point-to-point, narrowcast, and broadcast; handling of multiple concurrent problems; complexity of dialogues; and termination problems, etc.

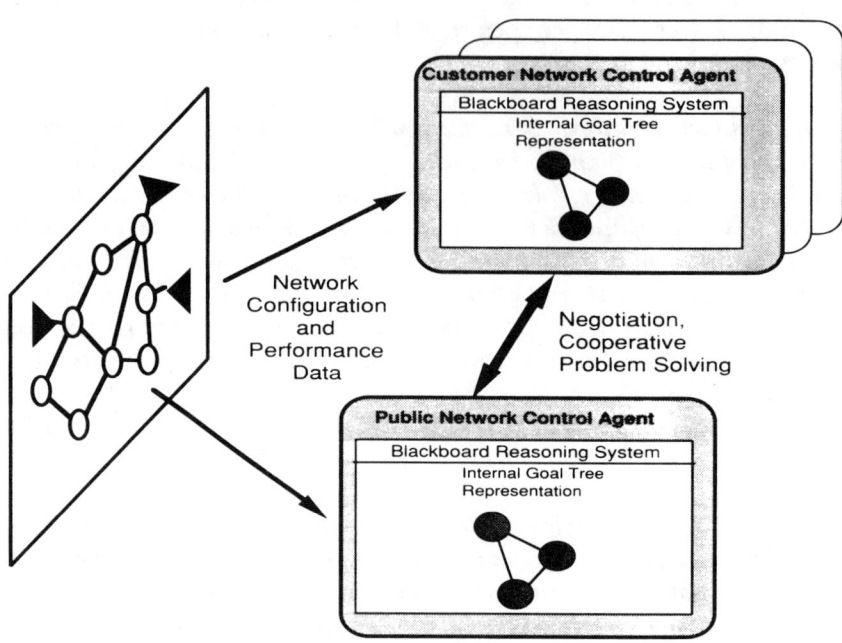

Figure 1. Cooperation in the customer network control domain.

### 4.3 New knowledge representations

A knowledge representation (KR) is a systematic way of codifying what an expert knows about some domain. Ultimately, a computer must be able to store, process, and utilize this coded knowledge. The main criteria for assessing the power of a representational framework are logical adequacy (ability to express the knowledge we wish to represent), expressive power (a language with well-defined and "complete" syntax and semantics), and notational convenience (agreed-upon conventions which make the information easy to write and read). Many representational schemes have been developed [24–25]. Most expert systems today use production rules or frames for knowledge representations. Rule-based paradigms offer adequate power for general-purpose work but seem to be insufficient for the evolving network requirements.

Model-Based Reasoning (MBR) [17] is particularly well suited to diagnosis and troubleshooting, and can provide an essential KR technology for the network domain in generating a "best guess" solution when all necessary information/data does not exist. MBR works through the interaction of observation (of the behavior of the actual device) and prediction (based on the model). It works on the presumption that if the model is correct, all the discrepancies between the observations and prediction arise from the defect in the device. Model-Based approaches can be practically used when the device or the system can be formally modeled and the problem domain does not contain too many device interactions. It is difficult to model a complete network on a consistent basis because of the wide variety of components it employs for diverse applications and their interactions. Individual devices can be modeled, however, to use this approach in the telecommunications domain. Although it is a serious area of current research, MBR applications to telecommunication systems await more technical developments.

Different representations are appropriate for specific portions of the knowledge that is required in any complex operation. Hybrid representations may increase the robustness of expert systems, thereby overcoming the "brittleness" for which the expert systems are criticized when unable to perform even slightly beyond their explicit domains of expertise.

**Case-based reasoning for traffic management**

A prototype system, called NETTRAC (NETwork Traffic Routing Assistant using Cases), is being built at GTE Laboratories for traffic management [26]. The system receives network performance data from a (simulated) group of switches under its control, recognizes and interprets abnormal conditions that it observes, and develops plans for installing controls to alleviate network problems. With approval from the user, it installs the controls and monitors [27] their effects, recommending adjustments when needed. Figure 2 shows the functional diagram of NETTRAC.

NETTRAC currently handles the following four broad categories of network traffic problems:

- Trunk group overload (or "isolated-demand overflow")
- Focussed overload
- Partial facility (trunk or switch) failure
- Complete facility failure

In order for NETTRAC to know how to handle a particular type of problem, we provide it with a description of how to recognize, treat, and monitor the problem. These descriptions are the "cases," in the form of past experiences, used by the case-based reasoner. To use these cases for solving network problems, NETTRAC must be able to find a relevant case when confronted with a problem. NETTRAC accomplishes this by indexing its cases according to the crucial features of a situation that together indicate the possible applicability of each case. Final selection of the specific case on which to model its response is done by evaluating the details of a situation to determine which case is most similar and most likely to lead to a favorable outcome.

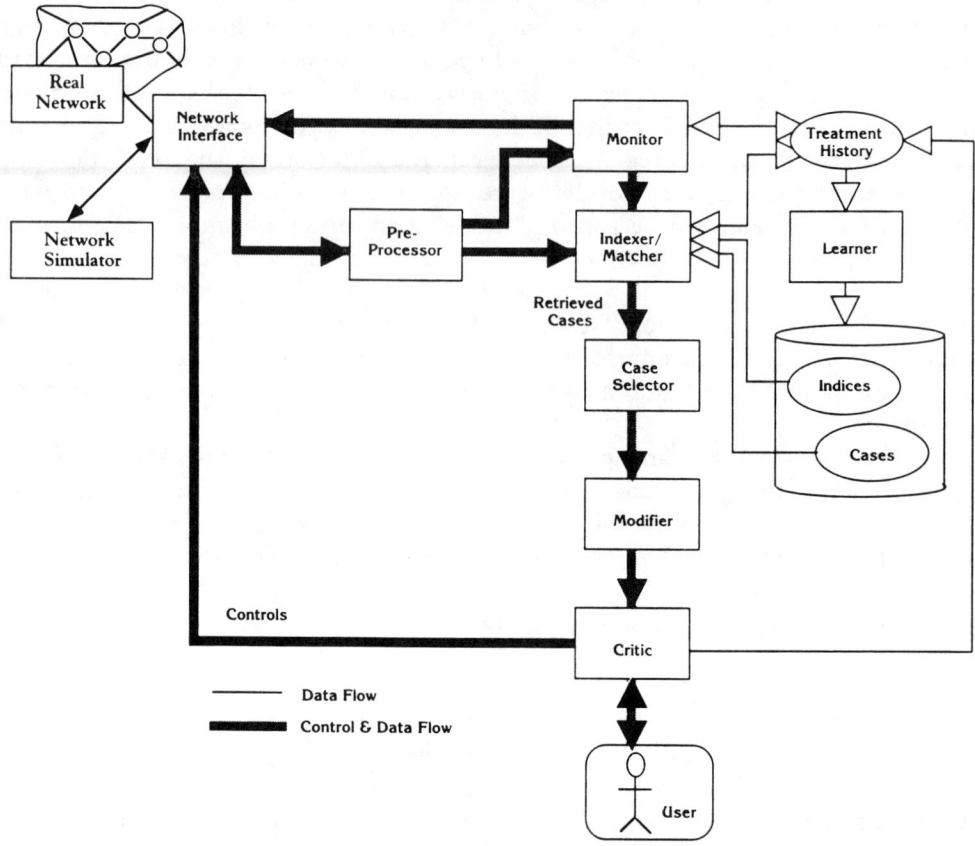

Figure 2. Case-based reasoning (NETTRAC) functional diagram.

Obviously, a large number of cases are required to describe all significant problems in a domain as complex as traffic management, and NETTRAC currently has only a (substantial) subset of the case knowledge it will ultimately need. We have, however, provided the system with a "soft matching" mechanism, the Modifier, that expands the class of problems for which a case is applicable. It does this by defining specific circumstances under which a case may "borrow" attributes from another somewhat similar case. In the example above, a CODE-BLOCK control could be "borrowed" from some other case for any switch types that don't support the GAP control. This avoids the need to explicitly encode every possible combination of features in separate cases.

There are several advantages to be gained from this case-based approach when dealing with complex problems such as network traffic management. Through incorporating a simple learning or case acquisition mechanism, the system can accumulate new cases as it gains experience. This makes CBR especially useful in evolving domains, or where much domain knowledge is missing or difficult to obtain, because the automatically acquired cases can "fill in the gaps" and track gradual changes in the problems of the domain. Also, CBR systems avoid the "brittleness" of other approaches: rather than having to match a precise set of conditions, CBR systems are designed to handle situations that are analogous to, but not exactly like, those of which they have explicit knowledge. This feature is a result of "soft-matching" to determine case applicability, and of adapting the case to apply to a broader range of problems. There are also some efficiencies to be gained through CBR; because the system outlines a complete treatment plan, only one matching and selection cycle may be required for each network problem, compared with dozens or more for a rule-based system. This is the origin of the oft-cited performance advantage of CBR for time-constrained applications.

A significant part of our continuing efforts is the construction of an automatic case-acquisition capability. This feature makes use of the user's expertise as well as the system's own experience to extend its knowledge. Initially, this will involve adding new cases to the system's experience base when the user changes the system's proposed solution. Later, the system may identify additional predictive features as a result of its own experience. As these predictors are identified, they will be used to further index the expanding set of stored cases, thus automatically expanding the experience/case base of the system.

## 4.4 Machine learning techniques

In order to keep up with the accelerating changes in telecommunication networks, future expert systems will need to be able to adapt themselves, without relying on the intervention of human knowledge engineers. Indeed, it is possible to imagine a rate of change in network technology that will exceed the ability of human organizations to digest the requisite new knowledge. At that point, machine learning will be not only an economic necessity, but a technological imperative for further advancement.

This high degree of pay-off has engendered an explosion of current research activities and a wealth of promising new techniques, encompassing both symbolic methods, and non-symbolic methods such as connectionism and genetic algorithms.

As with the need for multiple knowledge representations, we believe that no single machine learning approach will suffice for complex learning problems. It is much less clear, however, when a particular method is appropriate. Telecommunications applications have been proposed for connectionist networks, for example, from alarm correlation to network design. A pressing need, therefore, is to identify both the appropriate application of emerging techniques and the means by which these techniques can be used together.

One effort to address this issue of integrated learning is ongoing at GTE Laboratories, and is highlighted in the following section.

### The integrated learning system [28]

Machine learning is a rapidly growing sub-field of Artificial Intelligence, and a large variety of learning algorithms have been reported in the literature [29-34]. No one algorithm provides a totally satisfactory solution to a wide range of problems. An important issue is how to combine various learning paradigms, how to integrate different reasoning techniques, and how to coordinate distributed problem solvers. An Integrated Learning System (ILS) [28] has been implemented at GTE Laboratories to provide a framework for interpreting and evaluating a variety of learning algorithms distributed across a heterogeneous network of computers and languages. Network Traffic Control has been chosen as the application domain. Figure 3 shows the ILS architecture.

At present, ILS contains three learning paradigms: Inductive (FBI), search-based (MACLEARN), and knowledge-based (NETMAN). ILS also includes a central controller (TLC) which manages control flow and communication between the agents. The agents provide TLC with their own expert advice and critiques on other agents' advice. TLC chooses which suggestion to adopt and performs the appropriate actions. At intervals, the agents can inspect the results of the TLC's actions and use this feedback to learn, improving the value of their future advice. A network simulator (NETSIM) is used to provide a realistic environment to evaluate the learning architecture.

FBI and MACLEARN are written in Symbolics LISP and run on Symbolics Lisp Machines. NETMAN is written in Quintus Prolog and runs on SUN Microsystems workstations. ILS is completely distributed. Communication among instances of the agents and TLC is via TCP/IP streams with a text-based protocol.

*Inductive Learning.* FBI (Function-Based Induction) is an extension of Quinlan's ID3 [35]. FBI learns decision trees from large numbers of examples. Trees both compress and generalize the experience represented by sets of examples; the trees completely describe the examples. A decision tree can be expanded into a set of rules, one for each leaf of the tree, so that this approach generates classification rulesets from examples.

FBI is also able to discover potentially useful concepts that are combinations of existing functions by examining a tree and finding paths that lead to identical subtrees. The discovered concepts are then used to simplify the existing decision tree and are made available as building blocks in the construction of other decision trees. Often the concepts discovered in this way are useful because they reflect genuine features of the domain. In other cases, the concepts discovered are artifacts caused by random patterns in the example set. FBI can ask other elements of ILS, in particular NETMAN, to assess the utility of a discovered concept.

*Search-Based Learning.* MACLEARN currently performs best-first search in order to learn useful combinations of operators (called macro-operators or macros) that can be subsequently treated as a single operator. Macro-learning is a form of chunking which can improve search performance by enlarging the set of operators available for the search. The availability of a good set of macros will often drastically reduce the combinatorial explosive nature of a search problem. A key issue in macro learning is to be highly selective in choosing which macros to keep. MACLEARN uses various criteria to perform the filtering process.

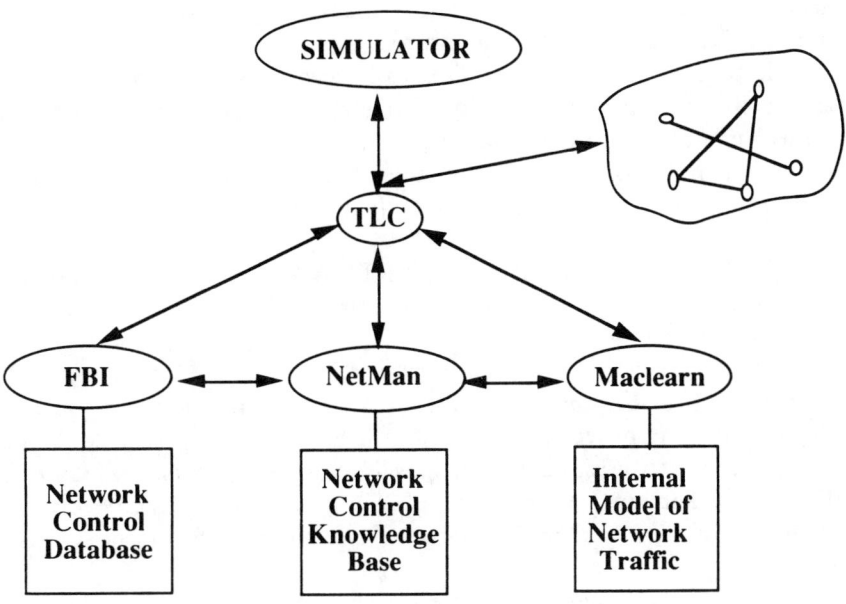

Figure 3. The integrated learning system.

On complex problems, MACLEARN may encounter combinational explosion as the search space of possible operators becomes too large. MACLEARN becomes bogged down in the search and may be unable to find a satisfactory solution. Other agents within ILS can provide assistance to MACLEARN by constraining the search and indicating which part of the search space should be examined.

*Knowledge-Based Learning.* NETMAN is an example of a knowledge-intensive learning system [34]. Such systems have a large amount of knowledge of the domain, similar to the knowledge base of an expert system. The knowledge need be neither complete nor totally accurate. As a result, NETMAN can make mistakes. (Human experts suffer from the same limitation, of course.)

Ideally, NETMAN would be able to distinguish accurately between situations in which an action will be successful and those in which it fails. Unfortunately, the computation involved, and the stochastic nature of the domain, make this impossible to do precisely. Instead, NETMAN heuristically differentiates the cases by calling on FBI, another component of ILS.

NETMAN learns four major types of information from experience:

- Stored caches: NETMAN stores as a macro the sequence of rule firings that led to advice that worked.

- Support list: The support list indicates how successful or unsuccessful a particular action proved to be. Those that have proved valuable in the past are more likely to be used in the future.
- Possible bugs: When an action fails to have the expected result, NETMAN can classify the cause and severity of this failure. This information is stored and will affect the future use of the action.
- Plans: A plan consists of a sequence of actions that have proved useful, together with the expected effect of each action.

When actions have unexpected results, NETMAN attempts to explain the cause of the unpredicted behavior. This analysis allows NETMAN to discover that sometimes an action will fail due to a bug. NETMAN is able to classify the type of bug and associate it with the action.

*The Learning Coordinator.* The TLC manages communication between agents and the decision-making process. It first asks the agents to propose a control action. It then asks the agents to critique the proposals of other agents. TLC then chooses among the proposed actions, and executes it. The process is repeated every five minutes when a new set of data and traffic statistics are received from the switches in the simulator.

The success of ILS will be demonstrated when ILS as a whole does better than each individual learning agent. Preliminary results, thus far, have been encouraging. The resulting knowledge/learning of each agent will be utilized more effectively. Efforts are also under way to improve the individual learning algorithms and add other learning paradigms to the ILS.

## 5. A VIEWPOINT ON THE FUTURE NETWORK

### 5.1 The ultimate network and its evolution

An obvious way to deal with a complex network is to build automatic controls in the network by building sensory points, reasoning, and control mechanisms—a task much easier said than done! There is still a long way to go before we can take this goal seriously, but limited automatic control functionality is beginning to appear in present systems.

Several generic categories of knowledge engineering applications have emerged in the last several years [6, 36]. Some of the categories of knowledge-based systems relevant to network management, capture, and use expertise in design, planning, interpretation, diagnosis, monitoring, prediction, and control. The intelligent system applications for networks can be mapped into two broad conceptual categories. The first category deals with design and planning issues in establishing and providing network facilities. Flexibility of the network is built into this phase. The second category supports operations, management, administration, and control (OMAC) functions and reflects on the reliability aspect of the network. There are strong pressures to integrate the existing optimizing and algorithmic methods and tools with the emerging intelligence in the network. A variety of stand-alone knowledge-based systems are in field trials or in commercial use in the network. Also, algorithmic design and planning tools such as EFRAP (The Exchange Feeder Route Analysis Program), cash flow, and traffic engineering tools are available today to the network designers. There is a need for building intelligent planning tools and integrating them with currently used databases, so that the same system can be used by different groups, including network planning, network engineering, and implementation planning. Expert system front ends will be providing the consolidated data environments for these groups to make intelligent decisions.

Network management and traffic control systems are currently used in decision support mode to manage networks. As traffic control expert systems become closely integrated with alarm surveillance systems and are tested sufficiently to verify the accuracy of their decisions, they can be trusted to make simple traffic rerouting decisions and to install controls, thus making networks more automatically controlled (autonomous). At the same time, as the systems are extended with more knowledge about operations and alternative controls, they will more closely support human experts in making complex decisions.

## 5.2 An autonomous network scenario

In an autonomous network, error-free operation is provided by hardware flexibility and intelligent diagnostic functions embedded into the network components and into the network management system. The network management system continuously monitors traffic demand and facility operation, adjusting the normal flow of traffic as needed. This system also has a learning component to permit it to come to anticipate the routine overloads and adjust to the slower shifts (hopefully growth) in traffic demands. One function of this system is to report on the capacity of the network to handle the demands and to warn the planning group when problems seem to be caused by design mismatch rather than temporary demand anomalies. Operators now work with the system to solve long-term operational threats—the system itself handling the small problems.

The autonomous network will also request and direct repair and maintenance functions. The overall system will have a wide variety of sensors and status display systems distributed and integrated in the network. The actions are taken by a collection of processors, with some of the monitoring and analysis functions being performed at switch level, along with some repair and maintenance actions; the rest of the repair actions will take place at regional centers serving a subset of the network (and a single roving repair crew) along with more monitoring and analysis and facility error detection and diagnosis. Regional centers will also be the first line of attack on traffic management functions. For the sake of improved reliability and load sharing, the regions covered by a center will overlap. The centers will be individually responsible for coordinating their actions so that work is not duplicated and that answers to requests from other functions are complete. For the major operational functions, such as diagnosis of network-wide problems and overall coordination of complex problem solutions, there may be one or more central coordination centers. The function of these centers is to monitor the overall performance of the network and the other control centers, and to initiate action when it seems appropriate and is lacking. For this reason, the line between operation and design is less distinct. Operation and design are merged into one process, directing the hardware and software evolution of the network. These centers will also be responsible for interacting with the network owner to provide needed information on network operation and performance. The network owner is now a strategist, orchestrating the decision priorities to meet business objectives.

## 6. SUMMARY AND CONCLUSIONS

Despite many of the major initiatives in the industry and several high powered developments taking place, it is a fair question to ask, "Are the knowledge systems real?" "Can they perform any 'worthwhile' task with reliability?" Feigenbaum [37] conducted an exhaustive survey of expert systems in day-to-day production use. At the AAAI Conference address in 1988, he reported over 3000 systems supposedly in production use. This number may well have doubled by now. DEC, Dupont, American Express, and IBM reported that their expert systems save ten to hundreds of millions of dollars per year. The advantages of knowledge systems were also established in interviews with the user groups. In many cases, these systems, besides storing the much needed corporate expertise permanently and improving quality and performance, provide up to an order of magnitude productivity increase and 1-2 orders of magnitude speedup of operations. These gains are significant and are being recognized by the corporate management. Some companies have concentrated on building large systems for a complete task. Other companies, like Dupont, built a very large number of small systems to perform minor day-to-day tasks.

In telecommunications, knowledge systems are emerging, but slowly, primarily in diagnosis and maintenance areas. AT&T is using NEMESYS for network management and control. Many more powerful systems are in field trial stage and ready to be launched into day-to-day operations. Integration of these individual systems into a larger system is the natural next step.

Some final questions to ask are, Where might this new technology (AI) lead us? Will there be real benefit by using it? Should there be an autonomous network or a network without human control? Can a communication network control itself effectively, using its own intelligence? These are interesting questions whose answers will emerge through further research. For now, integration of expert systems in network management and operations is paving the way for more reliable, functionally rich, and intelligent networks, and much more is expected as the technology advances.

## ACKNOWLEDGMENTS

Much of the work reported in this paper is being conducted in several projects at GTE Laboratories. The author would like to acknowledge the contributions of the staff of these projects. Suggestions and comments of Richard Brandau and Robert Weihmayer have been valuable in the preparation of this paper and are gratefully acknowledged. Larry Bernstein, Pradeep Sen, Rodney Goodman, and John Vittal reviewed the manuscript and gave insightful suggestions. Thanks are due to Wilfredine Chiasson, who shaped the paper in the present form. Finally, the author would like to thank William Griffin for encouragement and support of this work and its publication.

**REFERENCES**

1. "Expert Systems in Network Management," *IEEE Network Magazine*, Vol. 2, No. 5, September 1988.
2. S. Goyal, "Future of OSSs," Panel, *IEEE Supercom. ICC '90*, Atlanta, GA, April 1990.
3. S. Goyal and L. Kopeikina, "The Evolution of Intelligent Network," ICC'87 Workshop on the Integration of Expert Systems into Network Operations, June 11-12, 1987, Seattle, WA.
4. S. Goyal, R. Weihmayer, and R. Brandau, "Intelligent Systems in the Future Network," Proceedings of *IEEE Networks Operations and Management Symposium*, San Diego, CA, February 11-14, 1990.
5. R.M. Goodman, J. Miller, and P. Smyth, "Real Time Autonomous Expert Systems in Network Management," in *Integrated Network Management*, edited by B. Meandzija and S. Westcott, Elsevier Science Publishers, 1989.
6. S.R. Wright and G.T. Vesonder, "Expert Systems in Telecommunications," in *Expert Systems with Applications*, Vol. 1, pp. 127-136, 1990.
7. M. Thandasseri, "Expert Systems Application for TXE4A Exchanges," *Electrical Communication*, Vol. 60, No. 2, 1986.
8. D. Prerau, A.S. Gunderson, R.E. Reinke, and S. Goyal, "The Compass Expert System: Verification, Technology Transfer, and Expansion," in *Second Conference on Artificial Intelligence Applications*, pp. 597-602, IEEE, Washington, D.C., 1985.
9. P. Zeldin, F. Miller, E. Siegfried, and J. Wright, "Knowledge Based Loop Maintenance: The ACE System," *ICC'86*, pp. 1241-1243, June 1986.
10. G. Vesonder, et al., "ACE: An Expert System for Telephone Cable Maintenance," in *8th International Joint Conference on Artificial Intelligence*, pp. 116-121, AAAI, Menlo Park, CA, 1983.
11. S. Guattery and F. Villarreal, "NEMESYS: An Expert System for Fighting Congestion in the Long Distance Network," *Expert Systems in Government*, IEEE, October 1985.
12. J. Hannan, "Network Solutions Employing Expert Systems," *Phoenix Computers and Communications Conference* (PCCC-87), pp. 543-547, IEEE, Washington, D.C., 1987.
13. L. Mantleman, AI Carves Inroads: "Network Design, Testing, and Management," *Data Communications*, pp. 106-123, July 1986.
14. S. Bernstein, "DesignNet: An Intelligent System for Network Design and Modelling," in *International Communications Conference 1987*, edited by D.J. Sassa, New York: IEEE, Seattle, WA.
15. F. Ferrara, F. Giovannini, E. Paschetta, "IAS: An Expert System for Packet-Switched Network Monitoring and Repair Assistance," in *Proceedings of Conference on Artificial Intelligence, Telecommunications, and Computer Systems*, edited by R. Attard, pp. 185-197, Nanterre, France: ECCAI, 1989.
16. J.M. Ackroff, P.T. Surko, and J.R. Wright, "AutoTest-2: An Expert System for Special Services,"in *Proceedings of the Fourth Annual Artificial Intelligence and Advanced Computer Technology Conference*, edited by M. Teitell, pp. 503-508, 1988.

17. R. Davis and W. Hamscher, "Model Based Reasoning, Troubleshooting," AI Labs, MIT, May 1988.
18. E.H. Durfee, V.R. Lesser and D.D. Corkill, "Cooperative Distributed Problem Solving," in *The Handbook of Artificial Intelligence*, edited by A. Barr, P.R. Cohen and E.A. Feigenbaum, Vol. 4, Addison-Wesley, 1989.
19. R. Davis and R.G. Smith, "Negotiation As a Metaphor for Distributed Problem Solving," *Artificial Intelligence*, 20, 1, 1983.
20. R. Weihmayer and R. Brandau, "A Distributed AI Architecture for Customer Network Control," *Proceedings of Globecom'90*, San Diego, CA, December 2-5, 1990.
21. L. Kopeikina, R. Brandau and A. Lemmon, "Case-Based Reasoning for Continuous Control," in *Proceedings Case-Based Reasoning Workshop*, Clearwater Beach, FL (Morgan Kaufmann, Palo Alto, CA), pp. 250-259, 1988.
22. R. Brandau and R. Weihmayer, "Heterogeneous Multi-Agent Cooperative Problem Solving in a Telecommunications Network Management Domain," *AAAI 9th DAI Workshop*, September 12-14, 1989, Orcas Island, Washington, December 1989.
23. R. Weihmayer, R. Brandau, and H.S. Shinn, "Modes of Diversity: Issues in Cooperation Among Dissimilar Agents," *Proceedings of Tenth Distributed AI Workshop, AAAI-sponsored*, October 1990.
24. *"Readings in Knowledge Representation,"* edited by R.J. Brachman and H.J. LeVesque, Morgan Kaufmann, 1985.
25. J. Kolodner, R. Simpson, Jr., and K. Sycara-Cyranski, "A Process Model of CASE-Based Reasoning in Problem Solving," in *Proceedings IJCAI-85*, AAAI, Menlo Park, CA, 1985.
26. A.B. Davis, C.V. Lafond, and A.V. Lemmon, "A Proof-of-Concept Network Traffic Management System Using Case-Based Reasoning," December 1989.
27. L. Kopeikina, R. Brandau, and A. Lemmon, "Extending Cases Through Time," Workshop on Case Based Reasoning, *AAAI 1988*, St. Paul MN. Aug 23, 1988.
28. B. Silver, J. Vittal, B. Frawley, G. Iba, and K. Bradford, "ILS: A Framework for Integrating Multiple Heterogeneous Learning Agents," *Proceedings of the Second Generation Expert Systems, 10th International Workshop on Expert Systems and Their Applications*, Avignon 1990.
29. W.J. Frawley, "Using Functions to Encode Domain and Contextual Knowledge in Statistical Induction," in *Knowledge Discovery in Databases (IJCAI-89 Workshop)*, edited by G. Piatetsky-Shapiro and W.J. Frawley, pp. 99-108, International Joint Conference on Artificial Intelligence, 1989.
30. G.A. Iba, "A Heuristic Approach to the Discovery of Macro-Operators," *Machine Learning 3(4)*, pp. 285-317, 1989.
31. R.S. Michalski, J.G. Carbonell, and T.M. Mitchell (editors), *Machine Learning: An Artificial Intelligence Approach*, Vol. 1, Tioga Press, 1983.
32. R.S. Michalski, J.G. Carbonell, and T.M. Mitchell (editors), *Machine Learning: An Artificial Intelligence Approach*, Vol. 2, Morgan Kaufmann, 1986.
33. B. Silver, "Precondition Analysis: Learning Control Information," in *Machine Learning: An Artificial Intelligence Approach*, edited by R.S. Michalski, J.G. Carbonell, and T.M. Mitchell, Vol. 2, pp. 647-670, Morgan Kaufmann, 1986.

34. B. Silver, "NetMan: A Learning Network Traffic Controller," in *Proceedings of Third International Conference on Industrial & Engineering Applications of Artificial Intelligence and Expert Systems*, edited by M. Matthews, pp. 923-931, Association for Computing Machinery, 1990.
35. J.R. Quinlan, "Induction of Decision Trees," *Machine Learning 1*, (1) pp. 81-106, 1986.
36. S. Goyal and R. Worrest, "Expert System Applications to Network Management," in *Expert Systems Applications to Telecommunications*, edited by J. Liebowitz, pp. 3-44, New York: John Wiley & Sons, 1988.
37. E. Feigenbaum, P. McCorduck, and P. Nii, *The Rise of the Expert Company*, TimeBOOKS, 1988.

# Chapter 2: Management Information

The foundation of any network management system is a database containing information about the elements to be managed. In both the SNMP and OSI environments, the database is referred to as a management information base (MIB). Each resource to be managed is represented by an object. The MIB is a structured collection of such objects. Each node in the system will maintain a MIB that reflects the status of the managed resources at that node. A network management entity can monitor the resources at that node by reading the values of objects in the MIB and may control the resources at that node by modifying those values.

For the MIB to serve the needs of a network management system, it must meet several objectives:

1. The object or objects used to represent a particular resource must be the same at each node. For example, consider information stored concerning the TCP entity at a node. The total number of connections opened over a period of time consists of active opens and passive opens. The MIB at the node could store any two of the three relevant values (number of active opens, number of passive opens, total number of opens), from which the third could be derived when needed. However, if different nodes select different pairs for storage, it is difficult to write a simple protocol to access the required information. As it happens, the MIB definition for TCP/IP specifies that the active and passive open counts be stored.

2. A common scheme for representation must be used to support interoperability.

The papers in this chapter examine the issues relating to management information design and look at the approaches used for both SNMP and OSI systems management. In this part of the chapter, we introduce two key underlying concepts: ASN.1 and object-oriented design.

Abstract Syntax Notation One (ASN.1), defined in ISO standard IS 8824, is the language used to define the syntax of objects in the management information base for both SNMP and OSI systems management. In addition, the syntax of application-level protocol data units for both SNMP and OSI systems management is defined using ASN.1. While ASN.1 is not required to define management information elements, its use in both the SNMP and OSI realms means that it is essential that the student of these standards have the ability to "read" ASN.1. Furthermore, ASN.1 has gained widespread acceptance for use in a whole range of standards in both the TCP/IP and OSI architectures. To be "network literate," one needs an understanding of ASN.1.

Both SNMP and OSI management information is represented as a collection of "objects." In the case of SNMP, an object is simply a typed scalar variable, and a simple hierarchical structure of objects forms the MIB. In the case of OSI systems management, the term object is used in the sense of object-oriented design. Object-oriented design principles play a key role in the OSI structure of management information. It should be pointed out that the object-oriented approach is not the only way to represent management information. Both relational and hierarchical database technologies have been widely used in proprietary systems. However, as was pointed out in Chapter 1, with the increasing incorporation of object-oriented capability in operating systems, this technology should enjoy increased use in network management. Furthermore, because OSI systems management relies heavily on object-oriented concepts, a basic understanding of these concepts is needed before approaching the OSI systems management standards.

## Abstract Syntax Notation One (ASN.1)

The basic building block of an ASN.1 specification is the module. We begin this section by looking at the top-level structure of the module. Then, we introduce some lexical conventions used in ASN.1 definitions. Next, the data types defined in ASN.1 are described. Finally, an example of the use of ASN.1 is given.

**Module definition.** ASN.1 is a language that can be used to define data structures. A structure definition is in the form of a named module. The name of the module can then be used to reference the structure.

Modules have the basic form:

```
<modulereference> DEFINITIONS ::=
    BEGIN
        EXPORTS
        IMPORTS
        AssignmentList
    End
```

The modulereference is a module name followed optionally by a numeric object identifier to identify the module. The EXPORTS construct indicates which definitions in this module may be imported by other modules. The IMPORTS construct indicates which type and value definitions from other modules are to be imported into this module. Neither the IMPORTS nor the EXPORTS constructs may be included unless the object identifier for the module is included. Finally, the assignment list consists of type assignments and value assignments. Type and value assignments have the form:

```
<name> ::= <description>
```

The easiest way to describe the ASN.1 notation is by example. First, we need to specify some lexical conventions.

**Lexical conventions.** ASN.1 structures, types, and values are expressed in a notation similar to that of a programming language. The following lexical conventions are followed:

1. Layout is not significant; multiple spaces and blank lines can be considered as a single space.

2. Comments are delimited by pairs of hyphens (--) at the beginning and end of the comment, or by a pair of hyphens at the beginning of the comment and the end of the line as the end of the comment.

3. Identifiers (names of values and fields), type references (names of types), and module names consist of upper- and lowercase letters, digits, and hyphens.

4. An identifier begins with a lowercase letter.

5. A type reference or a module name begins with an uppercase letter.

6. A built-in type consists of all capital letters. A built-in type is a commonly used type for which a standard notation is provided.

**Abstract data types.** ASN.1 is a notation for abstract data types and their values. A type can be viewed as a collection of values. The number of values that a type may take on may be infinite. For example, the type INTEGER has an infinite number of values.

We can classify types into four categories:

- *Simple*: These are atomic types, with no components.
- *Structured*: A structured type has components.
- *Tagged*: These are types derived from other types.
- *Other*: This category includes the CHOICE and ANY types, defined below.

Every ASN.1 data type, with the exception of CHOICE and ANY, has an associated tag. The tag consists of a class name and a nonnegative integer tag number. There are four classes of data types, or four classes of tag:

- *Universal:* Generally useful, application-independent types and construction mechanisms; these are defined in the standard and are listed in Table 2-1.
- *Application-wide:* Relevant to a particular application; these are defined in other standards.
- *Context-specific:* Also relevant to a particular application, but applicable in a limited context.
- *Private:* Types defined by users and not covered by any standard.

A data type is uniquely identified by its tag. ASN.1 types are the same if and only if their tag numbers are the same. For example, UNIVERSAL 4 refers to OctetString, which is of class UNIVERSAL and has tag number 4 within the class.

**Simple types.** A simple type is one defined by directly specifying the set of its values. We may think of these as the atomic types; all other types are built up from the simple types. The simple data types in the UNIVERSAL class can be grouped into several categories, as indicated in Table 2-1; these are not "official" categories in the standard but are used here for convenience.

The first group of simple types can be referred to, for want of a better word, as basic types. The Boolean type is straightforward. The Integer type is the set of positive and negative integers and zero. In addition, individual integer values can be assigned names to indicate a specific meaning. The BitString is an ordered set of zero or more bits; individual bits can be assigned names. The actual value of a BitString can be specified as a string of either binary or hexadecimal digits. Similarly, an OctetString can be specified as a string of either binary or hexadecimal digits. The Real data type consists of numbers expressed in scientific notation (mantissa, base, exponent); that is:

$$M \times B^E$$

The mantissa (M) and the exponent (E) may take on any integer values, positive or negative; a base (B) of 2 or 10 may be used.

Finally, the Enumerated type consists of an explicitly enumerated list of integers, together with an associated name for each integer. The same functionality can be achieved with the Integer type by naming some of the integer values; but, because of the utility of this feature, a separate type has been defined. Note, however, that although the values of the enumerated type are integers, they do not have integer semantics. That is, arithmetic operations should not be performed on enumerated values.

Object types are used to name and describe information objects. Examples of information objects are standards documents, abstract and transfer syntaxes, data structures, and managed objects. In general, an information object is a class of information (for example, a file format) rather than an instance of such a class (for example, an individual file). The Object identifier is a unique identifier for a particular object. Its value consists of a sequence of integers. The set of defined objects has a tree structure, with the root of the tree being the object referring to the ASN.1 standard. Starting with the root of the object identifier tree, each object identifier component value identifies an arc in the tree. The Object descriptor is a human-readable description of an information object.

ASN.1 defines a number of character string types. The values of each of these types consist of a sequence of zero or more characters from a standardized character set.

There are some miscellaneous types that have also been defined in the UNIVERSAL class. The Null type is used in places in a structure where a value may or may not be present. The Null type is simply the alternative of no value being present at that position in the structure. An External type is one whose values are unspecified in the ASN.1 standard; it is defined in some other document or standard and can be defined using any well-specified notation. UTCTime and GeneralizedTime are two different formats for expressing time. In both cases, either a universal or a local time may be specified.

**Structured types.** Structured types are those consisting of components. ASN.1 provides four structured types for building complex data types from simple data types:

### Table 2-1. Universal class tag assignments.

| Tag | Type Name | Set of Values |
|---|---|---|
| **Basic Types** | | |
| UNIVERSAL 1 | BOOLEAN | TRUE or FALSE |
| UNIVERSAL 2 | INTEGER | The positive and negative whole numbers, including zero. |
| UNIVERSAL 3 | BIT STRING | A sequence of zero or more bits. |
| UNIVERSAL 4 | OCTET STRING | A sequence of zero or more octets. |
| UNIVERSAL 9 | REAL | Real numbers. |
| UNIVERSAL 10 | ENUMERATED | An explicit list of integer values that an instance of a data type may take. |
| **Object Types** | | |
| UNIVERSAL 6 | OBJECT IDENTIFIER | The set of values associated with information objects allocated by this standard. |
| UNIVERSAL 7 | Object descriptor | Each value is human-readable text providing a brief description of an information object. |
| **Character String Types** | | |
| UNIVERSAL 18 | NumericString | Digits 0 through 9, space |
| UNIVERSAL 19 | PrintableString | Printable characters |
| UNIVERSAL 20 | TeletexString | Character set defined by CCITT Recommendation T.61 |
| UNIVERSAL 21 | VideotexString | Set of alphabetic and graphical characters defined by CCITT Recommendation T.100 and T.101. |
| UNIVERSAL 22 | IA5String | International alphabet five (equivalent to ASCII) |
| UNIVERSAL 25 | GraphicString | Character set defined by ISO 8824 |
| UNIVERSAL 26 | VisibleString | Character set defined by ISO 646 (equivalent to ASCII) |
| UNIVERSAL 27 | GeneralString | General character string |
| **Miscellaneous Types** | | |
| UNIVERSAL 5 | NULL | The single value NULL. Commonly used where several alternatives are possible but none of them applies. |
| UNIVERSAL 8 | EXTERNAL | A type defined in some external document. It need not be one of the valid ASN.1 types. |
| UNIVERSAL 23 | UTCTime | Consists of the date, specified with a two-digit year, a two-digit month, and a two-digit day, followed by the time, specified in hours, minutes, and optionally seconds, followed by an optional specification of the local time differential from universal time. |
| UNIVERSAL 24 | GeneralizedTime | Consists of the date, specified with a four-digit year, a two-digit month, and a two-digit day, followed by the time, specified in hours, minutes, and optionally seconds, followed by an optional specification of the local time differential from universal time. |
| UNIVERSAL 9-15 | Reserved | Reserved for addenda to the ASN.1 standard. |
| UNIVERSAL 28- | Reserved | Reserved for addenda to the ASN.1 standard. |
| **Structured Types** | | |
| UNIVERSAL 16 | SEQUENCE and SEQUENCE OF | Sequence: Defined by referencing a fixed, ordered list of types; each value is an ordered list of values, one from each component type. Sequence-of: Defined by referencing a single existing type; each value is an ordered list of zero or more values of the existing type. |
| UNIVERSAL 17 | SET and SET OF | Set: Defined by referencing a fixed, unordered list of types, some of which may be declared optional; each value is an unordered list of values, one from each component type. Set-of: Defined by referencing a single existing type; each value is an unordered list of zero or more values of the existing type. |

- SEQUENCE
- SEQUENCE OF
- SET
- SET OF

The SEQUENCE and SEQUENCE OF types are used to define an ordered list of values of one or more other data types. This is analogous to the record structure found in many programming languages, such as Cobol. A SEQUENCE consists of an ordered list of elements, each specifying a type and, optionally, a name. The notation for defining the SEQUENCE type is as follows:

```
SequenceType ::= SEQUENCE {ElementTypeList} | SEQUENCE { }
ElementTypeList ::= ElementType | ElementTypeList, ElementType
ElementType ::=
    NamedType                    |
    NamedType OPTIONAL           |
    NamedType DEFAULT Value      |
    COMPONENTS OF Type
```

A NamedType is a type reference with or without a name. Each element definition may be followed by the keyword OPTIONAL or DEFAULT. The OPTIONAL keyword indicates that the component element need not be present in a SEQUENCE value. The DEFAULT keyword indicates that, if the component element is not present, then the value specified by the DEFAULT clause will be assigned. The COMPONENTS OF clause is used to define the inclusion, at this point in the ElementTypeList, of all the ElementType SEQUENCES appearing in the referenced type.

A SEQUENCE OF consists of an ordered, variable number of elements, all of one type. A SEQUENCE OF definition has the following form:

```
SequenceOfType ::= SEQUENCE OF Type | SEQUENCE
```

The notation SEQUENCE is to be interpreted as SEQUENCE OF ANY; the type ANY is explained in a later subsection.

A SET is similar to a SEQUENCE, except that the order of the elements is not significant; the elements may be arranged in any order when they are encoded into a specific representation. A SET definition has the following form:

```
SetType ::= SET {ElementTypeList} | SET { }
```

Thus, a SET may include optional, default, and component-of clauses.

A SET OF is an unordered, variable number of elements, all of one type. A SET OF definition has the following form:

```
SetOfType ::= SET OF Type | SET
```

The notation SET is to be interpreted as SET OF ANY; the type ANY is explained in a later subsection.

**Tagged types.** The term *tagged type* is somewhat of a misnomer since all data types in ASN.1 have an associated tag. The ASN.1 standard defines a tagged type as follows:

> A type defined by referencing a single existing type and a tag; the new type is isomorphic to the existing type, but is distinct from it. In all encoding schemes a value of the new type can be distinguished from a value of the old type.

Tagging is useful to distinguish types within an application. It may be desirable to have several different type names, such as Employee_name and Customer_name, which are essentially the same type.

For some structures, tagging is needed to distinguish component types within the structured type. For example, optional components of a SET or SEQUENCE type are typically given distinct context-specific tags to avoid ambiguity.

There are two categories of tagged types: implicitly tagged types and explicitly tagged types. An implicitly tagged type is derived from another type by *replacing* the tag (old class name, old tag number) of the old type with a new tag (new class name, new tag number). For purposes of encoding, only the new tag is used.

An explicitly tagged type is derived from another type by *adding* a new tag to the underlying type. In effect, an explicitly tagged type is a structured type with one component, the underlying type. For purposes of encoding, both the new and old tags must be reflected in the encoding.

An implicit tag results in shorter encodings, but an explicit tag may be necessary to avoid ambiguity if the tag of the underlying type is indeterminate (for example, if the underlying type is CHOICE or ANY).

**CHOICE and ANY types.** The CHOICE and ANY types are data types without tags. The reason for this is that when a particular value is assigned to the type, then a particular type must be assigned at the same time. Thus, the type is assigned at "run time."

The CHOICE type is a list of alternative known types. Only one of these types will actually be used to create a value. It was stated earlier that a type can be viewed as a collection of values. The CHOICE type is the union of the sets of values of all of the component types listed in the CHOICE type. This type is useful when the values to be described can be of different types depending on circumstance, and all the possible types are known in advance.

The notation for defining the CHOICE type is as follows:

    ChoiceType ::= CHOICE {AlternativeTypeList}
    AlternativeTypeList ::= NamedType | AlternativeTypeList, NamedType

The ANY type describes an arbitrary value of an arbitrary type. The notation is simply:
    AnyType ::= ANY
This type is useful when the values to be described can be of different types but the possible types are not known in advance.

| Table 2-2. Applicability of subtype value sets. | | | | | | |
|---|---|---|---|---|---|---|
| Type (or derived from such a type by tagging) | Single Value | Contained Subtype | Value Range | Size Constraint | Permitted Alphabet | Inner Subtyping |
| Boolean | ✓ | ✓ | | | | |
| Integer | ✓ | ✓ | ✓ | | | |
| Enumerated | ✓ | ✓ | | | | |
| Real | ✓ | ✓ | ✓ | | | |
| Object Identifier | ✓ | ✓ | | | | |
| Bit String | ✓ | ✓ | | ✓ | | |
| Octet String | ✓ | ✓ | | ✓ | | |
| Character String Types | ✓ | ✓ | | ✓ | ✓ | |
| Sequence | ✓ | ✓ | | | | ✓ |
| Sequence-of | ✓ | ✓ | | ✓ | | ✓ |
| Set | ✓ | ✓ | | | | ✓ |
| Set-of | ✓ | ✓ | | ✓ | | ✓ |
| Any | ✓ | ✓ | | | | |
| Choice | ✓ | ✓ | | | | ✓ |

**Subtypes.** A subtype is derived from a parent type by restricting the set of values defined for a parent type. That is, the set of values for the subtype is a subset of the set of values for the parent type. The process of subtyping can extend to more than one level; that is, a subtype may itself be a parent of an even more restricted subtype.

Six different forms of notation for designating the values of a subtype are provided in the standard. Table 2-2 indicates which of these forms can be applied to particular parent types. The remainder of this subsection provides an overview of each form.

**Single value.** A single value subtype is an explicit listing of all of the values that the subtype may take on. For example:

    SmallPrime ::= INTEGER ( 2 | 3 | 5 | 7 | 11 | 13 | 17 | 19 | 23 | 29 )

In this case, SmallPrime is a subtype of the built-in type INTEGER. As another example:

    Months ::= ENUMERATED     {january (1),
                                             february (2),
                                             march (3),
                                             april (4),
                                             may (5),
                                             june (6),
                                             july (7),
                                             august (8),
                                             september (9),
                                             october (10),
                                             november (11),
                                             december (12) }

    First-quarter ::= Months ( january | february | march )
    Second-quarter ::= Months ( april | may | june )

First-quarter and Second-quarter are both subtypes of the enumerated type Months.

**Contained subtype.** A contained subtype is used to form new subtypes from existing subtypes. The contained subtype includes all of the values of the subtypes that it contains. For example:

    First-half ::= Months ( INCLUDES First-quarter | INCLUDES Second-quarter )

A contained subtype may also include listing explicit values:

    First-third ::= Months ( INCLUDES First-quarter | april )

**Value range.** A value range subtype applies only to INTEGER and REAL types. It is specified by giving the numerical values of the endpoints of the range. The special values PLUS-INFINITY and MINUS-INFINITY may be used. The special values MIN and MAX may be used to indicate the minimum and maximum allowable values in the parent. Each endpoint of the range is either closed or open. When open, the specification of the endpoint includes the less-than symbol (<). The following are equivalent definitions

    PositiveInteger ::= INTEGER (0<..PLUS-INFINITY)
    PositiveInteger ::= INTEGER (1..PLUS-INFINITY)
    PositiveInteger ::= INTEGER (0<..MAX)
    PositiveInteger ::= INTEGER (1..MAX)

The following are equivalent:

NegativeInteger ::= INTEGER (MINUS-INFINITY..<0)
NegativeInteger ::= INTEGER (MINUS-INFINITY..–1)
NegativeInteger ::= INTEGER (MIN..<0)
NegativeInteger ::= INTEGER (MIN..–1)

**Permitted alphabet.** The permitted alphabet constraint may only be applied to character string types. A permitted alphabet type consists of all values (strings) that can be constructed using a subalphabet of the parent type. Examples:

TouchToneButtons ::= IA5String ( FROM
   ( "0" | "1" | "2" | "3" | "5" | "6" | "7" | "8" | "9" | "*" | "#" ) )

DigitString ::= IA5String ( FROM
   ( "0" | "1" | "2" | "3" | "5" | "6" | "7" | "8" | "9" ) )

**Size constraint.** A size constraint limits the number of items in a type. It can only be applied to the string types (bit string, octet string, character string) and to SEQUENCE OF and SET OF types. The item that is constrained depends on the parent type, as follows:

| Type | Unit of Measure |
|---|---|
| bit string | bit |
| octet string | octet |
| character string | character |
| sequence-of | component value |
| set-of | component value |

As an example of a string type, Recommendation X.121 specifies that international data numbers, which are used for addressing end systems on public data networks, including X.25 networks, should consist of at least 5 digits but not more than 14 digits. This could be specified as follows:

ItlDataNumber ::= DigitString ( SIZE ( 5..10 ) )

Now consider a parameter list for a message that may include up to 12 parameters:

ParameterList ::= SET SIZE ( 0..12 ) OF Parameter

**Inner subtyping.** An inner type constraint can be applied to the SEQUENCE, SEQUENCE OF, SET, SET OF, and CHOICE types. An inner subtype includes in its value set only those values from the parent type that satisfy one or more constraints on the presence and/or values of the components of the parent type. This is a rather complex subtype, and only a few examples are given here.

Consider a protocol data unit (PDU) which may have four different fields, in no particular order:

PDU ::= SET { alpha   [0] INTEGER,
              beta    [1] IA5String OPTIONAL,
              gamma   [2] SEQUENCE OF Parameter,
              delta   [3] BOOLEAN }

To specify a test that requires the Boolean to be false and the integer to be negative:

TestPDU ::= PDU ( WITH COMPONENTS { ..., delta (FALSE), alpha (MIN...<0)})

To further specify that the beta parameter is to be present and either 5 or 12 characters in length:

   FurtherTestPDU ::= TestPDU (WITH COMPONENTS {..., beta (SIZE (5 | 12) PRESENT})

As another example, consider the use of inner subtyping on a SEQUENCE OF construct:

   Text-block ::= SEQUENCE OF VisibleString
   Address ::= Text-block ( SIZE (1..6) | WITH COMPONENT (SIZE (1..32)))

This indicates that the address consists of from 1 to 6 text blocks, and that each text block is from 1 to 32 characters in length.

**Data structure example.** Figure 2-1, taken from the ASN.1 standard, is an example that defines the structure of a personnel record. Figure 2-1a depicts the personnel record informally by giving an example of a specific record.

Figure 2-1b shows the formal description, or abstract syntax, of the data structure. In the notation, a structure definition has the form:

   <type name> ::= <type definition>

A simple example is:

   SerialNumber ::= INTEGER

There are no simple types defined in the example. A similar construction is:

   EmployeeNumber ::= [APPLICATION 2] IMPLICIT INTEGER

This definition makes use of the universal type Integer, but the user has chosen to give the type a new tag. The use of the term [APPLICATION 2] gives the tag (class and tag number) for this new type. Because the designation IMPLICIT is present, values of this type will be encoded only with the tag APPLICATION 2. If the designation were not present, then the values would be encoded with both the APPLICATION and UNIVERSAL tags. The use of the implicit option results in a more compact representation. In some applications, compactness may be less important than other considerations, such as the ability to carry out type checking. In the latter case, explicit tagging can be used by omitting the word IMPLICIT.

The definition of the Date type is similar to that of EmployeeNumber. In this case, the type is a character string consisting of characters defined in ISO 646, which is equivalent to ASCII. The double hyphen indicates that the rest of the line is a comment; the format of the Date type will not be checked other than to determine that the value is an ISO 646 character string.

The type of Name is the SEQUENCE type. In this case, each of the three elements in the sequence is named. ChildInformation is of the SET type. Note that no name is given to the first element of the set, but that the second element is given the name dateOfBirth. The second element is the data type Date, defined elsewhere. This data type is used in two different locations, here and in the definition of PersonnelRecord. In each location, the data type is given a name and a context-specific tag, [0] and [1] respectively. This follows the general rule: When an implicit or explicit tag is defined, but only the tag number is provided, then the tag's class defaults to context specific.

Finally, the overall structure, PersonnelRecord, is defined as a SET with five elements. Associated with the last element is a default value of a null sequence, to be used if no value is supplied.

Figure 2-1c is an example of a particular value for the personnel record, expressed in the abstract syntax.

| | |
|---|---|
| Name: | **John P Smith** |
| Title: | **Director** |
| Employee Number: | **51** |
| Date of Hire: | **17 September 1971** |
| Name of Spouse: | **Mary T Smith** |
| Number of Children: | **2** |

Child Information
    Name:    **Ralph T Smith**
    Date of Birth:    **11 November 1957**

Child information
    Name:    **Susan B Jones**
    Date of Birth:    **17 July 1959**

(a) Informal description of personnel record

```
PersonnelRecord ::= [APPLICATION 0] IMPLICIT SET{
    Name,
    title [0] VisibleString,
    number EmployeeNumber,
    dateOfHire [1] Date,
    nameOfSpouse [2] Name,
    childen [3] IMPLICIT SEQUENCE OF ChildInformation DEFAULT {}}

ChildInformation ::= SET {
    Name,
    dateOfBirth [0] Date }

Name ::= [APPLICATION 1] IMPLICIT SEQUENCE {
    givenName VisibleString,
    initial VisibleString,
    familyName VisibleString }

EmployeeNumber ::= [APPLICATION 2] IMPLICIT INTEGER

Date ::= [APPLICATION 3] IMPLICIT VisibleString — YYYYMMDD
```

(b) ASN.1 description of the record structure

```
{                           {givenName "John", initial "P", familyName "Smith"}
    title                   "Director"
    number                  51
    dateOfHire              "19710917"
    nameOfSpouse            {givenName "Mary", initial "T", familyName "Smith"},
    children
    { {                     {givenName "Ralph", initial "T", familyName "Smith"},
        dateOfBirth         "19571111"
      {                     {givenName "Susan", initial "B", familyName "Jones" },
        dateOfBirth         "19590717" }}}
```

(c) ASN.1 description of a record value

Figure 2-1: Example of use of ASN.1

**PDU example.** As another example, consider the ASN.1 specification of the format of the protocol data units for the SNMPv2 protocol (described in Chapter 3). The specification from the standard is reproduced in Figure 2-2.

```
SMP-PDU DEFINITIONS ::= BEGIN

PDUs ::= CHOICE {get-request           GetRequest-PDU,
                 get-next=request      GetNextRequest-PDU,
                 get-bulk-request      GetBulkRequest-PDU,
                 response              Response-PDU,
                 set-request           SetRequest-PDU,
                 inform-request        InformRequest-PDU,
                 trap                  SNMPv2-Trap-PDU      }

GetRequest-PDU          ::=PDU          [0] IMPLICIT PDU
GetNextRequest-PDU      ::=PDU          [1] IMPLICIT PDU
GetBulkRequest-PDU      ::=Bulk PDU     [5] IMPLICIT PDU
Response-PDU            ::=PDU          [2] IMPLICIT PDU
SetRequest-PDU          ::=PDU          [3 IMPLICIT PDU
InformRequest-PDU       ::=PDU          [6 IMPLICIT PDU
SNMPv2-Trap-PDU         ::=PDU          [7] IMPLICIT PDU

PDU::= SEQUENCE {request-id Integer32,
                 error-status INTEGER {                 --sometimes ignored
                     noError (0),
                     tooBig (1),
                     noSuchName (2),                    --for proxy compatibility
                     badValue (3),                      --for proxy compatibility
                     readOnly (4),                      --for proxy compatibility
                     genError (5),
                     noAccess (6),
                     wrongType (7),
                     wrongLength (8),
                     wrongEncoding (9),
                     wrongValue (10),
                     noCreation (11),
                     inconsistentValue (12),
                     resourceUnavailable (13),
                     commitFailed (14),
                     undoFailed (15),
                     authorizationError (16),
                     notWritable (17) },
                 error-index INTEGER (0..2147483647),   --sometimes ignored
                 variable-binding VarBindList }         --values are sometimes ignored

BulkPDU ::= Sequence {                                  --MUST be identical in structure to PDU
            request-id        Integer32,
            non-repeaters     INTEGER (0..max-bindings),
            max-repetitions   INTEGER (0..max-bindings),
            variable-binding  VarBindList    }          --values are ignored

VarBind ::= Sequence {name ObjectName,
                 CHOICE {value          ObjectSyntax,
                         unspecified    NULL,           --in retrieval requests
                         noSuchObject [0]   IMPLICIT NULL,
                         noSuchInstance[1]  IMPLICIT NULL,
                         endOfMibView [2]   IMPLICIT NULL }

VarBindList ::= SEQUENCE (SIZE (0..max-bindings)) OF VarBind

END
```

**Figure 2-2: SNMPv2 PDU format definitions**

One new construct in this example is the CHOICE type. This is used to describe a variable selected from a collection. Thus, any instance of the type PDUs will be one of seven alternative types. Note that each of the choices is labeled with a name. Six of the PDUs defined in this fashion have the same format but different labels. The format consists of a sequence of four elements. The second element, error-status, enumerates 18 possible integer values, each with a label. The last element, variable-binding, is defined as having syntax VarBindList, which is defined later in the same set of definitions.

The BulkPDU definition is also a sequence of four elements, but differs from the other PDUs.

VarBindList is defined as a SEQUENCE OF construct consisting of some number of elements of syntax VarBind, with a size constraint of up to 2,147,483,647, or $2^{31}-1$, elements. Each element, in turn, is a sequence of two values; the first is a name, and the second is a choice among five elements.

## Object-oriented design

Object-oriented concepts have become quite popular in the area of computer programming, with the promise of interchangeable, reusable, easily updated, and easily interconnected software parts. More recently, database designers have begun to appreciate the advantages of an object orientation, with the result that object-oriented database management systems (OODBMS) are beginning to appear. It is this latter area that is of relevance to OSI systems management.

Object-oriented programming and object-oriented database management systems are in fact different things, but they share one key concept: that software or data can be "containerized." Everything goes into a box, and there can be boxes within boxes. In the simplest conventional program, one program step equates to one instruction; in an object-oriented language, each step might be a whole boxful of instructions. Similarly, with an object-oriented database, one variable, instead of equating to a single data element, may equate to a whole boxful of data.

The attraction of object-oriented databases is their flexibility in representing a variety of concepts and facts. For basic text and numerical information, a conventional record-oriented database provides efficient storage, and a relational database provides simple and powerful access facilities. However, when the data are not, or cannot be, organized into neat rows and columns of words and numbers, these approaches are flawed. Some examples of applications that require other kinds of data representations:

- A chemical or pharmaceuticals company, whose data describe the structure and properties of molecules.
- An electronics shop, whose critical data are huge libraries of semiconductor designs.
- A petroleum company, storing huge numbers of geophysical maps.
- An ad agency, with large numbers of layouts, photographs, tapes, and films.

For these applications, a database that can reflect the structure of the things that it represents is vital. The object-oriented approach provides a convenient and natural way of capturing that structure.

The object-oriented approach is well-suited to representing network management information. The resources that are to be managed can be viewed as hierarchical, interrelated objects. For example, a modem has two physical interfaces and a set of properties, such as data rate. Each interface relates the modem to another device or communications facility, each of which has its own object representation.

**Object structure.** The central concept of object-oriented design is the *object*. An object is a distinct software unit that contains a collection of related data and procedures. Generally, these data and procedures are not directly visible outside the object. Rather, well-defined interfaces exist that allow other software to have access to the data and the procedures.

The data and procedures contained in an object are generally referred to as variables and methods, respectively. Everything that an object "knows" is expressed in its variables, and everything it can do is expressed in its methods.

The *variables* in an object are typically simple scalars or tables. Each variable has a type, possibly a set of allowable values, and may be either constant or variable (by convention, the term variable is used even for constants). Access restrictions may also be imposed on variables for certain users, classes of users, or situations.

The *methods* in an object are procedures that can be triggered from outside to perform certain functions. The method may change the state of the object, update some of its variables, or act on outside resources to which the object has access.

Objects interact by means of *messages*. A message includes the name of the sending object, the name of the receiving object, the name of a method in the receiving object, and any parameters needed to qualify the execution of the method. Note that the message can only be used to invoke a method within an object. The only way to access the data inside an object is by means of the object's methods. Thus, a method may cause an action to be taken or the object's variables to be accessed, or both.

The property of an object that its only interface with the outside world is by means of messages is referred to as *encapsulation*. The methods and variables of an object are encapsulated and available only via message-based communication.

This property offers two advantages:

1. It protects an object's variables from corruption by other objects. This protection may include protection from unauthorized access and protection from the types of problems that arise from concurrent access, such as deadlock and inconsistent values.

2. It hides the internal structure of the object so that interaction with the object is relatively simple and standardized. Furthermore, if the internal structure or procedures of an object are modified without changing its external functionality, other objects are unaffected.

**Object classes.** An object in a database represents some thing, be it a physical entity, a concept, a software module, or some dynamic entity such as a virtual circuit. The values of the variables in the object express the information that is known about the thing that the object represents. The methods include procedures whose execution affects the values in the object and possibly also affects that thing being represented.

In practice, there will typically be a number of objects representing the same types of things. For example, if a virtual circuit is represented by an object, then there will be one object for each virtual circuit currently open in a system. Clearly, every such object needs its own set of variables. However, if the methods in the object are re-entrant procedures, then all similar objects could share the same methods. Furthermore, it would be inefficient to redefine both methods and variables for every new but similar object.

The solution to these difficulties is to make a distinction between an object class and an object instance. An *object class* is a template that defines the methods and variables to be included in a particular type of object. An *object instance* is an actual object that includes the characteristics of the class that defines it. The instance contains values for the variables defined in the object class.

**Inheritance.** The concept of an object class is powerful because it allows for the creation of many object instances with a minimum of effort. This concept is made even more powerful by the use of the mechanism of inheritance.

Inheritance enables a new object class to be defined in terms of an existing class. The new class, called the *subclass*, automatically includes the methods and variable definitions in the original class, called the *superclass*. A subclass may differ from its superclass in a number of ways:

1. The subclass may include additional methods and variables not found in its superclass.

2. The subclass may override the definition of any method or variable in its superclass by using the same name with a new definition. This provides a simple and efficient way of handling special cases.

3. The subclass may restrict a method or variable inherited from its superclass in some way.

The inheritance mechanism is recursive, allowing a subclass to become the superclass of its own subclasses. In this way, an *inheritance hierarchy* may be constructed, as illustrated in Figure 2-3. Any object class inherits all of the characteristics of its superclass, including those characteristics that the superclass inherited from higher up the hierarchy. For example, object class C-A2 includes all of the methods and variables in C-A that are not overridden in the definition of C-A2, and object class C-A2b includes all of the variables defined in C-A that are not overridden in either C-A2 or C-A2b, plus all of the variables defined in C-A2 that are not overridden in C-A2b.

Conceptually, we can think of the inheritance hierarchy as defining a search technique for methods and variables. When an object receives a message to carry out a method that is not defined in its class, it automatically searches up the hierarchy until it finds the method. Similarly, if the execution of a method results in the reference to a variable not defined in that class, the object searches up the hierarchy for the variable name.

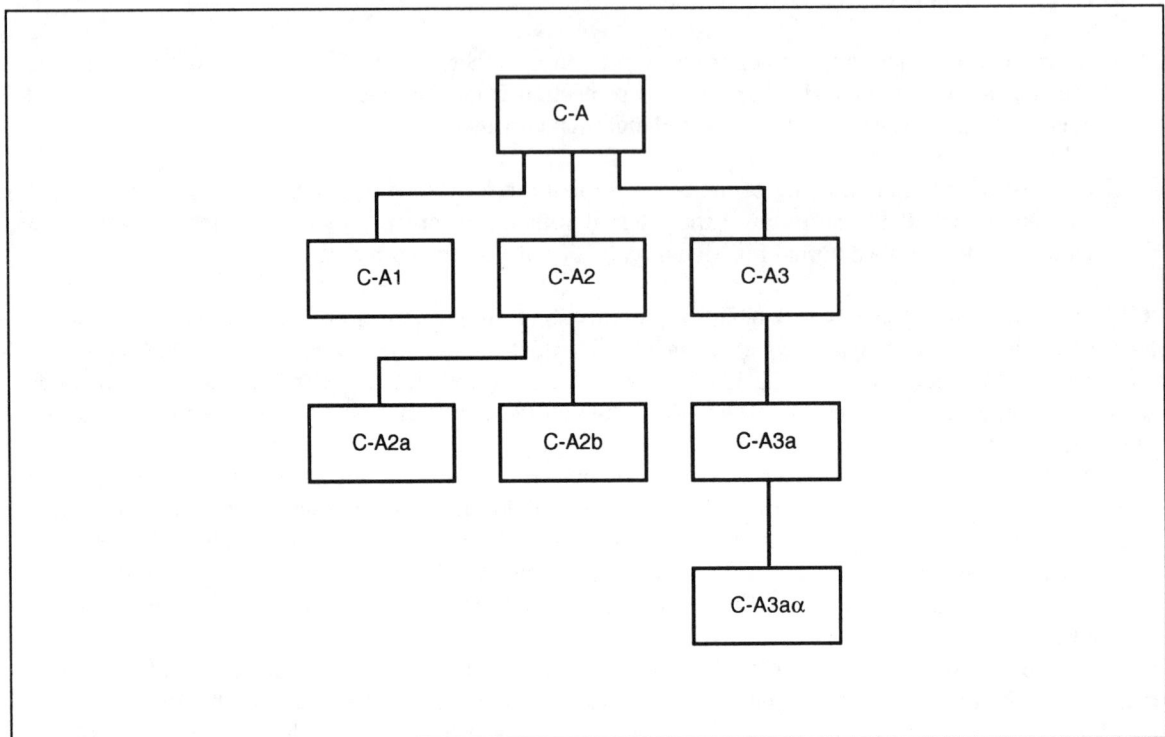

**Figure 2-3: An inheritance hierarchy of object classes**

**Polymorphism.** Polymorphism is an intriguing and powerful characteristic that makes it possible to hide different implementations behind a common interface. Two objects that are polymorphic to each other utilize the same names for methods and present the same interface to other objects. For example, there may be a number of print objects for different output devices, such as printDotmatrix, printLaser, printScreen, and so forth, or for different types of documents, such as printText, printDrawing, and printCompound. If each such object includes a method called *print*, then any document could be printed by sending the message *print* to the appropriate object, without concern for how that method is actually carried out.

It is instructive to compare polymorphism to the usual modular programming techniques. An objective of top-down, modular design is to design lower-level modules of general utility with a fixed interface to higher-level modules. This allows the *one* lower-level module to be invoked by *many* different higher-level modules. If the internals of the lower-level module are changed without changing its interface, then none of the upper-level modules that use it are affected. By contrast, with polymorphism, we are concerned with the ability of *one* higher-level object to invoke *many* different lower-level objects using the same message format to accomplish similar functions. With polymorphism, new lower-level objects can be added with minimal changes to existing objects.

**Containment.** Object instances that contain other objects are called *composite objects*. Containment may be achieved by including the pointer to one object as a value in another object. The advantage of composite objects is that they permit the representation of complex structures. For example, an object contained in a composite object may itself be a composite object.

Typically, the structures built up from composite objects are limited to a tree topology; that is, no circular references are allowed, and each "child" object instance may have only one "parent" object instance. Figure 2-4 illustrates the type of hierarchical structure that results.

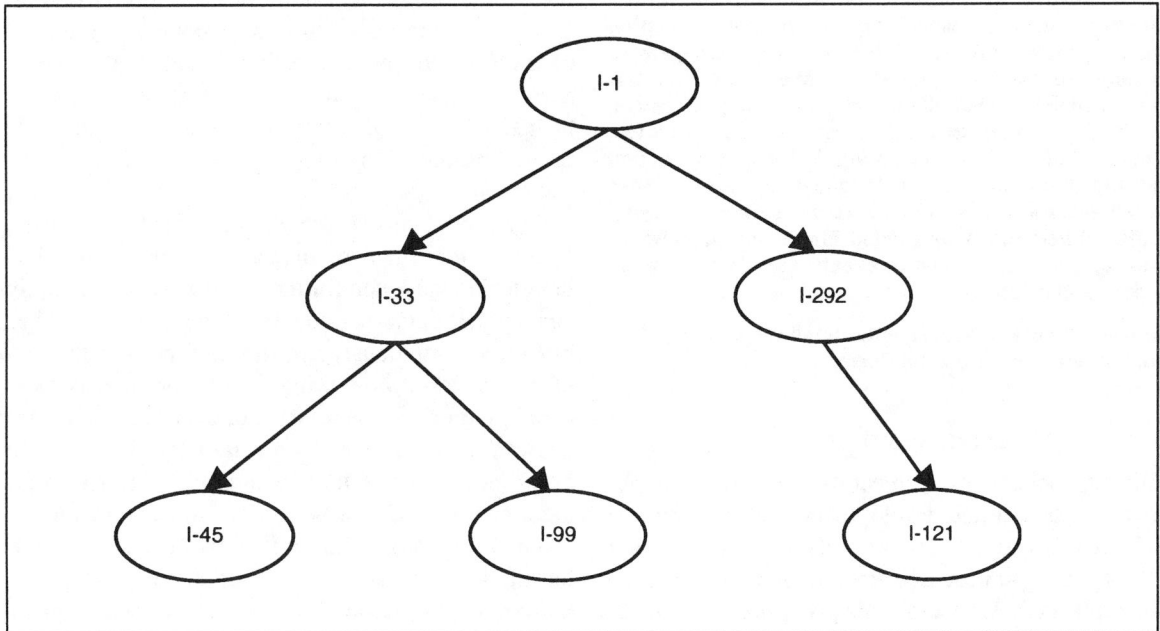

Figure 2-4: A containment hierarchy of object instances

It is important to be clear about the distinction between an inheritance hierarchy of object classes and a containment hierarchy of object instances. The two are not related. The use of inheritance simply allows many different object types to be defined with a minimum of effort. The use of containment allows the construction of complex data structures.

## Paper summary

"Managing Communication Networks by Monitoring Databases" considers the problem of managing large networks using statistical tests, alerts, and correlation among alerts. The authors propose a model of these network management functions as data-manipulation operations. This approach guides the design of the management information base. "Network Information Modeling for Network Management" provides a specific example of the use of management information to model managed resources, with a detailed breakdown of the key elements of the model.

"Development and Integration of a Management Information Base" discusses MIB development for SNMP. The article looks at the evolution of the MIB, and some of the design and development issues.

In a number of network management systems, including OSI, management information is represented and manipulated using object-oriented technology. "Understanding Network Management with OOA" is a tutorial on the use of object-oriented concepts in network management. "System Management Information Modeling" provides an overview of object-oriented modeling principles used in OSI systems management. "Distribution of Managed Object Fragments and Managed Object Replication: The Data Distribution View of Management Information" describes techniques for coping with object-oriented management models in a distributed environment. "OSI Management Information Base Implementation" discusses issues involved in implementing the MIB in an OSI-based network management system product.

# Managing Communication Networks by Monitoring Databases

Ouri Wolfson, Soumitra Sengupta, and Yechiam Yemini

*Abstract*—We consider the problem of managing large communication networks using statistical-tests, alerts, and correlation among alerts. We propose a model of these network management functions as data-manipulation operations. We argue that this approach can improve the flexibility of network management systems by providing a language that is declarative and set-oriented. These are properties of existing data-manipulation languages, and we show that any data-manipulation language, augmented with several new capabilities, can serve as a language for specifying the aforementioned network management functions. The new capabilities required are specification of events, correlation among events, and change-tracking.

*Index Terms*— Network management, database systems, language features, events, real-time databases.

## I. INTRODUCTION

NETWORK management has recently emerged as an active area of research and development [19]; it is mainly concerned with management functions in large communication networks [3], [1]. The purpose of such functions is to handle faults and performance bottlenecks. This paper presents a data-oriented approach to network management in which network management functions are specified as data manipulation statements. Thus the expressive power of current database languages is exploited to construct many of the network management functions (tests, alerts, etc.) in an interactive, declarative, and set-oriented fashion. This approach has the potential of improving the flexibility of network management systems in which management functions usually cannot be specified in an *ad hoc* fashion and are limited to a restricted set of operations. For example, suppose that a network operator wants to be notified when the delay on 20% of the communication links in the network exceeds 5 s. If this alert (called, say, OVERLOAD) is provided *a priori* by the network management system, then it probably also allows the operator to interactively change the 20% and 5 s as parameters. However, if such an alert is not provided, then setting it up may involve extensive applications programming which cannot be done in a few minutes (at least not in existing systems). Using our approach, this is possible, assuming familiarity of an operator with a data-manipulation language such as SQL, designed for *ad hoc* interactive access to databases by naive users. Our proposed language features also enable the definition of multiple management functions in a single statement.

Our model focuses on the data for the following reasons. Network management in general consists of two activities: monitoring and controlling the network or, equivalently, a conceptual database-model of the network. The database-model is continuously updated to represent the current status of the network. Monitoring the network means "watching" for certain important phenomena, or events, to occur. In our model an event is represented by a data-pattern, and watching for the event means the continuous retrieval of this data-pattern from the network database. So, for example, watching for the event "Number of packets transmitted by processor 75 is higher than the number of packets transmitted by processor 20" means the continuous retrieval of the two values from the network database. Similarly, network control means the activation of processes that directly or indirectly change the status of the network or some of its components. These process activations may be triggered by insertion in the database of certain data items. Thus both network monitoring and network control can naturally be represented using database manipulation.

For the purpose of specifying network management functions (specifically, statistical tests, alerts, and correlation among alerts) we propose new language features which enable real-time monitoring of database changes. The additional language features constitute a contribution to the database field in the following sense. Database systems provide the capability of data definition and data manipulation and, through the data dictionary, meta-data concerning the data-definition. However, they do not provide meta-data concerning the data-manipulation. In other words, existing systems lack a facility that describes the data-manipulation in the same way the data-dictionary describes the data definition. We propose such a facility. Our proposal is independent of the underlying data model; it may be object-oriented or relational.

For example, the proposed language features allow the user to request that whenever the value of a certain attribute changes, the old value is appended to a trace. This may be requested for each object in a class, or just for objects that satisfy some selection predicate. Furthermore, a separate trace may be requested for each object, or several objects (e.g., all the ones with COLOR = "yellow") may be monitored in the same

---

Manuscript received September 20, 1990; revised May 28, 1991. Recommended by M. Jarke. This research was supported in part by DARPA through Grant F-29601-87-C-0074, by the Center for Advanced Technology of Columbia University through Grants NYSSTF-CAT(89)-5 and NYSSTF CU01207901, and by the NSF through Grant IRI9003341.

O. Wolfson was with the Department of Computer Science, Columbia University, 450 Computer Science Building, New York, NY 10027. He is now with the Department of Electrical Engineering and Computer Science, University of Illinois, Chicago, IL 60680.

S. Sengupta and Y. Yemini are with the Department of Computer Science, Columbia University, 450 Computer Science Building, New York, NY 10027.

IEEE Log Number 9102391.

trace. Another example of a new language feature is event correlation. For example, the user may request a certain action when two different changes occur simultaneously or when one occurs before the other but the events are not more than 50 s apart. As we shall demonstrate, our proposed language features are particularly important in database management systems which receive an automatic inflow of data from various sensors in real-time.

More precisely, we propose three new language features. They all address temporal monitoring of database changes. First, the specification of basic events. An example of a basic event that can be specified using the proposed language feature is the following: "There exist tuples that satisfy a certain predicate, and this condition persists for a period of 10 minutes." Second, the specification of correlated events. A correlated event is triggered by the occurrence of several events which satisfy certain temporal constraints. Third, the specification of trace-collections. A trace records the way an attribute changes over time, and a trace-collection is a set of traces, all of which have the same characteristics (e.g., the same start-time and same end-time).

The network information (configuration, status, etc.) is usually represented at any point in time by data residing at various elements in the network. This whole data collection can be conceptualized as a distributed database which models the network. In practice, for performance reasons only part of this information is managed by the network management system, since management involves an overhead in accessing the information. For example, in OSI terminology the managed part is called the "Management Information Base" (or MIB) [16]; and in [11] it is called the "Network Model."

In this paper, we call this part the "Network Database," to emphasize that our discussion is independent of whether or not its exact content is the same as that of the MIB or any other model. The fact that the network management system manages the network database implies, in the present paper, that accessing the network database must be done by a request (of a user or of a program) to the network management system. Consequently, the network management system can be instructed to monitor the requests to access the Network Database.

The extent to which our approach is applicable will be influenced by the Network Database scheme and its distribution throughout the network. For example, if the link-delay information is not part of the network database, then setting up the alert OVERLOAD in an interactive fashion is impossible. Similarly, if the delay information is part of the network database but is dispersed throughout the network, then the processing of OVERLOAD may put an intolerable load on the network. We present a proposed interface language between the network management system and the outside world. This language enables the specification of management functions, but the expressive capabilities and the performance depend on the implementation and architecture. The performance also depends on the algorithms for processing the data manipulation language proposed, but these algorithms are beyond the scope of this paper.

Before concluding this introduction we make the following important remark about the scope of this paper. We discuss here multiple issues with the purpose of providing the "big picture" of the required interfaces and the relationships between network management and databases. However, we do not attempt to study in-depth any single issue. For example, we ignore the issue of transactions and database consistency. The reason for doing so is that the data representing the status of the network may be inaccurate when generated (e.g., one processor may report that a communication link is up, whereas another may report that the same link is down). In other words, for much of the data, preserving consistency may not be worthwhile.

The rest of this paper is organized as follows. The next section discusses the main components of a network management system; namely, the network database and functions for fault and performance management. In Section III we discuss the modeling of a key element in our proposal; namely, events. In Section IV we discuss the definition of traces and trace classes. Traces often enable prediction of faults and performance bottlenecks. In Section V we return to events and discuss events that are data patterns in traces. In Section VI we demonstrate how automatic fault and performance management can be based on the previously defined concepts. In Section VII we compare this work to the relevant literature, and in Section VIII we summarize and discuss future work.

## II. THE NETWORK MANAGEMENT COMPONENTS

A Network Management System (NMS) consists of the *network database* and a set of *management functions*. The NMS manages the network database the same way a database management system manages the data, and additionally, it executes management functions either automatically or in response to requests by human operators.

### A. The Network Database

There are two types of data in the network database. One is the *configuration* data, and the other is the *history* data. The configuration data represents the current status of the network and is further divided into *static* and *dynamic* data. The static configuration database consists of the representation of permanent objects in the network such as computers, communication links, software layers, groups of nodes, local area subnetworks, and users, and, obviously, the relationships among these objects. The dynamic configuration database consists of the representation of transient objects such as virtual circuits, user-sessions, delays, routing tables, etc. The configuration database is used for normal network operation (such as message routing) in addition to its usage for fault management.

The history database consists of information about the evolution of the network and its status over time (possibly in summary form), such as the virtual circuits between a certain pair of processors between 3 and 5 P.M., the number of packets transmitted by certain processors in each minute for the last hour, etc. This information is generated by statistical tests (see the next subsection), it is mainly based on the dynamic configuration database, and it is used for fault and performance management and for capacity planning.

## B. The Network Management Functions

There are three basic types of management functions: actions, alerts, and inferences. *Actions* are management functions that execute in the real network. Each action is associated with one or more network objects. There are two types of actions: interventions and tests.

An *intervention* is an action aimed at overcoming a problem by changing something in the way the network or some of its components operate. Several examples of interventions are: "Reboot a computer," "deactivate the interface between a gateway and a local area network," "call the technician indicating a faulty equipment," and "change some parameters of a protocol layer." A *test* is an action that monitors the network. In contrast to an intervention, it is nonintrusive; i.e., it does not change the operation of the network. There are two types of tests. One is a definitive test, and the other is a statistical test. A *definitive test,* when applied to a network object (say a modem), determines whether or not the object is functioning properly. A definitive test is usually supplied by the equipment manufacturer, and may be associated with an intervention; the intervention is invoked if the test determines improper functioning. For example, "reboot" is an intervention associated with a definitive test which determines that the status of a processor is "down."

Statistical tests are used when definitive tests are insufficient for problem diagnosis and isolation, or when the problem is not with a particular device but with the overall network status. Congestion in a local area subnetwork is an example of a network-status problem. A *statistical test,* when applied to an object or a set of objects, generates a trace (a history-database object). Traces can be analyzed in order to generate alerts (these are discussed below). An example of a statistical test called, say, MESSAGE_TIME($A, B$) is one that generates a record for each message from the processor at network address $A$ to the processor at network address $B$; the record specifies how long it took until the message was acknowledged.

An *alert* is a management function which indicates an abnormal condition. An alert is triggered either by the state of the network (as reflected in the database) or by one or more tests. An example of an alert triggered by the network state is OVERLOAD: "the delay on 20% of the communication links exceeds 5 s." An example of an alert called, say, SPIKE($A, B$) that is triggered by the test MESSAGE_TIME($A, B$) is the following: "There is an increase of more than 10 s in the acknowledgment time of two consecutive messages from $A$ to $B$." Generally, an alert may be triggered by multiple tests, and multiple alerts may be triggered by the same test. Therefore there is a many-to-many relationship between tests and alerts.

An *inference* is a management function which maps one or more alerts to a set of tests, alerts, and interventions. For example, an inference may map the alert SPIKE($A, B$) to the set of definitive tests UP_DOWN($Z$) for each processor $Z$ that is on a path from $A$ to $B$ (presumably UP_DOWN determines whether $Z$ is "up" or "down").

A *fault management state* is the collection of tests, interventions, and alerts that are active in the network at some point in time. *Fault management* is the continuous activity of inferencing from the current management state to the next, such that faults and performance bottlenecks in the network are either predicted and prevented, or detected, isolated, and eliminated.

## III. EVENTS

An event is "something" of importance to network management. For example, the alert OVERLOAD discussed previously is an event. In general, most alerts are simply events. Additionally, events serve as the building blocks for the specification of other management functions such as the statistical tests discussed in the next section.

An event is either basic or correlated. A correlated event is a combination of multiple events; it occurs if they all occur simultaneously. One of the primary purposes of such a grouping of events is to enable correlation of alerts. Intuitively, the user may specify that if alerts A and B occur at the same time, and alert C does not occur, then alerts A and B are probably related to the same problem source; the occurrence of A and B, but not C, will then be called D. The inference mechanism may then treat D differently than either A or B.

In order for an event to *occur,* i.e., be noticed (otherwise, as far as the network management system is concerned, it has not occurred), it must be *specified* and then *activated.* Event monitoring consumes resources; therefore a specified event may be active or inactive. An event is instantaneous and does not persist over time. After the event occurs the specification has to be reactivated in order for the event to occur again. Next we discuss the specification of events.

### A. Basic Events

A *basic event* is either: (i) a data-pattern in the network database; or (ii) a data manipulation operation, namely, a retrieve, add, delete, or update of the network database; or (iii) Calendar-time.

A *data-pattern* event occurs when a certain data-pattern appears in the database; for example, when the delay on 20% or more of the communication links exceeds 5 s (OVERLOAD). A data-pattern event is specified using a data-retrieval operation which supposedly executes continuously (in practice, the network management system executes it only if at least one of the retrieved objects changes). The event occurs when the retrieval returns at least one element, and for this reason an event of this type is also called a *nonempty-retrieval* event. If the data pattern exists in the database at event activation, then the event will occur immediately. Otherwise, it will occur when the data pattern appears in the database.

For example, assume that there is a relation LINKS that has a tuple for each communication-link in the network, and that one of the attributes of this relation is DELAY (on the link). The nonempty-retrieval event OVERLOAD can be specified by the following data retrieval statement, which, for the sake of simplicity, is written in SQL:

SELECT X = Y/Z
FROM
WHERE 0.2 $\leq$
[SELECT Y=COUNT(*)

```
       FROM LINKS
       WHERE DELAY > 5 ]
   /
   [ SELECT Z=COUNT(*)
     FROM LINKS ]
```

In the case of retrieval from object classes, an object-oriented retrieval language (e.g., the one in [2]) can be used for specifying data-pattern events.

A parameter of a data-pattern event is the following: PERSISTENCE $\geq$ "time-interval." It indicates that the event is to occur only if the data-pattern persists in the database at least for the specified time-interval. The purpose of this parameter is to enable ignoring data-patterns which are transient. For example, if PERSISTENCE $\geq$ 10 min is associated with the data-pattern event OVERLOAD, then the resulting event, which we call PERSISTENT-OVERLOAD, will occur when the delay on 20% or more of the communication links exceeds 5 s and this condition persists for more than 10 min. Note that it is not required that the percentage of slow links remains constant for 10 min; just that the percentage exceeds 20% for this duration.

The time-interval sometimes cannot be determined *a priori*. Then a procedure $P$ may be specified instead of a time-interval. $P$ is invoked when the data-pattern is detected and it will compute the persistence interval (possibly by communicating with the network operator).

A *data-manipulation* event occurs when a certain data-manipulation operation is performed in the system. It is obviously specified by a data-manipulation operation. For example, ADD to LINKS, and OLD LINKS WHERE DELAY > 5 are two events. The first occurs when some tuples are added to the relation LINKS; the other occurs when the tuples of LINKS which have a DELAY > 5 are either replaced or deleted. In general, we adopt the definition of an event in POSTGRES version 2 [27] to serve as our data-manipulation event. Thus a data-manipulation event consists of an operation—i.e., ADD, DELETE, REPLACE, RETRIEVE, OLD (DELETE or REPLACE) or NEW (ADD or REPLACE)—together with an object class or a subset of the class (e.g., LINKS WHERE DELAY > 5).

A data-pattern event can obviously be implemented by a data-manipulation event. For example, PERSISTENT-OVERLOAD can be implemented by examining each modification to LINKS, and when the 20% limit is exceeded, verifying that the condition persists. However, we feel that often the data-pattern event provides a higher level of abstraction, as is the case for PERSISTENT-OVERLOAD. Specifically, the network operator may specify this event directly instead of "programming" its occurrence using the data-manipulation events.

The specification of a *Calendar-time* event consists of a time hierarchy value. Three examples of time-hierarchy values are: 1 min, 3 h, and 12 A.M. January 8. For the first specification the event occurs every minute; for the second, every 3 h; and for the third, every year on January 8th at 12 A.M.

The *occurrence time* of an event is simply the time at which the data-retrieval succeeds, or the data manipulation event completes, or the calendar time is reached. If PERSISTENCE $\geq v$ is specified for a data-pattern event, then the occurrence time increases by $v$. In other words, if the pattern is required to persist for at least some time interval, then, assuming that it does, the occurrence time is the time at the <u>end</u> of the interval.

In addition to the occurrence time, correlation of events (see the next subsection) may refer to the *valid time* of an event. Intuitively, this is the time at which the event occurred in the real world. For a calendar time event it is the same as the occurrence time. For a data-pattern event or a data-manipulation event, the valid time is an attribute of the data being retrieved or manipulated. Presumably the attribute stores the time at which the event occurred in the real world. For example, suppose that the relation LINKS has a STATUS attribute that can have the value "up" or "down," and a TIME attribute which indicates when the status became "up" or "down." Then consider the data-manipulation event:

   NEW LINKS WHERE STATUS='down'.

If $valid - time$ = TIME is specified, then the valid time of the event is taken from the attribute TIME of the tuple being added or replaced. However, since multiple objects may be retrieved or manipulated in a single operation, then some aggregate function (average, minimum, or maximum) of all the attribute values must be specified (e.g., $valid - time$ = max(TIME)). For a data-pattern event, if PERSISTENCE is specified, then the valid time is the value of the aggregate function at <u>end</u> of the time interval.

*B. Correlated Events*

Basic events can be grouped into correlated events. For example, a correlated event may occur if the basic event OVERLOAD (a data-pattern event) occurs at the same time as the basic event 12 A.M. (a calendar-time event). Formally, a *correlated* event is a disjunction of conjunctions of events and is specified using correlation rules. Two parameters are associated with a correlation rule to capture the temporal relationships among the events in the specification. These parameters, namely, time order and time constraints, will be discussed after the presentation of rules.

*1) Correlation Rules:* An *atom* is an event symbol (e.g., OVERLOAD), possibly preceded by the symbol "¬"; if it is, then the atom is *negative*, otherwise it is *positive*. A *correlation rule* consists of a positive atom designated as the *head*, and a set of one or more atoms designated as the *body*. The body of a rule must contain at least one positive atom. The head is the *correlated* event being defined by the rule, and its symbol must be different than that of a basic event. An event in the body of a rule may be basic or correlated. Syntactically, the head and the body of a rule are separated, in the Prolog tradition, by the symbol ":-".

A correlation rule has the following semantics. If all the positive-atom events in the body occur simultaneously, and at that time none of the negative atom events occurs, then the rule is *fireable*. In practice, simultaneity means a default time-interval of some length $\varepsilon > 0$. More precisely, our computational model assumes a database consisting of time-stamped events (the time stamp is the occurrence time). These are the events which have *occurred*. At each step of the "computation" a fireable (in the current database) rule is chosen nondeterministically and the correlated event in the head of the rule is added to the database (i.e., it occurs). The occurrence time of the correlated event is the last occurrence time of a positive event in the body of the rule.

For example, consider the following correlated event:

OVERLOAD-AT-12 :- OVERLOAD, 12 A.M.

This event occurs if the OVERLOAD event occurs in conjunction with the 12 A.M. calendar-time event.

If there is another basic event, UNDERUTILIZED, which means that 20% of the links are underutilized, then the following event:

OVERLOAD-UNDERUTILIZED :-
OVERLOAD-AT-12, UNDERUTILIZED.

may be specified. OVERLOAD-UNDERUTILIZED occurs if 20% of the links are overloaded at 12 A.M., and 20% of the links are underutilized at the same time.

To demonstrate the use of negative atoms, consider the event:

D-NEG :- OVERLOAD-AT-12, ⁻ UNDERUTI-
LIZED.

It occurs if 20% of the links are overloaded at 12, but UNDERUTILIZED does not occur then.

It is possible to define a correlated event consisting of a disjunction of two events $A$ and $B$ by having two rules with identical heads and with the bodies $A$ and $B$, respectively. For example, the event OVERLOAD-$OR$-12 which occurs when OVERLOAD occurs or at 12 A.M., whichever is first, can be specified by the following two rules:

OVERLOAD-$OR$-12 :- OVERLOAD.
OVERLOAD-$OR$-12 :- 12am.

*2) Temporal Order:* The events represented by the positive atoms in the body of the rule may be required to occur in a certain temporal order—say $G$—in order for the event in the head to occur. If so, then this is specified by the keyword $order = G$ associated with the rule. $G$ is a directed acyclic graph, which in our case represents the time-precedence requirements for the specification of the correlated event. The nodes of $G$ are the positive atoms in the body of the rule, and the arcs represent the time-precedence requirements. If there is a path from node $a$ to node $b$, then $a$ is required to occur before $b$; only then the event in the head of the rule can occur. If there is no path from $a$ to $b$ nor from $b$ to $a$, then there is no requirement as to the order in which these two events occur.

For example, consider the rule specifying the event OVERLOAD-UNDERUTILIZED, and assume that $order = G$ is associated with the rule. Suppose that $G$ is the graph:

OVERLOAD-AT-12 → UNDERUTILIZED

Then the event OVERLOAD-UNDERUTILIZED occurs only if the event OVERLOAD-AT-12 occurs before the event UNDERUTILIZED. If $G$ does not have have any arcs, then OVERLOAD-UNDERUTILIZED occurs if both events in the body occur, regardless of the order.

There may be a required order for valid times and a different required order for occurrence times.

*3) Temporal-Constraints:* The events represented by the atoms in the body of the rule are required by the keyword *time-constraints* to satisfy certain temporal constraints $C$. This is specified as $time - constraints = C$ associated with the rule where $C$ is a set of constraints. Each constraint is represented by a subset $S$ of the atoms in the body of the rule and a time hierarchy value $v$. $S$ must contain at least one positive atom. The constraint indicates that in order for the rule to be fireable, the time-interval of length $v$ starting at the occurrence of the first event from $S$ will contain the occurrence time of all the positive events in $S$, and will not contain the occurrence time of the negative events. For example, consider the definition of OVERLOAD-AT-12. A constraint, {OVERLOAD, 12 A.M.} = 5 s, says that OVERLOAD-AT-12 will occur only if OVERLOAD and 12 A.M. are at most 5 s apart. For another example, consider the rule specifying D-NEG. A constraint:

{OVERLOAD-AT-12, ⁻ UNDERUTILIZED} =
5 s

associated with the rule says that D-NEG occurs if OVERLOAD-AT-12 occurs, and UNDERUTILIZED does not occur within 5 s after the occurrence of OVERLOAD-AT-12. The intersection of two constraints may be nonempty.

The time-interval of a temporal constraint often cannot be determined *a priori*. Then a procedure $P$ may be specified instead of a time-interval. Then $P$ is invoked at the first occurrence of an event in the body of the rule, and it will compute the interval for the constraint (possibly by communicating with the network operator).

Notice that the two rule parameters, order and time-constraints, are independent. The $order = G$ parameter may be specified independently of whether or not $time - constraints = C$ is specified. If both are specified, then any set of constraints is consistent, and any combination of values for $C$ and $G$ is consistent. By consistency we mean that there are occurrence times for the (positive and negative) events in the body, such that the precedence order specified is satisfied, and so are all the temporal-constraints. This is proven in the appendix.

There may be a set of temporal constraints that pertains to valid times and a different set of constraints that pertains to occurrence times.

*4) Variables:* Each data-pattern and data-manipulation event is associated with a variable which is instantiated when the event occurs. The variable is instantiated to the set of tuples whose retrieval or manipulation triggered the event. For example, the variable associated with OVERLOAD denotes the percentage of links that have a long (> 5) delay. The variable associated with the event:

ADD LINKS WHERE STATUS='down'

is the set of tuples being added.

The variables associated with events may be used to further constrain the occurrence of correlated events to the cases in which the variables associated with the positive events in the body of a rule satisfy a certain predicate. For example, suppose that the variable associated with UNDERUTILIZED denotes the percentage of links that is underutilized. Then the correlated event defined as

OU :- OVERLOAD($X$), UNDERUTILIZED($Y$),
$X < Y$.

occurs only if the percentage of underutilized links exceeds the percentage of overloaded links. In general, the variables associated with the positive events can be used to construct relational algebra expressions and arithmetic expressions; in turn, these can be combined into predicates using set- and arithmetic-comparison operators. Then the correlated event occurs only if the relational and arithmetic predicates so constructed are satisfied. The variable associated with a data-pattern event that has a PERSISTENCE interval is instantiated at the end of the time-interval.

The correlated event at the head of the rule may also be associated with a variable—e.g., $X$—as follows:
OU($X$) :- OVERLOAD($X$), UNDERUTILIZED($Y$), $X < Y$.
In general, the variable associated with the correlated event in the head of the rule is some relational algebra expression or arithmetic expression involving the variables associated with the positive events in the body of the rule.

We require that in a rule, a variable associated with a negative atom must also be associated with a positive one.

## IV. TRACES

We model a statistical test in network management by a trace. A *trace* is a sequence which tracks the changing of an attribute value of an object, and it is part of the history database. Each member of a trace is a triple $(t, o, a)$, where $t$ is a time-stamp (e.g., 2:45 A.M.), $o$ defines the position of the member in the trace (e.g., 117th), and $a$ is an attribute-value. For example, a trace may track the acknowledgment time of messages from processor 101 to processor 102. Each trace has an identifier $i$ that uniquely identifies the trace (e.g., 101, 102). $i$ may be an object-id or a relational key. Each trace also has a start point, which is defined by an event and a time duration.

It is relatively simple to specify a trace; however, often the user will want to define a set of traces, all of which have the same characteristics. For example, suppose that the user wants to specify a statistical test, that, say, monitors the acknowledgment time of messages from each IBM processor to each DEC processor. Therefore the topic of the rest of this section is specification of a *trace collection*. Intuitively, each trace collection is defined with respect to a *monitored class* or relation scheme; i.e., a set of objects that is being monitored. Each trace records the changes in an attribute of the monitored class called the *monitored attribute*. Usually, each trace records the sequence of changes to the monitored-attribute for one object in the monitored-class, but it can record the sequence of changes to more than one object. For example, there may be a trace for the "yellow" objects and one for the "green" objects, although there may be more than one object of the same color. Then the "yellow" trace consists of the values of the yellow objects, and if two such objects are changed simultaneously, then the two values are recorded in the trace in a nondeterministic order. An object which is neither green nor yellow will not have its monitored attribute traced. In other words, the traces (or their identifiers) partition the set of monitored objects. The changes to the monitored attribute in each partition are recorded in one trace, and one (possibly empty) partition consists of the objects which are not traced at all.

Next, we formally present the specification parameters for a trace collection, and then we shall provide a detailed example.

- *Monitored class*: The class of objects being monitored. It may be an extensional object class; for example, the class of nodes in the network or an intentional (also called virtual, or view) object class.
- *Monitored attribute*: This is an attribute name of the monitored class. It identifies the attribute whose change is being tracked.
- *Trace-identifiers class*: The key-word OBJECT-ID, or an intentional or extensional class of trace-identifiers.
- *Trace identifier*: A subset of the attributes of the monitored class. It should be specified only if the Trace-identifiers class is not OBJECT-ID.
- *Sampling event*: A basic or correlated event. Upon its occurrence, the monitored attribute is sampled.
- *Change only*: An indication to ignore sampling if the current value of the attribute is identical to the one in the previous occurrence of the sampling event.
- *Start event*: An event which determines when the trace collection is activated.
- *Duration*: A time interval during which the trace collection is active.

Now we discuss the above parameters. The operational semantics of the trace-collection specification are as follows. At each point in time there is a *Trace-identifiers class*, or a set of identifiers that we denote $S$. Each identifier corresponds to a unique trace in the collection and each trace has a unique identifier. For the example in the beginning of this section, (101, 102) is a member of the Trace-identifiers class. If *Trace-identifiers class* = 'OBJECT-ID', then $S$ is the set of object identities of the *Monitored class*. Otherwise, $S$ is an (extensional or intentional) relation. Obviously, $S$ changes in time (for example, because objects are added and deleted). Whenever the *Sampling event* occurs, each object $o$ in the *Monitored class* is examined; if $o$'s *Trace identifier*, say $i$ (e.g., the value of the attributes {FROM, TO} in the message-acknowledgment example), appears in $S$, then the current value of the *Monitored attribute* is appended to the end of the trace which has the identifier $i$. If *Change-only* is "on," then appending is done only if the current value of the attribute is different than the one in the previous occurrence of the *Sampling event*. The *Start event* activates the trace collection for the *Duration* specified. The trace collection can be referred to (using trace based events, as discussed in the next section) only while the collection is active. If the *Start event* reoccurs while the trace collection is active, its effect is to keep the collection active for the time-interval *Duration* starting at that point in time.

Notice that the members of the *Trace-identifiers class* may change over time. For example, the color "red" may be added. In this case a trace is started. In general, the addition of a trace-identifier to the class starts a trace, and its deletion stops it. Also, if for an object $o$ the value of the attribute(s) *Trace identifier* changes—e.g., from "yellow" to "green," then the monitoring of $o$ switches traces.

For a comprehensive example of a trace-collection specification, consider the problem of tracing the acknowledgment time of each message between a DEC and an IBM computer. The example is somewhat complicated to demonstrate various subtleties of the trace collection specification. Suppose that there exist two extensional object classes: (i) PROCESSOR, having, among others, the attributes ID (e.g., 117658), NETWORK_ADDR (e.g., A12), and TYPE (e.g., DEC), and (ii) a wrap-around relation MESSAGE having, among others, the attributes SOURCE_ADDR, DEST_ADDR, and ACK_TIME. The relation MESSAGE is assigned a fixed amount of storage and addition of tuples wraps-around. When a message is acknowledged a tuple is added to the relation MESSAGE. Notice therefore that there may be more than one tuple having the same pair of SOURCE_ADDR and DEST_ADDR values.

The trace-collection that we call MESSAGE_TIME is specified as follows:
- *Monitored-class*: MESSAGE.
- *Monitored-attribute*: MESSAGE.ACK_TIME.
- *Trace-identifier class*: Is a relation having a tuple for each pair of addresses such that the first is an IBM and the second is a DEC. The relation can be defined as a view, using SQL, as follows:
  SELECT SOURCE_ADDR =p1.NETWORK_ADDR,
    DEST_ADDR = p2.NETWORK_ADDR
  FROM PROCESSOR p1, PROCESSOR p2
  WHERE p1.TYPE=IBM, p2.TYPE=DEC
- *Trace-identifier*: SOURCE_ADDR, DEST_ADDR.
- *Sampling-event*: NEW tuple of MESSAGE.
- *Change-only*: On.
- *Start-event*: OVERLOAD
- *Duration*: 1 h.

With each active trace-collection we associate a *corresponding* object-class; i.e., a class having the same name as the collection (e.g., MESSAGE_TIME). Each object in this class consists of one trace. For example, the trace for the pair of addresses $A23$ and $B45$ in the MESSAGE_TIME trace collection is denoted: MESSAGE_TIME (ID = (SOURCE_ADDR=A23, DEST_ADDR=B45)).

Next we argue that there is a need for an additional parameter in the trace-collection specification. Consider the trace-collection MESSAGE_TIME. If the type of the processor at address A55 changes from IBM to HP, then each trace that has an identifier A55,x (for some x) is either disabled or erased from the trace collection MESSAGE_TIME. If it is disabled, and subsequently the type of the processor at address A55 changes back to IBM, then each disabled trace can be enabled—namely, resumed. Otherwise, new traces having the identifier A55,x are started. Namely, the trace collection has an additional attribute:

  Status = either 'resume' or 'anew'.

## V. TRACE-BASED EVENTS

We have mentioned that in network management alerts may be triggered by the evolution of the network-configuration over time. Now that we have defined trace collections we can precisely explain this statement. Similarly to basic events which are represented by nonempty retrievals from the network database, basic events may also be represented by nonempty retrievals from the history database. The history database is the set of traces, and each trace is simply a relation with three attributes, as explained at the beginning of Section IV. Consequently, nonempty retrievals from traces are not different than any other retrieval and can be defined as basic events.

For example, consider the trace collection MESSAGE_TIME. Following is the specification of an event, called SURGE, which occurs when two messages in a trace that are acknowledged within 5 s of one another have an increase in the attribute value (acknowledgment time) which is greater than 17.
  SELECT SOURCE_ADDR, DEST_ADDR
  FROM MESSAGE_TIME p1, MESSAGE_TIME p2
  WHERE p1.ID = p2.ID, and p2.t < p1.t + 5, and p2.a > p1.a + 17

Clearly, more than one data-pattern event can be specified for a trace collection, and such an event may be triggered by multiple trace collections. In other words, the relationship between trace collections and events is many-to-many.

## VI. SPECIFICATION OF INFERENCES

An inference maps the occurrence of one or more alerts to the activation of one or more tests, alerts, and interventions. The mapping depends on the contents of the configuration database, and like many diagnosis problems, it is naturally expressible in a rule-language program. Rule languages for knowledge bases [10], [14], [22], [33] are designed to efficiently handle the large amounts of data encountered in network management. Such a language, when combined with the data reduction paradigm [35], [12], [34], can be processed in parallel at multiple computers of the network while minimizing the amount of interprocessor communication.

For inferencing we adopt RDL1, the rule language proposed in [14]. Next, we briefly discuss this language (the interested reader can find further details in [14]) and then we demonstrate it by an example. An RDL1 program consists of a set of *inference rules*. The syntax of an inference rule is: IF *condition* THEN *action*. The condition is a data-retrieval statement, and the action is a set of data-modification (i.e., insert, delete, or update) statements. Each variable which appears in the action part must also be selected in the condition part. An RDL1 program has a (possibly empty) set of relations declared as TEMPORARY. An event is associated with each program.

The semantics of the language are as follows: An RDL1 program is activated upon the occurrence of the associated event. The variable that is instantiated when the event occurs is a relation or a set of constants, and the rules of the program can refer to this variable. At activation time, the TEMPORARY relations are empty. An active RDL1 program executes in steps. At each step a fireable rule is chosen nondeterministically and is fired. This continues until no more rules are fireable. A rule is *fireable* if its condition part retrieves a nonempty set of objects (or tuples); i.e., the condition succeeds. Firing a rule means modifying the database using the action part of the rule; if the modification triggers the execution of one or more management functions such as tests (see the example below), then the execution of these functions is part of the firing of the rule.

The following is an example of an RDL1 program. For simplicity and uniformity we will write the rules in the PROLOG notation, separating the condition and action parts by the ":-" symbol. The insert operation is denoted by "+", and the delete operation by a "−". The program consists of two rules and is activated when the event SURGE occurs.

r1: +UP_DOWN($Z$), −CONNECTION
(SURGE.SOURCE,
$Z$, SURGE.DEST) :-
CONNECTION(SURGE.SOURCE, $Z$,
SURGE.DEST)
r2: +REBOOT($Z$), −DOWN($Z$) :- DOWN($Z$),
TYPE($Z$,
"processor")

r1 should be read as follows: if there is a tuple (SURGE.SOURCE, $Z$, SURGE.DEST) in the relation CONNECTION, then delete it and add to the relation UP_DOWN the tuple $Z$. CONNECTION is a database relation, and if the tuple $a$, $b$, $c$ is in CONNECTION, then $b$ is on the path from $a$ to $c$ (in the graph representing the communication network). SURGE.SOURCE and SURGE.DEST are the two processor-identifications in the variable which is instantiated when the event SURGE occurs. This RDL1 program treats them as constants. UP_DOWN is the name of a control relation (meaning that insertion of a tuple in UP_DOWN triggers the execution of a program) and also the name of a definitive test. We assume that the test UP_DOWN receives as parameter an object $Z$ and indicates whether the status of $Z$ is "up" or "down."

Intuitively, rule r1 orders to test every object that is on the path from SURGE.SOURCE to SURGE.DEST to determine its status. The execution of r1 deletes all the tuples of the form CONNECTION(SURGE.SOURCE, $Z$, SURGE.DEST) for some $Z$; therefore in the next execution-step rule r1 is not fireable.

Assuming that some $Z$'s are "down," in the next execution step of the program rule r2 is fired. The DOWN predicate in r2 denotes a relation holding the objects that the UP_DOWN test diagnosed as "down." TYPE is a relation having in the first column the identification of an object, and in the second column its type. REBOOT is a control-relation name, and also the name of an intervention (program performing the reboot).

Intuitively, the rule r2 orders to perform a REBOOT for every object that tested faulty, and is a processor. UP_DOWN and DOWN are temporary relations.

## VII. COMPARISON TO RELEVANT LITERATURE

This paper is related to works which propose network management languages. For example, [36] proposes an extension to SQL to facilitate writing network management programs, and [4] proposes a new language, with descriptive and prescriptive components, for the same purpose. In contrast, we propose the extension of data management capabilities, and this extension is useful for network management as well as other applications. Additionally, this extension is independent of a particular data manipulation language. This paper also suggests that modeling upon existing platforms can significantly reduce the necessary amount of network-management application-program development. The OSI network management specification effort [5], [6] provides an interface at a lower level than ours.

The work on active databases (e.g., [7]), on triggers (e.g., [9], [20]), and on rule-languages (e.g., [14], [22], [27], [33], [13]) has also addressed the specification of events (we recommend [20] for a comprehensive discussion of related work). However, temporal constraints among events, an issue arising in real-time systems, has not been discussed in these works. In contrast, the specification of such constraints has been a main topic of this paper. As we have seen, even the definition of basic events is more complex when one wants to smooth out the effects of transient conditions (as enabled by the PERSISTENCE parameter). On the other hand, the work on real-time databases (e.g., [23], [15]) concentrates on concurrency control issues, a topic which is outside the scope of this paper.

The present proposal of traces is related to work on temporal databases (e.g., [29], [30], [25], [31]). However, the emphasis in that research is on the *manipulation* of traces, whereas we discussed their specification. This work is also related to temporal logic (e.g., [18]) and interval logic (e.g., [17], [21]), maintenance of temporal databases in Artificial Intelligence (e.g., [8]), and temporal extensions to the relational model (e.g., [24]). However, the emphasis in such research is on the *inference* of temporal knowledge rather than the *specification* of temporal constraints. The specification of correlated events can be done in various logic formalisms which are often more powerful. However, we feel that the important constructs for the specification of correlated events are conjunction and disjunction, partial ordering, and time interval. In our opinion, these are most naturally specified as rules, directed acyclic graphs, and set-constraints, respectively, as we proposed.

## VIII. CONCLUSION AND FUTURE WORK

We showed how statistical-tests, alerts, and correlation among alerts can be represented as trace collections, events, and correlated events, respectively, and as such they can be specified using data-manipulation languages augmented with two new language-constructs that we defined. These language constructs will prove useful in any application of real time databases for monitoring and control.

The first language construct defines events and is based on a data manipulation language (such as SQL). We also proposed the features necessary for temporal correlation of events. The second language construct defines traces which track the way attribute values evolve over time in a database which represents a continuously changing system.

The next step in network management research is to define the content, architecture, and distribution scheme of the network database, and the algorithms for processing the language constructs proposed.

Additionally, we intend to extend the proposed language into a complete event-trace model, in which the basic building blocks are events and traces, as schemas and tuples are in the relational model. The work in [29] and [30] can serve as a starting point for a language to manipulate events and traces. We will study the processing of such a language, particularly in a distributed environment. We will also study the static analysis of an event-trace specification to answer questions such as: can this correlated event occur?, what is the maximum time between the occurrence of two correlated events?, what is the minimum length of a trace that guarantees that no events based on the trace will be lost?

## APPENDIX

We will prove that any set of temporal constraints is consistent with any order graph. Let $A$ be the set of atoms appearing in the body of an instantiated correlation rule (an instantiated rule is a rule in which all the variables are replaced by constants). OVERLOAD and ¬OVERLOAD(0.3) are examples of atoms. We assume that an event and its negation do not both appear in the body of the rule. The *occurrence time* is a function that maps each atom $a \in A$ to a non-negative real number $o(a)$. Intuitively, the occurrence time of a negative atom is the occurrence of the positive event. Denote by $P \subseteq A$ the subset of positive atoms. Let $E$ be a set of ordered pairs, each of which has two members of $P$. The pair $(P, E)$ is an *order* graph if it is acyclic. A *constraint*, $c$ is a pair $(s, b)$, where $s$ is a subset of $A$ which contains at least one positive atom, and $b$ is a positive real number. $b$ is called the *interval* of the constraint. The next proposition states that for any given set constraints and for any order-graph there is an assignment of occurrence times that satisfies the constraints and the order.

*Proposition*

Let $C$ be a set of constraints, and $G = (P, E)$ an order graph. Then there exists an occurrence-time function $o$, such that: (i) for any pair of positive atoms $e$ and $f$ and for any constraint $c = (s, b)$ of $C$ such that $e$ and $f$ are in $s$, $|o(e) - o(f)| \leq b$; (ii) for any negative atom $e$ and for any constraint $c = (s, b)$ of $C$ such that $e$ is in $s$, there is a positive atom $f \in s$ such that $o(e) - o(f) > b$; and (iii) for any pair of positive atoms $e$ and $f$, if $(e, f) \in E$, then $o(e) < o(f)$.

*Proof:* The proof is constructive, demonstrating an occurrence time function with the desired properties. Intuitively, we "squeeze" all the positive atoms in the smallest interval, which starts from 0, and postpone all the negative atoms until very late. Formally, let us first assign occurrence time to the positive atoms. Let $b_1$ be the smallest bound of a constraint in $C$. For an atom $a \in P$, that does not have any predecessors in $G$, $o(a)$ is 0. For the other positive atoms we assign occurrence times as follows: Let $a$ be an atom for which all the immediate predecessors in $G$ have been assigned occurrence times; assume that $m$ is the maximum occurrence time of such a predecessor. Then we assign $o(a) = m + \varepsilon$, where $0 < \varepsilon < b_1 - m$. Since $G$ is acyclic after at most $|P|$ iterations, all the positive atoms are assigned occurrence times. Let $b_2$ be the biggest bound of a constraint in $C$. All the negative atoms of $A$ are assigned the occurrence time $2 \cdot b_2$.

Now it is easy to see that our occurrence time function satisfies the three requirements of the proposition. The first requirement is satisfied, since all occurrence times of the positive atoms are within the smallest interval. The second requirement is satisfied, since the occurrence time of a positive atom is smaller than $b_1$, and $2 \cdot b_2 - b_1 \geq b_2$. The third requirement is satisfied by the way the occurrence-time function $o$ was defined. □

If the occurrence time of an atom must be a natural (rather than real) number, then the above proposition does not hold. For example, if $G$ is the graph $a \to b \to c \to d$, then the single constraint $o(d) - o(a) < 2$ cannot be satisfied.

## REFERENCES

[1] F. E. Boland, Ed., *Working Implementation Agreements for Open Systems Interconnection Protocol.* Los Alamitos, CA: IEEE Computer Soc., 1989
[2] F. Cacace, S. Ceri, S. Crespi-Reghizzi, L. Tanaka, and R. Zicari, "Integrating object oriented data modeling with a rule-based programming paradigm," in *Proc. ACM-Sigmod Int. Conf. on Management of Data*, 1990.
[3] J. D. Case, J. R. Davin, M. S. Fedor, and M. L. Schoffstall, "Simple network management protocol," Network Inform. Ctr., SRI Int., Menlo Park, CA, Request for Comments 1067, Sept. 1988.
[4] D. L. Cohrs and B. P. Miller, "Specification and verification of network managers for large internets," in *Proc. ACM-Sigcomm*, 1989.
[5] Information Process. Syst., OSI Common Management Inform. Protocol, ISO/IEC DIS 9596-2, Dec. 1988.
[6] Information Process. Syst., OSI Common Management Inform. Service, ISO/IEC DIS 9595-2, Dec. 1988.
[7] S. Chakravarthy *et al.*, "HiPAC: a research project in active, time-constrained database management," Xerox Advanced Inform. Technol., TR XAIT-89-02 (this reference subsumes several publications on the HiPAC project).
[8] T. Dean, "Using temporal hierarchies to efficiently maintain large temporal databases," *JACM*, vol. 36, no. 4, Oct. 1989.
[9] M. Darnovsky and J. Bowman, "TRANSACT-SQL USER'S GUIDE" Sybase Inc., Doc. 3231-2.1, 1987.
[10] L. M. L. Delcambre and J. N. Etheredge, "A self-controlling interpreter for the relational production language," in *Proc. ACM-Sigmod Int. Conf. on Management of Data*, 1988.
[11] A. Dupuy, S. Sengupta, O. Wolfson, and Y. Yemini, "Design of the Netmate Network Management system," in *Integrated Network Management*, vol. 2, I. Krishnan and W. Zimmer, Eds. Amsterdam, The Netherlands: Elsevier Science–North Holland, 1991.
[12] S. Ganguly, A. Silberschatz, and S. Tsur, "A framework for the parallel processing of datalog queries," in *Proc. ACM-Sigmod Int. Conf. on Management of Data*, 1990.
[13] A. Kotz, K. Dittrich, and J. Mulle "Supporting semantic rules by a generalized event/trigger mechanism," in *Proc. EDBT'88*. New York: Springer-Verlag, 1988.
[14] G. Kiernan, C. de Maindreville, and E. Simon, "Making deductive database a practical technology: a step forward," in *Proc. ACM-Sigmod Int. Conf. on Management of Data*, 1990.
[15] H. Korth, N. Soparkar, and A. Silberschatz, "Triggered real-time databases with consistency constraints," in *Proc. VLDB*, Aug. 1990.
[16] Management Information Library—Rev. 1.0, OSI MIB Working Group of NMSIG of NIST/OSI Implementation Workshop, Mar. 1989.
[17] B. Moszkowski, "A temporal logic for multilevel reasoning about hardware," *IEEE Computer*, vol. 18, Feb. 1985.
[18] A. Pnueli, "The temporal logic of programs," in *Proc. 18th Symp. on FOCS*. New York: IEEE, 1977.
[19] C. Partridge, Ed., "Special issue on network management," *IEEE Network*, vol. 2, Mar. 1988.
[20] T. Risch, "Monitoring database objects," in *Proc. VLDB*, Aug. 1989.
[21] R. R. Razouk and M. M. Gorlik, "A real time interval logic for reasoning about executions of real-time programs," in *Proc. ACM-SIGSOFT Conf.*, 1989.

[22] T. Sellis, Ed., "Special issue on rule management and processing in expert database systems," *SIGMOD Rec.*, vol. 18, no. 3, Sept. 1989.
[23] S. H. Son, Ed., "Special issue on real-time database systems," *ACM SIGMOD Rec.*, Mar. 1988.
[24] R. Snodgrass, "The temporal query language TQuel," *ACM Trans. Database Syst.*, vol. 12, no. 2, June 1987.
[25] R. Snodgrass, Ed., "Special issue on temporal databases," *Data Eng.*, Dec. 1988.
[26] M. Stonebraker, Ed., "Special issue on database prototype systems," *IEEE Trans. Data and Knowledge Eng.*, vol. 2, Mar. 1990.
[27] M. Stonebraker, A. Jhingran, J. Goh, and S. Potamianos, "On rules, procedures, caching and views in database systems," in *Proc. ACM-Sigmod Int. Conf. on Management of Data*, 1990.
[28] M. Stonebraker *et al.*, "Third Generation Data Base System Manifesto," Univ. California, Berkeley, Memo. UCB/ERL M90/28.
[29] A. Segev and A. Shoshani, "Logical modeling of temporal data," in *Proc. ACM-Sigmod Int. Conf. on Management of Data*, 1987.
[30] A. Segev and A. Shoshani, "The representation of a temporal data model in the relational environment," presented at the 4th Int. Conf. on Statistical and Scientific Data Manage., June 1988.
[31] A. Segev and H. Gunadhi, "Event-join optimization in temporal relational databases," in *Proc. VLDB*, Aug. 1989.
[32] J. D. Ullman, *Principles of Database and Knowledge-Base Systems*, vols. 1/2. Rockville, MD: Computer Sci. Press, 1989.
[33] J. Widom and S. Finkelstein, "Set-oriented production rules in relational database systems," in *Proc. ACM-Sigmod Int. Conf. on Management of Data*, 1990.
[34] O. Wolfson, H. Dewan, S. Stolfo, and Y. Yemini, "Incremental evaluation of rules and its relationship to parallelism," in *Proc. ACM-Sigmod Int. Conf. on Management of Data*, 1991.
[35] O. Wolfson and A. Ozeri, "A new paradigm for parallel and distributed rule processing," in *Proc. of the ACM-Sigmod Int. Conf. on Management of Data*, 1990.
[36] U. S. Warrier, P. A. Relan, O. Berry, and J. Bannister, "A network management language for OSI networks," in *Proc. ACM-Sigcomm*, 1988.

**Ouri Wolfson** received the B.Sc. degree in mathematics from the University of Tel-Aviv in 1976, and the Ph.D. degree in computer science from the Courant Institute of Mathematical Sciences, New York University, in 1984.

Before joining the Department of Electrical Engineering and Computer Science of the University of Illinois, Chicago, he was a Research Scientist in the Computer Science Department of Columbia University, New York City. Before then, he had been the American Broadcasting Co., AT&T Bell Laboratories, and the Technion. His research interests are in databases, communication network management, and rule processing, and he has published extensively in these areas. At Columbia University he was the co-founder of the Paradiser project, and one of the principal architects of the Netmate project. Paradiser aims to research and develop an environment for parallel and distributed rule processing that takes into consideration real-time constraints. Newmate is a prototype set of software tools for the management of very large communication networks (hundreds of thousands of interconnected computers).


**Soumitra Sengupta**, photograph and biography not available at the time of publication.


**Yechiam Yemini**, photograph and biography not available at the time of publication.

# NETWORK INFORMATION MODELING FOR NETWORK MANAGEMENT

H. Yamaguchi, S. Isobe, T. Yamaki and Y. Yamanaka

Network Operations Laboratory
NTT Network Information Systems Labs.
3-9-11 Midori-cho
Musashino-shi, Tokyo, 180 Japan
Telephone +81-422-59-2925
Facsimile +81-422-59-3628

## Abstract

This paper describes the methodology and results of an information model for managing telecommunication networks.

In recent years, the network management of an operating company has been changing to global and multi-functional network operations for providing the best telecommunication services.

To support such network operations, it is important to develop an integrated network operation system which comprises distributed and harmonized operation support systems sharing a global network management information and interacting with each other. For the environment of the integrated network operation system, the common master database concept is important. To establish a common master database, it is essential to define the unified global network management information.

The most fundamental domain for network management information is the network configuration information domain which represents the fundamental resources of operating companies. The other network management information should be combined to the network configuration information with some relationships.
The presentation discusses the layered view of the telecommunications network and provides a global information model of the network. The model can be utilized directly for conceptual design of the common master database.

# What is Information Modeling ?

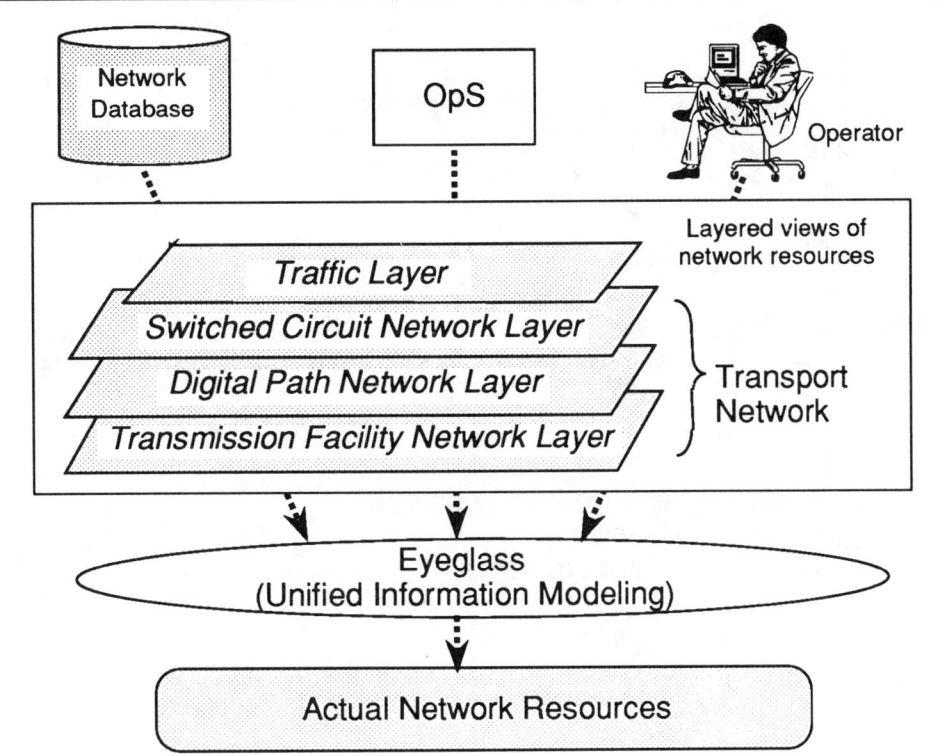

## What is Information Modeling ?

Adopting a data oriented approach is useful for developing an integrated network operation environment. In this approach, a unified view of the network resources is essential which is represented by a network information model. The network information model means network representation by data. The unified network information model and data schema definitions are implemented in a common master database.

This paper presents some network information modeling results. In this model, four layers are defined: a transmission facility layer, a digital path layer, a switched circuit layer and a traffic layer. The aggregate of the transmission facility, digital path and switched circuit layers is called the transport network layer. Above the transport network layer is the traffic layer. The characteristics of each layer will be described later.

# Model Definition Methodology
## (Entity-Relationship diagram)

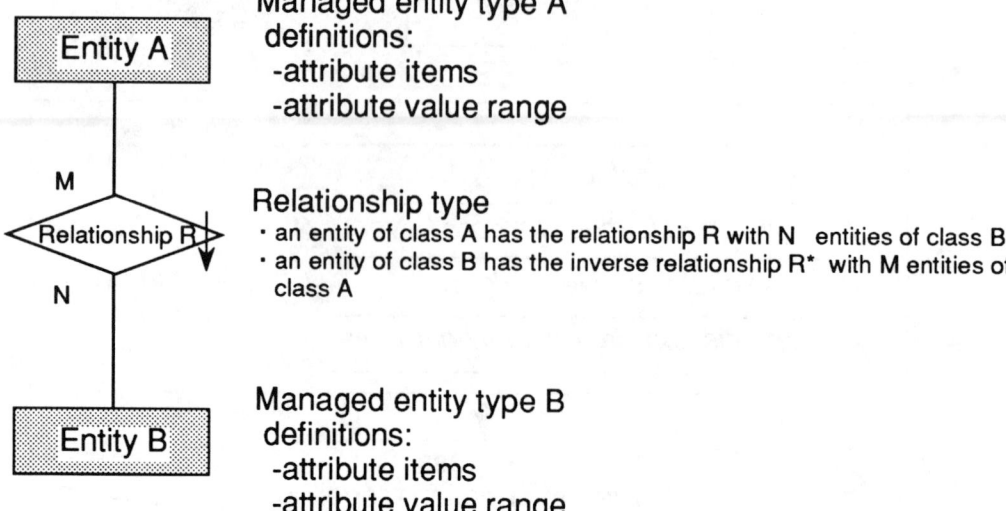

Managed entity type A definitions:
- attribute items
- attribute value range

Relationship type
- an entity of class A has the relationship R with N entities of class B
- an entity of class B has the inverse relationship R* with M entities of class A

Managed entity type B definitions:
- attribute items
- attribute value range

## Model Definition Methodology

It is important to make network resources visible by data to realize an integrated network operations. For obtaining the visibility, it is necessary to define managed entities and relationships among those entities because a network is a system which combines various network elements.

The Entity-Relationship (ER) modeling methodology is used for the network information modeling. This methodology first identifies managed entities (MEs), and then defines relationships between those entities. An ER diagram defines entities and relationships as shown in the above figure.

Information of the model consists of the following definitions :
1) Managed entity type definition:
   Things which exist physically or logically in the telecommunications network and are recognized for network management.
2) Relationship type definition:
   Relationships which are recognized between two of managed entities.
3) Attribute definition:
   Features which characterize a managed entity type which include definitions involving data types, data lengths and value ranges of attributes.

The ER model definition is directly used for the conceptual design of the database.

# Generalized Entities and Relationships

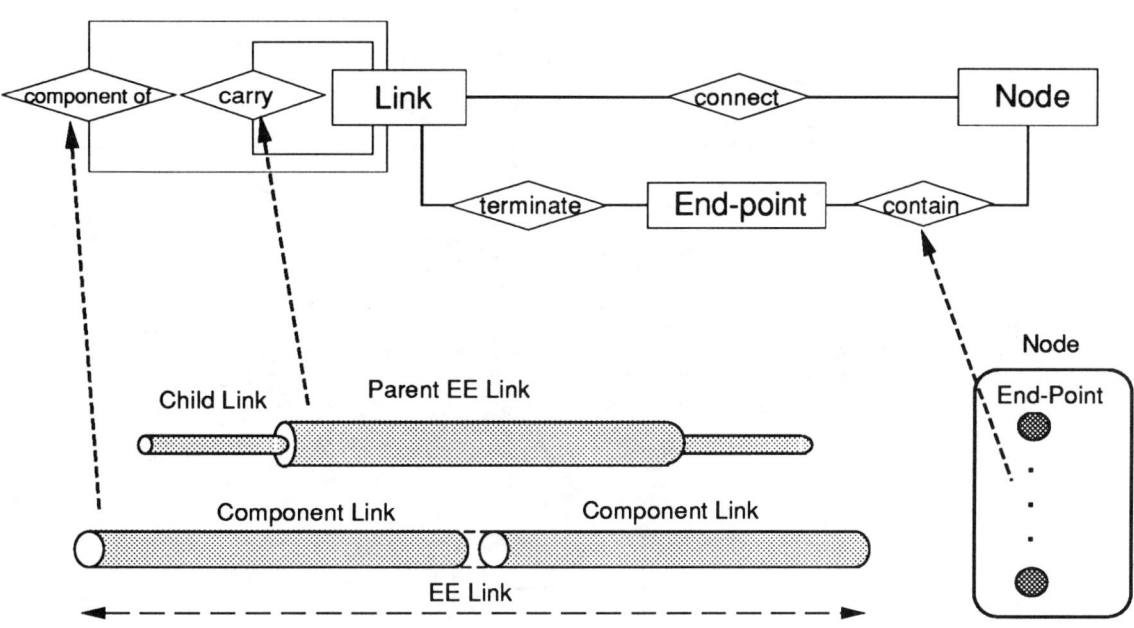

EE Link : End to End Link

# Generalized Entities and Relationships

A network is a system for providing services by connecting network elements. Topologically, it can be represented by a set of nodes and a set of links. These nodes and links are recognized as managed entity types. A link connects two nodes, and a node terminates one or multiple links.

An end-point entity type is defined in addition to node and link entity types. An end-point entity is considered to address a link allocation point of the node.

The fundamental relationships between these three entity types are as follows:
 - A link connects two nodes and a node connects multiple links.
 - A node contains endpoints.
 - An end-point terminates a link.
 - A link may be a component of another link which is an EE(End to End) link.
 - A link may be carried by another link which is a parent link.

Those generalized entity types, a link, a node and an end-point, will be specialized when they are applied in each layer of a network model.

## Specialization of Node and Link

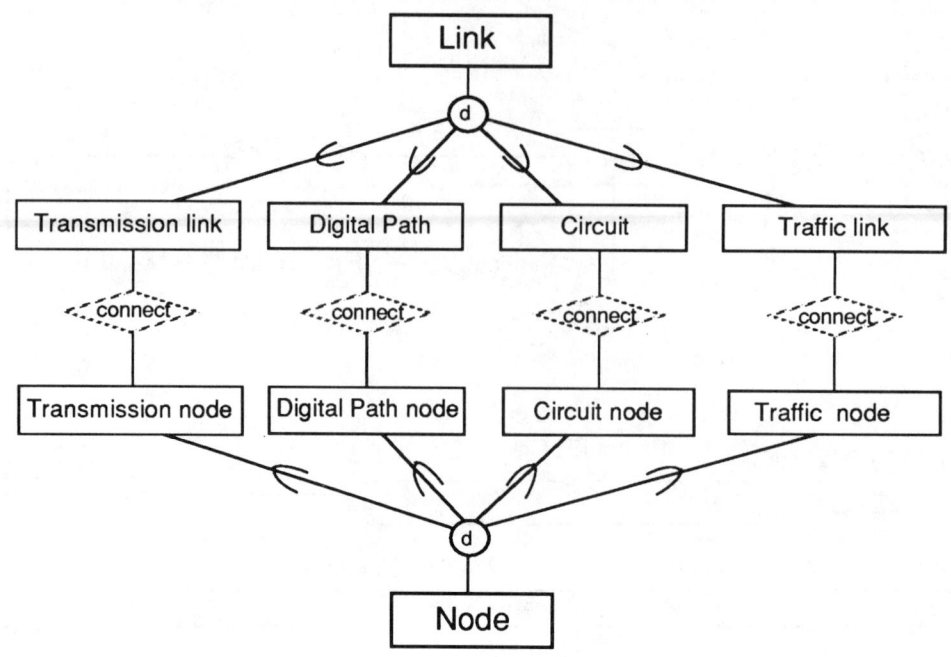

## Specialization of Node and Link

Specialization is the process of defining a set of subtypes for an generalized entity type. A diagrammatic technique for displaying this concept has already been proposed in an enhanced-ER model. In the above figure which employs the technique, each of a generalized node and a generalized link entity types is specialized to four types, and each corresponding pair of entity types has the "connect" relationship.

Specialized link entity types are: a transmission link, a digital path, a circuit and a traffic link. Specialized node entity types are: a transmission node, a digital path node, a circuit node and a traffic node.

There are "connect" relationships between a link entity type and a node entity type in the same layer. For example, a transmission link connects two transmission nodes.

# Layered Model of Transport Network

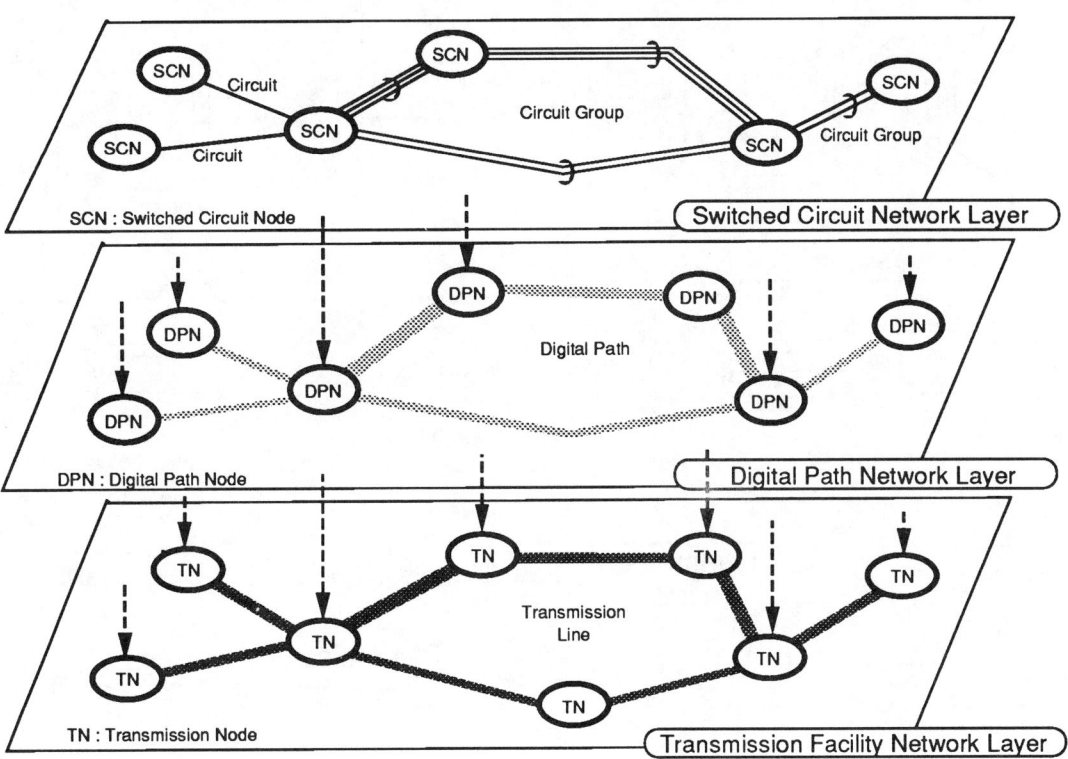

## Layered Model of Transport Network

In order to develop a global network information model, it is necessary to define the relationships between entity types in the different layers.

Three layered views of the transport network are shown in the above figure. As for link entities, it is recognized that a lower layer link carries upper layer links. The carrying link is an EE link of the lower layer and the carried link is a component/EE link of the upper layer.

The upper layer can access the lower layer transmission capability at the nodes which are indicated associated arrows in the above figure.

Those layered views of the network are reflected by the layered operations and management activities, that is, most of those activities are carried in the single layer. In the case of the integrated network operations, the global information model which includes information of all layers is required.

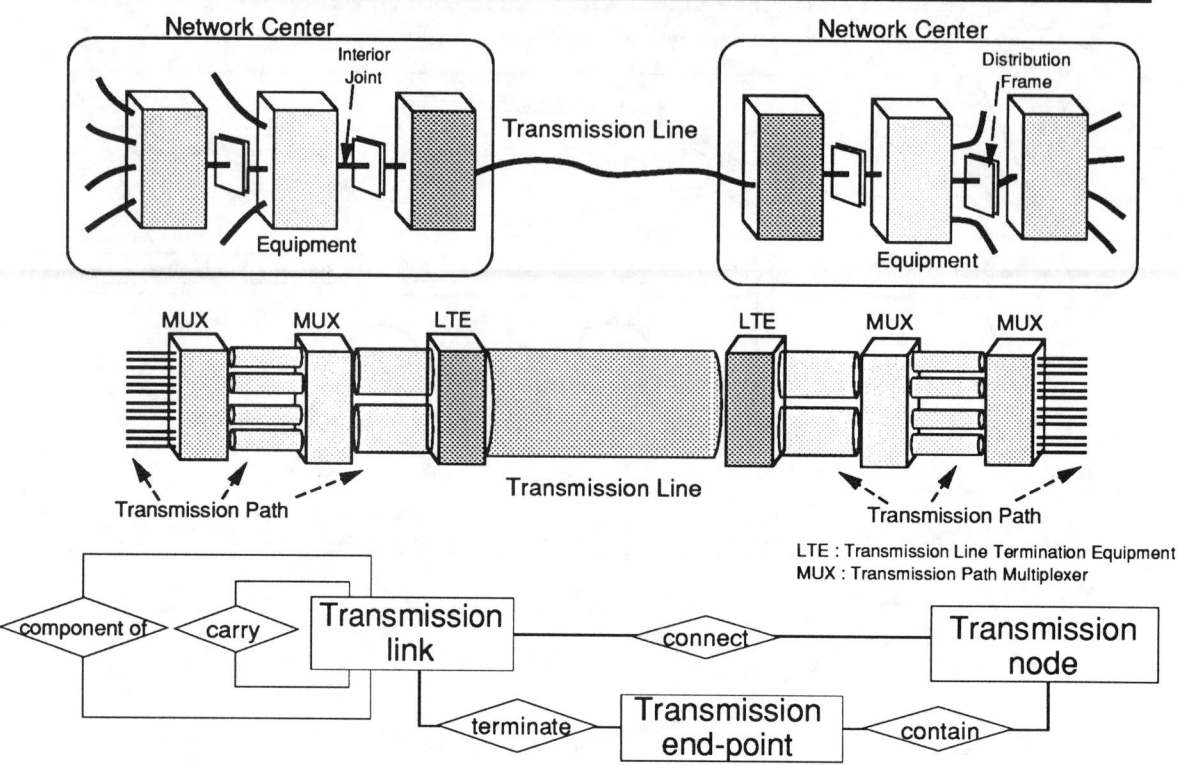

## Transmission Facility Network Layer View

This figure illustrates the transmission facility network layer view. In this layer, a transmission link entity type includes a transmission line and a transmission path. A transmission node refers to network centers. A transmission end-point corresponds to the terminating equipment of the link which is in the network center.

A transmission line connects between two network centers and is terminated by two transmission end-points each of which is a line termination equipment(LTE), whereas a transmission path connects between two network centers and is terminated by two transmission path multiplexers(MUXs).

The ER diagram of the facility network layer is shown in the above figure. Although a distribution frame and an interior joint are recognized as managed entity types in this layer, we will not consider these supplementary types in this paper.

# Digital Path Network Layer View

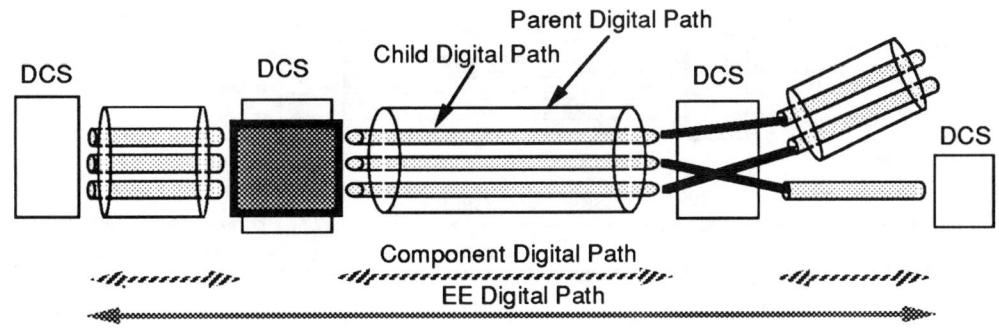

DCS : Digital Cross-connect System

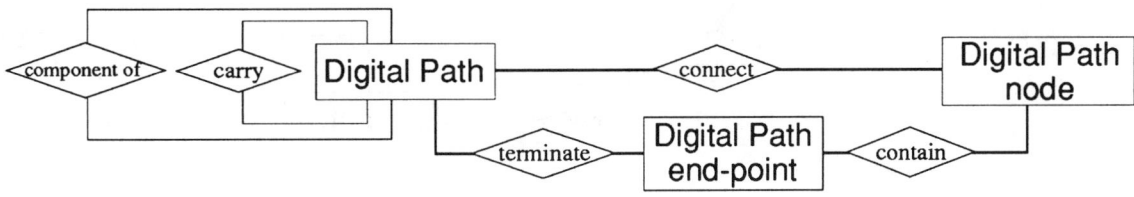

# Digital Path Network Layer View

The path network layer view is illustrated in this figure. In this layer, a digital path, a digital path node and a digital path end-point are recognized as entity types. A digital path node refers to digital cross-connect systems. A digital path means a transmission capability between two digital path nodes. A digital path end-point indicates a digital path allocation point on a digital path node.

An EE digital path is composed of the chain of component digital paths which are connected by the digital cross-connect system.

The ER diagram of the digital path network layer is obtained as shown in the above figure. For the path entity type, "carry" and "component of" relationship types are recognized.

# Switched Circuit Network Layer View

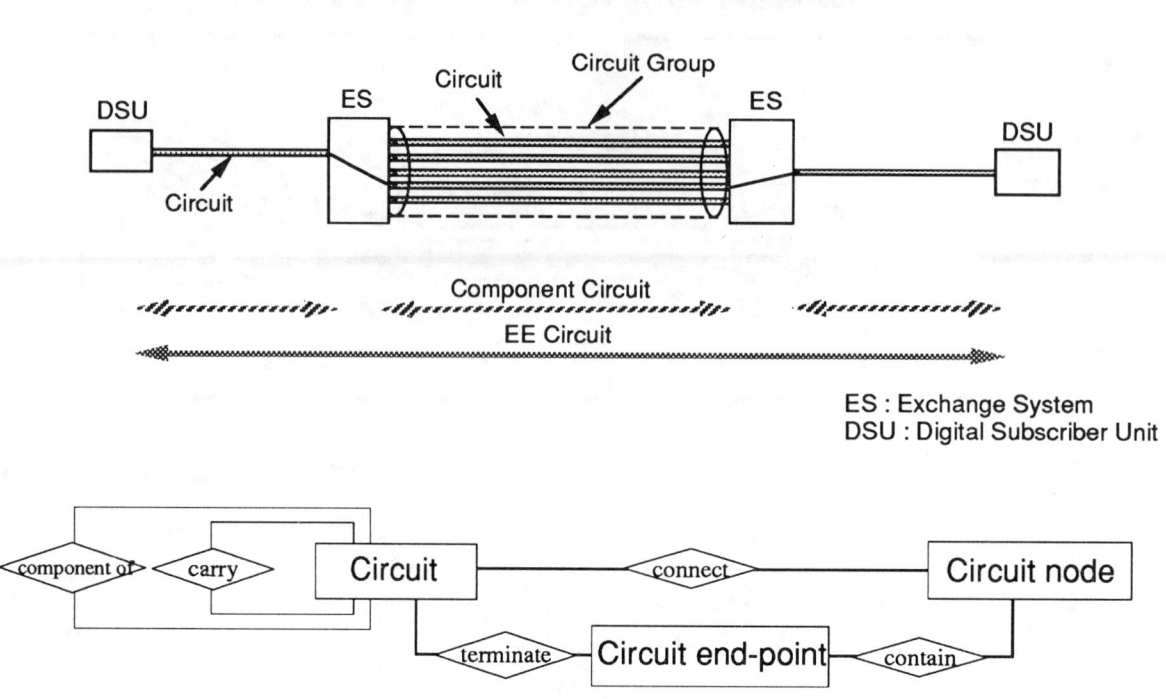

## Switched Circuit Network Layer View

This figure illustrates the switched circuit network layer view. In this layer, a circuit, a circuit node and a circuit end-point are recognized as entity types. A circuit node refers to an exchange system. A digital subscriber unit is also classified into the circuit node. A circuit end-point indicates an allocation point in a circuit node.

An EE circuit connects two customer nodes such as the digital subscriber unit and consists of component circuits connected by exchange systems. A circuit group contains multiple circuits which are handled as an operational unit.

The ER diagram of the switched circuit network layer is obtained as shown in the above figure. For the circuit entity type, "carry" and "component of" relationship types are recognized.

# Traffic Network Layer View

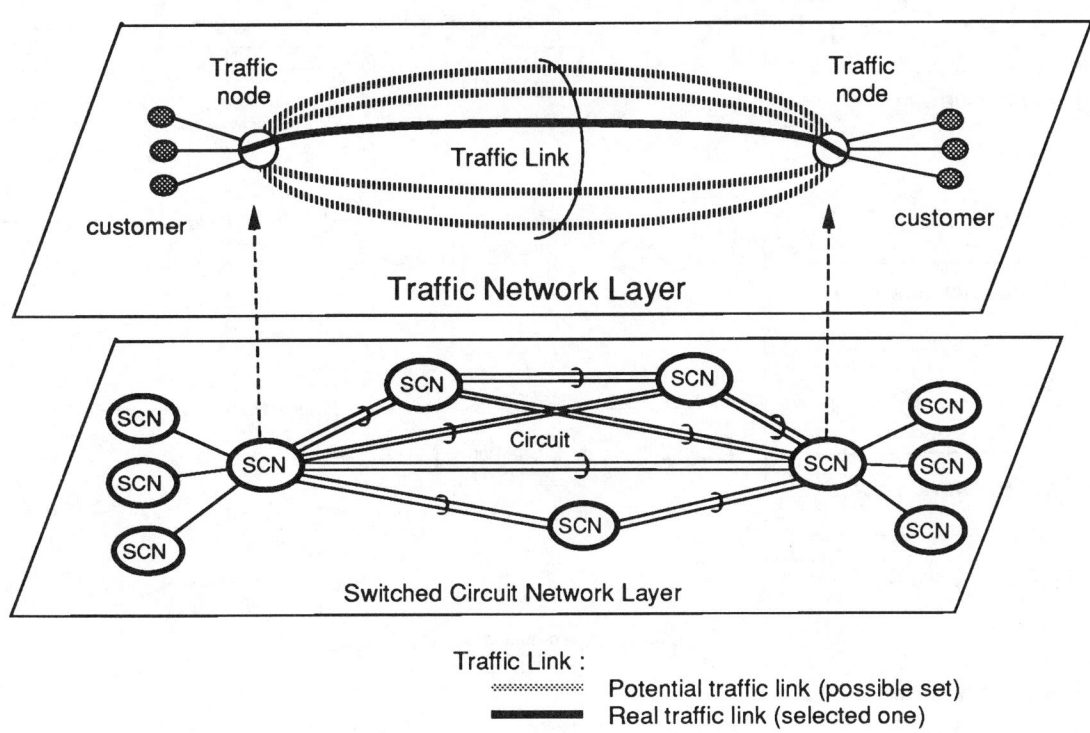

## Traffic Network Layer View

This figure illustrates the traffic network layer view. In this layer, a traffic node, a traffic link and a traffic end-point are recognized as entity types. A traffic node refers to an exchange system. A traffic link means a routing path between selected two nodes. A traffic end-point indicates a traffic link allocation point on a traffic node.

The traffic link connects two traffic nodes each of which acts originating or terminating node for a telephone call. A traffic link between two nodes is recognized as a potential routing path which can be used for transmitting a traffic between two nodes. Traffic link information is stored in the circuit nodes related to the traffic routing. When a telephone call connection is set up, a traffic link selected from potential traffic links is called a real traffic link. An EE traffic link is composed of a chain of component traffic links.

## Global Network Information Model

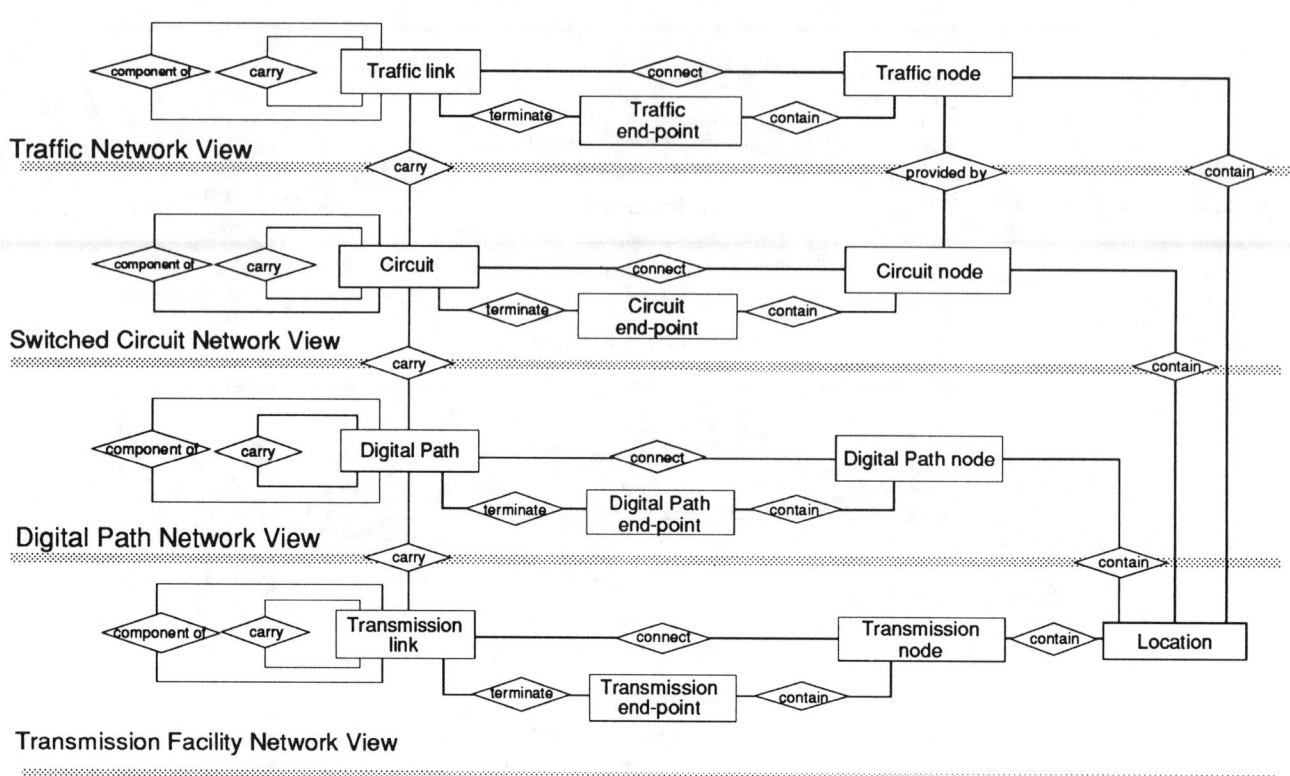

## Global Network Information Model

This figure shows a global network information model for the telecommunications network management which is obtained by combining four network layer views.

There is defined "carry" relationship between two link types in the different layers. In the global model, a location entity type is defined as an entity type which has geographical information.

## Summary

This paper presents the layered network information model which includes four layered views of telecommunications network configuration. It is discussed that every layer can be modeled by the same structure which has three generalized entity types: a node, a link and an end-point. The specializations of those generalized entity types are presented for each layers.

The global information model can be utilized as a conceptual network model for the integrated telecommunications network operations.

# Development and Integration of a Management Information Base

## by Bob Stewart, Xyplex

**Abstract**  With the Internet's SNMP as the primary example, and references to OSI's CMIP, this article positions the MIB concept in Network Management. It examines the growth of the SNMP MIB from first version through the current explosion of standard experimental and private MIBs. It discusses the reason, means, and problems of that growth, and propose a solution to the some of the problems.

**Introduction**  A protocol to carry monitoring and control information is necessary to realize distributed network management, but the process of defining what the protocol carries encompasses far more effort and difficulty. Following, we will examine a process by which such information, termed a *Management Information Base* (MIB), is defined and provided to the network manager, using the *Simple Network Management Protocol* (SNMP) as the example. The discussion comprises the following major sections:

- Design—the origin, philosophy, and structure of SNMP.
- Development—the principles and process of MIB development.
- Future—the projected evolution of network management protocols and a proposal for improved interoperability.

**History**  In 1988, recognizing the need for interoperable, distributed network management, the *Internet Activities Board* (IAB), overseeing body for the Internet protocol suite (commonly known as TCP/IP), commissioned work on the necessary protocol definitions [1]. The IAB chose a short-term plan for a simple protocol, with possible longer term replacement by an international standard protocol. To facilitate that evolution, the protocols were to share basic definitions.

The short term part of the plan lead to creation of SNMP, based heavily on the already-proven *Simple Gateway Monitoring Protocol* (SGMP) [3]. The long term part of the plan was to use the *Common Management Information Protocol* (CMIP) as defined by the *International Organization for Standardization* (ISO) in the *Open Systems Interconnection* (OSI) framework. For early Internet implementations, CMIP was to use the *Transmission Control Protocol* (TCP) as its transport mechanism, a combination known as "CMIP over TCP/IP" (CMOT) [4].

Work on SNMP progressed rapidly, but the CMOT work did not. Furthermore, attempts to coordinate the two paths were impeding progress, so in 1989 the IAB decoupled the efforts [2]. At this point, SNMP assumed the position of long-term solution. CMOT work continues in the Internet community, and CMIP work proceeds in the international community, but by far the most complete, interoperable network management implementation is found in SNMP. At this time, SNMP's base documents [5, 6, 7] compose a standard, recommended Internet protocol.

**Philosophy**  The SNMP design philosophy is of major importance, as it drastically affects the protocol structure and evolution. The philosophy's two overriding principles are *simplicity* and *extensibility* [5]. Not only can we discuss the intent of these goals, but experience since they were chosen allows us to consider their merit and realization.

*Simplicity* is important to encourage implementation and foster correctness. Distributed network management is not possible unless the systems to be managed implement the protocol. Such implementations will not be present with the necessary ubiquity if such an implementation is too costly. Furthermore, they will not be useful if they are not robust and accurate. SNMP is therefore strongly biased toward simplicity in the managed systems, which far outnumber the managing systems.

For the most part, the design met the goal of simplicity, although simplicity in one area can lead to complexity in others (discussed later with regard to SNMP as a protocol). Such specifics notwithstanding, the widespread implementation of SNMP, versus the relative lack of practical CMIP implementations, indicates that SNMP's simplicity helped encourage its acceptance, while CMIP may have been hindered by its more extensive capability, but resulting complexity.

*Extensibility* is necessary to allow immediate, useful implementation while assuming that all necessary capabilities cannot be included at the outset. SNMP succeeds reasonably well in extensibility of MIB design, as shown by the proliferation of MIB extensions. It has been less effective in incorporating certain functions, such as actions to be taken, or efficient manipulation of large, complex databases. Nevertheless, this does not necessarily imply a shortcoming on the part of SNMP's designers, as the additional complexity accompanying such capabilities would most likely have violated the requirement for simplicity, resulting in a far more disastrous failure to be accepted as a standard. Furthermore, the "MIB explosion" was inevitable, as availability of interoperable, distributed network management lead to raised consciousness and expectations which turned into demands on commercial system vendors for extensive SNMP management capabilities.

**Structure**  Documentation of the SNMP design comprises three major components:

- The generic Structure of Management Information (SMI) [5].
- The Management Information Base [6].
- The protocol itself [7].

Overall, the approach to distributed network management follows the now-classic client-server model as shown in Figure 1. The client runs at the *managing system*. It makes requests and is typically called the *Network Management System* (NMS) or *Network Operation Center* (NOC). The server is in the *managed system*. It executes requests and is called the *agent*.

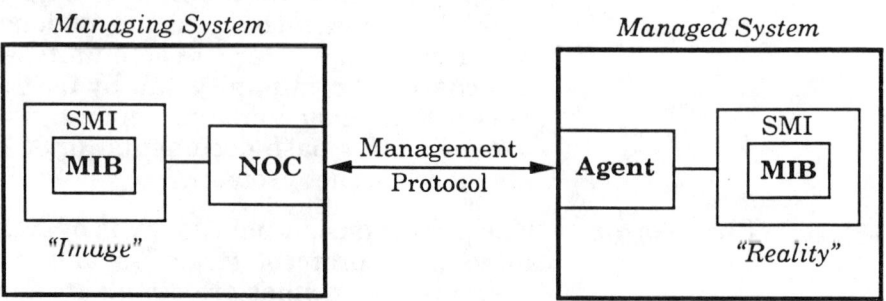

Figure 1: SNMP Management Architecture

# MIB Development and Integration

**SMI** The *SMI* sets down the elemental structure and form of management information, thereby limiting the universe of choices. Overall, it defines the concept of a MIB as an abstract tree, with individual data items as the leaves. (See Figure 2). It provides a basis for MIB extensibility, in the form of "experimental" and "private" branches to the tree. It establishes *Abstract Syntax Notation One* (ASN.1) as the standard for documenting MIBs [8] and encoding protocol messages [9], picking a small subset of ASN.1's rich supply of data representations. It institutes the basic format for MIB documentation, in the form of an ASN.1 "macro." Finally, it defines the means of identifying individual data items, termed *objects,* for both single instance (scalar) and multiple instance (table) objects, using ASN.1 object identifiers.

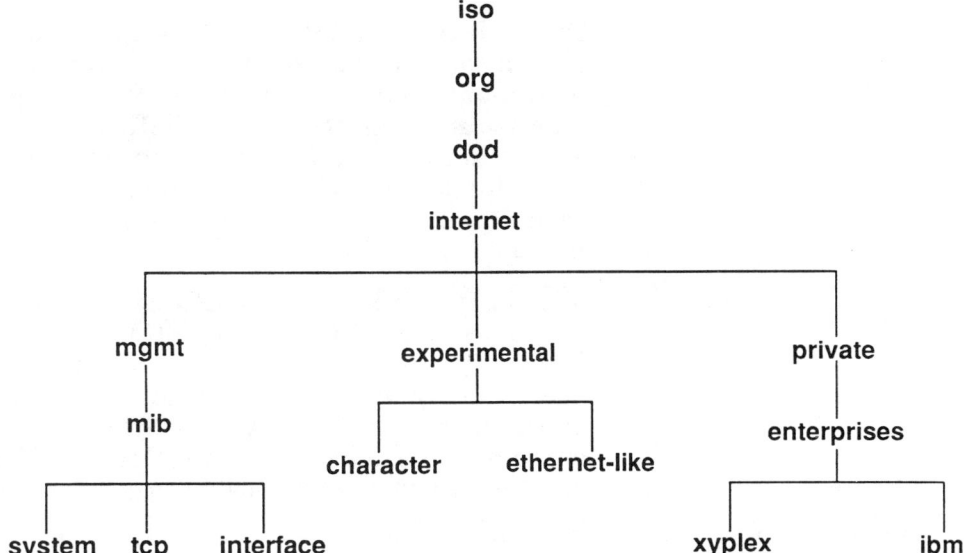

Figure 2: MIB tree

The concept of "tables" deserves special mention, as it has become an area of some controversy. Strictly speaking, tables do not exist in a MIB; the concept was not part of SGMP, and was added for compatibility with CMIP. Abstractly, each data item is an independent entity, in some cases sharing the instance part of their identification. On the other hand, documentation and implementation techniques implied that multiple instance objects exhibit an organization of rows and columns, leading to the desire, and need, to create or delete entire rows. Later documentation [10], attempts to remedy some of the confusion between abstract architecture and practical implementation, but the conflict between the original, pure architecture and the table concept, which has become firmly ensconced in the minds of most MIB designers, remains an area of confusion and awkwardness.

Experience with the SMI proves it as a strong base. It has some readily admitted deficiencies (such as lacking bit strings, integers greater than 32 bits, and text strings distinguishable from binary strings), but as yet the desire for such extensions has not overpowered the desire for continued stability.

**MIB** The *MIB* was, in fact, just the starting point for MIB definition. It formed a useful base of management information, and set a tone for future MIB development. The original MIB contains objects for observation and limited control of the Transport, Network, and Data/Physical Link layers of an internet.

Subsequent events show that the MIB designers behaved wisely in severely limiting MIB contents. Although it is easy to find complaints about missing information, the original MIB was interesting in its contents while remaining reasonable to implement, resulting in a sufficient number of implementations to prove the utility of SNMP as a management protocol.

**Protocol**

The *protocol* defines how to exchange messages containing MIB objects, and exactly how to identify instances for the original MIB. The protocol is the level where one chooses either SNMP or CMOT as the carrier for the MIB. As with the SMI and the MIB, the designers kept SNMP simple, preferring a few general purpose functions: *get, get-next, set,* and *trap,* and specifying it as a request-response protocol using a datagram transport service.

These intentional limitations have considerable impact on MIB design, sometimes keeping the protocol simple at the expense of additional complexity in the MIB. The *get-next* function (often called "the *powerful get-next*") is SNMP's key function, as it gives a NOC the ability to explore a MIB without pre-knowledge of its contents, doing so with a single, relatively simple mechanism in the agent; although MIB designers must take *get-next* into account for efficient access to instanced information.

This is in contrast to CMIP's somewhat more complex mechanisms called *scoping and filtering.* SNMP's *set* function seems simple, but has the painful (for the agent) characteristic that a *set* request can specify many unrelated objects in any order, and the *set* must succeed or fail as a unit. Finally, the *trap* function (for reporting events) is currently the least used and least understood, with considerable controversy over correct event logging operation.

**MIB Development**

The original MIB, now known as *MIB-I,* set the tone for subsequent MIB development, in terms of its form, contents, and the process used to develop it. It originated the following conventions of MIB design:

- *Limited number of objects:* The designers chose a somewhat arbitrary limit of 100 objects for MIB-I. The MIB contains a few more, but the limit imposed discipline, forcing careful evaluation of objects for general utility. This principle leads to the corollary that objects are not duplicated within or across MIBs, and that objects are not defined if the NOC can calculate them more-or-less readily from other objects.

- *Limited computational impact:* The designers accepted a constraint that no more than one counter should appear in critical paths of operation. This constitutes no absolute requirement, but imposes a worthwhile discipline, important in implementing high performance systems. In practice though, it can be difficult to follow, as the definition of "critical path" varies depending on system requirements and implementation models.

- *Limited use of optional objects:* MIB-I contains no optional objects. Instead, entire object groups are implemented if and only if the system has the related capabilities. For example, if the system does not implement TCP, it does not implement the TCP MIB group, but if it does implement TCP, it must implement the complete TCP MIB group. Defining objects as optional allows indecision and compromise on the part of MIB designers with differing opinions, and is at odds with consistency of implementation.

# MIB Development and Integration

- *Style of organization and definition:* Conventions in this area are less clear, but MIB-I certainly serves as a model in ways that may not have been intended. For example, its approach to identification of network interface instances with a small, densely-spaced integer that does not change has carried over into various other MIBs, both in reference to those interfaces, and the identification technique used in similar tables. Suffice it to say that the erstwhile MIB designer would do well to understand the reasons behind the organization of the original MIB.

**MIB II**  The second version of the basic MIB, known as *MIB-II* [11], contains incremental changes to MIB-I. Its contributions include:

- *Incremental extensions:* Although the SMI implies that new versions of the MIB were to be new branches in the tree, with retained objects in both the old and new branches, practical experience indicated that the better plan was to make compatible changes to MIB-I, leaving existing objects intact and adding new objects on the ends of the existing branches.

- *Object deprecation:* Some changes required removing old objects, thus MIB-II added the concept of "deprecated" objects to soften the transition to "obsolete" as defined by the SMI. For the convenience of existing NOCs, such objects must be implemented as if "mandatory," but are subject to removal in a later version of the MIB.

- *Use of textual conventions for object syntax:* Short of adding data types to the SMI, MIB definitions needed a way to indicate common data types, such as an octet string that is to contain only printable ASCII. For this purpose, MIB-II added the use of "textual conventions," ASN.1 mappings of an object syntax to an existing SMI encoding. For example, `DisplayString` implies an all ASCII octet string for documentation purposes, but the actual ASN.1 encodings for a `DisplayString` and an `OCTET STRING` are the same.

**Concise MIB form**  During its development cycle, MIB-II became an early example of a new form of MIB definition called *Concise MIB form* [10, 12]. This eliminated much redundancy in MIB definitions, removing opportunities for contradictions and reducing typical document size by over 40%. It established a new convention that techniques for instance identification can appear in the MIB document, rather than the protocol document (for example, SNMP) as the first such did; although instance identification remains architecturally a protocol-specific matter. Also importantly, Concise MIB form extended the ASN.1 macro so more information can readily be parsed by computer programs, further improving the potential for direct integration of new MIBs into existing NOCs with less custom programming.

**Private MIBs**  The largest body of MIB development is in private MIBs. From the *Internet Assigned Numbers Authority,* organizations can obtain a unique number that defines their private branch of the overall MIB. Within that branch they can do anything they wish, with complete freedom as to process and documentation; although a private MIB should not stray too far from the accepted standards and conventions if it is to have any hope of interoperation with a generic NOC. The typical private MIB defines hundreds of additional objects, and often works only with a NOC customized to match.

In an attempt to help integrate private MIBs into generic NOCs, an individual on one of the SNMP working mailing lists instigated creation of an *Internet MIB Repository*. The result is a public collection of MIB documents, available on the Internet at a neutral, central site, documenting the private MIBs of any organization wishing to submit a document that will pass scrutiny by a MIB syntax checking program (a MIB compiler). In particular, system vendors who implement private SNMP MIBs can now easily supply documentation that can be processed by a growing number of NOCs.

**Experimental MIBs** The experimental branch of the overall MIB contains a growing number of experimental MIBs. As with private MIBs, each has its own branch of the tree, obtained from the Internet assigned numbers authority. Such MIBs often are developed by Internet working groups under the auspices of the *Internet Engineering Task Force* (IETF). The section on MIB process, following, describes such development in more detail. Experimental MIBs are subject to considerable discussion by interested experts and represent a common agreement that is assumed subject to change based on experience in implementation and use. They can thus be widely implemented in a common way with the understood risk that they will be replaced, nicely blending interoperability with the flexibility to learn and improve.

Some examples of experimental MIBs include various flavors of IEEE 802 devices, including Ethernet/802.3, Token Ring/802.5, and bridges. Other experimental MIBs cover the proposed Point-to-Point Protocol (PPP), and character stream devices. As experimental MIBs mature, they may move to the management branch and become Proposed Standards.

**MIB Process** For discussion purposes, the following steps describe a development process for a new standard MIB branch. The process for a private MIB would be less formal, and typically internal to its developing organization. The process described here does not reflect documented, official IAB or Internet procedure, as such does not yet exist; instead, the following is based on the author's ongoing experience in developing a MIB.

**Establish working group** Internet standards development is the task of the IETF. The IETF is divided into Areas, such as Applications, User Services, and Network Management, each with an *Area Director*. Area Directors oversee *Working Groups* that exist for the duration of specific tasks, such as development of an experimental MIB. Anyone who can demonstrate sufficient interest can cooperate with the appropriate Area Director to establish a working group. Subject to approval by the Area Director, a working group writes its own charter, which describes its task and sets milestones to plan and measure progress.

For a MIB extension, the working group should attract the participation of multiple parties with expertise and interest in the subject area, usually representing an assortment of businesses and educational institutions. Indicative of Internet community spirit, and the strong commercial interest in Internet protocols, such a working group typically exhibits remarkable cooperation among businesses that otherwise are ardent competitors.

**Develop Draft** The major part of a MIB working group's task is to develop an *Internet Draft* defining the MIB. Typically the draft will have one or two editors, with starting technical contributions from several group members. As each draft appears, the group reviews it, comes to sufficient consensus on issues, and the editor issues a new draft.

## MIB Development and Integration

Once the group has general consensus, the document becomes an Internet Draft, publicized and readily available within the IETF, supporting broader review and comments by IETF members who did not participate in the working group. The draft may position the MIB extension in the management branch of the MIB or, more commonly for development purposes, in the experimental branch.

Most of a working group's task is coordinated and carried out via electronic mail on the Internet. Final decisions are usually made at open IETF meetings, held three to four times a year. Although it is possible to participate in a working group without electronic access to the Internet, such participation would be severely handicapped.

For a MIB, the working group must find those objects that are of general interest and use to network managers without excessive impact on implementations, either in complexity or efficiency. Object design must avoid assuming particular implementation models; instead design must proceed from a sound architectural base. Experience with existing implementations or standards provides important input, but cannot be followed blindly, as design requirements and goals may differ.

To help assure acceptance, the MIB must be pared to the bone. A big, complex MIB will not enjoy the widespread implementation necessary to prove its utility. The working group will have to agonize over inclusion of each object, often omitting objects that would be interesting but are too costly or not sufficiently representative of differing implementations. Even so, such objects are not lost, as they can easily be included in private MIBs. Also, the group must be aware of other MIBs that exist or are in development, so as to avoid duplication.

The working group must anticipate how information is to be used, especially with tabular information. For example, table access may require searching for individual entries or sequential access to all entries. In the former case, SNMP's *get* and *get-next* functions work best with an instance identification that directly selects the desired instance, such as the destination internet address of a routing table entry. In the latter case, *get-next* is the likely function of choice, and a direct identification may force the agent into a complex search for each entry as the NOC requests it. In this case, the best instance identifier may be a simple, sequential integer that bears no direct relationship to other instance parameters. If both types of access are anticipated, the MIB may need both organizations, or the working group may have to make a hard choice.

**Implement** Once the working group has a stable Internet Draft, the MIB must be implemented. The first implementation does not have to be a carefully designed commercial product. It may be a prototype, sufficiently functional for interaction with a NOC or two, but not intended for open public use. Its purpose is to prove that the MIB can be reasonably implemented and has none of the flaws that only become obvious when a programmer attempts committing abstract architecture to hard code. Clearly, if implementation uncovers problems, the working group must reiterate enough of the process to fix the shortcomings, and the corrections must in turn be implemented.

**Publish RFC**  The IAB decides when an Internet Draft is to enter the Internet standards track as a *Proposed Standard* in the form of a *Request For Comments* (RFC). Several steps lead to this point. Given a preliminary implementation and resolution of all outstanding comments, the working group presents their explicit recommendation to the Area Director. The Area Director is responsible for first approval, then passes the package to the *Internet Engineering Steering Group* (IESG). A positive consensus in the IESG results in submission to the IAB for final approval. Upon approval by the IAB, the IESG Secretary gives the RFC text to the RFC Editor for publishing. At this point, several experimental MIBs have also been moved into the management branch.

**Implement widely and use**  Once available as an RFC the MIB must be widely implemented and used in real-life network management. If this does not occur and the causes of such lack of interest are not fixed, the MIB is dead. If this does occur, the experience gained will indicate any changes that must occur before the next step, from Proposed Standard to *Draft Standard*. If the necessary changes are extensive, the MIB goes back to the working group and Internet Draft status.

**Declare Standard**  When a MIB has survived the test of widespread implementation and use, the IAB can promote it to Draft Standard and eventually to Internet Standard, with additional status of Recommended or Required.

**Protocol future**  SNMP and the SMI will change slowly, if at all. Although pressure exists now to consider changes to both, the desire for stability and deeper experience with what we already have continues to override the desire to fix even the admitted problems, much less open the door for change in more controversial areas.

The SNMP MIB will expand. New MIBs, in the management, experimental, and private branches, continue to appear at an astounding rate. The rate of MIB invention outstrips the ability of the management community and the NOC developers to employ the MIBs for the most benefit of network managers. Instead, too many NOCs concentrate on a few functions and superficially impressive graphics, leaving the hapless network manager with relatively primitive means to use even the standard MIB, on an object by object basis. Most needed is a better way to integrate new MIBs into existing NOCs. The following section on interoperation addresses this.

**CMIP ?**  Finally, what of OSI and CMIP? Networking vendors continue to express support for CMIP while implementing SNMP. Given its weight as an International Standard, use of CMIP seems inevitable, but timing remains unclear. As with SNMP, the biggest problems facing CMIP are MIB definition and widespread implementation in managed systems. MIB definition is hard in the friendly, informal Internet standards environment, and that difficulty increases in the more political OSI environment. Furthermore, it may be that CMIP's additional complexity could delay widespread implementation indefinitely. The SNMP community continues to develop new MIB objects although many of them remain unimplemented, and this is in the face of a design discipline not imposed on CMIP, thus CMIP's problems can only be worse.

Part of the answer for practical OSI network management may lie in incorporation of some SNMP concepts, but, as yet, no one from the SNMP community has found the time and energy to take SNMP into the international standards process.

# MIB Development and Integration

**Interoperation**

The MIB explosion must continue to make necessary information available, but NOC and agent suppliers need a way to reconcile their products. NOC suppliers cannot track every MIB development, and agent suppliers cannot do or expect custom programming for every NOC. The answer to this dilemma may be implied by the current practices, that is, standard, machine-readable MIB descriptions have proven to be valuable resources for minimal integration of a new MIB into an existing NOC. A growing number of NOC vendors supply a means to directly read such information.

Although the current MIB format can supply a computer program with most of the information needed to interoperate, it falls far short of the information needed to provide useful monitoring and control to a network manager. This does not imply that such information should be added to the basic form. To do so would adversely impact the time needed to get a new MIB implemented. Rather such information should be available from supplemental documents. The following proposal is still in embryonic form. It has enjoyed a bit of discussion, but does not represent work in progress. The supplemental information is in two categories:

- *Common Supplement:* The Common Supplement provides information applicable across implementations. Its primary purpose is to assist in formatting displays. It has clear, full-word labels for objects, groups objects logically, both within a display and into different displays, and provides help text aimed at network managers rather than MIB implementors. It defines how to create table entries, and indicates what objects in such an entry are required. Further, it might go into analysis of how to recognize problems and what to do next when they occur, although attempting this level of utility could make the idea too complex for practical realization.

- *Implementation Supplement:* The Implementation Supplement adds implementation-specific information to the common supplement. It further refines the Common Supplement, possibly adding additional labels or groupings, and it indicates what objects are actually implemented for those cases where objects are optional, or for non-standard implementations that do not include mandatory objects. It provides a means for the vendor to document the behavior of a particular agent implementation, in a form that should be shipped as part of the product.

**Summary**

We have examined the origin, philosophy, and structure of SNMP to support understanding of the MIB and its place, both in design and in use. Our examination of MIB evolution lead to a detailed description of the process for developing a MIB extension. Finally, after predictions of protocol futures, and recognition of the growing problem of new MIBs, we proposed additional standard-format, machine-readable documentation as an approach to improving interoperability.

**Acknowledgements**

In the little more than a year I've been involved with SNMP, I owe much to Jeff Case, Chuck Davin, Keith McCloghrie, Marshall Rose, and numerous other individuals on the Internet for their help and patience in my education regarding SNMP.

**References**

[1] V. Cerf, "IAB Recommendations for the Development of Internet Network Management Standards," RFC 1052, April 1988.

[2] V. Cerf, "Report of the Second Ad Hoc Network Management Review Group," RFC 1109, August 1989.

[3] J. Davin, J. Case, M. Fedor, & M. Schoffstall, "A Simple Gateway Monitoring Protocol," RFC 1028, April 1989.

[4] U. Warrier & L. Besaw, "The Common Management Information Services and Protocol over TCP/IP," RFC 1095, April 1989.

[5] M. T. Rose & K. McCloghrie, "Structure and Identification of Management Information for TCP/IP-based internets," RFC 1155, May 1990.

[6] K. McCloghrie & M. T. Rose, "Management Information Base for Network Management of TCP/IP-based Internets," RFC 1156, May 1990.

[7] J. D. Case, M. S. Fedor, M. L. Schoffstall, & J. R. Davin, "Simple Network Management Protocol," RFC 1157, May 1990.

[8] Information Processing Systems, Open Systems Interconnection—Specification of Abstract Syntax Notation One (ASN.1), ISO, International Standard 8824, December 1987.

[9] Information Processing Systems, Open Systems Interconnection—Specification of Basic Encoding Rules for Abstract Syntax Notation One (ASN.1), ISO, International Standard 8825, December 1987.

[10] M. T. Rose, K. McCloghrie (editors), "Towards Concise MIB Definitions," Internet Draft, IETF, December 1990.

[11] "Information Base for Network Management of TCP/IP-based Internets: MIB-II," RFC 1158, May 1990.

[12] "Information Base for Network Management of TCP/IP-based internets," Internet Draft, IETF, December 1990.

[13] *ConneXions*, Volume 3, No. 3, March 1989, Special issue on Network Management.

[14] *ConneXions*, Volume 4, No. 8, August 1990, Special issue on Network Management and Network Security.

[15] Marshall T. Rose, "The Simple Book—An Introduction to Management of TCP/IP-based internets," Prentice-Hall, 1990, ISBN 0-13-812611-9.

[16] Paul Brusil, "Components of OSI: Systems Management," *ConneXions*, Volume 5, No. 4, April 1991.

[17] Lee LaBarre, "Management By Exception: OSI Event Generation, Reporting, and Logging," Invited Paper in Proceedings of the IFIP *Second International Symposium on Integrated Network Management*, Washington, D.C., North-Holland Publisher, April 1991.

*[Ed. This article is based on a paper presented at the 1991 Silicon Valley Networking Conference. Printed with permission].*

**BOB STEWART** has been designing and implementing network and system management software since 1969. He was the DECnet network management architect from 1976 to 1982, took a break to write the initial architectural specification for the IEEE 802 MAC bridge, then barely kept his shirt after helping found a home computer software company in 1984. Since then he has designed and implemented software for Xyplex, where his title is Network Architect and his name plate says *Architectural Theologian*. He is active in the IETF SNMP working group, and is chairman of the Character MIB and Special-purpose Hosts working groups. He collects guns, swords, and puns, and has opinions on almost everything. He can be reached as: `rlstewart@eng.xyplex.com`.

# Understanding Network Management with OOA

*Lisa Olson*
*Alan Blackwell*

An integrated network management system is a complex application system that allows end-users to integrate, control, and manage heterogeneous networks involving a multiplicity of vendor processing and communication products. This type of system normally includes fault management, performance management, configuration management, network-user administration, service-order processing, inventory management, and accounting-software applications. Analysis of such systems reveals an extraordinary level of computational, behavioral, and data complexity. This complexity introduces a need to employ a powerful analysis paradigm that transcends the limitations of traditional analysis and design methodologies.

Object-Oriented Analysis (OOA) is a powerful methodology for understanding and documenting complex software applications. The methodology supports and promotes the fullest possible understanding of the integrated network management problem domain. These benefits of OOA are attributable to its ability to support integrated and consistent analysis of software systems containing informational, behavioral, and computational complexities.

## What is OOA?

OOA focuses on the essential requirements of a software system. The essential requirements of a system are characterized as the requirements that would persist in an environment of perfect implementation technology. This feature allows OOA to present a static and concise description of the problem domain. The imperfections of any specific implementation technology are considered in the design phase of the software system development cycle. The separation of technology imperfection requirements from essential application requirements allows OOA to be survivable and portable in the presence of constantly evolving technology.

The limitations normally encountered with respect to traditional methods are that they concentrate on a particular aspect of system requirements: information modeling [1] [2] focuses on the data characteristic of an application, behavior modeling [3] studies the real-time characteristics of an application, and process modeling [4–6] analyzes the computational characteristics of an application. OOA synergistically merges information, process, and behavior modeling into a powerfully comprehensive and unified analysis methodology. It provides two important views of system requirements: an object class view and a communication view. Object classes detail the essential entities of the system while the communication model details the object communications.

Information modeling focuses on the entities, or rather on the object classes in a system and the relationships among them. The information model illuminates the data aspect of the object class. Object classes are an abstraction of similar entities that may be either physical or logical. An object class contains attributes. An attribute of an object class is an abstraction that identifies or describes an instance of the object class, or refers to an instance of another object class. Referential attributes express the relationship between object classes. This is expressed in an Entity Relationship Diagram (ERD). The ERD is accompanied by a data dictionary that defines the attributes of an object class. The ERD documents a normalized view of the object classes, the cardinality, and the conditionality of the relationships between them. The ERD and the data dictionary constitute the information model. The behavior model focuses on the lifecycle of object classes in the system, and it is documented via a State Transition Diagram (STD). The STD reveals the states, events, transitions, and actions associated with an object class. Process modeling examines the actions (or rather the operations) of an object class, as well as examining inputs and outputs. This is expressed in a Data Flow Diagram (DFD). The unification of the ERD, the STD, and the DFD occurs via an interesting set of nexuses. For instance, states of an object class in a STD are discovered in the domain of a "state" attribute of the object class, and certain processes can only be invoked when the value of a "state" attribute of an instance of an object class has attained a certain value.

OOA makes a significant departure from more traditional methods of system analysis. Since the basic unit of analysis is the object class, this analysis methodology provides a platform for subsequent object-oriented design and programming. Object-oriented analysis, design, and programming permits systems to benefit from encapsulation, polymorphism, and inheritance.

- *Encapsulation*: In object oriented design, only the operations of an object class have access to its internal data. Data is private. Operations are invoked by sending a message to the object class. This feature is known as encapsulation. The principal benefit of this approach is that the implementation of the object is independent of the applications that use the object class.
- *Polymorphism*: The polymorphism quality is based on the fact that many object classes respond differently to the same message. This permits rapid addition of new object classes to evolving applications.
- *Inheritance*: Inheritance allows the designers to specify a new object class that is similar to an existing object class without having to specify the known similarities. The new object class inherits the operations of the existing object class. This feature implements code reusability and positively impacts the system development lifecycle.

## OOA and Network Management Applications

There are many ways to model a network using OOA. However, the analyst must take into consideration how the applica-

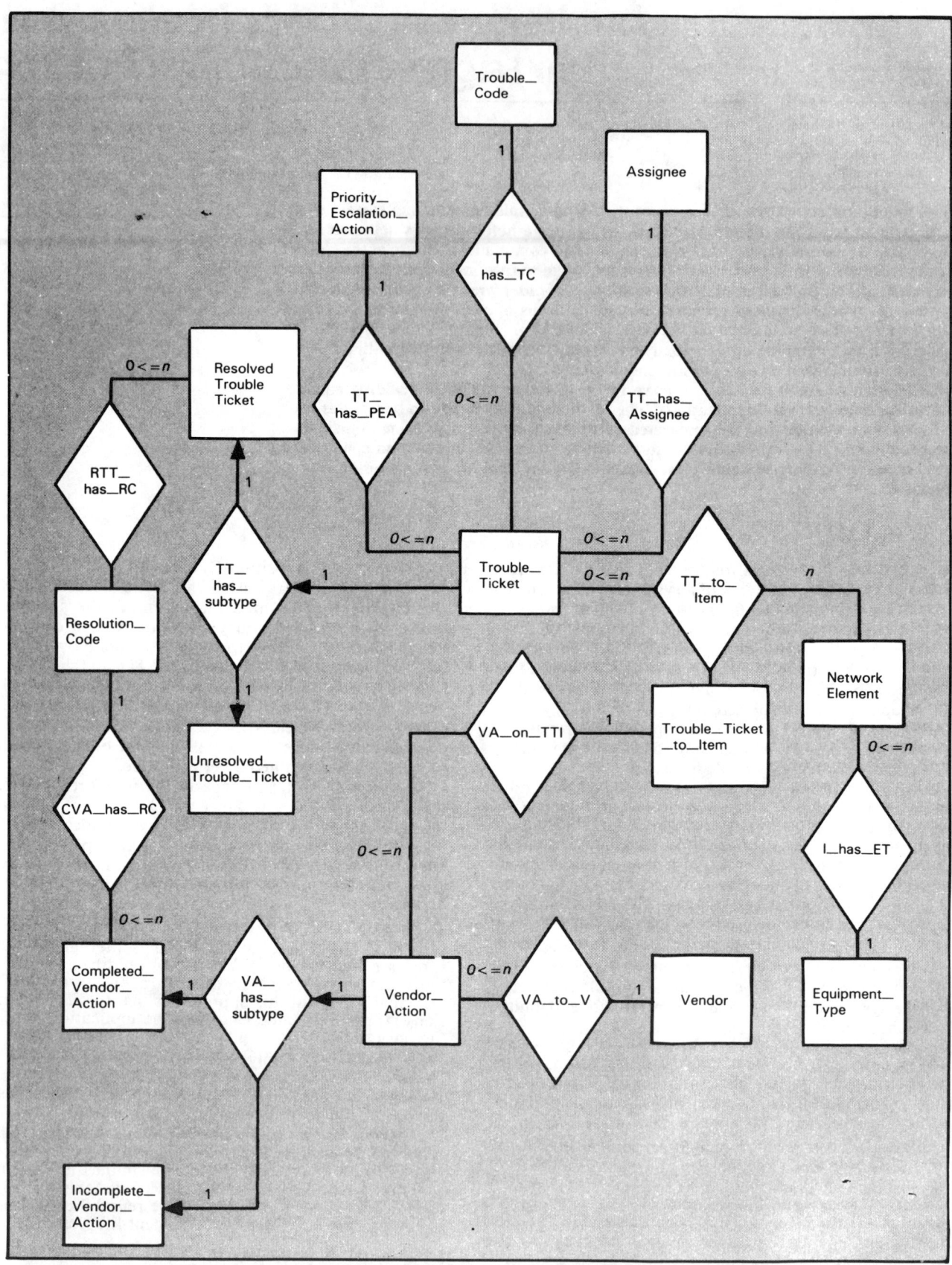

Fig. 1. Entity relationship diagram.

```
Trouble_Ticket (store) =
@ticket_number +
opened_date +
opened_time +
user_name +
user_telephone +
user_site +
problem_description +
tt_state.
--------
A Trouble Ticket is used to track problems reported
by people. A Trouble Ticket is created every time someone
calls in to report a problem.
Other identifiers: opened_date+opened_time+user_name+user_telephone
```

*Fig. 2. Data dictionary entries.*

tion is to use the model. Modeling the hardware alone is straightforward, but modeling the logical aspects of devices can be very complicated. Interesting objects are often generated by the requirements of the business enterprise. In order to manage a network, objects are necessary to reflect installed configuration, to plan network resources, to troubleshoot network problems, and to control network equipment costs.

When modeling network management administrative applications, the primary focus is not on the specific devices in the network but on the business process. For example, in a trouble ticketing system, the process of recording a problem does not change if the broken device is a PC or a Private Branch Exchange (PBX). The objects that are identified in administrative applications are mostly logical in nature. For example, a trouble code or a vendor action represent logical object classes. The objects that are physical are generic. For example, the network element object represents any device that fails. In a business application, transitions need to be recorded and reconciled so management can learn when changes were made, why they were made, and who made them. Thus, an integrated network management system will contain object classes that represent physical entities in the network as well as logical entities that support the management information needs of the business enterprise.

# How to Use OOA
## The Entity Relationship Diagram

The following ERD represents a trouble ticketing application. The objective of the trouble ticket application is to re-

```
TT_has_TC(store) =
@ticket_number +
@trouble_code.
--------
Every trouble ticket has exactly one trouble code. Every
trouble code may be used on zero or many trouble tickets.
```

*Fig. 3. Data dictionary relationships.*

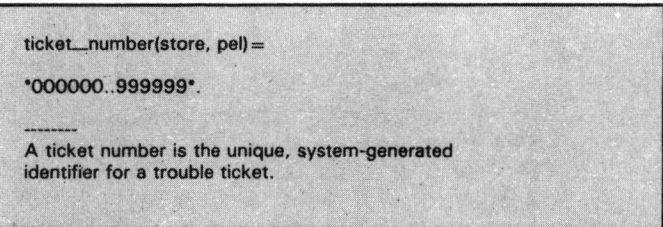

*Fig. 4. Data dictionary attributes.*

cord, manage, and control service problems associated with items supplied by vendors. In the notation used, a rectangle represents an object, and a diamond represents a relationship. The numbers on the lines represent the conditionality and cardinality. For example, the relationship between Trouble_Ticket and Trouble_Code is "for every Trouble_Code there are between zero and $n$ Trouble_Tickets assigned to it (one to many, conditional), and for every Trouble_Ticket there is one Trouble_Code associated with it (one to one, unconditional)." In OOA object classes may participate in many relationships. Figure 1 shows that Trouble_Ticket has an Assignee, a Trouble_Code, Priority_Escalation, and Item relationships. The figure also shows that the Trouble_Ticket is a supertype. It has two subtypes: a Resolved_Trouble_Ticket and an Unresolved_Trouble_Ticket.

The supertype/subtype notation in OOA allows for the specialization of generalized object classes. The supertype contains attributes that are common to all the subtypes. The subtypes carry the attributes that are unique to its specialized object class. This is the notational construct that provides for the specification of inheritance.

## Data Dictionary Entries

The data dictionary defines the objects and relationships shown in the ERD. Each object is defined by enumerating and describing the attributes (see Figure 2). Those attributes which uniquely describe the object are denoted by the @ sign. Each

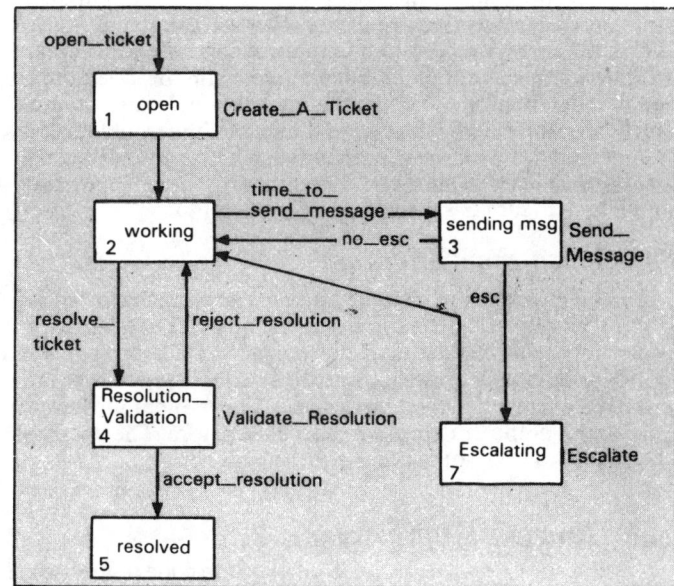

*Fig. 5. State transition diagram.*

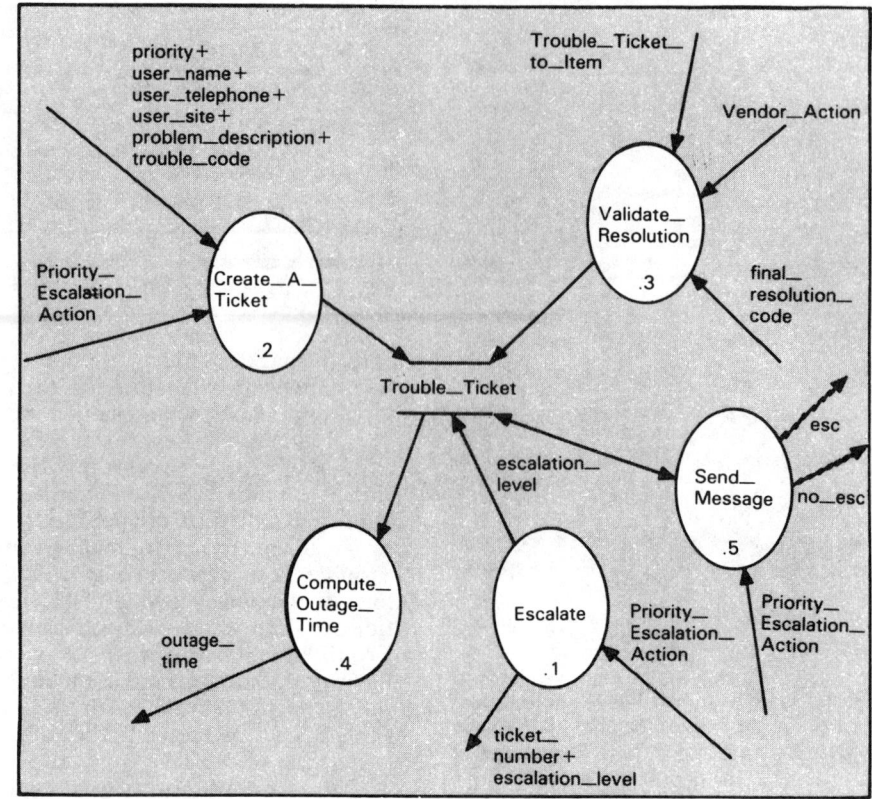

*Fig. 6. Data flow diagram.*

relationship is defined by specifying those attributes which relate the objects (see Figure 3). The relationship is described in terms of its conditionality and cardinality. Each attribute of an object is defined in the data dictionary by specifying its domain and including a description (see Figure 4).

### The State Transition Diagram

The STD is used to show the different states of an object. The sequence of states that an object can enter defines its lifecycle. In Figure 5, the boxes represent the different states, the arrows represent the transitions between states, and the labels on the arrows represent communication needed to make the transition. An unbolded label names the process that describes the transition. For example, an external source communicates an open_ticket message, the state of the trouble ticket is "open," and the process to accomplish the transition into the state is called "Create_A_Ticket." The various processes shown in Figure 5 are described in the DFD.

### The Data Flow Diagram

The DFD is used to show the processes that occur because of state transitions. In Figure 6, the bubbles represent processes and can be expanded upon by another DFD or a process specification which contains pseudo code. The arrows represent data flowing between processes. The two parallel lines in the center of the drawing represent a data store. The data store is defined by the attribute list for the object class.

### The Process Specification

The Process Specification (PS) is pseudo code that is associated with a DFD process bubble. Figure 7 lists the procedural steps to create a ticket.

### The Communication Model

The communication model describes the data and/or the messages that are passed between the objects of the system. In Figure 8, the bubbles represent the objects, the straight lines represent data, and the jagged lines represent events. Not all objects must be represented in this model, only those with significant interaction with others.

## Relationship of OOA with Industry Standards

A significant percentage of the object classes to support integrated network management systems are mandated by indus-

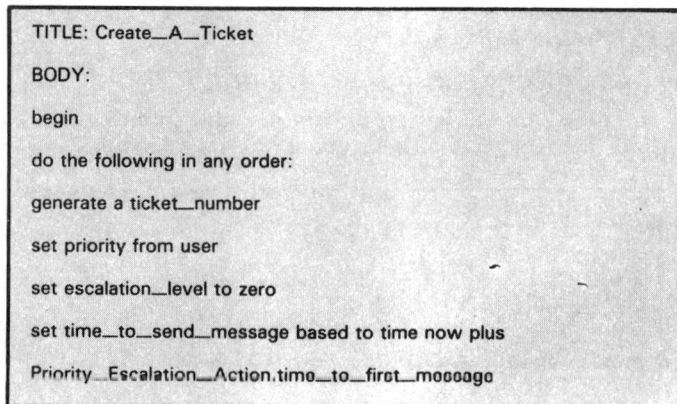

*Fig. 7. Ticket creation.*

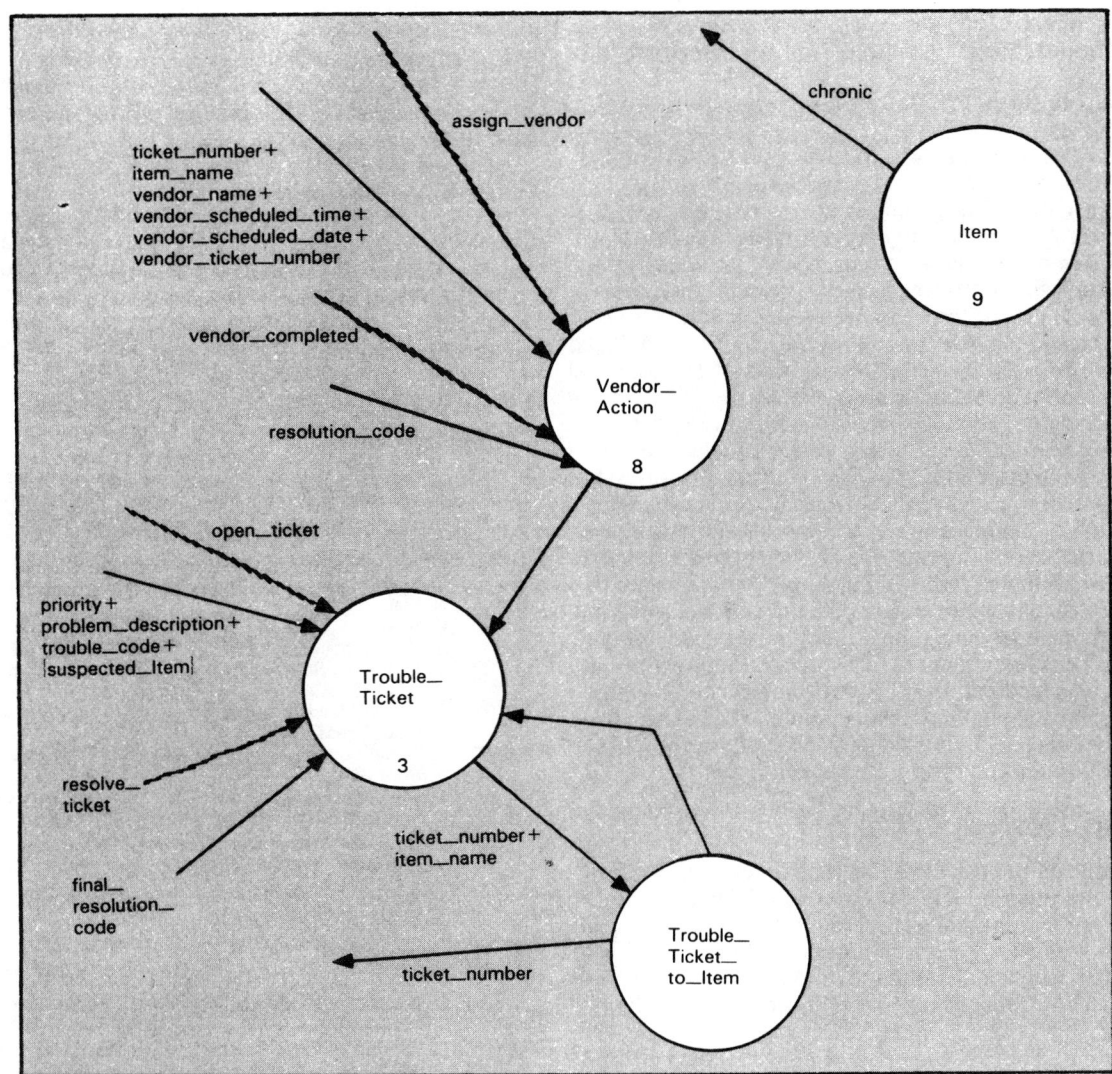

Fig. 8. Communication model.

try standards for network interoperability. Analysis and design of an integrated network management system should be guided by the specifications of the Open Systems Interconnection/Network Management (OSI/NM) Forum [7–9]. The Forum provides standards for application services, protocol specifications, and object specifications. These standards provide the means for truly open systems.

The Forum has proposed many of the objects and operations necessary to support network management activities. Network management system requirements consist of standards-related object classes and enterprise object classes. Enterprise specific object classes are needed to support specific business requirements. Thus, the role of the system analyst is to examine the Forum object classes and develop object-oriented models that encompass the full scope of business requirements.

The Forum specifies a containment strategy. The containment strategy entails the hierarchical arrangement of managed objects in the Managed Information Base (MIB). This arrangement is known as the Management Information Tree (MIT). The MIT contains the decomposition of any "complex" managed object. For instance, the containment of a Printed Circuit Board (PCB) in a telephone switching system is illustrated as follows:

PBX_ID/CABINET_ID/SHELF_ID/SLOT_ID/PCB_ID

As the example shows, the representation of containment is provided by the naming strategy. It shows that a particular card is in a particular slot. Additionally, that slot is in a particular shelf, within a particular cabinet of a telephone switch. This naming strategy enhances the modeling of device configuration and connectivity.

The Forum specified object classes serve as an excellent point of departure for the development of an OOA model. The object classes in the standards are specified by the means of a template. The template contains many clauses. The "Derived From" clause is used to specify the inheritance of an object class. In OOA, this essence is represented by the supertype/subtype notation. The object classes also have operations that are defined by the standards bodies. They specify operations associated with object classes. This is accomplished via the specification of Common Management Information Service Element (CMISE) primitives.

The Forum has specified a generic state model. The system analyst should carefully scrutinize the object classes in order to discern the need for additional state attributes for any object class. This is necessary because additional states will impact the state transition matrix. Each new state might require actions to be performed on state entry. These actions will indicate a need for additional operations and thereby impact the process model.

In order to conduct an OOA, the Forum specifies that object classes must be normalized. This is necessary because the standards permit null and multivalued attributes. In OOA, these types of attribute are suspect. The presence of null and/or multivalued attributes in the object class often indicates that the object class may in actuality represent more than one object class. When object classes are combined, the negative effects ripple through the ensuing phases of behavior and process modeling. The STDs of the behavior model and the DFDs of the process model become more complex. Fully normalized object classes promote better understanding of the essential object classes and their relationships within the problem domain. Additionally, when objects are normalized in such a fashion, they can be readily prototyped using a relational database management system. By disallowing null attributes, the prototype usually requires fewer disk resources and promotes ease of database management. Moreover, by disallowing multivalued attributes, the prototype can be implemented in a system with a standard relational algebra.

Notwithstanding the body of work completed by the Forum and other standards organizations, there is still considerable work ahead. The commitment to OOA fosters an in-depth understanding and specification of essential object classes within the network management problem domain. When the standard specifications are completed and accepted, the ability to assimilate any undefined object classes is assured.

## Pros and Cons of OOA

OOA is much more maintainable than other methods. Adding a new requirement or feature usually results in one or more new objects which are related to existing objects. The objects are added to the ERD. The behavior and processes of the new objects are analyzed. The communication model may be updated to reflect any changes the new objects present. The impact on the existing work is minimal. OOA also transitions well into object-oriented design and programming. This method of developing systems produces reusable code with fewer chances for error than more traditional methods.

OOA is a new methodology, and the tools to support OOA are still maturing. The building blocks of OOA are included in most Computer Aided Software Engineering (CASE) tools but linking them together in the way that the OOA method dictates is not yet straightforward. There is on-going work with the vendors to develop CASE tools that will adequately support the methodology.

In conclusion, OOA is a consistent and comprehensive method for decomposing complex network management applications into understandable units. It encourages the analyst to consider all aspects of the application, starting at the most important data level and expanding to the behavior and processing aspects in an integrated manner. It provides an analysis of essential application system requirements that are static and understandable by a diverse audience.

## References

[1] P. Pin-Shan Chen, "The Entity-Relationship Model: Toward a Unified View of Data," *ACM Trans. on Database Systems*, vol.1, Mar. 1976.
[2] M. Flavin, *Fundamental Concepts of Information Modeling*, Yourdon Press, 1981.
[3] D. Harel, "Statecharts: A Visual Approach to Complex Systems," CS86-02, Dept. of Applied Math., The Weizman Inst. of Science, Israel, Mar., 1986.
[4] C. Gane and T. Sarson, *Structured Systems Analysis: Tools and Techniques*, Prentice-Hall, 1979.
[5] T. DeMarco, *Structured Analysis and System Specification*, Yourdon Press, 1981.
[6] S. M. McMenamin and J. F. Palmer, *Essential Systems Analysis*, Yourdon Press, 1984.
[7] "OSI/Network Management Forum—Protocol Specification," issue 1, Jan. 1989.
[8] "OSI/Network Management Forum—Application Services," issue 1, June 1989.
[9] "OSI/Network Management Forum—Object Specification Framework," issue 1, Sept. 1989.

## Biography

**Lisa Olson** graduated with a math degree from Wellesley College in 1982. She has been working in the computer industry since that time. For the last five years she has been working for Boeing Computer Services in Bellevue, Washington. Currently she is managing a group which is creating applications for an integrated network management system.

**Alan Blackwell** is a Senior Consulting Engineer of Unify Corp. on assignment to Boeing Computer Services. He has extensive background in telecommunications, software engineering, and information engineering.

## OSI Modeling

# System Management Information Modeling

OSI techniques and tools successfully model telecommunications equipment, networks, and services — and enhanced capabilities are on the way.

S. Mark Klerer

S. MARK KLERER is supervisor of the network management protocols and standards group in AT&T Bell Laboratories.

The end of the twentieth century marks the onset of the information age. Increasingly, it is information that moves financial markets and industry, provides entertainment to the masses, and forms the core of communications between individuals. As this information has become more valuable to an enterprise, at the same time it has also become more voluminous. With the emergence of global enterprises, this information also is distributed throughout that enterprise and communications and information storage resources become critical to everyday functioning. These developments have led to a critical need in managing communications and information resources. Furthermore, since the information needs of users are provided by multiple service providers and vendors, a common infrastructure is required over which this information can be communicated. The Open Systems Interconnection (OSI) systems management project in ISO provides such a common infrastructure. This infrastructure also has been adopted by CCITT and is used for the specification of the telecommunications management network (TMN).

One of the critical components of a comprehensive system's and network management framework is the management information model to be used.

As applied to systems and network management, information essentially plays two roles: information associated with management processes, and information representing physical and logical resources subject to management.

Information associated with management processes is concerned with such entities as customer records, trouble records, log records, etc. Representing this information involves the modeling of the process and defining the information associated with that process. The information associated with a management process generally is manipulated only by management operations.

Information representing physical and logical resources is concerned with such entities as the abstraction of communications equipment, physical logs, event discriminators, etc. Representing this information first requires modeling those aspects of the resource that are of interest to management. Once this abstraction has been made, the totality of the resource from the management's viewpoint is represented by that information. For the model to be useful, linkage must be provided between the physical reality and the model components. This implies that manipulations performed on the model will result in real effects on the resources represented. Similarly, information that represents dynamic characteristics of the resource is expected to be consistent in the model and in the resource it represents. Therefore, information representing resources is manipulated by both the management process and the resource. Indeed, there may be a significant amount of information about a resource that the manager can only monitor as it changes, without being able to manipulate that information directly.

This article provides an overview of OSI modeling principles and concepts as contained in the systems management information model [1]. There is an overview of object-oriented modeling principles as applied for OSI systems management. The notions of inheritance, compatibility, and allomorphism are included. There is a description of how managed objects (MOs) are named. A reference to notational tools for OSI management is provided.

## Object-oriented Modeling

The amount of information that must be managed for a large system or network requires that a structured approach be taken to model and represent that information. Since many entities in communications and information networks share common characteristiqs, a way had to be found to exploit this characteristic in order to maximize commonality and minimize implementation efforts and diversity. These considerations have led to the adoption of the object-oriented paradigm for OSI management. This paradigm allows the modular development of specifications and implementations.

### Encapsulation

Encapsulation is intrinsic to object-oriented design and ensures that the operational integrity of an object is preserved. Encapsulation refers to the principle that the object can be impacted only by means of messages that it receives. It should be noted that this does not necessarily mean only management messages, but also refers to "messages" that may be generated internal to the system from other objects. Encapsulation requires clear specification of the message interface and clear specifications of the expected and allowed results in response to a message.

Encapsulation also allows the object designer and implementer to change and modify the internal design of his objects without impacting the users of the services provided by the object.

In the case of OSI management, clear specification is required of the management messages that may be sent, however, no explicit specification is required for other messages. For a complete description of the object, some of these matters may have to be specified as part of the object behavior.

### Anatomy of an OSI MO

In defining an MO class, the characteristics of each instance that is a member of that class must be specified. The characteristics that are necessary to fully specify an object follow:
- Superclasses of the MO.
- Visible attributes of the object.
- Operations that can be performed on an MO.
- Notifications that may be emitted by an MO as a result of internal events.
- Behavior that an MO exhibits.

To allow additional flexibility in modeling resources, these characteristics (except for the superclasses) are collected into modular packages. MOs are modeled as collections of packages. Packages may be mandatory or conditional. Mandatory packages contain those characteristics that are essential and must be possessed by every instance that is a member of that class. Conditional packages reflect those characteristics that are deemed to be nonessential and may be present in some class members, but not all. When present, these characteristics are of interest to management and generally provide some additional capability. These packages are referred to as conditional in that the class definition includes a specification of the conditions under which these packages must be present. However, it is important to note that these packages may be present in an object instance even when the condition is not satisfied.

In general, conditional packages within a class should be used in those cases where the presence or absence of a characteristic is a configuration decision at the time of object instantiation or of some nonessential management functionality where subclassing would lead to additional complexity. Separate subclasses should be defined in those cases where essential differences are manifest in object behavior.

It should be noted that the basic building construct in the OSI management information schema is the MO and that packages only introduce additional modularity in providing class definitions. Packages themselves are not instantiable on their own and individual behavioral characteristics of a conditional package may vary depending on the object in which they are installed.

The following discussion focuses on the characteristics that the MO has as a whole, although the reader should realize that all these characteristics are defined as parts of packages.

### Packages

As mentioned previously, packages are the modular construct of which objects are composed. Mandatory packages always are a part of each instantiated object. Conditional packages, however, may be absent when an object is instantiated. A conditional package must be instantiated at the same time as the object is created; it cannot be instantiated at a later time. Once instantiated the conditional package cannot be deleted without deleting the MO.

### Attributes

Attributes are named characteristics of an MO. A value is associated with each attribute of an MO. Such values may be read or modified through internal system or network activity or through management actions. The modifications that may be performed on such attributes are subject to the internal constraints imposed by object and attribute behavior.

OSI management supports all common data types and also supports set-valued attributes. Set-valued attributes are attributes that contain multiple elements that are indistinguishable except by value. Individual elements may be added or removed from such a set, subject to consistency constraints.

Note that attributes can represent static variables occupying storage or may represent computational processes that yield a value in response to a read operation referencing the attribute identifier. For instance, the "age" of an employee may be an attribute of a craftsperson's record, however, the actual variable stored may be the birthdate and the age may be computed by taking the difference between that date and the date of the query. Similarly, "current monthly charges" could be represented as an attribute of a billing record, yet this attribute may be computed based on unit charges, distances, and usage time when the inquiry is made. Thus, no direct relationship need exist between the amount of storage required and an attribute. For instance, if in a majority of cases an attribute has identical values, absence of that value may be used to indicate that as a default value.

In short, attributes may either be implemented as stored values that can be read or modified, or may be interpreted as being references to methods that will return values in response to a get statement and will put the computational process in the right state in response to a set statement.

In addition to attributes, the concept of an attribute group is introduced. An attribute group is a named group of individual attributes. It provides a shorthand reference to multiple attributes that are semantically related. All operations on attribute groups are performed as if each attribute had been referenced separately. An attribute group may be extensible, that is, the group may have a different number of members in different classes.

### Behavior

The behavior specification for an MO specifies the dynamic characteristics of an object and its attributes, notifications, and actions. It includes the semantics of attributes and describes the way in which management operations affect the object and its attributes. Behavior also describes the internal events that occur and result in observable changes in the object. This includes conditions under which attribute values may change and under which noti-

*The behavior specification for an MO specifies the dynamic characteristics of an object and its attributes, notifications, and actions.*

*In OSI management the create and delete operations are not defined as part of the object class definition but as a part of the name binding.*

| Purpose of the operation | Systems management name of the operation | Corresponding CMIS service | Applicable entities |
|---|---|---|---|
| Retrieve the value of one or more attributes | Get attribute value | M-GET | All single-valued, set-valued attributes and attribute groups |
| Overwrite the existing value of one or more attributes with specified values | Replace attribute value | M-SET with the modify operator in the service primitive indicating "replace" | Single-valued and set-valued attributes only |
| Overwrite the existing value of one or more attributes with a predefined default value | Replace with default | M-SET with the modify operator in the service primitive indicating "set to default" | All single-valued, set-valued attributes and attribute groups |
| Add a member to a set-valued attribute | Add member | M-SET with the modify operator in the service primitive indicating "add values" | Set-valued attributes only |
| Delete a member from a set valued attribute | Remove member | M-SET with the modify operator in the service primitive indicating "remove values" | Set-valued attributes only |

■ **Table 1.** *Attribute-oriented management operations.*

fications may be emitted by the object. Generally, the behavior may be specified in terms of preconditions that must exist for some event or action to occur, the postconditions that will exist after an action or event occurs, and the invariants of the MO.

### Operations on MOs

MOs generally represent active entities that exhibit behavior and move through some state space. As such, there is a requirement to be able to control the entities represented by the MOs by means of operations performed on the MO. Since MOs are encapsulated, operations to be performed on them can only by affected by passing messages to the object. These messages must also contain all parameters/information necessary to determine the nature of the operation, the manner in which it is to be performed (e.g., best effort or synchronized), and the conditions that must exist for it to be performed. Similarly, the results of an operation can only be known when the MO emits an indication with the appropriate results. In general, this requires an indication of whether the operation executed successfully or failed, the parameters associated with success, and any identifiable causes of failure.

The above represents general requirements for proper functioning in an object-oriented environment. Since the management information model is optimized for functioning in the CMIS/CMIP environment, some specific requirements are placed on the types of errors that the object must be able to detect for particular operations. This assures that managers using CMIS will receive the error resolution they expect.

In addition, since CMIS/CMIP supports the accessing and selection of multiple objects by means of scoping and filtering, a design decision had to be made as to how to allocate the responsibility in determining whether the filtering characteristics are satisfied and whether, therefore, the MO has been selected for the operation. Conceptually, the responsibility for managing the scope of the selected objects rests with the management agent process in determining the depth of the naming tree over which filtering will be performed. However, the responsibility for determining whether the filtering criteria have been satisfied rests with the MO. Thus, the attribute-value assertions that constitute the filter are made available to the MO.

Finally, since operations that operate on multiple objects may be requested to operate synchronously, an indication whether or not the particular operation is to execute in such a manner must be available to each selected MO. This is required to assure that the object can revert to its previous state if some of the selected objects cannot perform the operation.

OSI management operations are categorized into attribute-oriented operations and whole object-oriented operations. It is important to recognize that even attribute-oriented operations obey the encapsulation principle. The user does not directly manipulate attributes, but requests that the MO perform these operations and if the appropriate preconditions exist the attribute will be operated upon.

### Attribute-oriented Operations

The attribute-oriented operations and their mapping onto CMIS services are summarized in Table 1. Generally these operations allow for the retrieval and setting of attribute values. It must be noted that these operations, even when supported by an MO, are subject to policy constraints. These constraints may include security and access privilege limitations.

### Whole Object-oriented Operations

The second category of operations consists of those operations that impact an object's behavior as a whole without being targeted or specifically aimed at setting or retrieving attribute values, although attribute value changes may occur as a side effect. The whole-object-oriented operations and their mappings onto CMIS are summarized in Table 2.

A feature of OSI management is the fact that the create and delete operations are not defined as part of the object class definition but as a part of the name binding. That implies that whether or not an MO can be created or deleted by management action will depend on the "container" in which the new instance is to be created or from which

| Purpose of operation | Name of systems management operation | Corresponding CMIS service | Applicable entities |
|---|---|---|---|
| Create and initialize an instance of an MO class | Create | M-CREATE | MO classes for which name-bindings that allow object creation have been defined |
| Delete one or more instances of an MO | Delete | M-DELETE | MO classes for which name-bindings that allow object deletion have been defined |
| Specify a specific operation to be performed by MOs. | Action | M-ACTION | All MOs that require specialized operations |

■ **Table 2.** *Whole-object-oriented management operations.*

> *OSI management operations are categorized into attribute-oriented operations and whole object-oriented operations.*

it is to be deleted. Furthermore, it is possible to define two different name bindings within the same container (i.e., to the same object) of which one allows the create or delete operation and the other does not. This also requires that an object must keep track of the name binding under which it was created in order to determine its deletion behavior.

The create operation is different from other operations in the sense that it is not handled by the MO (as it does not yet exist), but by the systems management process in the creating system. At creation time all conditional packages that are to be instantiated must be specified. All attribute values that require assignment must be available at creation time. The source for the attribute values may be mandatory explicit values that cannot be overridden by the manager, values specified explicitly by the manager, values obtained by reference to a reference object specified by the manager, values obtained from a known initial value MO, default values specified by the object class, or local assignment mechanisms. If, after all these mechanisms have been exhausted, a value remains unspecified, the create operation will fail. Also note that a managed system, when responding to a create request, may instantiate additional conditional packages that had not been requested by the manager. Additionally, an instance from a compatible class may be instantiated rather than a member of the actual class requested by the manager if allomorphism is supported. In the latter case the manager will be informed of the actual class of the object that has been instantiated.

When executed, the deletion operation is fatal to MOs that are contained in that MO instance. The behavior associated with MO deletion must, therefore, specify whether deletion will succeed if the MO still contains other objects. In those cases where such deletion is not allowed, the manager will have to proceed by first deleting the contained objects and then deleting the respective containing objects. For example, if a model of a network has been constructed by defining a "network" MO which contains several "crossconnect" MOs and several "connection" MOs, then if automatic deletion is allowed, deletion of the "network" MO will result in deletion of every MO contained in the model. If automatic deletion is not allowed then the manager will have to delete all contained objects prior to deletion of the "network" MO.

The action operation allows for extensibility of operations that can be performed by MOs that cannot be accomplished by the predefined operations. Examples of such operations are the performance of tests and operations that involve the creation of multiple objects of different object classes.

### Notifications Emitted by an MO

Since MOs frequently represent active resources, internal and external events occur that impact the operation modeled by the MO and must result in corresponding behavior in the MO. Many of these events are of interest to systems management. Such events are made visible to the local management process as notifications that are emitted by the MO whenever such an event occurs. The visibility of these internal notifications outside the local system depends on the overall system configuration and is configurable by means of standardized OSI management services [2].

In addition to events that occur as autonomous activity of the object and its environment, the object also may be impacted by management operations (e.g., values may be modified by a manager, MOs may be deleted, etc.). These events are of interest to resource users and to other managers, and also give rise to notifications. Standard notifications for the common life-cycle events of an MO have been defined within OSI management [3].

### Inheritance Rules

Object-oriented modeling allows specialization of one MO class from another. A class derived from another class is referred to as a subclass of that class, which in turn is referred to as its superclass. A subclass may be specialized from a superclass by modifying the characteristics of the superclass. For OSI management such modifications may include only the following:
- The addition of new management operations and notifications.
- The addition of new attributes and attribute groups.
- The addition of new compatible behavior.
- The compatible extension of characteristics present in the superclass.

Description of the conditions imposed by compatibility follow.

A class derived by means of specialization is said to inherit the characteristics of its superclass. MOs must obey the inheritance and compatibility rules defined in this section. Inheritance with these restrictions imposed is referred to as strict inheritance. The relationship between subclasses and superclasses results in a hierarchy referred to as the inheritance hierarchy or the inheritance tree.

The MO inheritance hierarchy begins with a class called top which is the superclass for all MOs. This class is not instantiable, however, it has

| Property of attribute value | Extended MO | Compatible MO | Relationship |
|---|---|---|---|
| Required value set | Set of values = A | Set of values = B | A must be a superset of B |
| Permitted value set | Set of values = X | Set of values = Y | X must be a subset of Y |
| Initial and default values | Initial value m Default value n | Initial value p Default value r | No relationship required |

■ Table 3. *Compatibility requirements for attribute values.*

| Notification parameters | Extended MO | Compatible MO | Relationship |
|---|---|---|---|
| Presence of parameters | Parameter set = A | Parameter set = B | A must be a superset of B and extension is possible only if the definition in the compatible class allowed such extension |

■ Table 4. *Compatibility requirements for notification parameters.*

| Action Parameters | Extended MO | Compatible MO | Relationship |
|---|---|---|---|
| Mandatory parameters | Parameter set=A | Parameter set=B | A must be a superset of B and defaults must be defined for *all* mandatory parameters not supported by the compatible class |
| Optional parameters | Parameter set=X | Parameter set=Y | X must be a superset of Y and extension is possible only if the definition in the compatible class allowed such extension |
| Response parameters | Parameter set=R | Parameter set=S | R must be a superset of S and extension is possible only if the definition in the compatible class allowed such extension |

■ Table 5. *Compatibility requirements for action parameters.*

important characteristics that support the acquisition of management knowledge.

In addition to supporting the specialization of one object class from a single superclass, OSI management allows derivation of a subclass by means of specializing multiple superclasses; this is referred to as multiple inheritance. When multiple inheritance is used, then in addition to obeying the rules of strict inheritance with respect to each of its superclasses, the resulting subclass characteristics must be internally consistent without introducing behavioral contradictions.

## Object Compatibility

As already discussed, one of the advantages of the object-oriented approach is the capability it provides for the reusability of specifications, software, and implementation. Also, through the mechanisms provided to support allomorphism, it allows the reuse of knowledge one possesses about a resource. To ensure that these goals can be realized in a sensible and realistic manner, OSI management introduces the notion of compatibility.

To discuss the notion of compatibility, the concepts of an extended MO and a compatible MO are introduced. Generally, the extended MO is an object that shares some of the characteristics of the compatible MO, but provides some additional capabilities. Two MOs are said to be compatible with each other if they obey the rules described below. In general, the rules for compatibility attempt to assure that interactions between the manager and agent do not result in unexpected results that cannot be interpreted by the manager.

In order for an MO to be a compatible extension of another MO, the following relationships must hold between the two objects.

All characteristics supported by the compatible MO must be supported by the extended MO, when instantiated under the same conditions.

Additional characteristics may be available in the extended MO class.

The conditions for the presence of conditional packages in the extended MO class must be such that the package will be instantiated in the extended MO whenever it would be instantiated in the compatible class.

Extensible attribute groups must include all the attributes that would be included in the compatible MO.

The general constraint on the relationship between the behavior of the extended MO and the compatible MO is that the behavior of the extended MO shall not contradict that of the compatible MO. Some specific requirements that will help ensure this are given in Table 3.

In addition, Tables 3 through 5 show relationships that apply to the attribute values, action parameters, and notification parameters of the extended and compatible MOs.

## Allomorphism

Allomorphism refers to the ability of an MO instance that is a member of one class to be managed as an instance of an object of one or several other MO classes. In its most general form OSI allows members of arbitrary classes to be related allomorphically as long as they exhibit compatible behavior. In its most useful format allomorphic behavior will result in the object fully emulating the behavior and characteristics of a member of that MO class to which it currently is allomorphic. Two types of allomorphism may be distinguished: static and dynamic. Static behavior involves an object being created allomorphically and representing that class to all its users. Dynamic allomorphism allows the same object to represent different class characteristics to different managers.

Static allomorphism is useful in allowing a managed system to substitute a more refined MO, generally representing a more sophisticated resource, for the one that the user or manager requested. The more useful case is, however, that of dynamic allomorphism. Dynamic allomorphism allows managing systems and managed systems to evolve independently, thus providing for backward compatibility. It also allows for an elegant way of handling proprietary extensions. Backward compatibility is provided by allowing the manager to request that the MO behave as if it were an instance of a class of which the manager has full knowledge. The manager need not have any other information about the object.

Allomorphism accommodates proprietary extensions by allowing vendors to create subclasses (or otherwise compatible classes) while retaining the

| Behavioral property | Extended MO | Compatible MO | Relationship |
|---|---|---|---|
| Invariants | Set of invariants = A | Set of invariants = B | A must be a superset of B |
| Preconditions | Set of preconditions = X | Set of preconditions = Y | The relationship must be such that if the preconditions of the extended MO are such that an operation or event would be allowed then the preconditions in the compatible MO would also allow that operation to proceed |
| Postconditions | Set of postconditions = P | Set of postconditions = R | The relationship must be such that the postconditions in the extended MO will include all the postconditions that apply to the compatible MO under the same circumstances |

■ **Table 6.** *Compatibility requirements for MO behavior.*

capability of being managed as an instance of a standard class. A management system customized to cope with the proprietary extensions can exploit the vendor-specific features, while a standard management system still can be assured of interoperability.

As defined in SMI, allomorphism is a property of an instance not of the class as a whole. This allows members of the same class to exhibit different allomorphic behavior. The more usual case is the case of every member of a class being allomorphic to some superclass. However, the capability of allowing individual instances to be allomorphic to other compatible classes is useful in creating customized views of MO instances. For instance, if a service provider wishes to hide certain attributes and events from some users, a compatible class may be defined that is identical to the MO class except that it is lacking the characteristics that are to be hidden from the user. The user is then granted access to only instances of that "view" class, thus essentially masking the characteristics that are to be kept private.

Allomorphism is the one property that potentially makes class relationships visible to the user and of importance to the implementor. Allomorphism is not free; however, it is an important property that will prove its usefulness in the marketplace.

### Making the MO Anatomy Visible

Since instances of the same MO class may differ in some of their properties, the capability is provided within OSI management for exploring these properties. This capability is provided by attributes defined as part of the object "top" and thus inherited by all MO classes. The attributes can be read and provide information on:
- The actual MO class of the instantiated MO.
- The allomorphic classes supported by the MO, excluding its actual class.
- The registered packages that are a part of the instantiated MO.
- The name binding with which the MO has been instantiated.

It is important to realize that these attributes can only provide information about MOs that have been instantiated. Information cannot be obtained by this method concerning the capabilities of a system with respect to MO classes and conditional packages for which instances do not exist in the system.

## Containment and Naming

Since many instances of a particular MO class may exist, and since each instance must be accessible and uniquely distinguishable, names must be assigned to all instantiated objects.

To allow the construction of unique names without requiring a universal name server for each object, a hierarchical naming structure has been chosen for OSI management naming. The naming structure is compatible with that of the directory. The hierarchy chosen is based on containment. That is, an MO is named in terms of the MO representing the resource that contains the resource represented by the MO to be named. Choice of this relationship implies that MOs must be instantiated top-down (i.e., first the containing object and then the contained object). This relationship was chosen since it represents a natural real world relationship. The containment relationship used for naming may represent either physical resource containment or logical containment.

### The Naming Tree

Names constructed in accordance with the above criteria give rise to a naming tree of MO instances. The naming hierarchy culminates in an object called root, which always exists and has no properties other than serving as the origin of the naming tree.

The object with reference to which a particular MO is named is known as the superior object. The object that is being named by that object is known as the subordinate object. The relationship that identifies a possible class from which superior objects for naming the subordinate object may be selected is known as a name binding. The attribute that is used for naming an object with respect to its superior must have a unique value assigned to it for each MO that uses the same superior object. The attribute and its associated value that specifies the name of the subordinate MO with respect to its superior is known as the relative distinguished name of the object.

Unambiguous, universally unique names are constructed by recursively specifying relative distinguished names until the root is reached. A name constructed by this method will be unique in every context in which it is used. Therefore, the name is suitable for use in integrating systems and information gateways where information concerning multiple systems and networks may be stored.

*Allomorphism refers to the ability of an MO instance that is a member of one class to be managed as an instance of an object of one or several other MO classes.*

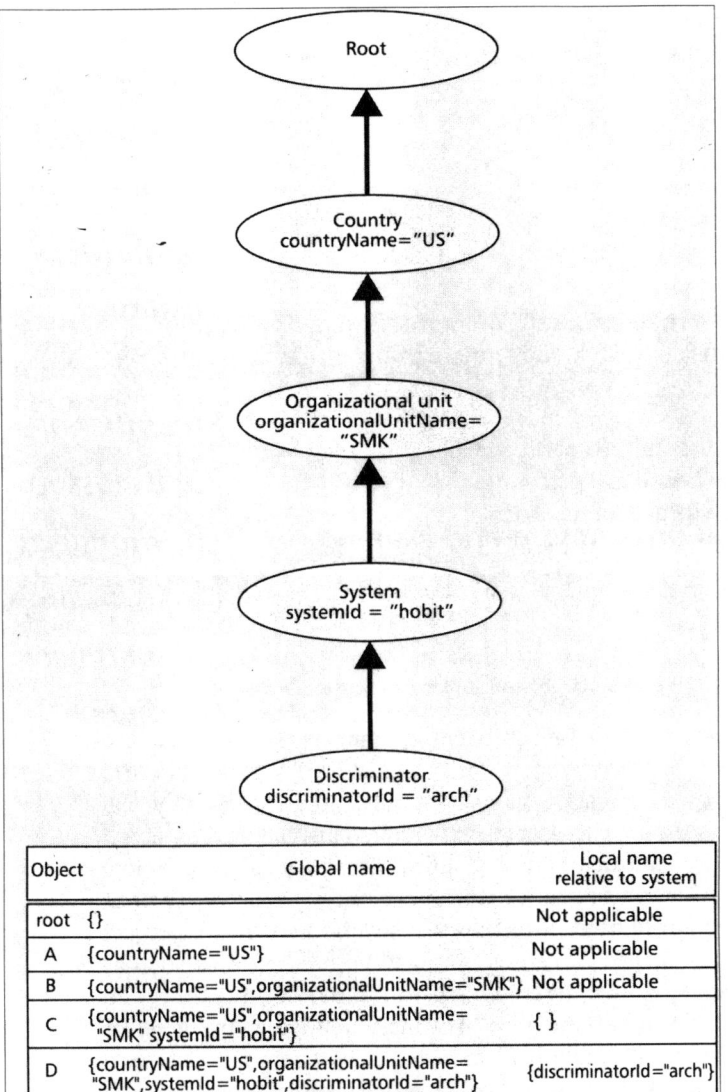

**Figure 1.** *Example of global and local name forms.*

However, since such names can be lengthy, the overhead of having to carry these names may be excessive, therefore, the concept of local distinguished names is introduced. Such names are unique only up to a certain point in the MO hierarchy. Structurally these names are the same as distinguished names, however the topmost parts of the naming hierarchy are not specified. Such names are unique and suitable for use when communicating with systems that do not contain information about similar objects in other parts of the naming hierarchy or when the context has been limited by other means. For OSI management the default context for local names is assumed to be the MO that plays the role of the system MO. This means that when communicating with a system in order to manage those entities that comprise the system, local distinguished names can be used. Examples of local and global names are shown in Fig. 1.

### Making MO Name Bindings Visible

As noted earlier, the create and delete behavior of MO may depend on the name binding with which the MO was instantiated. Therefore, in order to understand the create/delete behavior it is necessary to be able to determine an MO's name binding. To allow this, the object top has an attribute called "name binding" that contains the identifier for the name binding with which the object was instantiated. This attribute is mandatory and is inherited by all subclasses. It can be read, but cannot be set to another value after the object has been created.

## OSI Tools for MOs Definition

*O*SI management provides notational tools for those developing MO specifications for use in implementation and standards. The use of a uniform notational method is designed to facilitate the exchange of information. The detailed description of these tools is beyond the scope of this article. The tools make use of the ASN.1 [4] notation and of a set of templates defined in GDMO [5] for the specification of MO classes, packages, attributes, actions, notifications, behavior, and parameters.

## Conclusion

*T*he OSI systems management information model has emerged as an object-oriented paradigm for the modeling systems and network resources for use in management. The model is designed to meet the needs of end customers and service providers. The OSI techniques and tools have found acceptance within CCITT and regional standards bodies for the modeling of telecommunications equipment, networks, and services. These techniques have allowed for a systematic assessment of network and systems management needs and allow network management to move into the twenty-first century. Based on experience with the existing techniques, work is currently in progress on enhancing the OSI capabilities to provide for improved support of distribution and synchronization of management information, to provide a more comprehensive model for relationships among MOs, and to provide additional tools for the manipulation of management information involving complex queries and operations.

### References

[1] ISO/IEC 10165-1:1992, Information Technology Open Systems Interconnection Structure of Management Information, Part 1: Management Information Model (also CCITT Recommendation X.720:1992).
[2] ISO/IEC 10164-5:1992, Information Technology Open Systems Interconnection Systems Management, Part 5: Event Report Management Function (also CCITT Recommendation X.734:1992).
[3] ISO/IEC 10164-1:1992, Information Technology Open Systems Interconnection Systems Management, Part 1: Object Management Function (also CCITT Recommendation X.730:1992).
[4] ISO 8824:1990, Information Technology Open Systems Interconnection—Specification of Abstract Syntax Notation One (ASN.1) (also CCITT Recommendation X.208:1992).
[5] ISO/IEC 10165-4:1992, Information Technology Open Systems Interconnection Management Information Services Structure of Management Information. Part 4: Guidelines for the Definition of MOs (also CCITT Recommendation X.722:1992).

### Biography

S. MARK KLERER received the M.Sc. degree in systems engineering from Stanford University. Currently, he is supervisor of the network management protocols and standards group in AT&T Bell Laboratories. Mark is systems management rapporteur in ISO SC21/WG4 and was editor of the Systems Management Information Model (ISO 10165-1).

# Distribution of Managed Object Fragments and Managed Object Replication: The Data Distribution View of Management Information

S. Mark Klerer and Roberta S. Cohen
AT&T Bell Laboratories
Crawfords Corner Road
Holmdel, New Jersey 07733

## 1. Introduction

This paper describes techniques for coping with object oriented management models in a distributed environment. We assume an environment in which CMIP[1] and the ISO management functions are used as the specific management protocols. Logical and physical resources (e.g., circuits, applications, modems, processors) are modelled as managed objects[2] in this environment, each represented by data that can be manipulated by local and remote application programs and communicated among open systems. Complex resources, such as networks, can be modelled as a collection of individual resources, as well as a managed object with a unique data representation. But concepts for object aggregation, relationships such as the IS-PART-OF relationship, have been slow to emerge for use within object modelling. To the extent that such concepts are available today, they are invariably applied at the level of the defined object. Such an approach, while valuable for conceptualizing complex resources, does not allow for units of aggregation below the object level, as, for example, when the data elements of a single object are maintained in a distributed fashion.

Network Management places unique requirements on managing systems, requirements which can often be met by optimally using data distribution and data reduction techniques. Maintaining data close to where it will be used, for example, is a useful technique of management, but one that often creates unusual data distribution needs when the same data are needed in multiple places. At times, the need for widely distributed data is counter balanced by the need for very small, efficient implementations of network resources-- implementations that can offer only minimal data maintenance. Both of these needs, data distribution and highly efficient, small implementations are addressed here through our proposal for object replica and object fragment handling capabilities.

Two types of users are defined for the network management information base (the MIB); the network management staff (NMS) and the database administration staff (DAS). The network management staff is the primary user of the MIB, and the MIB should, therefore, be designed primarily to meet this user's requirements.

The database administration staff (DAS) is responsible for the distribution of data and the maintenance of the database. The DAS is also responsible for assuring that the MIB meets the performance requirements as determined by the network management staff. To accomplish these tasks the DAS must be able to distribute and/or replicate information as dictated by performance and reliability requirements.

Ideally the design choices made by the DAS should be transparent to the network management staff. Specific replicas accessed and specific distribution of management information is of no interest to the network management staff.

The paper discusses a technique that allows distribution and replication of management information so as to preserve transparency to the network management staff while at the same time allowing the network management information base administration staff to gain access to individual object fragments and specific replicas of object information.

## 2. The Data Distribution View of Managed Objects

In many cases practical implementation considerations will dictate that managed objects be visible from more than one system. Such considerations result in requiring that systems be able to act as virtual locations of managed objects. This can be accomplished by supporting multiple replicas of a managed object and by providing capabilities that will allow a system to assemble object information if not contained within the system.

The use of replicas may be required for performance reasons. The speed with which retrievals or modifications can be made will be improved when multiple replicas are available. Similarly, reliability is enhanced by having multiple replicas of managed objects. However, maintaining multiple replicas requires additional care to assure that the views offered by different replicas are consistent and it also requires management capabilities that allow for the identification of consistency problems.

Replication of management information might be avoid if one allowed systems to create chained management requests and obtain managed object information on behalf of managers. This would allow maintenance of a centralized distributed database but would impose potentially serious performance penalties and may not be feasible for large networks.

### 2.1. Managed Object Replicas

#### 2.1.1. Characteristics of Replicas

A replica is a copy of the managed object specification. For network management purposes it is desirable that the number of replicas that exist or the particular replica that has been accessed be transparent to the network management staff. However, the network management information base administrator (DAS) must have the ability to access a particular replica and manage it.

This gives a replica a dual nature. On the one hand, it serves as a window to the managed object; on the other, it acts as a data structure.

When used as a window to the managed object, a particular replica need not be identified. The managed object is accessed by specifying the managed object class and its instance. The network management authority may provide access to the managed object through any replica available. When accessed in this mode each replica provides a means of obtaining information about the resource, as represented by the managed object, or exercising control on the resource, as represented by the managed object. In this way, each replica acts as if it were the managed object.

It also should be possible to access a particular replica of the managed object in this mode. If a specific replica is specified, the DAS or NMS has the ability to verify that control can be exercised through that particular replica.

In order to allow manipulation of replicas as data structures, all managed object replicas are considered to be allomorphic to a new object class, called the *"Data Object Class"*. In this view replicas must be identified individually and can be managed as parts of a distributed database.

Individual replicas can be identified by specifying the managed object name and an associated replica suffix as part of the name. When accessed in this mode all operations pertain to the data structure and not the resource as represented by managed object. In this way, CMIS[3] services can be used to manage replicas. The following semantics are associated with operations on replicas:

    i.    In response to a create operation, a replica duplicating the managed object description will be created. No real resources required to support the managed object will be allocated. Also a "shadowing" mode and "shadow" source will have to be specified (see below) as part of the create request.

           The create request will also have to identify the destination of any control information that is sent to the replica. This destination can be another intermediate system or the system that contains the actual resource to be controlled.

    ii.   In response to a delete operation, the data structure and identifier associated with a particular replica is deleted. This operation has no impact on the underlying resource.

           When the last replica is deleted, the resource that was represented by the managed object still exists and provides service, however, all management knowledge of that resource has been lost; that is, from an open systems viewpoint the resource has become unmanageable.

iii. In response to get operation, a read of the current values as available in this particular replica is obtained.

iv. In response to a set operation, the values stored in the replica will be changed without impacting the managed object. This service may be used to force an update in a replica.

In essence, when accessed as a data object, the relationship between the replica and the resource is severed.

## 2.2. The MIB Directory

In order to allow management users to locate and access managed objects, a directory type of service must be available that supports determination of the location of all managed objects. This directory service may itself be a distributed application.

The MIB directory should make available at least one address for each managed object that has been instantiated. When the address of a specific managed object is requested, the MIB directory may return the address of a particular replica, without identifying which replica was chosen. When data structures are requested, the MIB directory should provide the capability for locating specific replicas, thus when the address of a specific replica is requested, this address should be returned.

The MIB directory can be optimized for the use of management. Such optimization can include the ability to determine the replica closest to the application inquiring about its location, the ability to avoid replicas that have become inconsistent and the ability to select a replica that can presently provide the best service. It should be noted that such optimization requires that the MIB directory have some knowledge of the state of each replica and that this functionality allows the MIB directory to take on the characteristics of a *"trader"* as defined in ODP[4].

Figure 1 shows how use may be made of the MIB directory to locate particular managed objects and replicas. The figure also shows how a front end system may be used to make the full complexity of the management data distribution transparent to the user. The front end system is serving a particular user and is designed so as to appear as the virtual location of all the managed objects that are of interest to that user. Management requests are sent to the front end system which automatically uses the MIB directory to access the managed object or replica, as required.

## 2.3. Updating of Replicas (Shadowing)

Two modes of updating replicas can be defined. One is event driven and the other relies on polling.

### 2.3.1. Event Driven Shadowing

Where replicas are to be kept tightly synchronized, an event report based shadowing service should be provided. This requires that event reports be sent from a replica that is already closely coupled to the resource, whenever an attribute in the object changes. The object emitting these notifications, thus, serves as master copy for that particular replica.

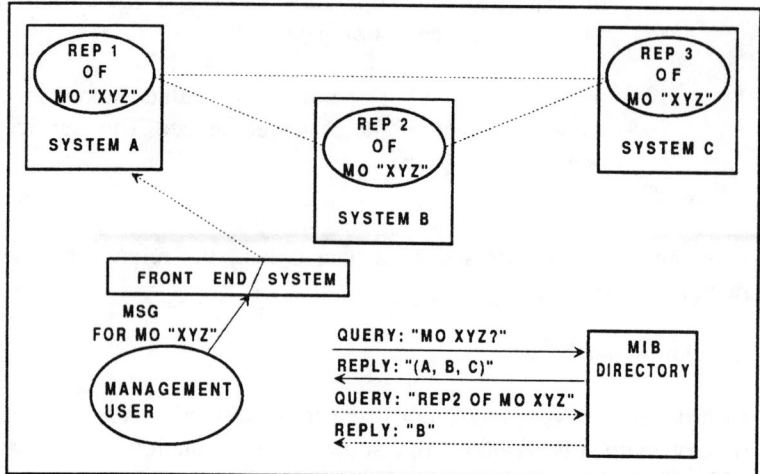

Figure 1. Access to Managed Objects and Replicas

In event driven shadowing it is the responsibility of the system receiving the event reports to assure that the MIB is updated on the basis of the information contained in the event report. It must be noted that this is more complicated and different than mere logging of event reports. To provide a reliable shadowing service, confirmed event reports should be used. If no confirmation is received, an event may be generated and sent to a DAS location to indicate that the database may have become inconsistent. The DAS may then take steps to assure that that particular replica is put in an appropriate state.

Since all replicas may provide access to the managed object, it is possible to have more than one place through which a change may be initiated. Therefore, to avoid looping of "shadow" messages it may be desirable that each replica only have one source from which it obtains shadow information and that shadow information not be sent to a system that was the source of the information on the basis of which the replica was updated.

Figure 2 shows an example of a change on managed object "XYZ" that is accessed via replica 2, resulting in event reports being sent to the systems containing replicas 1 and 3 and in the updating of these replicas.

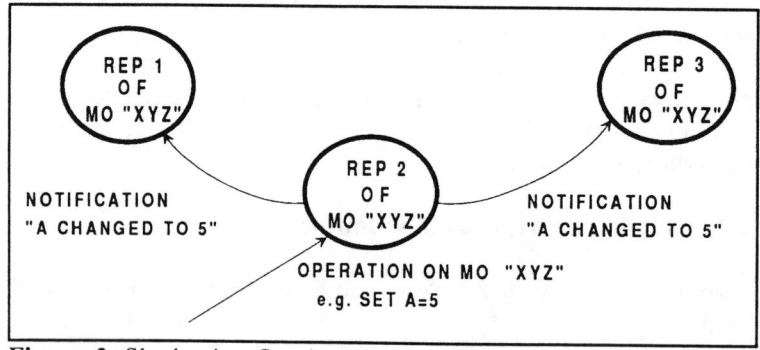

Figure 2. Shadowing Services for Replicas

### 2.3.2. Shadowing via Polling

An alternative method is for the system storing the replica to periodically poll a master copy for the latest values of the attributes. Notice that if the polling is done in response to an incoming request for information about this object, then this service becomes similar to "*chaining*". This kind of shadowing is more likely to be used where near real time (as distinct from actual real-time) alignment is acceptable, (e.g. collecting of billing information).

In shadowing via polling it is the responsibility of the system doing the polling to assure that the requested updates are received. The system being shadowed is unaware that it is being shadowed. If a response is not received, an event report must be sent to a DAS location indicating that the database may have become inconsistent.

Finally, a combination of polling and event driven shadowing may be used. Some attributes may be updated based on attribute change notifications, and others will only be updated if polled.

## 3. Object Fragment Distribution

In some cases, implementation consideration may dictate that less than a whole managed object instance (i.e. less than a whole replica) be stored in a single open system. In those cases where this is done, one or more than one open system may appear to be the virtual location of the managed object definition. An open system that appears to be a location of a managed object specification will be called a "*Managed Object Server* (MOS)." Any system that either stores or can assemble a whole replica can assume the role of a MOS.

A network management user may access any system that is a MOS in order to obtain information about or control the underlying resources for which the MOS has access to managed object specifications.

### 3.1. Object Fragments

In order to allow distribution of characteristics of a managed object the concept of an object fragment is introduced. Object fragments may themselves be viewed as objects, however, they differ from managed objects in that no specific object class is associated with a fragment. Instead a fragment type is defined as being merely a piece of an object class specification that has an identifier associated with it.

Object fragments can be used to accommodate the need to allow the storage of attributes, behavior and the exercise of control in the most appropriate system. This distribution, may for example, allow the definition of a fragment that contains only a behavior specification. Such a fragment would be useful when a simple device is to be controlled, in which the attributes must have a specific relationship to each other, but where the device itself cannot enforce this relationship. A fragment, stored in a more complex front end, could be responsible for enforcing these consistency constraints.

Figure 3 shows three cases where it may be useful to break a managed object into fragments and to distribute the fragments in different systems.

Case 1 represents the case of a modem that has been modeled as a managed object. The modem managed object has parameters that can be set and monitored and also requires that certain relationships be maintained between parameter values for different modes of operation. To support the implementation of simple modems, the modem managed object has been split into two fragments; one acting as sink for control information and the other fragment enforcing consistency constraints.

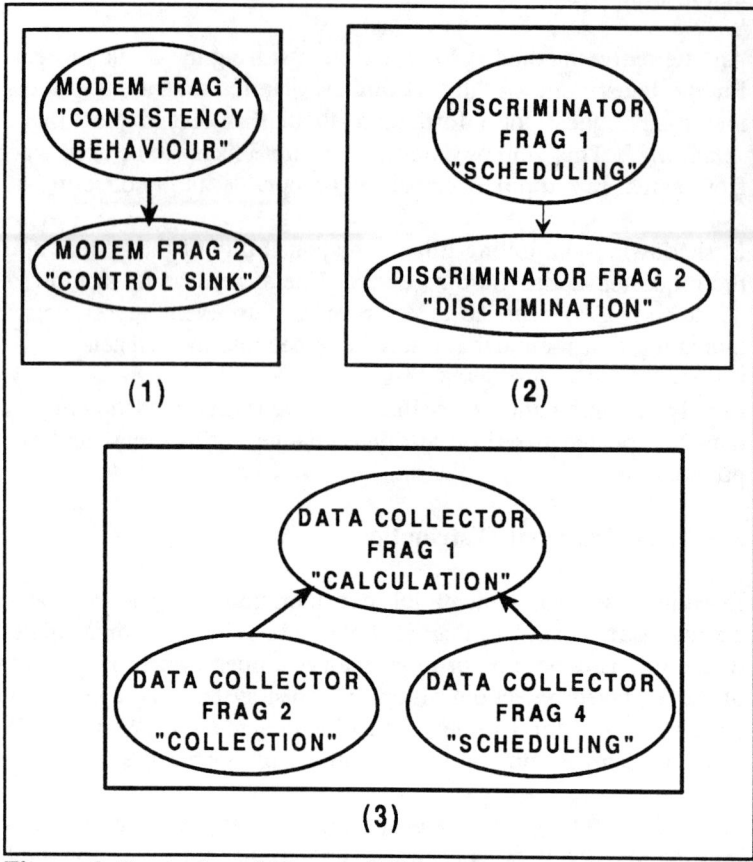

**Figure 3**. Examples of Managed Object Fragments

Allowing the consistency constraint fragment to be located remote from the basic control fragment allows the design of modems that due not enforce any constraints and allows the behavior to be controlled remotely. This particular fragmentation of an object is of special interest as it results in a fragment that only contains a behavior specification. It should be noted that in order to enforce the constraints the behavior fragment must have access to the attribute values of the control fragment. This may imply that a single management operation, i.e. a set, may have to be decomposed into a get and set operation or converted to a filtered set or may require that a complete replica be kept at the system that maintains the behavior fragment.

Case 2 represents a discriminator managed object that has been split into two fragments. One fragment provides the capability to filter event reports based on specified criteria to be satisfied by the content of the potential event report; the other fragment provides the capability of scheduling the activity time of the discriminator. Again, this fragmentation allows the design of simple discriminators that do not perform scheduling and whose scheduling is determined by the remote fragment. Note that this implies that the remote fragment has access to the state attributes of the discriminator and can manipulate these to obtain the desired behavior.

Case 3 represents a statistical data processing managed object that allows for the collection and scheduled summarization of management information. This managed object has been split into three fragments. One fragment schedules the activity, the other fragment collects the appropriate parameter values and the third fragment performs the statistical computation.

### 3.1.1. Characteristics of Object Fragments

Object fragments provide the DAS with the capability of distributing managed object replicas in an arbitrary fashion. The key characteristic of a fragment is that the fragments constitute a decomposition of the managed object and that any customized behavior that has been associated with an attribute or other managed object characteristic is retained as part of a fragment.

Objects fragments can be standardized or proprietary (possibly defined dynamically).

Standardized fragments can be defined ab-initio, or may correspond to already existing building blocks. Existing building blocks that can be used as fragments are:

i. Conditional packages in which the package object identifier used for the package would serve the purpose of fragment type identifier. The detailed behavior of the fragment type is, thus, determined by the package identifier and the managed object class in which the package is installed.

ii. Inherited or allomorphic object classes in which the object class of the allomorphic object is used to identify the fragment type. The behavior of the fragment is determined by the allomorphic object class identifier and the managed object that includes the characteristics of the managed object class.

   Notice that this is not equivalent to an allomorphic invocation of the object. In an allomorphic invocation the object exhibits the behavior of the allomorphic class; when invoked as fragment of a managed object, the actual managed object behavior is exhibited. Also when a managed object is required to act as an allomorph, the managed object class field is used to request that allomorphic behavior be exhibited. When fragments are accessed the actual object class is used.

Proprietary fragments may defined by assigning unique identifiers to arbitrary decompositions of object classes. Schema management could allow dynamic decomposition of object classes, the only requirement being that a system acting as MOS must be able to determine where all fragments are located and which set of fragments constitute the managed object in its entirety.

## 3.2. Naming of Object Fragments

In order to allow the DAS to manage individual fragments, individual fragments must be identifiable. In general it is possible not to assign identifiers to individual fragments, but to access a system and request all information that it has about the object. This approach is possible as long as only one fragment of the managed object acts as an assembler of fragments. If more than one fragment has that ability, provision must be made for suppressing such assembly in order to avoid looping. This can be accomplished by assigning identifiers to individual fragments or requiring that all the attributes to be retrieved are explicitly identified. Where fragment naming is used, a fragment instance can be identified by appending the fragment type to the managed object instance name. This provides for a consistent naming plan across managed objects, replicas and fragments.

## 3.3. MOS Functions

In order to be able to function as a MOS an open system must be able to provide the following functionality:

i. determine which open systems contain object or fragment specifications for all objects for which the system is a MOS;

ii. distribute control information to relevant objects and fragments.

iii. assemble all relevant object fragments.

### 3.3.1. The Object Fragment Directory (OFD)

In order to enable the MOS to assemble all relevant object fragments the MOS must have an Object Fragment Directory (OFD). The OFD must contain the decomposition of each object into its actual fragments and the identification of the open system(s) that provides access to that fragment.

### 3.3.2. Assembly and Distribution of Information

For retrieval operations, the MOS must retrieve information about each object fragment it does not store by obtaining that information from a system that has that information. This is accomplished by using the OFD to determine which fragments are to be assembled and the systems to be accessed. Of course, for a particular management operation it may not be necessary to access all fragments.

In order to allow network managers to control the resource, the MOS must distribute the control information to the appropriate object fragments.

Figure 4 shows the relationship between the managed object, its fragments and the OFD.

## 3.4. Fragments and Objects

It should be noted that fragments <u>are</u> objects and are manipulated as objects from the standpoint of the data administrator. However, from the viewpoint of management they are viewed as fragments of a larger object - i.e. the managed object.

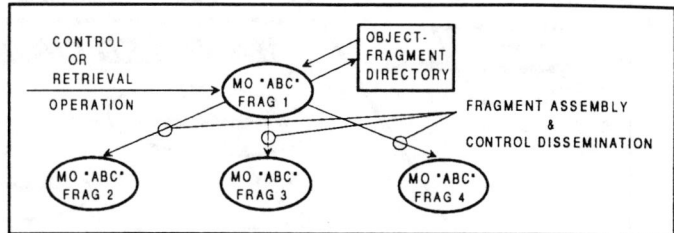

**Figure 4**. Fragment Assembly

The reasons for adopting this approach is to make clear that there are some key differences between the requirements for the definition of managed objects and those for the definition of fragments.

First, and most important, managed objects can be instantiated by themselves. Fragments are meaningless except when instantiated as part of a managed object.

As a consequence of the above, the final behavior of a fragment type is determined by the object class of which the fragment is a part. In essence, this implies that when fragments are modeled as object classes, these classes themselves are not directly instantiable but require that the managed object as a whole be instantiated and that the appropriate behavior is assured. A managed object class may be viewed as a composition of fragment types with customized behavior added to make these fragments into a coherent whole. When the fragments are then again distributed, these fragments maintain their customized behavior.

In terms of ODP definitions, a managed object with fragments may be viewed as a set of distributed objects with specific interfaces and contracts defined among these objects to assure correct behavior.

Second, the reason for defining fragments as a concept separate from managed objects is to make it clear that these objects are subservient to the managed object view and to allow the definition of the generic relationship that exists between managed objects and fragments. The existence of fragments must be transparent to the management user. Therefore, the naming of fragments is hidden from the network management user; and for ease of maintaining the name space, a naming strategy derivative from the managed object name is employed.

## 4. Conclusion

This paper proposes an approach that allows separation of network management and database administration concerns in a distributed management environment. The resulting model allows the data distribution aspects of the MIB to remain invisible to the network manager user. The relationship between replicas and managed objects is shown in Figure 5 and the relationship between fragments and managed objects is shown in Figure 6.

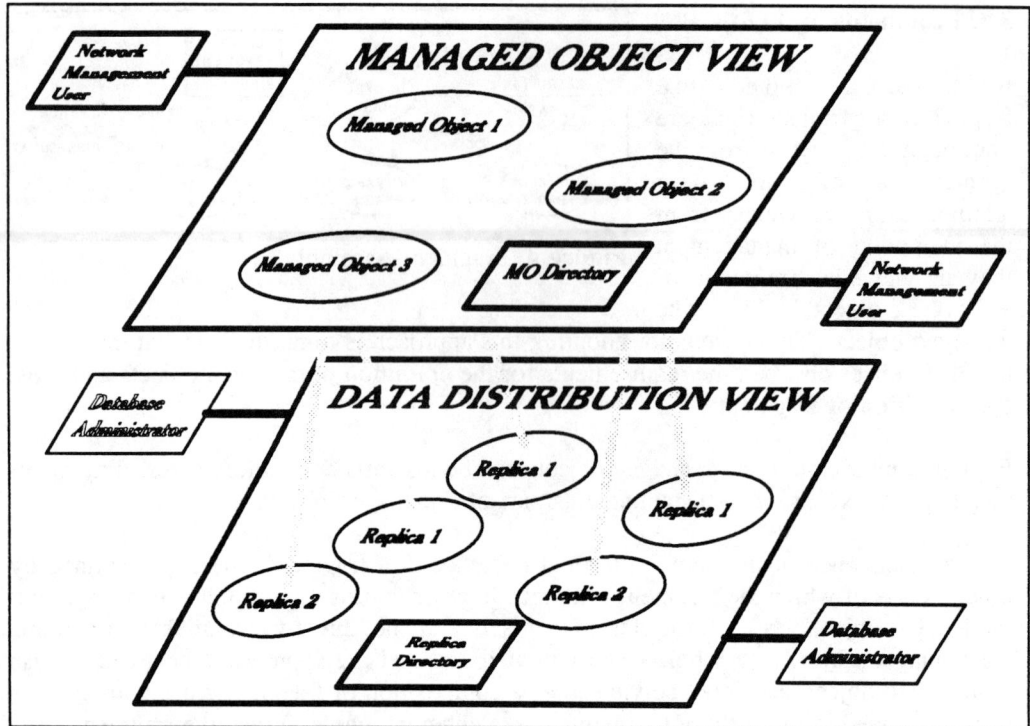

**Figure 5**. Managed Objects and their Replicas

Replicas must be as numerous as the need for near-instaneous information demands. A resource may be represented by managed object specifications that are found on a number of different open systems, and several schemes for shadowing the information contained in managed object replicas were discussed here. Satisfaction of the need for information nearness, however, does not meet the requirement within some management enterprises for very simple implementations. This need is met by object fragments shown in Figure 6.

Object fragments, like object replicas, are also associated with managed objects but represent only a portion of each managed object specification. Fragments are distributed on the basis of efficiency of implementation and local custom.

Needless to say, fragments may be used to represent replicated managed object specifications. Although complex from the standpoint of the database administrator, the principles of object fragmentation and object replication lend themselves to use in concert and together, provide a powerful arsenal of modeling tools.

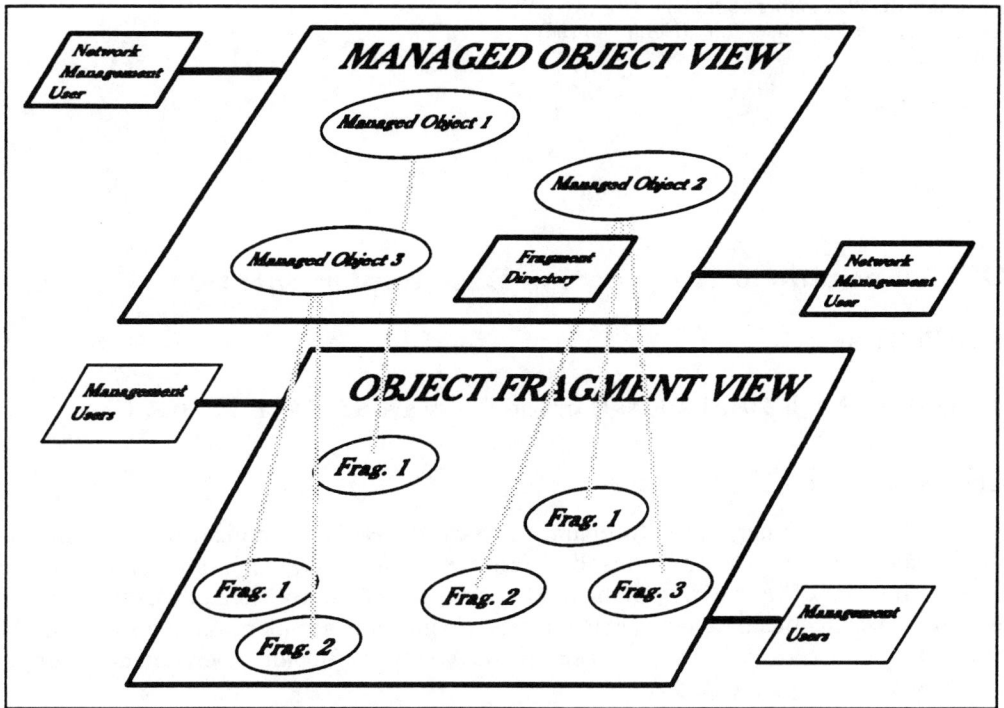

**Figure 6**. Managed Objects and Their Fragments

## 5. References

[1] ISO/IEC 9596 : 1990, *Information technology - Open Systems Interconnection - Management Information Service Definition - Common Management Information Protocol*

[2] ISO/IEC 10165-2, *Information technology - Open Systems Interconnection - Structure of Management Information - Part 2: Definition of Management Information*

[3] ISO/IEC 9595 : 1990, *Information technology - Open Systems Interconnection - Management Information Service Definition - Common Management Information Services*

[4] ISO/IEC JTC1/SC21 N4888, *Draft Basic Reference Model of Open Distributed Processing - Part 2: Descriptive Model*

# OSI Management Information Base Implementation

Subodh Bapat

Racal-Milgo, MS E-204, 1601 N. Harrison Parkway, Sunrise, FL 33323, USA

**Abstract**

The Management Information Base (MIB) is the conceptual repository of all management information stored in an OSI-based network management system. The definition of a MIB, which is the subject of many standardization efforts, describes a conceptual schema containing information about managed objects, their attributes, and relationships between them. A MIB definition does not describe how a MIB may be implemented.

This paper addresses and highlights issues involved in implementing the Management Information Base in an OSI-based network management system product. Aside from the object model framework itself, many other considerations are important in a MIB implementation. These include suitability of the MIB platform for the selected object model, the architecture for distributing MIB information, mechanisms for ensuring MIB data integrity, extensions of the standard MIB object model to allow value-added applications, maintenance issues including MIB schema changes, as well as MIB backup and recovery. This overview may provide some benefit to MIB designers of network management system products.

## 1. INTRODUCTION

The Management Information Base (MIB) is the conceptual repository of all management information stored in an OSI network management system. The MIB defines the set of all managed objects visible to a network management entity.

The MIB is in general an interface definition - it defines a conceptual schema which contains information about specific managed objects, which are instantiations of managed object classes. Further, the schema embodies relationships between these managed objects, specifies the operations which may be performed on them, and describes the notifications which they may emit. The definition of a MIB, which is the subject of many standardization efforts [1], [2], does not in any way specify how such a MIB may be implemented.

This paper presents the considerations involved in implementing the Management Information Base in an OSI network management system product. The term *Management Information Base* will be used interchangeably to mean both the abstract model of management information which is visible at the interface, as well as its implemented form which allows the persistent storage of this information.

## 2. THE OBJECT MODEL

For a MIB to be implemented, its object model must be well-defined and complete. The process of modeling involves the following steps:

1. Selection of a modeling paradigm
2. Identification of resources that need to be modeled as objects for management purposes
3. Identification of attributes of the managed objects
4. Identification of relationships between the managed objects
5. Description of object behavior, i.e. operations on managed objects and the notifications emitted by them.
6. Formalization of the above information in an unambiguously defined syntax.

In addition to the above, a diagrammatic representation of the object model, or subsets thereof, is often found in practice to be a useful aid to comprehension.

### 2.1 The Modeling Paradigm

An important modeling paradigm that is used in the definition of a MIB is *Object-Oriented (OO) Modeling*. The benefits of object-oriented modeling are many[3], chief among which is the imposition of a formal conceptual framework to guide the thought process of the system designer. In an OO model, MIB objects are organized in a class hierarchy, such that they exhibit an *Inheritance Relationship* from the superclass to the subclass.

*Entity-Relationship (ER) Modeling* is another modeling paradigm [4] which can be used in a MIB definition. The ER paradigm is highly suited for defining generalized relationships between MIB objects. Parts of the OO model can be subsumed within the ER model - the OO notion of inheritance can be modeled through the **is-a** relationship. For example, if the `lanMACBridge` object class is a subclass of the `equipment` object class (such that it inherits all its attributes in the OO model), it can be represented as a `lanMACBridge is-a equipment` relationship in the ER model. However, the OO notion of methods which operate upon objects is not modeled in the ER framework. On the other hand, the ER concept of a generic relationship is not explicitly available in an OO model; it is nevertheless meaningful and often necessary to introduce such relationships as a semantic constructs [5].

Both object-oriented modeling and entity-relationship modeling are well-understood concepts and have been dealt with at length in many excellent references in the literature [3], [4], and will not be described here. Current OSI-based standardization efforts concentrate largely on OO modeling, with supplementary information being supplied through ER diagrams.

From a productization standpoint, however, each has specific advantages and disadvantages in its ease of implementation in an actual MIB; this is discussed in a later section.

## 2.2 Object Identification

This phase consists of explicitly identifying the resources which need to be modeled as objects for management purposes. The choice of what constitutes an object is often obvious; at other times, it is not always clear. Generally, every resource that is used in communication, and which must be described in order that its behavior be monitored or influenced, must be modeled as an object. This may be a network communications resource, or may be a logical or physical resource not involved in communicating data, but is still required for management purposes (such as a `location` or a `vendor` object). In general, object decomposition is performed in a manner so as to permit as much independence between objects as possible.

## 2.3 Attribute Identification

This phase consists of explicitly identifying what aspects of the above resources need to be modeled as object attributes for management purposes. Even though a particular apsect may be part of the complete description of the resource (e.g. the color of the exterior), it may not be necessary to model it as an object attribute for management purposes if such an attribute is either not useful, not relevant or not meaningful in management activities.

## 2.4 Object Relationships

The OO notion of superclasses and subclasses naturally stems from the *Inheritance Relationship* between objects, in which the subclass inherits attributes and methods from its superclass, and may further refine and specialize the methods. Such inheritance relationships can be modeled and implemented in a MIB using a well-understood, rigorous framework.

In addition, networks require the modeling of *Containment Relationships*, in which some object instances may be physically or logically contained within other object instances. Containment relationships are different from inheritance relationships, because they do not imply inheritance of attributes from the containing object class to the contained object class. For example, an `equipment` object instance may be contained within a `location` object instance; this models containment, and does not imply that the `equipment` object class inherits attributes from the `location` object class. Further, the `equipment` object instance may itself contain a `portCard` object instance, which may contain a `port` object instance; in no case are attributes passed down as they would be in a superclass/subclass relationships. Containment relationships need to be explicitly identified for purposes of object addressing and naming. The OSI Directory [6] could be used to store names and addresses of managed object instances, though such a mapping between containment hierarchies and The Directory has not yet been defined or standardized.

Other types of relationships between objects are also important and need to be modeled as well. *Connectivity Relationships* between objects are important in modeling network topology and for determining routing. *Domain Relationships* must be modeled for clearly defining object boundaries and administrative responsibility. *Authority Relationships* are necessary in defining roles of management entities, for example, a management entity acting in a manager role participates in an *Authority Relationship* with a management entity acting in an agent role. Several other types of relationships exist and are useful for management purposes; these must all be modeled and reflected in a MIB implementation.

## 2.5 Actions

The specification of an object includes a description of what methods may act upon the object. In the MIB object model, the methods constitute operations, such as **CREATE**, **DELETE**, and **ACTION**, which may be performed on the managed object. A MIB implementation must have the capability of storing this information so that the validity of a requested type of **ACTION**, for example, may be checked against the targeted managed object class.

## 2.6 Formalization

All object modeling information above must be presented in a formal manner, either notational or pictorial. The formal presentation of a MIB's object model must clearly identify every informational element such that it unambiguously translates into whatever implementational form is selected.

The technique chosen to formalize OO object definitions and inheritance relationships is ASN.1 macro notation [7], which has successfully been applied in many standards efforts [8].

The technique used to formalize ER relationships has generally been pictorial [4], which assists in defining the schema to implement those relationships in a MIB.

## 3. IMPLEMENTATION OF THE MIB

### 3.1 Platforms for Hosting a MIB Implementation

A MIB implementation, which essentially is a store of persistent information required for management purposes, can be hosted on several types of platforms:

1. Object-oriented databases
2. Relational databases
3. Flat-file databases
4. Proprietary format databases
5. Firmware

6. Volatile memory

7. Combinations of the above

Generally, MIB information in a system product is distributed. A typical configuration may include a disk-based relational database on a central management station, static object attributes stored in a PROM contained within the managed resource, and dynamically changing information in RAM memory accessible to software processes. These processes could be system management applications, agents, or proxy agents, and could be resident in either the central management station, in intermediate management devices, or within the managed resource itself. Figure 1 depicts a typical such configuration.

### 3.2 Architectural Principles for Partitioning MIB Information

An important architectural issue which must be resolved during the system design of the product, is the partitioning of MIB information across the entire management solution. The following discussion assumes that a minimal configuration for a network management system product consists of a management station with some persistent storage capability (referred to as a central management station database), and that this management station is connected to network resources of interest, which are modeled as managed objects.

In many cases, network resources are capable of being downloaded or strapped for certain management attributes (e.g. configuration management parameters, fault management parameters). Further, they are capable of being queried as to current settings of those parameters. In such cases, it is not strictly necessary to store this information in the central management station, although it may be desirable to do so from a redundancy perspective.

Certain other network resources may be capable of storing MIB information, not just about themselves, but about other managed objects as well. For example, the internal database in a PBX or an intelligent multiplexer may already possess some information about its immediate topology, and about the communication capabilities of its nearest neighbors. If such a resource can be queried for this information, then this information need not be stored in a central database. In other instances, information may already be stored within a managed resource (e.g., a management entity may choose to store an `eventReportingSieve` object within a managed communications resource, so that sieving may be done locally). Such information, too, may or may not be stored in a central database.

On the other hand, there are pieces of information which are most optimally stored in a central database - this typically includes system-wide information, such as a complete directory of managed objects, and network-wide topology information. While this information could possibly be distributed, the access speeds required for such applications as graphical depiction, zooming and panning of network topology, often necessitate the storage of this information in the central database.

The following architectural principles, then, may be applied towards distributing MIB information in a product implementation:

1. The internal information storage capabilities of every managed object instance must be determined. If the network resource can store non-volatile information (e.g. either in firmware, via hardware straps, or on an internal disk, etc.) and is capable of being queried for that information, those attributes need not be stored in the central database on the management station.

2. If the managed object can store only volatile information which needs to be supplied to it (e.g. through its front panel or downloaded on boot-up) then copies of this information must be stored in a central database (as it may be lost in an unreliable situation.)

3. System-wide information, such as the Directory, network-wide connectivity, high-level security management functions for administrative authentication, historical data to generate performance and trending statistics, as well as usage information required for triggering accounting management applications, is most optimally stored in the central database.

4. In a hierarchy of management entities (e.g. proxy agents in software, mediation devices in hardware), where the intermediate entity also has the capability of storing persistent information, consideration should be given to storing MIB data in the intermediate entity if such data is not frequently required by management applications. This is so that the number of queries the intermediate entity needs to make of the central database in the course of its normal operation is minimized, thus reducing traffic on that link, and the transaction load on the central database.

5. Reliability and fault-tolerance requirements of the network management system product may require that redundant copies of MIB information be stored in both a managed object's internal database as well as the central management station. The tradeoff for this redundancy could be an increase in the requirements of database capacity and processing power on the central management station, affecting product cost.

In several productized network management systems, a combination of the above techniques is used, with some degree of redundant storage of MIB information. Redundancy is often desirable for the purposes of recovery and backup of the entire MIB. However, the MIB then essentially becomes a distributed database, and this leads to the concomitant problem of maintenance of consistency between replicated copies of information. It is then incumbent on the application entities to ensure atomic updates of each copy of MIB information. Further, either an access control mechanism or a deadlock detection and recovery mechanism must be in place, in the event that conflicting updates are simultaneously applied to different replicated copies of the same MIB information.

Determining the optimal partitioning of MIB information in an actual network management system product is best accomplished after analysis results obtained from actual experimentation. Such analysis should consider the tradeoffs between application response time, bandwidth cost, the nature of application queries, and the frequency of queries. Different heuristics will emerge depending on the primary use the network management system product is subjected to. In addition, the reliability and redundancy requirements on the product will also influence the partitioning of MIB information.

### 3.3 Management Station Databases

The choice of database type on the central management station is important. Some issues involved here are described:

### 3.3.1 Object-Oriented Databases

Object-oriented databases are a strong candidate platform type for storing the MIB object model. The advantages are as follows:

1. Object-oriented databases are naturally suited for storing MIB information, because the MIB itself is formally described as a set of abstract data types in an object-oriented class hierarchy.

2. In addition to the ability to model object description through storage of attributes, they also have the ability to model interface behavior, through the ability to store methods.

However, there are some drawbacks with this choice:

1. Although object-oriented database technology is expected to achieve stability soon, it may not be mature enough at this point to be considered in a product implementation.

2. The definition of an access language for querying and manipulating object-oriented databases is not a standard.

3. The MIB object class hierarchy, as defined in several standards documents [8], [9], when graphed in an inheritance tree, is rather broad and shallow. This means that the depth of superclass/subclass relationships between MIB object classes is of low order (and typically is about 2 or 3), whereas the number of high-level MIB object classes that derive from {top} is large. Therefore, although inheritance relationships are important, the number of such inheritance relationships in the current OSI-based MIB models may be low enough so as not to make an object-oriented database implementation an absolute necessity.

4. Performance characteristics of object-oriented databases are not well documented. Techniques such as *Class-Hierarchy Flattening* to improve performance have been used to improve performance, but are not particularly advantageous to MIBs because the MIB class hierarchy is itself shallow. No standard benchmarks are available for measuring performance of object-oriented databases embedded within a productized application system.

### 3.3.2 Relational Databases

Relational databases are a popular choice for central management station implementations of MIBs. The advantages of relational technology are many:

1. Relational database technology is mature, stable, and enjoys the support of several large companies.

2. Relational databases are usually accessed using a standard access language (SQL) [10].

3. Well-defined mechanisms exist to translate an Entity-Relationship model into normalized schema within a relational database.

4. Application activities, such as report generation and ad-hoc querying, are easily prototyped and implemented in a relational database.

On the other hand, relational databases suffer from the drawbacks that:

1. They are not well-suited to storing Object-Oriented models. Both inheritance relationships and containment relationships are essentially tree structures, which must be "flattened" into tabular relations for storage within a relational database. Although this is certainly possible, tree traversal through relational tables involves a sequence of several join operations, which are awkward to perform in SQL.

2. Many other types of relationships also require joins, which can cause performance degradation unless the ancillary access structures (such as indexes and clusters) are finely tuned for the type of queries made.

### 3.3.3 Other Database Types

Flat-file databases and other proprietary format databases can be tailored very specifically to a MIB object model or a subset thereof, and can be optimized for performance. However, the disadvantage is that network management applications are more complex to develop, since now they must be aware of the physical layout of the data under the proprietary format in order to manipulate it. This increases not just development time, affecting the productized system's time-to-market, but may also further complicate the maintenance effort.

### 3.4 Translation of MIB Object Model into Schema

A crucial step for arriving at a MIB implementation from an object model, is the translation of the object model into a set of data structures (collectively termed *schema*) which are understood by the platform on which the MIB is implemented.

An object-oriented database is well suited to storing both the attributes and methods that define a MIB object; however, a translation is necessary from the ASN.1 macro notation (e.g. **M-OBJECT-CLASS** macros defining a managed object, **ATTRIBUTE** macros for defining object attributes, **NAME-BINDING** macros to define addressing [8]), into the corresponding data definition language of the object-oriented database system. This will define the object schema which will contain instances of each managed object class.

For relational databases, such a translation results in SQL **CREATE** commands to generate the relational tables and views for storing MIB object classes. Depending on the level of normalization desired, some attribute information could be stored redundantly in order to avoid excessive joins while traversing the class hierarchy. A limitation of most relational database products is that they do not have the capability for storing methods (actions which may be performed on object instances, expressed as code fragments) associated with the object class.

### 3.5 Attribute Integrity Issues

An area of concern in a MIB product implementation is integrity of attribute data, which must be assured to minimize the potential for MIB corruption. Attribute integrity can be assured by many different mechanisms, some of which are described below.

### 3.5.1 Consistency of Replicated Attributes

Many MIB implementations contain replicated attribute data. In some situations, replication occurs within the scope of a single management domain - for example, managed object attributes may be stored both internally within the managed object as well as in the central management database. In this situation, consistency can be assured by having a well-defined concurrency control mechanism, which assures simultaneous and atomic updates of all copies of attributes. This can be achieved by appropriate advisory or mandatory locking mechanisms. Alternatively, if it is tolerable to allow minor windows of inconsistency, a periodic polling mechanism can be instituted where the subordinate instance of the attribute frequently queries the superordinate instance to determine whether they are synchronized; if an inconsistency is detected, the subordinate instance of the attribute will update itself.

In a situation where attributes are replicated in the central management databases of peer-level management entities sharing the same conceptual schema[11], [12], consistency can be effected by the use of CMIS primitives. When a managed object changes state, the management entity responsible for that object issues an **M-SET** primitive [13] to the peer management entity, thus causing it to update its internal copy of the attribute. This message may be confirmed or unconfirmed depending on the specific CMIS service used.

Sometimes it is necessary to create redundant copies of information within the same central management database. Although this violates principles of normalization, selective replication often helps run-time performance. In this instance, consistency must be assured by appropriately constructing the application code responsible for maintaining this information, or through mechanisms supported by the host database platform.

### 3.5.2 Dependency Integrity

Often, object instances have dependencies on each other, an example of which is an *Existence Dependency*. This concept formalizes the notion that a contained managed object instance participating in a containment relationship, is existence-dependent on the containing managed object instance (e.g a `t1AggregateCard` object instance cannot exist unless its containing `t1Multiplexer` object instance exists.) This implies that the contained managed object instance cannot be created, until the containing managed object instance has been created (e.g. with an **M-CREATE** CMIS primitive [14]).

In a MIB implementation, such dependencies can be enforced using *Referential Integrity* mechanisms. These mechanisms assure that references between objects (semantically understood to be relationships, e.g. a containment relationship in this example) are consistently maintained. This is usually accomplished with the aid of *triggers*, which provide the ability to manipulate data across a set of instances over the entire schema, in a cascaded manner. Thus, when a `t1Multiplexer` managed object instance is deleted following the receipt of an **M-DELETE** CMIS primitive, triggers can be used to ensure that all other managed object instances (e.g. `t1AggregateCard`) contained within that `t1Multiplexer` are automatically deleted.

More complicated dependencies can be enforced using *stored procedures* within the MIB implementation - for example, the ability to detect and prevent cyclical or reflexive containment relationships.

### 3.5.3 Domain Integrity

Some object attributes are required to possess only one of a finite, enumerable set of values. For example, T1 Multiplexer ports may only operate at speeds at the T1 rate or one of a restricted set of predefined subrates. A MIB implementation must therefore enforce that its representation of the **speed** attribute of all `t1AggregatePort` object instances can only possess one of the acceptable set of values. This can be accomplished using *Domain Integrity*, which instructs the host database to check that any attempts to set the attribute to an unacceptable value (outside its domain) are flagged as error conditions. This requires that the domain of acceptable values for the attribute be specified at schema definition time, and requires the translation of the ASN.1 macro notation for attributes **WITH ATTRIBUTE SYNTAX `<syntax-name>`** into the appropriate schema definition construct for attribute domain integrity.

# 4. EXTENSIONS TO THE STANDARD MIB

In addition to the managed object classes defined by various standards, a real MIB implementation may require other types of information to be stored in order to increase the power or usefulness of the product. The following are examples of such extensions.

## 4.1 Extended Security Management

A MIB may be required to include security information about access to various managed object instances, as well as mechanisms for performing authentication for operations on specific managed object instances. Also necessary may be security information for access control to the network management system itself, including direct control and manipulation of the MIB itself. This is especially necessary if the system is a multiple user system, and involves defining to the MIB the judicious grant of authorizations to query and manipulate stored information.

## 4.2 User Configuration

The storage of administrative information about users of the communications network in the MIB may add additional value to the system. For example, when several different mutually exclusive groups of users are using the same communications resources (as in an X.25 packet switched environment), *Closed User Groups* must be configured and maintained within the MIB. Users and user groups can themselves be managed objects which must be created, maintained and deleted in the MIB.

## 4.3 Configuration Histories and Profiles

An extended MIB may maintain past configurations of object instances, so that a history of configuration changes (manual or automatic) can be determined for selected object instances, objects can be restored to their previous configuration states from the current state.

It may also choose to store typical configuration profiles for managed object classes, whether or not current instances of that object class actually conform that profile. This would provide a Configuration Management application the ability to merely select one of a set of predefined profiles, while configuring a specific managed object instance. It would also allow automatic scheduling of configuration changes for managed objects, which may take place at predefined times in a programmed manner. For example, a managed object could conform to one configuration profile for peak hours of operation, and another configuration profile for offpeak operation. Storing the various possibilities for configuration profiles for the object in the MIB, makes it possible to schedule this reconfiguration in an automated manner.

## 4.4 Problem Management

A network management entity choosing to implement a complete Problem Management, Tracking and Resolution system, linked to Fault Management information, would require an augmented MIB. This would include the ability to translate Event Reports into trouble tickets or incident reports, assign job codes based on those reports, recognize and categorize types of problems, group related incidents together, institute automatic escalation of problem severity with time, track progress of problem resolution, interface with Accounting Management applications which provide credit for lost service, and close out, delete, and/or archive past problems for historical purposes.

### 4.5 Extended Performance Management

Some users of a network management system may require a complete Performance Management system, including tracking resource utilization, predicting potential overload situations, allocating and managing bandwidth, generating trending statistics, and funneling this information to appropriate network planning applications. The storage of such information within a MIB would facilitate these functions.

## 5. MAINTENANCE OF THE MIB

Maintenance of the MIB is an ongoing process in the lifecycle of a network management system product, and maintenance issues must be considered during the MIB implementation phase.

### 5.1 MIB Information Redistribution

As the network management system evolves, it may become necessary to redistribute MIB information within the system. This could become necessary for performance and architectural reasons as well as to take advantage of new technology.

If a new version of a managed object class is introduced, whose instances can now locally store attribute information previously located in the central management database, it may be desirable to redistribute the location of this information in order to reduce traffic between agent and manager processes.

Excessive traffic patterns or query loads on the central management database can cause performance degradation, and may require that MIB information be repartitioned to alleviate this problem. This could be achieved by devolving some subset of the MIB schema down to an intermediate management entity, such as a proxy agent, which would then be responsible for maintaining that information.

### 5.2 MIB Schema Modification

MIB schema modification is required in situations where the evolution of the system requires that new managed object classes be supported, or new capabilities and functions are added to existing managed object classes.

When a new managed object class is introduced, the schema must be augmented to support the new managed object. This requires updating appropriate Directory information to recognize the new object class as a supported type. The Directory must be architected in a manner that minimizes the impact on application software of additions and deletions of supported object types, and attempts to maintain as much backward compatibility as possible.

In a situation where new functionality is added to an existing managed object class, the schema could be impacted in various ways, which include new attributes to be added to the object's representation, or a change in the attribute's domain of values, etc. For example, if a communications resource is upgraded to operate at higher speeds, the domain of acceptable values for its **speed** attribute needs to be changed. Dynamic schema modification may also occur during the process of schema negotiation between peer management entities.

The impact of such a change is not restricted to the MIB schema alone, because the application processes concerned with configuring, validating and using this information will also need to be upgraded to reflect the new attributes or new range of allowable values for existing attributes.

## 6. PERFORMANCE

A MIB implementation must ensure that it meets adequate performance criteria, i.e. the response time required for a MIB-oriented transaction must be well within the system specifications. The performance criteria a MIB must satisfy vary with the nature of the managed objects, the size of the managed network, its distribution architecture and its connectivity with peer management systems.

### 6.1 MIB Transaction Load Mix

Most MIBs will experience different types of transactions depending on the network management primitive received. Figure 2 shows the types of MIB transactions resulting from CMIS requests. The following are examples of the type of MIB transaction triggered based on the CMIS primitive received:

1. **M-GET**: MIB information retrieval
2. **M-SET**: MIB attribute value update
3. **M-CREATE**: MIB object instance creation
4. **M-DELETE**: MIB object instance deletion
5. **M-EVENT-REPORT**: MIB event instance creation or attribute value update
6. **M-ACTION**: may result in a MIB attribute value update as a side-effect

Other CMIS primitives may also result in MIB transactions being generated as side-effects.

### 6.2 Performance Tuning

The response characteristics of MIB operations are very sensitive to the transaction mix. For example, a network system prone to frequent failures will generate a large number of event reports to its management system, requiring the MIB to perform a large number of event instance creations. On the other hand, a management system whose primary use is to generate reports, will be frequently subject to information retrieval queries from the MIB. A MIB tuned to deliver optimal performance under one type of transaction mix will in general not be optimally suited for another type of transaction mix. In tuning a relational database, for example, appropriate placement of indexes on tables can be very effective for a large number of retrieval operations; but these same indexes may hamper performance if the system is subject to frequent object instance creations and deletions.

The MIB performance must be sized for the maximal possible load on the system. During occasions of catastrophic network-wide failure, a burst of a very large number of alarms can be expected simultaneously from many managed objects; the corresponding load on the MIB will display the characteristics of high-demand OLTP (On-Line Transaction Processing) activity. The MIB as well as its access interface must be designed to handle such bursty, high-volume peak demands without loss of significant operational data.

## 7. BACKUP AND RECOVERY

Like the managed network, network management systems themselves are not immune to failure; this makes it critical to have in place a mechanism for backing up and recovering information in the MIB.

The backup mechanism consists of two distinct parts: (i) Schema Recovery, and (ii) Content Recovery. Schema recovery consists of retrieving from an implemented MIB merely the data structures which provide the templates within which information stored. Content recovery consists of recovering the actual information stored in the MIB, e.g. specific instances of managed objects. In a distributed MIB, content recovery involves querying every distributed element of the MIB - whether in the central management database, agent entities or within the managed object itself - in order to capture the complete picture of the network in a regeneratable form.

Schema recovery need not be performed unless the schema has changed. Schema changes could occur during system software upgrades, and are not expected to happen frequently. On occasions like incremental backups, only content recovery is sufficient. On the other hand, when it is desired to create another instance of the network management system for controlling a different set of managed objects, only schema recovery is sufficient, because the second system will presumably create a different set of managed objects within the same schema.

## 8. CONCLUSION

This paper has attempted to address and highlight some of the important issues in implementing a MIB in an OSI-based network management system product.

Aside from selecting an object model framework for the MIB, many other issues become important for a MIB implementation. These include suitability of the MIB platform for the selected object model, the architecture for distributing MIB information, mechanisms for ensuring MIB data integrity, extensions of the standard MIB object model to allow value-added applications, maintenance issues including MIB schema changes, as well as MIB backup and recovery. This overview may provide some benefit to MIB designers of network management system products.

## *REFERENCES*

1. ISO 10165, "Information Processing Systems - Open Systems Interconnection: Management Information Services - Structure of Management Information"

2. OSI/NM Forum Release 1, "Object Specification Framework", Forum 003

3. "Object-Oriented Concepts, Databases and Applications", ed. Won Kim and Frederick Lochavsky, Addison-Wesley/ACM Press, 1989.

4. "Fundamentals of Database Systems", Ramez Elmasri and Shamkant Navathe, Benjamin/Cummings, 1989.

5. Proceedings of OOPSLA 87, "Relations as Semantic Constructs in an Object-Oriented Language", Rumbaugh, James, Pages 466-481, Oct 1987.

6. CCITT Draft X.501 / ISO DIS 9594, "The Directory."

7. ISO 8824, "Information Processing Systems - Open Systems Interconnection: Specification of Abstract Syntax Notation One (ASN.1)".

8. OSI/NM Forum Release 1, "Library of Managed Object Classes, Name Bindings and Attributes", Forum 006

9. Committee T1M1.5, "A Generic Network Model", T1M1.5/89-010R2

10. "An Introduction to Database Systems", C.J. Date, Addison-Wesley.

11. OSI/NM Forum Release 1, "Forum Architecture", Forum 004

12. OSI/NM Forum Release 1, "Shared Management Knowledge", Forum 009

13. OSI/NM Forum Release 1, "Protocol Specification", Forum 001

14. OSI/NM Forum Release 1, "Application Services", Forum 002

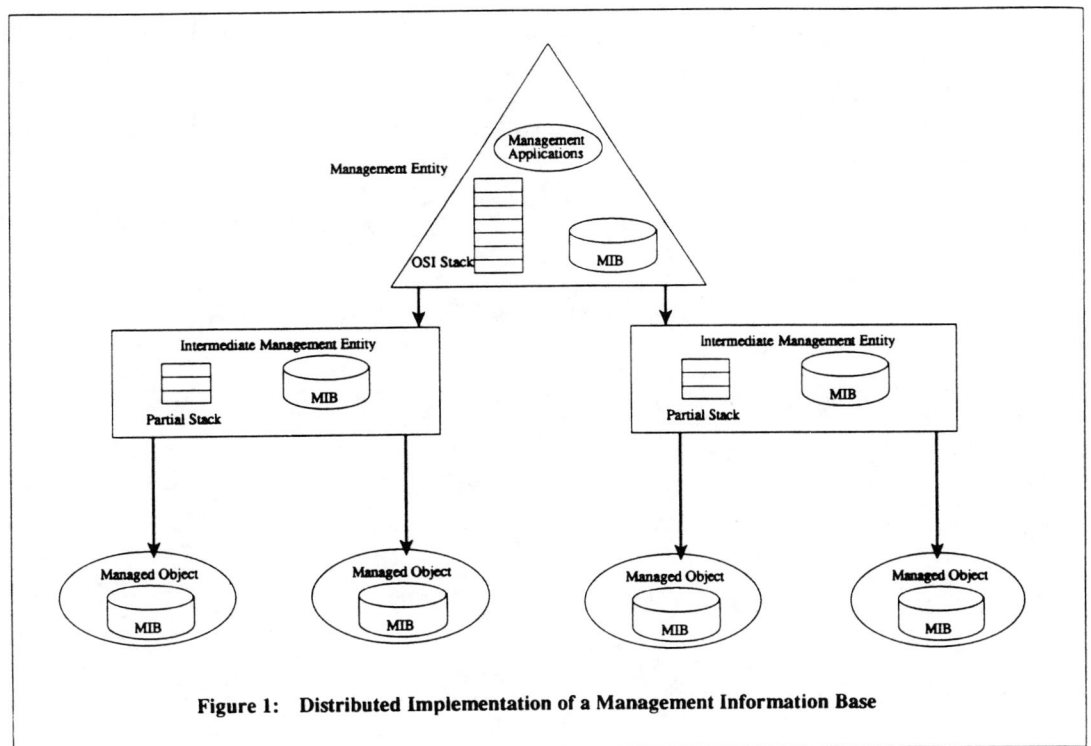

Figure 1: Distributed Implementation of a Management Information Base

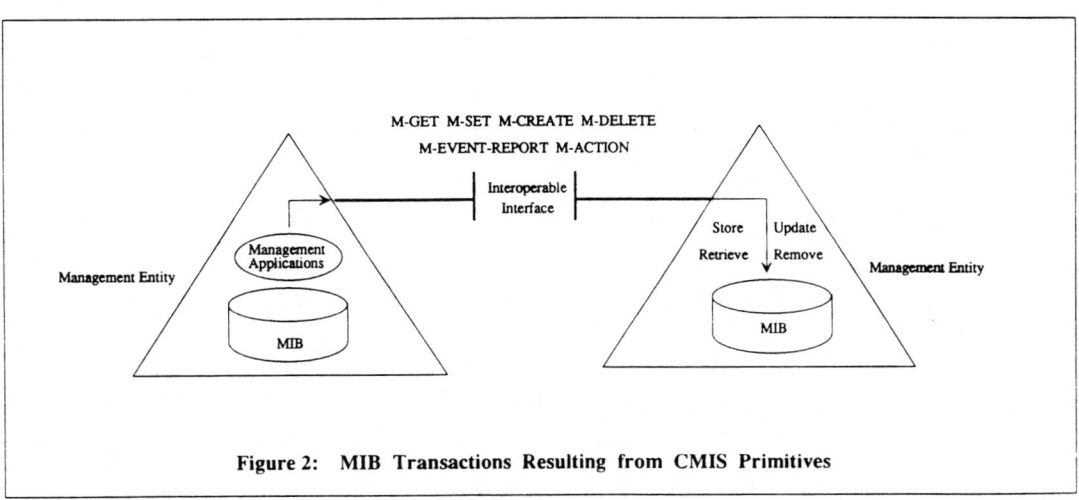

Figure 2: MIB Transactions Resulting from CMIS Primitives

# Chapter 3: Simple Network Management Protocol (SNMP)

In recent years, the simple network management protocol (SNMP) has come to dominate the market for interoperable network management tools. A number of vendors offer stand-alone network management workstations based on SNMP, and most vendors of bridges, routers, workstations, and PCs offer SNMP agent packages that allow their products to be managed by an SNMP management station.

The set of specifications that define SNMP and its related functions and databases is comprehensive and growing. Table 3-1 lists the nonobsolete specifications issued in the request-for-comment (RFC) series as of the time of this writing. The three foundation specifications are:

- Structure and Identification of Management Information for TCP/IP-based Internets (RFC 1155): Describes how managed objects contained in the MIB are defined.
- Management Information Base for Network Management of TCP/IP-based Internets: MIB-II (RFC 1213): Describes the managed objects contained in the MIB.
- Simple Network Management Protocol (RFC 1157): Defines the protocol used to manage these objects.

The remaining RFCs define various extensions in one of these three areas.

As the name suggests, SNMP is a simple tool for network management. It defines a limited, easily implemented management information base (MIB) of scalar variables and two-dimensional tables, and it defines a streamlined protocol to enable a manager to get and set MIB variables and to enable an agent to issue unsolicited alerts, called traps. This simplicity is the strength of SNMP. SNMP is easily implemented and consumes modest processor and network resources. Also, the structure of the protocol and the MIB is sufficiently straightforward so it is not difficult to achieve interoperability among management stations and agent software from a mix of vendors. As a result, SNMP has, since its publication in 1988, been quick to expand into widespread use.

Simplicity is also SNMP's weakness. Now that customers are used to the basic monitoring and control features made possible by SNMP, they want more: more efficiency, more functionality, and more security.

This is where SNMPv2 comes in. This recently announced second-generation standard enables more efficient retrieval of large amounts of management information, provides functional enhancements to SNMP, and provides a security facility for SNMP.

In this part of this chapter, we begin with a brief history of the evolution of SNMP from version 1 to version 2. Since the first reprinted paper in this chapter covers version 1 in ample detail, it is not covered in this part. Instead, the next section provides an overview of SNMPv2. Finally, since SNMP was originally developed for use over TCP/IP-based networks and internets, and since the most popular architecture for both SNMP and SNMPv2 is TCP/IP, a brief introduction to TCP/IP is provided.

## The history in a nutshell

A bit of history is in order here. The starting point was the simple gateway monitoring protocol (SGMP) issued in November 1987. The SGMP provided a straightforward means for monitoring TCP/IP gateways (equivalent to OSI level-3 routers). When the need for a more general-purpose network management tool was identified, SGMP was taken as the baseline and adapted to produce the simple network management protocol (SNMP), first issued in August 1988. SNMP provided a minimal but powerful set of facilities for monitoring and control of network elements using a straightforward structure of management information (SMI), management information base (MIB), and protocol. One notable deficiency in SNMP was the difficulty of monitoring networks, as opposed to nodes on networks. Remarkably, a quite substantial functional enhancement to SNMP was achieved simply by the definition of a set of standardized management objects referred to as the remote network monitoring (RMON) MIB, first issued in November 1991. RMON represented the first, and last, major functional enhancement to the first version of SNMP.

### Table 3-1. SNMP-related RFCs.

| | Date | Title |
|---|---|---|
| **Full Standards** | | |
| 1155 | May 1990 | Structure and Identification of Management Information for TCP/IP-based Internets |
| 1157 | May 1990 | A Simple Network Management Protocol (SNMP) |
| 1212 | March 1991 | Concise MIB Definitions |
| 1213 | March 1991 | Management Information Base for Network Management of TCP/IP-based Internets: MIB-II |
| **Draft Standards** | | |
| 1398 | January 1993 | Ether-like Interface Type MIB |
| **Proposed Standards** | | |
| 1229 | May 1991 | Extensions to the Generic-Interface MIB |
| 1230 | May 1991 | IEEE 802.4 Token Bus MIB |
| 1231 | May 1991 | IEEE 802.5 Token Ring MIB |
| 1239 | June 1991 | Reassignment of Experimental MIBs to Standard MIBs |
| 1243 | July 1991 | Appletalk MIB |
| 1253 | August 1991 | OSPF Version 2 Management Information Base |
| 1269 | October 1991 | Definitions of Managed Objects for the Border Gateway Protocol (Version 3) |
| 1271 | November 1991 | Remote Network Monitoring Management Information Base |
| 1285 | January 1992 | FDDI Management Information Base |
| 1286 | December 1991 | Definitions of Managed Objects for Bridges |
| 1289 | January 1992 | DECnet Phase IV MIB |
| 1304 | February 1992 | SMDS Interface Protocol (SIP) MIB |
| 1315 | April 1992 | Management Information Base for Frame Relay DTEs |
| 1316 | April 1992 | Definitions of Managed Objects for Character Stream Devices |
| 1317 | April 1992 | Definitions of Managed Objects for RS-232-like Hardware Devices |
| 1318 | April 1992 | Definitions of Managed Objects for Parallel-Printer-like Hardware Devices |
| 1354 | July 1992 | IP Forwarding Table MIB |
| 1368 | October 1992 | IEEE 802.3 Repeater MIB |
| 1381 | November 1992 | X.25 LAPB MIB |
| 1382 | November 1992 | X.25 PLP MIB |
| 1389 | January 1993 | RIPv2 MIB |
| 1406 | January 1993 | DS1/E1 Interface Type MIB |
| 1407 | January 1993 | DS3/E3 Interface Type MIB |
| 1414 | January 1993 | Identification MIB |
| **Experimental** | | |
| 1187 | October 1990 | Bulk Table Retrieval with the SNMP |
| 1224 | May 1991 | Techniques for Managing Asynchronously Generated Alerts |
| 1227 | May 1991 | SNMP MUX Protocol and MIB |
| 1228 | May 1991 | SNMP-DPI; SNMP Distributed Program Interface |
| 1238 | June 1991 | CLNS MIB |
| 1283 | December 1991 | SNMP over OSI |
| 1298 | February 1992 | SNMP over IPX |
| **Informational** | | |
| 1215 | March 1991 | A Convention for Defining Traps for Use with the SNMP |
| 1303 | February 1992 | A Convention for Describing SNMP-based Agents |

| Table 3-2. SNMP Version 2 (SNMPv2) documents. ||
|---|---|
| *Introduction to SNMPv2*<br><br>Provides an overview of version 2 of the Internet-standard Network Management Framework, termed the SNMP Version 2 framework (SNMPv2). This framework is derived from the original Internet-standard Network Management Framework (SNMPv1). | *Manager-to-Manager MIB*<br><br>Defines managed objects that describe the behavior of an SNMPv2 entity acting in both a manager role and an agent role. |
| *Structure of Management Information for SNMPv2*<br><br>Defines the subset of Abstract Syntax Notation One (ASN.1) use to define the SNMPv2 MIB. The document also defines the module types and ASN.1 macros used to define the MIB. | *Conformance Statements for SNMPv2*<br><br>Defines the acceptable lower bounds of implementation, and the notation to be used to specify the actual level of implementation achieved. |
| *Textual Conventions for SNMPv2*<br><br>Defines the initial set of textual conventions available to all MIB modules. | *SNMPv1/SNMPv2 Coexistence*<br><br>Describes coexistence between SNMPv2 and SNMPv1. The document covers management information and protocol operations. |
| *Protocol Operations for SNMPv2*<br><br>Defines the protocol data units (PDUs) for SNMPv2 and the protocol operations for those PDUs. | *SNMPv2 Administrative Model*<br><br>Presents an elaboration of the SNMP administrative model. This model provides a unified conceptual basis for administering SNMP protocol entities to support authentication and integrity, privacy, access control, and the cooperation of multiple protocol entities. |
| *Transport Mappings for SNMPv2*<br><br>Defines how SNMPv2 maps onto an initial set of transport domains. The mapping onto UDP is the preferred mapping. | *SNMPv2 Security Protocols*<br><br>Defines protocols to support three data security services: (1) data integrity, (2) data origin authentication, and (3) data confidentiality. |
| *Management Information Base for SNMPv2*<br><br>Defines managed objects that describe the behavior of an SNMPv2 entity. | *SNMPv2 Party MIB*<br><br>Defines a portion of the management information base (MIB) for use with network management protocols in TCP/IP-based internets. It describes a representation of the SNMP parties as objects, consistent with the SNMP security protocols. |

Another deficiency in SNMP was the complete lack of security facilities. To remedy this problem, a set of documents referred to as secure SNMP (S-SNMP) was issued as proposed standards in July 1992. In that same month, the simple management protocol (SMP) was issued outside the internet standards structure. SMP was produced by a collaboration of four key "SNMP players," one with a university and three in private industry. The SMP announcement was accompanied by four interoperable implementations from the four organizations. SMP provided functional enhancements to SNMP and incorporated, with minor modifications, the security enhancements of S-SNMP. SMP also incorporated some of the concepts from RMON, including the specifications of alarms and events, and a simple technique for row creation and deletion in tables. SMP was accepted as the baseline for developing a second-generation SNMP, known as SNMP Version 2 (SNMPv2). The first generation came to be called SNMPv1.

To produce SNMPv2, two working groups were set up. The SNMPv2 working group was charged with all nonsecurity aspects, including SMI, MIB, protocol, conformance statements, and coexistence strategies with SNMPv1. This work was substantially based on SMP. After many iterations, this working group completed its work in December 1992 and issued a set of nine internet draft documents that were ready to enter the standardization process as proposed internet standards.

The second working group, known as the SNMPv2 security working group, proceeded at a slightly slower pace to develop the security aspects of SNMPv2. This work was substantially based on S-SNMP, as revised for SMP. After many iterations, this group produced three internet draft documents in early 1993.

The entire package of 12 documents has now been published as proposed Internet standards (Table 3-2). This means that the specification can be considered technically stable, and many vendors are hard at work to bring out products as soon as possible. Given that the specification now totals over 400 pages, some might question the "Simple" in SNMPv2. Nevertheless, SNMPv2 does represent a natural progression from SNMPv1 and does retain, to some extent, the characteristics of ease of implementation and clarity of that earlier specification.

## SNMP Version 2

Surprisingly, SNMPv2 does not provide network management at all! SNMPv2 instead provides a framework on which network management applications can be built. Those applications, such as fault management, performance monitoring, accounting, and so on, are outside the scope of the standard.

What SNMPv2 does provide is — to use a contemporary term — the infrastructure for network management. Figure 3-1 is an example of a configuration that illustrates that infrastructure.

The essence of SNMPv2 is a protocol that is used to exchange management information. Each "player" in the network management system maintains a local database of information relevant to network management, known as the management information base (MIB). The SNMPv2 standard defines the structure of this information and the allowable data types; this definition is known as the structure of management information (SMI). We can think of this as the language for defining management information. The standard also supplies a number of MIBs that are generally useful for network management. In addition, new MIBs may be defined by vendors and user groups.

At least one system in the configuration must be responsible for network management. It is here that any network management applications are housed. There may be more than one of these management stations, to provide redundancy or simply to split up the duties in a large network. Most other systems act in the role of agent. An agent collects information locally and stores it for later access by a manager. The information includes data about the system itself and may also include traffic information for the network or networks to which the agent attaches.

SNMPv2 will support either a highly centralized network management strategy or a distributed one. In the latter case, some systems operate in the roles of both manager and agent. In its agent role, such a system will accept commands from a superior management system. Some of those commands relate to the local MIB at the agent. Other commands require the agent to act as a proxy for remote devices. In this case, the proxy agent assumes the role of manager to access information at a remote agent, and then assumes the role of an agent to pass that information on to a superior manager.

All of these exchanges take place using the SNMPv2 protocol, which is a simple request/response type of protocol. Typically, SNMPv2 is implemented on top of the user datagram protocol (UDP), which is part of the TCP/IP protocol suite.

The final ingredient noted in Figure 3-1 is that of party. The actual exchange of information takes place between two parties. The use of parties allows systems to define access control and security policies that differ depending on the combination of manager, agent, and desired information. This gives the user considerable flexibility in setting up a network management system and assigning various levels of authorization to different persons.

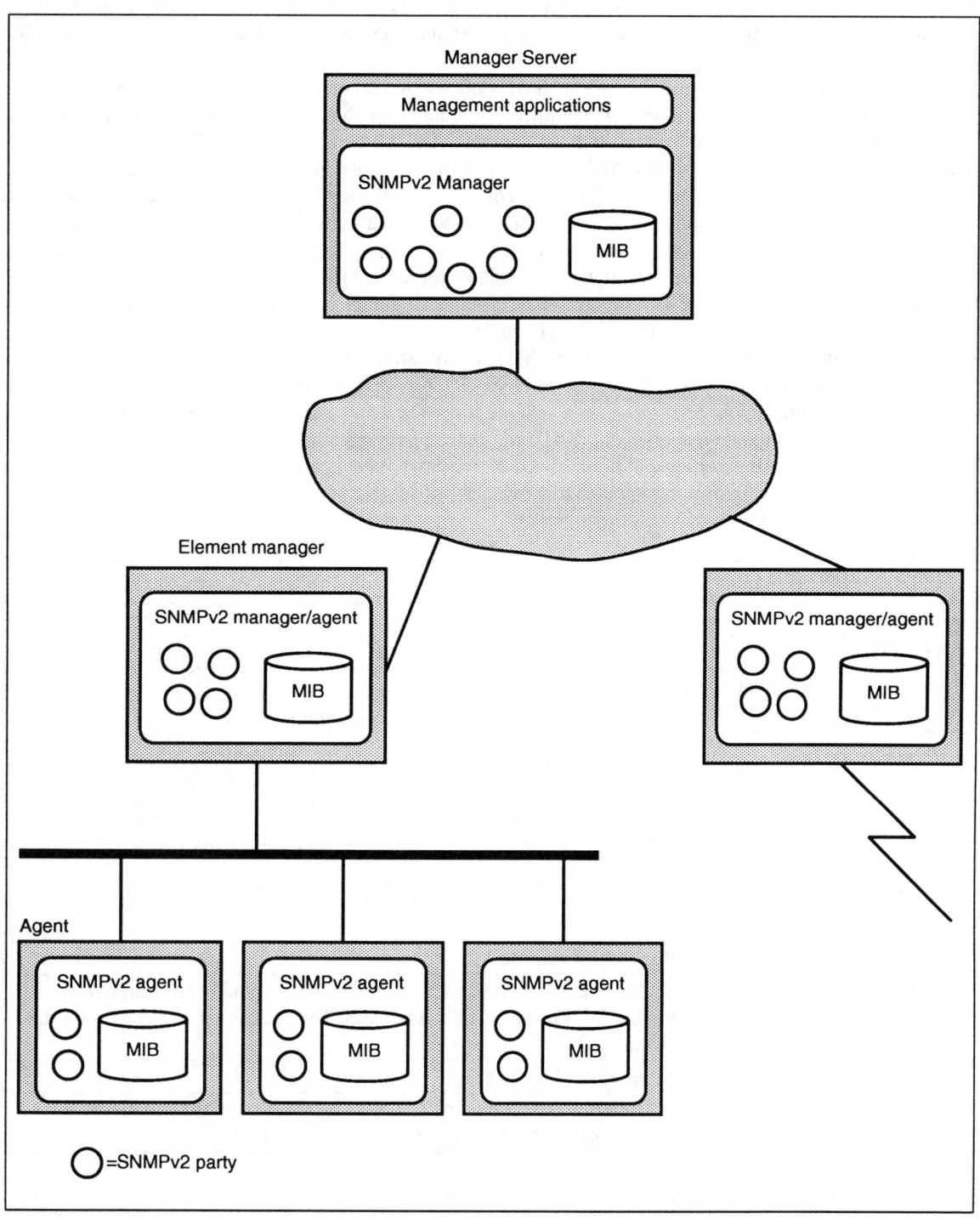

Figure 3-1: SNMPv2-managed configuration

**Structure of management information.** The means by which resources in the network may be managed is to represent these resources as objects. Each object is, essentially, a data variable that represents one aspect of the managed agent. The collection of objects is referred to as a *management information base* (MIB). The MIB functions as a collection of access points at the agent for the management station. These objects are standardized across systems of a particular class (for example, bridges all support the same management objects). A management station performs the monitoring function by retrieving the value of MIB objects. A management station can cause an action to take place at an agent or can change the configuration settings of an agent by modifying the values of specific variables.

The structure of management information (SMI) defines the general framework within which a MIB can be defined and constructed. The SMI identifies the data types that can be used in the MIB, and how resources within the MIB are represented and named. The philosophy behind SMI is to encourage simplicity and extensibility within the MIB. Thus, the MIB can store only simple data types: scalars and two-dimensional arrays of scalars, called tables. The SMI does not support the creation or retrieval of complex data structures. This philosophy is in contrast to that used with OSI systems management, which provides for complex data structures and retrieval modes to support greater functionality. SMI avoids complex data types and structures to simplify the task of implementation and to enhance interoperability. MIBs will inevitably contain vendor-created data types and, unless tight restrictions are placed on the definition of such data types, interoperability will suffer.

There are actually three key elements in the SMI specification. At the lowest level, the SMI specifies the data types that may be stored. Then, the SMI specifies a formal technique for defining objects and tables of objects. Finally, the SMI provides a scheme for associating a unique identifier with each actual object in a system, so that data at an agent can be referenced by a manager.

Table 3-3 shows the data types that are allowed by the SMI. This is a fairly restricted set of types. For example, real numbers are not supported. However, it is rich enough to support most network management requirements.

| Table 3-3. Allowable data types in SNMPv2. | |
|---|---|
| **Data Type** | **Description** |
| INTEGER | Integers in the range of $-2^{31}$ to $2^{31} - 1$. |
| UInteger32 | Integers in the range of 0 to $2^{32} - 1$. |
| Counter32 | A nonnegative integer that may be incremented modulo $2^{32}$. |
| Counter64 | A nonnegative integer that may be incremented modulo $2^{64}$. |
| Gauge32 | A nonnegative integer that may increase or decrease, but shall not exceed a maximum value. The maximum value cannot be greater than $2^{32} - 1$. |
| TimeTicks | A nonnegative integer that represents the time, modulo $2^{32}$, in hundredths of a second. |
| OCTET STRING | Octet strings for arbitrary binary or textual data; may be limited to 255 octets. |
| IpAddress | A 32-bit internet address. |
| NsapAddress | An OSI address. The first octet contains a binary value in the range of 0 to 20 that indicates the length of the address. The remaining octets contain the actual address. |
| BIT STRING | An enumeration of named bits. |
| OBJECT IDENTIFIER | Administratively assigned name to object or other standardized element. Value is a sequence of up to 128 nonnegative integers. |

The SNMPv2 specification includes a template, known as an ASN.1 (Abstract Syntax Notation One) macro, which provides the formal model for defining objects. Figure 3-2 shows how this template is used to define objects and tables of objects.

The first three productions serve to define a table, grokTable, stored at an agent. As with all SNMPv2 tables, grokTable is organized as a sequence of rows, or entries, each of which has the same sequence of objects; in this case, each row consists of four objects. The INDEX clause specifies that the object grokIndex serves as an index into the table; each row of the table will have a unique value of grokIndex.

The access type of grokIPAddress is read-create, which means that the object is read-write and that the object may be assigned a value by a manager at the time that the row containing this object is created by a manager. Each row of the table maintains a counter for the number of grok packets sent to the grokIPAddress specified for that row. The grokCount object is read-only; its value cannot be altered by a manager but is maintained by the agent within which this table resides. The grokStatus object is used in the process of row creation and deletion. The algorithm for row creation and deletion is rather complex. In essence, a RowStatus type of object is used to keep track of the state of a row during the process of creation and deletion.

Each object definition includes a value, which is a unique identifier for that object. For example, the value for grokEntry is {grokTable 1}, which means that the identifier for grokEntry is the concatenation of the identifier for grokTable and 1. The objects in a MIB are organized in a tree structure, and the identifier of an object is found by walking the tree from its root to the position of the object in the tree structure. For scalar objects, this scheme provides a unique identifier for any given object instance. For objects in tables, there is one instance of each object for each row of the table, so a further qualification is needed. What is done is to concatenate the value of the INDEX object to the identifier of each object in the table.

```
grokTable OBJECT-TYPE
    SYNTAX    SEQUENCE OF GrokEntry
    MAX-ACCESS   not-accessible
    STATUS    current
    DESCRIPTION
        "The (conceptual) grok table."
    ::= { adhocGroup 2 }

grokEntry OBJECT-TYPE
    SYNTAX        GrokEntry
    MAX-ACCESS   not-accessible
    STATUS        current
    DESCRIPTION
        "An entry (conceptual row) in the
        grok table."
    INDEX        { grokIndex }
    ::= { grokTable 1 }

GrokEntry ::= SEQUENCE {
        grokIndex         INTEGER,
        GrokIPAddress     IpAddress,
        grokValue         Counter32,
        grokStatus        RowStatus }

grokIndex OBJECT-TYPE
    SYNTAX        INTEGER
    MAX-ACCESS   not-accessible
    STATUS        current
    DESCRIPTION
        "The auxiliary variable used to
        identify instances of the columnar
        objects in the grok table."
    ::= { grokEntry 1 }

grokIPAddress OBJECT-TYPE
    SYNTAX        IpAddress
    MAX-ACCESS   read-create
    STATUS        current
    DESCRIPTION
        "The Ip address to send grok packets
        to."
    ::= { grokEntry 2 }

grokCount OBJECT-TYPE
    SYNTAX        Counter32
    MAX-ACCESS   read-only
    STATUS        current
    DESCRIPTION
        "The total number of grok packets
        sent so far."
    DEFVAL { 0 }
    ::= { grokEntry 3 }

grokStatus OBJECT-TYPE
    SYNTAX        RowStatus
    MAX-ACCESS   read-create
    STATUS        current
    DESCRIPTION
        "The status object used for creating,
        modifying, and deleting a conceptual
        row instance in the grok table."
    DEFVAL { active }
    ::= { grokEntry 4 }
```

**Figure 3-2: An example of an SNMPv2 table**

**Protocol operation.** The heart of the SNMPv2 framework is the protocol itself. The protocol provides a straightforward, basic mechanism for the exchange of management information between manager and agent.

The authInfo field is used to carry information required if this is to be an authenticated exchange. If authentication is used between this pair of parties, then a message digest is computed over the message using a secret key by the source party. The destination party computes the same digest; if there is a match, this verifies that the message was indeed sent by the party that is indicated in the srcParty field.

The authInfo field also includes two time stamps used to maintain synchronization between party clocks at source and destination. These clocks assure the timeliness of the message (i.e., it has not been captured and replayed).

An additional feature of SNMPv2 is that communication between two parties may be protected from eavesdropping, using encryption. For this purpose, the entire message with the exception of the privDst field is encrypted. The privDst field simply repeats the dstParty field. This value must remain in the clear to enable delivery to the intended party.

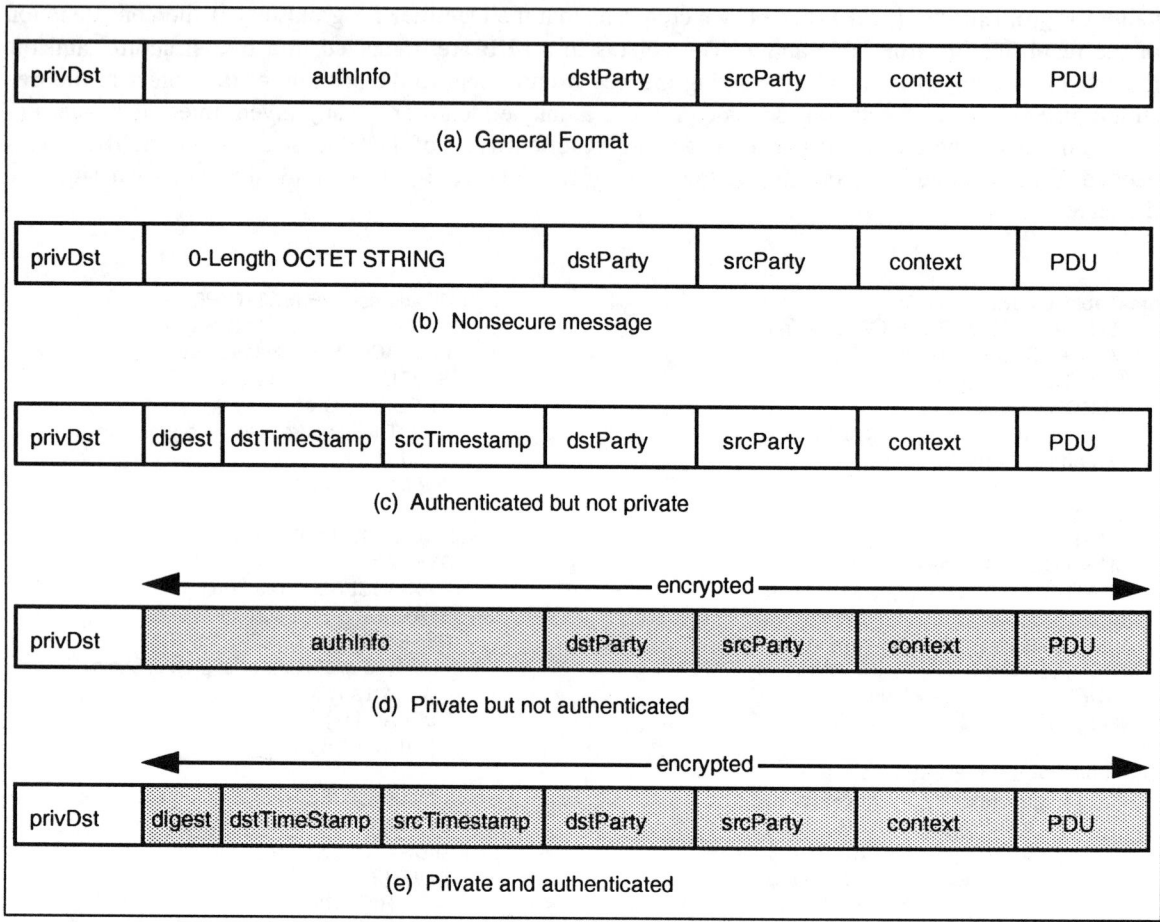

Figure 3-3: SNMP message formats

As Figure 3-3 indicates, the communication between two parties may be nonsecure, or may provide either authentication or privacy, or may provide both.

Seven types of PDUs may be carried in an SNMP message. The general formats for these are illustrated in Figure 3-4; the formal ASN.1 definition was provided in Figure 2-2. Several fields are common to a number of PDUs. The request-id field is an integer assigned such that each outstanding request can be uniquely identified. This enables a manager to correlate incoming responses with outstanding requests. It also enables an agent to cope with duplicate PDUs generated by an unreliable transport service. The variable-bindings field contains a list of object identifiers; depending on the PDU, the list may also include a value for each object.

The GetRequest-PDU, issued by a manager, includes a list of one or more object names for which values are requested. If the get operation is successful, then the responding agent will send a Response-PDU. The variable-bindings list will contain the identifier and value of all retrieved objects. For any variables that are not in the relevant MIB view, its identifier and an error code are returned in the variable-bindings list. Thus, SNMPv2 permits partial responses to a GetRequest, which is a significant improvement over SNMP. In SNMP, if one or more of the variables in a GetRequest are not supported, the agent returns an error message with a status of noSuchName. To cope with such an error, the SNMP manager must either return no values to the requesting application, or it must include an algorithm that responds to an error by removing the missing variables, resending the request, and then sending a partial result to the application.

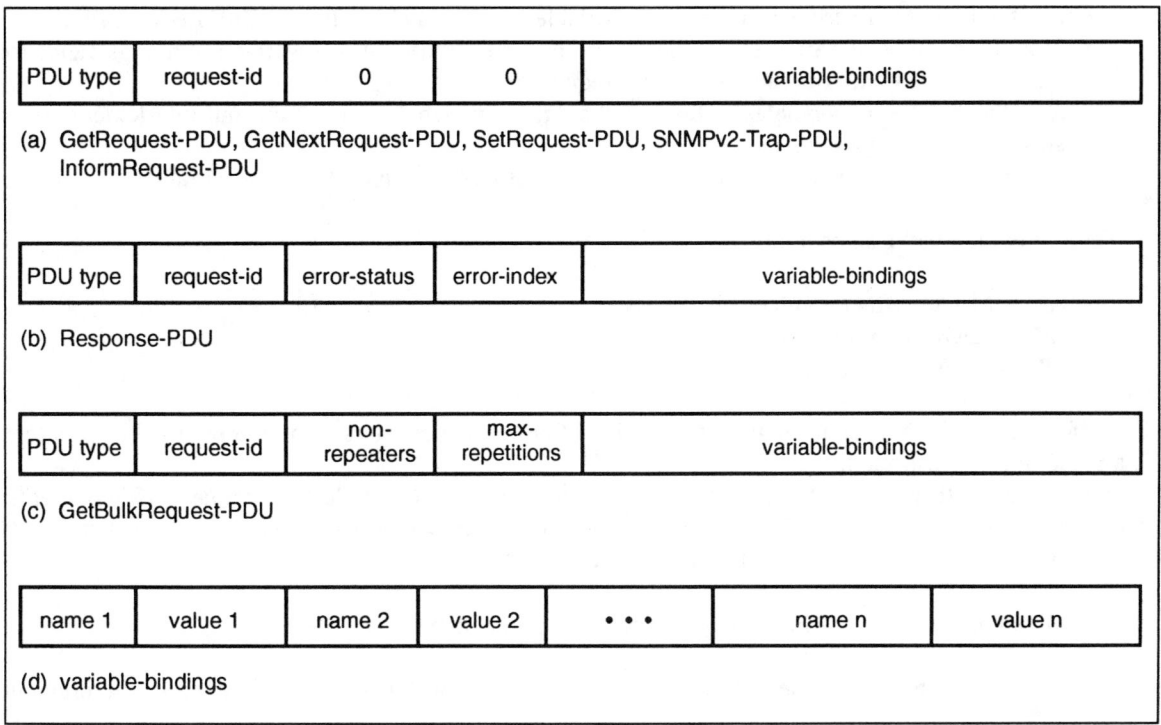

Figure 3-4: SNMPv2 PDU formats

The GetNextRequest-PDU also is issued by a manager and includes a list of one or more objects. In this case, for each object named in the variable-bindings field, a value is to be returned for the object that is next in lexicographic order, which is equivalent to saying next in the MIB in terms of its position in the tree structure of object identifiers. As with the GetRequest-PDU, the agent will return values for as many variables as possible. One of the strengths of the GetNextRequest-PDU is that it enables a manager entity to discover the structure of a MIB view dynamically. This is useful if the manager does not know a priori the set of objects that are supported by an agent or that are in a particular MIB view.

One of the major enhancements provided in SNMPv2 is the GetBulkRequest-PDU. The purpose of this PDU is to minimize the number of protocol exchanges required to retrieve a large amount of management information. The GetBulkRequest-PDU allows a SNMPv2 manager to request that the response be as large as possible given the constraints on message size.

The GetBulkRequest operation uses the same selection principle as the GetNextRequest operation; that is, selection is always of the next object instance in lexicographic order. The difference is that, with GetBulkRequest, it is possible to specify that multiple lexicographic successors be selected.

In essence, the GetBulkRequest operation works in the following way. The GetBulkRequest includes a list of $(N + R)$ variable names in the variable-bindings list. For each of the first $N$ names, retrieval is done in the same fashion as for GetNextRequest. That is, for each variable in the list, the next variable in lexicographic order plus its value is returned; if there is no lexicographic successor, then the named variable and a value of endOfMibView are returned. For each of the last $R$ names, multiple lexicographic successors are returned.

The GetBulkRequest-PDU has two fields not found in the other PDUs: nonrepeaters and max-repetitions. The nonrepeaters field specifies the number of variables in the variable-bindings list for which a single lexicographic successor is to be returned. The max-repetitions field specifies the number of lexicographic successors to be returned for the remaining variables in the variable-bindings list. To explain the algorithm, let us define the following:

- $L$ is the number of variable names in the variable-bindings field of the GetBulkRequest-PDU.
- $N$ is the number of variables, starting with the first variable in the variable-bindings field, for which a single lexicographic successor is requested.
- $R$ is the number of variables, following the first $N$ variables, for which multiple lexicographic successors are requested.
- $M$ is the number of lexicographic successors requested for each of the last $R$ variables.

The following relationships hold:

$$N = \text{MAX} [ \text{MIN (nonrepeaters, L), 0}]$$
$$M = \text{MAX} [ \text{max-repetitions, 0} ]$$
$$R = L - N$$

The effect of the MAX operator is that if the value of either nonrepeaters or max-repetitions is less than 0, a value of 0 is substituted.

If $N$ is greater than 0, then the first $N$ variables are processed as for GetNextRequest. If $R$ is greater than 0 and $M$ is greater than 0, then for each of the last $R$ variables in the variable-bindings list, the $M$ lexicographic successors are retrieved. That is, for each variable:

1. Obtain the value of the lexicographic successor of the named variable.

2. Obtain the value of the lexicographic successor to the object instance retrieved in the previous step.

3. Obtain the value of the lexicographic successor to the object instance retrieved in the previous step.

4. And so on, until $M$ object instances have been retrieved

If, at any point in this process, there is no lexicographic successor, then the endOfMibView value is returned, paired with the name of the last lexicographic successor or, if there were no successors, with the name of the variable in the request.

Using these rules, the total number of variable-bindings pairs that can be produced is $N + (M \times R)$. The order in which the last $(M \times R)$ of these variable-bindings pairs are placed in the Response-PDU can be expressed as follows:

**for** $i := 1$ **to** $M$ **do**
    **for** $r := 1$ **to** $R$ **do**
        retrieve $i$th successor of $(N+r)$th variable;

The effect of this definition is that the successors to the last $R$ variables are retrieved row by row, rather than retrieving all of the successors to the first variable, followed by all of the successors to the second variable, and so on. This matches with the way in which conceptual tables are lexicographically ordered, so that if the last $R$ values in the GetBulkRequest are columnar objects of the same table, then the Response will return conceptual rows of the table.

The GetBulkRequest operation removes one of the major limitations of SNMP, which is its inability to efficiently retrieve large blocks of data. Moreover, the use of this operator can actually enable reducing the size of management applications that are supported by the management protocol, realizing further efficiencies. There is no need for the management application to concern itself with some of the details of packaging requests. It need not perform a trial-and-error procedure to determine the optimal number of variable-bindings to put in a Request-PDU. Also, if a request is too big, even for GetBulkRequest, the agent will send back as much data as it can, rather than simply sending a tooBig error message. Thus, the manager simply has to retransmit the request for the missing data; it does not have to figure out how to repackage the original request into a series of smaller requests.

The SetRequest-PDU is issued by a manager to request that the values of one or more objects be altered. The receiving SNMPv2 entity responds with a Response-PDU containing the same request-id. The SetRequest operation is atomic: either all of the variables are updated or none are. If the responding entity is able to set values for all of the variables listed in the incoming variable-bindings list, then the Response-PDU includes the variable-bindings field, with a value supplied for each variable. If at least one of the variable values cannot be supplied, then no values are returned, and no values are updated. In the latter case, the error-status code indicates the reason for the failure, and the error-index field indicates the variable in the variable-bindings list that caused the failure.

The SNMPv2-Trap-PDU is generated and transmitted by a SNMPv2 entity acting in an agent role when an unusual event occurs. It is used to provide the management station with an asynchronous notification of some significant event. The variable-bindings list is used to contain the information associated with the trap message. Unlike the GetRequest, GetNextRequest, GetBulkRequest, SetRequest, and InformRequest-PDUs, the SNMPv2-Trap-PDU does not elicit a response from the receiving entity; it is an unconfirmed message.

The InformRequest-PDU is sent by an SNMPv2 entity acting in a manager role, on behalf of an application, to another SNMPv2 entity acting in a manager role, to provide management information to an application using the latter entity. As with the SNMPv2-Trap-PDU, the variable-bindings field is used to convey the associated information. The manager receiving an InformRequest acknowledges receipt with a Response-PDU.

For both the SNMPv2-Trap and the InformRequest, various conditions can be defined that indicate when the notification is generated, and the information to be sent is also specified.

**SNMPv2 management information base.** The objects defined as part of SNMPv2 are organized into three MIBs: the SNMPv2 MIB, the manager-to-manager MIB, and the party MIB. Each MIB is in turn organized into a number of groups. A group is simply a related collection of objects. Typically, implementations are characterized in terms of which groups they implement. An implementation is said to include a group if all of the objects in that group are supported. This provides a concise way for vendors and customers to gain a mutual understanding of what management information is supported by the vendor's product.

The SNMPv2 MIB defines objects that describe the behavior of an SNMPv2 entity. This information enables a manager to monitor the amount of SNMPv2-related activity at an agent and the amount of dedicated SNMPv2-related resources at the agent. This MIB contains five groups: SNMPv2 statistics, SNMPv1 statistics, object resources, traps, and set.

The SNMPv2 statistics group provides basic instrumentation of the SNMPv2 entity. It consists of counters used to record the number of incoming and outgoing SNMPv2 messages, broken down into successful messages plus those that suffered various error conditions. The SNMPv1 statistics group includes several objects that are useful if an SNMPv2 entity also implements SNMPv1. The object resources group enables a SNMPv2 entity acting in an agent role to describe its dynamically configurable object resources; essentially, this group consists of a table with one entry for each resource, with a text description of the resource. The trap group consists of objects that allow the SNMPv2 entity — when acting in an agent role — to be configured to generate SNMPv2-Trap-PDUs.

Finally, the set group consists of a single object, snmpSetSerialNo, that is used to solve two problems that can occur with the use of the set operation. First, multiple set operations on the same MIB object may be issued by a manager, and it may be essential that these operations be performed in the order that they were issued, even if they are reordered in transmission. And second, concurrent use of set operations by multiple managers may result in an inconsistent or inaccurate database. The snmpSetSerialNo is an integer-valued object that obeys the following rules. If the value of the object is $K$ and a set operation is received that attempts to assign $K$ to this object, then the object is incremented to $(K + 1) \mod 2^{31}$, and the operation succeeds. If any other value is used, the operation fails.

The snmpSet object can be used in the following way: When a manager wishes to set one or more object values in an agent, it first retrieves the value of snmpSet object. It then issues a SetRequest-PDU whose variable-bindings list includes the snmpSet object with its current value. If two or more managers issue SetRequests using the same value of snmpSet, the first to arrive at the agent will succeed (assuming no other problems exist), resulting in an increment of snmpSet; the remaining set operations will fail due to an inconsistent snmpSet value.

**Manager-to-manager MIB.** The manager-to-manager (M2M) MIB is specifically provided to support the distributed management architecture. It enables a superior manager to define events that a subordinate manager will use as triggers for sending alert-type messages to the superior manager. The M2M MIB may be used to allow an intermediate manager to function as a remote monitor of network media traffic. It may also be used to allow an intermediate manager to report on activities at the intermediate manager or at subordinate agents. This MIB consists of two groups: the alarm group and the event group. The alarm group is used to define a set of threshold alarms. Each threshold alarm specifies some object in the local MIB that is to be monitored. When the value of that object crosses a threshold, then an event is triggered. Typically, the triggered event is an InformRequest-PDU that is to be sent to a superior manager. Each alarm in the alarm group points to an entry in the event group, which in turn defines the information that is to be sent with that InformRequest-PDU.

**Party MIB.** The party MIB is concerned with the security-related aspects of SNMPv2. This MIB consists of four groups: party database, contexts, access privileges, and MIB view. The best way to describe the purpose of each of these groups is to consider their use during message transmission.

Consider that a message is sent from a manager to an agent. The message header includes the fields srcParty, dstParty, and context. The party database group at the agent contains information about each local and remote party known to the agent. The party information includes authentication parameters that need to be applied to srcParty, and privacy parameters that need to be applied to dstParty. The context group consists of a table with one entry for each context known to the agent. Each entry specifies whether the context is local, in which case the appropriate MIB view must be used, or remote, in which case the proxied device is indicated. The MIB view group is referenced by the contexts group. The appropriate entry defines a subset of the local MIB that is accessible through this context. Finally, the access privileges database group contains the aclTable. Each entry in the table has a unique combination of srcParty, dstParty, and context, and indicates which management operations are allowed for this combination.

**Coexistence with SNMPv1.** With all of the benefits of SNMPv2, there is bound to be a strong demand on the part of customers, and we can expect to see a flood of announcements of SNMPv2-based products in the near future. But customers and vendors are faced with the same fact on the ground: There is a huge installed base of SNMPv1-based products. As usual, the problem of migrating a large installed base to a new generation is a vexing one. Fortunately, the developers of SNMPv2 have given much thought to this problem.

In all cases, an existing SNMPv1 installation consists of one or a small number of SNMPv1 management stations and a larger number of SNMPv1 agents. The easiest way to accomplish migration on an existing network is to upgrade the manager systems to support SNMPv2 in a way that allows coexistence of SNMPv2 managers, SNMPv2 agents, and SNMPv1 agents.

The task of transition is eased by the fact that the SMI defined for SNMPv2 is nearly a proper superset of that defined for SNMPv1. Therefore, it is an easy matter for an SNMPv2 management station to understand the MIB at an SNMPv1 agent. The major technical problem is that the protocol itself is different.

Two approaches are described in the SNMPv2 standard: the use of proxy agents and the use of bilingual managers.

The simplest way to achieve coexistence at the protocol level is to reach existing SNMPv1 agents from a SNMPv2 manager by means of a proxy agent. A SNMPv2 entity acting in a SNMPv2 agent role can be implemented and configured to act in the role of a proxy agent on behalf of SNMP agents. This would allow conversion between the SNMPv2 and SNMPv1 protocols. The proxy agent needs to perform two mappings. SNMPv2-PDUs coming from a SNMPv2 manager are converted to SNMPv1-PDUs to be sent to an SNMPv1 agent according to the following rules: GetRequest, GetNextRequest, and SetRequest PDUs are passed unchanged, and a GetBulkRequest-PDU is converted to a GetNextRequest-PDU with the same variable-bindings list. The effect of this mapping is that only the first "row" of the max-repetitions portion of the variable-bindings list will be retrieved. SNMPv1-PDUs coming from a SNMPv1 agent are converted to SNMPv2-PDUs to be sent to a SNMPv2 agent according to the following rules: A Response-PDU is passed unchanged, and a Trap-PDU is converted into a SNMPv2-Trap-PDU; the latter conversion involves a small format change.

An alternative way to achieve coexistence is to employ management stations that "speak" both SNMPv2 and SNMPv1. When a management application needs to contact a protocol entity acting in an agent role, the entity acting in a manager role uses either SNMPv2 or SNMPv1 PDUs based on information in a local database that assigns each correspondent agent to one of the two protocols. This dual capability in the management station should only be visible at the SNMPv2/SNMPv1 level. Management applications can be written as if they were using only SNMPv2. For communication with SNMPv1 agents, the manager can map operations as if it were acting as a proxy agent.

## The TCP/IP protocol suite

Based on protocol research and development conducted on its experimental packet-switched network, ARPANET, the US Department of Defense (DoD) has issued a set of military standards for computer communications protocols. Although there are five of these protocols (Table 3-4), the entire set is known by the names of two of them: transmission control protocol (TCP) and internet protocol (IP). These protocols are in widespread use within the US defense community. But what is more interesting is that they have been quietly building up a following in the commercial arena during a time when much attention has been focused on the international standards based on the Open Systems Interconnection (OSI) model. Currently, there are over 200 vendors that provide TCP/IP products, and these are the most widely available and most widely used set of standardized computer-communications protocols.

| Table 3-4. The TCP/IP protocol suite. |
|---|
| MIL-STD-1777 *Internet Protocol (IP)* |
| Provides a connectionless service for end systems to communicate across one or more networks. Does not assume the network to be reliable. |
| MIL-STD-1778 *Transmission Control Protocol (TCP)* |
| A reliable end-to-end data-transfer service. Equivalent to OSI transport protocol. |
| MIL-STD-1780 *File Transfer Protocol (FTP)* |
| A simple application for transfer of ASCII, EBCDIC, and binary files. |
| MIL-STD-1781 *Simple Mail Transfer Protocol (SMTP)* |
| A simple electronic mail facility. |
| MIL-STD-1782 *TELNET* |
| Provides a remote logon facility for simple scroll-mode terminals. |

**The basic protocol set.** The TCP/IP architecture, like the OSI model, is layered. In the case of TCP/IP, four layers are involved: network access, internet, transport, and application. This architecture is compared with that of OSI in Figure 3-5. The network access layer contains the protocols that provide access to a communications network, such as a local area network (LAN). Protocols at this layer are between a communications node and an attached host. The TCP/IP suite does not include any unique protocols at this layer. Rather, the protocol appropriate for a particular network (for example, Ethernet, IEEE 802, X.25) is used.

The internet layer consists of the procedures required to allow data to traverse multiple networks between hosts. Thus it must provide a routing function. This protocol is implemented within hosts and routers. A router is a processor connecting two networks, whose primary function is to relay data between networks using an internetwork protocol. The protocol at the layer is the *internet protocol (IP)*. A typical use of IP is to connect multiple LANs within the same building or to connect LANs at different sites through a wide area packet-switching network.

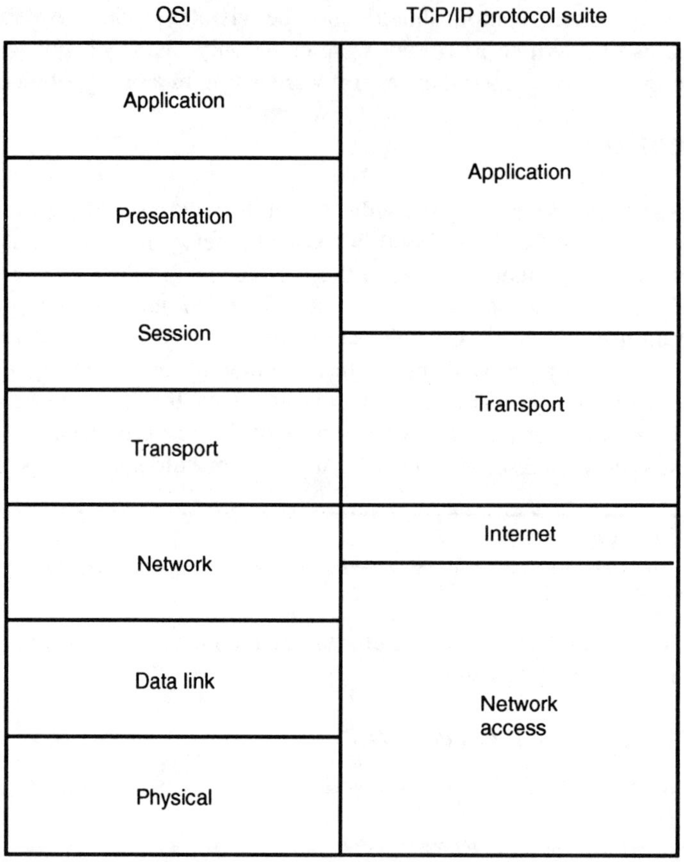

| OSI | TCP/IP protocol suite |
|---|---|
| Application | Application |
| Presentation | |
| Session | Transport |
| Transport | |
| Network | Internet |
| Data link | Network access |
| Physical | |

**Figure 3-5: A comparison of the OSI and TCP/IP communications architectures**

The transport layer provides the logic for assuring that data exchanged between hosts is reliably delivered. It also is responsible for directing incoming data to the intended application. The protocol at this layer is the *transmission control protocol (TCP)*.

Finally, the application layer contains protocols for specific user applications. For each different type of application, such as file transfer, a protocol is needed that supports that application. Three such protocols are included in the TCP/IP protocol suite: SMTP, FTP, and TELNET.

**User datagram protocol (UDP).** In addition to TCP, there is one other transport-level protocol that is in common use as part of the TCP/IP protocol suite: the user datagram protocol (UDP) specified in RFC 768. The UDP provides a connectionless service for application-level procedures. Thus it enables a procedure to send messages to other procedures with a minimum of protocol mechanism. SNMP makes use of UDP.

UDP sits on top of IP. Because it is connectionless, UDP has very little to do. Essentially, it adds a port addressing capability to IP.

## TCP/IP standards

As was mentioned, the five protocols that make up the core of the TCP/IP protocol suite have been issued as military standards. However, the family of protocols that make up the protocol suite extends far beyond these five core protocols. By universal agreement, an organization known as the Internet Activities Board (IAB) is responsible for the development and publication of these standards, which are published in a series of documents called Requests for Comments (RFCs).

This section provides a brief description of the way in which standards for the TCP/IP protocol suite are developed.

**The Internet and Internet standards.** The Internet is a large collection of interconnected networks, all of which use the TCP/IP protocol suite. The Internet began with the development of ARPANET and the subsequent support by the Defense Advanced Research Projects Agency (DARPA) for the development of additional networks to support military users and government contractors.

The IAB is the coordinating committee for Internet design, engineering, and management. Areas covered include the operation of the Internet itself and the standardization of protocols used by end systems on the Internet for interoperability. The IAB has two principal subsidiary task forces:

- Internet Engineering Task Force (IETF)
- Internet Research Task Force (IRTF)

The actual work of these task forces is carried out by working groups. Membership in a working group is voluntary; any interested party may participate.

It is the IETF that is responsible for publishing the RFCs. The RFCs are the working notes of the Internet research and development community. A document in this series may be on essentially any topic related to computer communications, and may be anything from a meeting report to the specification of a standard.

The final decision of which RFCs become Internet standards is made by the IAB, on the recommendation of the IETF. To become a standard, a specification must meet the following criteria:

- be stable and well-understood;
- be technically competent;
- have multiple, independent, and interoperable implementations with operational experience;
- enjoy significant public support; and
- be recognizably useful in some or all parts of the Internet.

The key difference between these criteria and those used for international standards is the emphasis here on operational experience.

**The standardization process.** Figure 3-6 illustrates the series of steps, called the *standards track*, that a specification goes through to become a standard. The steps involve increasing amounts of scrutiny and testing. At each step, the IETF must make a recommendation for advancement of the protocol, and the IAB must ratify it.

The white boxes in the diagram represent temporary states, which should be occupied for the minimum practical time. However, a document must remain a proposed standard for at least six months and a draft standard for at least four months to allow time for review and comment. The gray boxes represent long-term states that may be occupied for years.

A protocol or other specification that is not considered ready for standardization may be published as an experimental RFC. After further work, the specification may be resubmitted. If the specification is generally stable, has resolved known design choices, is believed to be well-understood, has received significant community review, and appears to enjoy enough community interest to be considered valuable, then the RFC will be designated a proposed standard.

For a specification to be advanced to draft standard status, there must be at least two independent and interoperable implementations from which adequate operational experience has been obtained.

After significant implementation and operational experience has been obtained, a specification may be elevated to a standard. At this point, the specification is assigned an STD number as well as an RFC number.

Finally, when a protocol becomes obsolete, it is assigned to the historic state.

As of this writing, the following SNMP-related specifications are Internet standards:

| Name | RFC | STD |
|---|---|---|
| Simple Network Management Protocol | 1157 | 15 |
| Structure of Management Information | 1155 | 16 |
| Management Information Base-II | 1213 | 17 |

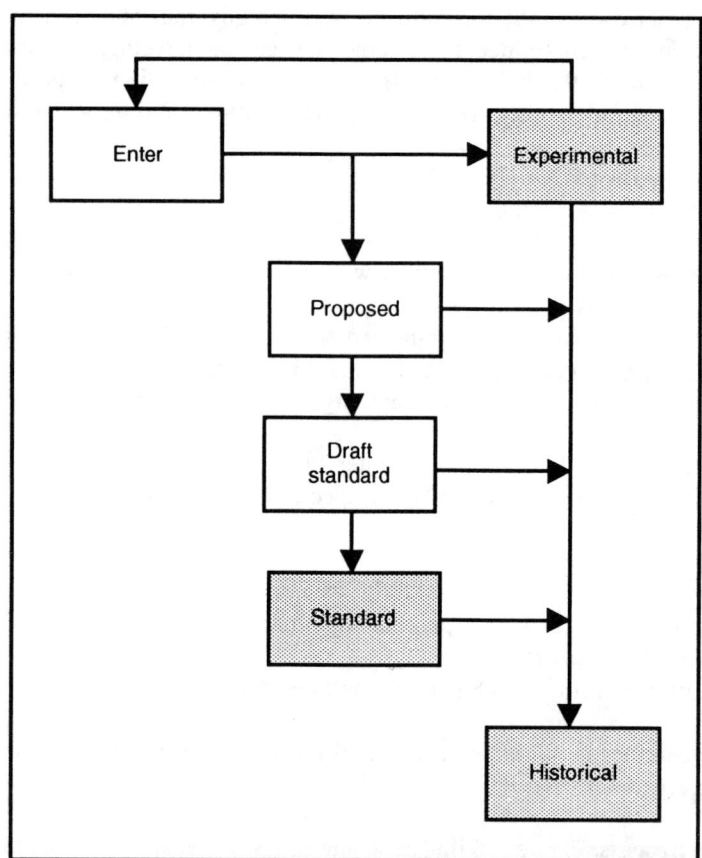

Figure 3-6: Standards track diagram

## Paper summary

The first three papers in this chapter describe the basic SNMP framework and capabilities. An overall introduction to SNMP is provided by "Network Management in the TCP/IP Protocol Suite." "An Integrated Architecture for LAN/WAN Management" provides an example of the use of SNMP to build a distributed network management architecture. "MIB II Extends SNMP Interoperability" discusses the most important MIB defined for use with SNMP.

The remaining papers examine various extensions and enhancements to the original SNMP. "SNMP Security" provides an overview of the recent enhancement of SNMP to include security features; although this paper discusses the security enhancements in the proposed Secure SNMP of July 1992, the same features are present in the new SNMPv2. Finally, "Coming Soon to a Network Near You" provides an assessment of SNMPv2. Although the article was written at a time when only the SMP specification was available, its conclusions remain valid.

# 7

# Network Management in the TCP/IP Protocol Suite

*Craig Partridge\* and Keith McCloghrie*

Support for network management is often an afterthought in the development of a protocol suite. Certainly, network management research has lagged behind research in other areas of networking. Indeed, it is probably fair to say that research on network management is nearly a generation behind research on other topics.

In this chapter we examine the current and developing management protocols for networks using the TCP/IP protocol suite.

## 7.1 HISTORY OF NETWORK MANAGEMENT IN THE TCP/IP PROTOCOL SUITE

"Comprehensive" network management protocols, protocols designed to serve most or all of a protocol suite's management needs, are a new addition to the TCP/IP protocol suite. To understand why these protocols have been developed, it is worth taking a brief look at how TCP/IP networks were managed before formal management protocols were developed.

When the initial work on the protocol suite was finished in the late

\*Mr. Partridge would like to acknowledge the assistance of Bolt Beranek Newman, Incorporated, which provided him the time to contribute to this book.

1970s, the only "management" protocol included was the Internet Control Message Protocol (ICMP). ICMP was designed to allow hosts and gateways to exchange control messages, in particular, messages indicating errors in datagram processing and routing, and warning of the presence of congestion. However, ICMP also includes a few basic messages that can be used for error diagnosis. The most important of these diagnostic messages are the *Echo/Echo Reply* messages. An Echo message sent to an IP system (host or gateway) requires an Echo Reply message to be sent back to the originating system. The Echo Reply message must also return any data included in the Echo message.

Using the Echo and Echo Reply messages along with various IP header options such as *Source Routing* and *Record Route* and given the ability to set some IP header fields such as the *Time-To-Live*, a very powerful program can be written to analyze network problems. Indeed, such a program is widely used throughout the ARPA Internet and is known as *ping* for Packet Internet Groper, a name coined in 1979 by Dr. David Mills of the University of Delaware. Ping can be used to observe variations in network round-trip times and loss rates which allow a manager to discover the presence of and isolate the source of network congestion in a network path. Fragmentation and reassembly problems can be traced by sending large Echo messages. Other more sophisticated observations are also possible.

Once a problem is discovered using ping, further investigations can be carried out with more specialized tools. Packet printers such as the Packet Filter [MOGUL87] can be used to examine local network traffic. Most gateways allow remote operators to log in and examine log files. Furthermore, most of the TCP/IP application protocols use ASCII data formats, which make it possible to telnet to an application port and type in commands by hand. (This last trick is particularly useful when debugging *e-mail* problems.)

In fact, the combination of ping and various auxiliary tools worked so well that for many years there was no pressure to develop new management protocols. Researchers who developed more powerful management protocols discovered that the community felt no need for them; a case in point is the Host Monitoring Protocol (HMP), which was used to manage *backbone* gateways, but never implemented in *non-backbone* gateways. There was no pressure to develop more powerful management tools until the Internet growth rate exploded in the late 1980s. This pressure resulted not just from the increased number of hosts and gateways, but also from the more complex network topologies introduced by the rapid growth.

Figure 7.1 shows how the Internet has grown. It graphs the number of IP networks attached to the Internet over time, starting in 1983. Observe that in late 1986 the growth rate suddenly became much faster. In 1987 the Internet doubled in size, from 175 to 350 active IP networks. We

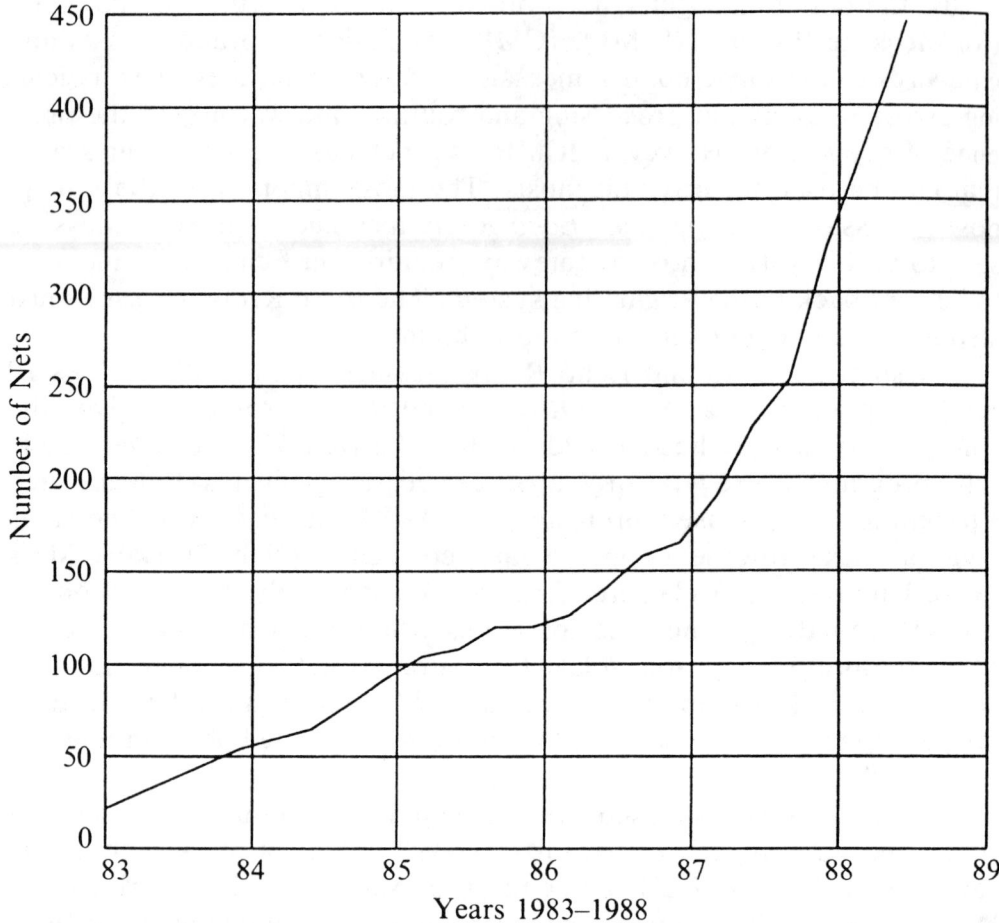

**Figure 7.1.** Internet growth in networks.

should also note that this number does not fully convey the impact of growth. Concurrent with the increase in IP networks has been an increase in the use of *subnetting,* the practice of combining several distinct networks together into one logical IP network. (For an example of a well-developed subnetted network, see G. Trewitt's paper on the Stanford University network [TREW88].) One way to measure the increase in subnetting is to look at the average number of hosts per network. A higher average implies increased use of subnetting. In 1983 the average number of hosts per network was about 8. By late 1987, the average was nearly 100 hosts per network. Clearly, the boom in IP networks went hand-in-hand with a boom in subnetting. This growth rate, although it has moderated slightly, continues today and is putting extraordinary management demands on the TCP/IP community.

The key management problem in a fast-growing network is training people to run it. By 1987 the training problem in the TCP/IP community had become severe. Management tools like ping are designed to be used by network experts with several years of training. They are not suitable for use by computer operators. By 1987 there was an acute shortage of experts to run networks and the community began to see cases where organizations had built networks and then had great difficulty operating those networks due to the lack of experienced personnel.

In response to the need for better and easier network management, the community encouraged several researchers to develop proposals for more comprehensive network management protocols which could be used to develop network management applications requiring less user expertise. By early 1988, three promising approaches had been developed. In February of that year, the Internet Activities Board (the group responsible for directing research on TCP/IP protocols) convened a meeting to select a future TCP/IP standard from among the three protocols. The three candidates were: The High-Level Entity Management System (HEMS) [PART 88]; the Simple Network Management Protocol (SNMP), an enhanced version of the Simple Gateway Management Protocol (SGMP); and the use of OSI's CMIP protocol over TCP/IP (CMOT).

In the end, the participants in the meeting proved unable to choose between the three proposals; each protocol had features and limitations (technical and political) that made it about equal to the other two. As a result, a compromise was fashioned. (A complete description of the meeting and its decisions may be found in RFC 1052.) The developers of HEMS volunteered to withdraw their proposal in the interest of finding a solution. The other two proposals were chosen as potential standards. The SNMP, whose developers chose to compromise on functionality and flexibility in the interest of developing a protocol that could be quickly deployed and efficiently implemented, was chosen as the current network management protocol in order to get the community out of the immediate network management crisis. The other protocol, CMOT, was an attempt to take the still-developing ISO Common Management Information Protocol (CMIP) and adapt it for use in managing networks using TCP/IP protocols. CMOT was designated the long-term management solution, contingent on demonstrations that it was suitable for extremely large datagram networks. The meeting participants further decided that, in order to aid in the eventual transition from SNMP to CMOT, both protocols would be required to use the same database of managed objects. In other words, both protocols would use the same monitoring and control variables within any host or gateway. A working group was established to define this common database.

The rest of this chapter looks at SNMP and CMOT and their common management base in more detail. We begin by introducing some basic network management concepts which are common to both protocols. We will then look at the common Management Information Base (MIB) and conclude by examining each protocol in some detail.

## 7.2 NETWORK MANAGEMENT CONCEPTS

### Models of Network Management

As a result of the recent activity in network management and the importation of some OSI management concepts (via CMOT), the current TCP/IP model of network management is a melange formed by researchers with different perspectives.

The TCP/IP community has traditionally thought of network management in terms of the abstract operations used to support it, in particular, the monitoring and control model. The OSI community has focused more on the activities that network management is designed to support. The current TCP/IP model, influenced by CMOT, is a mix of the traditional view and the OSI approach.

The TCP/IP community has historically chosen to divide network management into two parts. *Monitoring* is the process of observing the behavior of the network and its components, both to detect problems and to support research into understanding and possibly improving the network's performance. *Control* is the process of changing the network's behavior in real-time by adjusting parameters while the network is up and running in order to improve performance or repair faults.

This dichotomy reflects the community's research background. Monitoring is generally considered a very open activity. In principle, anyone on the network should be able to monitor the network's performance or ask for information from any host or gateway. (As the TCP/IP protocol suite has became more popular commercially, there has been some pressure to reconsider this open access policy. Companies do not want their internal traffic patterns available to competitors. There is, however, an advantage to the open access policy. Experience suggests that a network in which monitoring information is universally available is much easier to keep running because more people can locate and examine a problem.) Control, on the other hand, involves changing the state of the network. Clearly, control is a privileged activity and requires some authentication that the person or system exercising control is both qualified and entitled to make changes.

In contrast, the OSI community has treated network management as an activity subdivided into a number of *functional areas*, where a functional area is a class of activities devoted to a particular purpose such as fault management or accounting. The focus of the OSI network management activity has been to identify the management needs of each functional area and standardize ways to meet those needs.

Interestingly, in practice, the methods for implementing the OSI model of functional areas and the methods for implementing the TCP/IP model of monitoring and control turn out to be very similar. Both models work in terms of application-level protocols used to effect transactions or procedure calls between managing and managed systems.

In the current TCP/IP model, management is effected through an interaction between a management application on the managing system and a management *agent* on the managed system. The agent maintains an object database of access points in the management system. These objects are standarized across systems of a particular class (e.g., hosts all support the same management objects). The management application effects monitoring and control by reading and writing (or getting and setting) the management objects in the agent using a standard management protocol. In other words, the object database provides an abstract representation of the managed system to the management application and it is the agent's responsibility to translate operations on this abstract database into real operations upon the managed system. For example, if a managing system sets an object corresponding to a *reload button* in the object database, the agent must cause the managed system to reload its networking software.

Note that although the model does not place any constraints on how many agents can be managed by one management station, the community generally would like the number to be rather high. (For example, the HEMS designers felt, after discussions with the networking community, that a single management station should comfortably be able to manage as many as a thousand agents.)

## Events

One problem with managing a large number of devices from a single system is that if the number of managed devices gets very large, it is no longer possible for the management station to regularly poll each managed system. This observation naturally leads to the idea that managed systems should asynchronously notify management stations of potential problems, using special management messages called *events*. (The TCP/IP community orginally referred to such messages as *traps* and sometimes still uses this term.)

An appealing characteristic of events is that they are only sent when a problem occurs, whereas management systems that use polling find that most of their management traffic is devoted to sending polls to "healthy" systems. In other words, a lot of network bandwidth is consumed getting management information that the management station probably does not need.

All of the TCP/IP management protocols support some sort of event mechanism. They differ in how often they expect events to occur.

## Methods for Managing Special Devices

Typically, the agent model described above is thought of as an exchange between two application-level processes: the management application and the management agent. Therefore, management is thought of as occurring only between systems which support the complete TCP/IP protocol suite up to the application layer.

In practice, that model has proved too limiting. Network managers want to manage all the components in their network, not just hosts and gateways. In particular, system managers want to manage specialized network devices such as modems and bridges, which do not support a full protocol suite.

There are various ways to incorporate such specialized devices into a management scheme that is based on application-level interaction. Both CMOT and SNMP use a scheme called *proxy* which was first proposed by the designers of HEMS. In the proxy approach, specialized devices are managed through a management agent on a proxy system. The proxy agent acts as an intermediary between the management application and the actual device. When requested by the management application, the proxy management agent instructs the device to perform the desired operation using the device's own management protocols. The device then returns the result to the proxy agent which in turn repackages the result into the management protocol and sends it to the management application. For example, if a management application wishes to control a modem attached to host $A$, the application sends a request to the management agent on host $A$. The agent converts the request into an instruction over the modem's control channel, gets the result of the request, and converts that result into a suitable reply to the management application. A similar approach can be used for *bridges*. By designating a *host* on the same network as the bridge, as the *proxy* for the bridge, applications can perform management operations on the bridge, even if the application is on a host several networks away.

How the agent converts the standard management protocol instructions into operations or instructions for the specialized device is left unspecified. The only requirement is that the agent support an object database that includes manageable objects for the devices for which the agent is a proxy.

In practice, proxies have been implemented in several different ways. Some proxies do protocol conversion, converting a request in the standard management protocol into a request in the device-specific protocol used by the special devices. Other proxies simply re-encapsulate the management request in a lower-level protocol. For example, the SNMP protocol can be sent over Ethernet MAC layer frames to bridges that support SNMP (RFC 1089). As a result, an SNMP proxy for a bridge can simply strip off the UDP and IP packet headers and resend the SNMP query unchanged to the bridge. Handling the reply from the bridge is simply a matter of re-encapsulating the Ethernet frame into UDP and IP for delivery to the managing application.

More recently proxy schemes have also been used to *off-load* expensive computation tasks from devices dedicated to key network functions. In particular, the SNMP community has used proxy to cache answers to commonly asked queries and to handle (expensive) authentication. Management stations ask a proxy agent for information about a device; if the proxy agent has a cached answer to the query, it uses the cache, otherwise it asks the device. Similarly, queries requiring significant processing for authentication or access-control checks can be sent to a proxy agent which does the authentication check before passing the query on to the managed agent. These different uses of proxy can be used in combination or individually.

## External Data Formats

One of the key assumptions underlying the MIB or object database approach to network management is that a universal external representation of a managed system exists. In other words, there exists a way to provide a standardized system representation for management.

This assumption actually has two parts. First, it assumes that we can find an abstract representation, in the form of a MIB, for any system. This assumption is examined in more detail in the next section. The other assumption, which we look at here, is that given an abstract representation, there is a concrete way to implement that representation, which all the different systems on the network can understand and exchange. This process is called *externalization* and is achieved through the use of *external data formats*.

An external data format is a standard representation of a data object, a representation that can be understood by any machine. To use an external data format, a sending system must convert its internal representation of the object into external form before sending it to another machine. In turn, a receiving system must convert the data object from the external format it receives into its own internal representation for processing.

In the worst possible case, this representation problem is $n \times m$. All $m$ receivers must know the $n$ different data formats used by the senders. An $n \times m$ approach is obviously prohibitively expensive and thus almost all external data formats use a single canonical form which all systems must convert into and out of.

There are several well-known data formats suitable for this purpose, but both SNMP and CMOT use the Abstract Syntax Notation One (ASN.1), the external data format developed by CCITT and ISO.

ASN.1 is a *tagged* data format. Each data item is transferred as a triple of <type, length, value>. The *type* identifies what type of datum is encoded: integer, character, structure, boolean, etc. The *length* is the length of the value section. The *value* is the actual value itself, in a well-defined bit order. More complex data types are built recursively from simple types (e.g., to create a record, one uses a structure type whose data field contains ASN.1 objects corresponding to the fields in the record). For example, a socket type, in ASN.1, might look like Figure 7.2 where IpAddress is an ASN.1 type to represent a four-octet IP address. This is necessarily a cursory introduction. For more detail on ASN.1 and data encoding in general, see [PART88b].

## 7.3 INTERNET MIB AND SMI

The definition of the managed object base for TCP/IP protocol networks is divided into two parts, a Structure of Management Information (SMI) and a Management Information Base (MIB). OSI defines its object database the same way; this is not a coincidence.

### The SMI

The SMI defines the general framework within which a MIB can be defined. The SMI identifies the data types that can be used in the MIB, how objects within the MIB are named and specified, and guidelines for extending the MIB. The SMI does not define any actual objects in the MIB.

In the TCP/IP protocol community, the SMI is of special importance because it has been designed to ensure that if a MIB is defined according to the SMI guideliness the MIB can be used by both SNMP and CMOT. The community was especially interested in being able to design and write applications that could be used with either SNMP or CMOT, thus easing the eventual transition from SNMP to CMOT.

Defining an SMI that accommodated both protocols proved a real challenge (see [McCL89]). For example, SNMP is designed, for efficiency reasons, to support only a very limited set of data types. As a result, the SMI is limited to four of ASN.1's eight primitive types (INTEGER, OCTET STRING, OBJECT IDENTIFIER, and NULL) and permitted only one constructed type, SEQUENCE, and further stipulates

```
TcpSocket ::= SEQUENCE {
    tcpLocalAddress -- the local IP address
        IpAddress,
    tcpLocalPort -- the local TCP port
        INTEGER (0..65535),
    tcpRemoteAddress -- the remote IP address
        IpAddress,
    tcpRemPort    -- the remote TCP port
        INTEGER (0..65535)
}
```

**Figure 7.2.** Example of ASN.1.

that SEQUENCES may not be nested within SEQUENCES and prohibits constructed octet strings. It required considerable deliberation to determine that those five types were sufficient to build a useful MIB.

The OBJECT IDENTIFIER type is particularly important. It is a structured name and is used by management protocols to name objects in the MIB. An OBJECT IDENTIFIER is a specially encoded sequence of integers which uniquely indentifies a node in a unique naming tree defined by ISO. OBJECT IDENTIFIERS are typically written as a sequence of dot-separated digits. For example, 1.3.6.1.2.1.3 identifies the type for sysUpTime.

In the MIB, OBJECT IDENTIFIERS are used to uniquely indentify object types. An object type defines how a piece of information is abstractly encoded for transmission between managed systems (for example, that a particular field of a route structure is represented as an IP address). In both SNMP and CMOT, the OBJECT IDENTIFIERS are also used to name objects in the MIB (for example, to request that the interface structure be returned). However, the protocols use different mechanisms to identify which instance of an object is to be retrieved (i.e., to determine which interface's *interface structure* is to be returned).

The SMI further defines some application-specific types, built from the five permissible ASN.1 types. The need for some of these is obvious. For example, a standard representation for an IP address was clearly required and an *opaque* type, allowing consenting applications to exchange arbitrary types, is clearly useful. But some of the types have more subtle characteristics.

The *counter* type is perhaps the most interesting. A counter is a 32-bit integer that is always increasing and which rolls over from *0xffffffff* back to 0. Counters are used for counting packets, bytes processed, and the like. Some network managers prefer a mechanism called *latch counters*, which stick at *0xffffffff* until reset. However, the TCP/IP community felt very strongly that latch counters are inconsistent with allowing several applications to monitor a device simultaneously. The logic is as follows: if multiple applications are observing a counter that latches, then one of them must be responsible for resetting it to 0 so that all the managing applications can continue to read useful data from the counter. Unfortunately, if that application fails to detect that the counter has latched and reset it, the other applications will find the counter offers no information (the latched value never changes). If the other applications try to reset the counter themselves, they will reset over each other's resets, causing the count to be mistakenly reset to 0 more than once, thus losing information. *Roll-over counters* do not have this problem, they never need to be reset. The disadvantage of roll-over counters is that after they have rolled over a few times, it is difficult for a managing application to learn if the counter value of 1 means that one packet has been seen or $2^{32}+1$ packets have been seen. The only way a management application can distinguish between the two values is to occasionally check the counter after the agent is started. This continuous checking is a bit of a nuisance, but because the SMI defines a large counter size, it can be done infrequently.

The SMI also defines a *gauge* type which can increase or decrease and which latches *0xffffffff*. Gauges are used to measure levels, such as the current number of packets stored in a queue. As such, the latched value is useful even if it is not reset (it tells you that at some point in time the queue was larger than the system can count) and is not inconsistent with having multiple managers.

Finally, the SMI defines a timer value, called *TimeTicks*, which measures time in hundredths of a second since a given epoch. The epoch is defined on a per object basis. This type is used for timestamps and clock values and is somewhat controversial. Many experts would prefer that the MIB use absolute time values and the standard ASN.1 representations for those absolute times. Unfortunately, most systems running the TCP/IP protocol suite do not support a time synchronization protocol; the only time synchronization protocol is experimental (see RFC 1059). In the absence of synchronized time, relative timestamps are considered more useful (they provide unambiguous timestamps within a system) and with some effort such relative times can be used to construct an accurate sequence of events system-wide by comparing timestamps for known events among different machines.

The SMI also leaves out a couple of important types. One obvious limitation is the restriction on *nesting* structured types within structured types. This prohibition was intended to allow SNMP to interoperate with the MIB. The designers of SNMP felt strongly that nested structures were too expensive to process in a real-time management agent.

Another type that was left out was *thresholds*. Thresholds are values, which if exceeded, cause the agent to send events to one or more management applications. Although both SNMP and CMOT can deliver events, the working group defining the SMI felt strongly that the idea of sending events based on threshold values was, as yet, poorly understood. In particular, the group feared that threshold would cause *event floods*, situations where a managed system's threshold is repeatedly exceeded and the system sends out a continuous stream of events which inundates the network. Such event floods have been observed on several networks, most notably the ARPANET. Event floods have the perverse characteristic that they are generally caused by network congestion and, because the event floods cause more data to be sent, usually make the congestion problem even more severe.

It is possible that additional types will be added, and a relaxation of some of these restrictions could occur in future versions of the SMI, as lessons are learned through implementation experience.

## The MIB

The MIB defines the actual management objects which are operated upon by the management protocol. It also defines what protocol operations may be applied to each object. For example, it defines an object that represents TCP Connections Blocks (TCBs) and decrees that remote applications can read this object, but not change it. (Changing a TCB is forbidden because allowing third parties to change TCP connection states while a connection is in progress can invite disaster.)

The first version of the MIB (which is currently the standard) is intentionally small; only 126 management objects are defined. Most of the objects are required of all systems; a few are required only of gateways.

The MIB was limited in size because the TCP/IP community believed that it was important to get the MIB deployed as soon as possible to deal with the looming network management crisis. A smaller MIB was considered to be less of an imposition on TCP/IP protocol vendors, who had to re-instrument their systems to support the MIB. In retrospect this decision appears to have been correct. Most major manufacturers deployed a MIB within six months of the release of the specification.

Many people are suprised by the notion of a MIB that is required of all systems. They find it difficult to believe that very different implementations can be made to provide a consistent MIB. However, experience with the TCP/IP MIB suggests this is not as difficult as it sounds. A careful reading of the protocol standards makes it clear that all implementations must provide certain types of functionality (routing tables and protocol control blocks are two good examples). It is then possible (although not easy) to define a MIB representation of that common functionality which can be used across all implementations.

In part because of the decision to limit the size of the MIB, the MIB working group set strict guidelines to ensure that the objects included in the standard were, indeed, useful. In particular, the group required that any object in the MIB be shown to be:

1. Essential for either fault or configuration management.
2. Useful in some implementations of the protocol suite (an experimental implementation was considered acceptable).
3. General in its utility. In particular, implementation-specific objects were excluded.

The working group further agreed to limit the MIB's effect on protocol efficiency by avoiding objects which were redundant (e.g., a value that could be derived from another in the MIB) and limiting the number of counters or objects that had to be updated by critical sections of code (for example, the primary path through any layer of the network stack).

The MIB is divided into eight groups: the *System Group*, the *Inter-*

*faces Group*, the *Address Translation Table*, the *IP Group*, the *ICMP Group*, the *TCP Group*, the *UDP Group*, and the *EGP Group*.

The System Group is used to represent information about the system on which the protocol suite is running, in particular, information about the system's manufacturer and software revision, as well as how long the system has been up. At some point in the future this group will probably be expanded to include information about system load level and memory management.

The Interface Group presents generic information about each network interface on the system. A large amount of information is stored about each interface, including the number of inbound and outbound data errors found, the number of broadcast, multicast, and unicast packets sent, the number of packets received and sent, and the maximum transmission unit of the device. In practice, this definition has proved useful but inadequate and there are plans to enchance it so that device specific information (such as Ethernet frame errors and FDDI interval timers) can be represented.

The Address Translation group contains the mappings between IP addresses and subnetwork-specific addresses that all IP systems must support. Examples of such tables include the ARP table on Ethernets and the X.121 mapping table needed on X.25 networks that support IP.

The IP Group stores information about the IP layer. This information is generally much the same as the information kept for interfaces: datagrams received and sent, counts of datagrams with errors, and the like. In addition, the layer contains addressing information as well as control variables that permit remote applications to adjust the default IP Time-To-Live and manipulate the IP routing tables.

The ICMP Group, the TCP Group, and the UDP Group all store information about their particular protocol. This information includes aggregate counts of datagrams received and sent, counts of particular types of messages received, and in the case of TCP, protocol control blocks. One interesting problem with control blocks that the current MIB does not address is what to do with a control block after the connection is closed. Currently, the MIB provides no mechanism for representing inactive control blocks, but this is known to be inadequate. If a user complains to a network manager that his or her connection failed, the information the manager wants most is the old control block for the broken connection because it contains all the state information for the connection at the time it failed.

The EGP Group is required only of these systems (i.e., gateways) which support the Exterior Gateways Protocol, the routing protocol used to link autonomous systems.

The MIB does not include any management information for applications such as TELNET, FTP or SMTP. Management information for applications was left out for a variety of reasons, of which two were paramount. First, requiring vendors to instrument applications for the MIB would have made it substantially more difficult to implement. Most implementations of the TCP/IP protocol suite already collected management information for the transport layer and below and had some mechanism for retrieving management information that could be adapted to support the MIB. The MIB designers knew of no system which instrumented its applications, perhaps because lower-layer protocols are typically part of the operating system and therefore relatively easy to access, whereas applications can have multiple instantiations in processes, which are harder to manage. Second, because the community had no experience with managing applications, the MIB working group felt that defining standard objects for managing applications would clearly violate its "prior experience" rule.

## Case Diagrams

One interesting by-product of the development of the TCP/IP MIB was a method of diagramming MIBs, a method termed *Case diagrams* for Prof. Jeffery D. Case of the University of Tennessee, Knoxville, who developed them.

A key problem in defining a MIB is making sure that all the error conditions will be tracked so that if there is an error, somewhere in the MIB, some object will reflect the fact that the error occurred. Unfortunately, a tedious list of MIB object definitions is an inefficient way to make sure that the errors are recorded. What is really needed is a *flow* or *state diagram*, with each path labeled with the name of the object that records information about that path. Another problem is ensuring that all implementations record the same information at the same place in the processing sequence (if they record information at very different places, the values from two implementations will not be comparable). Case diagrams attempt to solve both problems.

An example Case diagram is shown in Figure 7.3. It illustrates the inbound IP layer of the TCP/IP MIB. There is a main path from the interface layer to the transport layer. An arrow leaving the main path indicates an error condition or flow (in the case of fragmentation) that must be accounted for. Arrows into the main path indicate cases where data is re-injected into the main path and should be counted. The arrows also show the relative positions at which an object is updated, which allows us to keep implementations consistent.

The figure also illustrates one drawback of Case diagrams, as they are currently designed—there is no way to represent global errors or transitions. For example, datagrams may be dropped at any point in the main processing path, not just at the point indicated on the diagram.

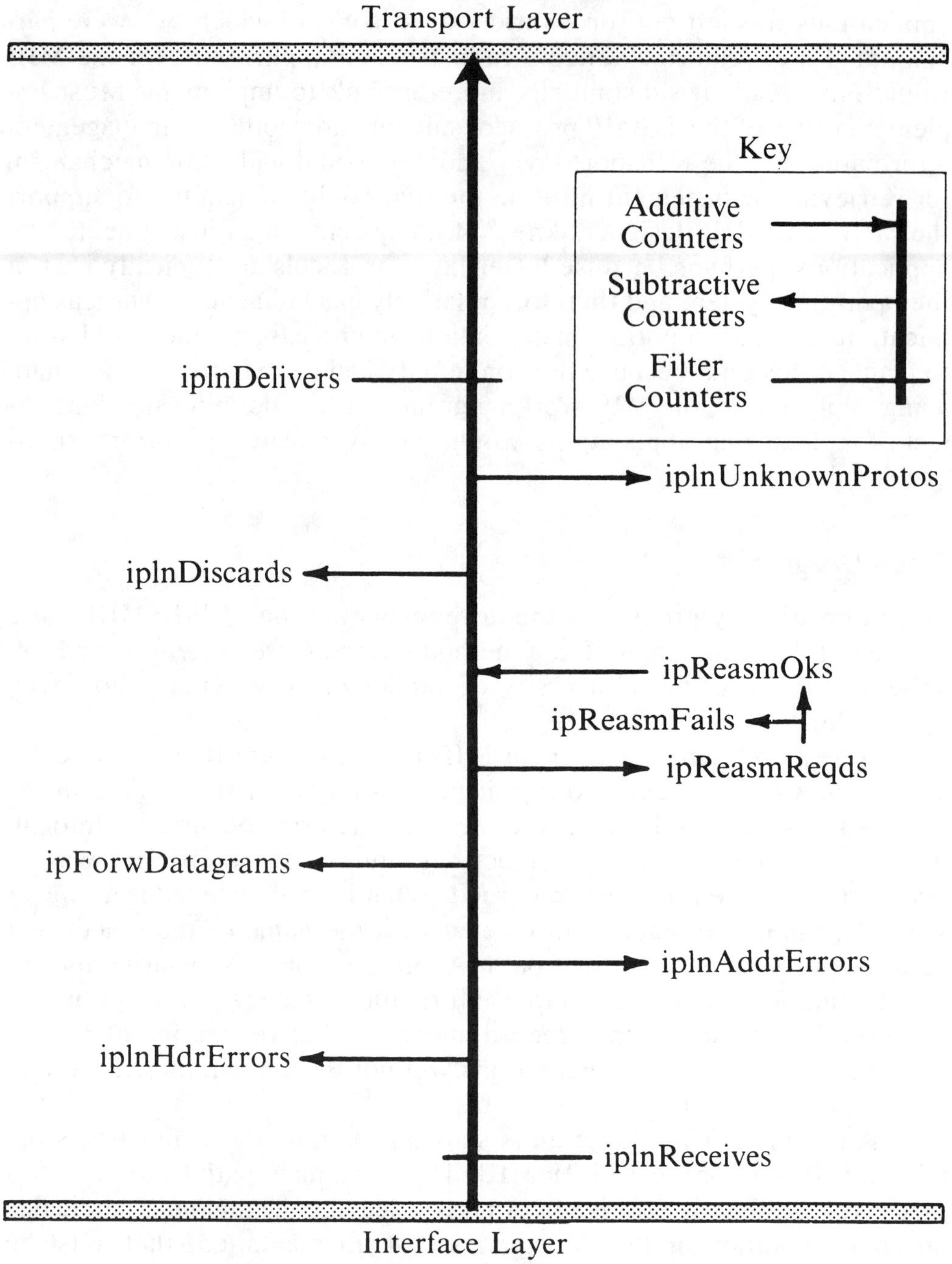

**Figure 7.3.** Case diagram for IP Input.

## 7.4 SNMP

### Philosophy

The Simple Network Management Protocol (SNMP) is specified in RFC-1098. It was designed, as its name implies, to optimize the processing of a few simple operations upon which network management can be built. Initially, the primary motivation for keeping SNMP simple was to allow network management implementations to be implemented quickly to meet the immediate needs of the Internet, but other benefits have also been realized through this approach.

Simplicity allows management implementations in agents to be smaller and more efficient. This allows agents to spend the majority of their (often) limited memory and processing resources on performing their primary functions, rather than on the processing of management requests.

As and when management requires more complexity, the designers' philosophy was to burden the management station, rather than the agents, with implementing that complexity. In this way, any significant management processing needs are performed in management stations for which network management is a primary function.

Another design goal of SNMP was to be robust under adverse network conditions. In fact, in contrast to the goals of non-management protocols, it is more important for network management to work under adverse conditions than under normal conditions, particularly for fault and performance management when diagnosing and rectifying the causes of the adverse conditions. Network management protocols are most valuable and need to work efficiently when a network is performing poorly.

These goals led to SNMP being *transaction-based* and *datagram-oriented*. Being datagram-oriented removes any need for a set-up phase prior to requesting protocol operations, and datagram-oriented SNMP has no "connection" that can fail under adverse conditions. Also, management applications have full control over retransmitting requests; therefore, different applications can employ different strategies. A vitally important request can be retransmitted many times until (hopefully) it eventually succeeds, as opposed to a routine periodic query for which a single failure is of little consequence.

However, because it is datagram-oriented, SNMP requires protocol messages to be sent wholly contained within a single datagram. In practice, this imposes a size restriction on requests. The size restriction follows the general TCP/IP model of limiting datagrams to fit within an 576 byte IP datagram, unless it is somehow known that a larger size can be accomodated.

In SNMP, the asynchronous messages generated by agents and sent to management stations on specific occurrences (e.g., link down) are called *traps*. SNMP defines only a limited number of traps because they are intended to alert a management station to a problem area. It is the responsibility of the management station to intensify its management operations on that or other nearby agents, to diagnose what conditions exist, and to monitor for improvement or deterioration. This philosophy is called *trap-directed polling*.

## Protocol Stack

The standard method of encapsulating SNMP requests for transmission across a TCP/IP-based network is to use the User Datagram Protocol (UDP). An alternative would have been to have SNMP run on top of a transaction-based protocol, but no such standard existed in 1988.

The option of using TCP was rejected on several grounds: TCP is more complicated than UDP; TCP is not datagram-based; TCP requires connection-state information to be maintained if connections are long-lived; and TCP requires more overhead if connections are set-up/torn-down as and when required.

SNMP uses two UDP ports: 161 and 162. Port 161 is the agent's port to which the management station sends requests; port 162 is the port at a management station to which an agent sends traps.

The SNMP protocol is specified using ASN.1; that is, the format of the protocol messages exchanged between protocol entities is described using the ASN.1 specification language, and the data portion of UDP datagrams which carry the protocol messages contains ASN.1 encodings. However, care was taken in specifying the ASN.1 syntax in order to simplify the requirements on the ASN.1 parser needed by an implementation; in particular, there are no context-specific tags.

## Conformance with SMI

SNMP conforms to the requirements placed on a management protocol by the TCP/IP-standard SMI. The variables which can be manipulated by SNMP are those which occur as instances of non-aggregate object types specified according to the rules set out in the SMI. This includes not only versions of the TCP/IP-standard MIB, but also experimental or proprietary extensions to the MIB which can be specified using object identifiers.

SNMP does not allow access to aggregate object types (i.e., access to a whole table); rather, access must be to instances of the individual object types within the aggregate object. Thus, to retrieve a whole table, all elements of that table must be retrieved individually. In effect, SNMP views the MIB as a flat space and provides access only to the individual leaves of the MIB tree.

The SMI also requires that a conformant management protocol provide a means of identifying object instances. SNMP does this by appending an instance identifier at the end of the object identifier. For those object types which do not occur within an aggregate object type, there can be only one instance; SNMP uses an instance identifier of "0" for such objects. For example, the MIB object sysUpTime has the object identifier 1.3.6.1.2.1.3; because there is only one instance of this object, the object identifier used to identify its object instance for SNMP is 1.3.6.1.2.1.3.0.

In contrast, there can be multiple instances of those object types which occur within an aggregate object. For these objects, SNMP defines a sequence of one or more values as the instance identifier. The particular sequence used is dependent upon the object to be identified. For example, the MIB object ifDescr has the object identifier 1.3.6.1.2.2.2.1.2; this object occurs within an entry in the Interfaces Table. There is an instance of this object for each agent's interfaces. The object identifier used to identify the object instance for the first interface is 1.3.6.1.2.2.2.1.2.1.

## Protocol Data Units

All SNMP protocol messages begin with two fields of header information followed by a message-type specific format (see Figure 7.4). The header fields are the protocol version number and the community name. The

```
snmpMessage Message ::=
    {
        version version-1,
        community "public",
        data {
            get-response {
                request-id 42,
                error-status noError,
                error-index 0,
                variable-bindings {
                    {
                        name 1.3.6.1.2.1.1.0,    -- sysDescr
                        value {
                            simple {
                                string "unix",
                            }
                        }
                    }
                    {
                        name 1.3.6.1.2.1.3.0,    -- sysUpTime
                        value {
                            application-wide {
                                ticks 360000,    -- one hour
                            }
                        }
                    }
                }
            }
        }
    }
```

**Figure 7.4.** Example of an SNMP message.

protocol version number is handled exactly as in any other protocol. The community name will be explained later.

SNMP defines five message types: Get-Request, Get-Next-Request, Get-Response, Set-Request, and Trap. There is, by design, some commonality between these types. For example, there is only one "response" type message, even though there are three "request" type messages. This is because the same response message type is used for each of the request types.

The commonality is also evident in the content and format of the different message-type specific formats. In particular, each of them contains a sequence of variable bindings, where each binding consists of the name and value of an object (the name of an object is its object identifier including the appended instance identifier). Note that because SNMP views the MIB as flat, there is no restriction on what combinations of objects may be named in the variable bindings of a single request.

In addition, all but the Trap type contain a request-id, an error-status, and an error-index. The value of request-id in a request serves to distinguish it from other requests in progress. When generating a response, the value of request-id in the response is set equal to the value of request-id in the request; this serves to resolve ambiguity in matching responses with requests when a management station has multiple concurrent requests in progress.

Some of these common fields (the error-status, the error-index, and the value fields in the variable bindings) are redundant in request messages. In these cases, the fields are present but their values are ignored. Their presence provides for greater similarity of syntax between the message types, which allows for more optimal parsing techniques in the agents, and may provide the opportunity for agents to generate responses in situ (i.e., in the same buffer as the incoming request). They also help when composing requests for many objects, by knowing how many objects can be included in the variable bindings of each request without causing the error condition which results from a response being larger than can be sent in a single datagram.

Another commonality is that each of the requests are atomic; that is, the specified operation is to be applied either to all or to none of the objects named in the variable bindings. Therefore, before the operation is put into effect, all error-checking must be performed for all the objects named in the request.

## Lexicographical Ordering

Because of the dynamics of the set of objects in an agent's MIB, a management protocol needs a mechanism by which a management station can search for and retrieve objects without specifying them by name. SNMP provides this through its concept of having a lexicographical ordering of all object instances in the agent's MIB. This ordering is by object identifier (including the appended instance identifiers). By having an ordering, the management station can supply an object identifier and ask for the object instance which occurs next in the ordering.

For example, the first few objects defined in the standard MIB (version 1), for an object with two interfaces, are shown in Table 7.1 listed in their lexicographical order, with their SNMP instance identifiers appended.

Thus, a management station can obtain lexicographically next values as shown in Table 7.2.

Note that because SNMP views the MIB as having no hiearachy, the lexicographical ordering takes no account of the end of tables in the MIB. There is only one object which does not have a lexicographically next object (the object which is lexicographically last in the agent's MIB).

## Message Types

The Get-Request operation names a set of objects and requests that the agent generate a Get-Response containing the values of those objects.

Table 7.1. LEXICOGRAPHICAL ORDERING OF OBJECTS

| Object | Object Identifier |
|---|---|
| sysDescr | 1.3.6.1.2.1.1.0 |
| sysObjectID | 1.3.6.1.2.1.2.0 |
| sysUpTime | 1.3.6.1.2.1.3.0 |
| ifNumber | 1.3.6.1.2.2.1.0 |
| ifIndex.1 | 1.3.6.1.2.2.2.1.1.1 |
| ifIndex.2 | 1.3.6.1.2.2.2.1.1.2 |
| ifDescr.1 | 1.3.6.1.2.2.2.1.2.1 |
| ifDescr.2 | 1.3.6.1.2.2.2.1.2.2 |

Table 7.2. LEXICOGRAPHICAL-NEXT OBJECTS

| Object Identifier | Lexicographical-Next Objects |
|---|---|
| 1.3.6.1.2 | 1.3.6.1.2.1.1.0 |
| 1.3.6.1.2.1.1 | 1.3.6.1.2.1.1.0 |
| 1.3.6.1.2.1.1.0 | 1.3.6.1.2.1.2.0 |
| 1.3.6.1.2.1.1.1 | 1.3.6.1.2.1.2.0 |
| 1.3.6.1.2.1.3 | 1.3.6.1.2.1.3.0 |
| 1.3.6.1.2.1.3.0 | 1.3.6.1.2.2.2.1.1.1 |
| 1.3.6.1.2.2 | 1.3.6.1.2.2.2.1.1.1 |
| 1.3.6.1.2.2.2.1.1.1 | 1.3.6.1.2.2.2.1.1.2 |
| 1.3.6.1.2.2.2.1.1.2 | 1.3.6.1.2.2.2.1.2.1 |

Each object named must exactly match an object instance available in the agent's MIB.

The Get-Next-Request operation also requests that the agent generate a Get-Response containing the values of a set of objects. However, in this case the objects are not specifically named. Instead, for each of the object names in the variable bindings, it is the (name and) value of the lexicographically next object which is returned in the Get-Response.

The Set-Request operation requests that each of the objects named in the variable bindings be set to the values specified. After success (or failure) the agent generates a Get-Response to confirm (or deny) that the new values were set (see Table 7.3). Only some of the objects in the MIB can be set to new values. For objects which are parameters, the purpose of the Set-Request is to give them new values. Action-type objects, which can be set to a particular value to request a specific action, are also possible with SNMP. For example, an object called reBoot could be defined in an agent's MIB, which when set to the value 1, would cause the agent to restart itself.

There are three special circumstances which occur when setting object instances within an aggregate object type. First, SNMP provides no way to differentiate between the creation of a new object instance and the modification of an existing object instance. The typical way this is implemented is that an *agent* assumes a *modify* is requested if the instance already exists, and a *create* otherwise. Second, when creating a new instance (e.g., a new entry in the IP Routing Table), some agents require that values be supplied (in the one Set-Request) for all objects within the new entry; other agents may be able to supply default values for some of the objects. Third, for deletion of an entry in a table, an object instance of any object within an entry can be set to the ASN.1 type NULL.

The final message type is the Trap. It is generated by an agent to send an asynchronous notification to a management station of the occurrence of some significant event. The message includes a number of fields to identify which agent generated the trap and when, and what type of event occurred (see Table 7.4). The ubiquitous variable bindings are also present; in this case, the objects and their values are used to supply additional information about the event. For example, a Link-Down trap re-

**Table 7.3. SNMP ERROR CODES**

| Error-type | Value | Description |
|---|---|---|
| noError | 0 | Success |
| tooBig | 1 | Response too large to fit in single datagram |
| noSuchName | 2 | Requested object unknown/unavailable |
| badValue | 3 | Object can not be set to specified value |
| readOnly | 4 | Object can not be set |
| genErr | 5 | Some other error occurred |

Table 7.4. SNMP TRAP CODES

| Trap-type | Value |
|---|---|
| coldStart | 0 |
| warmStart | 1 |
| linkDown | 2 |
| linkUp | 3 |
| authenticationFailure | 4 |
| egpNeighborLoss | 5 |
| enterpriseSpecific | 6 |

quires that the first object in the variable bindings be the ifIndex object instance identifying the particular interface which went down. However, for the most part, the contents of the variable bindings on traps are agent-specific.

## Community Names

One of the fields in the header of an SNMP message is the community name. SNMP uses the community name for three separate purposes: authentication/privacy, access control, and proxy identification.

In concept, a network management system based upon SNMP consists of overlapping communities. An agent belongs to a set of such communities. Different communities use different authentication and privacy techniques. The agent may provide access for a specific community to only a subset of its MIB, and the agent may belong to a community only in its role as being a proxy agent for some other device(s).

In practice, all that is required is to determine how many different combinations of authentication/privacy, access control, and proxy are required for SNMP access to the agent, and then assign a community name to each. All of these are then configured into the agent, and the appropriate subsets into the management station(s) for which SNMP access to the agent is valid, together with the appropriate parameters. Except for *proxy* (see below), any commonality of community names between different agents is merely coincidental and irrelevant.

Typically, an agent will use the same community name in generating a response as was used in the corresponding request. In addition, the agent needs to be configured with a community name for each management station to which it will send traps.

## Authentication and Privacy

Authentication and privacy is an area for which a complete solution could not be devised within the time frame in which SNMP needed to be deployed. *Hooks* were provided in the protocol for an initial "trivial" scheme and provision was made for the later addition of more sophisticated schemes. This was proved to be adequate while the majority of management is concerned with monitoring. The more sophisticated schemes will be required before network adminstrators are likely to allow a significant amount of control via network management.

To implement authentication and privacy, received SNMP messages are passed to an authentication procedure together with the message's community name, source, and destintation addresses. The authentication procedure's role is to determine if a message is authentic, perform any authentication related transformations on the query, and return the resulting message. Processing would then continue using the message in its revised form. Note that in the event that privacy were in use, the data passed to the authentication procedure would be encrypted, and the data returned would be unencrypted. Another procedure performs the role in reverse during the generation of a SNMP message.

At the time of this writing, the only authentication and privacy mechanism defined is *trivial* authentication. Any community name which indicates trivial authentication has no privacy and is always declared authentic. Thus, any SNMP message with a valid community name is authentic. Effectively, the community name becomes a password (which appears unencrypted in every message).

It is expected that other authentication mechanisms will be defined, possibly including a method based on the Kerberos system [STEI88].

## Access Control

The purpose of access control is to provide different management capabilities to different management stations. The details of defining the number of differentiations and what they allow is an agent-specific implementation matter. The protocol provides the concept that the community name indicates the subset of the MIB to which the request can have access and the type of access allowed. Different types of access are *read-only, read-write, write-only,* and *not-accessible*. Note that write-only can actually be useful in a few situations; for example, storing a password into a MIB variable.

Some fairly sophisticated access control policies are possible using the schemes outlined above. In keeping with SNMP's simple model, it is not appropriate to burden an agent with any such schemes requiring significant processing or memory resources. However, such a capability can be provided by having requests processed through an intermediate proxy agent. In this scenario, the authentication scheme(s) used between the originating entities and the proxy agent would be different from that used between the proxy agent and the real agent. The proxy agent would have the superset of capabilities to individual network operators or interested network users, and would only pass on requests to the agent which passes the sophisticated access control.

## Proxy

The uses for proxy have already been mentioned: protocol translation, offloading of repetitive queries, and offloading of sophisticated authentication and access control. In each of these circumstances, the proxy agent acts as an intermediary between the entity originating a request and the agent whose MIB is being accessed. Typically, such a proxy agent will be acting as an intermediary for many agents and will also have its own MIB. So it needs to be able to determine which MIB a received request is trying to access.

The use of an intermediary proxy agent does not change the originating entity's procedures; it still generates the request using the community name appropriate for the agent whose MIB the request is to access. Therefore, by using different community names for different agents, the proxy agent can use the community name to determine which agent's MIB is being accessed.

## Loss of Protocol Messages

With the standard encapsulation of SNMP messages within UDP datagrams, the underlying protocol stack provides no protection against the loss of SNMP messages. With the request and response type messages, recovery can be handled by the management station because it can detect loss by the lack of response (after some time-out period). For Get-Requests and Get-Next-Requests, the management station can simply retry by re-transmitting the request for some number of times; if none of these succeeds, it can assume that either the agent has gone down or that connectivity to the agent has been lost.

Recovery from no response to a Set-Request is also possible, although a little more tricky, in that the station should probably (depending on what objects are being set) issue a Get-Request to determine if the sets took effect before re-issuing the Set-Request.

In contrast, traps are unreliable; that is, there is no protocol message sent in response to a trap, and there is no way to know if they ever arrived at the management station. This is an important point to realize when planning a network management system based on SNMP. Effectively, traps can be used only as an early warning system; there must be a secondary way to discover that a significant event occurred. One way to do this is to have the management station poll the agent for status at an appropriate frequency.

## Thresholds

Thresholds are really a MIB issue, rather than a protocol issue, and there is provision in SNMP to allow enterprise-specific extensions to the set of traps. A trap could be generated when a Counter increases by more than some threshold value within some time period or a Gauge reaches some threshold value. However, the use of thresholds in agents is contrary to the spirt of SNMP which endeavours to keep the agent's network management role simple. Thresholds are still possible within the SNMP spirit though, if the inspection of values for a threshold exceeded condition is done in the management station. In this case, the additional network traffic will generally be of more concern than the additional load on the agent.

# AN INTEGRATED ARCHITECTURE FOR LAN/WAN MANAGEMENT

Sameh Rabie, Xi-Nam Dam

**Bell-Northern Research**

P.O. BOX 3511, Station C
Ottawa, Ontario, K1Y 4H7
Canada

Telephone: (613) 765-2587

## Abstract

The effective management of LAN/WAN distributed networks poses several challenges: collection and homogenization of management information from diverse network elements, applying local and networkwide intelligence for correlating network events and isolating problems, and the ability of creating a flexible management structure which reflects the growing and changing organizational needs. Furthermore, the management architecture should be expandable for supporting today's increasingly large sized networks, and must not allow the management information to impose an excessive overhead on the network resources.

The paper presents a distributed management architecture which is capable of meeting the above requirements. The architecture consists of three principal components: network elements supporting a standard management protocol, mediation elements which perform local intelligence in addition to protocol conversion and data distribution functions, and management workstations which perform global data analysis and provide operators with an integrated view of the network functioning. The paper also reports on our progress with applying the described architecture to the intelligent and integrated management of large data communication networks.

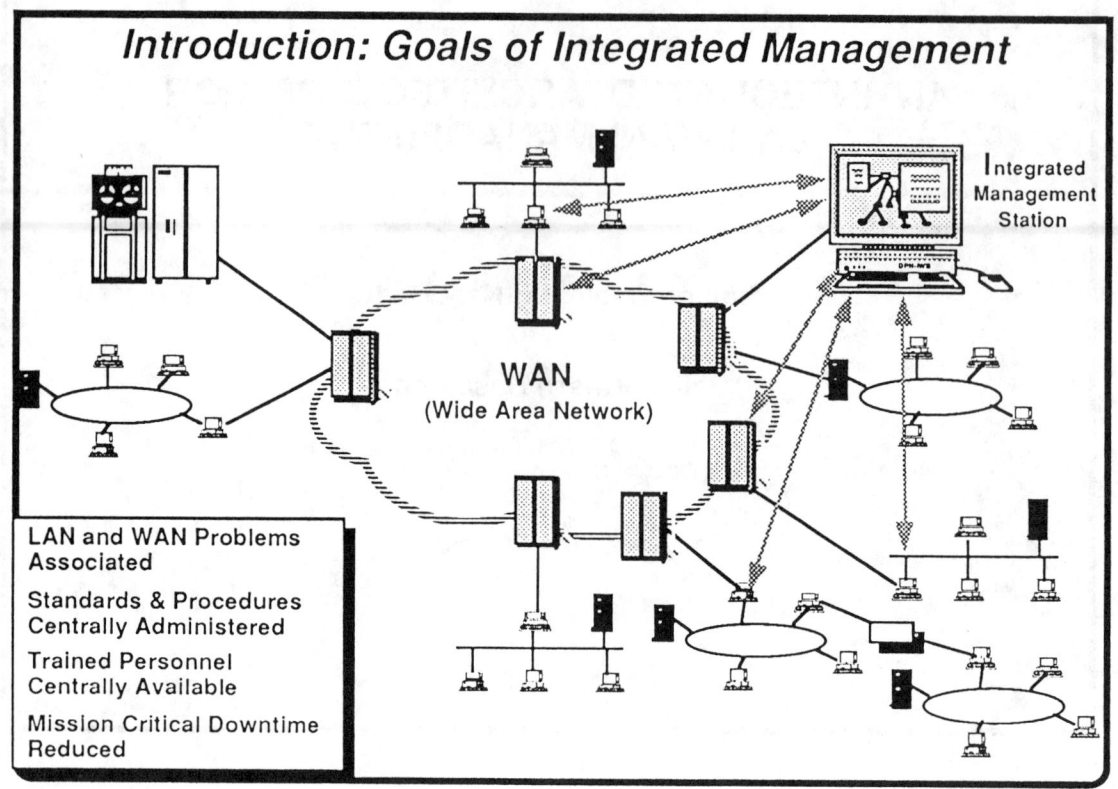

Local area networks are growing in popularity at a rapid rate. Linking corporate computers is becoming an essential element in today's corporate communications environment. Furthermore, organizations are moving beyond isolated islands of Local Area Networks (LANs) into a globally interconnected environment, where the many corporate LANs and attached devices are capable of exchanging information irrespective of geographical boundaries.

With LAN interconnection comes the problem and opportunity of managing the entire LAN/WAN network from some centralized location(s) in an integrated fashion. The goals of integrated management include improved operational efficiency, applying uniform and standard procedures, and improved fault resolution and network performance through the correlation of information from the multiplicity of devices which make up the entire network.

The next section describes the structure and components of our proposed architecture for integrated LAN/WAN management. This is followed by several fault management scenarios which illustrate the advantages of adopting an integrated management approach. Finally, the paper describes our progress with applying the described concepts to evolution of the DPN* (Data Packet Networks) for use in the integrated multivendor network management environment.

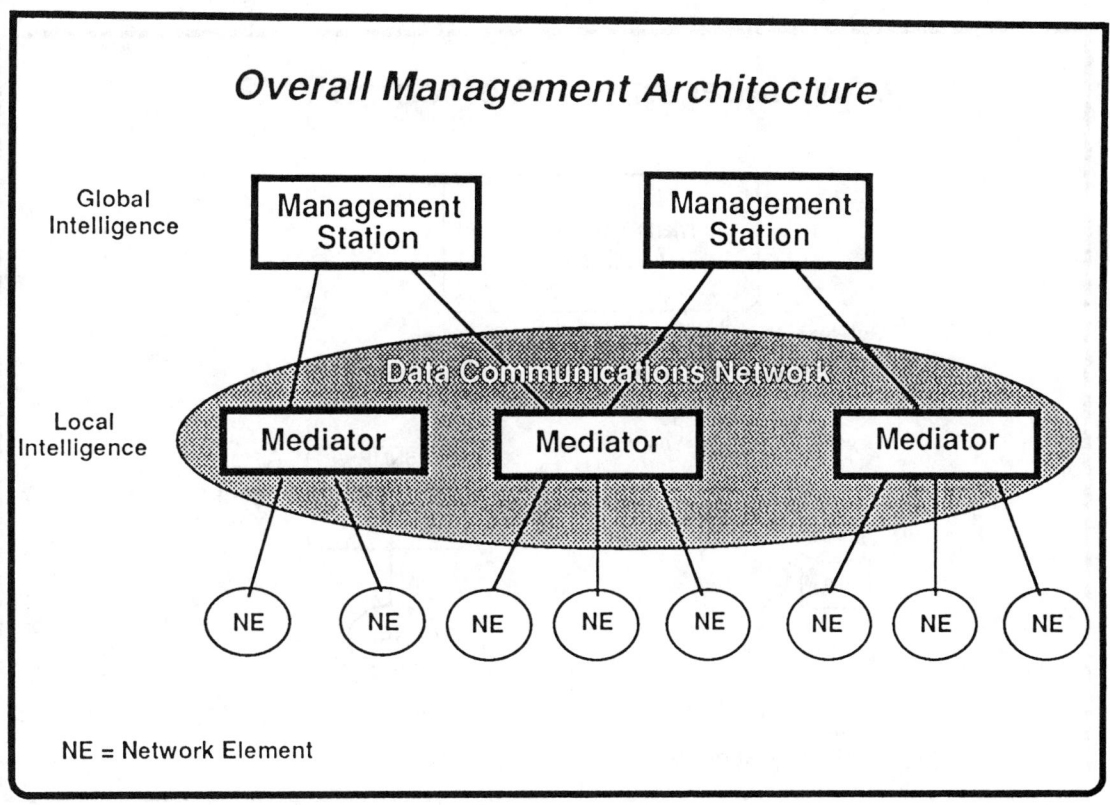

The proposed management architecture consists of three principal components:

- **Network elements** which include LAN and WAN devices such as application servers, bridges, routers, packet switches and multiplexers

- **Mediators** which perform protocol conversion between the (potentially many) network element management protocols and a single uniform WAN management protocol supported by the management station applications. In addition, the mediators perform other important functions such as the filtering and thresholding of information before sending it to the management stations, and the distribution of management information events to multiple management positions.

- **Management stations**, which receive, analyze and present the entire network information to the operators in a concise and clear manner, and also enable the operators to effect remote control of any of the network devices.

The proposed architecture has several advantages over the traditional two tier architecture involving network elements and management stations. The advantages include design modularity through the functional partitioning between local and networkwide management entities, the conservation of network bandwidth through local filtering by the mediators, and the scalability to very large networks because of the use of distributed computing techniques. The following slides describe each element of the architecture in some detail.

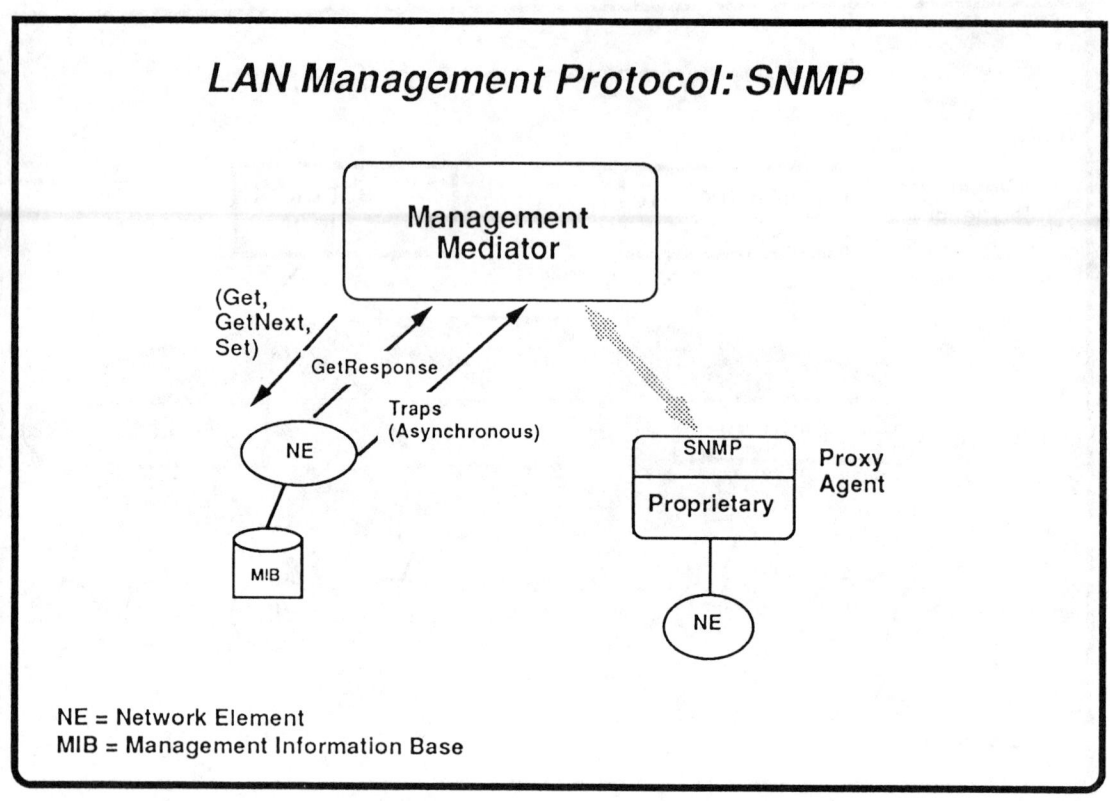

A majority of modern LAN network elements are (or will be) supporting the SNMP (Simple Network Management Protocol) communications protocol [1]. The SNMP runs typically on top of the UDP (User Datagram Protocol/IP Internet Protocol. However, the management protocol is designed to be independent from the transport network protocol mechanism.

The SNMP protocol assumes a Manager to Agent communication using five message types:

- Get and GetNext are used by manager to query a variable in the agent's Management Information Base.
- Set is used by manager to set a variable in the agent's Management Information Base.
- GetResponse is used by the agent to provide the requested information.
- Traps are used by agents to asynchronously inform the manager of significant and critical events (e.g. linkdown, linkup)

Abstract Syntax Notation One (ASN.1) (ISO 8824) is used to describe SNMP protocol data units and managed information base, and the Basic Encoding Rules (ISO 8825) are used to produce the transfer syntax.

Proxy agents can be used to translate proprietary management protocols into SNMP.

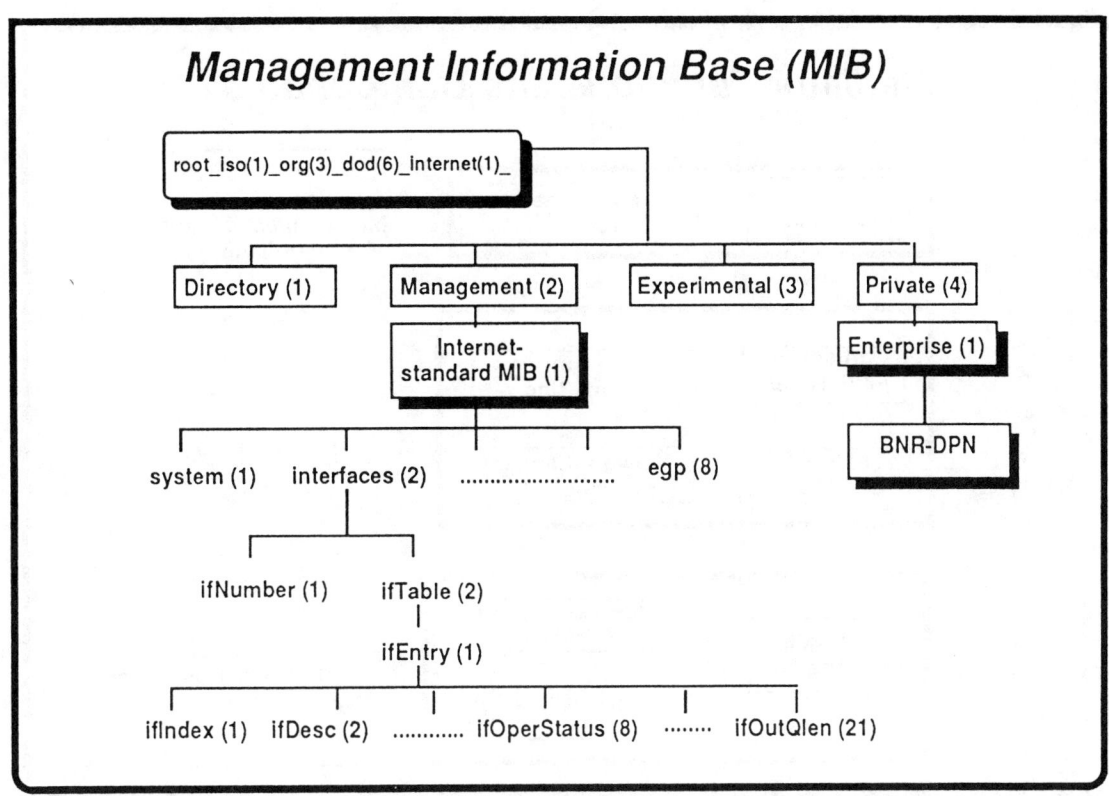

A standard communications mechanism is not by itself sufficient for realizing multivendor integrated network management. The structure and semantics of the management information must also be standardized. For example there must be an agreement on what counters or measurements are taken for a particular service, and how this information can be addressed in the network element.

SNMP addresses these issues in two additional standards:
- the Internet-standard Structure of Management Information (SMI) [2]; and
- the Internet-standard Management Information Base (MIB) [3].

The SMI is organized hierarchically. Each object has a unique name which is derived by appending its own identifier to that of its parent. The hierarchical organization facilitates the design of modular MIBs, since objects belonging to the same functional area can be grouped together under the same parent. The second standard defines the particular core objects for the management of the TCP/IP Internet suite of protocols (111 objects in total which are organized into 8 groups, later extended to 170 objects in MIB-II).

The SMI provides several extensibility mechanisms which allow for the addition of "experimental" and private objects, as well as the definitions of new versions of the Internet-standard MIB. In fact, at the time of writing, there are over 20 experimental MIB modules under development, which provide for standardized management of various services and technologies such as Frame Relay, FDDI, OSI protocols, LAN Hubs, and the Switched Multi-Megabit Data Services (SMDS).

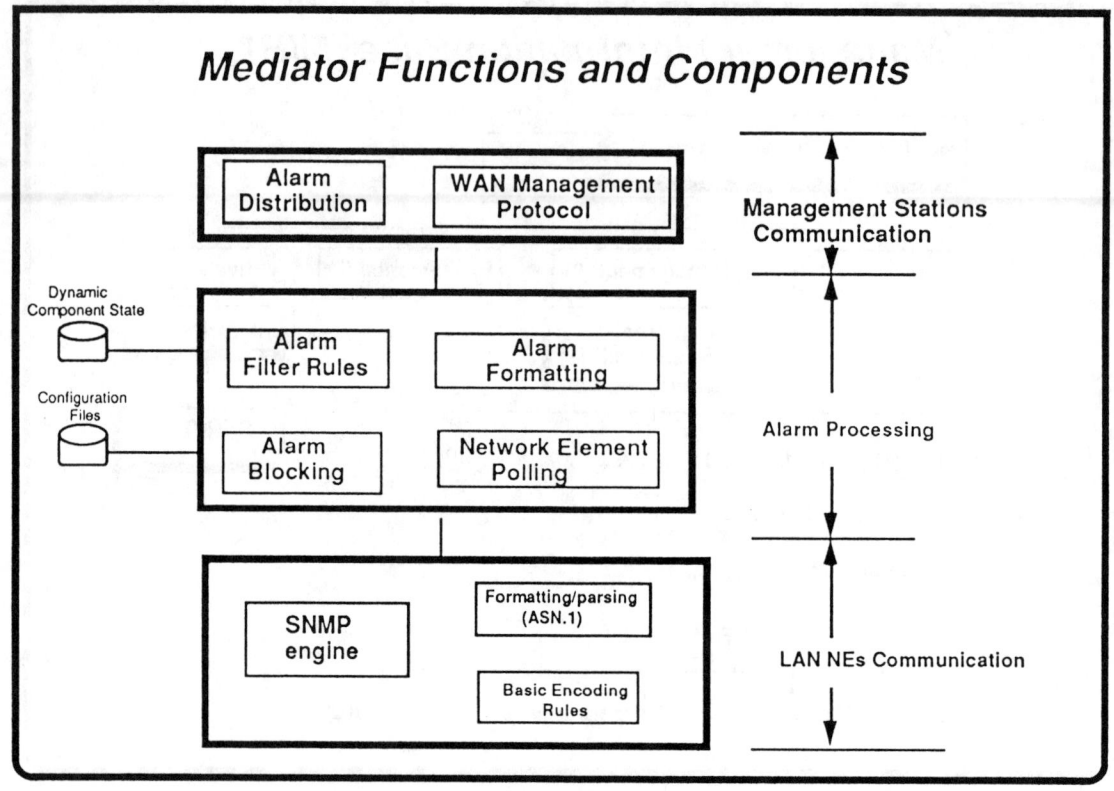

The second component of the architecture, the LAN Mediator, performs an intelligent protocol conversion function between the low level SNMP device data and the high level operations-oriented information suitable for processing and display by the management stations. For example, for fault management function, the mediator periodically polls selected variables in the network elements' MIBs and watches for abnormal behaviors such as an inoperational state or a queue overflow condition. It also receives asynchronous traps from the devices which usually indicate a faulty operational condition.

The mediator software consists of three major components:
- a network element communication module using the SNMP protocol;
- an Alarm Processing module which interrogates the LAN devices and generates alarms according to user-specified rules; and
- a Management station communications module which forwards alarms to and receives control information from concerned managers.

The mediator decision making about when to signal an alarm to the management stations is controlled by a set of user-customized rules. These rules specify the nature and frequency of device polling, and the MIB values and thresholds for raising an alarm. Furthermore, the user is also able to specify the criticality, problem code, and explanatory text which is included in each alarm generated by the mediator. Other mediator configuration information include the list of maintenance-mode devices for which no alarms should be generated, and the MIB variables which are periodically measured for subsequent analysis and display by performance management applications.

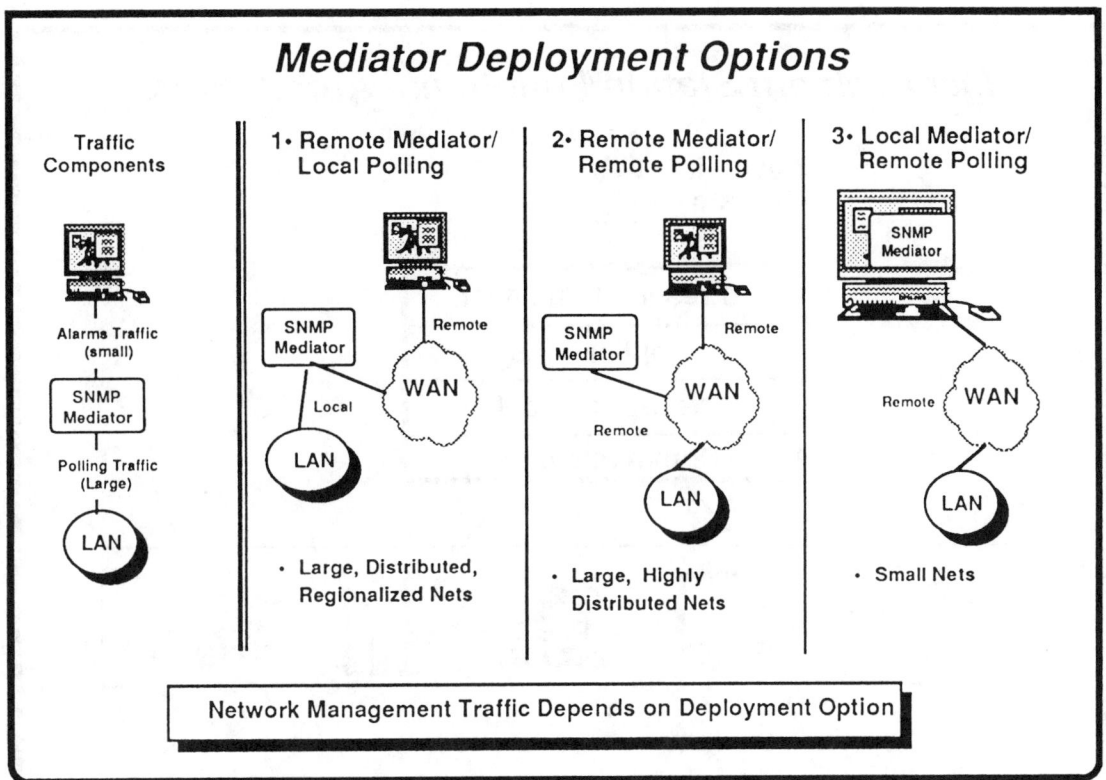

The described architecture provides a large degree of flexibility in selecting the number and locations of the management mediators. This enables making tradeoffs between the amount and nature of network management traffic on the one hand and the cost of the mediators deployment on the other.

The management traffic consists of two major components: the SNMP traffic between the LAN devices and mediator, which tends to be relatively large because of the polling-oriented nature of the SNMP protocol; and the alarm and control traffic between the management stations and the mediator, which tends to be relatively small because this traffic is generated only on an exception or as-needed basis.

The following basic deployment scenarios are typical, depending on the geographic make up and size of the network.

1• Large, regionalized networks. The Mediators will be deployed locally at each campus/region, with each Mediator polling its devices through high speed LAN links. This configuration optimizes facility cost, since only the traffic between the Mediators and management stations will be carried on expensive WAN facilities.

2• Large, highly distributed networks. In this case, the Mediators will be remote from both the management stations and the LAN devices which are being polled.

3• Small networks. The Mediator can co-reside on the same management system(s) platform, with the SNMP polling traffic carried across the WAN.

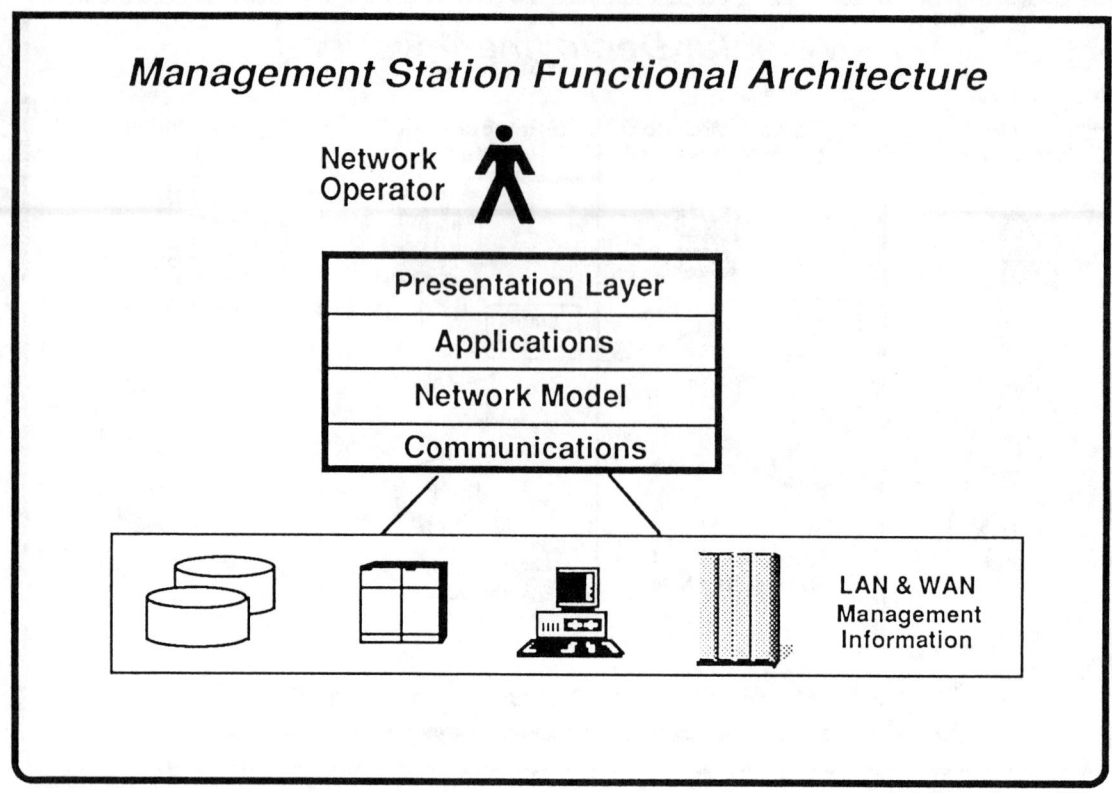

The last key component of the architecture is the management station. The management stations contain the integrated applications and provide the interface to the network operators. We propose a layered architecture for the management stations, which consists of four distinct layers.

The user interface layer is responsible for presentation of information to the operator and obtaining his/her requests in a natural and consistent way. In addition to providing common and reusable facilities to the applications layer below, the user interface layer ensures a common look and feel for the different applications within the network management system.

The application layer contains the different tools that make up the network management system. The tools will draw on the entire networkwide operation and configuration data, and should be able to perform conventional as well as intelligent analysis and correlation functions [4].

The network model layer implements an object-oriented representation of network entities and their relationships [5]. In addition to representing static information, the model objects are updated in real-time with the alarm and status information received from the mediators.

The communications layer is responsible for the protocol function with other management entities such as the LAN mediators and WAN facilities.

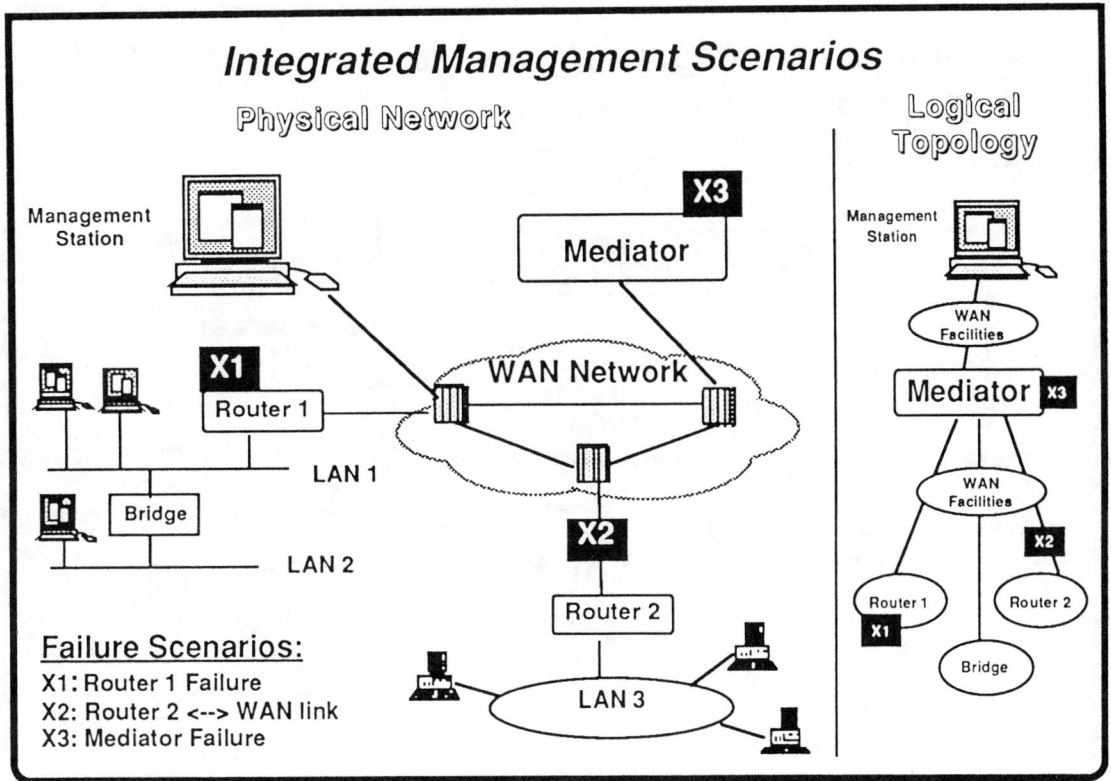

We present here several fault management scenarios which illustrate the advantages of the described integrated management approach. Consider the network shown above, which consists of three LANs and a wide area packet switching network. LAN 1 and LAN 2 are connected through a local bridge, while LAN 1 and LAN 3 are connected through the WAN network using router devices. The management architecture consists of a remote mediator, which communicates with the LANs and the management station through the WAN facilities. Consider the following fault scenarios:

1- Router 1 failure. As a result, the Mediator will loose contact with all the devices in both LAN 1 and LAN 2. Rather than signalling a failure in all the devices, the use of an intelligent alarm analysis application at the management station (supplemented by a graphics display) would explain to the operator that Router 1 is the *cause* of failure, and that the bridge and other LAN 1/2 devices are isolated as a *result* of this failure.

2- Failure in the link between Router 2 and the packet network. Again, the integrated alarms analysis application at the manager should be able to correlate the generated LAN and WAN alarms to point to the failing link.

3- Mediator failure. The management station should flag the cause of failure, and indicate that all the LAN devices are probably functioning alright, although their state cannot be monitored (unless a back up mediator takes over).

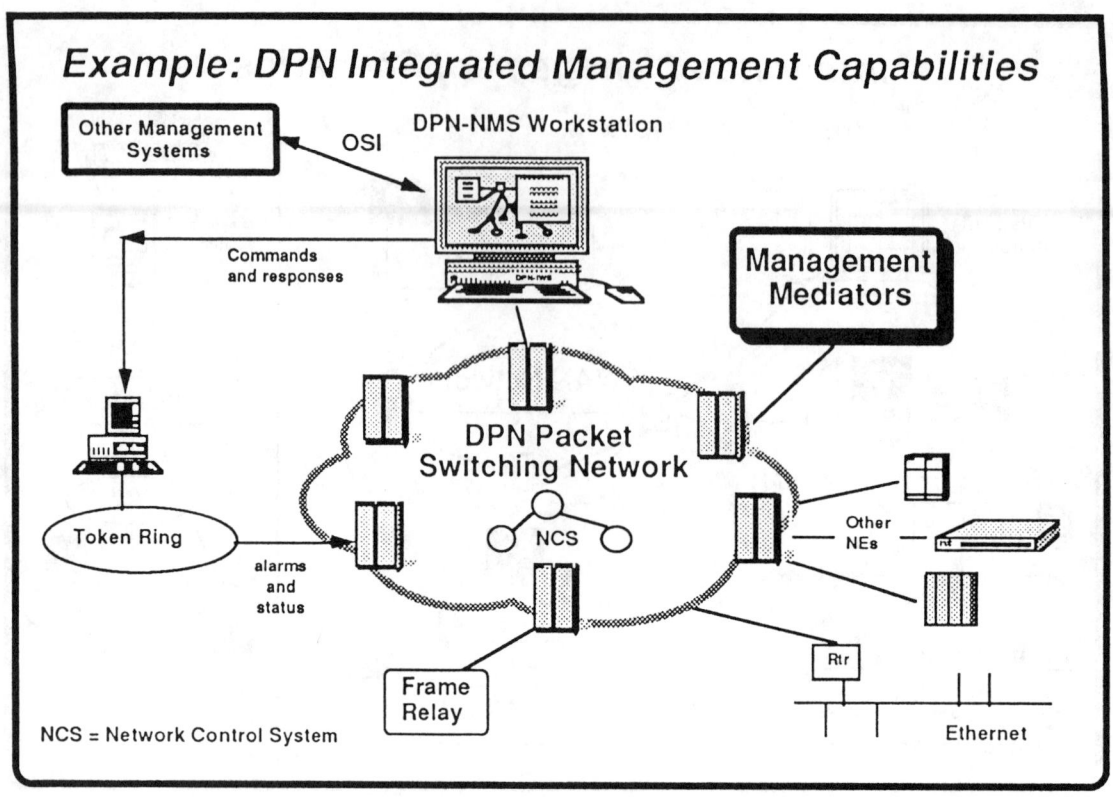

DPN is a well known packet switching system produced by Northern Telecom. The product is already used in more than 100 public and private data networks in over 60 countries [6]. The DPN system supports major international and industry standard protocols such as X.25, X.75, Frame Relay, IBM SNA** and Token Ring LAN interface. The element management capabilities of DPN networks are quite extensive in all five management areas: fault, configuration, performance, security, and accounting management. The management applications run on the DPN-NMS (DPN Network Management System) Workstation, a Unix***-based platform with high-resolution color graphics, multitasking, and an input pointing device [7].

Currently, the DPN management system is being extended for supporting standards-based multivendor management. In particular, the DPN has implemented a LAN/WAN integrated architecture with similar capabilities to those described in the paper: intelligent and distributed mediators, support of the SNMP as well as proprietary device protocols, and providing intelligent and integrated applications at the integrated workstation. Furthermore, the architecture exploits the DPN Network Control System (NCS) capabilities of hierarchical distribution, redundancy and advanced recovery features to provide a very flexible and robust LAN/WAN management system which is equally adaptable to managing networks with sizes varying from a handful to tens of thousands of nodes.

In addition to supporting the SNMP protocol, the DPN is also committed to supporting the OSI standards and Network Management Forum specifications [8], and currently provides a link to other major interoperability industry standards such as the NetView** interface for communicating with the IBM NetView host applications.

## Summary & Conclusions

**The Challenge**
- Large networks
- Multivendor
- Multi-technology
- Geographic distribution
- LAN/WAN dependence
- Mission critical
- Different mgmt systems
- Costly local resources

**Integrated Management**
- Data Consolidation
- Intelligent Applications
- Remote Access

**Benefits**
- Centralized & Regionalized resources
- Faster repair
- Optimized Net performance
- Common user interface
- Uniform procedures

Modern communication networks are growing in complexity because of increased connectivity and diversity of the network elements which make up these networks. Integrated network management can improve the effectiveness of managing these networks in a number of ways, including centralized resources, integrated and intelligent applications, and common operational procedures and user interface.

The paper presented a flexible integrated architecture, which is adaptable for managing LAN/WAN networks of varying sizes and geographical distributions. Key features of the architecture include the distribution of management intelligence between local and networkwide entities, the adoption of open and standard protocols, and the provisioning of extensive user customizability of the various management entities. Our experience with implementing the proposed architecture to the management of corporate communication networks confirm both the soundness of the design and the benefits to the user organizations.

## References:

1. "A Simple Network Management Protocol (SNMP)", Internet RFC 1157, 1990.

2. "Structure and Identification of Management Information for TCP/IP-based Internets", Internet RFC 1155, 1990.

3. "Management Information Base Network Management of TCP/IP-based Internets", Internet RFC 1156, 1990

4. S. Rabie, "Intelligent Tools for Network Management", Proceedings of International Switching Symposium (ISS), 1990.

5. S. Rabie, "Object-Oriented Network Operations for Packet Switching Networks", Proceedings of IEEE Network Operations and Management Symposium, NOMS 1990.

6. D. Jeanes, J. Peleato, M. Unsoy, "Packet Switching for Global Networks", Proceedings of International Conference on Computer Communications, ICCC 1990.

7. B. Shastry, M. Unsoy, G. Wilbur, "DPN-IWS: New Platform for DPN-100 Network Management", Telesis (BNR), vol. 91, December 1990.

8. S. Rabie, P. Ng, X. Dam, "Management of Corporate Communication Networks in the OSI Environment", Proceedings of IEEE Global Communications Conference, Globecom 1991.

\* DPN is a trade mark of Northern Telecom
\*\* SNA and NetView are trade marks of IBM
\*\*\* Unix is a trade mark of AT&T

## SNMP NETWORK MANAGEMENT

By Chris VandenBerg, Advanced Computer Communications

# MIB II Extends SNMP Interoperability

Vendors Are Adding Proprietary Extensions to SNMP's Management Information Base, Compromising the Standard. MIB II Can Change That

Since the first generation of products supporting the simple network management protocol (SNMP) was introduced last year, some 128 vendors have rallied to the cause. In just a short while, this TCP/IP-based standard for managing inter-network routers has gained unrivaled acceptance among both vendors and users.

Now SNMP is being called upon to manage an ever-increasing variety of network devices, ranging from terminal servers and workstations through concentrators and bridges. And there's no end in sight, although it's too early to say whether the exhibitor at this month's Interop Conference and Exhibition who plans to use an SNMP management station to bring up a toaster on the Internet is onto something big (see this month's EOT).

What is clear, however, is that the trend is toward expanding SNMP's scope in bringing network and systems management to customers.

One of the key ways that SNMP can be extended is by adding to its management information base (MIB), the repository of information needed to manage devices on a network. The MIB contains a list of network objects and their attributes, such as the number of packets sent to a network interface, routing table entries, and protocol-specific variables for IP routing.

The MIB originally specified in the SNMP standard, commonly referred to as MIB I, includes a limited list of objects dealing with IP internetworking routing variables. MIB II, currently under consideration as an Internet standard, extends SNMP capabilities to a variety of media types and network devices. SNMP developers are working to add support for T1 transmission equipment, token ring, token bus, and Fiber Distributed Data Interface (FDDI) media, Microsoft LAN Manager networks, Digital Equipment Corp. DECnet Phase V systems, bridges, and terminals. Eventually, the MIB will include objects that manage applications as well as networks. When that happens, users will be able to manage their applications across the network and dynamically reallocate such system resources as processing capacity and storage.

SNMP already provides a way for a vendor to add proprietary extensions to its MIBs, but such extensions can limit interoperability with other vendors' SNMP implementations. One of the goals

**Chris VandenBerg** is the network management product manager for Advanced Computer Communications (Santa Barbara, Calif.). He can be reached through the Internet at chris@salt.acc.com.

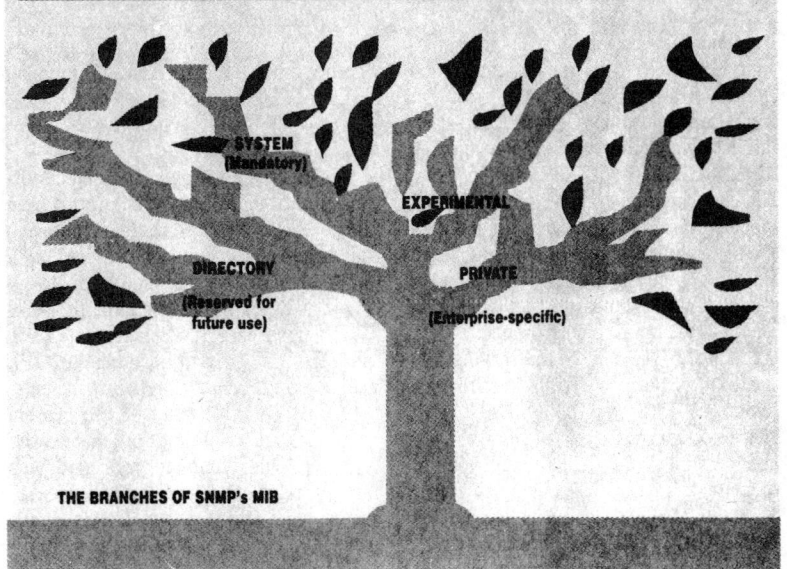

**Figure 1: The SNMP MIB Structure**

The SNMP MIB repository is divided into four branches. The system branch contains MIB I objects and attributes. The private branch contains proprietary vendor-specific variables. The experimental branch contains object variables being tested. The directory branch is reserved for future use.

THE BRANCHES OF SNMP's MIB

## MIB II Expands SNMP

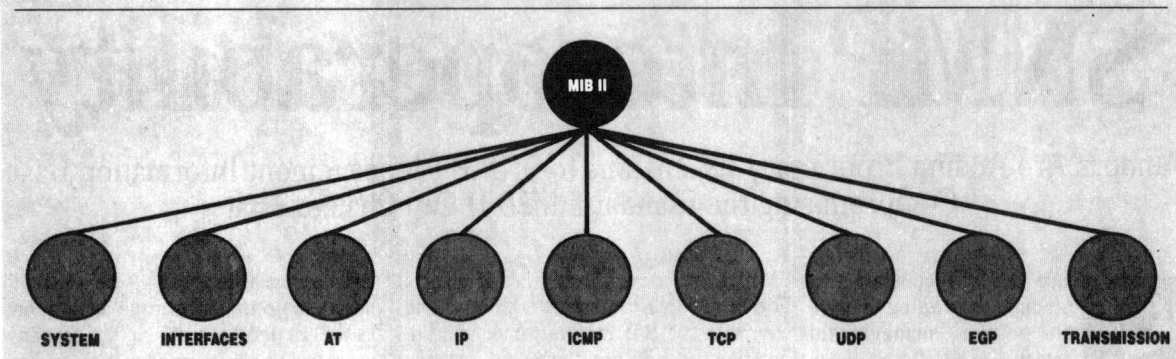

**Figure 2: MIB II Functional Groups**
MIB II includes the MIB I functional groups and two additional categories. These, the SNMP and transmission groups, handle systems administration and network media, respectively.

of MIB II is to ensure that Vendor A's SNMP agent can communicate with Vendor B's SNMP management station. MIB II also seeks to guarantee that all vendors uniformly implement SNMP for a particular class of equipment, such as FDDI cards, by delineating that equipment in the standard. As a result, MIB II should help eliminate incompatibilities and extend the benefits of standards-based management across corporate internetworks. While there will always be a need for vendor-specific additions to SNMP, standardization on key technologies will ease the job of heterogeneous management.

### LOOKING UNDER THE HOOD

The MIB architecture looks something like a tree with four branches (see Figure 1): a directory branch, a system branch, an experimental branch, and a private branch. The system branch contains both MIB I and MIB II object groups. The experimental branch contains media-specific objects. The private branch supports proprietary vendor extensions to the MIB. Once the media-specific objects become SNMP standards, they will be included in the management branch.

The MIB is a virtual store of information contained within a managed device—also known as the SNMP agent. This information base is made up of objects consisting of name, syntax, and encoding information. The name is called the Object Identifier and is unique for each object. Syntax is the means by which a value, such as the number of packets sent, is displayed. Syntax types include counter, gauge, octet string, network address, and integer. MIB II specifies a new type of octet string called a display string, which allows a string of information to be displayed to an operator without requiring the management system to execute the string. The encoding mechanism converts machine code into English, allowing a programmer or network administrator to interpret information that the network management station is collecting. The MIB adheres to the American National Standards Institute's ASN.1 Basic Encoding Rules. The encoding specifies whether an object is designated read-only, read-write, write-only, or not accessible. In addition, status information specifies whether an object is mandatory, optional, obsolete, or decremented.

### MIB EXTENSIBILITY

MIB I includes over 100 objects organized into eight functional groups (see Figure 2): system, interface, address translation (AT), internet protocol (IP), internet control message protocol (ICMP), transmission control protocol (TCP), user datagram protocol (UDP), and exterior gateway protocol (EGP). These groups allow a network management system (NMS) to poll the system group for a description of the device, the object ID specifying the type of device being queried, and how long the device has been up and running. The interface group, for example, contains such information as a text description of the interface, and its type (Ethernet, point-to-point, FDDI), maximum packet size, speed, and operational status. Each group collects protocol parameters, such as the number of active TCP connections, number of packet redirects received, and number of user datagram packets flowing through a device.

MIB II adds new objects to these existing groups. It also incorporates two new object groups: transmission and SNMP. MIB II marks a shift in focus for SNMP from an Ethernet and wide-area orientation toward a much broader focus on all media types used in both LANs and WANs. This reflects current market trends away from isolated LANs to a world of widely linked internets consisting of an assortment of network technologies.

The transmission group was created to move beyond the Ethernet-centric orientation of MIB I by adding support for IEEE 802.2, 802.5, FDDI, and T1 networks. For example, the Internet Engineering Task Force FDDI working group is developing the specification for FDDI to be managed by an SNMP system. The group, which consists of FDDI vendors, users, and academicians, created a preliminary set of FDDI objects that are compatible with the ANSI X3T9.5 Station Management spec, which is the management utility for FDDI devices in LANs. SNMP will extend this management format to WANs and possibly to metropolitan-area networks as well.

The SNMP group contains new object identifiers that provide statistical in-

# SNMP NETWORK MANAGEMENT

## MIB II Expands SNMP

**Figure 3: MIB II's Added Functionality**
New system objects added under MIB II give network administrators text information on location, system contact, and system services in the event of a network failure.

```
                        SYSTEM
     /      /      /      |      \      \      \
SYSDESCR SYSOBJECT ID SYSUPTIME SYSCONTACT SYSNAME SYSLOCATL SYSSERVIC
```

SYSCONTACT = System contact
SYSDESCR = System description
SYSLOCATL = System location
SYSNAME = System name
SYSOBJECTID = System object identification
SYSSERVICE = System service
SYSUPTIME = System uptime

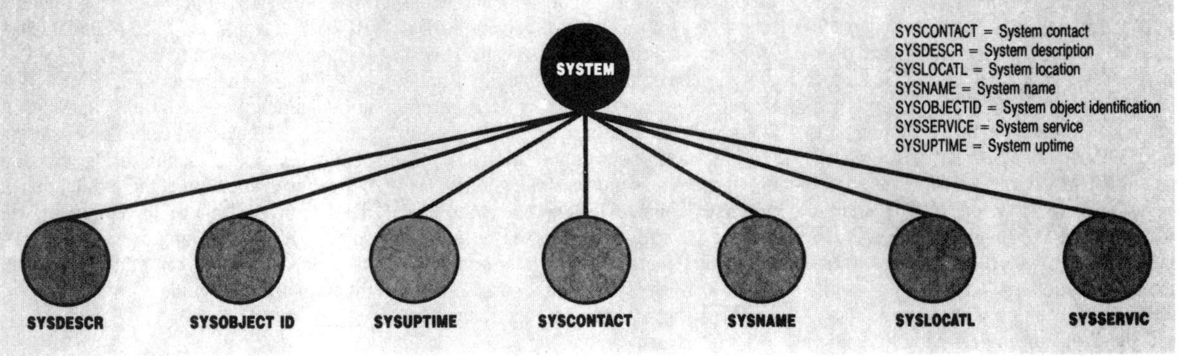

formation about network performance to the network administrator. The objects allow the NMS to track the amount of management traffic being responded to by a device. Parameters such as the number of SNMP packets into and out of a device, number of packets with bad community names, number of packets that didn't conform to the ASN.1 encoding specification, and total number of requests for information are provided by the SNMP group. Having this type of information at hand is becoming increasingly important as the size and complexity of networks increase exponentially.

Under MIB II, the system group added four new objects to provide information, such as the name of a person to contact in the event of a network failure (see Figure 3). The new objects also include the physical location of the system, system name, and services provided by the device in question. This last object offers the ability to query a device supporting MIB II to determine the levels of functionality supported, with values for physical, data link/subnetwork, internet (supports IP), end-to-end connectivity (supports TCP), and applications. This feature resembles the OSI common management information protocol, which provides management information at each of the seven layers of the OSI protocol stack.

Several other object groups were enhanced by the MIB II spec, including the interfaces group, which gained support for six new media/protocol types, including point-to-point protocol, 3-Mbit/s Ethernet, and the serial line internet protocol (SLIP). An additional table entry, ifSpecific, was added to provide the NMS with media-specific information such as that kept in the address translation table.

Other tables that were changed in MIB II were the TCP group and the IP group. Two objects were added to the TCP group, tcpInErrs and tcpOutRsts; these allow the NMS to monitor error packets passed up from the IP layer to TCP and the number of resets generated by a TCP layer. These objects are tools that allow a network administrator to manage the end-to-end connectivity of a network connection, not merely the physical connection.

### VENDOR-SPECIFIC ADDITIONS

While the industry awaits formal standardization of MIB II, vendors continue to implement their own proprietary extensions to SNMP while adhering to the generalized approach necessary in MIB I and MIB II. The enterprise portion of the MIB allows vendors to enhance the management of their devices using SNMP and to share this information with other users and vendors who might need to interoperate with their systems.

A branch within the enterprise group is allocated to each vendor that registers with the Information Sciences Institute (Marina Del Rey, Calif.). The vendor is assigned an enterprise number denoting its location in the enterprise portion of the MIB. This mechanism allows vendors to customize their management applications with product-specific MIB objects. This approach, for example, lets users view how a concentrator is configured, which boards are installed, and how they are operating.

Of course, additions to specific agent MIBs don't benefit users unless their NMSs know about vendor-specific extensions and have the ability to take full advantage of them. Within the SNMP structure, an NMS can get only the information it knows how to ask for. This approach was deemed essential to prevent the network from being clogged with management information that devices were mindlessly broadcasting on LANs or WANs. This "speak only when spoken to" philosophy allows a management station to ask for and receive only the information it requires to perform a specific operation, thus conserving network bandwidth for the task of moving traffic.

Along with this trend toward MIB versatility and extensibility in management agents must come an associated versatility in the management station. NMS users who cannot easily change management software to incorporate MIB extensions may find themselves with a Ferrari that has no engine—nice to look at but useless.

Similarly, an NMS trying to manage a device without understanding and taking advantage of the device's MIB extensions cannot offer the user the full benefits of those extensions. Users may have only partial functionality at best and lack some of the essential tools needed to ade-

## SNMP NETWORK MANAGEMENT

## MIB II Expands SNMP

quately manage their network.

Most vendors are more than willing to supply both SNMP-compliant and readable text versions of their MIB extensions. It should be noted that format is essential here to avoid having to type hundreds of object definitions into an NMS. There are several compilers currently used by vendors to check syntax and overall adherence to the ASN.1 specification. A flexible NMS should offer the ability to read an MIB file from disk (assuming it is in SNMP-compliant format) and compile it into the NMS library of objects. As the new media objects under MIB II begin to emerge from the testing phase, this feature will become more and more essential. As specifications add capabilities to the standard MIB, users will want to be able to add those enhancements without waiting for their NMS vendors to do so.

Users can access the MIB repository at the Information Sciences Institute through the anonymous file transfer protocol, which does not require that the user have an account number and password. This permits the transfer of MIBs for general viewing and for use in adding functionality to an NMS. User demand for management interoperability has resulted in open cooperation among vendors to establish a neutral site to publish MIBs. More and more vendors are realizing that there is no competitive advantage gained by refusing to release their MIB extensions to other vendors.

This attitude of cooperation has benefited users as vendors make good on the promise of open management. In the end, users purchase equipment based not on the management information it offers but on how it performs. Of course, users want assurances that the equipment they buy will be manageable.

Vendors soon will begin offering MIB utilities that let users take a more active role in determining which device capabilities are beneficial in their environments. Instead of waiting for a vendor to grind out a new software release, users will be free to set their own pace for adding functionality. The day is not far off when a new piece of equipment will come with a floppy disk containing the vendor's MIB extension. Being able to read the file off the floppy and add to an MIB database brings more control to the user.

The second-generation NMSs that are beginning to appear on the market offer some of these features. The evolution of this technology should bring with it a better understanding of the capabilities of SNMP. And with this development will come a corresponding increase in the benefits that SNMP can offer the user in the network management arena. ■

**REQUEST FOR COMMENT**
If you would like to see more articles on this subject please circle **402** on the Reader Service Card.

# SNMP Security

by

Keith McCloghrie, James R. Davin and James M. Galvin

**Background**

The *Simple Network Management Protocol* (SNMP) [2] was an outgrowth of SGMP, the Simple Gateway Monitoring Protocol [1]. SGMP was a grass roots effort to define a network management protocol to meet the need to monitor IP gateways, a need which in 1987 had become critical for maintaining the Internet. Because of the immediate need, the SGMP was designed with the minimum set of features required. Among the features not considered immediately required were the ability to control gateways and security. Without full support in the SGMP for the control of gateways, the lack of security was considered acceptable. However, a hook was included to enable the later addition of authentication.

Both because of the SGMP's ability to fulfill the narrow focus of its goals, and because of the lack of an alternative, SGMP was successful. So successful in fact, that the recommendation of the first *ad hoc* committee meeting to set direction for network management protocols in the Internet [3], was that SNMP, as a successor to SGMP, should be the "short-term" standard. The subsequent definition of SNMP included support for controlling as well as monitoring any/all network devices, not only IP gateways. However, security still gained no more than another hook for its later addition. This hook used a "community" field to identify the administrative relationship between the sender and the receiver, including the authentication algorithm being used. For the time being, only the "trivial" authentication algorithm was defined, in which any community name known to the receiver was automatically authentic. [Note that because the community field identifies, among other things, an algorithm, it is more than just a "password."]

Subsequently, several members of the SNMP community began thinking about how to define additional authentication algorithms to provide a reasonable level of security protection. With the growth of SNMP such that it has now become the *de facto* standard for management of not just TCP/IP networks, but increasingly of other networking regimes also, the lack for security is fast becoming a problem. At last (two years later), the effort to define additional algorithms has now resulted in the publication of Internet Draft documents [7, 8, 9], ready for trial implementations. The length of time it has taken is an indication of how hard security can be, especially for network management which has the need to continue operating under adverse network conditions.

**The threats**

As in all security work, the threats that may be encountered must be identified. For SNMP Security, the identified threats are:

- *Modification of Information:* The threat that an in-transit message from an authorized source may be modified. For example, a *Set-Request* to further tighten the filtering in a bridge could be modified to specify no filtering.

- *Masquerade:* The threat that management operations not authorized for some source may be attempted by that source by assuming the identity of another source that has the appropriate authorizations. For example, any network user pretending to be the NOC's management station.

- *Message Stream Modification:* The threat that messages may be re-ordered, delayed or replayed to cause unauthorized management operations to be performed. For example, capturing an authorized request to reboot a router, for replay at a later date.

- *Disclosure:* The threat of eavesdropping on the exchanges between managed agents and a management station. Protection against this threat is mandatory when SNMP is used to administer private parameters on which its security is based. It would also be appropriate when setting passwords in, say, a terminal server.

**Goals and constraints**

To protect against these threats, SNMP Security must provide: message integrity, data origin authentication, replay protection, and privacy.

In addition, the design was influenced by the following constraints:

- When requirements of effective management in times of network stress are inconsistent with those of security, the former are preferred.

- Neither SNMP nor its underlying security mechanisms should depend upon the ready availability of other network services (e.g., *Network Time Protocol* (NTP) or secret/key management protocols).

- A security mechanism should entail no changes to the basic SNMP network management philosophy.

**Mechanisms**

Three basic mechanisms are used to meet the goals: use of the *MD4* message digest algorithm, use of the DES cryptographic algorithm, and use of loosely synchronized clocks.

The MD4 [4] message digest algorithm is used to support message integrity. The MD4 calculation is performed on the concatenation of a secret value and a portion of an SNMP message, and the resultant 128-bit digest is included as part of the message sent to the recipient. Thus, a modified message is only valid if the digest it contains is correspondingly modified, but the correct digest cannot be calculated without knowing the secret (which, of course, is not transmitted as part of the message).

Data origin authentication is provided by the same MD4 digest calculation, since if only the originator of the message and its intended recipient know the secret value used in the calculation, and if the recipient did not send it, then it must have been generated by the originator.

Replay protection is provided by including in each message a timestamp value indicating the time of the message's generation according to the clock maintained by the originator. The recipient uses the timestamp to determine both that the message is recent, and that it was generated subsequently to all previous messages received.

The *Data Encryption Standard* (DES) [5] in the Cipher Block Chaining mode of operation [6] is used to provide privacy. An appropriate portion of the message is encrypted prior to being transmitted to its recipient.

**Problems of integrating the mechanisms**

Identifying these basic mechanisms was the easy part of the task. What turned out to be much harder was resolving the issues of how to make them usable by SNMP implementations.

# SNMP Security

First, consider that data origin authentication and message integrity are based on the *source* of the message, but encryption is based on the *destination* of the message. Access control needs to be based on which source is trying to access what target, and the target is based on the destination. Thus, there is a need to differentiate between source and destination, a need which the existing "community" field does not provide. Second, how are the loosely synchronized clocks maintained, especially if they cannot be based on NTP? Third, how are the secrets distributed and maintained?

**Introducing the SNMP Party**

After much consideration, it was decided that SNMP's Administrative Framework needed to be refined to be able to distinguish between source and destination. This has been done with the introduction of the concept of an SNMP "Party." An SNMP party is defined as an execution context of a SNMP protocol implementation. Whenever a SNMP protocol implementation processes a message, it does so by acting in the role of one of the SNMP parties defined for it. Each SNMP party executes at a specific transport address, and has specific authentication parameters, privacy parameters, proxy information, and a MIB view. The authentication parameters include an algorithm, a secret, and the state information needed to maintain its clock and ensure proper message ordering. The privacy parameters include an algorithm and a secret. The proxy information either indicates no-proxy, or "points" to another SNMP party where the real-agent executes. The MIB view specifies the subset of an agent's MIB that the party can access.

By including an algorithm in both the authentication and privacy parameters, multiple parties with different capabilities can be defined for execution at a single SNMP protocol entity. One party can use no-authentication and no-privacy; another can use MD4-authentication and no-privacy; and another can use MD4-authentication and DES-privacy. However, for security reasons, the use of privacy requires the use of authentication.

In this model a SNMP message is originated by one party and destined for another party. The message is authenticated according to the authentication information of the source party. The message is encrypted (or not) according to the privacy information of the destination party. Access control specifies that a specific source party is allowed to originate a particular set of SNMP operations (e.g., *Get-Request* and *Set-Request,* or just *Get-Request*) to a specific destination party. In practice, each SNMP protocol implementation needs to keep a local database of party information, both for parties that execute locally and for remote parties with which local parties communicate.

While this model requires the format of a SNMP message to change in order that both the destination and source parties and the appropriate authentication information (e.g., the digest and the timestamp) can be sent with the message, it does not (fortunately) entail any change to the SNMP PDU. In fact, an agent implementation which followed the guidelines in the original SNMP protocol specification, should be able to implement the new message format with little more than changes to the authentication service function.

**Maintaining clocks**

Each SNMP party has a (relative) clock. In order to be authentic, a message received by the party must have a timestamp which, when added to an administratively defined "lifetime," is greater or equal to the value of the clock at the time of receipt.

Thus, in order to communicate with a remote party, a SNMP protocol entity must retain in its local database a clock value which is (loosely) synchronized with the remote value. Since clocks tend to drift, it is necessary for the clocks to be inspected periodically, and re-synchronized if necessary. This chore is delegated to the management station. However, a few features are included in the protocol to enhance the synchronization through the regular exchange of messages, and the party clocks are purposely positioned in the MIB to support easy read access to them through unauthenticated and authenticated *Get-Requests*, so that a manager does not need to maintain synchronization with all its agents all of the time, but can let some lapse, and later re-synchronize when necessary.

The lifetime value must be carefully chosen. It must be large enough to accommodate variations in communications delay as well as to accommodate a small amount of drift. On the other hand, it is the lifetime value which provides the window in time during which a message is valid, and so lifetimes must be kept within the bounds which an administration wants protection against replay attacks (e.g., a few minutes).

The constraint that network management must continue to operate even under conditions of network stress, even if this impacts the level of security, was mentioned above. One way this can be achieved, is by a manager artificially advancing its notion of the party clock in an agent, so that even though communication delays may have increased dramatically, a message will still be considered authentic when it arrives at an agent.

**Distributing secrets**

The use of both the MD4 authentication and the DES privacy algorithms rely on secrets, which are shared by the originator and the recipient. If these algorithms are to maintain their level of security, their secrets must remain secret and not be available to would-be attackers. Thus, they cannot be transmitted over the network, except in an encrypted form. So, once the two SNMP protocol entities share a secret used for encryption, that secret can be used to encrypt new (changed) secret values for that or any other party. Such changing of secrets on a regular basis is very desirable from a security standpoint.

However, the initial distribution of secrets cannot be done over the network. Instead, it must be done manually as a piece of initial configuration information entered into the manager and the agent, before secure communication is possible. Subsequent distribution of secrets can be done via SNMP access to appropriately secured MIB objects, unless one or both entities loses its knowledge of the secret (or if it is known that the secret has been comprised).

**Identifying SNMP Parties**

Since each SNMP party is unique to the particular SNMP protocol implementation where it executes, many parties need to be defined. A convenient way to do this is to identify them by *Object Identifiers* (OIDs), of which there is an infinite supply! This allows each network administration to obtain its own branch in the OID tree, and allocate OIDs for its agents from there.

However, to simplify matters, a set of six "initial" OIDs have been assigned for use with each IP address, three for local execution at an agent, and three for the agent to communicate with. The three have different settings of authentication and privacy algorithms, with an appropriate MIB view and access control parameters defined for each. The extension of these six to the number actually required in an agent can, of course, be done through the use of SNMP requests acting on appropriate MIB objects.

# SNMP Security

**Summary**  Security of management operations is a feature which has been overdue for inclusion in SNMP. Due to the operational necessity, use of SNMP for monitoring has flourished even without security. However, some vendors and network administrators have been slow to use SNMP for controlling their devices until security is in place. Now that specifications of the SNMP Security Protocol outlined above are available for experimental implementations, we will be able to determine how practical these specifications are, and (hopefully) can look forward to secure network management becoming a reality in the not-too-distant future.

**References**

[1] J. R. Davin, J. D. Case, M. S. Fedor, & M. L. Schoffstall, "A Simple Gateway Monitoring Protocol," RFC 1028, November 1987.

[2] J. D. Case, M. S. Fedor, M. L. Schoffstall, & J. R. Davin, "Simple Network Management Protocol," RFC 1157, May 1990.

[3] V. Cerf, "IAB Recommendations for the Development of Internet Network Management Standards," RFC 1052, April 1988.

[4] Ronald L. Rivest, "The MD4 message digest algorithm," RFC 1186, October 1990.

[5] FIPS Publication 46–1, "Data Encryption Standard," National Institute of Standards and Technology (NIST), US Department of Commerce, January 1977.

[6] FIPS Publication 81, "DES Modes of Operation," NIST, Dec. 1980.

[7] J. R. Davin, K. McCloghrie, J. M. Galvin, "SNMP Administrative Model," RFC in preparation.

[8] J. M. Galvin, K. McCloghrie, J. R. Davin, "SNMP Security Protocol," RFC in preparation.

[9] K. McCloghrie, J. R. Davin, J. M. Galvin, "Experimental Definitions of Managed Objects for Administration of SNMP Parties," RFC in preparation.

**KEITH McCLOGHRIE** is an Associate Director of Engineering at Hughes LAN Systems, Inc. where he is responsible for the development of network management products. He is a member of the IETF's Network Management Directorate and has been an active member of the SNMP working group since its inception, involved in the development of many MIB specifications. He is a member of the IFIP Working Group 6.6 on network management, involved in the organization of the International Symposiums on Integrated Network Management. He gained his B.Sc. in Mathematics from Manchester University in England.

**JAMES R. DAVIN** currently works in the Advanced Network Architecture group at the M.I.T. Laboratory for Computer Science where his recent interests center on protocol architecture and congestion control. He serves on the steering group of the IETF where he contributes to the evolution of standards for network management. In the past, he has been engaged in router development at Proteon, Inc., where much of his work focused on network management. He has also worked at Data General's Research Triangle Park facility on a variety of communications protocols. He holds the B.A. from Haverford College and masters degrees in Computer Science and English from Duke University.

**JAMES M. GALVIN** is a Senior COMSEC Scientist at Trusted Information Systems, Inc, in Glenwood, Maryland. Dr. Galvin's responsibilities emphasize communications security, especially computer networks, architectures, policies, and procedures. He is a principal in the development of TIS' soon to be openly available implementation of Privacy Enhanced Mail. He is very active in the IETF Security Area Advisory Group and Chair of the OSI Implementor's Workshop Security Special Interest Group, hosted quarterly by the NIST. He received his Ph.D. and M.S. degrees, both in Computer Science, from the University of Delaware in 1988 and 1986, respectively. In 1982, he received is B.S. in Computer Science and Mathematics from Moravian College in Bethlehem, PA.

## NETWORK MANAGEMENT

# Coming Soon to a Network

**B**atman Returns, Alien 3, Star Trek VI: Sequels are a sure sign of success in Hollywood. Now one of the networking industry's hottest properties is getting a sequel of its own: SNMP 2, the first revision of the hugely popular multivendor management protocol, is slated for release early next year.

The upgrade, which comes just four years after the introduction of SNMP, is the handiwork of Internet Engineering Task Force (IETF) members Jeffrey D. Case, Keith McCloghrie, Marshall T. Rose, and Steven Waldbusser.

An IETF working group is evaluating their proposal, which the authors call the simple management protocol (SMP).

But don't expect to see that name in lights: According to Bob Stewart, chairman of the SNMP Version 2 working group and network architect at Xyplex Inc. (Boxborough, Mass.), the final cut will go by the title SNMP 2.

That choice of names is meant to indicate the close connection between the revision and the original management protocol. Still, until the IETF approves the spec (slated for early 1993), SMP is the simplest—and most accurate—designation.

Given SNMP's enormous success, the upgrade might look like a case of "if it ain't broke, don't fix it." Today, roughly 25 percent of all network management systems worldwide use the protocol, and SNMP vendors are growing at up to 75 percent annually. Even more impressive, the number of network devices that can be overseen by SNMP has increased by two orders of magnitude in the past two years or so.

But critics have never shied away from pointing out inherent limitations in the SNMP framework. For instance, while the protocol's connectionless transport and small set of simple commands allow it to be put on devices with limited memory, like bridges and routers, they also generate an excessive number of packets on most networks, slowing response time. The larger the network, the more packets generated and the more bandwidth consumed.

Reprinted from November 1992 *Data Communications Magazine*, pp. 66-76. Copyright © 1992 McGraw-Hill, Inc. All rights reserved.

By Mary Jander, Data Communications

# Near You

SMP, in contrast, delivers an array of messaging options that enable agents to communicate more efficiently with management stations. Further, SMP's bulk retrieval mechanism lets management stations obtain reports from agents about a range of variables without issuing repeated requests. These features alone should dramatically improve the performance of SMP systems by reducing the number of packets in messages.

One of SMP's most significant contributions is manager-to-manager communications, which allows a station to act as either manager or agent. This allows SNMP systems to offer hierarchical management—a significant first—including midlevel managers that offload tasks from the central management station.

SMP also ends its forerunner's reliance on TCP/IP. The upgrade runs over Appletalk, Internet Packet Exchange (IPX), and OSI protocol stacks, clearly a boon in this age of multiprotocol corporate backbones. It also should help boost SNMP's popularity overseas, where OSI is on the rise.

## A SECURITY BLANKET

For many users and vendors, though, SMP's chief attribute is the way it addresses the long-standing problem of SNMP security—or rather, lack of security. This may well be the original protocol's primary flaw, limiting applications to simple monitoring and fault detection instead of the configuration and task automation SNMP is truly capable of.

The security shortfall also has kept SNMP out of certain networks. Most carriers, for example, refuse to offer SNMP for their network services.

The IETF already addressed this issue with Secure SNMP, a set of specifications approved in March 1992 that adds user validation, message protection, and data encoding to SNMP systems (see "Securing the Message"). But Secure SNMP's repetitive messaging structure consumes even more bandwidth than SNMP alone, clearly a problem.

SMP modifies Secure SNMP, making it far more efficient. Tests conducted by SMP's authors indicate that their proposed protocol processes significantly more variables per second than SNMP (see Figure 1). And when Secure SNMP's authentication and DES encryption are added, SMP still outperforms its forerunner, even though security features slow the performance of both.

At this point, the IETF is evaluating the changes to Secure SNMP suggested by SMP's authors. But the IETF task force has opted to keep its evaluations of SMP and Secure SNMP separate, although every effort will be made to finish them at the same time to hold to a minimum any disruptions to SNMP's installed base.

## NO PAIN, NO GAIN?

SMP's authors envision a smooth transition to the new spec (see "SMP—Straight From the Source"). First, they say, management systems will change, then agents. When SMP has been universally implemented, SNMP can be eliminated.

Others are skeptical. "Even though SMP will be widely accepted, all of this won't synchronize early on as easily as the SMP proponents say it will," says Asheem Chandna, senior product manager at Synoptics Communications Inc. (Santa Clara, Calif.). "No technical document can answer the question of how users are going to implement SMP or support the migration from SNMP to SMP or the coexistence of the two protocols."

Some of those questions can be answered now, at least in theory. New software will be needed that lets SNMP stations manage devices equipped with both SNMP and SMP agents. And network devices once managed with SNMP will need to be outfitted with SMP agents if they are to take full advantage of the upgrade.

A few device vendors will be able to install bilingual agents on new products that have the memory to handle the extra SMP software—though this approach isn't likely. Many vendors will wind up offering two versions of the same product, one with SMP, the other with SNMP.

As Chandna cautions, "the year 1993 will be confusing. But in 1994, we'll start to see SMP pay off." And William J. Yeager, computer systems specialist at the Knowledge Systems Laboratory at Stanford University (Stanford, Calif.), notes: "SMP and its suggested improvements are good tools, but they are only tools. It's software, not management protocols, that stands to provide really significant wins for users."

The first SMP upgrades should begin to reach the market late in 1993 (some vendors are readying prototypes for coming trade shows), but most vendors say shipments will start after the IETF standardizes SMP.

The sheer volume of those shipments is likely to reach staggering proportions. SNMP is the de facto standard for managing LANs and internetworking equipment. Thomas Nolle, president of market research consultancy CIMI Corp. (Voorhees, N.J.), says users' worldwide investment in SNMP in 1992 should hit $28 million, compared with the roughly $215 million spent on proprietary man-

---

**Mary Jander** is network management and new products editor for DATA COMMUNICATIONS.

## NETWORK MANAGEMENT

## SNMP 2 Preview

# SMP—Straight From the Source

It's hard to argue with success. SNMP put simple, straightforward network management in the hands of users, and users put SNMP to work with a vengeance. In the four years since its introduction, SNMP has been implemented virtually everywhere: PCs, Macs, bridges, routers, hubs, file servers, and hosts (as well as other networking devices). It's now the premier protocol for overseeing multivendor internetworks.

Given SNMP's track record, why would anyone want to tinker with it—especially four of its leading proponents?

Well, no one (least of all the four of us) ever claimed the protocol is perfect. In fact, SNMP's enormous popularity has meant that its supporters have concentrated more on keeping the installed base stable rather than on refining the protocol. Enhancements have been made in the least intrusive way possible, by adding new objects to the management information base (MIB).

But other problems (such as speed, security, and system management) aren't addressed as easily.

Last year, succumbing to mounting pressure from users and vendors, the Internet Engineering Task Force (IETF) decided that security was too important an issue to delay any longer—even if adding it meant changing the protocol. This spring the IETF approved Secure SNMP—the first significant change to the protocol's framework.

At the same time, the IETF issued a request for proposals to address other SNMP shortcomings.

But as Eastern Europe has made all too clear, change can be very difficult to control. In order to ensure orderly change rather than anarchy, the four of us teamed up to create, document, and implement our proposed revision to SNMP—the simple management protocol (SMP) and its framework. We included Secure SNMP in our specification so that only one upgrade would be needed across the industry. In so doing, we felt it would be possible to boost performance and enhance security while keeping disruptions to a minimum.

**DESIGNED FOR SUCCESS**

The design of SMP was motivated by the same architectural considerations key to SNMP: minimizing the cost and complexity of network management agents and putting net management in centralized stations.

Because there will always be more agents on a network than management stations, it's essential that the former consume fewer system resources. A guiding principle of SNMP and SMP is to shift the burden of processing from agent to manager whenever possible. This ensures that the device hosting the agent will remain free to do its primary job. Giving agents too many management duties can result in a range of network anomalies, from reduced response times to full-blown broadcast storms.

SMP, as noted, builds on Secure SNMP as defined in RFCs 1351, 1352, and 1353—with two major exceptions.

First, SMP makes Data Encryption Standard (DES) encoding optional instead of mandatory. This was done because the U.S. government does not allow DES-encrypted source code to be exported.

Second, SMP allows SNMP packets to arrive at a management station out of their transmitted order. Secure SNMP requires packets to be delivered in order, since those that don't may have been intercepted and copied by an unauthorized party. But most networks reorder packets in the course of regular data transmissions, especially during times of stress, precisely when net management is needed most. In order to meet the requirements of Secure SNMP, messages would have to be re-sent until received in order. This slows response time.

**THE JOY OF SETS**

SMP improves the operation of control functions via the SET command in two ways. For one thing, it introduces a locking scheme that gives a management station uninterrupted access to a device while it is being configured. When invoked, the lock ensures that only one station can access an agent or group of agents at a time.

For another, SMP clarifies the procedures to be followed when creating, modifying, and deleting rows from tables. The ROWSTATUS mechanism borrowed from the RMON MIB allows a management station to create new variables, such as a routing table entry, in a standardized way.

Further, Secure SNMP and the improved SETs open the door to applications that demand extensive configuration capabilities, such as the administration of users on a file server.

SMP makes a small change to SNMP that yields a major improvement in performance. The new GETBULK command activates a bulk retrieval mechanism that allows a management station to retrieve a range of variables simultaneously. This mechanism uses a minimum amount of system resources and is easy to implement. Formerly, most vendors programmed their SNMP stations to send a GETNEXT for each variable to be retrieved. This slowed response time considerably. SMP transfers using GETBULK typically run more than 10 times faster than SNMP transfers.

SMP defines a few new data types, including 64-bit counters. A counter is a type of SNMP variable that (as its name suggests) counts the number of times an event occurs on a system, such as the number of packets received. SNMP already offers 32-bit counters, but as networks get faster and more complex, these are becoming outmoded in some environments. If the number of events recorded by a 32-bit counter exceeds 32 bits, the counter starts over from zero without notifying the management station—in effect losing track of the actual number of packets passed.

SMP also introduces a data type for OSI addresses that will help extend management to OSI networks.

In addition, SMP subtypes allow data to be defined in different ways, depending upon context. An IPX address can be created using the SMP OCTET STRING data type; a timestamp can be defined using SMP's TIMETICKS data type.

If an SNMP agent can't respond to some portion of a station's request for information because it isn't equipped with a particular MIB, it will reject the entire request. SMP addresses this problem by introducing "exception conditions." If an SMP agent can respond only to part of a station's request because it is missing a particular MIB variable, it can flag the missing piece as an "exception" and return the rest of the data.

SMP also furnishes a richer set of error codes that agents can use to explain their inability to respond to a management station's requests. For example, an SMP agent can tell a station that a SET request contains a value that is too long or that makes no sense.

Such error messages offer management applications more information about the nature of agent failures, so they can determine if failures are permanent or temporary and take corrective action. This gives SMP applications a better opportunity to respond to an error without involving a human operator or to provide an operator with more information to solve the problem.

**COMMUNICATIONS CONCERNS**

SMP builds support for manager-to-manager communications, a feature that is missing from SNMP. First, SMP adds acknowledged information transfers between two management stations, including reliable event notifications. With the INFORM command, one management station can send information to another—which was not possible under SNMP—and request confirmation of message receipt.

Second, an SMP MIB has been defined that controls how events at a management station may be generated and transmitted to another SMP management station.

Besides allowing information transfer between management stations, manager-to-manager communications lets a hierarchical network management system be built. On such a system, a midlevel management station local to a LAN would poll the devices on that LAN. When a fault is detected, the midlevel station could transmit an event notification to a higher-level station on the backbone. This reduces the net management traffic flowing over the backbone while retaining the reliability inherent in a polled environment.

SMP gives developers a way to add machine-readable annotations (called "macros") to MIBs. Although it is possible to annotate a MIB under SNMP, most comments are lost when the MIB is compiled because they aren't machine-readable. Five new macros have been defined: object-type definitions, object-group definitions, module-compliance definitions, agent-capabilities definitions, and trap definitions. These macros also establish a structure for MIB annotations. For instance, a macro can detail how well a vendor's MIB matches the standard MIB. It might indicate, among other things, how many of the nine groups of the RMON MIB a network monitor agent implements. Macros will help ensure interoperability, and users will be able to point to macros when making requests of vendors.

Several of SMP's features eliminate many of the TCP/IP biases of SNMP. Transport mappings are specified for multiple protocol stacks, including TCP/IP, IPX, Appletalk, and OSI's connectionless network protocol (CLNP). Others can be specified as necessary.

These transport mappings furnish a simple way to describe how to place SMP messages into these stacks. Proxy agents (conversion software) allow TCP/IP management stations to talk to other protocols on non-TCP/IP networks and to incorporate SMP without assigning IP addresses to large numbers of systems.

One of SMP's design goals is backward compatibility with SNMP whenever reasonably possible: SNMP MIB definitions are fully compatible with the SMP framework.

The SMP proposal includes one document devoted entirely to coexistence and transition. Two primary approaches are suggested: bilingual management stations and the use of proxy agents.

Bilingual management stations implement both SNMP and SMP. A bilingual manager sends SNMP queries to SNMP agents and expects SNMP responses; it also sends SMP queries to SMP agents and expects SMP responses. This means changing the management station's software but makes it possible to take full advantage of SMP. Bilingual agents are discouraged because they can add too much of a burden to their host devices.

Alternatively, a proxy agent may be used to convert from one message format to another. For example, a management station might support only SNMP, converting SMP messages via proxy agent. This approach allows management station software to remain unchanged but limits the degree to which it can exploit SMP.

We have implemented both of these approaches and found both to be workable.

—*By Jeffrey D. Case, Keith McCloghrie, Marshall T. Rose, and Steven Waldbusser*

---

**Jeffrey D. Case** is president of SNMP Research Inc. (Knoxville, Tenn.) and the co-author of several management standards, including SNMP. **Keith McCloghrie** is a director of engineering at Hughes LAN Systems Inc. (Mountain View, Calif.). He has written a number of Internet standards and is the co-author of MIB II. **Marshall T. Rose** is a principal at Dover Beach Consulting Inc. (Mountain View, Calif.), a computer communications consultancy. He has developed source code for TCP/IP and OSI and is a co-author of MIB II. **Steven Waldbusser** is a consultant and the manager of network development at Carnegie-Mellon University (Pittsburgh) and the author of the RMON MIB and Appletalk MIB.

## SNMP 2 Preview

agement systems like IBM's Netview and less than $2 million on systems with CMIP (common management information protocol). The number of MIB (management information base) objects defined by users and vendors for SNMP rose from about 100 at the start of 1990 to roughly 23,000 in 1992, according to The Yankee Group (Boston). And SNMP sales are on the rise. International Data Corp. (IDC, Framingham, Mass.) estimates that there will be 20,780 SNMP systems installed worldwide by the end of 1992, compared with 9,695 at the end of 1991.

### PARING DOWN PACKETS

One of the ways that SMP reduces the number of packets sent over a network is with a bulk retrieval mechanism activated by its new GETBULK command. Most SNMP systems, in contrast, repeatedly invoke the GETNEXT request to obtain reports on a range of variables in an agent. To retrieve router address tables or other lists from SNMP devices, for example, a management station must issue a GETNEXT for every item on the list.

"The real processing load in an SNMP system comes from the number of packets passed between management station and agents, not the size of the packets or the polling frequency of the station," says Yeager. "The bulk retrieval mechanism in SMP will cut down on the number of packets processed, reducing the amount of bandwidth consumed by the protocol."

SNMP's messaging vocabulary also is limited. For instance, if a management station asks a device to report on a feature it doesn't possess, such as a particular MIB variable, the device returns an empty packet. Upon receipt of the blank message, the manager often repeats its original request, wasting bandwidth in an attempt to ascertain information the device cannot supply.

What's more, SNMP management stations can't distinguish among the many reasons that empty packets may be returned to them. The device may not be able to supply any information on a particular variable. Or it could be out of service. In either event, an empty packet is sent.

SMP's answer is to improve communications between agents and managers with new data types, event messages, and so-called exception conditions. With them, an agent can tell a management station why it can't respond. For example, the agent may not be equipped with the desired MIB. Or it may have the right MIB but be missing a specific variable. Or it may be doing other tasks and unable to respond when asked. In each case, though, the SMP agent is not reduced to returning empty packets.

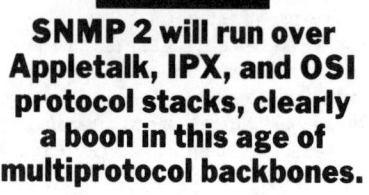

**SNMP 2 will run over Appletalk, IPX, and OSI protocol stacks, clearly a boon in this age of multiprotocol backbones.**

Another way that SMP improves communications is with manager-to-manager exchanges. To date, SNMP systems have been fairly inflexible when it comes to configuration: Management stations can communicate only with their agents, rather than with other stations.

SMP, however, makes it possible for a management station to act as either manager or agent. By using the new INFORMREQUEST command, stations can communicate with one another. This feature opens the way to the first midlevel managers on SNMP systems, which will add a layer of management between central stations and agents.

Midlevel managers could be set up to poll several agents on a particular LAN segment and pass their findings along to the central console. This would be a godsend to a large organization, since midlevel managers at remote sites could oversee bridges and routers on individual segments, reporting back to corporate headquarters as needed (see Figure 2). And because midlevel managers free central stations from having to poll all the agents in a network, they open the way to far larger SNMP installations. In the same vein, midlevel managers could relieve agents from having to store large amounts of Secure SNMP information, such as passwords and validation codes.

SMP's manager-to-manager communications are augmented by Secure SNMP's Party MIB, which lets one station talk to multiple agents at one IP address. In other words, SMP lets more than one agent occupy one computer plat-

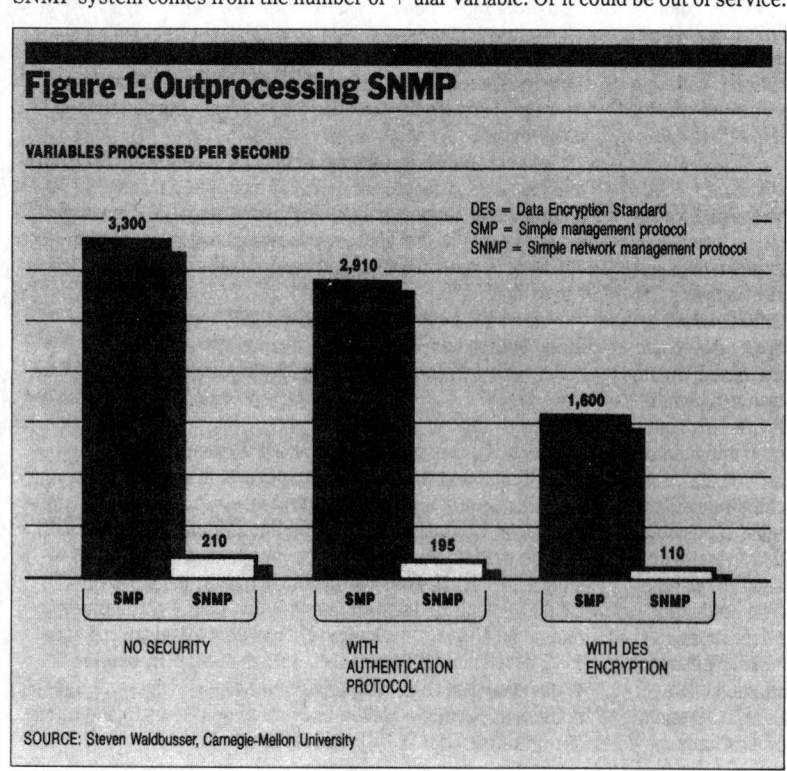

**Figure 1: Outprocessing SNMP**

VARIABLES PROCESSED PER SECOND

DES = Data Encryption Standard
SMP = Simple management protocol
SNMP = Simple network management protocol

| | SMP | SNMP |
|---|---|---|
| NO SECURITY | 3,300 | 210 |
| WITH AUTHENTICATION PROTOCOL | 2,910 | 195 |
| WITH DES ENCRYPTION | 1,600 | 110 |

SOURCE: Steven Waldbusser, Carnegie-Mellon University

## SNMP 2 Preview

form. This means SMP can be used to manage not just devices but all the components of a computer system, including applications, storage, and communications software. Apple Computer Inc. (Cupertino, Calif.) and Sunconnect (Mountain View, Calif.) already say that SMP will help them build system management applications. SNMP, in contrast, lets only one agent be placed on a platform.

SMP's approach to putting multiple agents on a platform is not the first to be tried. Other techniques have been proposed, and many vendors have engineered their own solutions. SNMP Multiplexer (SMUX), published as an experimental document by the IETF, attempts to do the same thing, but has proven cumbersome. And proprietary solutions aren't always compatible with standard SNMP.

### STATIONS FIRST

Vendors of management stations will probably be first out of the gate with SMP upgrades. Several strategies are open to them. For starters, they could simply scrap SNMP entirely and move to SMP—impractical as long as devices and systems in multivendor networks support SNMP.

Accommodating both protocols during the transition period is the path most vendors will follow, either with proxy software or with bilingual devices.

The proxy approach is the easiest to implement, though by no means the best choice. A proxy installed on a management station or subsystem translates messages from SMP into SNMP. This technique eases the transition to the new protocol but does not allow SNMP installations to fully exploit either SMP or Secure SNMP. Instead, SNMP agents coexist with SMP agents, taking basic management information from them. Also, introducing a proxy between a management station and agent adds complexity and another potential point of failure to net management systems. Still, some vendors may elect to offer proxies until they are satisfied that users really intend to move to SMP.

The bilingual approach requires vendors to build management stations that can support both SNMP and SMP agents. The advantage to this technique is that it lets stations reap the full benefits of SMP while supporting older products as well.

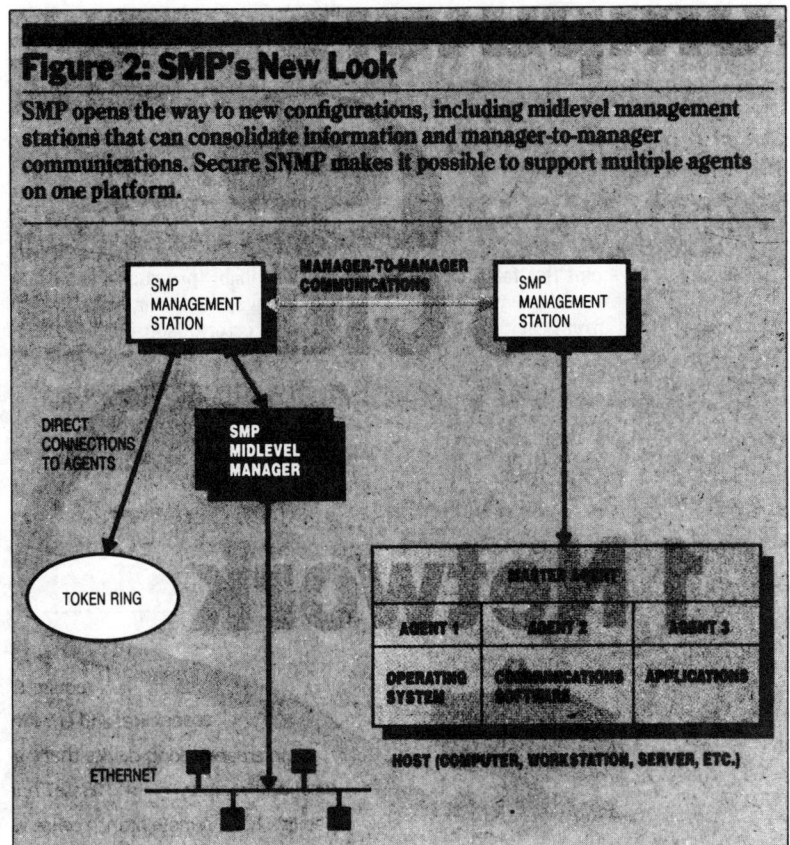

**Figure 2: SMP's New Look**
SMP opens the way to new configurations, including midlevel management stations that can consolidate information and manager-to-manager communications. Secure SNMP makes it possible to support multiple agents on one platform.

The drawback is that designing a bilingual manager means re-engineering the management station, a more complex task than merely adding a proxy.

Still, this may not be as daunting as it sounds. The basic structure of SMP and SNMP is the same, which allows them to share underlying components and services.

Specifically, SMP and SNMP have a traditional hierarchical database structure in common, including an indexing mechanism for naming network entities and listing their specific attributes. SNMP uses simple commands like GET or SET to retrieve information from network devices and report it to the management station.

In most commercial SNMP systems, the information collected by a management station is translated into another format, such as a relational database like Ingres or Oracle, before it is displayed or used. Thus, changing the type of information that is fed to the relational database will not alter the overall design of the system. Typically, the upgrade from SNMP to SMP will involve adding to the definitions, commands, and error codes that can be used. The management interface and applications can remain intact.

Given this, it's easy to see why some vendors believe an upgrade to SMP may even go unnoticed by users. Mike Erlinger, director of network development at Lexcel (Fullerton, Calif.), says "SMP will provide a more efficient capability for moving MIB data around a system," but it won't alter the actual way that MIBs are handled. Actually, some vendors expect third-party developers of SMP applications to face the biggest challenge, since SMP needs new APIs (application program interfaces).

"The interface between management applications and SNMP or SMP can be the same for many systems," says James Herman, a vice president of Northeast Consulting Resources Inc. (Boston). He points out that the same MIBs can be used with either SNMP or SMP.

Herman says it may be considerably easier to add SMP to systems that deploy

## NETWORK MANAGEMENT

## SNMP 2 Preview

what he calls a "network management platform" geared to multiple protocols. Such systems usually contain a core set of services that include a graphical user interface, communications software, and a set of object-oriented APIs. Since the APIs establish the links between management protocols and the core services, these systems are more or less indifferent to the source of the input.

Among the systems that fall into the management platform category are the DECmcc Director from Digital Equipment Corp. (Maynard, Mass.), HP Openview from Hewlett-Packard Co. (Palo Alto, Calif.), AIX Netview/6000 from IBM, Netlabs/Manager from Netlabs Inc. (Los Altos, Calif.), Novell Netware Management System from Novell Inc. (Provo, Utah), and Sunnet Manager from Sunconnect.

The quintessential management platform, the Distributed Management Environment (DME) being developed by the Open Software Foundation (OSF, Cambridge, Mass.), will embody much of the technology found in current systems. All of the aforementioned vendors, and the OSF, say they plan to upgrade to SMP when it is approved and users demand it.

### DOUBLE AGENTS

Vendors whose network devices are equipped with SNMP agents—like suppliers of management stations—have several options when it comes to upgrading to SMP. Here again, they may choose to do nothing, create two versions of their products, or create bilingual agents.

Many will likely choose the first path, leaving it to station suppliers to support SMP and waiting to see how it sells before adding new agents. Others—particularly those that support the RMON (remote network monitoring) MIB—may move to SMP along with the station vendors.

Agent vendors also may offer proxy translation software, which would run on their devices or attached computers. Once again, though, proxies add another potential point of failure without delivering the benefits of SMP. Vendors also may opt to create bilingual agents. SMP's authors, however, don't recommend taking that tack, believing that the burden of supporting two protocols should be put on the management station, not the agent.

The choice of agent strategy will depend largely on the resources available to the device and memory available in the agent. Some bridges and routers, for instance, are very tightly engineered and may not have the horsepower to support a bilingual agent. But most hubs have plenty of extra processing power, and their modular architectures should make adding another agent relatively easy.

"We'll probably provide a switchable SNMP/SMP agent for our hubs," says Roger Dev, director of software development at Cabletron Systems Inc. (Rochester, N.H).

Karl Auerbach, president of Empirical Tools and Technologies Inc. (Santa Cruz, Calif.), estimates that 50 percent to 75 percent of SNMP agent code will be reused for SMP agents. "The SMP agents can use the same memory, the same code that translates MIBs, and the portion of the agent that processes variables."

Despite such duplication, SMP agents, he indicates, will typically be twice as large as their SNMP counterparts, chiefly because of Secure SNMP code. But he points out that doubling the size may still yield an agent that uses less than 64 kbytes of memory. Some vendors are toying with the idea of implementing SMP without Secure SNMP. This scheme could severely limit a device's ability to work with other SMP systems.

### CMIP RESURFACES

In all the excitement surrounding the move to SMP, it's easy to lose sight of

---

### Securing the Message

Although SMP and Secure SNMP are being studied by separate working groups of the Internet Engineering Task Force (IETF), the two are very closely linked.

Some of SMP's most important innovations stem from its use of Secure SNMP as a foundation. Further, the changes to the Secure SNMP standard (first approved by the IETF in March 1992) that the authors of SMP have proposed will make security easier to implement and more efficient. They also will make the upgrade to SMP far easier.

SNMP's lack of security has kept it off certain kinds of networks. Carriers, for instance, felt that SNMP wasn't up to snuff when it came to protecting central office switches and other sensitive gear from intruders.

Secure SNMP is changing that. Long-distance carrier MCI Communications Corp. (Washington, D.C.) recently announced it would allow customers to use their own SNMP systems to monitor and configure MCI frame relay service subscriptions. And regional Bell operating company Ameritech (Chicago) is running a similar trial for SMDS (Switched Multimegabit Data Service).

But Secure SNMP does more than offer a safe backdrop for SMP. The upgrade uses the Party MIB first introduced in Secure SNMP to support multiple agents on a single platform (one of SMP's chief innovations).

The Party MIB allows a management station to communicate with multiple agents through one IP address—as long as those agents are properly registered as "parties" with the management station. SNMP allows only one agent to access an IP address, which was usually assigned to the operating system of the device hosting the agent.

In essence, the Party MIB allows all the elements of a computer system—OS, storage, and even applications—to be equipped with their own agents. When combined with SMP's manager-to-manager communications, the Party MIB enables a LAN server or workstation to act as a master agent, monitoring itself and other workstations.

Besides SMP, commercial products have started to emerge that address the issue of multiple agents. The most significant so far is Enhanced Management Agent Through Extensions (Emanate) from SNMP Research Inc. (Knoxville, Tenn.). Emanate equips an SNMP agent with a protocol that lets it link with other agents on the same platform or on different platforms. —*M.J.*

## SNMP 2 Preview

the fact that SNMP was originally seen as an interim protocol on the way to CMIP. In fact, the IETF planned to replace SNMP with CMIP once the International Organization for Standardization (ISO) finished its work on the latter.

But users were understandably impatient for nonproprietary management for their internetworks, and SNMP—unlike CMIP—was ready to implement and easy to use. A skilled programmer can master the basics in one sitting. Best of all, SNMP was freely available on the Internet, where for the price of a phone call, users could exchange implementation tips with the top software development laboratories in the U.S.

The rest, as the saying goes, is history. Today, CMIP remains a shadowy promise on the periphery of industry development; SNMP is a de facto standard. What's more, SMP will bring the protocol closer to CMIP. And there's even talk among SMP backers of lobbying the ISO through the International Telegraph and Telephone Consultative Committee (CCITT) or the American National Standards Institute (ANSI) to make SMP an accepted alternative to CMIP.

For most CMIP supporters, though, close isn't close enough.

Tony Jeffree, a principal consultant with the Sema Group Ltd. (London) and chair of the IEEE 802.1 Network Management Task Group, which approved CMIP over Logical Link Control protocol (CMOL) this year, is among the naysayers. He believes that CMIP is more efficient and flexible than SNMP and better suited to international use because of its endorsement by groups like the ISO and the IEEE.

"I think the choice between SNMP or SMP and CMIP is clearer than that between SNMP and SMP. There are many advantages to CMIP; it's more object-oriented and goes beyond a simple database approach."

He points out that CMIP easily deploys functions beyond the reach of SNMP. For example, a reset button can be directly programmed into a CMIP agent; SNMP, to do the same thing, needs to have a MIB element created that turns on and off in the presence of certain conditions.

But moving to CMIP from SNMP won't be as smooth as going from SNMP to SMP. According to Herman, the shift to SMP "really isn't that big a deal, since you're using the same MIBs in both cases. But going to CMIP is more difficult since the structure of its management information is different from that of SNMP or SMP." That means that the software used to translate CMIP into the format used by the management station would have to be revamped. Also, applications would have to be changed to accommodate the broader range of information available in CMIP MIBs.

Ultimately, it looks as if the future of network management belongs to both CMIP and SMP—albeit not in equal measure. The general feeling in the industry is that the SMP upgrade won't put a damper on SNMP's popularity. But devotion to SNMP hasn't made users and vendors forget CMIP. In government and carrier applications, and in the international market, CMIP is growing, albeit slowly.

The strategies of some of the leading management platform vendors bear this out. IBM and HP, for example, are committed to SNMP and CMIP. Both recently added support for CM-API (consolidated management application program interface) to their systems—IBM to AIX Netview/6000 and HP to Openview.

Other vendors are adding SNMP to their CMIP systems. Data General Corp. (Westborough, Mass.) and Digital Analysis Corp. (Reston, Va.) have codeveloped a management system called OS/Eye Node designed for CMIP that also uses SNMP. And the Concert system developed by British Telecommunications PLC (London), which is now being used mainly to manage its own networks, also delivers SNMP as an add-on to CMIP.

"We live in a multiprotocol world, and we'll continue to do so," asserts Elizabeth K. Adams, managing director of the Network Management Forum (Bernardsville, N.J.), a consortium of vendors, users, and industry and government groups working to define implementation parameters for management systems based on international standards. Adams says the forum will follow the progress of the IETF closely and will add SMP to its Omnipoint series of specification documents when the standard is approved. ∎

---

### To Obtain Copies of the SMP Specs...

On the Internet, at the following address: lancaster.andrew.cmu.edu, get files: pub/smp/smp-*.txt. Alternatively, obtain the following individual files, in the suggested order of reading: smp-intro.txt; smp-smi.txt; smp-tc.txt; smp-proto.txt; smp-tm.txt; smp-mib.txt; smp-m2m.txt; smp-coex.txt.

To obtain copies of the SMP specification documents from the IETF on the Internet: connect via anonymous FTP to the nnsc.nsf.net host and request the following eight documents from the internet drafts subdirectory: draft-rose-smp-tm-00.txt; draft-rose-smp-tc-00.txt; draft-rose-smp-proto-00.txt; draft-rose-smp-smi-00.txt; draft-rose-smp-intro-00.txt; draft-rose-smp-mib-00.txt; draft-rose-smp-m2m-00.txt; draft-rose-smp-coex-00.txt.

**TO OBTAIN SAMPLE SMP CODE...**

Code is available free on the Internet from Marshall T. Rose and Steven Waldbusser. For Rose's code contact: ics.uci.edu. Access the mrose/isode-smp subdirectory. The file is isode-smp.tar.Z.

For Waldbusser's code contact: lancaster.andrew.cmu.edu. Access the smp-dist subdirectory. Open Readme file for further instructions. All files should be downloaded in binary form. Rose's code is compressed.

Code also is available for sale from Jeffrey D. Case at SNMP Research Inc., 3001 Kimberlin Heights Rd., Knoxville, Tenn. 37920-9716; 615-573-1434.

---

**REQUEST FOR COMMENT**
If you would like to see more articles on this subject please circle **543** on the Reader Service Card.

# Chapter 4: OSI Systems Management

We begin this chapter with a brief overview of the OSI model, for which OSI systems management is designed. Next, we look at two key application-level capabilities, ACSE and ROSE, which are part of the OSI architecture and are used by OSI systems management. Next, the organizations involved in developing OSI-related standards are discussed. This is followed by an introduction to OSI systems management.

## The OSI model

With the widespread use of communications networks and distributed computing, standards are needed to promote interoperability among vendor equipment and to encourage economies of scale. Because of the complexity of the communications task, no single standard will suffice. Rather, the functions should be broken down into more manageable parts and organized as a communications architecture. The architecture would then form the framework for standardization.

This line of reasoning led ISO in 1977 to establish a subcommittee to develop such an architecture. The result was the Open Systems Interconnection (OSI) reference model. Although the essential elements of the model were in place quickly, the final ISO standard, ISO 7498, was not published until 1984. A technically compatible version was issued by CCITT as X.200.

**The concept of open systems.** Open Systems Interconnection is based on the concept of cooperating distributed applications. In the OSI model, a system consists of a computer, all of its software, and any peripheral devices attached to it, including terminals. A distributed application is any activity that involves the exchange of information between two open systems. Examples of such activities include:

- A user at a terminal on one computer is logged onto an application such as transaction processing on another computer.
- A file management program on one computer transfers a file to a file management program on another computer.
- A user sends an electronic mail message to a user on another computer.
- A process-control program sends a control signal to a robot.

OSI is concerned with the exchange of information between a pair of open systems, and not with the internal functioning of each individual system. Specifically, it is concerned with the capability of systems to cooperate in the exchange of information and in the accomplishment of tasks.

The objective of the OSI effort is to define a set of standards that will enable open systems located anywhere in the world to cooperate by being interconnected through some standardized communications facility and by executing standardized OSI protocols.

An open system may be implemented in any way, provided that it conforms to a minimal set of standards that allows communication to be achieved with other open systems. An open system consists of a number of applications, an operating system, and system software such as a database management system and a terminal handling package. It also includes the communications software that turns a closed system into an open system. Different manufacturers will implement open systems in different ways, in order to achieve a product identity that will increase their market share or create a new market. However, virtually all manufacturers are now committed to providing communications software that behaves in conformance with OSI in order to provide their customers with the ability to communicate with other open systems.

**The model.** A widely accepted structuring technique, and the one chosen by ISO, is layering. The communications functions are partitioned into a hierarchical set of layers. Each layer performs a related subset of the functions required to communicate with another system. It relies on the next lower layer to perform more primitive functions and to conceal the details of those functions. It provides services to the next higher layer. Ideally, the layers should be defined so that changes in one layer do not require changes in the other layers. Thus we have decomposed one problem into a number of more manageable subproblems.

The task of ISO was to define a set of layers and the services performed by each layer. The partitioning should group functions logically, and should have enough layers to make each layer manageably small, but should not have so many layers that the processing overhead imposed by the collection of layers is burdensome. The resulting reference model has seven layers, which are listed with brief definitions in Table 4-1.

**Table 4-1. The OSI layers.**

| Layer | | Definition |
|---|---|---|
| 1 | Physical | Concerned with transmission of unstructured bit stream over physical link; involves such parameters as signal voltage swing and bit duration; deals with the mechanical, electrical, and procedural characteristics to establish, maintain, and deactivate the physical link. |
| 2 | Data link | Provides for the reliable transfer of data across the physical link; sends blocks of data (frames) with the necessary synchronization, error control, and flow control. |
| 3 | Network | Provides upper layers with independence from the data transmission and switching technologies used to connect systems; responsible for establishing, maintaining, and terminating connections across networks. |
| 4 | Transport | Provides reliable, transparent transfer of data between end points; provides end-to-end error recovery and flow control. |
| 5 | Session | Provides the control structure for communication between applications; establishes, manages, and terminates connections (sessions) between cooperating applications. |
| 6 | Presentation | Performs generally useful transformations on data to provide a standardized application interface and to provide common communications services; examples: encryption, text compression, reformatting. |
| 7 | Application | Provides services to the users of the OSI environment; examples: transaction server, file-transfer protocol, network management. |

Figure 4-1 illustrates the OSI architecture. Each system contains the seven layers. Communication is between applications in the two computers, labeled application X and application Y in the figure. If application X wishes to send a message to application Y, it invokes the application layer (layer 7). Layer 7 establishes a peer relationship with layer 7 of the target computer, using a layer-7 protocol (application protocol). This protocol requires services from layer 6, so the two layer-6 entities use a protocol of their own, and so on down to the physical layer, which actually transmits bits over a transmission medium.

Note that there is no direct communication between peer layers except at the physical layer. That is, above the physical layer, each protocol entity sends data down to the next lower layer to get the data across to its peer entity. Even at the physical layer, the OSI model does not stipulate that two systems be directly connected. For example, a packet-switched or circuit-switched network may be used to provide the communication link.

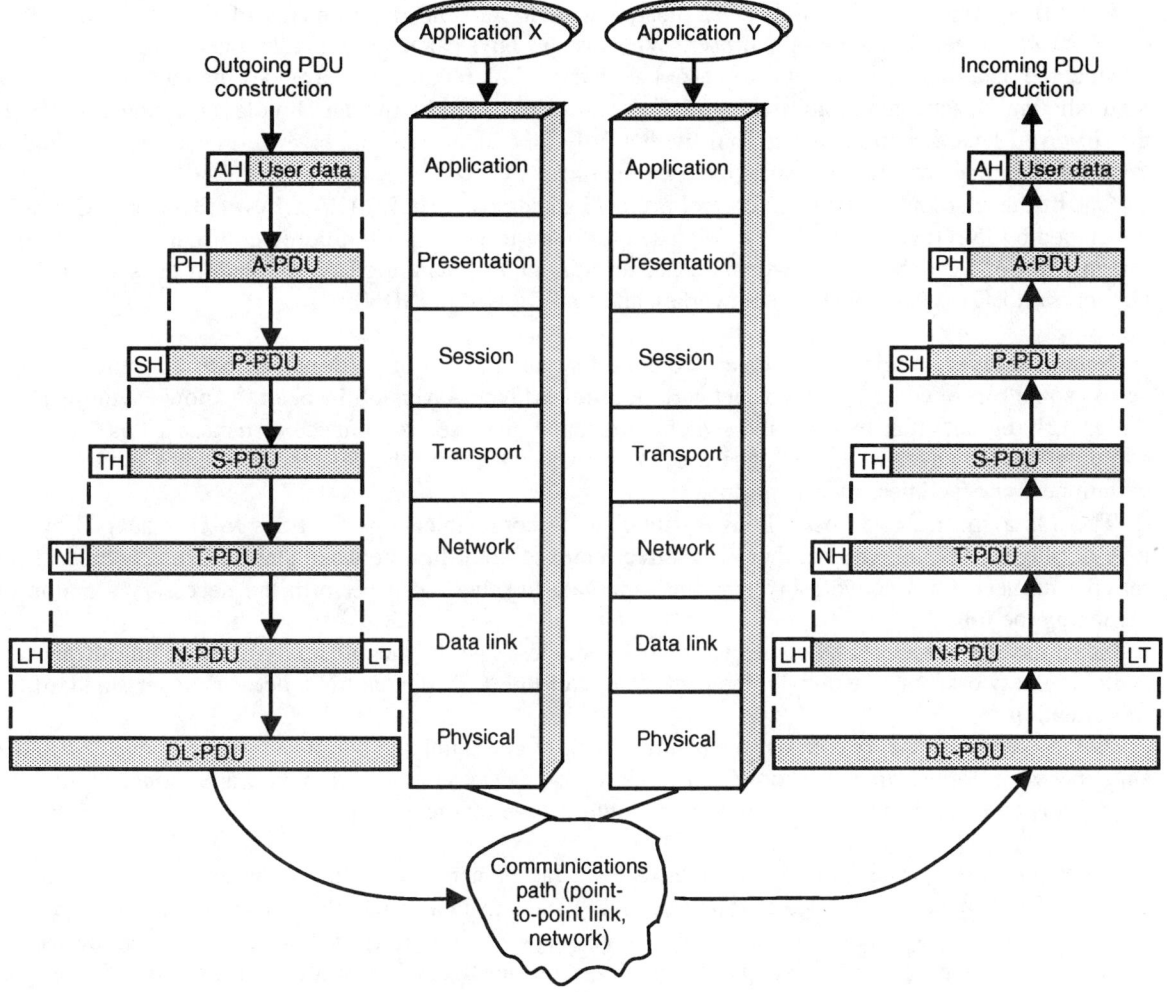

Figure 4-1: The OSI environment

## The OSI layers

**Physical layer.** The physical layer covers the physical interface between devices and the rules by which bits are passed from one to another. The physical layer has four important characteristics:

- *Mechanical:* Relates to the physical properties of the interface to a transmission medium. Typically, the specification is of a pluggable connector that joins one or more signal conductors, called circuits.
- *Electrical:* Relates to the representation of bits (for example, in terms of voltage levels) and the data transmission rate of bits.
- *Functional:* Specifies the functions performed by individual circuits of the physical interface between a system and the transmission medium.
- *Procedural:* Specifies the sequence of events by which bit streams are exchanged across the physical medium.

The physical layer differs from the other OSI layers in that it cannot rely on a lower layer to transmit its PDUs. Rather, it must make use of a transmission medium whose characteristics are not part of the OSI model. There is no physical layer PDU structure as such; no header of protocol control information is used. The PDU simply consists of a block or stream of bits.

**Data link layer.** The data link layer must deal with both the requirements of the communications facility and the requirements of the user. Whereas the physical layer provides only a raw bit stream service, the data link layer attempts to make the physical link reliable and provides the means to activate, maintain, and deactivate the link. The principal service provided by the data link layer to higher layers is that of error detection and control. Thus, with a fully functional data link layer protocol, the next higher layer may assume error-free transmission over the link.

One of the best-known data link control protocol standards is HDLC (High-Level Data Link Control), developed by ISO (ISO 4335). It is widely used for point-to-point and multidrop configurations. It is also the ancestor of a number of other data link control protocols, including LAPB (used in packet-switching networks), LLC (used in local area networks), and LAPD (used in ISDN).

**Network layer.** The network layer provides for the transfer of information between end systems across some sort of communications network. It relieves higher layers of the need to know anything about the underlying data transmission and switching technologies used to connect systems. At this layer, the computer system engages in a dialogue with the network to specify the destination address and to request certain network facilities, such as priority.

There is a spectrum of possibilities for intervening communications facilities to be managed by the network layer. At one extreme, there is a direct point-to-point link between stations. In this case, there may be no need for a network layer because the data link layer can perform the necessary function of managing the link.

Next, the systems could be connected across a single network, such as a circuit-switching or packet-switching network. As an example, the packet level of the X.25 standard is a network layer standard for this situation.

At the other extreme, two end systems might wish to communicate but are not even connected to the same network. Rather, they are connected to networks that, directly or indirectly, are connected to each other. This case requires the use of some sort of internetworking technique.

**Transport layer.** The transport layer provides a mechanism for the exchange of data between end systems. The connection-oriented transport service ensures that data are delivered error-free, in sequence, with no losses or duplications. The transport layer may also be concerned with optimizing the use of network services and providing a requested quality of service to session entities. For example, the session entity may specify acceptable error rates, maximum delay, priority, and security.

The size and complexity of a transport protocol depend on how reliable or unreliable the underlying network and network layer services are. Accordingly, ISO has developed a family of five transport protocol standards, each oriented toward a different underlying service.

**Session layer.** The lowest four layers of the OSI model provide the means for the reliable exchange of data and provide an expedited data service. For many applications, this basic service is insufficient. For example, a remote terminal access application might require a half-duplex dialogue. A transaction-processing application might require checkpoints in the data-transfer stream to permit backup and recovery. A message-processing application might require the ability to interrupt a dialogue in order to prepare a new portion of a message and later to resume the dialogue where it was left off.

All these capabilities could be embedded in specific applications at layer 7. However, since these types of dialogue-structuring tools have widespread applicability, it make sense to organize them into a separate layer: the session layer.

The session layer provides the mechanism for controlling the dialogue between applications in end systems. In many cases, there will be little or no need for session layer services, but for some applications, such services are used. The key services provided by the session layer include:

- *Dialogue discipline:* This can be two-way simultaneous (full duplex) or two-way alternate (half duplex).
- *Grouping:* The flow of data can be marked to define groups of data. For example, if a retail store is transmitting sales data to a regional office, the data can be marked to indicate the end of the

sales data for each department. This would signal the host computer to finalize running totals for that department and start new running counts for the next department.

- *Recovery:* The session layer can provide a checkpointing mechanism, so that if a failure of some sort occurs between checkpoints, the session entity can retransmit all data since the last checkpoint.

ISO has issued a standard for the session layer that includes as options services such as those just described.

**Presentation layer**. The presentation layer defines the format of the data to be exchanged between applications and offers application programs a set of data transformation services. The presentation layer defines the syntax used between application entities and provides for the selection and subsequent modification of the representation used. Examples of specific services that may be performed at this layer include data compression and encryption.

**Application layer**. The application layer provides a means for application programs to access the OSI environment. This layer contains management functions and generally useful mechanisms to support distributed applications. In addition, general-purpose applications such as file transfer, electronic mail, and terminal access to remote computers are considered to reside at this layer.

---

**Table 4-2. Application layer terms.**

*Application association*

A cooperative relationship between two application entities formed by the exchange of application protocol control information through their use of presentation services.

*Application context*

A set of rules shared in common by two application entity invocations in order to enable their cooperative operation. An application association has only one application context.

*Application entity invocation*

A specific utilization of part or all of the capabilities of a given application entity in support of the communication requirements of an application process invocation.

*Application process invocation*

A specific utilization of part or all of the capabilities of a given application process in support of a specific occasion of information processing.

*Application process*

A set of resources, including processing resources within a real open system, that may be used to perform a particular information processing activity.

*Application service element*

A part of an application entity that provides an OSI environment capability, using underlying services where appropriate.

*Application entity*

The aspects of an application process pertinent to OSI.

## Association control service element

One set of services that is a common requirement of almost all applications is that of establishing, maintaining, and terminating connections between application entities. Accordingly, service (ISO 8649; X.217) and protocol (ISO 8650; X.227) standards for an association control service element (ACSE) have been developed.

**Basic concepts.** Two concepts are essential to an understanding of the association control facility: application association and application context. These are defined in Table 4-2. The concept of *application association* needs to be contrasted with that of presentation connection. The application association and the presentation connection are actually two different aspects of the same thing, namely the relationship that exists between two application entities that are performing a shared task. From the point of view of the connection mechanisms needed to support information exchange, the relationship is a presentation connection. The presentation connection provides a pipe for the transfer of abstract data values with no constraints on the way these values are used. From the point of view of the information exchange itself, the relationship is an application association, which supports agreed-on procedures and shared semantics for the use of the corresponding presentation connection.

The application association supports the meaningful cooperative exchange between application entities within a defined *application context*. An application context is a mutually agreeable relationship between application entities in different open systems. The relationship exists for a period of time during which a cooperative task is performed. The relationship includes an agreement as to which application service elements will be employed, and the options and procedures related to those ASEs.

| Table 4-3. Association control protocol data units and parameters. ||
|---|---|
| **APDU** | **Parameters** |
| A-ASSOCIATE-REQUEST (AARQ) | Protocol version, application context name, calling AP title, calling AE qualifier, calling AP invocation-identifier, calling AE invocation-identifier, called AP title, called AE qualifier, called AP invocation-identifier, called AE invocation-identifier, implementation information, user information |
| A-ASSOCIATE-RESPONSE (AARE) | Protocol version, application context name, responding AP title, responding AE qualifier, responding AP invocation-identifier, responding AE invocation-identifier, result, result source-diagnostic, implementation information, user information |
| A-RELEASE-REQUEST (RLRQ) | Reason, user information |
| A-RELEASE-RESPONSE (RLRE) | Reason, user information |
| A-ABORT (ABRT) | Abort source, user information |

**Association control service.** Table 4-3 lists the primitives and parameters for the ACSE service. The purpose of this service is to provide for the establishment and termination of application associations.

The A-ASSOCIATE service is used to set up an application association. A one-to-one correspondence exists between an application association and a presentation connection and, therefore, between an application association and a session connection. The A-ASSOCIATE primitives are supported by the P-CONNECT primitives. The added value of the association control service is represented by those parameters that are carried in APDUs and not mapped onto the lower layers:

- Application context name
- Calling, called, and responding application process (AP) titles
- Calling, called, and responding application entity (AE) qualifiers
- Calling, called, and responding AP invocation-identifier
- Calling, called, and responding AE invocation-identifier
- User information
- Result, result source
- Diagnostic

Application context names identify the context; the responder may propose a different application context than the requester. The result of this negotiation is not defined in the standard but is application specific. Names may be assigned to application contexts by standards organizations as part of the application layer standards.

The next four bullet entries are parameters that unambiguously identify application processes, application entities, and the invocations of application processes and entities.

Either the requester or the accepter may optionally include user information. Its meaning depends on the application context that accompanies the primitive.

The result parameter indicates the result of using the A-ASSOCIATE service, and takes one of the following values:

- Accepted
- Rejected (permanent)
- Rejected (transient)

If the association is accepted, then an application association is created simultaneously with the underlying presentation and session connections.

The result source parameter indicates that the result is provided by the responding ACSE user, ACSE, or the presentation service provider.

The diagnostic parameter is used only if the result parameter has the value rejected (permanent) or rejected (transient). If the result source parameter has the value ACSE service provider, then the diagnostic parameter takes on one of the following values:

- No reason given
- No common ACSE version

If the result source parameter has the value ACSE service user, then the diagnostic parameter takes on one of the following values:

- No reason given
- Application context name not supported
- Calling AP title not recognized
- Calling AE qualifier not recognized
- Calling AP invocation-identifier not recognized
- Calling AE invocation-identifier not recognized
- Called AP title not recognized
- Called AE qualifier not recognized
- Called AP invocation-identifier not recognized
- Called AE invocation-identifier not recognized

Of the A-ASSOCIATE parameters, only the application context name, the result, and the result source parameters are mandatory. The others may be assumed to be set by prior agreement to simplify implementation.

The A-RELEASE service is used for the orderly release of an association. If the session negotiated release functional unit was selected for the association, the responder may respond negatively, thus causing the unsuccessful completion of the release service and the continuation of the association. For the request and indication primitives, the reason parameter takes on one of the following values: normal, urgent, or user-defined. On the response and confirm primitives, it takes on one of the following values: normal, not finished, or user-defined. The result parameter indicates acceptance or rejection of the release request. If the release is successful, then the application association is released simultaneously with the underlying presentation and session connections.

The A-ABORT and A-P-ABORT services cause the termination of the application association simultaneously with the underlying presentation and session connections. With A-ABORT, the abort source parameter indicates that the abort was initiated by either the ACSE or the other service user. With A-P-ABORT, the provider reason parameter is mapped directly from the P-P-ABORT service.

## Remote operations service element

The remote operations service element (ROSE) is one of the most widely used of the general-purpose application service entities. ROSE is intended to support interactive types of applications, which are characterized by a request by one application for another application to perform some operation. In the programming field, a common example of this mechanism is the remote procedure call.

**Principles.** The basic service provided by ROSE is the facility for invoking an operation on a remote open system. The application entity (AE) invoking the operation issues a request to the peer AE, specifying a particular operation to be performed. The other AE attempts to perform the operation and may report the outcome of the attempt. The interchange between the two entities is carried out in the context of an application association.

**Operation class.** Operations invoked by one application entity (*the invoker*) are performed by the other application entity (*the performer*). The interaction between two entities that results in an operation being attempted is characterized by an operation class, which is agreed on between the two entities for each separate invocation. The operation class is defined by two characteristics of the interchange: the reporting behavior of the AE attempting the operation, and whether the interchange is synchronous or asynchronous (Table 4-4).

| Table 4-4. ROSE operation classes. | | | |
|---|---|---|---|
| | | **Operation Mode** | |
| | | Synchronous | Asynchronous |
| **Reporting Mode** | If success, return result reply<br>If failure, return error reply | Operation class 1 | Operation class 2 |
| | If success, no reply<br>If failure, return error reply | | Operation class 3 |
| | If success, return result reply<br>If failure, no reply | | Operation class 4 |
| | If success, no reply<br>If failure, no reply | | Operation class 5 |

The performing AE may observe one of four types of reporting behavior:

- Always report a result, whether it is success or failure.
- Only report a failure.
- Only report a success.
- Do not report the result.

If a result, success or failure, is always reported, then the invoking AE has the option of waiting for a report before continuing, or not. With synchronous operation, the invoker requires a reply from the performer before invoking another operation. For asynchronous operation, the invoker may continue to invoke further operations without awaiting a reply.

**Association class.** ROSE may be used by two application entities that share an application association to invoke one or more operations. The AE that initiates an application association (by issuing an A-ASSOCIATE.request to ACSE) is called the *association initiator*, while the AE that responds to the request is called the *association responder*. The two AEs must agree on one of three association classes that will hold for the life of the association:

    Association class 1:    Only the association initiator can invoke operations.
    Association class 2:    Only the association responder can invoke operations.
    Association class 3:    Both the association initiator and the association responder can invoke operations.

The association class is an attribute of an application context and must be selected at the time that the association is set up using ACSE.

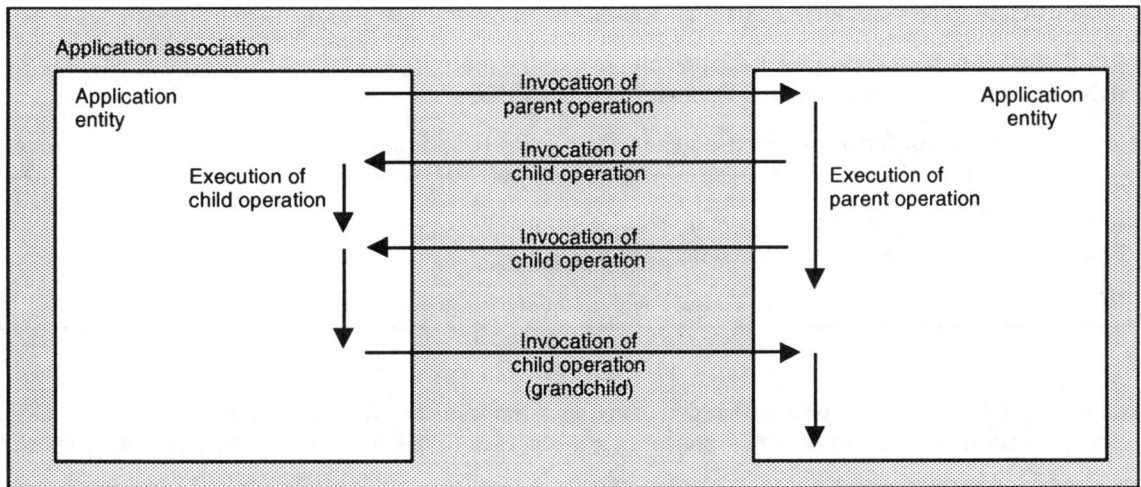

Figure 4-2: Linked operations

When association class 3 is selected, it is possible to group operations into a set of linked operations, which is formed by one parent operation and one or more child operations. The sequence is as follows:

1. One AE invokes an operation on the peer AE, referred to as the parent operation.

2. The performer of the parent operation may invoke zero, one, or more child operations during the execution of the parent operation. Thus, each of these child operations is performed by the AE that is the invoker of the corresponding parent operation.

3. Each child operation may in turn function as a parent operation to trigger zero, one, or more child operations in a recursive fashion.

Figure 4-2 illustrates the concept of linked operations.

**Remote operations service definition**. Table 4-5 lists the remote operation service primitives and parameters. The RO-INVOKE primitive is used for the invoker to request an operation of the performer. The parameters of this primitive are:

- Operation value: This identifies the operation to be performed. The identity and nature of the operation are beyond the scope of ROSE and must be agreed on between the two application entities.
- Operation class: Indicates one of the five operation classes (Table 4-4).
- Argument: The argument or list of arguments that accompanies the operation. Again, the nature of these arguments is beyond the scope of ROSE.
- Invoke-ID: Identifies the request of a RO-INVOKE service and is subsequently used to correlate this request with the corresponding replies. This parameter is needed for asynchronous operation.
- Linked-ID: If this parameter is present, the invoked operation is a child operation and the parameter is the invoke-ID of the linked parent operation.
- Priority: Identifies the priority of the transfer of the corresponding APDU relative to other APDUs to be exchanged between the AEs.

| Table 4-5. Remote operations service primitives and parameters. |
| --- |
| RO-INVOKE.request (operation value, operation class, argument, invoke-ID, linked-ID, priority)<br>RO-INVOKE.indication (operation value, argument, invoke-ID, linked-ID) |
| RO-RESULT.request (operation value, result, invoke-ID, priority)<br>RO-RESULT.indication (operation value, result, invoke-ID) |
| RO-ERROR.request (error value, error parameter, invoke-ID, priority)<br>RO-ERROR.indication (error value, error parameter, invoke-ID) |
| RO-REJECT-U.request (reject reason, invoke-ID, priority)<br>RO-REJECT-U.indication (reject reason, invoke-ID) |
| RO-REJECT-P.indication (invoke-ID, returned parameters, reject reason) |

The RO-RESULT primitives are used to provide a reply in the case of a successful operation. The result parameter provides information concerning a successfully performed operation and is beyond the scope of ROSE.

The RO-ERROR primitives are used to provide a reply in the case of an unsuccessfully performed operation. The error value parameter indicates the type of error, and error parameter provides additional information about the error. Both parameters are beyond the scope of ROSE.

The RO-REJECT-U service is used by a ROSE user to reject a request (RO-INVOKE) if the user has detected a problem. It may also be used to reject a reply (RO-RESULT, RO-ERROR).

## OSI systems management

Of all the areas of OSI (Open Systems Interconnection) standardization, the set of standards developed for OSI systems management is the most voluminous and most complex. The term *systems management* is used for what is generally referred to as network management in non-OSI literature.

The first standard related to network management issued by ISO was ISO 7498-4, which specifies the management framework for the OSI model. This document dictates that OSI management support user requirements for:

| Table 4-6. OSI systems management standards. | | |
|---|---|---|
| Title | ISO | CCITT |
| **OSI Management Framework and Overview** | | |
| OSI Basic Reference Model Part 4: Management Framework | 7498-4 | X.700 |
| Systems Management Overview | 10040 | X.701 |
| **CMIS/CMIP** | | |
| Common Management Information Service Definition | 9595 | X.710 |
| Amendment 4: Access Control | 9595 DAM 4 | X.710 |
| Amendment X: Allomorphism | 9595 PDAM X | X.710 |
| Common Management Information Protocol Specification Part 1: Specification | 9596-1 | X.711 |
| Amendment X: Allomorphism | 9596 PDAM X | X.711 |
| Part 2: Protocol Implementation Conformance Statement (PICS) Proforma | 9596-2 | X.712 |
| **Systems Management Functions** | | |
| Part 1: Object Management Function | 10164-1 | X.730 |
| Part 2: State Management Function | 10164-2 | X.732 |
| Part 3: Attributes for Representing Relationships | 10164-3 | X.733 |
| Part 4: Alarm Reporting Function | 10164-4 | X.734 |
| Part 5: Event Report Management Function | 10164-5 | X.735 |
| Part 6: Log Control Function | 10164-6 | X.736 |
| Part 7: Security Alarm Reporting Function | 10164-7 | X.737 |
| Part 8: Security Audit Trail Function | 10164-8 | X.740 |
| Part 9: Objects and Attributes for Access Control | 10164-9 | X.741 |
| Part 10: Accounting Meter Function | 10164-10 | X.742 |
| Part 11: Workload Monitoring Function | 10164-11 | X.739 |
| Part 12: Test Management Function | 10164-12 | |
| Part 13: Summarization Function | 10164-13 | |
| Part 14: Confidence and Diagnostic Test Categories | 10164-14 | |
| Accounting Management | SC 21 N 4971 | |
| Part s: Scheduling Function | SC 21 N 6021 | |
| OSI Software Management | SC 21 N 6040 | |
| General Relationship Model | SC 21 N 6041 | |
| Management Domains | SC 21 N 6047 | |
| Management Knowledge | SC 21 N 6048 | |
| Synchronization | SC 21 N 6049 | |
| Performance Management | SC 21 N 6306 | |
| **Management Information Model** | | |
| Part 1: Management Information Model | 10165-1 | X.720 |
| Part 2: Definition of Management Information | 10165-2 | X.721 |
| Part 4: Guidelines for the Definition of Managed Objects | 10165-4 | X.722 |
| Part 5: Generic Managed Information | 10165-5 | |
| Requirements for Implementation Conformance Statement Proformas | 10165-6 | |
| **Layer Management** | | |
| Elements of Management Information Related to OSI Network Layer Standards | 10733 | |
| Transport Layer Management | 10737 | |

- Activities that enable managers to plan, organize, supervise, control, and account for the use of interconnection services.
- The ability to respond to changing requirements.
- Facilities to ensure predictable communications behavior.
- Facilities that provide for information protection and for the authentication of sources of and destinations for transmitted data.

Subsequently, ISO issued a set of standards and draft standards for network management. CCITT is the joint sponsor of this effort, and has set aside the X.700 series of numbers for its recommendations. Table 4-6 lists the current set of management standard documents. The standards fall into five general categories:

- *OSI management framework and overview:* This category includes ISO 7498-4, which provides a general introduction to management concepts, and ISO 10040, which is an overview of the remainder of the documents.

- *CMIS/CMIP:* These standards define the common management information service (CMIS), which provides OSI management services to management applications, and the common management information protocol (CMIP), which provides the information exchange capability to support CMIS.

- *Systems management functions:* Standards in this category define the specific functions that are performed by OSI systems management.

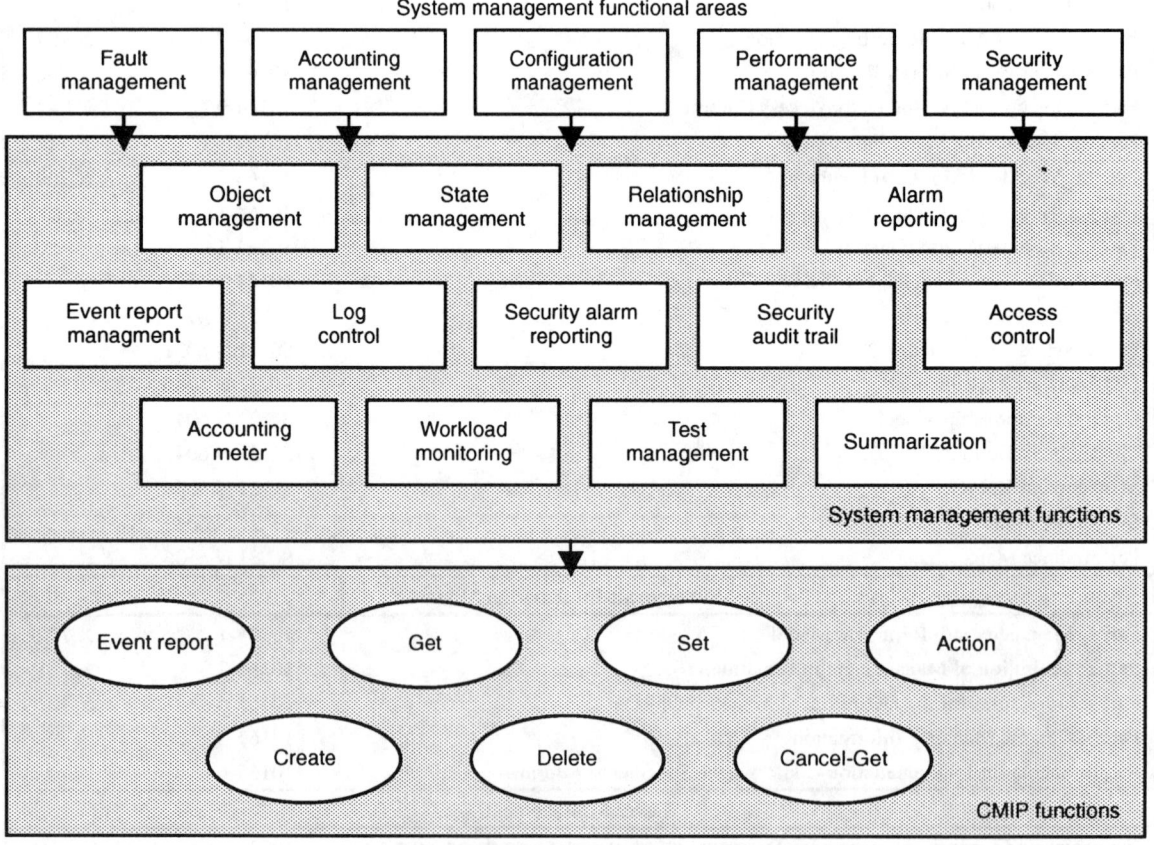

Figure 4-3: OSI network management architecture

- *Management information model:* These standards define the management information base (MIB), which contains a representation of all objects within the OSI environment subject to management.
- *Layer management*: These two standards define management information, services, and functions related to specific OSI layers.

Figure 4-3 indicates the way in which the OSI systems management standards are organized. The network management protocol is referred to as the common management information protocol (CMIP). Like SNMP and SNMPv2, it provides retrieval, set, and alert operations, although with more features and more flexibility.

The true strength of OSI systems management, however, is the detailed specification of a set of network management applications. The strategy involves a two-layer specification. The standard includes the definition of a number of system management functions (SMFs), each of which performs a specific related set of network management functions, such as functions related to workload monitoring. The SMFs are in essence modules that can be combined to construct major network management applications in five system management functional areas (SMFAs): fault management, accounting management, configuration management, performance management, and security management. These five SMFAs cover virtually all conceivable network management applications.

The appeal of the OSI approach is that, on the one hand, a powerful and flexible set of modules have been standardized that support any desired network management operation, and on the other hand, the facility has been designed to allow a user to select only required modules to build a system no larger than needed for a given environment.

There are two drawbacks to the OSI approach. First, because a significant portion of the standard is still evolving, there are few products on the market right now. And second, even with its modular design, an implementation of OSI systems management is a complex resource hog. Furthermore, the MIB structure in OSI systems management relies heavily on object-oriented technology. So far, few operating systems support object-oriented features. As a result, the object-oriented capability must be provided at the application level or in the database management system, adding more complexity and resource consumption.

## Paper summary

"OSI Systems Management" provides an overview of the OSI network management standards. "An Implementation of an OSI Network Management System" provides an example of the use of OSI network management standards.

"The OSI Network Management Model" discusses the rationale and approach of OSI systems management. This work aligns with the OSI network management standards. "Management By Exception: OSI Event Generation, Reporting, and Logging" provides a detailed discussion of the functions in OSI network management used for managing the timely transfer and manipulation of information in the form of events. "Optimizing OSI Management System Performance" examines the performance issues related to OSI systems management and discusses optimization techniques.

Finally, the SNMP and OSI approaches to network management are compared in "Network Management of TCP/IP Networks: Present and Future."

# Components of OSI: Systems Management
*Standards at mid life; Neo Natal Products*

**by Paul J. Brusil, The MITRE Corporation**

**Introduction**

Management is a critical core capability that will have major impact upon viable operational acceptance and deployment of OSI systems and networks. ISO has been developing a broad set of globally accepted management standards for management of general distributed information processing resources, including networks. Recently, CCITT, with focus on the telecom/telephony environment, and ISO, with computing industry emphasis, have agreed to progress common standards applicable to both environments. These standards have been based on object-oriented technology since their inception and are among the earliest international standards using this technology.

The broad mix of standards from increasingly diverse communities is making OSI systems management the world wide basis for multi-vendor, interoperable, integrated management. With interest growing in organizations like OSF and X-Open, the span of OSI integrated management will widen from today's integrated management of network elements in public (carrier-provided) and private LANs and WANs to include system and application software.

A large number of these standards are now stable and mature. Some have taken the volume of standards to mean high implementation costs. Others will leverage rapidly increasing memory availability and CPU power, as well as falling costs, to implement these standards in traditionally resource-constrained bridges and modems.

**Early adopters**

The commercialization of these standards has begun. The first multi-vendor demonstration of early OSI management standards occurred at INTEROP 88 (see Marshall in [2]). Numerous Japanese firms including NEC, Fujitsu, Hitachi, Toshiba, IBM-Japan and several others are now completing efforts to demonstrate mature OSI management and advanced OSI protocols such as *Transaction Processing* and *Remote Database Access*. OSI management products can be bought now; some were available for purchase at *ComNet '91*. Many industry giants will offer products soon. Those leading the commercialization charge include IBM, Digital, AT&T, British Telecom, Hewlett-Packard, Unisys, NCR, as well as the other 100+ international vendors in the OSI/Network Management Forum and the other 150+ international organizations within the *Network Management SIG* (NMSIG) of the Department of Commerce's *OSI Implementors Workshop*. Vendors and testing firms in nearly 20 countries are committed to OSI management as the method for enabling networks to access and manipulate management information on a worldwide basis.

This article provides the basic concepts associated with OSI systems management. It gives a tour through the various associated CCITT and ISO joint standards. It also considers work of organizations contributing to commercialization of this technology.

**Basic System Management concepts**

General concepts of OSI management have been described in several contexts, e.g., [1, 2], and are summarized in Figure 1. Basic components of management include *manager* and *managed* (often called *agent*) systems. These systems may contain the actual resources that provide the "useful work" in the distributed system being managed. For example, protocols provide the useful work in network elements. Sometimes these systems are management *proxies* that act as intermediaries between actual resources and management systems.

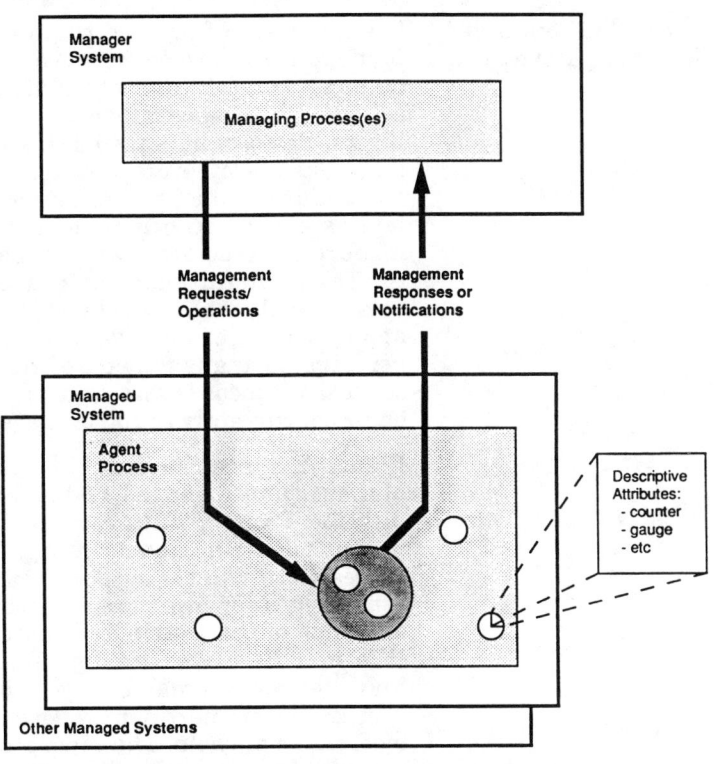

Figure 1: OSI Systems Management Framework

**Managed Objects**    Management activities may occur via application layer, manager processes in manager systems interacting with remote managed objects in managed systems. Through such interactions, one manipulates or retrieves management information pertinent to the resources being managed. The interactions occur via remote agent processes in managed systems. According to object-oriented paradigms, resources are modeled as *Managed Objects*. Managed objects logically characterize the actual resources for purposes of managing the resources. That is, a managed object models the permissible management operations (e.g., read, replace) on the managed object, permissible notifications that the object may wish to send, and descriptive attributes (e.g., counter, gauge) associated with the managed object. Managed objects may contain other managed objects.

For meaningful interoperation, manager and agent processes must share the same schema of knowledge about the managed objects in which they are mutually interested. Different schemata are possible so that different manager processes can have different management views of the same managed object.

Agent processes perform the management operations requested by manager processes, e.g., reading attributes of a specific object, setting object attributes, or returning a response to the corresponding requesting manager process. They may forward, according to specifiable rules, certain notifications (events) asynchronously generated by their associated managed objects. Agent processes may interact with their associated managed objects in ways not subject to standardization since such interactions may take place completely within one implementation.

## OSI Systems Management

**Example: Managing networks**

For a system of layered communication protocols, the OSI Systems Management framework recognizes three management approaches: management within a communications protocol, management within a layer (with several protocol instances) and management across layers. Protocol management, such as transport flow control windowing, consists of protocol-internal mechanisms needed to control a particular instance of communication. Layer management consists of layer-specific activities and networking services needed to manage resources associated with a particular layer, e.g., network layer routing mechanisms or link layer token control. Layer management acts directly at a single layer and does not necessarily rely on application layer manager and agent processes. Systems management pertains to management of networking resources associated with several protocol layers and protocol instances. All approaches may occur concurrently in the management of network systems.

Figure 2 conceptualizes OSI management for network elements. Manager and managed system elements contain the stack of communication *Protocol Entities* (PE) that provide networking services, as well as managing and agent application processes, respectively. These processes can access local managed objects and can communicate with remote partner processes to access remote managed objects. The PEs are some of the distributed resources to be managed. Associated with PEs may be *Layer Managers* (LMs) and management information. Managed objects may be layer objects specific to PEs; or, they may be system objects pertinent to several layers of PEs and/or the network element as a whole. The conceptual aggregate of all such management information is called a *Management Information Base* (MIB).

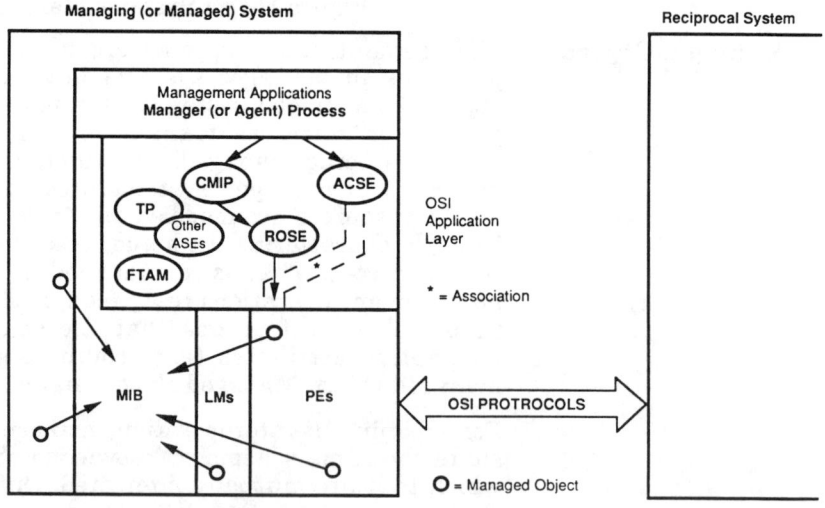

Figure 2: Architectural Model of OSI Management in Manager and Managed System Network Elements

Managing and agent processes rely on numerous OSI *Application Service Elements* (ASEs) which work together, calling upon each other as described in [3], to effect management communications. Typical of OSI, communications are connection oriented. An *Association Control Service Element* (ACSE) establishes and terminates associations (application-to-application "connections") between the managing and agent processes.

Management service requests and responses between the processes are then effected by the *Common Management Information Protocol,* CMIP, whose packet data units are sent over such connections. A *Remote Operations Service Element* (ROSE) provides a transaction-oriented, request/response service (similar to SNMP's Top-level Message) to carry the CMIP operations over the association. ROSE also provides for linking multiple replies to a single request. It has a parameter for indicating which CMIS operation is carried in the Remote Operations request or response.

Managing and agent processes may use services of other ASEs. For example, a transaction processing ASE could provide coordination and concurrency control of distributed management transactions if managers choose to synchronize changes across distributed resources. A file transfer ASE could provide bulk transfers for software configuration loads or transmission of aggregated management reports.

The context of which set of ASEs can be used by remote cooperating management applications is established at the time that an association is set up between the applications.

Operationally, the manager process may receive inputs from local administrative personnel or their software agents, from local LMs, from remote agent processes, and/or from remote LMs. Decisions made by the manager process are either effected by local mechanisms to the local managed objects, or they are communicated to remote agent processes or LMs.

**Standards overview**

The process of developing OSI standards has swung from codification of dejure, industry-wide approaches to international amalgamation of the autonomous research results of standards' participants. Furthermore, OSI System Management standards are being produced by many national and international standards organizations, including ANSI, several ISO sub committees and working groups, several CCITT study groups, and the IEEE. (Chappell [4] overviews relationships among these organizations.) Accordingly, the various standards are progressing at different rates, often perceived as slow. Some justify a deliberate pace because of the broad scope, complexity and intricacy of the subject, which cuts across all protocols, layers, numerous devices, and various technological disciplines, organizations, countries and laws. Others view the pace as arising from the difficult organizational problems and language barriers attendant in creating worldwide standards. ISO standards themselves represent a compromise among 87 countries representing more than 95% of the world's industrial production. Open consensus-building in such diverse forums is truly difficult. Accordingly, OSI standards in general, and systems management standards in particular, are often as much political achievements as they are technical compromises.

OSI Systems Management has four groups of standards: (a) those summarizing basic management concepts and models as well as the other standards that further specify details, (b) those relating to the specification of managed objects, (c) those specifying systems management functions that provide value-added capabilities beyond basic management communication services, and (d) those pertaining to the basic application layer services and protocols for communicating management information. In brief, these standards specify managed objects and attributes, as well as rules for defining, manipulating, sending information about, and controlling the sending of information about managed objects and attributes.

## OSI Systems Management *(continued)*

Within each group there are several standards. Currently, over 100 international standards are being developed. ISO is developing over 30 standards pertaining to OSI Systems Management; CCITT is developing over 60, 23 of which are identical to corresponding ISO standards; IEEE 802 and P1003 are developing at least 7. Figure 3 shows the standards being developed within one ISO *Sub Committee* (SC). They form the core set upon which most of the other standards are based. Their contents, inter-relationships and inter-dependencies are summarized in the next section.

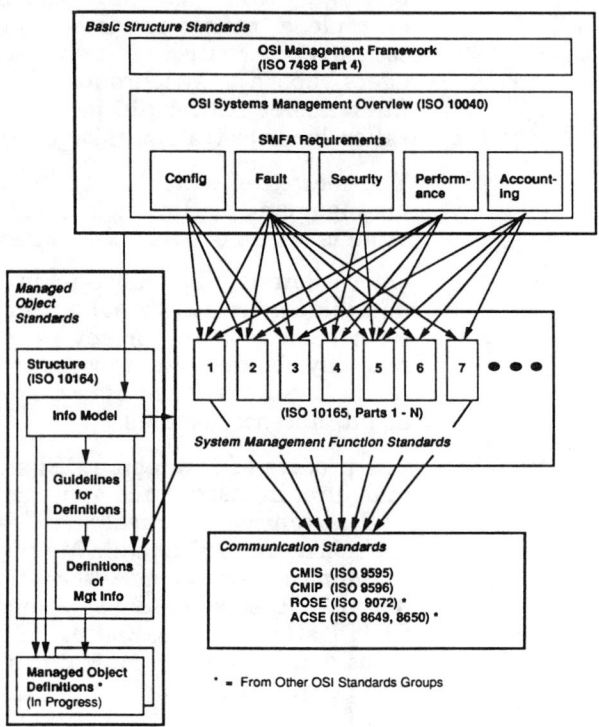

Figure 3: Core OSI System Management Standards (From ISO SC21)

Good news: there are now 18 stable ISO international systems management standards at the *Draft International Standard* (DIS) or *International Standard* (IS) levels. All 11 DISs are scheduled to reach IS by mid 1991. These 18 standards provide such a sufficiently rich and stable set of management tools that implementations of OSI management systems can safely begin without fear that they may be obviated due to changes in evolving standards.

A number of the less mature standards, *Committee Drafts* (CDs), are planned to be technically stable enough to become DISs in 1991. Today's major short-coming for OSI management is that stable, internationally-standard definitions of many managed objects, such as those progressing in CCITT, IEEE and ISO, are not yet in hand.

**Guide to standards**

Details within the core standards are too voluminous to summarize here. Only salient features and a guide to the standards are given here. Indicated with each standard's description are the ISO document number, the current standardization level, the anticipated IS date, and the corresponding CCITT recommendation number.

These documents are available from the *American National Standards Institute* (ANSI) in New York City, or *Omnicom, Inc.* in Vienna, Virginia.

**Management Structure standards**

*Management Framework* (ISO IS 7498-4, OSI Basic Reference Model; CCITT X.700). This and ISO standard 10040 provide the architectural information required to guide development of all the system management standards. The framework defines major elements of OSI management: *System Management Functional Areas* (SMFAs), MIB, basic managed object concepts, and different methods of management information interaction, i.e., system, layer and protocol management.

SMFAs enumerate generic requirements for management in several areas (see, e.g., Stine et al in [1]). For example, requirements to enable identification or negotiation of mechanisms for associating and collecting communication resource usage charges, to initiate or deactivate charging algorithms, and to monitor or report account relevant information are given in an *Accounting Management SMFA*. The *Security Management SMFA* requirements include capabilities to combat threats by providing audit trails of security-relevant events, capabilities to analyze such audit trails, and tools for supporting the control of security services and mechanisms as well as the associated decision making, e.g., when to redistribute keys, when to reinitialize encipherment algorithms and when to isolate infected nodes. Other SMFAs—*Fault Management, Performance Management and Configuration Management*—contain obvious requirements to detect and to isolate problems, to monitor and to tune networks, and to monitor and to maintain continuous operations, respectively.

*Systems Management Overview* (ISO DIS 10040, IS in '91; CCITT X.701). This standard expands the framework's concepts via a systems management model. The model refines managed objects concepts and provides a brief guide on how to use the management-information-related standards to define managed objects. The model addresses functional aspects of systems management by describing the relationships between SMFA requirements and the system management functions standards (ISO 10164). It addresses communication aspects such as management processes acting in either a managing or an agent role. It also addresses application layer concepts relating to systems management and the establishment of shared knowledge about the intrinsically distributed elements of a management system. Lastly, it addresses organizational concepts, such as management domains, that describe ways management can be distributed for reasons of management scale, security, accounting, or the need to provide administrative autonomy over an organization's resources. This standard also provides a brief overview of the other systems management standards.

**Management Information standards**

Standards defining management information pertain to the *Structure of Management Information* (SMI) and the managed object descriptions applicable to real resources. Rules guiding those developing the definition, structure and identification of managed objects are specified in the former (ISO 10165)—a multi-part standard. Having objects defined according to a common structure is perhaps the single most important notion that will facilitate integration of management across a variety of heterogeneous resources and system environments. This notion transcends the significance of a single common management communication protocol within such heterogeneous environments.

## OSI Systems Management

*SMI—Part 1: Management Information Model* (ISO DIS 10165-1, IS in '91; CCITT X.720). This standard defines (a) a model governing logical organization of management information and relationships into which managed objects can enter (inheritance, specialization, allomorphism, containment), (b) consistent and versatile naming and containment principles so that managed objects and their attributes can be identified in, and accessed by, management protocols, and (c) so-called Managed Object Knowledge tools to allow dynamic discovery of which managed objects have been instantiated in a given system.

The information model is heavily based on object-oriented design principles. Accordingly, it permits easy extensibility to incorporate new classes of managed objects and functions as they emerge, modularity and extensibility of management protocol and procedures, and reuse of pieces of management information specifications.

Attributes, the properties of managed objects, may be either *singlevalued,* as in some of today's other management approaches, or *setvalued.* Set-valued attributes are those whose value is a set of members of a given datatype. For retrieval purposes a group of attributes may be referenced by a single "group" attribute. Attributes determine or reflect behavior of managed objects. They may be collected together with notifications, operations and behavior to form conditional packages that can be conditionally instantiated in managed objects.

Objects can be extensions of other objects by inheriting characteristics, such as operations, attributes, behavior, from superclass objects, and by adding new characteristics such as attributes, actions, action arguments, and/or extending/restricting, e.g., attribute and argument ranges. Allomorphism, a technique to extend object classes to support new equipment and technology types without making older management systems obsolete, is specified so that migration between versions of management is possible.

The model allows two types of management operations. The first can be applied to object attributes (get/replace/set-to-default attribute value and add/remove members of set-valued attributes). The second apply to whole objects (create/delete/action).

Lastly, principles of containment and naming are specified to identify managed objects uniquely. Managed object identifiers are of two components: one identifying the class of objects to which a managed object belongs (e.g., a transport entity object class defined by an ISO standards body), the other identifying the specific instance of the managed object (e.g., the transport object in a specific network element). The former is an ASN.1 object identifier, a sequence of integers that navigate through a hierarchical registration tree to the class of the managed object (see, McCloghrie et al in [2]). The latter is a distinguished name based on the concatenated sequence of relative distinguished names of object instances in a containment tree (see, e.g., [7]).

*SMI—Part 4: Guidelines for the Definition of Managed Objects* (ISO DIS 10165-4, IS in '91; CCITT X.722). This standard, generally referenced by its acronym GDMO, specifies a set of guidelines and templates to be used by individuals defining managed object classes. It, therefore, encourages consistency among object definitions, ensures definitions compatible with all appropriate OSI management standards, and reduces duplication of effort among object definers by identifying commonly useful documentation layouts, procedures and definitions.

By using these templates and the grammar and rules of the ASN.1 specification language, managed object definitions will consist of enumeration of:

- the object's attributes,
- the operations that can be applied to the object,
- any conditions/constraints that may affect execution of each operation (e.g., any synchronization constraints within the object and criteria for supporting operation requests for atomic synchronization with other objects),
- the effects (exhibited behavior) that these management operations have upon the object and its attributes as well as upon related objects,
- the notifications that can be emitted by the object,
- the behavior and syntax associated with specific action type of operations,
- the conditional packages which can be present in the object,
- the position of the object class in the inheritance hierarchy,
- alternative naming structures/bindings that define possible naming relationships with superior objects and the managed object classes from which subordinate objects may be instantiated, and;
- the objects that are allomorphic with this object class.

This standard also summarizes requisite registration concepts for object definers. Contrary to other management approaches, OSI managed object naming and registration are independent.

*SMI—Part 2: Definition of Management Information* (ISO DIS 10165-2, IS in '91; CCITT X.721). This standard defines generic attribute types, specific attributes, and packages, including their syntax, behavior, valid operations, as well as name bindings for object classes. These definitions are specified via GDMO templates.

This standard enumerates a set of support managed object classes, most of which are fully specified in the system management function standards (ISO 10164). These support objects, attributes and packages may in principle be reusable components within definitions of other managed objects in a wide variety of classes. Examples of such support management information definitions include:

- a discriminator object for controlling the filtering of notifications that may be reported as events to a remote manager or log,
- generic attribute types such as counter, gauge, counter threshold, gauge threshold and tidemarks, and
- generic packages for daily or weekly scheduling of, e.g., notification filtering.

**Managed Object definitions**

In addition to support managed objects discussed above, every standards group that specifies a protocol or a component of a communications system is responsible for specifying, according to SMI rules, the managed object(s) and attributes associated with that resource. The number of such standards groups is very large.

## OSI Systems Management

Those actively engaged in defining objects according to the SMI/GDMO include ISO's transport and network layer bodies, ANSI's FDDI committee, CCITT's and ANSI's telecommunication management network bodies, IEEE's 802 group (work is underway in 802.2, 802.3, 802.5, 802.6 and 802.10) and IEEE's P1003 POSIX group.

Many industry consortia are also using SMI/GDMO to define system objects required for multi-vendor interoperability, as well as experimental, pre-standards, layer objects. Active groups include *INTAP* (Interoperable Technology Association for Information Processing—Japan) defining objects for ISDN and FDDI internets, *CNMA* (Communications Network for Manufacturing Applications) defining OSI upper and lower layer objects for European experimentation, the *OSI/Network Management Forum* defining objects for manager-to-manager interactions, and NMSIG defining objects for high level management of internets with heterogeneous lower layer protocols.

To encourage early and quick, interim managed object implementations, some in ISO are considering to define generic managed objects. Comparable to ongoing NMSIG initiatives, these would be high level overview definitions of key system and networking resources. They would be developed before the detailed standard managed objects are internationally hammered out by the various resource-specific standards bodies. Early management implementations could include these generic managed objects. By themselves, they could accommodate high level, "surface" management. Additional interim refinements by vendors could provide more meaningful objects incorporating resource-specific details. Only software pertinent to the interim refined definitions would need to be swapped out when standard refined definitions become available. This would permit early fielding of objects without significantly hampering commercial transition to subsequent standard objects.

**IMIL** To encourage open and non-redundant definitions and refinements of these and/or other vendor-specific objects, the NMSIG has been working with its regional sister organizations, the OSI Workshops in Europe and Asia, to develop notions of an *International Management Information Library* (IMIL). The IMIL is to be a widely and readily accessible repository that lists or points to all object definitions in the standard GDMO syntax. Standards governing establishment and maintenance of the IMIL would need to be developed.

Near term uses of the IMIL would be many. It would give wide spread public disclosure to managed objects of all sorts, including those to manage multi-vendor interoperable applications, such as spread sheets and graphics, and multi-vendor interoperable system software such, as data base management systems. It would be used to reduce proliferation of comparable object definitions by screening for, and potentially working to harmonize, such similarities before definitions are entered into, or referenced by, the IMIL. In true object oriented fashion, the IMIL would promote reuse and refinement of existing management information definitions. Once the IMIL becomes richly populated, vendors will be able to manage both standard and, at least to some extent, proprietary resources of other vendors. Additionally, users will have a single complete directory and dictionary of OSI manageable objects from which procurement selections can be made. There is already discussion about using profiles of IMIL objects as part of emerging US government federal information processing standards to be mandated soon for government management procurements.

**System Management Functions standards**

The multi-part, *System Management Functions* (SMF) standards define functionality to support SMFA requirements. A SMF may support requirements in many SMFAs, e.g., the *Event Report Management Function SMF* may be applicable to all SMFAs. Conversely, a SMFA may require several SMFs. Each SMF standard provides mappings between services provided by the SMF and CMIS. Initial SMFs being progressed are as follows.

*Object Management Function* (ISO DIS 10164-1, IS in '91; CCITT X.730). This standard specifies services for creating, deleting, examining and changing sets of management information. It specifies services for reporting creation/deletion of managed objects, name changes to managed objects, and changes to attribute values.

*State Management Function* (ISO DIS 10164-2, IS in '91; CCITT X.731). This standard models and specifies the states which managed objects may have. It defines nine generic attribute types useful for inquiring about and changing the management state of a managed object. One notification (event) type is defined for reporting management state changes when they occur either through internal operation of, or management action upon, the resource. Operational, usage and administrative viewpoints are addressed. Services are defined for monitoring operability and usage of system resources, for administratively restricting their availability, and for restricting receipt of state change notifications.

*Attributes for Representing Relationships* (ISO DIS 10164-3, IS in '91; CCITT X.732). This standard models and identifies types of relationships which can exist among managed objects representing different parts of a system. It specifies ten generic attribute types and one notification type, together with their applicable parameters and semantics for importation into managed object definitions when relationships with other managed objects are to be specified. Services are defined for establishing, examining and monitoring the relationships among managed objects, and therefore for observing how operation of one part of a system depends on other parts.

*Alarm Reporting Function* (ISO DIS 10164-4, IS in '91; CCITT X.733). This standard models alarm reporting. It specifies five generic alarm notifications (events), together with their parameters and semantics. These notifications are associated primarily with fault management.

*Event Report Management Function* (ISO DIS 10164-5, IS in '91; CCITT X.734). This standard provides a model for event reporting and the control of event reporting. It specifies means for controlling selection and distribution of events to manager-specifiable destinations. It specifies an event forwarding discriminator managed object that defines manager-creatable/setable criteria by which managed object notifications may be conveyed remotely as event reports, as well as the time periods during which such event forwarding discrimination can occur. LaBarre [5] gives an excellent tutorial. Event-driven management is deemed particularly crucial in WANs with premium transmission costs and in bandwith-constrained aeronautical and military environments.

*Log Control Function* (ISO DIS 10164-6, IS in '91; CCITT X.735). This standard provides a model for logging events and other management information. It specifies a log, and services by which records associated with event reports can be logged.

## OSI Systems Management

Similar to concepts associated with event forwarding discrimination, records can be logged according to numerous manager-setable schedules and only if manager-creatable/setable logging criteria are passed. See [5].

*Security Alarm Reporting Function* (ISO DIS 10164-7, IS in '91; CCITT X.736). This standard models reporting of security-related events (e.g., attacks on, or breaches of, system security) and misoperations in security services and mechanisms. It specifies generic security alarm notifications, together with their parameters and semantics, as well as facilities for creating, deleting and modifying event forwarding discriminators for controlling selection and distribution of security alarms to manager-specifiable destinations.

*Security Audit Trail Function* (ISO CD 10164-8, IS in '92; CCITT X.740). This standard provides extension of the log control function standard, with its discriminator concepts, to security relevant event logging. It specifies how to control starting/stopping of security auditing and creating/modifying auditing criteria. It specifies generic security audit trail notifications and their applicable parameters and semantics.

*Objects and Attributes for Access Control* (ISO CD 10164-9, IS in '93; CCITT X.741). This standard models access control for management communication associations, as a whole, as well as for individual management operations within an association. It specifies managed objects and attributes (to be associated with those objects to be managed and protected in a system) to be used to grant or to deny access according to the access control policy represented by this access control management information.

*Accounting Meter Function* (ISO CD 10164-10, IS in '92; CCITT X.742). This standard provides a model for accounting meters and logs, and for the control of such objects. It specifies services for retrieving, reporting, and recording resource usage data and for selecting which usage data are to be collected and under what conditions they are to be reported.

*Workload Monitoring Function* (ISO CD 10164-11, IS in '92; CCITT X.739). This standard models gauges to be used for resource utilization monitoring, for rejection rate monitoring and for resource request rate monitoring. It specifies gauge managed objects, a mean monitor metric object for deriving the instantaneous mean value of an associated gauge object, the notifications that can be emitted, and operations for initiating, terminating, suspending, resuming and modifying metric monitoring.

*Test Management Function* (ISO CD 10164-12, IS in '92; CCITT X.745). This standard supports remote control of tests involving open systems and the specification of tests which exercise OSI resources in such systems. Individual tests may be used in the context of several different SMFAs, such as both fault and performance management.

*Measurement Summarization Function* (ISO CD 10164-13, IS in '92; CCITT X.738). This standard provides a model for sampling and aggregating (in manager-specifiable ways), optionally buffering, and reporting (according to manager-specifiable schedules) various summarizations of values of manager-specifiable attributes of (a) specific object instances across time (time averages), or (b) a set of object instances at a particular time (ensemble averages).

It specifies managed objects and attributes that indicate which objects and attributes are to be considered for inclusion in summary reports, scheduling of observations upon these objects/attributes, scheduling of summary reports, lists of observations to be included in summary reports, and summarization algorithms to be used. It specifies services for reporting such summaries and for initiating/terminating summarization activities.

*Confidence & Diagnostic Test Classes* (ISO WD 10164-y; CCITT X.737). This standard allows activation of manager-specifiable diagnostic tests (connectivity, data integrity, protocol integrity, data saturation, connection saturation, response time, loopback, function, etc.) on managed objects. These test classes permit determination of the quality of services being provided by the system being managed.

Other SMF standards that are still in their early development include the Time Management Function (ISO WD 10164-z, IS in '93; CCITT X.743), Software Management Function (10164-q, IS in '94; CCITT X.744), and Performance Management Function ( CCITT X.746).

## Management Communications standards

*Common Management Information Service* (ISO IS 9595, including IS Amendments 1,2, and CD Amendment 4 [scheduled for IS in '92]; CCITT X.710) and *Common Management Information Protocol* (ISO IS 9596, including IS Amendments 1 and 2; CCITT X.711). These standards provide the building blocks that define operations needed to perform the System Management Functions. The former, CMIS, defines services invokable by management processes when they communicate remotely. The latter, CMIP, defines the protocol to provide these services, as well as the mapping of this protocol onto the OSI remote operations service. CMIP is a powerful protocol that allows several operations to be performed in few commands, thereby minimizing management communication traffic.

CMIS services are based on the management information model. They include initialization service, information transfer service, and synchronization and linked reply services.

The initialization service supports the exchange of information about managed objects, management functions, and CMIS services supported by each end of a management association established by ACSE.

Information transfer services provide management operations services that (a) create and delete instances of managed objects (the CMIP CREATE and DELETE operations provide these services), (b) retrieve attributes of managed objects (provided by the CMIP GET operation), (c) cancel previously requested retrieval services (CMIP CANCELGET), (d) modify attributes of managed objects (CMIP SET), and (e) perform actions that may be specific to a managed object, such as initiate a diagnostic self test (CMIP ACTION). Also included are notification services that transfer events emitted by managed objects (CMIP EVENT-REPORT).

Synchronization service provides best effort or atomic synchronization of an operation across multiple objects. Linked reply service provides for multiple replies to be returned as a result of a single request and to be linked with the appropriate single specific request.

Some CMIS services have "modes": confirmed and unconfirmed. The former requires remote management process to send a response to indicate receipt and success or failure of the operation requested. The latter doesn't use responses.

## OSI Systems Management

CMIS also describes operations that can be performed upon multiple objects, i.e., some single service requests may be concurrently applied across many managed objects. In particular, CMIS provides capabilities of selecting which objects are to be operated upon through a process of "scoping" and "filtering." Scoping identifies the pool of managed objects that are candidates to be operated upon, whereas filtering specifies which objects from the "scoped" pool will actually be operated upon. Scoping identifies candidate objects by specifying the root of a subtree in the containment hierarchy as well as the number of levels down from this root in the subtree that are to be screened (filtered). Filtering applies tests to each candidate (scoped) object to extract the particular subset that match filter criteria.

*Protocol Implementation Conformance Statement* (CD Amendment 5 [scheduled for IS in '92] of ISO IS 9596; CCITT X.712). This standard provides tables to be used by vendors to indicate implementation specifics, such as (a) what aspects of OSI management communication protocols were implemented, e.g., which protocol version, roles (manager, agent or both), modes and functional units, (b) application contexts and abstract syntaxes supported, and (c) limitations or ranges on values, etc.

**From standards to products**

Just like with other international standards, obtaining broad consensus among numerous constituencies has made many OSI management standards rife with potentially incompatible options, gaps and ambiguities. This can lead to incompatible implementations. Chappell [4] describes the commercialization process to overcome this hurdle. It fosters development of multi vendor products competitively available in any country and interoperable with comparable products from any other world region. Milestones are regionally harmonized implementation agreements profiles, called *International Standard Profiles* (ISPs), that clarify ambiguities, fill gaps and specify interoperable subsets of OSI standards. ISPs themselves become ISO standards.

OSI management ISPs are being completed in parallel with activities needed to complete remaining OSI management standards. Constituencies collaborating in ISP harmonization include the three *Regional OSI Workshops,* in which users heavily participate, as well as major vendor consortia such as the OSI/Network Management Forum, X-Open and the Japanese INTAP group. Reference [6] are North America's regional agreements serving as inputs to this international harmonization.

**Procurement and testing**

Other factors assisting convergence to interoperable products include recent discussions among countries to coordinate their individual network management procurement mandates. Compatible US and UK government procurement directions, based on harmonized implementation agreements, are likely by the end of 1991. Other European governments will follow suit shortly thereafter. Furthermore, to assure product conformance and interoperability, testing organizations such as the Corporation for Open Systems will begin to roll out testing products and services for these harmonized agreements also at the end of 1991.

The emerging combined pull of government and user demand, with the push of product availability, testing and interoperability, as well as public catalogues and dictionaries of managed objects, will likely be a major impetus to foster rapid fielding of all OSI technology in general.

**References**

[1] *ConneXions,* Special Issue: Network Management and Network Security, Volume 4, No. 8, August 1990.

[2] *ConneXions,* Special Issue: Network Management, Volume 3, No. 3, March 1989.

[3] Rose, Marshall T., "Components of OSI: The Application Layer Structure," *ConneXions,* Volume 4, No. 1, January 1990.

[4] Chappell, David, "Components of OSI: A Taxonomy of the players," *ConneXions,* Volume 3, No. 12, December 1989.

[5] LaBarre, Lee, "Management By Exception: OSI Event Generation, Reporting, and Logging," Invited Paper in Proceedings of the *Second International Symposium on Integrated Network Management,* Washington, D.C., North-Holland Publisher, April 1991.

[6] Stable Implementation Agreements for OSI Protocols: Part 18—Network Management, Version 4, Edition 1, NIST Special Publication 500-183, December 1990; Working Implementation Agreements for OSI Protocols: Part 18—Network Management, December 1990, NIST IR document in publication.

[7] Benford, Steve, "Components of OSI: The Directory Service," *ConneXions,* Volume 3, No. 6, June 1989.

[8] Marshall T. Rose, "The Simple Book—An Introduction to Management of TCP/IP-based internets," Prentice-Hall, 1990, ISBN 0-13-812611-9.

**PAUL J. BRUSIL** is a Principal Scientist in The MITRE Corporation's Distributed Processing Systems Division, Network Management Specialty Group and OSI Specialty Group. He is the organizer, convener and first chair of OIW's Network Management SIG and IFIP's *First International Symposium on Integrated Network Management.* He is the OIW's OSI User Representative to North America's four man delegation to the Regional Workshop Coordinating Committee working to eliminate regional incompatibilities in OSI implementations and thereby to bring globally interoperable OSI products to market as quickly as possible. Paul received his Ph.D from Harvard's Division of Engineering and Medical School in 1973.

# An Implementation of an OSI Network Management System

*Fred Halsall*
*Nasser Modiri*

The overall goal of the work reported in this article has been to investigate the software tools that are necessary to enable an Open Systems Interconnection (OSI) network, based on International Standards Organization (ISO) protocols, to be monitored and managed. To achieve this goal, the network manager system has been developed to allow the communication subsystems associated with all of the nodes connected to an OSI network to be managed in a dynamic way.

When there are a number of systems operating and manipulating many complex jobs interconnected by a network, the need for some network management facility is essential. The network manager developed is based on the ISO standards for OSI management. It is concerned primarily with the management of the communication subsystems in each node connected to an OSI network. The developed system does not attempt to implement all the management functions (that is, Management-Specific Application Service Elements—MSASEs) but rather shows how the developed framework can be used to provide these functions.

As applications of OSI are evolving, the topics not covered by the ISO Basic Reference Model [1–3] are manifesting themselves. These include network security, naming, and addressing, and (more recently) network management. Since one of the components of the system developed as part of this article is concerned with network management, a more detailed discussion of this topic is now presented.

## Network Management

The network management framework [4] has been defined to provide the means for the communication subsystems in all the nodes connected to a network to be remotely monitored and controlled. The general structure of the proposed management framework is shown in Figure 1. The network manager interacts with the Management Application Process (MAP) to monitor and control the communication subsystems in all network nodes. In practice, to allow for large—perhaps multisite—systems to be managed, the management framework is divided into a number of domains, each with its own domain manager. Within the scope of this article, however, only a single management domain is considered. Associated with each domain are MSASE(s) and a Common Management Information Service Element (CMISE) [5] [6]. The CMISE interacts with the set of Local Management Application Entities (LMAEs) on a peer-to-peer communication basis—one per communication subsystem—according to the Common Management Information Protocols (CMIPs) [7] [8]. To respond to a query, each LMAE interacts with the various protocol layers of the communication subsystem (that is, for the ISO Reference Model, layers 1 through 7) to obtain and transfer management data from and to the CMISE.

The bulk of the intelligence (and hence processing) associated with the management of a subnetwork is in the MSASEs and

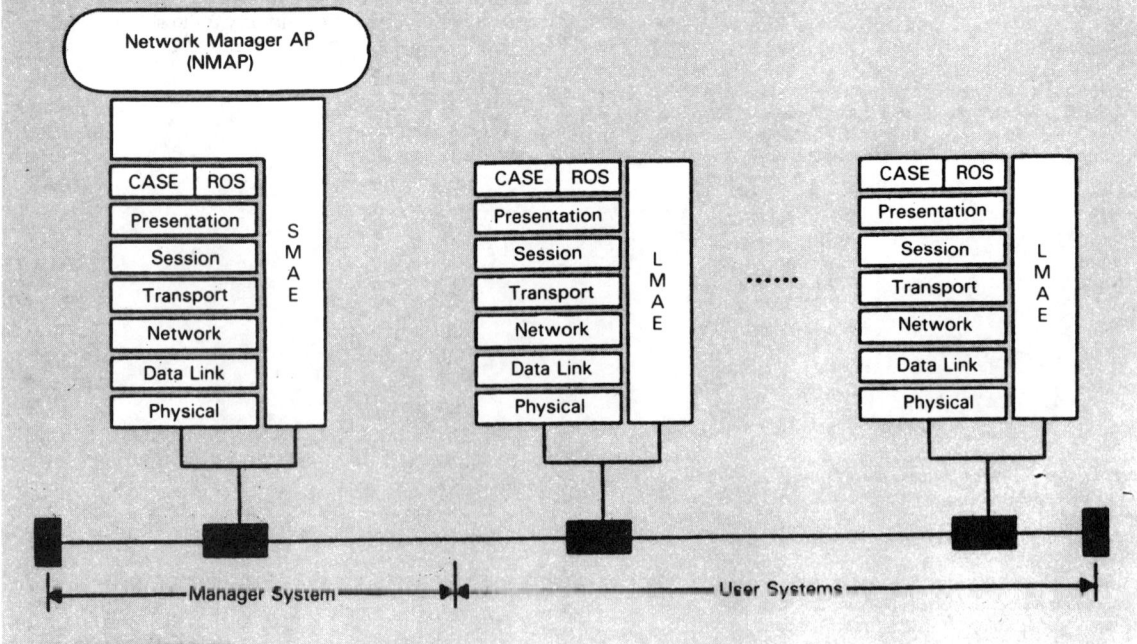

*Fig. 1. Network management framework.*

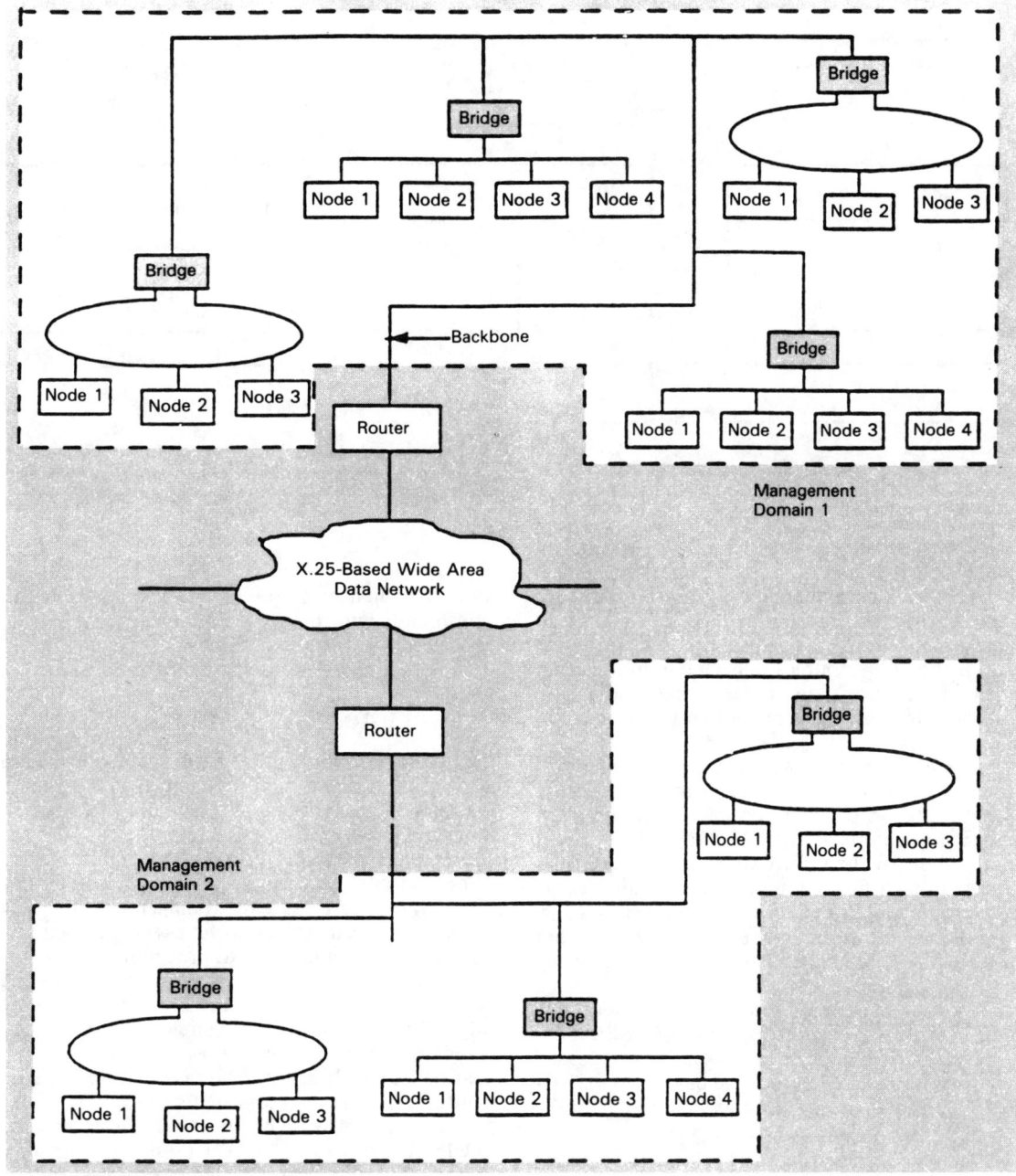

*Fig. 2. Typical LAN configuration.*

CMISE; the LMAEs simply provide the means for obtaining or controlling operational parameters used within each protocol layer of a communication subsystem. In this way, only a minimum set of functions need be added to each protocol layer (that is, extensions to the protocol layer's state-machine implementation in the form of additional incoming service primitives); hence, the processing overheads associated with the management aspects of an operational system are kept to a minimum.

Not every communication subsystem need have an LMAE, and the simpler its operations, the less there is a need for one. However, for complete control of a subsystem's operation, the LMAE must respond to commands from the MSASEs. There are five MSASEs residing on top of the CMISE that may be invoked by the network manager. These are: Fault Management (FM), Accounting Management (AM), Configuration and name Management (CM), Performance Management (PM), and Security Management (SM).

In response to a query from a network manager, the appropriate MSASE component will use the services supported by the CMISE to obtain or transfer the related management data from or to an LMAE. To perform these services, the CMISE, in turn, uses the services first of the Association Control Service Element (ACSE) [9] [10][1] application entity to establish an association with the appropriate LMAE, and then uses the services provided by a second sublayer, the Remote Operation Service Element (ROSE) [11] [12], to obtain or transfer the related data.

The manageable resources in an OSI network are known as the OSI resources (that is, managed objects). These comprise

---

[1]The implementation described in this article is based on the ISO/DIS CMIS, January 1989, in which the CMISE uses the services of ACSE for association establishment. However, in September 1989 there was a revision to the CMISE services in which the ACSE services are not directly used for association establishment.

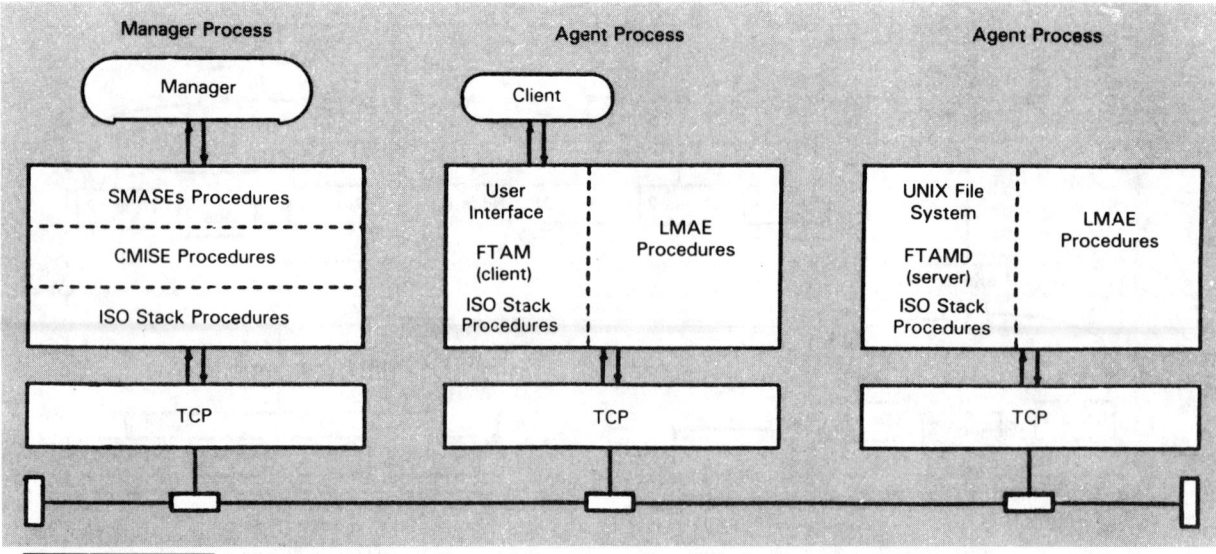

*Fig. 3. Experimental system.*

the protocol layers in each communication subsystem that are being used in the specific OSI Environment (OSIE). Hence, in order to manage an OSI network, the network manager must be able to monitor the OSI resources in each communication subsystem to obtain real-time data on performance and data traffic so as to be able to diagnose problems and optimize network usage.

Associated with each resource is a set of actions (directives) that enable a network manager to remotely carry out specific management operations on selected variables maintained by each layer and hence accessible through the attached LMAE interface. Normally, most of the information is maintained by means of simple counters whose contents may be requested by a CMISE in response to an MSASE request. However, if a particular event occurs (i.e., a threshold is reached) in a layer that indicates a possible fault, the layer may inform the CMISE directly.

After an association has been established between the CMISE and an LMAE (using the services of the ACSE), management data can start to flow until the association is released (or aborted). Management data is exchanged between a manager (through the CMISE) and an agent (that is, an LMAE) for the following purposes:

- *Event reporting*—used by the LMAE to initiate the transfer of event data back to the CMISE
- *Information transfer*—used by the CMISE to request statistical data from an LMAE
- *Control*—used by the CMISE to initiate selected actions by an LMAE

An example of a large but typically interconnected set of Local Area Networks (LANs) is shown in Figure 2. Although the management of this type of network can be carried out as a single entity, in practice it is more likely that it is considered as a linked set of LANs (domains), each managed by a different manager. The network management system that has been developed is therefore intended to investigate a single management domain.

The article comprises ten sections. After this section, we describe the experimental system that has been used. The section after that describes the MSASE services. Then, we describe the CMISE service primitives. The next section describes the CMISE protocol functions that the manager tool uses. The LMAE protocol, which is used to response to the remote operations requested by the CMISE services, is then covered, and the interfaces devised for the network manager system after that. We then give some examples of the network manager commands with their associated responses. The section after that describes the network manager system development environment. Finally, we discuss our conclusions.

## Experimental System

Before describing the results obtained, it is necessary to first describe the experimental system that has been used to carry out these investigations. A schematic of the system is shown in Figure 3.

Essentially, it comprises three systems—Sun Workstations® in practice. Two systems communicate using File Transfer Access and Management (FTAM) [13], and a third system is then used to act as the manager station. The latter contains a set of MSASE procedures that provide the manager with the means of controlling and accessing parameters associated with the ISO stacks in the other two stations. The MSASEs achieve this by using the services of the CMISE, which in turn communicates with the LMAEs in the other two stations, according to the Network Management (NM) protocol to carry out the requested service.

The NM software has been written to be compatible with the ISODE software [14]. The ISODE comprises a set of procedures that collectively implement the transport, session, presentation, and application layers of the ISO model.[2] These are then liked to the particular application software to form a single application process that runs under the UNIX® operating system. Communication between application processes is then carried out through Transmission Control Protocol (TCP) [15].

The approach has been to write additional procedures to implement the various MSASEs, and these have then been linked with the other software in that node to form a single, expanded application process. In this way, all the parameters associated with the ISO stack procedures are readily accessible by the LMAE procedures. Thus, as the FTAM client and server processes communicate through the ISO stack, operational pa-

---

®Sun Workstation is a registered trademark of Sun Microsystems, Inc.

[2]This software is not an implementation of a specific OSI protocol suite.

®UNIX is a registered trademark of AT&T Bell Laboratories.

rameters relating to the latter can be accessed or changed by the network manager via the MSASEs, CMISE, and CMIPs.

## MSASE Services

The various services available to the network manager are listed in Table I along with their mapping to the various

Table I. Mapping of MSASE Commands to CMISE Services

| Service | Command | CMISE Service |
|---|---|---|
| FM | TCP | Local |
|  | event | M-EVENT-REPORT |
|  | cevent | M-EVENT-REPORT-CONFIRMED |
|  | linked | M-LINKED-REPLY |
|  | cget | M-GET |
|  | set | M-SET |
|  | cset | M-SET-CONFIRMED |
|  | action | M-ACTION |
|  | caction | M-ACTION-CONFIRMED |
| AM | Finirq | Local |
|  | Ainirq | Local |
| CM | mn | Local |
|  | reset | Local |
|  | load | Local |
|  | time | M-GET |
|  | syspr | M-GET |
| PM | get | M-GET |
|  | put | M-GET |
| SM | Username | M-ACTION-CONFIRMED |
|  | Password | M-ACTION-CONFIRMED |
| Others | bell | Local |
|  | help | Local |
|  | quit | Local |

CMISE services. These are grouped into six categories: FM, AM, CM, PM, SM, and others. Normally, a command will be mapped into a corresponding CMISE service primitive and, in turn, the CMISE communicates with an LMAE (according to the CMIPs) to perform the appropriate remote operation.

Table II. CMISE Primitives with their Corresponding PDUs

| Service Primitive | CIMP Operation (PDUs) |
|---|---|
| M-INITIALIZE | INIRQ |
| M-EVENT-REPORT | m-EventReport |
| M-EVENT-REPORT-CONFIRMED | m-EventReport-Confirmed |
| M-LINKED-REPLY | m-Linked-Reply |
| M-GET | m-Get |
| M-SET | m-Set |
| M-SET-CONFIRMED | m-Set-Confirmed |
| M-ACTION | m-Action |
| M-ACTION-CONFIRMED | m-Action-Confirmed |
| M-CREATE | m-Create |
| M-CANCEL | m-Cancel |
| M-DELETE | m-Delete |
| M-TERMINATE | TERRQ |
| M-UABORT | UABRQ |

Some commands, however, have only local significance—for example, "TCP," which returns true if the local TCP is running, and "mn," which returns the name of the network manager system.

## CMISE Services

The user services available at the CMISE interface are of two types: confirmed and nonconfirmed. It should be noted, however, that in the implemented system with the confirmed services it is the remote LMAE that generates the response Protocol Data Unit (PDU) directly, rather than a response primitive being generated. In general, prior to passing or obtaining data to or from a remote LMAE, an association must first be established between the CMISE and the particular LMAE involved. This is done by means of the M-INITIALIZE service. Similarly, after the particular management operation, the association must be closed and this is done by means of the M-TERMINATE service.

Table III. States - CMISE Regime Management

| Abbreviated | Description |
|---|---|
| INI-PD | Enter the wait association confirmation state (wait for INIRP PDU). |
| TER-PD | Enter wait termination confirmation state (wait for TERRP PDU). |
| INITIALIZED | CMISE association establishment is invoked. |
| IDLE | CMISE regime ended. |

Within the MSASEs, a routine is used to a get a line from the keyboard and process it against the table of commands available. Thus, when a command is issued the appropriate CMISE service primitive is invoked, with relevant data being passed to the CMISE in the form of parameters. As an example, the "PM.get" MSASE service primitive is mapped into the M-GET CMISE service primitive with parameters:

ObjectClass = PM  
ObjectInstance = name of account  
Result = returned result

On receipt of a CMISE service primitive (incoming event), the local CMISE protocol machine will create a corresponding CMIP PDU. A list of the PDUs corresponding to each CMISE service primitive is given in Table II.

## CMIPs

On receipt of a CMISE service primitive, the CMISE protocol machine will generate an appropriate PDU and send this to

Table IV. Specific Actions - CMISE Regime Management

| [1] | Send the PDU constructed as user data using the services of the ACSE Application Entity. |
|---|---|
| [2] | Initialize all additional state information. |
| [4] | Output an error message. |

the peer LMAE protocol machine using the services of either the ACSE or ROSE sublayer. The CMISE uses the services of the ACSE Sublayer for connection establishment (and termi-

Table V. Predicates - CMISE Regime Management

| P1 | M-INITIALIZE.REQUEST primitive acceptable. |
|---|---|
| P2 | Result parameter of the A-ASSOCIATE.CONFIRM primitive indicates success of the operation. |

nation) to the required LMAE and ACSE, in turn, makes use of the presentation layer services as described in ISO/DIS 8650/2.

After an association, the CMISE uses the services of the ROSE sublayer to carry out the appropriate operation.

On receipt of a CMISE primitive, the state-machine implementation for the CMISE uses the parameters provided by the service primitive to encode the corresponding PDU, which is then transferred to the LMAE as the user data field of the ACSE or ROSE service primitive. The procedure of the association establishment of the CMISE with an LMAE is outlines as follows.

Table VI. Incoming Events - CMISE Regime Management

| Name | Incoming Event |
|---|---|
| M-INIRQ | M-INITIALIZE.REQUEST service primitive. |
| M-TERRQ | M-TERMINATE.REQUEST service primitive. |
| M-UABRQ | M-U-ABORT.REQUEST service primitive. |
| M-PABIN | M-P-ABORT.INDICATION service primitive. |
| INIRP | INITIALIZE response PDU. |
| TERRP | TERMINATE response PDU. |
| UABRP | U-ABORT response PDU. |

## CMISE Invocation

On receipt of and M-INITIALIZE.REQUEST service primitive:
- Construct an INIRQ PDU.
- Send the INIRQ PDU as user data on the A-ASSOCIATE.REQUEST service primitive.
- Enter the initialize pending state.

Table VII. Outgoing Events - LMAE Regime Management

| Name | Outgoing Event |
|---|---|
| M-INICF | M-INITIALIZE.CONFIRM service primitive. |
| M-TERCF | M-TERMINATE.CONFIRM service primitive. |
| A-UABIN | A-U-ABORT.INDICATION service primitive. |
| A-PABIN | A-P-ABORT.INDICATION service primitive. |
| UABRQ | U-ABORT request PDU. |
| INIRQ | INITIALIZE request PDU. |
| TERRQ | TERMINATE request PDU. |

## LMAE Responding

On receipt of an INIRQ PDU:
- Check the access parameters.
- Check the functional unit to determine capability; if OK, construct an INIRP PDU with the same functional unit; if NOTOK, construct an INIRP PDU with reason for failure.
- Send INIRP PDU as user data on an A-ASSOCIATE.RESPONSE service primitive.

Table VIII. Initiating Entity State Table: CMISE Association

| Event/State | IDLE | INI-PD | INITIALIZED | TER-PD |
|---|---|---|---|---|
| M-INIRQ | 1 | | | |
| INIRP | | 2 | | |
| M-TERRQ | | | 3 | |
| TERRP | | | | 4 |
| M-UABRQ | 5 | 5 | 5 | |
| UABRP | 6 | 6 | 6 | |
| M-PABIN | 7 | 7 | 7 | |

## CMISE Confirmation

On receipt of an INIRP PDU:
- If the result parameter is success, construct and issue an M-INITIALIZE.CONFIRM (that is, from its parameters establish association).
- If the result parameter is failure, issue an M-INITIALIZE.CONFIRM (that is, from its parameters, deduce that the association cannot be established).

Table IX. Initiating Entity State Table: Detailed Entries

| 1: | P1: | INIRQ, [1], [2] | - | INI-PD |
|---|---|---|---|---|
| | P̂1: | M-INICF [4] | - | IDLE |
| 2: | P2: | M-INICF | - | INITIALIZED |
| | P̂2: | M-INICF [4] | - | IDLE |
| 3: | | TERRQ, [1] | - | TER-PD |
| 4: | | M-TERCF | - | IDLE |
| 5: | | A-PABIN, [3] | - | IDLE |
| 6: | | A-UABIN | - | IDLE |
| 7: | | A-PABIN | - | IDLE |
| 8: | | UABRQ, [1] | - | IDLE |

Collectively, Tables III to IX summarize the protocol state-machine devised for the CMISE to make a proper connection with an LMAE. When an association has been established, the initiator requests the responder to perform remote operations. The responder in turn attempts these operations, replying with either a result or an error. This process continues until the initiator decides to release the association. One of the most frequently used ROSE services by the CMISE is the RO-

Table X. Mapping of MSASE Commands to CMISE Primitives and their Use of CMIP PDUs

| Command | CMISE Primitive | CMIP PDU | ROSE Service Used |
|---|---|---|---|
| get | M-GET.REQUEST | m-Get | RO-INVOKE.REQUEST |
| set | M-SET.REQUEST | m-Set | RO-INVOKE.REQUEST |
| action | M-ACTION.REQUEST | m-Action | RO-INVOKE.REQUEST |

INVOKE.REQUEST service primitive, which requests an operation to be performed remotely. This service may only be invoked by the network manager (the MSASEs and the CMISE). When a request is sent to an LMAE (agent) to perform a remote operation, the agent returns a result either of error or otherwise. As

Table XI. States - LMAE Regime Management

| Abbreviated | Description |
|---|---|
| INI-PD | Enter the wait association confirmation state (wait for INIRP PDU). |
| TER-PD | Enter the wait termination confirmation state (wait for TERRP PDU). |
| INITIALIZED | LMAE association establishment is invoked. |
| IDLE | LMAE regime ended. |

an example, Table X shows the mapping operation between typical MSASE services, first to the corresponding CMISE primitives, then to the CMIP PDUs, and finally to the ROSE services.

# LMAE Protocol

The LMAE uses the services of the ACSE sublayer for responding to a CMISE connection establishment or termination. After an association, the LMAE uses the services of the

Table XII. Specific Actions - LMAE Regime Management

| | |
|---|---|
| [1] | Send the PDU constructed as user data using the services of the ACSE Application Entity. |
| [2] | Initialize all additional state information. |
| [3] | Communications failure. |
| [4] | An error message. |

ROSE sublayer to return the results of the requested remote operations. On receipt of an ACSE/ROSE primitive, the state-machine implementation of the LMAE takes the PDU intended for it from the primitive received and locally generates an appropriate CMIP response PDU. The LMAEs do not generate service primitives. Hence, if a PDU is one of the confirmed type, the LMAEs reply with a CMIP to convey to the CMISE

Table XIII. Predicates - LMAE Regime Management

| | |
|---|---|
| P3 | Association is acceptable for establishment. |
| P4 | Association is acceptable for termination. |

the result of the remote operation carried out. A summary of the LMAE protocol is presented in Tables XI to XVII. After an association has been established, the LMAE PDUs, shown in Table XVIII, relating to remote operations are transferred to the CMISE on the data field of the ROSE service primitives. Table XIX shows examples of the mapping of the LMAE PDUs to the ROSE primitives.

Table XIV. Incoming Events - LMAE Regime Management

| Name | Incoming Event |
|---|---|
| INIRQ | INITIALIZE request PDU. |
| TERRQ | TERMINATE request PDU. |
| A-PABIN | A-P-ABORT.INDICATION service primitive. |
| A-UABIN | A-U-ABORT.INDICATION service primitive. |
| UABRQ | U-ABORT request PDU. |

On receipt of an RO-INVOKE.INDICATION service primitive, the LMAE will perform the remote operation and return a result or an error response. In the former case, RO-RESULT.REQUEST is used and in the latter case, RO-ERROR.REQUEST is used to return the outcome of the operation.

Table XV. Outgoing Events - CMISE Regime Management

| Name | Outgoing Event |
|---|---|
| INIRP | INITIALIZE response PDU. |
| TERRP | TERMINATE response PDU. |

# Network Manager Operation

Before describing the features of the experimental network manager system devised, it is useful to first describe in detail the MSASE display and the network agent display. The latter has been used for monitoring and debugging purposes. A description of these is now presented.

## MSASEs

The MSASE is the interface with the MAP. It thus forms the user interface where an association can be invoked with a network agent and remote operations initiated. A network manager cannot have multiple associations with agents concurrently, and single associations are only permitted in the experimental network manager system. The network manager can access dif-

Table XVI. Responding Entity State Table: LMAE Association

| Event/State | IDLE | INI-PD | INITIALIZED | TER-PD |
|---|---|---|---|---|
| INIRQ | 1 | | | |
| TERRQ | | | 2 | |
| A-PABIN | | 3 | 3 | 3 |
| A-UABIN | | 3 | 3 | 3 |
| UABRQ | | 3 | 3 | 3 |

ferent facilities (i.e., OSI resources) from around the network. There are two possible methods of invoking the MSASEs services:

- **Interactive:** The manager may execute the MSASE services interactively and invoke operations through commands (that is, either local or remote).
- **Embedded:** The MSASE program automatically forms an association and invokes operations as required. This can be used in cases when there is repetition, for example, when it is required to examine the network statistics for a number of nodes in a predefined sequence.

Table XVII. Responding Entity State Table: Detailed Entries

| 1: | P3: | [2] | - | INI-PD |
|---|---|---|---|---|
| | P̂3: | INIRP [4], [1] | - | IDLE |
| 2: | P4: | TERRP | - | IDLE |
| | P̂4: | TERRP [4], [1] | - | IDLE |
| 3: | | [3] | - | IDLE |

In the interactive mode, the manager is provided with a user-friendly interface, and when an operation is performed useful information is given about, for example, the state of a counter and whether it has reached a threshold level. Conceptually, the remote OSI resources can be considered analogous to a number of dial gauges, accessible only by the manager, that show the state of each network node. If the manager needs to know, or be reminded, about a certain operational parameter

Table XVIII. LMAE PDUs

| LMAE PDU | Type |
|---|---|
| INIRP | confirmed |
| m-EventReport-Confirmed | confirmed |
| m-Get | confirmed |
| m-Set-Confirmed | confirmed |
| m-Action-Confirmed | confirmed |
| m-Create | confirmed |
| m-Cancel | confirmed |
| m-Delete | confirmed |
| TERRP | confirmed |

associated with an OSI resource, then he/she should be presented only with the information requested rather than having to find his/her way through a large amount of data, most of

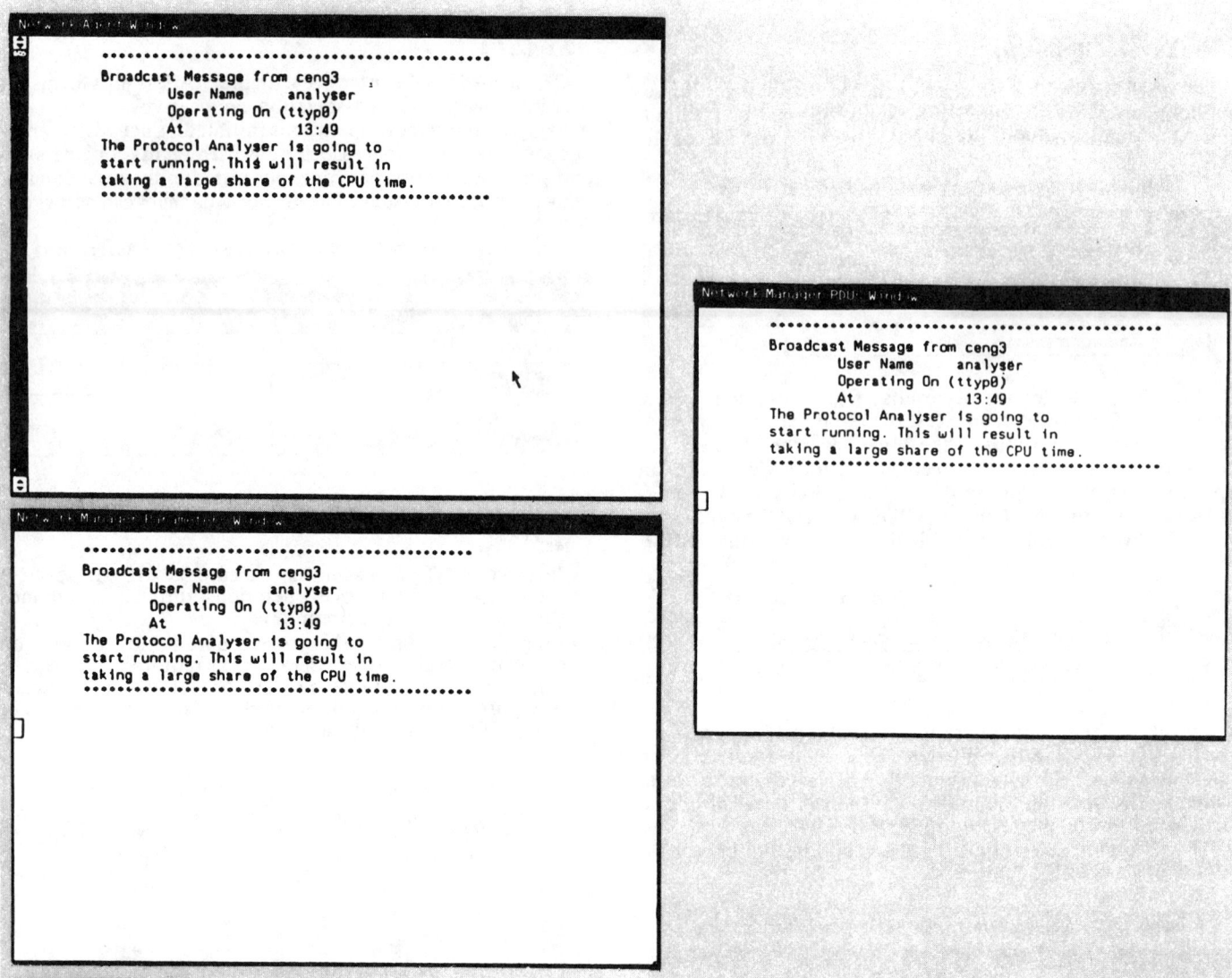

*Fig. 4. MSASE windows.*

which is irrelevant to him/her. Although in an operational NM system just a simple query-response type of interface will be used, in the experimental system three windows are used in order for the user to monitor the process. These are:

- *Network manager*—This window is a process with a scroll bar on its side to enable the manager to go back to the history of his/her work (i.e., commands issued). This window can take on-line commands from the manager and gives responses accordingly.
- *Network manager parameters*—This window has no history, and the parameters used with the CMISE primitives are displayed on it. Detailed information about the status of running the network manager program can be obtained from this window.
- *Network manager PDUs*—This window has no history, and it displays the encoded and decoded CMIP PDUs relating to each NM user command.

Thus, in practice, since a network manager is only interested in the result of the operations (commands) entered, the first window is the only place with which he/she is concerned. However, it is important to note that the windows do not have to all be executed on the same node and they could be running (in any combination), for example, on a dumb terminal connected to the node.

When the MSASE is invoked, it first checks the three operational windows to verify that they do exist by opening them. If they do not, association with a network agent is not established and the network manager is warned; otherwise, a message is sent all these windows. The type of message selected is the type to give useful information to the network manager about its node. A typical opening scene is shown in Figure 4. The message on each window comprises five parts: the host name, the user name, the window (that is, *tty*) from where the network manager's program is executed, the time of day, and a comment message. The message is kept in a file, and its contents can be easily changed.

Table XIX. Mapping of LMAE PDUs to ROSE Primitives

| LMAE PDU | ROSE Primitive |
| --- | --- |
| m-Get | RO-RESULT.REQUEST |
| m-Set | RO-RESULT.REQUEST |
| m-Action | RO-RESULT.REQUEST |

## Network Agent Display

In practice, it is unlikely for any display to be associated with the NM process on the agent system. Again, however, in the experimental system three windows are used on each system for development and debugging purposes. Each Network Agent Display (NAD) provides easy-to-understand short messages to indicate the operations taking place.

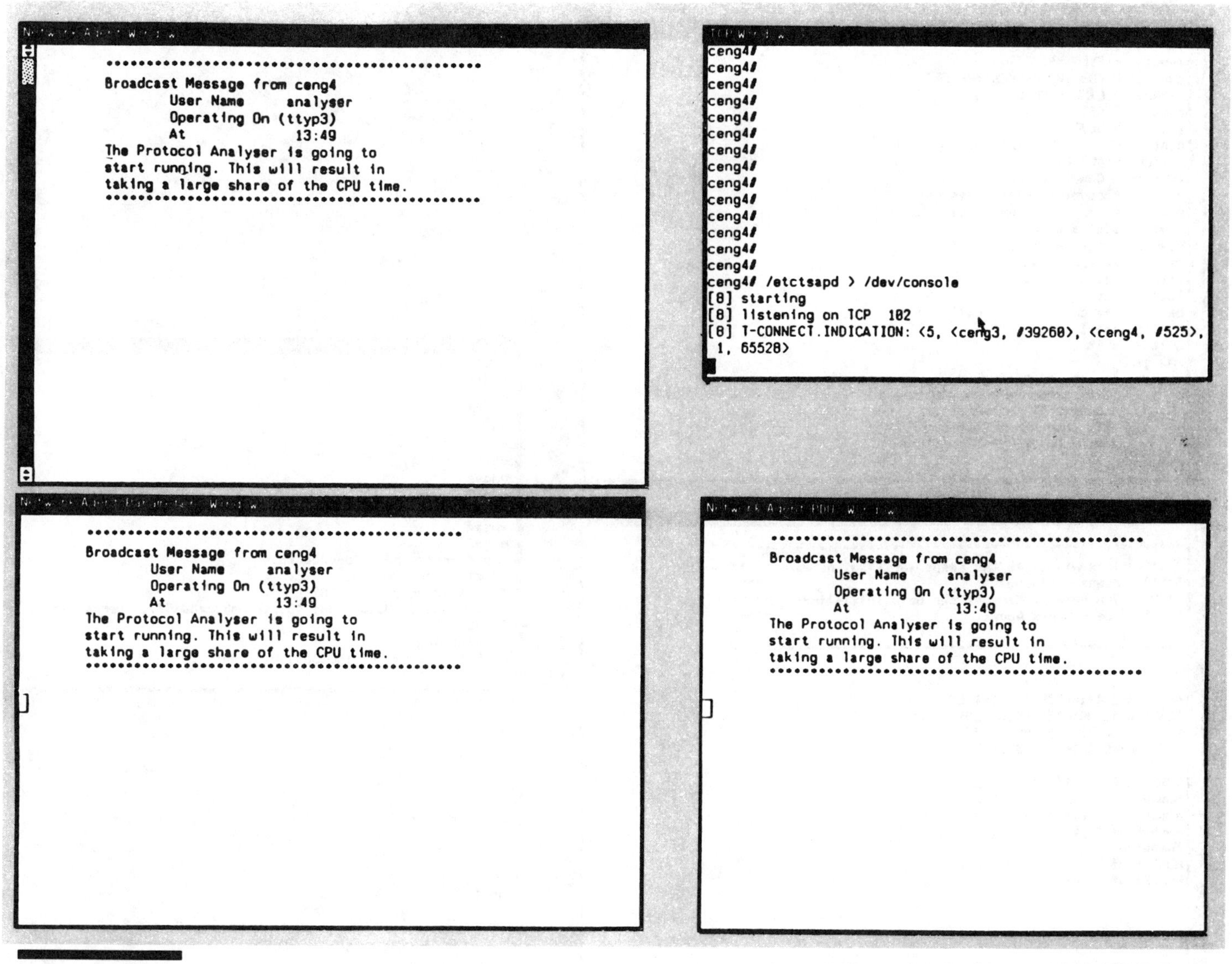

*Fig. 5. NAD windows.*

The NAD is similar in design to the MSASEs, and information has been divided into three categories: supervisory information relating to the operational commands issued by the manager, information relating to the CMISE primitives, and information regarding the encoding and decoding of the CMIP PDUs. The NAD comprises four windows, three of which are specific to the network agent. The fourth is for the usage of the underlying communication. They are:

- *Network agent*—This window has a scroll bar provided on its side to provide the history of the operations requested by the manager. Network-agent-specific information is only displayed in this window, that is, when the manager carries out an operation. The name or result of the operation is indicated in this window.
- *Network agent parameters*—This window has no history, and the LMAE primitive parameters are displayed on it. From the information provided in this window, the agent can gain a very detailed knowledge of the status and parameters used by the network agent program.
- *Network agent PDUs*—This window has no history, and CMIP operation PDUs (encoded and decoded) are displayed on it. The PDUs displayed in this window are shown in terms of Abstract Syntax Notation One (ASN.1).
- *TCP*—Communication-specific information is displayed in this window, and the access right of this window is that of the superuser. This is a command-type window with a scroll bar provided on it side to access it history.

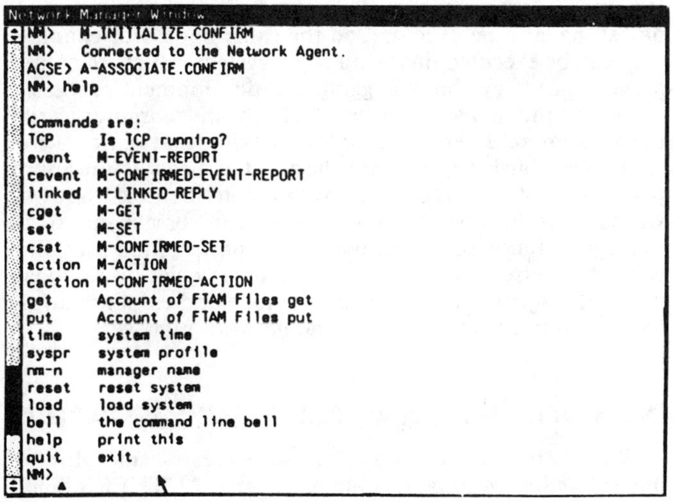

*Fig. 6. Help command.*

```
TCP      Is TCP running?
event    M-EVENT-REPORT
cevent   M-CONFIRMED-EVENT-REPORT
linked   M-LINKED-REPLY
cget     M-GET
set      M-SET
cset     M-CONFIRMED-SET
action   M-ACTION
caction  M-CONFIRMED-ACTION
get      Account of FTAM Files get
put      Account of FTAM Files put
time     system time
syspr    system profile
rm-n     manager name
reset    reset system
load     load system
bell     the command line bell
help     print this
quit     exit
NM> get
         You are operating on      --> ceng3
         This command allows you to get
         account of the number of files
         GET, when using FTAM and FTAMD
         under the ISODE-4.0 software.
NM>
```

a. MSASEs

```
***** This window is the responder (i.e. Network *****
***** Agent  Window).                            *****
***** The Network Manager can only initialise    *****
***** The Network Agent.                         *****

NA>    M-INITIALIZE.INDICATION
ACSE>  A-ASSOCIATE.INDICATION
NA>    M-INITIALISE.RESPONSE
ACSE>  A-ASSOCIATE.RESPONSE

Number of f-get() is --> 1
Number of f-get() is --> 2
Number of f-get() is --> 3
Number of f-get() is --> 4
Number of f-get() is --> 5
Number of f-get() is --> 6
Number of f-get() is --> 7
```

b. NAD

```
ceng4#
ceng4#
ceng4#
ceng4#
ceng4#
ceng4#
ceng4#
ceng4#
ceng4#
ceng4#
ceng4#
ceng4# /etctsapd > /dev/console
[8] starting
[8] listening on TCP 102
[8] T-CONNECT.INDICATION: <5, <ceng3, #39352>, <ceng4, #525>,
     1, 65528>
[8] starting
[8] ROS>  RO_INVOKE.INDICATION/5: get
```

*Fig. 7. PM.get command usage.*

An example of a typical set of windows is given in Figure 5. It is important to note that all the agent windows (processes) do not all have to be executed on the same node. For example, they can be executed on the manager system, which, of course, greatly speeds up the debugging and development process.

When the network agent, through the communication mechanism, receives a request for a service (that is, first a connection establishment), before the agent replies with the appropriate acceptance PDU of the association, it checks the NAD windows. If these windows do not exist, an abort is sent to the manager; otherwise, the response is a confirmation providing everything else is well. Hence, after an association establishment, the agent goes into a server mode and responds to the MSASE services requested by the network manager.

## Network Management Usage Example

To illustrate the use of the NM software, consider three of the MSASE commands, namely, the "OTHERS.help," "PM.get," and "PM.put" commands. The prompt "NM >" is displayed whenever the manager can type in a command. To get a listing of the table of commands shown earlier in Table I displayed, the network manager types in the command "help," as shown in Figure 6. In the experimental system, the two agents' systems are continuously communicating using FTAM; one is a client, and the other is a server. The two commands, PM.get and PM.put, have been selected to illustrate the interactions between the FTAM client and FTAMD server application programs of the ISODE software. The FTAM client and the FTAMD server are set up on two Sun Workstations, as was shown earlier in Figure 3.

Two commands that are available with the FTAM client are the "get" and "put" commands. The get command can be used to get a file from a source file and put it at a destination. The put command is similar to the get command but its operation is in reverse. A counter of the use of each command is kept and may be remotely accessed from the manager system. This is the example shown in Figure 7a. The PM.get command is issued to determine the number of usages of the FTAM get command. This is first mapped into an appropriate CMISE M-GET.REQUEST service primitive. Then, through the state-machine implementation devise, this generates the m-Get PDU. The ROSE service primitive RO-INVOKE.REQUEST is then used to transfer the m-Get PDU, as its data field, to the peer ROSE and subsequently to the LMAE to carry out the requested remote operation. An indication of the receipt of the m-Get PDU at the NAD is shown in Figure 7b.

Similarly, if the manager uses the PM.put command relating to the usage of the FTAM client put command, results similar to those of the PM.get command described will be obtained. Finally, the association termination of the network manager with an network agent is achieved through the use of the "quit" command.

## Development Environment

The development environment used for the network management is based on Sun Workstations, and all its software has been implemented using C [16], running under the UNIX operating system.

## Conclusions

The aim of the work described in this article was to develop a network management system to monitor, analyze, and manage the interactions between a network agent and the OSI resources that are used by the agent. The results of the analysis are presented in a suitable format, with complementary comments to aid the network manager in verifying the results obtained.

In addition to the network management system, two other software tools have been developed as the basis of some instrumentation available to a network manager. For example, a Dynamic Tester [17] is implemented that allows a suspected faulty system to be tested dynamically and the cause of the fault to be diagnosed automatically. Secondly, a Network Protocol Analyzer [18] is implemented that provides facilities to monitor, decode, and analyze the interactions taking place between two computers connected to an OSI network. The NM is capable of bringing either of these two instruments into the logical active network for the monitoring, testing, analysis, and management of a communication subsystem under consideration.

## Acknowledgments

The authors would like to acknowledge both the Wollongong Group and the Northrop Corporation for providing them with an early release of the ISODE-5.0 software.

## References

[1] ISO 7498, "OSI: Description of the Basic Reference Model for Open System Interconnections," 1983.
[2] ISO 7498 ADD 1, "OSI: Basic Reference Model for OSI—Connectionless-Mode Transmission," 1987.
[3] ISO 7498-1 PDAD 2, "OSI: Basic Reference Model for OSI—Multipeer Transmission," 1988.
[4] ISO/IEC JTC1/SC21/WG4 N, "OSI: System Management Overview," 1988.
[5] ISO/DIS 9595/1, "OSI: Management Information Service—Part 1, Overview," 1989.
[6] ISO/DIS 9595/2, "OSI: Management Information Service—Part 2, Common Management Information Service Definition," 1989.
[7] ISO/DIS 9596/1, "OSI: Management Information Protocol Specification—Part 1, Overview," 1989.
[8] ISO/DIS 9596/2, "OSI: Management Information Protocol Specification —Part 2, Common Management Information Protocol," 1989.
[9] ISO 8649/2, "OSI: Service Definition for Common Application Service Elements—Part 2, Association Control," 1988.
[10] ISO 8650/2, "OSI: Protocol Specification for Common Application Service Elements—Part 2, Association Control," 1988.
[11] ISO 9072/1, "OSI: Text Communication—Message-Oriented Test Interchange System (MOTIS)—Remote Operations, Part 1: Model, Notation and Service Definition," 1988.
[12] ISO 9072/2, "OSI: Text Communication—Message-Oriented Test Interchange System (MOTIS)—Remote Operations, Part 2: Protocol Specification," 1988.
[13] "OSI: File Transfer, Access and Management," final text: DIS 8571-1, "Part 1, General Introduction," DIS 8571-2, "Part 2, Virtual Filestore Definition," DIS 8571-3, "Part 3, File Service Definition," and DIS 8571-4, "Part 4, File Protocol Specification," 1988.
[14] M. T. Rose, *The ISO Development Environment, User's Manuals*, The Wollongong Group, 5.0 edition, 1989.
[15] Wollongong Group, "TCP/IP Software," 1988.
[16] B. W. Kernighan and D. M. Ritchie, *The C Programming Language*, Prentice-Hall, 1987.
[17] F. Halsall and N. Modiri, "A Dynamic Tester for Use With OSI Networks," submitted to *IEEE Net. Mag.*, 1989.
[18] F. Halsall and N. Modiri, "A Protocol Analyzer For The Monitoring And Analysis Of OSI Networks," submitted to *IEEE Net. Mag.*, 1989.

## Biography

**Fred Halsall** has been involved in data communications for nearly 20 years. He has written many articles in this field, and he has also published two books, *Introduction to Data Communications and Computer Networks* and *Data Communications, Computer Networks, and OSI*.

He is currently Professor of Communication Engineering at the University of Wells Swansea (UK). His current research interests, in addition to OSI network management, include various aspects of integrated multi-service communication networks.

**Nasser Modiri** received his B.S., M.S., and Ph.D. in electronics engineering from the University of Sussex (UK), the University of Southampton (UK), and the University of Sussex, in 1985, 1986, and 1989, respectively.

In 1988, he joined the Networking Centre of Hemel Hempstead, and, in 1989, he worked as a Principal Engineer with the High-level Design Authority to design ISO-based Network Management Systems at the STC Telecommunications (UK). He is currently Systems Engineer at the Teknekron Communications Systems in the United States. His current research interests include dynamically testing ISO-based systems, development of expert management systems, and testing of OSI/NM Forum systems.

## The OSI Model

# The OSI Network Management Model

Balancing the responsibilities of OSI's agents and platforms — and their interaction protocols — is complex, but OSI helps by offering functions lacking in Internet's SNMP.

Yechiam Yemini

There were dramatic shifts in the structure and role of networked systems within enterprises in the past decade. From isolated data-processing islands, networked computing systems have grown into complex mission-critical enterprise-wide systems. The network, the computer, and the very enterprise rapidly are becoming indistinguishable. These changes lead to significant risks and cost exposure associated with operations. For example, failures of a bank network can paralyze its operations, delays of security trades through brokerage system bottlenecks can cost in dollars and customers, and loss of hospital lab reports can prevent timely diagnosis and care. The goal of network management technologies is to reduce the risks and costs exposure associated with operations of enterprise systems.

Management systems are responsible to monitor, interpret, and control the network operations. A typical management system is depicted in Fig. 1. Vendors equip their devices with agent software to monitor and collect operational data (e.g., error statistics) into local databases, and/or detect exceptional events (e.g., error rates exceed threshold). Management platform workstations query device data, or obtain event notifications through management protocols. The management platform supports tools to display the data graphically, interpret it, and control operations.

This management paradigm is *platform centered*. Management applications are centralized in platforms, separated from the managed data and control functions in the devices. Platform-centered management reflects older network environments where devices lacked resources to run management software, management data and functions were relatively simple, and network organizations could devote the personnel needed to handle operations. The implications of these assumptions and their validity for current networks will be considered later.

The main challenge of management standardization is to develop conventions to support integrated management of heterogeneous networks. Platform-centered management requires a few standards. First, access by platforms to multivendor devices must be unified through a standard management protocol. Second, the structure of the agent's management databases, manipulated by the protocol, must be standardized. Together, these standards permit a platform to access and manipulate managed information at multivendor device agents. The OSI and Internet management models seek to standardize both areas.

Merely moving management information from devices to platforms, however, is insufficient to eliminate the curse of heterogeneity. Two additional barriers to integrated management arise: platform and semantic heterogeneity.

Platform heterogeneity means that management applications must be replicated for each major platform. For example, a device vendor wishing to offer six applications over five platforms may need to develop and maintain 30 product versions. Therefore, a number of recent consortia (e.g., OSF, XOPEN, POSIX) are pursuing management platform standards.

Semantic heterogeneity arises when different devices use different information to represent similar network behaviors. A management application program requires a uniform semantic model of the managed information it processes. It is necessary to standardize the very meaning of managed information. Various IEEE and CCITT protocol committees pursue this challenge, building managed information standards for protocol entities.

## Why Is Management Difficult?

Consider an example of a network "storm" to illustrate management complexities. Storms involving rapid escalation of cascading failures are not uncommon in networks. Figure 2 depicts

---

YECHIAM YEMINI is a member of the Computer Science Department at Columbia University, where he presently serves as the director of the New York State Center of Advanced Technology in computer and information systems.

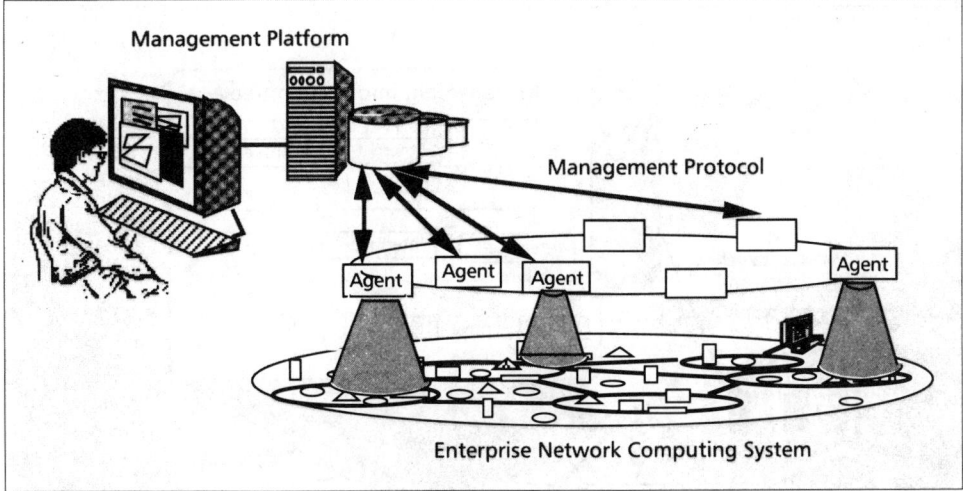

**Figure 1.** *Architecture of a network management system.*

a T1 link multiplexing a large number of connections (e.g., X.25 virtual circuits, or TCP) to a server/host. Suppose a long burst of noise disrupts the link causing packet loss (Fig. 2a). Logical link level protocols (above the physical layer) invoke automatic retransmission. They result in a burst of retransmission tasks at the interface processor queue (Fig. 2b) loading its queue and leading to its thrashing. Higher layer transport entities timeout and respond with a burst of corrective activities (e.g., reset connections). This burst processing of communications at host CPUs (Fig. 2c) leads to their thrashing, too.

Generally, protocol stack mechanisms handle lower-layer problems through corrective actions at higher layers. These mechanisms can escalate the very problems they intend to solve.

How can such complex network fault behaviors be monitored, detected, and handled? Suppose that relevant operational variables (e.g., T1 bit-error rates and the size of the interface processor queue) can be observed as depicted in Fig. 3. The storm formation could be detected from the correlation of the sudden growth in error rates and the resulting growth in queue size.

What management information should be used to capture these behaviors? The Simple Network Management Protocol (SNMP) uses a simple model for the structure of managed information (SMI) [2] involving six application-defined data types and three generic ones.

Temporal behaviors are described in terms of counters and gauges. An error counter represents the cumulative errors (integral) since device booting (the area under the error rate curve in Fig. 3). A gauge can model the queue length. The values of these managed variables can be recorded in an agent's management information base (MIB) [3], where they can be polled by a platform. An error counter, however, is not useful for detecting rapid changes in error rates to identify a storm. A platform must sample the counter frequently to estimate its second derivative, leading to unrealistic polling rates.

OSI management uses an object-oriented model of managed information [9, 10]. The behaviors of interest: noise, errors, and queue length are different forms of a time series. A generic managed

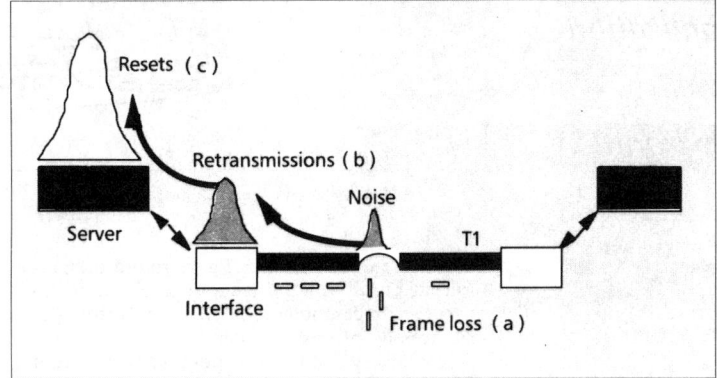

**Figure 2.** *Formation of a network storm.*

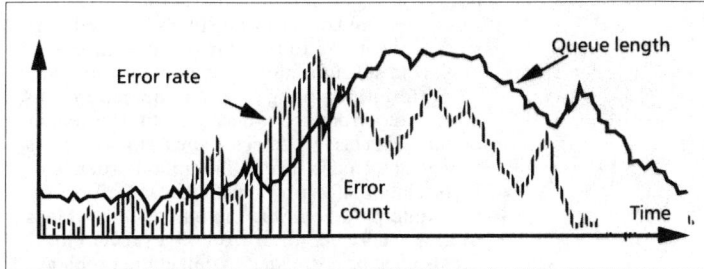

**Figure 3.** *Temporal behaviors correlation.*

object (MO) class may be defined to describe a general time series. This MO may include data attributes of the time series and operations (methods, actions) to compute functions of the time series (e.g., derivatives). This MO also may provide generic events notifications (e.g., whenever some function of time series exceeds threshold). The generic time series MO class may be specialized to define MO subclasses to model the bit-error rate of the T1 link and the queue length of the interface processor. A management platform can create instances of these MOs, within device agents' databases. The device agent can monitor the respective network behaviors and record the respective

*OSI management communications require connection-oriented transport and rely on the OSI application layer environment.*

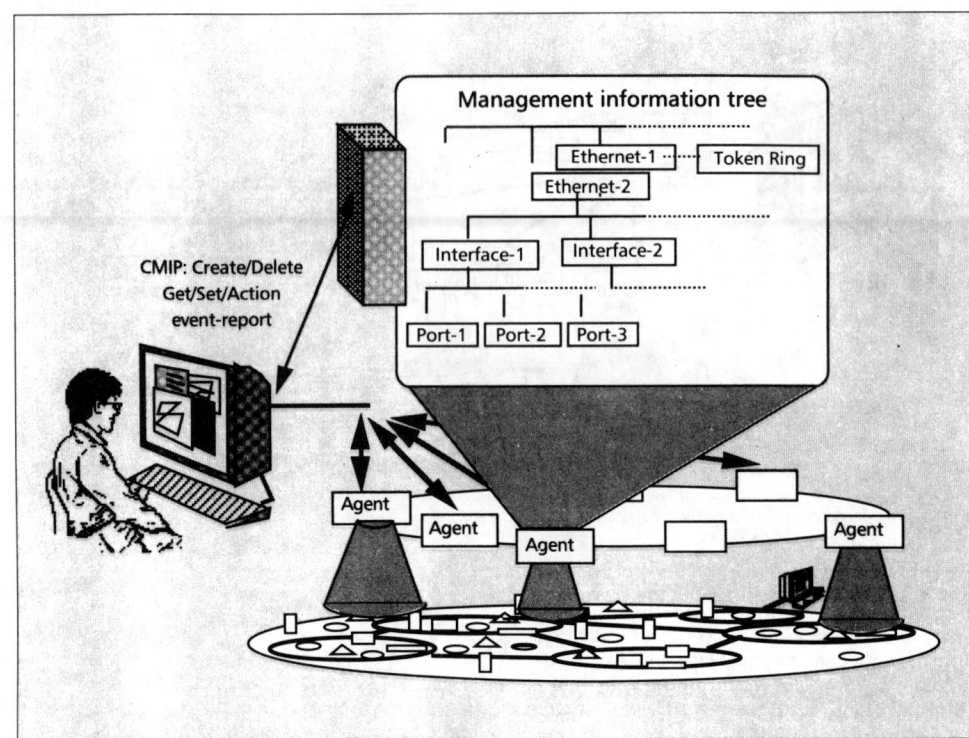
**Figure 4.** *Overall architecture of an OSI management system.*

values in these MO instances. Furthermore, the platform can enroll with the agent to receive notifications of events describing rapid changes of error rates and excessive processor queue.

To identify a storm it is necessary to detect not only error rate and interface queue threshold events, but to identify correlation among them. Unfortunately, the observation processes used for event detection may result in decorrelation of behaviors. Threshold excesses must be sustained over sufficient window to result in event notification and avoid spurious alerts. Implementation may use different sampling rates and detection windows for the error rate and queue length. Thus, either of the events may be detected singly, or the events may be detected in inverted temporal order. This decorrelating effect of observations can lead to erroneous interpretation. Often, hundreds or thousands of alerts may be generated by a fault. These events must be correlated to detect the problem's source. The results of such analysis may be very sensitive to the choices of managed information provided by devices and the implementation details of monitoring processes.

To make things worse, the devices involved in the storm formation are typically manufactured by different vendors. The managed data and its meaning may vary greatly among devices, rendering interpretation difficult. Moreover, networks often are operated by multiple organizations, each responsible for a different domain. Faults escalating across such domain boundaries may be particularly difficult to detect and handle. In the example, the T1 links may be managed by a telephone company while the layers above are operated by a user organization. The user may not be able to observe the behavior of the T1 layer and the telephone company may not be able to observe the behaviors of higher layers.

## OSI Management Model Overview

The OSI management model [5] is depicted in Fig. 4. The managing platform on the left uses the common management information protocol (CMIP) to access managed information, provided by an agent residing in a LAN hub on the right. The agent maintains a management information tree (MIT) database. The MIT models a hub using MOs to represent LANs, interfaces, and ports. A platform can use CMIP to create, delete, retrieve, or change MOs in the MIT; invoke actions; or receive event notifications.

The MIT contains instances of MOs organized on a hierarchical database tree, similar to the X.500 directory tree [12]. An MO instance includes attributes that serve as its relative distinguishing name (RDN). The RDN attributes uniquely identify the instance among the siblings of its MIT parent. In the hub example of Fig. 4, a port identification number may be used as the RDN to identify ports of a given interface MO. By concatenating RDNs along the MIT path from the root to a given node, a unique distinguishing name (DN) is obtained. This DN is used by CMIP to identify a node and access its managed information.

In contrast to SNMP MIB, the MIT is a dynamic database. SNMP also uses a tree [3] to store managed information. However, the structure of the MIB is static and is determined at its design time. CMIP provides CREATE/DELETE primitives to change the MIT dynamically. A dynamic database

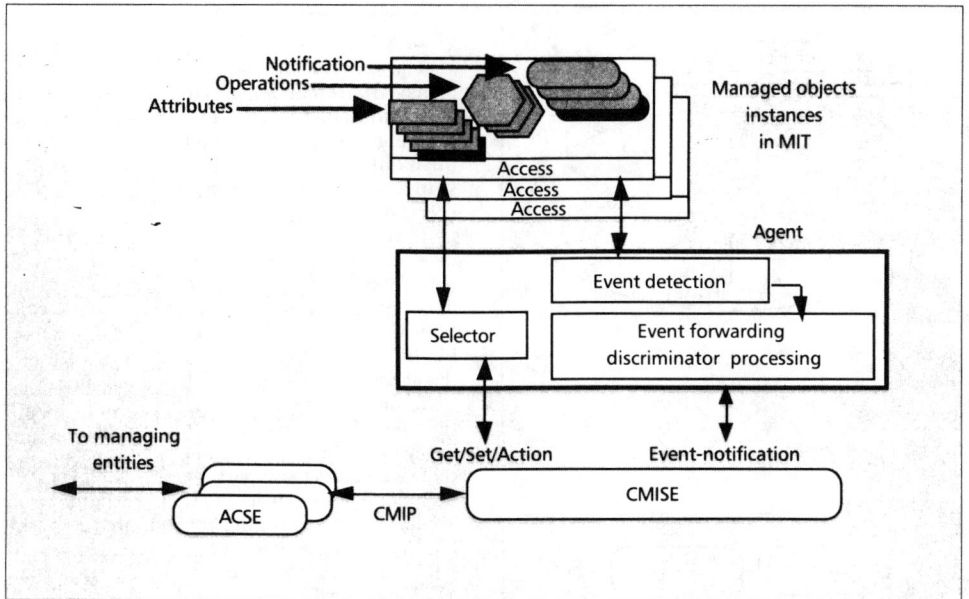

**Figure 5.** *Managed information communication architecture.*

can provide flexibility and efficiency in managed information access. Managing entities can control the contents and structure of the database. The database also may be flexibly organized to reflect specific device configurations. A static database structure may lead to difficulties in handling composite device structures. Different components may require their own database models. However, they cannot be unified into a single MIB due to its static structure. Therefore, complex hubs often include multiple SNMP agents (each handling a different component). A dynamic MIT permits these different database models to be easily unified.

A dynamic management database, however, presents significant implementation complexities. The resources required to store and process managed information cannot be predicted at design time. Managers may extend the MIT beyond available agent's resources. Changes in the MIT may result in corruption of the database. For example, an MO may be deleted while other MOs contain relationship pointers to it. Application software designers cannot share a single model of the MIT contents, as each application needs to build and maintain its own MIT subset.

## Management Communication Model

OSI management communications require connection-oriented transport and rely on the OSI application layer environment. (Consult Reference [12] for OSI application layer details.) Agents (managed entities) and managers (managing entities) are viewed as peer applications that use the services of a common management information service element (CMISE) to exchange managed information [6]. CMISE provides service access points (SAPs) to support controlled associations between managers and agents. Associations are used to exchange managed information

| Management communication services |
|---|
| M-INITIALIZE: Establish management association |
| M-TERMINATE: Terminate management association |
| M-ABORT: Unconfirmed termination |
| **Management information tree operations** |
| M-CREATE: Creates an MO instance record in the MIT |
| M-DELETE: Deletes an MO instance from MIT |
| **Managed information manipulation services** |
| M-GET: Retrieve information |
| M-CANCEL-GET: Cancel retrievals |
| M-SET: Change an attribute value |
| M-ACTION: Invoke an MO operation |
| M-EVENT-REPORT: Generate an MO event report to a manager |

**Table 1.** *SAPs provided by a CMISE entity.*

queries and responses, handle event notifications, and provide remote invocations of MO operations. CMISE utilizes the services of OSI's association control service element (ACSE) and the remote operations service element (ROSE) to support these services [12]. A typical structure of an agent communication environment is shown in Fig. 5. A symmetric organization governs the structure of peer managing entities.

The top section of Fig. 5 describes the structure of the MIT. MO instances and their attributes, operations, and event notifications are depicted as shaded rectangles at the top. The OSI agent provides selection functions to locate the MO records accessed by Get/Set/Action SAPs of CMISE. The agent also provides event detection and forwarding of notifications to managing entities enrolled (through MIT records) to receive them. A CMISE entity provides SAPs (depicted in Table 1) to support communications with the agent. It dis-

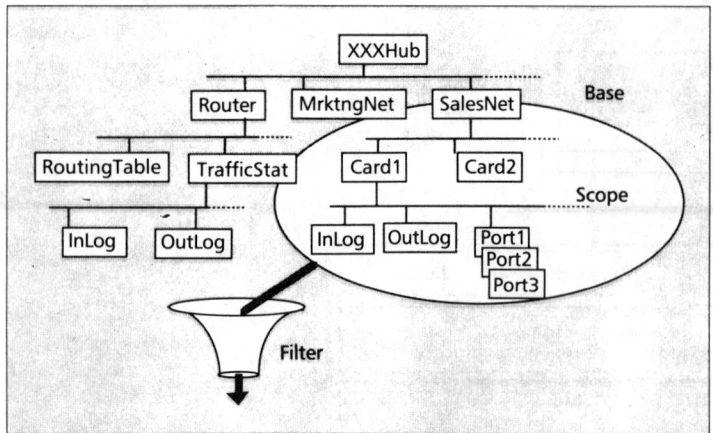

■ **Figure 6.** *Aggregated and selective retrieval.*

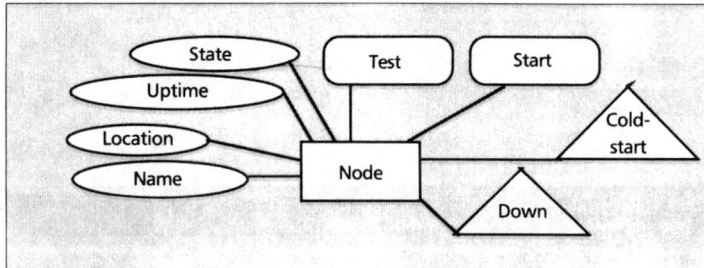

■ **Figure 7.** *Example of an MO.*

an ACSE and back to the originating manager.

The core services of CMISE provide access to managed information. The GET construct provides means for bulk retrieval and agent's information filtering. This is illustrated in Fig. 6. To accomplish bulk retrieval, a GET need only specify a subtree of the MIT from which data is to be retrieved. This subtree is specified by its base node and the scope of the GET request. To specify a selection criterion, a GET must provide a filter defined by a simple language. Retrieval of all port data on SalesNet whose error rates exceed some threshold is illustrated in Fig. 6. The GET request identifies the scope of the search and filter and the agent performs the search and selection.

Remote invocation of operations is accomplished through M-ACTION. It is necessary to specify the MO instance, the action to be invoked, and the parameters to be passed to it. The invocation is supported through the ROSE. Event notifications are handled by enrolling appropriate records on the MIT, using M-CREATE. A manager uses M-CREATE to place an event-notification-managed object on the MIT. Upon detection of an event, the agent uses the MIT to identify subscribers for notifications. An M-EVENT-NOTIFICATION is generated for each such subscriber.

## SMI Model

The structure of managed information (SMI) model plays a central role in the OSI standard. It is introduced in [8] and is elaborated in the guidelines for the definitions of managed objects (GDMO) [10]. This model is based on an extended object-oriented (OO) data model [16]. MOs, like OO classes, provide templates to encapsulate data and management operations (methods, actions) associated with managed entities. MO extends the class concept to include event notifications. Event notifications add a new dimension. Traditional OO software assumes a synchronous model of interaction between an object and its users (programs). Programs may invoke methods synchronously. On the other hand, events may occur independently and asynchronously with the manager computations that access them.

The MO model supports inheritance. An MO definition can include attributes, operations, and events of a more general MO. For example, a general MO describing an interface may be used to define specialized interfaces (e.g., Ethernet, Token-ring). The data, operations, and events associated

patches/receives CMIP PDUs to/from other service elements such as ACSE and ROSE. These PDUs are exchanges through a connection-oriented transport. CMIP PDUs are best viewed as carriers of requests and replies generated by respective CMISE primitives. For example, a CMISE M-GET accessed by a manager generates a CMIP GET-REQUEST PDU to the agent and respective GET-RESPONSE PDUs from the agent.

The interactions pursued by management applications peers are typically confirmed through the standard OSI request-reply model. For example, an invocation by a manager of the M-INITIALIZE SAP results in a CMISE invocation of the ACSE through a CMIP PDU. The manager ACSE sends an association request to a peer. The peer ACSE at the agent passes the CMIP request to the agent's CMISE. A confirmation PDU will then propagate back from the agent's CMISE through

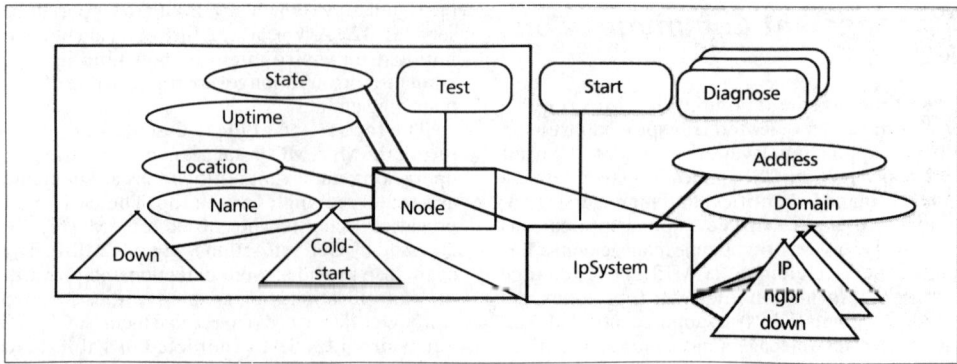

■ **Figure 8.** *A subclass of node.*

```
<class-label> MANAGED OBJECT CLASS
[DERIVED FROM <class-label> [,<class-label>]*;]
[ALLOMORPHIC SET   <class-label>  [,<class-label>]*;]
[CHARACTERIZED BY   <package-label>  [,<package-label>]*;]
[CONDITIONAL PACKAGES   <package-label>   PRESENT IF <condition-definitions>
        [,<package-label>PRESENT IF <condition-definitions>]*;]
[PARAMETERS <parameter-label> [, <parameter-label>]*;]
REGISTERED AS <object-identifier> ;
```

■ **Figure 9.** *Sample MO class template.*

```
eventLogRecord MANAGED OBJECT CLASS
DERIVED FROM logRecord;
CHARACTERIZED BY   eventLogRecordPackage PACKAGE
     ATTRIBUTES managedObjectClass GET, managedObjectInstance GET;;;
CONDITIONAL PACKAGES
     eventTimePkg PACKAGE ATTRIBUTES eventTime GET;;
     PRESENT IF the event time parameter was present in the CMIP event report;
REGISTERED AS {smi2MobjectClass 5};
```

■ **Figure 10.** *Example of eventLogRecord.*

with an interface MO will be inherited by these specialized subclasses. Inheritance is primarily a syntactic mechanism as one could simply include the definitions of the superclass in the subclass MO definitions to accomplish the same effect. To illustrate inheritance, consider an MO defining a class of node objects as depicted in Fig. 7. Ellipsoidal shapes describe data attributes. Rectangular shapes describe operations to test and start a node. Events are described by triangular shapes.

Consider now a specialization of a "node"—an IpSystem MO. An IpSystem can be defined as a subclass of node. It inherits all the node attributes, operations, and events. The IpSystem may replace some of these inherited components (e.g., a new start operation) and add new attributes, operations, and events.

### Relationships Are Significant in Management

Relationships among managed data items are of great importance in correlating information. In the earlier storm example, it was necessary to correlate observations of physical layer errors with those of an interface processor queue handling retransmission tasks. It would have been necessary to represent the relations among these objects to be able to correlate their behaviors. The managed information model of OSI, in contrast to SNMP, provides explicit means to represent relationships.

An MO may include relationship attributes with pointers to related MOs. For example, a port attribute representing the relationship "contained-in" may include a pointer to the interface object that contains it. The pointer value is the distinguishing name (DN) path identifier of the interface object on the MIT.

The OSI model includes a number of generic relationships that may be used in modeling MO such as "is-contained-in," "is-peer-of" (for protocol entities), and "is-backup-of" (for systems or components). The use of relationship attributes is similar to techniques used in the network model of databases [17]. It achieves great generality in representing, in principle, any entity-relationship model. For example, one can easily identify and retrieve

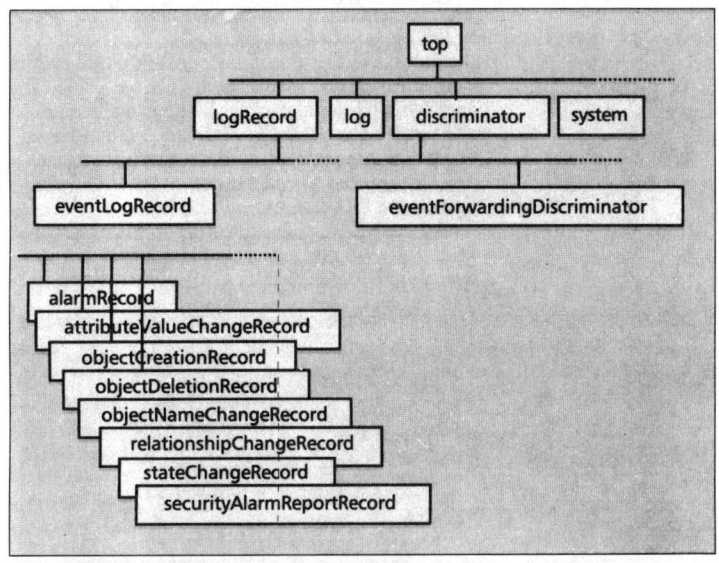

■ **Figure 11.** *The MO class hierarchy.*

information associated with all ports contained in a given interface, by traversing the respective relationship pointers. Of course, traversal may require substantial manager-agent interactions to retrieve and dereference pointers. This could have been simplified if the protocol included traversal primitives (GET-NEXT) to follow relationship pointers, similarly to network databases.

### GDMO Provides Syntax for MO Definitions

The GDMO introduces substantial extensions of ASN.1 to handle the syntax of managed information definitions. A new language structure (template), is introduced to combine definitions. Templates play a similar role as ASN.1 Macro, except they do not lend themselves to simple extensions of ASN.1 compilers. A sample template is the MO class template (Fig. 9). It is used to define MO structure and register the definitions on the ISO registration tree.

```
system MANAGED OBJECT CLASS
DERIVED FROM top;
CHARACTERIZED BY   systemPackage PACKAGE
    ATTRIBUTES systemID GET, operationalState GET, usageState GET,
    administrativeState GET REPLACE, managementState GET;
    ATTRIBUTE GROUPSstate, relationship;
    NOTIFICATIONS objectCreation, objectDeletion, objectNameChange,
    attributeValueChange, state Change, ......,environmentalAlarm;;;
CONDITIONAL PACKAGES
    dailyScheduling PRESENT IF both the weekly scheduling and
    external scheduler package  not present  in an instance
    ..........
    repairStatusPkg PACKAGE
    ATTRIBUTES...
    PRESENT IF both the weekly scheduling and external
    scheduler package are not present in an instance
................................
REGISTERED AS {smi2MOBJECTClass 14};
```

**Figure 12.** *Schematic subset of system MO.*

The <class-label> is a place-holder for an MO name. The "Derived from" section describes the superclasses whose definitions are inherited by the MO. The "Characterized by" part includes the body of data attributes, operations, and event notifications encapsulated by the MO. "Packages," "Conditional packages," and "Parameters" are templates used to combine definitions of attributes, operations, and event notifications. The "Registered as" part registers the MO definition on the ISO registration tree.

An example of definition of an eventLogRecord (Fig. 10) [9], using this template, follows. An eventLogRecord inherits attributes of a general logRecord (its superclass). It includes definitions taken from a package for eventLogRecordPackage and a conditional package eventTimePkg, and is registered on the OSI registration tree as the subtree labeled 5 under the label smi2MobjectClass. Attributes are followed with descriptors such as GET/REPLACE, denoting read/write access mode. Notice the informal statement of the condition under which the definitions by the conditional package are to be included. Thus, automated compilation of definitions, unlike SNMP MIBs, may be impossible.

The definitions of managed information (DMI) [9] define a class hierarchy as depicted in Fig. 11. Boxes represent different MO classes, while the tree represents inheritance relations among them.

These generic MOs focus on definitions of various forms of management logs. The system MO is the main tool in building MOs associated with a given system. It includes attributes to identify the system, represent its operational and administrative state, and provide generic notifications and packages of definitions for handling scheduled operations maintenance. A schematic subset of its definition is provided in Fig. 12.

For example, consider the problem of developing a class hierarchy to model typical networked systems, as a specialization of the system MO. A possible class hierarchy is illustrated in Fig. 13. This hierarchy considers two kinds of systems: complex systems (as on the left part of the tree) and simple systems, or elements (as on the right side of the tree).

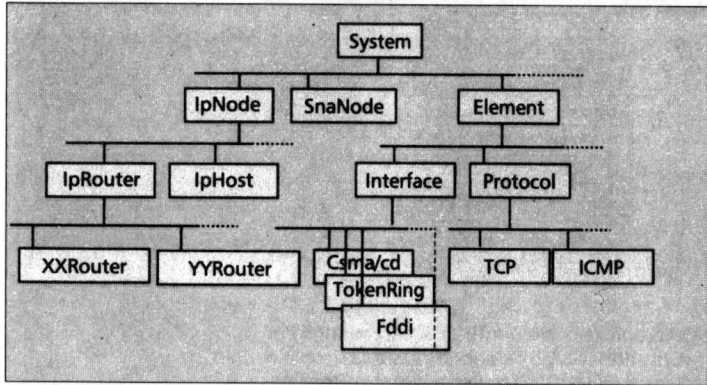

**Figure 13.** *An MO class hierarchy to represent networked devices.*

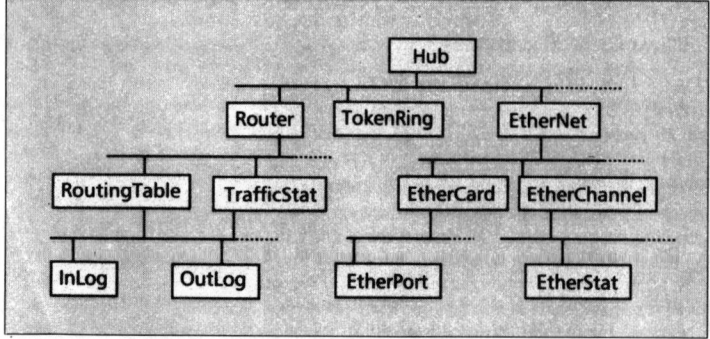

**Figure 14.** *Typical hub components and containment.*

## Putting It Together

### Building an OSI Managed Element

This section completes the picture through a brief sketch of OSI modeling of a LAN hub. Typical hub components and their containment relations are depicted in Fig. 14.

**Step 1: Identify Class Structure and Inheritance Relations Among MOs** — An MO must be designed for each managed component. The first step is to identify similarities of managed elements and capture them in MO classes, to use inheritance. A possible class inheritance hierarchy is depicted in Fig. 15. (For example, EtherPort and TokenPort components may share some attributes, operations, and events. The MO describing them may be developed as specialization of a generic port object.)

**Step 2: Design and Specify MO Syntactical Structures Using GDMO** — Using the GDMO, define managed attributes, operations, and event notifications for each of the MO classes needed. An example of port MO definitions is shown in Fig. 16. MO libraries defined by protocol committees (e.g., FDDI) may be used to capture standardized components.

**Step 3: Design Generic MIT Structure for the Device** — Design of the MIT follows the containment tree of Fig. 14. Each component is replaced by respective MO instances. For each MO, it is necessary to identify respective attributes forming a unique relative distinguishing name (RDN). For each device component, the respective MO instance must be created on the MIT (using a CMIP Create primitive). Dynamic managed objects (e.g., different logs) may be created and deleted by managers during network running time. Relationship attributes values are set after the respective MO instances are located on the MIT. For example, a "contained-in" relationship may be associated with port-card pairs. An instance of an etherPort MO may include a pointer to the etherCard MO instance. Similarly, an etherCard instance may point to an etherChannel instance (subnet) to represent the relationship "attached-to."

## Critical Assessment

The OSI model seeks to provide a comprehensive framework for handling management of arbitrarily complex systems. We will briefly evaluate some tradeoffs associated with this generality, and contrast the choices of OSI with those of the Internet SNMP.

### Managed Information Model

OSI provides an extended OO database framework to model managed information. It seeks to maximize the information modeling power to handle complex systems. Management information bases, however, need to balance conflicting requirements for functionality and real-time performance under resource constraints. It is not yet established whether the OSI design choices can strike such balance. For example, a dynamic MIT database can easily saturate agent's memory and/or processing resources. Demand for event notifications may tie agent's processing and communication resources, starving GET or ACTION requests (and vice versa).

Generally, the performance of OO databases is not yet understood [16]. Deletion of MO records may result in orphaned relationship pointers, requiring complex garbage collection at agents. Multiple managers pursuing CREATE/DELETE activities can lead to inconsistent views of the MIT.

Complexity of information model can lead to conformance difficulties. For example, the semantic of event notifications must be formally captured to permit specifications of conformance criteria. The meaning of events, however, is tied to device operations extrinsic to the MIT and its contents.

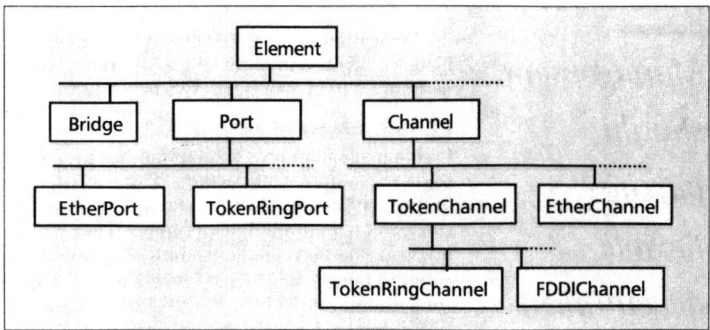

■ **Figure 15.** *A class hierarchy for hub MOs.*

```
port MANAGED OBJECT CLASS
DERIVED FROM  element;
CHARACTERIZED BY  portPackage PACKAGE
        ATTRIBUTES portNum GET, portStatus GET,...;
        OPERATIONS diagnose,disconnect,connect...;
        NOTIFICATIONS portFailure, portInitialized..;
................................
REGISTERED AS {......};
```

■ **Figure 16.** *Example of port MO definitions.*

In contrast, SNMP pursues a simple static MIB, seeking to minimize and constrain the agent's resource demand. The memory and processing resources needed to handle the MIB may be carefully evaluated and planned at design time. However, the data modeling power of SNMP is limited. For example, composite systems may need multiple MIB instances to represent their different parts. These MIBs cannot be combined into a single database nor be accessed from a single agent. Thus, a composite system requires as many SNMP agents as its components. As another example, lack of explicit modeling of relationships limits the ability of applications to correlate managed data. Recent proposals of SNMP V.2 [4] seek to resolve some of SNMP's information modeling limitations. The proper balance between modeling power and performance of managed information databases remains an elusive design goal.

### Managed Information Access Model

The OSI model introduces two important functionalities missing in SNMP: bulk and selective retrievals. Both capabilities are central in controlling the flow of management information. Without bulk retrieval, managers are forced to pursue a large number of polling requests. Without selective (filtered) retrieval, managers are forced to retrieve large amounts of irrelevant data.

Explicit invocation of agent's operations is another OSI capability missing from SNMP. Remote invocations are important for distribution of management computations to agents and improve manager control over agent's activities. They also can reduce the complexity of manager-agents interactions by limiting it to procedure interfaces. SNMP supports implicit invocations as side effects of SET requests. A diagnostic operation, for example, may be invoked by a "set" of a respective variable. Implicit invocations offer only limited capabilities in passing parameters and in synchroniz-

> *Management should pursue flexible decentralization of responsibilities to devices and maximal automation of management functions through application software.*

ing invocations with managers. Additionally, they increase agent's complexity since SET requests must be trapped to invoke respective procedures.

### Communication Model

OSI management uses connection-oriented transport and confirmed interactions. These provide reliability and enable bulk retrieval; a single GET can result in multiple-linked replies. They require, however, complex communication environment and result in failure-sensitivity. During network stress time, connections may not be sustainable over sufficiently long time to accomplish the management functions needed. Management entities may need to spend significant time and resources in handling lost connections. Connection-based transport may become an obstacle in accomplishing management interactions at a time when they are needed most.

Conversely, SNMP communications use a connectionless datagram transport (UDP) with confirmed GET/SET interactions and unconfirmed event notifications (TRAPs). The responsibility to ensure reliable communications is passed to agent/manager applications. For example, managers can detect loss of a GET/SET request when the GET-RESPONSE confirmation does not arrive. They can ignore the loss, reissue the request, or choose other alternatives to recovery. During stress time, managers may flexibly adjust their computations to handle loss, rather than confront an all-or-nothing choice of a reliable connection service. A datagram model requires a simple communication environment that is easy to implement. Managers, however, can only retrieve information that fits within a single UDP frame. This limits bulk retrieval mechanisms.

### The Platform-centered Management Paradigm

How useful is the OSI model in supporting platform-centered management? The OSI model prescribes powerful agents requiring substantial computational resources, on par with the resources available at the platform. This raises interesting questions concerning allocation of responsibilities among platforms and agents. If agents are to be as powerful, what functions should be removed from them and assigned to platform managers and why? If the platform is to play an incidental role in management, does it require a comprehensive, or even any, general management protocol? Why should it not limit exchanges with agents to application-specific APIs (e.g., using ROSE or an RPC)? How does a maximal access model, which exposes internal object details of managed entities to a platform, serve a minimal platform? However, if the platform is to be maximal, why are maximal agents required? The balance among the complexities and responsibilities of agents, platforms, and their interaction protocols is not yet understood.

How useful is platform-centered management? Platform-centered management suffers fundamental technical limitations [18]. First, it is unscalable. The rates at which device objects must be accessed and processed typically exceed the network/platform capacity. Platform processing and/or management communication resources can be quickly saturated as network size, speed, and complexity increase. Second, during stress times the platform must increase its interactions with agents, at a time when the network is least capable to handle these. Management response-time and reliability, furthermore, tend to stretch at a stress time, when fast and reliable response is most needed. Third, platform-centered management can lead to intense and unrealistic micromanagement of agents by platform applications. Fourth, platform heterogeneity and semantic heterogeneity, arising in the context of platform-centered management create barriers in the development of management applications.

Alternative management paradigms are needed to reflect the needs and opportunities of emerging networks and resolve the limitations of platform-centered management. Management should pursue flexible decentralization of responsibilities to devices and maximal automation of management functions through application software. Research toward such distributed management is described in Reference [18]. A management by delegation (MBD) paradigm is used to distribute management applications to device agents dynamically. Management application programs are delegated by platforms to device agents who execute them under remote platform control. MBD permits platforms to flexibly assign management responsibilities to devices, and even program devices to perform autonomous management. Additional research efforts to develop distributed management are described in References [13, 14].

## Conclusions

*I*t is useful to reconsider the central questions of network management: What should be monitored? How should it be interpreted? How should this analysis be used to control the network behavior? Management protocol standards provide syntactic structures to organize and access managed information. Such a syntactic framework can be useful in enabling systematic answers to these questions. However, the semantics of managed information, rather than its syntax, is the key to the answers. Clearly, the data that should be monitored needs to be derived from the model that is used to interpret the data. The model must be based on the semantics of the network operational behavior. Unfortunately, the manner in which interactions among network processes lead to faults or performance inefficiencies is not well understood. The storm example illustrated that, even when a fault behavior can be understood, it is unclear what symptoms need to be observed and how to correlate their respective data to handle it.

Significant research is needed to develop improved understanding of network operations and to build effective manageability. Standardization of managed information syntax is best viewed as a first step toward handling the semantics of network operations. Network management needs and scenarios are likely to continue and change as new types of networks, new applications, and better management technologies arise throughout the coming decade. As our understanding of the semantics of operations improves, new syntactic structures to support manageability will continue to emerge. Standardization of these mechanisms likely will continue and evolve in a manner not asimilar to the SNMP's evolution.

## Acknowledgments

The author gratefully acknowledges the research support provided by the National Science Foundation (NSF) under project number NCR-91-06127.

## References

[1] J. D. Case, et al., "A Simple Network Management Protocol (SNMP)," RFC 1157, May 1990.
[2] M. Rose and K. McCloghrie, "Structure and Identification of Management Information for TCP/IP-based Internets," RFC 1155, May 1990.
[3] K. McCloghrie and M. Rose, "Management Information Base for Network Management of TCP/IP-based Internets: MIB-II," RFC 1213, March 1991.
[4] J. D. Case, et al., "Introduction to the Simple Management Protocol (SMP) Framework," draft, July 1992.
[5] OSI, I.S.O., 10040 Systems Management Overview, 1991.
[6] OSI, I.S.O., 9595 Information Technology, Open Systems Interconnection, Common Management Information Services Definitions, 1991.
[7] OSI, I.S.O., 9596 Information Technology, Open Systems Interconnection, Common Management Information Protocol Specification, 1991.
[8] OSI, I.S.O., 10165-1 Information Technology, Open Systems Interconnection, Management Information Model, 1991.
[9] OSI, I.S.O., 10165-2 Information Technology, Open Systems Interconnection, Definition of Management Information, 1991.
[10] OSI, I.S.O., 10165-4 Information Technology, Open Systems Interconnection, Guidelines for the Definitions of Managed Objects, 1991.
[11] K. McCloghrie and M. Rose, "Common Management Information Services and Protocol over TCP/IP (CMOT)," RFC 1189, March 1991.
[12] M. T. Rose, The Open Book, A Practical Perspective on OSI (Prentice Hall, 1990).
[13] B. N. Meandzija and J. Westcott, ed., The First IFIP International Symposium on Integrated Network Management, (North Holland, May 1989).
[14] I. Krishnan and W. Zimmer, ed., The Second IFIP International Symposium on Integrated Network Management, (North Holland, April 1991).
[15] A. Kershenbaum, M. Malek, and M. Wall, eds., Network Management and Control Workshop, Tarrytown, N.Y. (Plenum Press, Sept. 1989).
[16] E. Horowitz, ed., Object-Oriented Databases and Applications (Prentice Hall, 1989).
[17] J. Ullman, Principles of Database & Knowledge Base Systems, vols. I & II, 3d ed. (Computer Science Press, 1988).
[18] Y. Yemini, G. Goldszmidt, and S. Yemini, "Network Management by Delegation," The Second International Symposium on Integrated Network Management, (North Holland, April 1991).

## Biography

YECHIAM YEMINI has been a member of the Computer Science Department at Columbia University since 1980, where he presently serves as the director of the N.Y. State Center of Advanced Technology in computer and information systems. His main research interests include computer networks, network management, high-speed networks, protocols, distributed systems, and performance analysis. He has published and lectured extensively in these areas. Research at his Distributed Computing and Communications (DCC) lab resulted in network design and management technologies that have been widely exported, applied by hundreds of sites, and commercialized by leading industry. He has been a co-founder, director, and chief scientific advisor of Comverse Technology Inc., a successful public high-tech manufacturer of multi-media message communication computers. He is also a co-founder of System Management Arts, Inc., a recent New York start-up building network and system management software.

# Management By Exception: OSI Event Generation, Reporting, and Logging

Lee LaBarre

The MITRE Corporation, Burlington Road, Bedford MA 01730

## 1. Introduction

Networks require near real-time monitoring and control of network resources to provide optimum use of available equipment and communication facilities and to provide the required performance in terms such as availability, bandwidth, delay, and error rates. However, the scale and complexity of today's networks, the stringent command and response time requirements, and the volume of status and traffic data are increasing to the point where network operators are unable to adequately handle the near real-time control of the networks. At the same time, the number and skill level of available network management personnel often is decreasing. Methods must be developed to reduce the volume of raw data offered to the operators, improve the information available for decision making, and assist the operator in making those decisions.

Most current network management systems overload network operators with raw data that is redundant and difficult to assimilate for problem diagnosis and determination of proper real-time control actions. They are usually based on polling for the transfer of significant volumes of raw data from managed systems to a central manager station. The information content relative to the total data transferred is usually very low, and is difficult to extract for the average network operator. This approach can put a significant drain on network resources, in terms of link and cpu bandwidth and does not provide network operators the timely information needed for near real-time control.

An alternate approach is to use management by exception as described below:

- Use infrequent polling to determine connectivity between managed systems and the management station. Such polling could be done using efficient lower layer protocol facilities, e.g., network layer echo.

- Maintain information about the network configuration, fault history, and "normal" levels of component and system performance as indicated by metrics derived from raw data sample measurements made at the managed system.

- Transfer information - not raw data - from the managed system to the manager station in the form of timely events containing notifications about significant occurrences in the network.

- Use the timely exception reports (event reports) about faults, configuration changes, and deviations from "normal" or desired performance, along with information about the network configuration, fault history and "normal" component and system performance levels to diagnose problems and make decisions to effect control actions. One such decision may be to request additional information from the affected devices to assist in the decision process.

Management by exception provides the information in the proper form needed for applying expert systems technology to network management. Expert systems can use the timely event and historical information to diagnose problems, recommend decisions, and in some cases automatically take control actions to effect those decisions.

This article concentrates on the functions developed by the International Standards Organization (ISO) to provide tools for managing the timely transfer and manipulation of information in the form of events. It provides a tutorial on ISO mechanisms for notification generation (section 5), the ISO system management functions related to reporting of notifications within event reports (section 6) and controlling their logging (section 7), and the services related to each (section 8). It also identifies the contents of standard events and log records defined in these and other system management functions (section 9), and describes ongoing work in defining metrics that may be used to characterize performance (section 10). Readers are expected to reference the ISO documents for complete definitions of the functions and associated ASN.1 syntax.

## 2. Management by Exception Approach

Figure 1 illustrates the management by exception approach to network management, including use of an expert system. Network components report events related to configuration changes, status changes, faults, security, and performance deviations to the network management control system (NMCS). Performance metrics are calculated within components from raw data measurements made on component resources. They characterize individual component and system performance in terms such as: availability, throughput, error rates, error ratios, and response time.

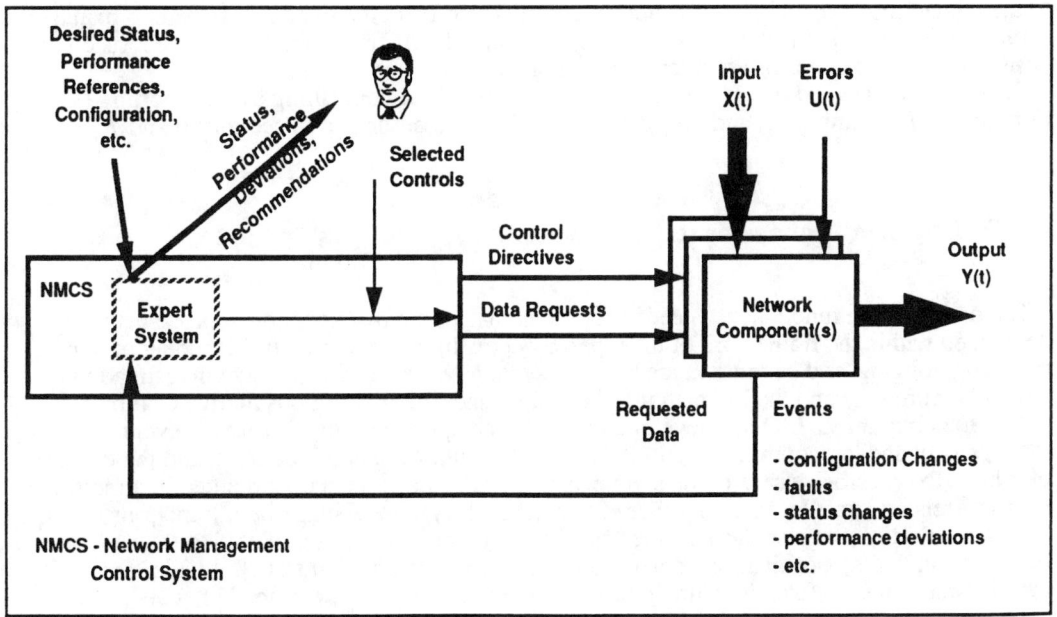

Figure 1: Management by Exception

These raw data measurements are samples taken at instances in time on random variables related to the component's status, traffic input $X(t)$, traffic output $Y(t)$, random inputs $U(t)$ due to errors. However, performance related events are generated only when the performance exceeds specified bounds.

The NMCS may display events directly to the operator, who must then use his knowledge of the desired status, performance bounds, network configuration, and experience to diagnose problems and determine appropriate control actions. For example, this may involve NMCS requests to the managed systems for detailed raw data to assist in the diagnosis. Alternatively, the events may be reported to an expert system in the NMCS that may diagnose problems and recommend control actions to the operator, and possibly even make those control actions automatically.

## 3. The OSI Structure of Management Information

Some knowledge of the OSI structure of management information (SMI) [1] is essential to understanding how notifications are generated, and their reporting and logging are controlled. The collection of management information that characterizes the resources in a managed system is called its management information base (MIB). The SMI uses an object-oriented approach to model the structure of management information. Physical and logical resources that may be contained within managed systems are modeled abstractly as managed object classes. Characteristics of the resource are modeled as attributes within a managed object class. A specific resource within a managed system is represented an an instantiation of an object class and is called a managed object. Managed objects may be created and deleted as resources are created and deleted within a managed system. Attribute values of a managed object may be retrieved and modified.

Managed objects may be designed to generate notifications when significant changes happen to the related resource. The notifications are transferred from the managed system to manager stations using management protocol event type protocol data units. Since event reports contain notifications, the two terms are often interchanged.

Two special managed object classes have been defined for controlling event reporting (Event Forwarding Discriminator) and logging (Log). They are described in sections 6 and 7.

## 4. OSI System Management Functions

The management functionality needed for the management by exception approach is being developed within the framework of the Open Systems Interconnection (OSI) model. Event reporting, logging, and generation are problems that have received extensive investigation in the ISO community and the International Telegraph and Telephone Consultative Committee (CCITT) community. ISO has developed models and specified objects for OSI event management and log control, and specified many useful events, their content, and the content of related log records. These models, objects and events have been documented in a multi-part series of related Draft International Standards, termed System Management Functions [ 2, 3, 4, 5, 6, 7, 8, 9]. ISO has also defined specific management information related to these functions, including notification contents and generation mechanisms [10]. In addition, ISO is defining mechanisms for calculating metrics that characterize performance [11, 12].

## 5. Notification Generation

ISO has defined several mechanisms for controlling the generation of notifications from managed objects if significant changes happen to the related resource. Some mechanisms are defined such that the change itself is the significant occurrence. Examples of such mechanisms are to emit a notification when:

- an object is created or deleted,

- a software or hardware processing failure happens that is peculiar to a resource,

- a state type attribute changes value, e.g., attributes indicating the operational or administrative state of the resource,

- a settable non-state type attribute value is changed, e.g., an attribute indicating an operational parameter such as the transport retransmission parameter.

However, changes to the most prevalent type of attribute in any MIB, counters and gauges, should not cause the generation of events. Such behavior would flood the network with traffic. The significant occurrence is not that the counter or gauge changed value, but that the value it changed to exceeded some specified bound. For example, when the ratio of the number of corrupted PDUs to the total number of received PDUs exceeds an acceptable value, a notification may be emitted as a fault indication. Or, when the count of users of a resource exceeds a defined number, the manager is informed so that some users may be shifted to another resource.

ISO [10] has defined generic mechanisms to generate notifications when a related counter or gauge exceeds a specified value.

### 5.1 Counter Thresholds

Counters may only increase until they reach their maximum value, and then they wrap to zero. Some counters may be reset to zero (though use of such counters is not recommended in multiple manager situations). The operation of the counter threshold is illustrated in figure 2.

A counter threshold attribute type has three associated values that must be specified by the manager. Those values and their associated semantics are as follows:

- comparison level: A notification is emitted when the value of the associated counter becomes equal to this value.

- offset value: If the value is not zero, then when a notification is generated, add the offset value to the comparison level. When the associated counter again equals the new comparison level, the process repeats. If the offset value is zero, the result is a "one shot", i.e., no more notifications are generated.

- notification switch: This determines whether notification generation is enabled.

The above three values define a single threshold level. Multiple threshold levels may be defined for a single counter threshold attribute.

### 5.2 Gauge Thresholds

Gauges associated with thresholds may increase and decrease in value. Consequently, if a gauge value oscillated about a comparison level, multiple notifications would be emitted. To prevent this, gauge threshold attribute types are defined with a hysteresis mechanism to prevent such repeated notifications. Figure 2 illustrates the operation of the gauge threshold attribute.

Gauge thresholds are defined as a pair of comparison levels: "notify high" and "notify low". The "hysteresis interval" is the difference between the values associated with the the notify high and notify low levels. A notification may be generated when the gauge value increases above the notify high value, or when it decreases below the notify low value. A notification switch defined for each level determines whether or not a notification is actually emitted.

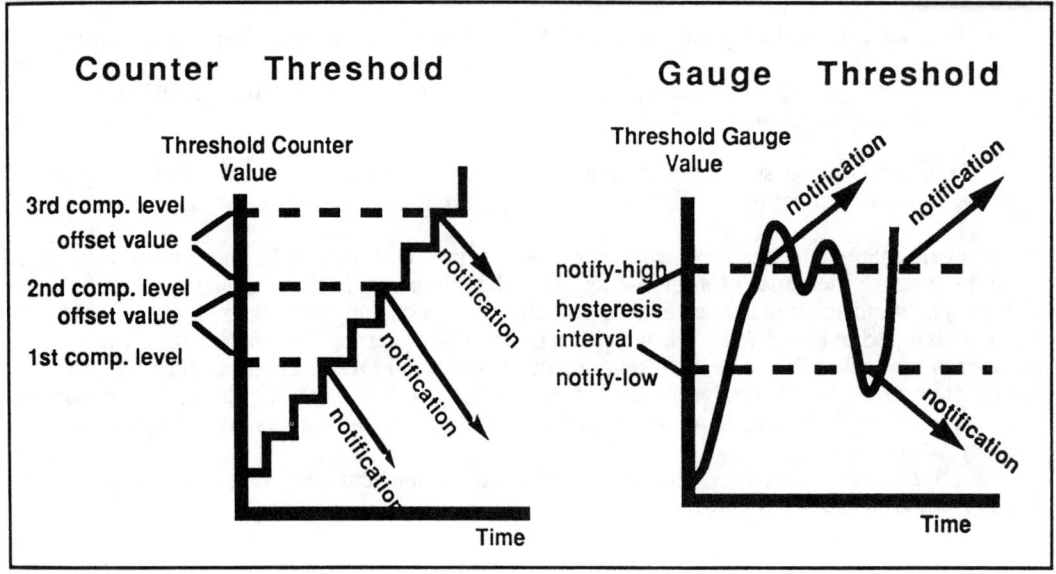

Figure 2: Counter and Gauge Threshold Operation

After generating a notify high notification, another one may not be generated until the gauge has decreased below the notify low level. Thus in figure 2, the second crossing of the notify high value does not cause a notification to be generated. Similarly, after generating a notify low notification, another one may not be generated until the gauge has increased above the notify high level.

The above two comparison levels and the associated enabling switches define a single threshold level. Multiple threshold levels may be defined for a single gauge threshold attribute.

## 6. Event Report Management Function

ISO has defined the Event Report Management Function [6] to schedule the distribution of event reports to one or more destinations, including logs. The destination selection is based on information contained in each event report. The function provides for the following:

- selection of (or filtering) event reports to be forwarded,

- distribution of the selected event reports to chosen destinations,

- ability to suspend and resume event reporting on a per destination basis,
- ability to create/destroy/modify selection criteria and destination indicators,
- ability to control the event report scheduling on a daily, weekly, or other basis.

The Event Report Management Function provides services by which event reports can be distributed. Event selections are done by a filtering process using the Event Forwarding Discriminator (EFD) managed object. Event Reporting Services are provided to initiate, terminate, suspend, resume, modify, and schedule event reporting through the manipulation of Event Forwarding Discriminator managed objects. These services are described in section 8.

### 6.1 Event Report Management Model
The Event Report Management Function conceptually behaves as follows (figure 3).

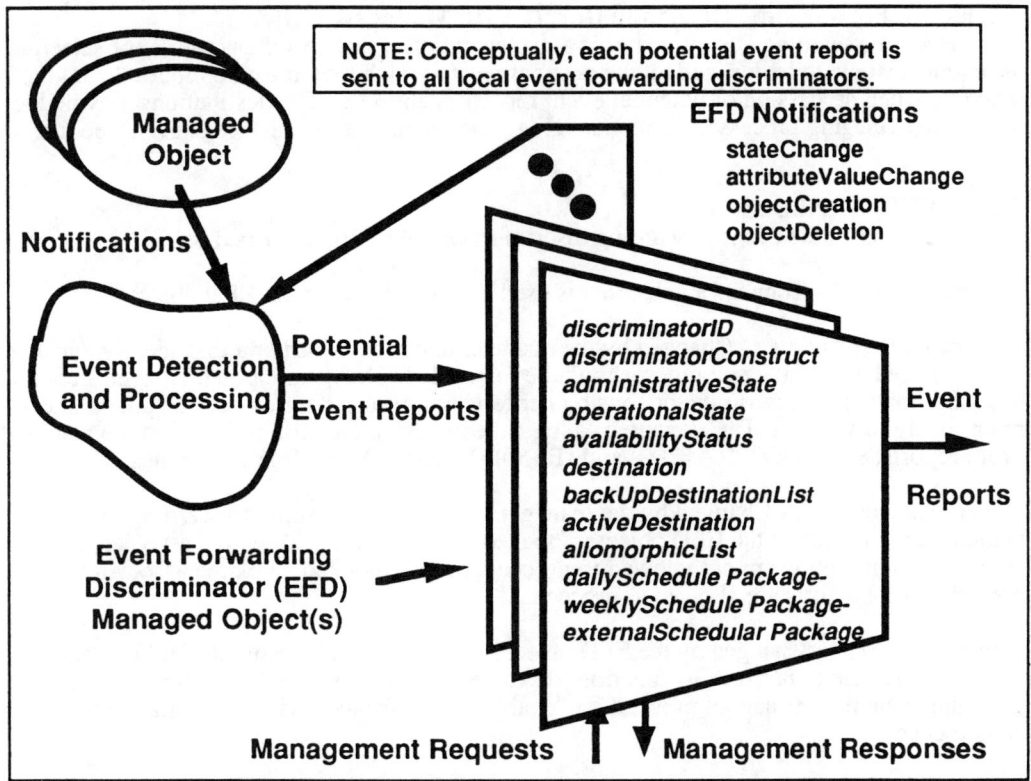

Figure 3: Event Report Management Model

- At least one managed object is capable of generating notifications that may be forwarded within an event report.

- A detection and processing module receives the locally generated notifications and forms potential event reports. Potential event reports contain all the information in the notification, plus information added by the detection and processing module, such as: event time, object class and instance.

- EFD managed objects provide the scheduling of event reporting and select the potential event reports that are forwarded to destinations as real event reports.

- EFDs actively forwarding events match attribute values in the potential event reports against criteria specified within the EFD by a manager. Potential event reports with attribute values that match those criteria are reported to the specified destination.

- Potential event reports are sent to all Event Forwarding Discriminators.

- Event reporting can be managed remotely by manipulation of the EFDs.

### 6.2 Event Forwarding Discriminator (EFD) Managed Object

The Event Forwarding Discriminator is a managed object that specifies criteria for selecting the events that are to be forwarded, the destinations to which they must be reported, and the schedule when processing of potential event reports is allowed. The destinations may be local or remote managing processes. The managing process may be one that logs event reports.

### 6.2.1 EFD Attributes

The attributes of the event forwarding discriminator object are described below.

*discriminatorID* - Contains a value that is used to uniquely name the EFD object.

*discriminatorConstruct* - Changed by the manager to define the criteria that specify whether the associated potential event report should be forwarded. Only those potential event reports that pass (match) the discriminator construct criteria will result in the associated potential event report being forwarded. The attribute is a logical expression on attributes within the potential event reports, e.g., {NOT {(A=100) and (B>50)}}, where A and B are attributes.

*administrativeState* - Changed by the manager to suspend or resume forwarding of events. Its value indicates whether the EFD object is "locked" by the manager, i.e., the associated potential event reports are not allowed to proceed, or is "unlocked", i.e., the associated potential event reports are allowed to proceed.

*operationalState* - Changed by the EFD object itself to indicate whether the EFD object is operationally able to perform its function. Its value may be "disabled", i.e., the associated potential event reports cannot proceed, or "enabled", i.e., the associated potential event reports can proceed.

*availabilityStatus* - Changed by the EFD itself to qualify the operational state. Its value may be "off-duty", indicating that the EFD is not processing potential event reports since it is "off-duty", i.e., the schedule currently inhibits processing of potential event reports. If the *availabilityStatus* is "off-duty" then the *operationalState* is "disabled".

*destination* - Identifies the title of the primary application to which the event reports are to be forwarded. This usually indicates an application in the managing system, but it may be the title of a local application or log.

*backUpDestinationList* - Is an ordered list of destinations to be tried in case the primary destination fails. This list is in priority order.

*activeDestination* - Identifies the title of the application to which the event reports are currently being forwarded. This is either the primary title specified in *destination* or one of the alternate application titles specified in *backUpDestinationList*.

*allomorphicList* - A managed object may behave as (i.e., be allomorphic to) one of its superclasses in the inheritance hierarchy [1]. Each managed object has knowledge of classes to which it is allomorphic, including itself, as an attribute called *allomorphs*. The *allomorphicList* attribute in the EFD contains an ordered list of managed object classes, one or more of which may be allomorphic to the object that emitted the notification. The object class associated with the event report will be the first object class encountered in EFD *allomorphicList* which is also a member of the *allomorphs* attribute of the object that emitted the notification.

### 6.2.2 EFD Scheduling Packages

Scheduling packages specify attributes and behavior used to control the automatic switching of the EFD between reporting-on, and reporting-off, i.e., "off-duty", conditions. Three conditional packages are specified to control reporting on a daily, weekly, or arbitrary basis.

*dailyScheduling Package* - Specifies a list of time intervals during a 24 hour time period when the EFD will be in the reporting-on condition.

*weeklyScheduling Package* - Specifies the date and time at which the EFD will start and stop the periodic weekly schedule, and the selected days of the week, relative to the starting date, and a list of intervals of the day, when the EFD may be allowed to be in the reporting-on condition.

*externalSchedular Package* - Specifies the name of an external schedular managed object that will control the reporting-on and reporting-off conditions of the EFD.

### 6.2.3 EFD Notifications

The EFD object may emit the following notifications, which are then themselves processed by an EFD object.

*objectCreation* - emitted when the EFD object is created.

*objectDeletion* - emitted when the EFD object is deleted.

*stateChange* - emitted by the EFD when the *administrativeState, operationalState, or availabilityStatus* attributes change value.

*attributeValueChange* - emitted by the EFD when settable non-state type attributes change.

## 7. Log Control Function

The Log Control Function [7] provides services by which records associated with event reports can be logged. Records can be logged according to a schedule. Record selection is done by a filtering process using mechanisms similar to those used by the EFD managed object. Log control provides the services to initiate, terminate, suspend, resume, modify, and schedule event logging through the manipulation of Log managed objects. These services are described in section 8.

## 7.1 Logging Model

The Log managed object (figure 4) contains storage for records. It adds information (e.g., unique record identifiers, logging time) to received event reports and transforms that information into potential log record objects. Attributes (shaded area of figure 4) associated with the log provide control over which potential log records are selected for storage, and control the availability of the logging activity. A subset of these attributes, as indicated in the trapezoid in figure 4, control the filtering of potential log records in the same way as the EFD object controls the forwarding of potential event reports. The filtered log records are stored and may be available for retrieval either via the management protocol or via other services such as file transfer.

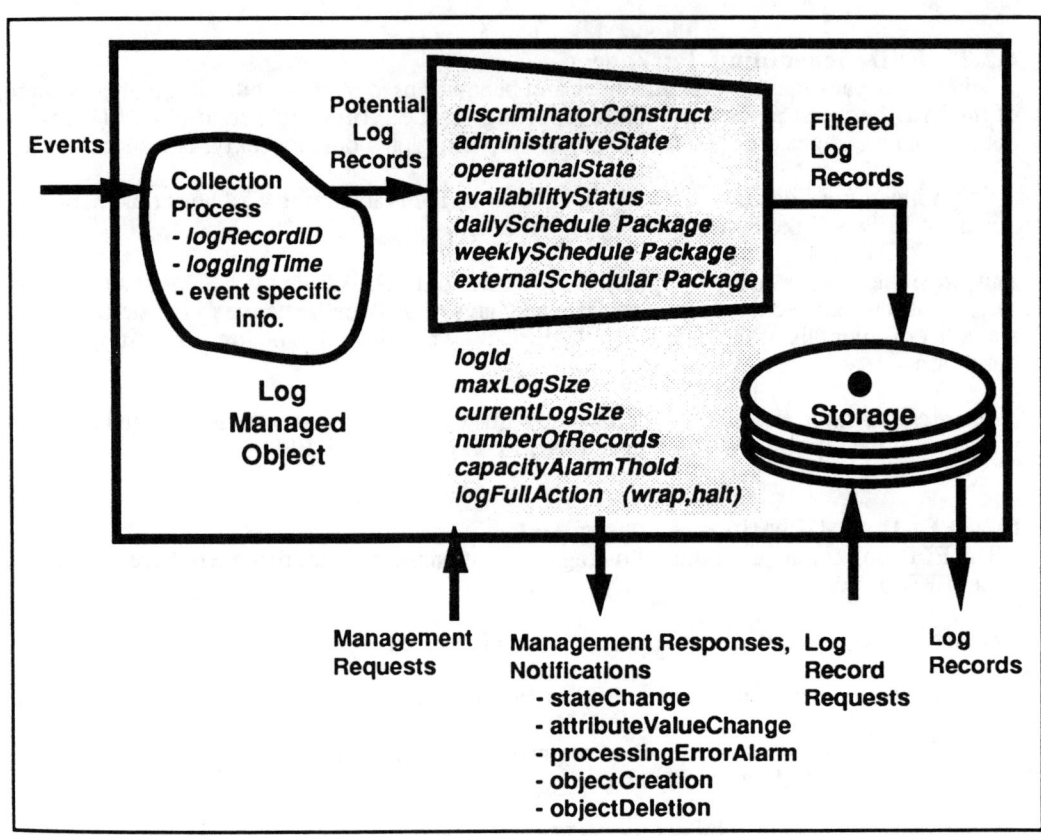

Figure 4: Log Control Model

## 7.2 Log Managed Object

The log's behavior is determined by its state attributes, discriminator construct attribute, and schedule attributes.

The log stores records in the order in which they are presented for logging. New records will be added to the log only if the log is:

- not in the "off-duty" condition due to scheduling,
- not in the "locked" administrative state,
- not in the "log-full" (for a log that halts) availability status,
- not in the "disabled" operational state, and
- the record passes the discriminator construct test criteria.

When the log has the "log-full" availability status, new records will not be entered into the log, but records currently in the log may be retrieved. Placing the Log object in the "locked" administrative state will prevent entry of new records into the log.

The log operational state and availability status reflect the internal activity of the log and cannot be changed by direct management action. Two options have been defined for the behavior of the log when it reaches the maximum log size. The log may either halt logging (discard new records) or wrap (discard old records). A log that halts will always generate a capacity threshold event. A log that wraps will discard an integral number of records, and may also generate a capacity threshold event indicating that a new wrap has occurred. Every log must be able to support the halt behavior; support of the wrap behavior is optional.

### 7.2.1 Log Attributes

The attributes of the Log object are described below.

*logID* - Uniquely identifies an instance of a Log managed object

*maxLogSize* - The maximum size in octets that the log can contain, exclusive of the system overhead involved in establishing the log.

*currentLogSize* - The current size of the log measured in octets.

*numberOfRecords* - The current number of records in the log.

*logFullAction* - Specifies the action to be taken when the maximum size of the log is reached. Options are: (a) Wrap - the oldest set of records in the log will be deleted to make room for new records. (b) Halt - no more record will be logged. Records already in the log will remain. All logs must support the Halt behavior.

*capacityAlarmThreshold* - See *logFullAction*. As a percentage of *maxLogSize*, the condition for which an event will be generated to indicate that a log full or log wrap condition is approaching. Support is mandatory for the Halt behavior.

The *discriminatorConstruct, administrativeState, operationalState,* and *availabilityStatus* function as defined for the event forwarding discriminator object, except that they control the logging of potential log records instead of the forwarding of potential event reports.

### 7.2.2 Log Scheduling Packages

The scheduling packages for the Log object are the same ones defined for the Event Forwarding Discriminator object. The scheduling packages control the times when the Log object may be active.

### 7.2.3 Log Notifications
*ProcessingAlarm* - emitted by the Log object when the *capacityAlarmThreshold* is generated with a probable cause of "storageCapacityProblem".

The *attributeValueChange, stateChange, objectCreation, and objectDeletion* notifications function as described for the Event Forwarding Discriminator object, except that they apply to the Log object.

## 8. Event Report Management and Log Control Services

Many of the attributes of the EFD and Log objects are the same, and the services used to control event reporting and logging are similar. Basic services have been defined to initiate and terminate, to temporarily suspend and resume, and to modify conditions for event forwarding or logging. The Event Forwarding Discriminator and Log attributes may be retrieved at any time through the normal use of the management protocol.

### 8.1 Initiation
A user at a managing system may desire that particular events generated at a managed system be reported to particular destination systems, or that logging should be initiated. This is accomplished by the creation of Event Forwarding Discriminator or Log managed objects at the managed system.

### 8.2 Termination
A user in a managing system can use this service to turn off the forwarding of events or logging at a specific managed system. This is accomplished by the deletion of the EFDs of the unwanted events, or Log objects, at the managed system. The absence of an EFD will not stop the generation of notifications from the managed objects; it simply prevents those particular notifications from being forwarded as event reports. Controlling the event generation mechanism, e.g., by setting to "off" the notify high and notify low switches on gauge thresholds, will prevent the generation of notifications.

### 8.3 Suspension/Resumption/Modification
This service enables the manager to temporarily suspend, and subsequently resume, the forwarding of event reports normally passed by an EFD, or logging of log records, and to modify conditions for event forwarding or logging.

To suspend event reporting, or logging, the EFD or Log *administrativeState* attribute is changed to "locked"; and to resume event reporting, or logging, it is changed back to "unlocked".

A managing system can modify the conditions of event forwarding for selected events, or logging of selected log records, by changing the values of the attributes which are used in the processing associated with event distribution and control, or with logging. For example, the user may want to modify the reporting of a specific type of event to a different destination, or change the schedule of the event reporting. To achieve such results, a managing system will need to modify the value of the EFD *destination* and/or *discriminatorConstruct* attributes and the appropriate scheduling attributes to reflect the new needs. Similarly, changes would be made to the *discriminatorConstruct* attribute and scheduling attributes in the Log object to control the selection of records to be logged.

## 9. Standard Event and Log Record Contents

The OSI system management functions have defined the contents for some standard event reports and log records. The contents, in addition to providing needed information about the event or log record, are used to select which events are to be forwarded or logged and for log record retrieval.

### 9.1 Standard Event Reports

The Event Report Management function uses the standardized information contained within an event report to select event reports that should be forwarded to specified destinations.

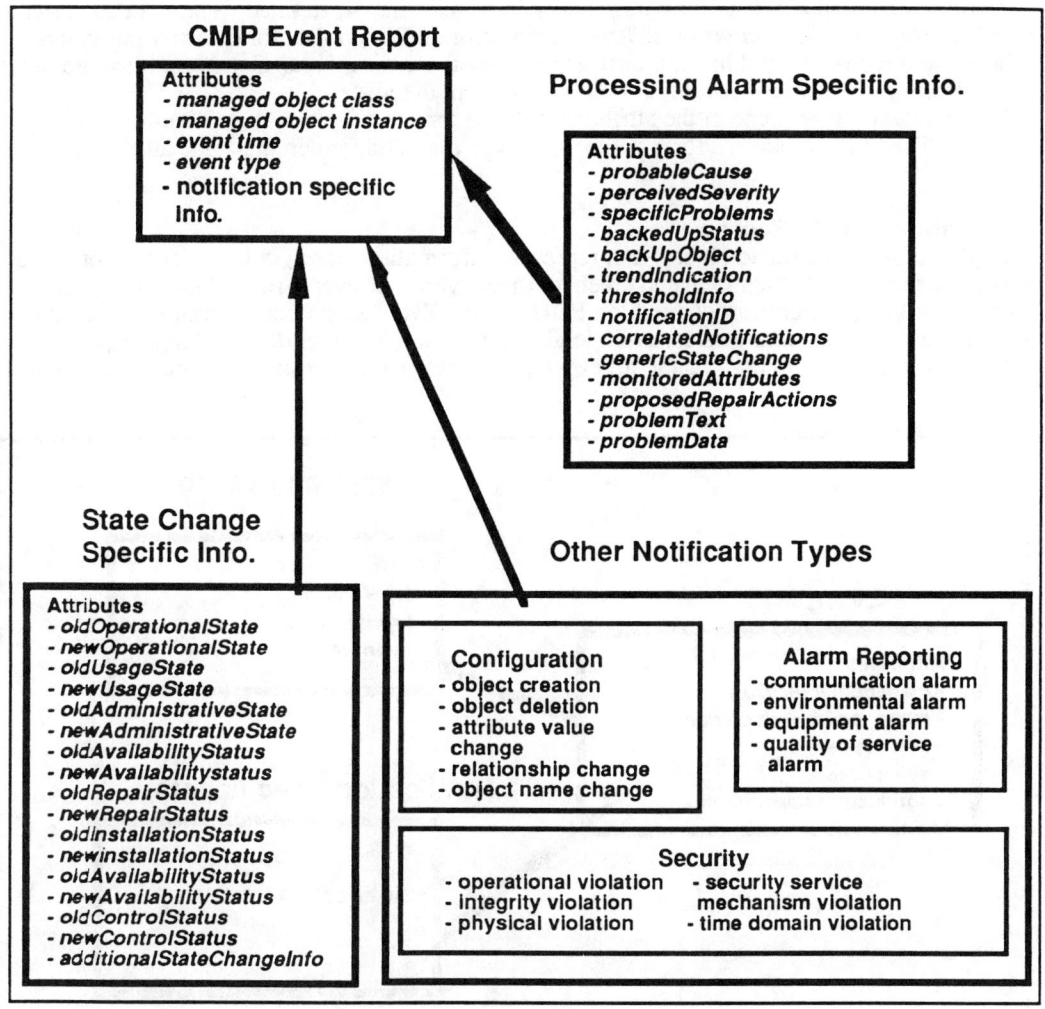

Figure 5: Event Report Contents

Several system management functions define standard information for notifications. This information is contained in the event report. For example the Alarm Reporting Function [5] capabilities, whether the condition is getting more or less severe, threshold related information, defines information to help with understanding the cause of the alarm, its severity, backup and other information for correlating the alarm to other alarms or providing additional diagnostic information.

Similarly the State Management Function [3] defines the information to be included in State Change notifications, and the Object Management Function [2] defines information to be included in notifications related to object creation and deletion.

All event reports also contain the additional information specified by CMIS [13] for event reports (event time is optional). Figure 5 illustrates the event (notification) specific information contained in the Processing Alarm event, and the State Change event.

Other notification types thus far defined in the standards for configuration management [2, 3, 4], alarm reporting [4], and security alarms [8], are also indicated in figure 5.

Attributes corresponding to the parameters of an event may be defined. These attributes can be referenced by a *discriminatorConstruct* attribute of an EFD object for determining if and where event reports should be sent, or referenced by the *discriminatorConstruct* attribute of a Log object to select which records should be stored in the log.

The standards allow some of the attributes defined for a notification to be conditionally present. Therefore, all events for a notification type may not contain the same attributes.

### 9.2 Standard Log Records

Log records are managed objects that represent information stored in logs. The records may contain information related to management defined events, or events related to protocol data units (PDUs) (e.g., transport connection PDUs). The Event Log Record (figure 6) managed object class contains attributes common to all log records (*logRecordID* and *loggingTime*), CMIS defined attributes common to all events, plus information specific to each notification

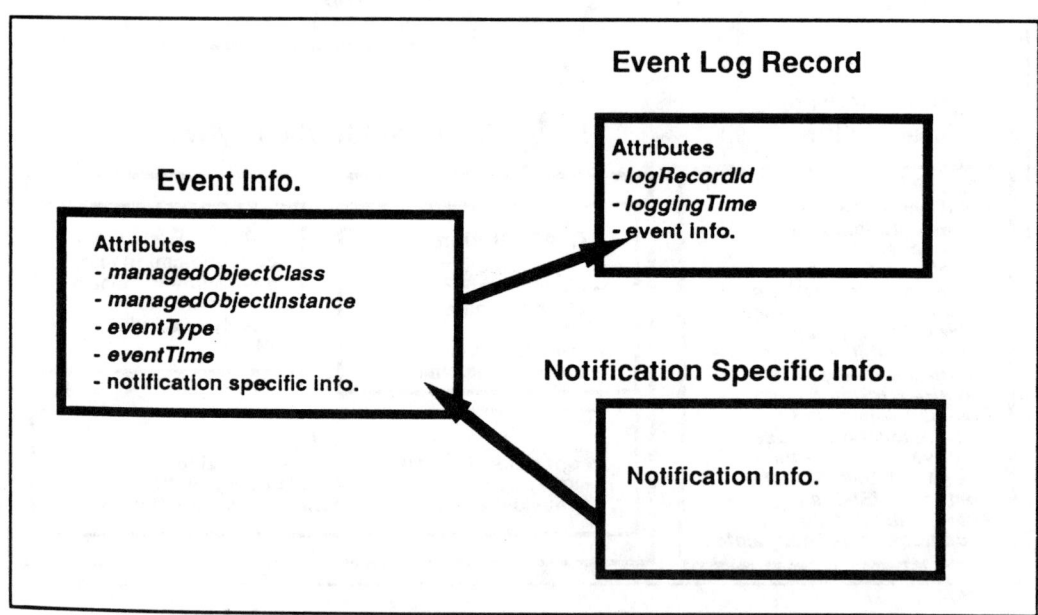

Figure 6: Log Record Contents

type. Standard information related to ISO notifications are defined in the system management functions, with their syntax defined in [10]. For example, the Alarm Record contains the attributes defined for the Event Log Record, including information specific to Alarm type notifications.

## 10. Performance Metrics

Classical performance models characterize system performance in terms of metrics that include: input traffic (offered load), output traffic (throughput), delays (e.g., service time), error rates, and fraction of system capacity in use (utilization). These performance metrics may be calculated from samples on the raw data contained in counters and gauges. For example, dividing the counter value that represent the number of input messages by the time between samples provides the metric for the offered traffic rate. Thresholds can be applied to the performance metrics and cause events to be reported to the manager station when acceptable performance bounds are exceeded.

### 10.1 Statistics on Performance Metrics

All of these performance metrics change over time, perhaps very rapidly from one short time interval to the next. These "instantaneous" performance metrics characterize the transient performance of the system components. But "instantaneous" metrics are often inadequate to characterize the performance of network components for the purpose of remote control across a communications network. By the time either the raw data samples, or the calculated "instantaneous" metrics, have been transmitted to the management station the component or system performance may have changed due to random fluctuations in the input traffic, or due to self-correcting algorithms in the individual components and protocols. Control actions based on the transient performance characterization may therefore be unnecessary or inappropriate to the changed conditions, and may even push the system into unstable operation.

Experience with control systems indicate that control decisions should be based on performance metrics derived from the weighted time-averaged distribution parameters of the performance metrics, which are random variables in time, calculated from many samples taken over a significant period of time. The weighted time-averaged distribution parameters, including the mean, variance, inter-quartile range, etc., of the metrics, tend to change slowly and filter out indications of transient behavior, thus adjusting to variations in traffic and the self-correcting behavior of components. Significant changes in these distribution parameters are more likely to be a true indication that a component's performance has altered. Thresholds applied to the time-averaged parameters of the performance metrics will result in fewer event reports being generated due to transient conditions that need no management action to correct.

ISO is developing standards that specify mechanisms for calculating the time-averaged statistics on counter type time differentials and gauge type attributes. The Workload Monitoring Function [11] defines algorithms for calculating the time-average statistics (mean, variance, percentiles) of counter differentials and gauges, defines thresholds on these statistics, and indicates how they may be applied to estimations of resource requests, resource rejections, and resource utilization that characterize the resource workload. The Summarization Function [12] specifies a method for scheduling the reporting of events that carry this summary statistical information and dynamically defining their contents.

## 10.2 Metric Objects

Managed objects are usually defined without specific consideration of the metrics that characterize the performance of the related resource, although their definers often define the counters and gauges that are the raw data measurements needed to calculate the performance metrics. Moreover, in most cases they should not include the metric calculations in the managed object, since which resources should be monitored for performance is usually a policy or system (or experimental) design decision.

A "meter", or metric object, that can be "attached" to the managed object to be monitored is needed to monitor the performance of resources represented by objects not designed with a requirement for performance monitoring - in much the same way that a voltmeter is attached to points in an electronic circuit (figure 7). The concept of metric objects defined in [11] fulfills that need. A metric object makes observations on one or more attributes in a monitored object according to a periodic schedule determined by the sample time. The observations may be used to calculate a value. If the calculated value represents a gauge value, as is the case with the metric objects defined in [11], then a gauge threshold may be associated with the calculated metric value.

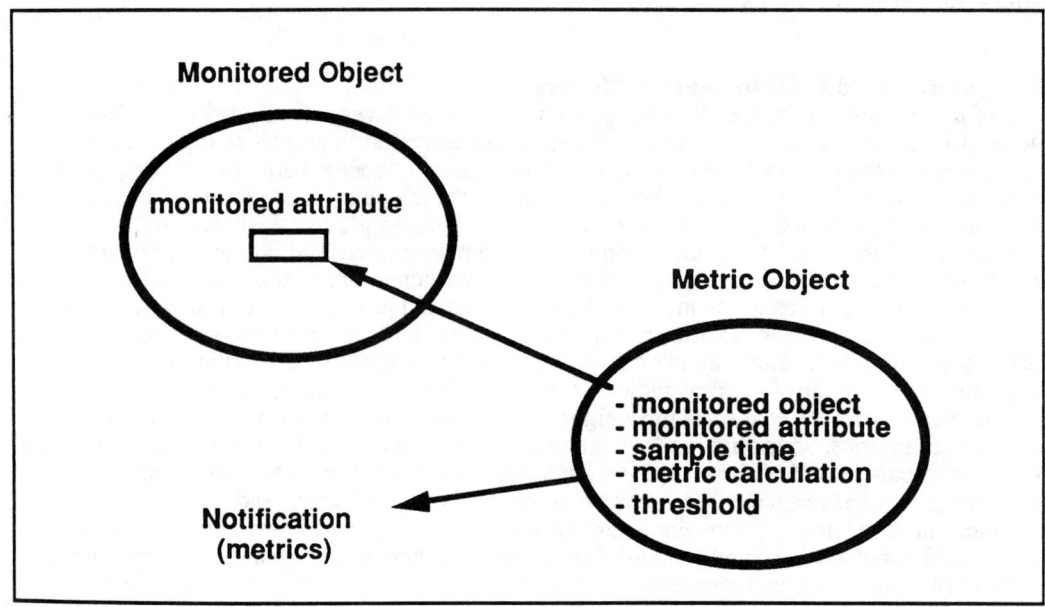

Figure 7: Metric Objects

## 11. Summary

One approach to network management is management by exception, where exceptions are reported via events. This paper has provided a tutorial on the standard tools being developed by ISO for event generation, event reporting, event logging, and performance monitoring. These tools are expected to become International Standards in 1991. Managed objects are currently being defined in the standards and implementors agreements communities that will use these tools for management of events. Implementors agreements on the system management function standards that define the event report and log control tools are now in progress within several communities. Future expert systems will use these tools to improve the timeliness and quality of information available to network operators and assist them in effecting control decisions.

## 12. References

1 ISO/IEC DIS 10165-1, Information Processing Systems - Open Systems Interconnection - Structure of Management Information - Part 1: Management Information Model.
2 ISO/IEC DIS 10164-1, Information Processing Systems - Open Systems Interconnection - Systems Management - Part 1: Object Management Function.
3 DIS 10164-2, Information Processing Systems - Open Systems Interconnection - Systems Management - Part 2: State management Function.
4 DIS 10164-3, Information Processing Systems - Open Systems Interconnection - Systems Management - Part 3: Attributes for representing Relationships.
5 ISO/IEC DIS 10164-4, Information Processing Systems - Open Systems Interconnection - Systems Management - Part 4: Alarm Reporting Function.
6 ISO/IEC DIS 10164-5, Information Processing Systems - Open Systems Interconnection - Systems Management - Part 5: Event Report Management Function.
7 DIS 10164-6, Information Processing Systems - Open Systems Interconnection - Systems Management - Part 6: Log Control Function.
8 ISO/IEC DIS 10164-7, Information Processing Systems - Open Systems Interconnection - Systems Management - Part 7: Security Alarm Reporting Function.
9 ISO/IEC DIS 10164-8, Information Processing Systems - Open Systems Interconnection - Systems Management - Part 8: Security Audit Trail Function.
10 ISO/IEC DIS 10165-2, Information Processing Systems - Open Systems Interconnection - Structure of Management Information - Part 2: Definition of Management Information.
11 ISO/IEC CD 10165-12, Information Processing Systems - Open Systems Interconnection - Systems Management - Part 12: Workload Monitoring Function.
12 ISO/IEC WP 10165-13, Information Processing Systems - Open Systems Interconnection - Structure of Management Information - Part 13 Summarization Function.
13 ISO 9595, Information Processing Systems - Open Systems Interconnection - Management Information Service Definition - Common Management Information Service.
14 ISO 9596, Information Processing Systems - Open Systems Interconnection - Management Information Protocol Specification - Common Management Information Protocol.

# OPTIMIZING OSI MANAGEMENT SYSTEM PERFORMANCE

Subodh Bapat

Racal Datacom
1601 N Harrison Parkway
Sunrise, FL 33323

## Abstract

This presentation will discuss techniques for optimizing the performance of a network management system.

The primary objective is to improve the response time of a network management system product, so that it may respond to external management requests (modeled using CMIP operations) within performance constraints imposed by specifications.

It is found that the performance characteristics of a given system product are dependent on the nature of primary use for which that system is employed. The distribution of MIB information for a given product is also important in determining overall system performance.

## Outline

* The architecture of a network management system determines the structure of the Management Information Base and the pattern of distribution of the information stored in it.

* The manner in which the network management system is utilized determines the nature of operations performed on the information stored in the Management Information Base

* The process of optimizing the performance of a network management system must take into account the nature of usage, and suitably tailor the information distribution in the MIB in accordance with such usage.

The Management Information Base (MIB) is the conceptual repository of all the information that is necessary for network management functions. Although the MIB is a virtual collection of information about managed objects, in a real implementation it is usually manifested as a distributed repository, consisting of various types of databases, memory and firmware elements.

Because the MIB is a distributed information store, the pattern of distribution determines the speed and ease of access of MIB information to network management operations. Therefore, it strongly affects the performance of a network management system.

In this presentation we will show that there is no single pattern of distribution of MIB information which will lead to optimal performance. Rather, the distribution must take into account the manner in which the network management is used. Each different utilization pattern gives rise to different considerations and priorities for distributing MIB information for optimal performance.

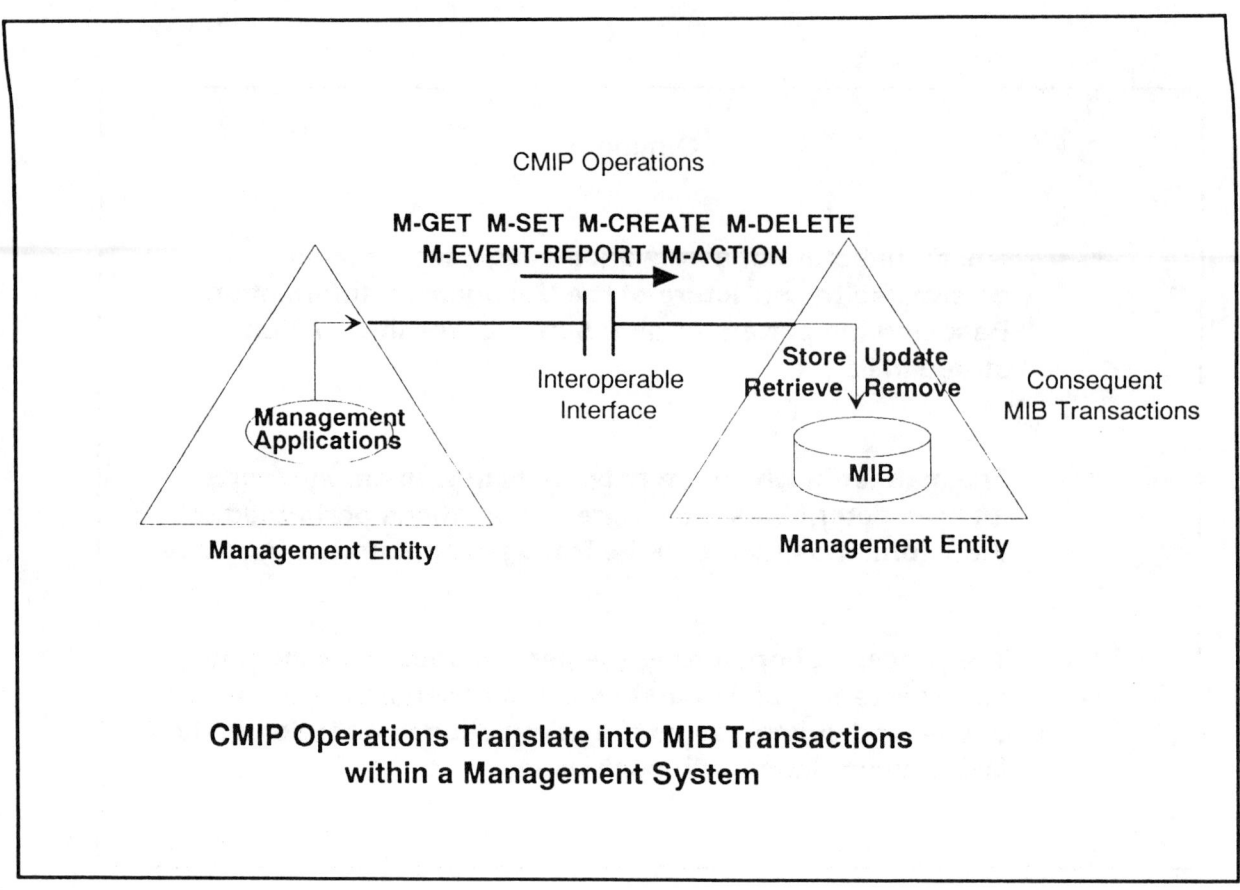

**CMIP Operations Translate into MIB Transactions within a Management System**

An OSI Management System receives stimuli from many external sources. Acting in an agent role, it may receive CMIP requests such as M-SET, M-GET, M-CREATE, etc. from peer management systems across an interoperable interface. Acting in a manager role, it may receive CMIP requests such as M-EVENT-REPORTs from agents associated with real resources in the managed network.

These requests perform abstract operations against a virtual MIB which is conceptually resident within the OSI Management System. In a real implementation, a MIB could be implemented as a distributed information store consisting of many database and memory elements. When CMIP operations are executed against the MIB, real operations such as Store, Update, Retrieve, and Remove are performed on these database and memory elements.

The performance of the OSI Management System depends to a great extent on the speed with which these operations can be executed. The objective of performance optimization therefore is to arrive at an optimal configuration for the internal distribution of this MIB information, which allows the fast processing of CMIP operations.

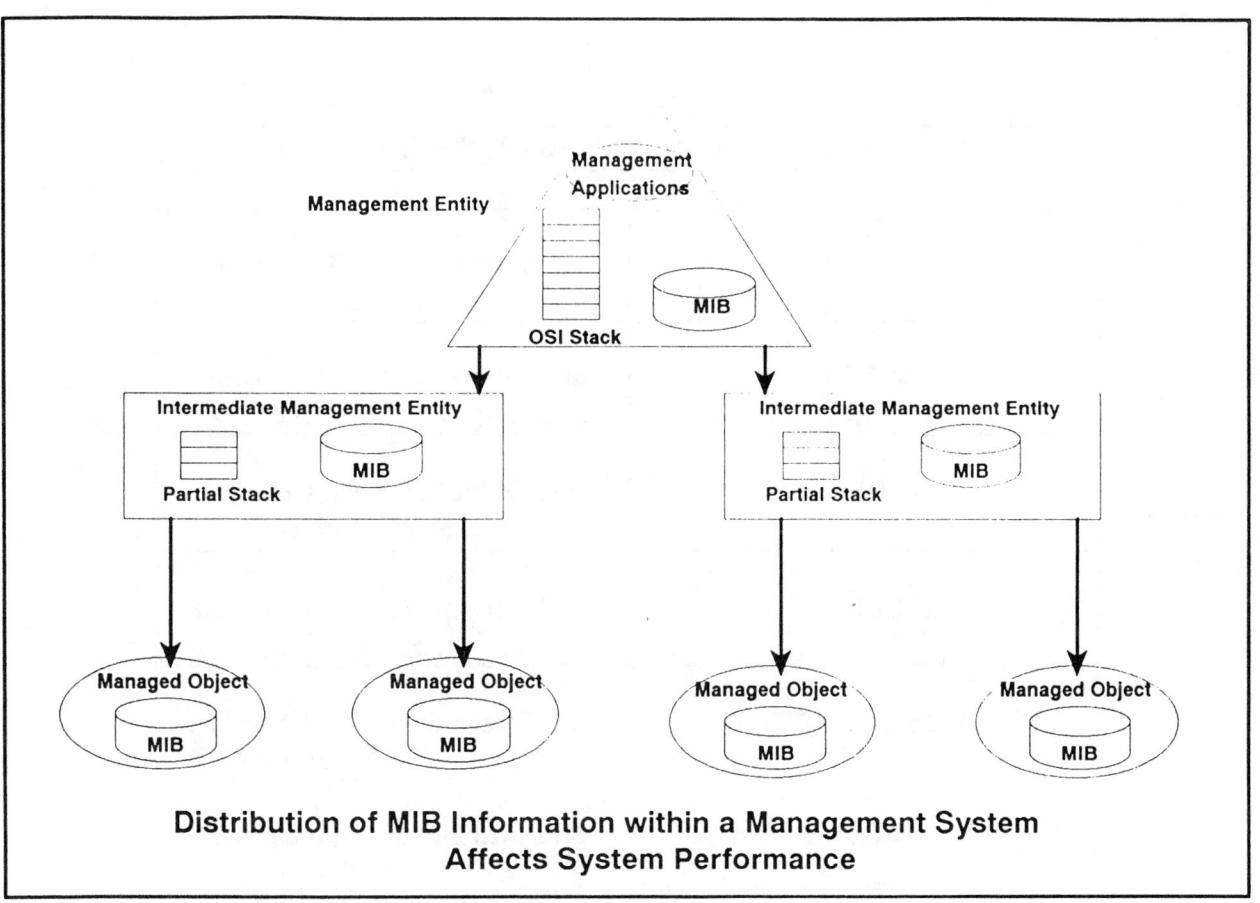

**Distribution of MIB Information within a Management System Affects System Performance**

The internal implementation of a MIB requires a mapping from the attributes of the abstract object model to real records, fields, registers and memory segments in the database, firmware, and software elements resident within both the network management station and real network resources.

Many network management stations contain an internal repository which stores MIB information in a persistent fashion. This repository may be a relational, object-oriented, flat-file or proprietary database. This database typically contains system-wide information (such as a directory of all managed resources and their network topology) and may also contain copies of information normally resident within the real resource, for purposes of redundancy.

MIB information may also be stored as firmware within the managed resource. Dynamic attributes, such as counters, are usually recovered from register values within real resources or memory locations within software entities. Such software-based representations of MIB information may include management application processes, layer entities, agent processes, or the local instrumentation of the resource. Occasionally such information may be stored in an intermediate management entity, such as a proxy agent, or a mediation device in a Telecommunications Management Network.

| MIB Transactions Resulting from CMIP Operations ||
|:---:|:---:|
| M-GET | MIB Information Retrieval (e.g. SQL SELECT) |
| M-SET | MIB Attribute Value Update (e.g. SQL UPDATE) |
| M-CREATE | MIB Object Record Creation (e.g. SQL INSERT) |
| M-DELETE | MIB Object Record Deletion (e.g. SQL DELETE) |
| M-EVENT-REPORT | MIB Event Instance Creation (e.g SQL INSERT) |
| M-ACTION | MIB Attribute Value Update (e.g. SQL UPDATE) |

To execute a CMIP operation, MIB information internally distributed within the management solution needs to be accessed. Since many attributes of a single object instance could be potentially available from different locations, all these locations must be accessed in order to reconstruct the entire object from its fragments. The speed of access, therefore, depends on the nature of the actual information distribution within the management solution.

Another important factor in performance optimization is the nature of the management station repository. This repository must be amenable and customizable for performance tuning. In particular, it must exhibit fast response times when frequent CMIP operations are executed against it.

The above visual uses the example of a relational database used as a MIB repository to show the effects of CMIP operation execution. A CMIP operation such as an M-GET, after being decoded by the CMIP protocol machine and mapped to the local information schema by a management application, may result in an SQL SELECT statement being issued against one or more tables within the relational repository. Similarly, other CMIP operations correspond to other SQL primitives being executed against the database schema. Therefore, optimizing the repository with respect to its primitive Read, Write, Update and Delete operations, has a significant effect on the processing rate for CMIP operations, and thus on the overall performance of the OSI management system.

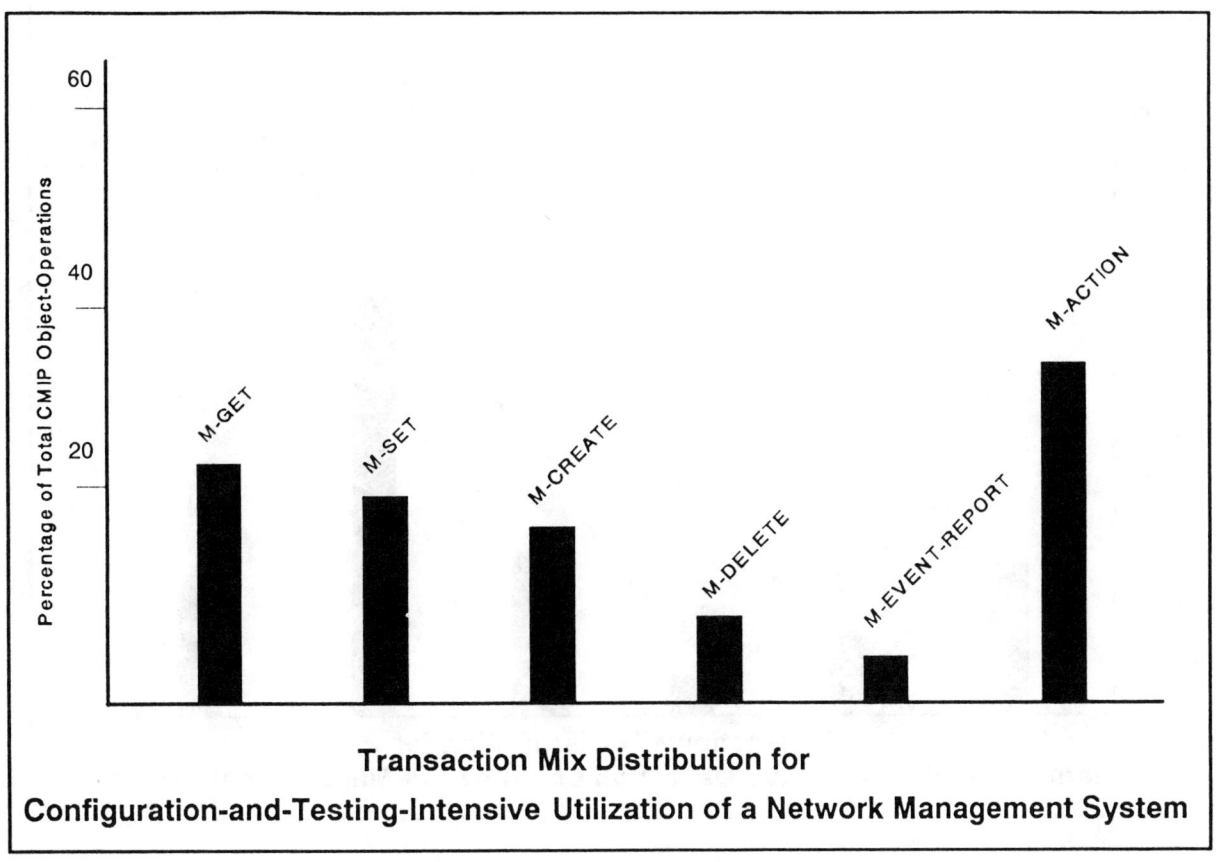

**Transaction Mix Distribution for Configuration-and-Testing-Intensive Utilization of a Network Management System**

The above visual plots the percentage of CMIP object-operations for each operation type. (A single operation request could result in many object-operations because of multiple objects scoped by it.) It demonstrates the transaction mix distribution for a network management system whose primary utilization is for network configuration, topology validation, and confidence and diagnostic testing.

Under this utilization pattern, a fairly even distribution of some CMIP operations is obtained. M-CREATE, M-SET, and M-GET operations constitute a significant percentage of the total number of operations during the phase where the network configuration is being defined. Managed objects are created within the network management system to represent real resources using M-CREATE operations. Although these could be created using Initial Value Managed Object templates, on several occasions their attribute values need to be refined using M-SETs. M-GETs are primarily used to validate configuration settings. Finally, a large number of M-ACTIONs could be used to invoke tests and other procedures to validate the resource's operation within the network. Under this utilization of a network management system, performance tuning would require fast processing of M-ACTION confirmation and linked replies. Also, since these procedures are usually conducted through a human user interface, a reasonable response time is required from the M-GET, M-SET and M-CREATE operations.

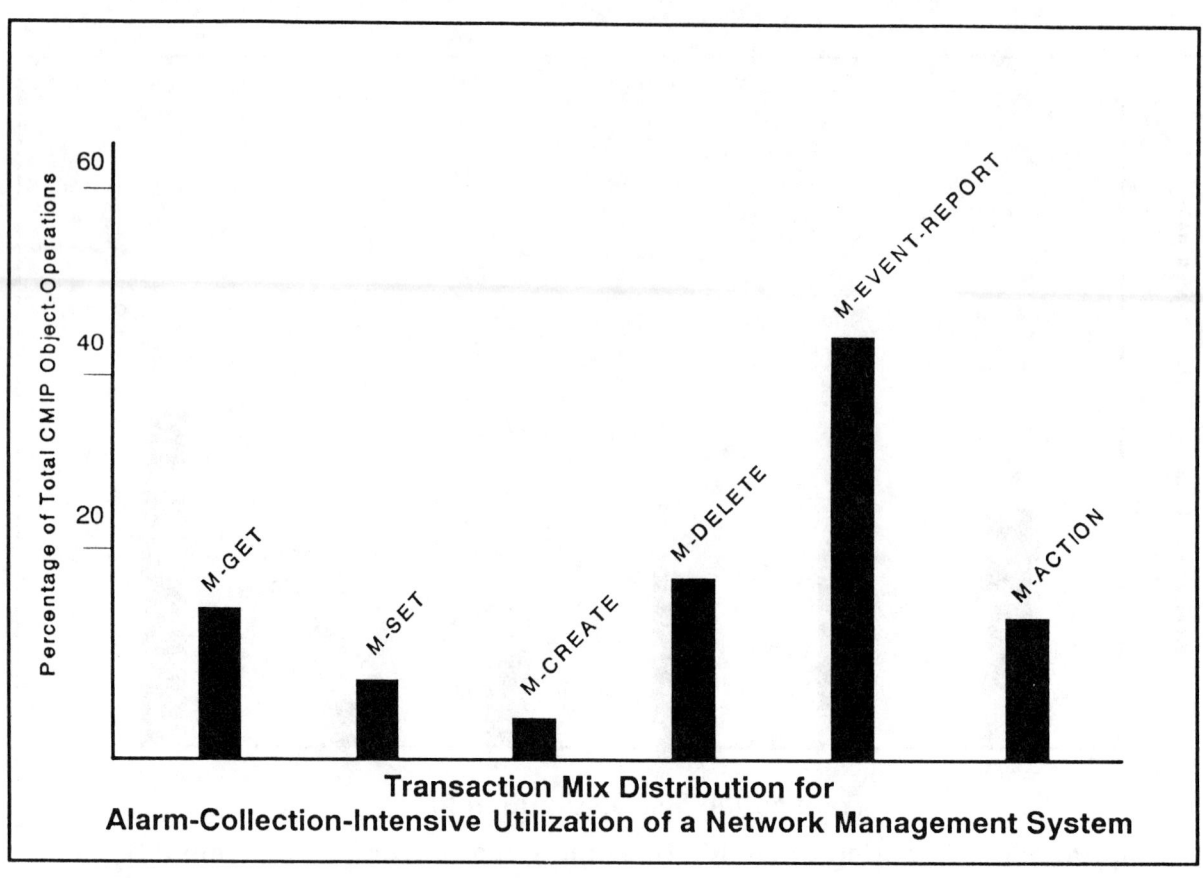

**Transaction Mix Distribution for
Alarm-Collection-Intensive Utilization of a Network Management System**

If the transaction mix distribution follows a different pattern, a different performance tuning strategy is required. The above example demonstrates the transaction distribution where alarm collection is the primary utilization.

Under this utilization pattern, an overwhelming number of CMIP operations are M-EVENT-REPORT operations arriving from agent processes. Since alarm collection could be a round-the-clock activity and often proceeds unattended by a human observer, alarm information must be stored in the management station repository for later inspection by a management operator or for report generation.

Performance tuning under this utilization pattern requires tuning the repository for fast insertion of event information. Under times of catastrophic network failure, a burst of M-EVENT-REPORT requests may be expected from many resources. In order not to lose any significant operational data, the repository must respond with performance similar to a high-demand OLTP (OnLine Transaction Processing) database.

Since alarm management through human interaction sometimes involves retrieving associated parameters, performing diagnostic testing, and deleting event instance records, some M-GET, M-DELETE and M-ACTION activity is also seen.

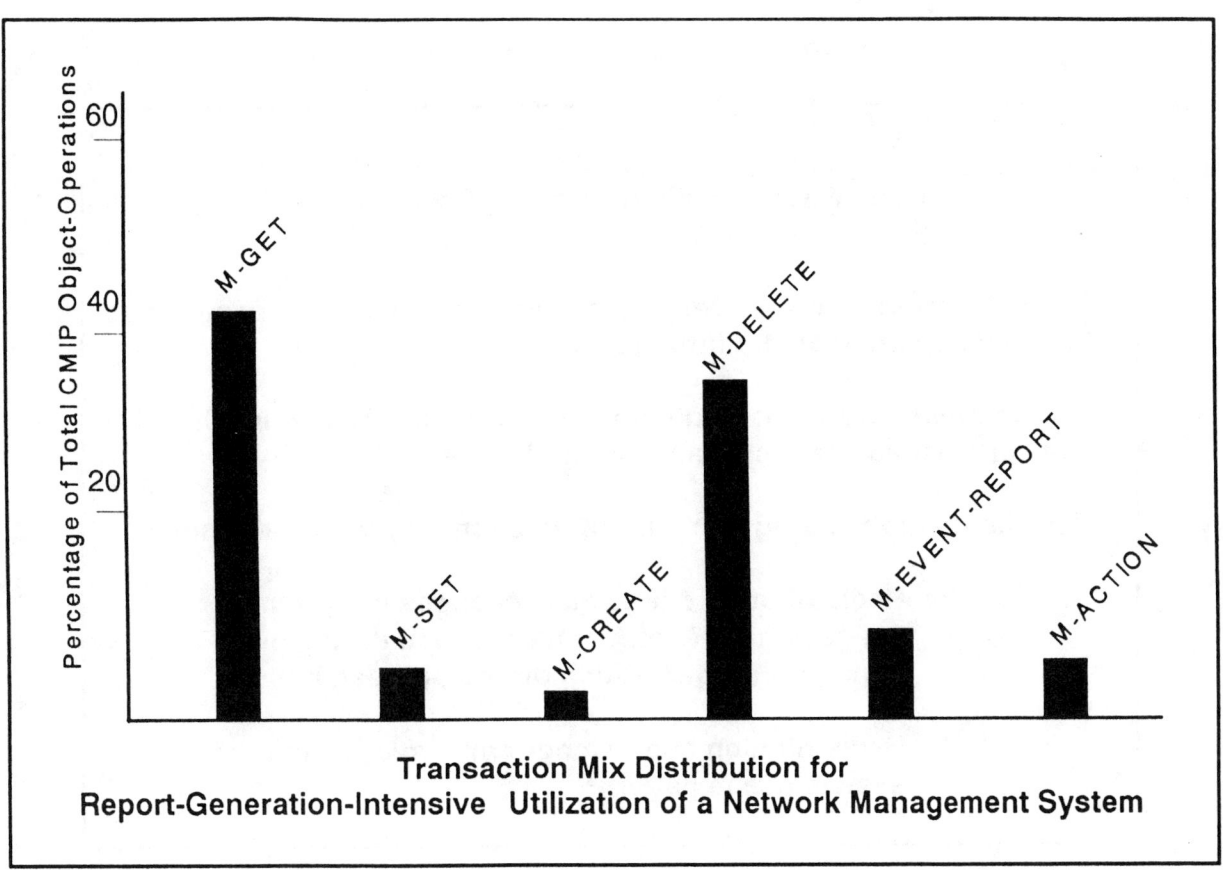

Some OSI Management Systems are used to periodically generate routine reports on network activity. Occasionally, these systems may not themselves be used for alarm collection, but may depend on a common networked repository, which is actually populated by another management system primarily used for alarm collection. The above visual depicts the transaction mix distribution one such report-intensive management system

Under this utilization pattern, the number of M-GETs is significantly high. Although routine reports often generate information about all objects in the network, it is often difficult to generate this report using a single M-GET scoping the entire containment hierarchy. This is because the parameters of interest in every class of managed object are different, and must be specified separately in multiple M-GET requests. Further, the order in which information is retrieved from the containment hierarchy is not necessarily the same order suitable for human presentation; thus, user-friendly report generation is best achieved using multiple M-GETs in a sequence approximating the format for report presentation.

Routine statistical information is often deleted from the repository, either immediately after report generation or after expiration following some aging policy. Therefore, a significant number of M-DELETEs is also seen.

> **Considerations in Performance Optimization**
>
> * **System performance and response characteristics are very sensitive to the distribution of MIB information**
>
> * **MIB information should be distributed to suit the manner in which the network management system is primarily used.**
>
> * **The distribution strategy for MIB information may vary with time:**
>
>   * **Redistribution due to daily changes in system usage pattern (e.g. Alarm collection during peak hours, report generation during off-peak hours)**
>
>   * **Redistribution due to long-term evolution in system usage patterns**

Because CMIP operations affect many aspects of a managed object instance, and because object fragments may be distributed over a management system, the nature of the actual distribution has a profound effect on system performance. By repartitioning managed objects to achieve a more optimal distribution of object fragments, system performance can be greatly improved.

It should be emphasized that a particular distribution of MIB information is only optimal relative to a given mix of CMIP transaction queries. Should the pattern of CMIP queries change, the MIB information needs to adapt itself to a different distribution in order to continue delivering optimal performance. Changes in the access pattern could occur with time. Such changes could be anticipated, such as daily or weekly changes in the pattern of use in a management system for peak and off-peak hours of operation. Also, long-term changes in the access pattern could occur with time as system operators become familiar with capabilities and begin exercising the system in different ways.

To maintain optimal performance under these circumstances, the system needs to adapt to these changes by using strategies such as caching off secondary storage and data migration.

> **Distribution-Based Performance Optimization Principles**
>
> * Perform an analysis to determine the nature of the CMIP operations performed within the system and the frequency patterns for each operation. (A system tuned to deliver optimal performance under one transaction mix will be non-optimal under a different transaction mix.)
>
> * Determine GET- and REPLACE- access frequencies for pertinent MIB attributes.
>
> * Store information closest to where it is most immediately useful.
>
> * If the delay associated with an OSI Management query by an application to the agent exceeds response requirements, store multiple copies of the information.
>
> * If Access Frequency Analysis shows high demand for some subset of the information, optimize that subset for fast access (e.g. in-memory caching.)

To arrive at an optimal distribution of MIB information, studies must be performed to analyze the transaction mix of CMIP operations. The studies must yield the nature and frequency of CMIP operations, and the actual attributes which are accessed during CMIP operations. Attributes which are frequently accessed for either GET or REPLACE must be identified. Further, the study must indicate which managed object classes are most frequently created and deleted.

Heuristics for optimal distribution of MIB information may be determined based on the above study. If an object is frequently accessed for reading attribute values, it should be ideally stored closest to where it is most often required, even if this means storing multiple redundant copies. For example, an eventReportingSieve object could be directly stored inside any real network resource which has the capability of local storage, so that sieving may be done locally. This will lead to optimal performance even if a second copy of the eventReportingSieve exists in the management station repository. On the other hand, if an object is frequently created or its attributes are frequently updated, performance will be improved if only one copy of that object exists. This is because multiple copies of information which is frequently written require the overhead of a synchronization protocol to assure consistency between the multiple copies.

> **Utilization-Based Performance Optimization Principles**
>
> * If the primary utilization is for alarm collection:
>   * Tune the repository for fast insertion
>   * Constraints to check uniqueness and consistency defined in database typically slow down insertion; remove them
>   * Garbage collection etc. must be postponed for a background, offline process.
>
> * If the primary utilization is report generation:
>   * Tune the repository for fast retrievals
>   * Enforce uniqueness and consistency checks to ensure consistent reports
>
> * If the primary use is configuration and testing:
>   * Tune the repository for fast creates, updates and deletes
>   * M-ACTIONs may produce many side-effects (state modifications, linked replies) which may need to be speedily recorded

The process of performance tuning for an OSI Management System needs to take into account the manner in which the system is utilized, since any single performance parameter profile is only optimal relative to a given transaction mix distribution.

If the primary utilization is for alarm collection, the management station repository must be tuned for fast insertion. For examples, in a relational database, a uniqueness index on a table assures consistency of information, but slows down insertion because every new record must be checked against every other record in the table. For fast insertion, indexes must be removed, with consistency checks done by an offline process. If the primary utilization is report generation, the repository must be tuned for fast retrievals, which may mean construction of hash tables based on attributes used as lookup keys. Since report generation is often concomitant with large M-DELETE sequences, and since instance deletion also requires lookup, such hash tables would speed up M-DELETEs as well. Reclaiming repository space freed up by M-DELETEs is best done by processes which run either offline or as low-priority background processes.

For configuration and testing, the repository must be tuned to respond to fast update operations due to the effects of reconfiguration and testing on attribute values.

# Network Management of TCP/IP Networks: Present and Future

*Amatzia Ben-Artzi*
*Asheem Chandna*
*Unni Warrier*

Transmission Control Protocol/Internet Protocol (TCP/IP) networking technology has come a long way since it was first conceived in the early 1970s. While the technology was originally used for research and interconnection at sites funded by the Department of Defense, recent years have witnessed its rapid acceptance and growth in the commercial networking sector. The current TCP/IP community network (popularly known as "the Internet"), spans the entire continental United States with international links to Europe, Japan, the Middle East, Australia, and South and Central America. The network includes about 150,000 connected hosts with user estimates running in the millions [1].

This recent growth of TCP/IP networking technology has led to the need for tools that provide for the management of interconnected TCP/IP networks. Regional network administrators need to be able to remotely configure and diagnose faults that relate to backbone networks and the gateways that interconnect them. Campus administrators need tools that allow them to monitor and control their internal campus networks, along with their links to the external world. Both the networking equipment and the connected computers (that need to be managed) are typically supplied by a variety of different vendors.

Recent network management activities in the TCP/IP community have focused on standardizing two network management protocols (Simple Network Management Protocol—SNMP, and Common Management Information Services and Protocol Over TCP/IP—CMOT) that provide for the exchange of management information. This article compares the current SNMP and CMOT approaches to TCP/IP network management, from several different perspectives. It provides comparisons based on both theory and knowledge gained from actual implementation experiences. The article also examines and explains the current level of user and vendor acceptance for these two protocols. Finally, it summarizes relevant ongoing work and provides a look at where we are headed over the next few years.

## Background

In early 1988, the Internet Activities Board (IAB)[1] held an ad-hoc meeting to determine a strategy for managing the nationwide TCP/IP-based Internet. The meeting's recommendation were officially endorsed and gave birth to two parallel standardization efforts: SNMP and CMOT [2]. It recommended that SNMP be deployed as a short-term solution, while CMOT be used as the eventual longer term solution.

The first effort has concentrated on producing standards for the implementation of the SNMP [3]. SNMP extends upon an earlier network management protocol called "Simple Gateway Monitoring Protocol" (SGMP) [4], which was designed for the monitoring of TCP/IP gateway systems (IP routers). The SNMP working group has been driven by the urgent need to provide network administrators with a better solution for remotely managing TCP/IP gateways and related network interfaces.

The second effort has been working to produce agreements for the implementation of CMOT [5]. CMOT is a protocol stack specification for deploying the International Standards Organization/Open Systems Interconnection (ISO/OSI) management protocol (Common Management Information Protocol—CMIP) [6] over existing TCP/IP environments. The CMOT working group has been motivated by the concept of using OSI management for TCP/IP network management [7].

Figure 1 shows the SNMP architecture. SNMP provides applications with a simple set of commands (Get, Set, and Get-Next) which are packaged using the Basic Encoding Rules (BER) associated with ISO Abstract Syntax Notation One (ASN.1) and sent over existing UDP/IP services. There is also a very limited trap message, which allows six standardized types of unconfirmed events to be reported asynchronously.

Current SNMP implementations are centered around a core set of three specifications: the SNMP protocol over a UDP/IP protocol stack [3], the rules for the Structure of Management Information (SMI) [8] for use with SNMP, and an initial collection of about 100 standardized SNMP objects [9]. The initial set of objects, termed "MIB-I," comprise a Management Information Base (MIB) that provides for limited fault and configuration management. MIB-I objects represent parameters that relate to TCP/IP protocols (TCP, IP, UDP, ICMP, and EGP), system address and interface tables, and system identification information.

Figure 2 shows the CMOT architecture. The application services provided by CMOT are defined by Common Management Information Services (CMIS), the service definition for the ISO CMIP protocol [10]. As shown in the figure, the application layer is based on OSI and contains Common Management Information Service Element (CMISE), Remote Operations Service Element (ROSE), and Association Control Service Element (ACSE). The transport and network layers are TCP/UDP and IP, respectively. The presentation layer consists of a Lightweight Presentation Protocol (LPP), and pro-

---

[1] The IAB sets policies for the nationwide Internet and serves as the official committee for TCP/IP-related standards (which are issued as Requests For Comments—RFCs). IAB standards and policies also form the basis for vendor product requirements and set the direction for the TCP/IP marketplace.

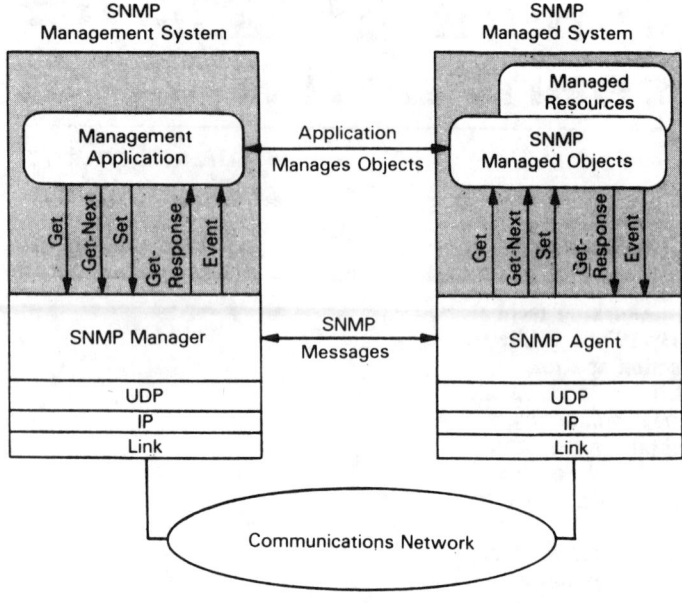

Fig. 1. SNMP architecture.

vides a mechanism for supporting OSI application services directly over TCP/IP environments [11].

## Technical Comparison

This section compares SNMP and CMOT from three perspectives: protocol services provided to applications, management paradigms, and implementation requirements.

### Protocol Services

In general, CMOT (via CMIS) provides management applications with a powerful object-oriented interface while SNMP offers an interface that is relatively primitive and more attribute-oriented. The following subsections compare the management communications models, functionalities offered, and information models, for SNMP and CMIP.

#### Management Communications

CMIP is an association-oriented protocol while SNMP is connectionless. Two CMIP application entities can exchange management operational messages, only if they set up and maintain an association with each other (i.e., an OSI association). SNMP application entities directly send messages to each other; they do not need to first establish and then maintain application level connections, as a prerequisite to operational communications.

This reduces the processing overhead, especially for infrequent SNMP communications. However, the trade-off is that the sender of a SNMP message can never be sure that the message has reached its destination. Thus, applications that utilize the SNMP protocol may need to build some sort of insurance that guarantees delivery (for example, an acknowledge strategy that works between applications).

#### Management Functionality

- *Multiple Object Selection*: CMIP provides for the implementation of sophisticated conditional commands, based on object type, value, and relative location in the managed network. SNMP does not provide these capabilities and requires one to specifically name the actual object instances being managed. (The one exception is the SNMP Get-Next message which allows a application to retrieve the next MIB object, relative to the current position.)

For example, a bridge management application on a CMIP-based management system, could directly request port information for all bridges in the managed network for whom *badpacketcount* ≥ 100. In comparison, an application using SNMP would have to know about all the bridges in the managed network, individually retrieve the information from all the bridges, and then check *badpacketcount* to determine which bridges are of interest.

- *Synchronization*: Both CMIP and SNMP can specify multiple operations (of the same type), within a single request. However, within a single request, CMIP operations on multiple object instances can be carried out on either a best effort basis or on an atomic basis. SNMP requests are always atomic—i.e., if for some reason, all the individual operations requested cannot be performed, then none are carried out and an error is returned.
- *Linked Replies*: CMIP allows an application to retrieve large amounts of data from multiple managed systems via a single request; the information is sent back in multiple linked replies. SNMP does not support linked replies. As a result, one is limited in the amount of information that can be retrieved through a single request. This limitation also makes SNMP inefficient for the retrieval of large amounts of information (for example, addressing tables).
- *MIB Browsing*: Both CMIP and SNMP can be used to browse new managed device MIBs. CMIP provides this feature via its multiple object selection capabilities and SNMP via the Get-Next message. However, with SNMP, retrieving a large MIB is a tedious and slow process, since one has to navigate the managed device's MIB in an ordered manner, retrieving one object at a time. With CMIP, one can use the multiple object selection capabilities with a wildcard and retrieve a new managed device's MIB much more quickly.
- *Actions*: CMIP provides for the definition and execution of object specific imperative commands (for example, "reboot system"). SNMP does not directly support imperative commands, but relies upon side-effects to achieve specific actions (for example, setting a boolean SNMP "reboot MIB" variable could cause the system to reboot).

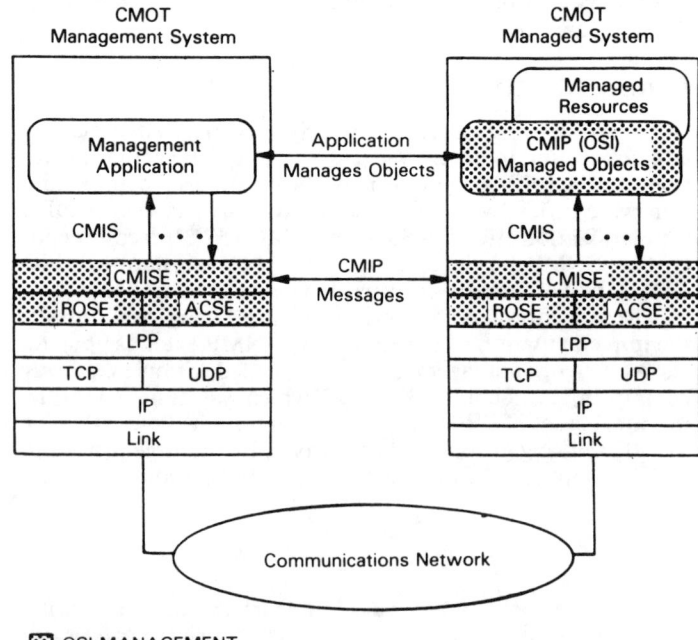

Fig. 2. CMOT architecture.

- *Event Confirmation*: CMIP events can be unconfirmed or confirmed while SNMP events are always only unconfirmed. As a result, a managed device that sends an SNMP event report can never be certain that the report was received by the destination management system.
- *Systems Management Functions*: A number of Systems Management Functions (SMFs) are being standardized to utilize the services offered by CMIS. (Examples of SMFs include error reporting, confidence and diagnostic testing, and log control.) In the case of SNMP, no equivalents of the SMFs exist, or are planned. It is also expected that future SMFs will empower CMIP to better support manager-to-manager communications. SNMP does not adequately support interactions that are specific to manager-to-manager communications.

**Management Information**

CMIP objects (i.e., OSI management objects) are more comprehensive than SNMP objects:

- *Object Definition*: CMIP objects are not the same as SNMP objects. CMIP object definitions include lists of attributes, events emitted, and the imperative actions that can be carried out. In addition, object types are structured in an inheritance hierarchy, and actual managed object instances are named through a containment hierarchy. In comparison, SNMP objects are similar to the attributes of CMIP objects and are additionally organized into groups. The additional detail and structure in CMIP objects directly support the sophisticated functionality provided by the CMIP service definition.
- *Object Naming*: The CMIP naming hierarchy is based on a highly flexible containment model, where managed objects are contained within one another. Multiple CMIP object instances of a given type can be remotely created, and deleted. As a result, applications can manage objects via names that are meaningful and are not tied to a particular network addressing mechanism. In contrast, SNMP-managed devices are named directly via IP addresses, and managed objects within devices are named via a static predefined naming trees.

  In addition, SNMP naming does not deal with the issue of proxy management where system $A$ manages device $B$ through system $C$. Proxy management is likely to be an important need in the management of large TCP/IP networks.
- *Object Representation*: CMIP objects are represented using the ISO defined ASN.1 and are encoded using ISO BER. SNMP objects are represented using a subset of ASN.1 and are encoded using the associated BER subset.

  Using a well-defined subset of ASN.1 and BER greatly reduces the code size and actual processing time. However, this also has the effect of restricting the types of objects that can be defined for use with SNMP. (For example, an address table entry could not be defined as a single SNMP object, but would be defined as a sequence of objects.)

## *Management Models*

There are two models (roughly corresponding to SNMP and CMIP/CMOT) that are widely used for network management:

- *Polling-based management*: Managed devices are polled for information of interest and return this information synchronously to the manager.
- *Event-based management*: Managed devices asynchronously send pre-configured information of interest to the manager.

The following paragraphs present simple examples for both models.

In a typical SNMP network, the SNMP manager is configured to poll managed devices at certain fixed intervals for critical SNMP MIB parameters. While polling at fixed intervals provides reliability, it tends to generate a large volume of network traffic [12]. It also limits the total number of devices that can be managed. The SNMP MIB-I specification does not include filter objects that would allow a manager to configure threshold-based events directly at the managed devices.

The analysis of polling protocols is a well-established science [13]. For the scenario where a single SNMP manager polls devices with a polling interval equal to $T$, the number of devices that can be managed is given by [13]:

$$N \leq T/\Delta \quad (1)$$

Here $\Delta$ is the minimum time required to perform a single poll, and includes time intervals required for the following (Figure 3):

$a$ = initiation of the poll at the manager (outgoing request)

$b$ = network delay from the manager to the agent

$c$ = receipt and interpretation at the agent (incoming indication)

$d$ = response at the agent (outgoing response)

$e$ = network delay from the agent to the manager

$f$ = receipt and interpretation at the manager (incoming confirmation)

$$\Delta = a + b + c + d + e + f \quad (2)$$

For simplification, if we assume that $a = c = d = f$ (for the internal message processing times) and that $b = e$ (for the network delays), then we have $\Delta = (4a + 2b)$. Thus:

$$\begin{aligned} N &\leq T/\Delta \\ &\leq T/(4a + 2b) \end{aligned} \quad (3)$$

For sake of example, let's consider the case in a single LAN, where each managed device is polled once every 15 minutes (typical at many TCP/IP sites today). Also, lets assume that $a = 50$ ms (for the internal message processing time), and that $b = 1$ ms (network delay for an Ethernet packet of about 1,000 bytes). With these numbers, we have:

$$\begin{aligned} N &\leq T/(4a + 2b) \\ &\leq (15 \times 60)/(4(0.05) + 2(0.001)) \\ &\leq 4,500 \end{aligned} \quad (4)$$

Thus, in the above LAN scenario, a single manager can manage a maximum of 4,500 devices with SNMP-based polling.

In Wide Area Networks (WANs), network delays tend to be much larger, due to longer transmitting distances, lower line capacities (typically 50 Kb/s as opposed to Ethernet 10 Mb/s), and incremental delays through gateways (100 ms is representative). Thus, having total network delays of 500 ms is not unusual. Using this as an example, we have:

$$\begin{aligned} N &\leq T/(4a + 2b) \\ &\leq (15 \times 60)/(4(0.05) + 2(0.5)) \\ &\leq 750 \end{aligned} \quad (5)$$

Thus, in the above WAN scenario, a single manager can manage a maximum of 750 devices with SNMP-based polling.

The event-based management model allows for filter objects to be specified at the devices. This allows a manager to

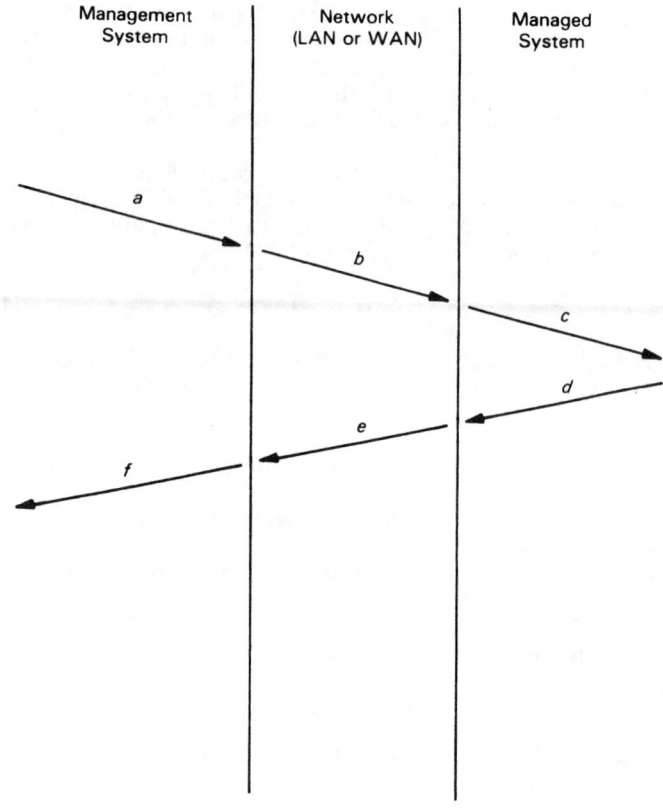

*Fig. 3. Time required for a single polling cycle ($\Delta$).*

configure managed devices to send threshold-based events. Event-based management is an intrinsic part of CMIP and was demonstrated at the CMOT multivendor demonstration at the the Interop'88 industry trade show. In comparison, the small number of events included in the SNMP standard specification have predefined triggers and do not provide managers the capability to configure thresholds.

With event-based management, managed devices only send information to the manager when there is something of interest to report. This implies that the earlier polling-based limitation is no longer applicable. However, this introduces a new bottleneck: the rate at which a manager can process incoming events.

For the scenario where a single CMOT manager receives event reports at the rate of $\Lambda$ and takes a time interval equal to $\Omega$ to internally process the message, the maximum number of devices that can be managed is given by [13]:

$$N \leq (1/\Lambda)(1/\Omega) \qquad (6)$$

Here $1/\Lambda$ represents the time interval between the generation of two consecutive event reports from a given managed device and can be expected to vary, depending on the filter thresholds. Also, $\Omega = f$, the time required to receive and interpret an incoming message at the manager. Using the same numbers as in the SNMP polling examples, we have:

$$\begin{aligned}N &\leq (1/\Lambda)(1/\Omega) \\ &\leq (1/\Lambda)(1/0.05) \\ &\leq (20/\Lambda)\end{aligned} \qquad (7)$$

If we set filtering such that the network traffic generated was equal to that in the polling model above, then in the LAN case we have $(1/\Lambda) = 15$ minutes (or 900 s). Thus:

$$\begin{aligned}N &\leq (20/\Lambda) \\ &\leq (20 \times 900) \\ &\leq 18,000\end{aligned} \qquad (8)$$

Thus, in the above LAN scenario, a single manager can manage a maximum of 18,000 devices with CMOT-based event management. Typically, however, we would expect the manager to use filters intelligently to reduce network traffic (relative to that generated via polling). For the case where $(1/\Lambda) = 10T$, we get $N \leq 180,000$ devices.

In the WAN case, we would expect the number to be approximately the same, since the maximum number of managed devices is no longer tied to network topology-related delays.

Here, we see a startling advantage of the event-based management model: a theoretical two orders of magnitude possible increase in the number of devices that can be managed. In the above LAN example, polling was only able to manage 4,500 devices, while the event-based model, using similar parameters, was able to manage a possible 180,000 devices. The difference is even larger for the WAN case (750 versus a possible 180,000).

The above examples can be varied to obtain specific numbers for given scenarios. However, it is worth noting that CMIP-based network management provides the above advantage intrinsically, while SNMP vendors need to add additional extensions to leverage threshold-based event management.

In a real network, determining the maximum number of managed devices is likely to require the consideration of several additional parameters not included in the above simple examples. Also, it is worth noting that the management of real networks requires a hybrid of both polling and event management schemes. The results obtained from the above examples lead us to point out that large networks should place a greater emphasis on including event-based network management mechanisms.

## Implementation Requirements

The implementation experience of Netlabs (a network management company), indicates that CMOT is significantly more complex (at least twice) to design and implement than SNMP. Unlike CMIP (in CMOT), the SNMP protocol machine does not need to keep state- or association-related information and hence occupies less code space than CMOT. The Netlabs manager software implements both SNMP and CMOT over existing TCP/IP services [14–16]. Excluding the code required for TCP/IP, SNMP occupies approximately one-third the total code-space required by CMOT (see Table I).

In addition, SNMP uses about 300 bytes per host data structure. Open CMOT associations require about 500 additional bytes per host, thus increasing the dynamic memory requirements. (In a virtual memory UNIX® system, the real bottleneck turns out to be the swap space available to the manager process, which is dependent on the other processes also running on the system. Real-time performance is also influenced by the amount of Random Access Memory—RAM available in the system.)

Applications utilize the network management protocols to execute management operations. From an application point of view, the relative performance of the two protocols can be measured by the number of management operations (for example, Get requests), that can be executed within a given time period. A convenient measure is Management Operations Per Second (MOPS). However, MOPS is dependent on a number of system specific parameters including the raw machine horsepower (commonly measured in Millions of Instructions Per

---

®UNIX is a registered trademark of AT&T Bell Laboratories.

**Table I. SNMP and CMOT Code Sizes**

| Module | SNMP | CMOT |
|---|---|---|
| Protocol | 8.7K | 127K |
| Protocol + Encode/Decode + Scheduler | 63K | 182K |

Second—MIPS). This leads us to propose an appropriate machine independent benchmark for network management protocols: the number of MOPS/MIPS.

Initial measurement with the Netlabs implementation indicates that SNMP provides 46 MOPS/MIPS, while CMOT provides 18 MOPS/MIPS. Several batches of 200 simple protocol Get requests were executed in a send loop with no user interactions, in order to obtain these averages. (It is worth noting that unlike SNMP, a small number of CMOT management operations can selectively retrieve large volumes of management information. Thus, more MOPS/MIPS is not necessarily better. A given management application may be able to utilize SNMP and CMOT management operations with different levels of efficiency.)

## Market Acceptance

At the last InterOp industry tradeshow (October '89), about 25 vendors demonstrated SNMP management systems and managed products while less than 5 vendors showed CMOT capability. Furthermore, the SNMP group demonstrated a basic level of multivendor interoperability while the CMOT vendors only showed standalone implementations within their individual booths.

As of mid-April this year, more than 90 vendors had obtained private enterprise subtrees from the Internet Registration Authority. Private enterprise subtrees provide vendors with a means for uniquely registering additional product specific managed object definitions. Most of these vendors will eventually publish their private MIB specifications [17–21] in order to enable multivendor management of their products. Although registration under private enterprise subtrees allows vendors to specify both SNMP and CMOT type objects, most vendors today are defining objects only for use with SNMP.

The SNMP standard specifies how SNMP messages can be carried over the UDP/IP stack (present in TCP/IP environments). However, SNMP messages have the potential to be carried over any transport mechanism that supports bidirectional flow and addressability. To date, SNMP has been directly implemented over Ethernet, LLC, Xerox Network Service (XNS), and Appletalk protocols.

It is clear that for new TCP/IP- and LAN-related products, most vendors have converged on today's de facto network management protocol (SNMP). This represents a step forward from existing proprietary management systems, where vendors utilized their own proprietary management protocols (see Figures 4 and 5). However, it is interesting to note that market pressure has not yet forced vendors to standardize on the detailed information that is managed via SNMP. Most of the vendors implementing SNMP today have not reached agreement regarding product-related MIBs. The overwhelming number of private MIB definitions underway suggests that future enterprise management systems have a challenge ahead of them; while the protocol is common, the information conveyed is still proprietary and is likely to mean different things for different managed systems (Figure 5).

This is especially true for vendors who are managing devices that do not have TCP/IP as a native part of their functionality (e.g., LAN bridges and Ethernet hubs). For these devices, managing the the TCP/IP-related resources included in MIB-I is not meaningful. All of the real management for these devices has to be enabled through vendor specific private MIBs.

This suggests that the market has settled on a quick-fix solution, which does not scale well when extended beyond its original focus (i.e., the management of TCP/IP gateway systems). Current SNMP implementations do not offer the level of interoperability likely to be provided by future ISO-based network management implementations (as shown in Figure 6) [22]. However, SNMP's market acceptance is easily explainable, once one understands current user and vendor positions.

From a user perspective, multivendor TCP/IP network management has been a crying need. Until SNMP, most vendors had failed to deliver on their promises to provide open TCP/IP network management. SNMP has been demonstrated as a working solution and has been presented as solving the problem of moving management information between products from different vendors. Thus, it has captured the imagination and hearts of users, who have extrapolated early demonstrations into personal visions of future network management. Due to the lack of vendor implementations, CMOT has missed the current window of opportunity in today's TCP/IP and LAN marketplaces.

From a vendor perspective, SNMP has provided vendors the opportunity to deliver on promises of open multivendor network management. SNMP is simple to implement and does not require vendors to launch large efforts into tracking rapidly evolving standards, nor does it require significant changes in internal research and development programs. Furthermore, since SNMP only imposes the network management protocol, vendors have been free to restructure their existing managed parameters into "SNMP speak"—thus leading to the current explosion of private MIBs discussed earlier. What was the result? SNMP has provided vendors a way to achieve a certain degree of openness while allowing them to implement MIBs which retain the essence of earlier proprietary systems.

## Ongoing Standardization Efforts

This section summarizes on-going work (through early April '90) in IAB-chartered TCP/IP network management standards groups. Also, important CMIP-based work efforts currently underway in several other national and international bodies are not discussed in this section.

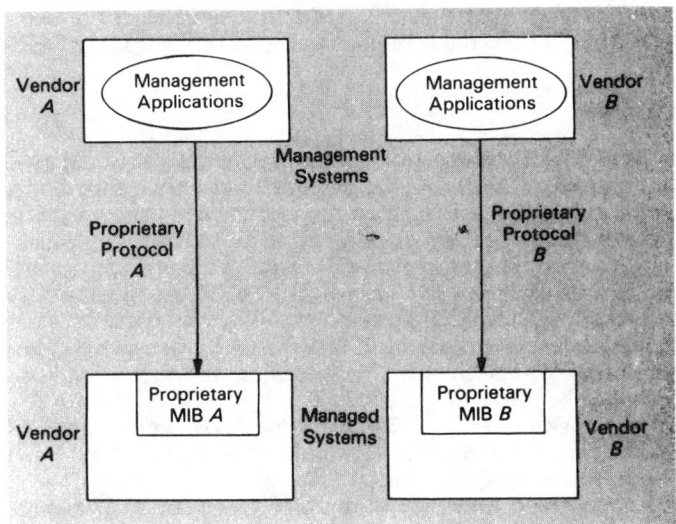

*Fig. 4. Existing proprietary network management systems.*

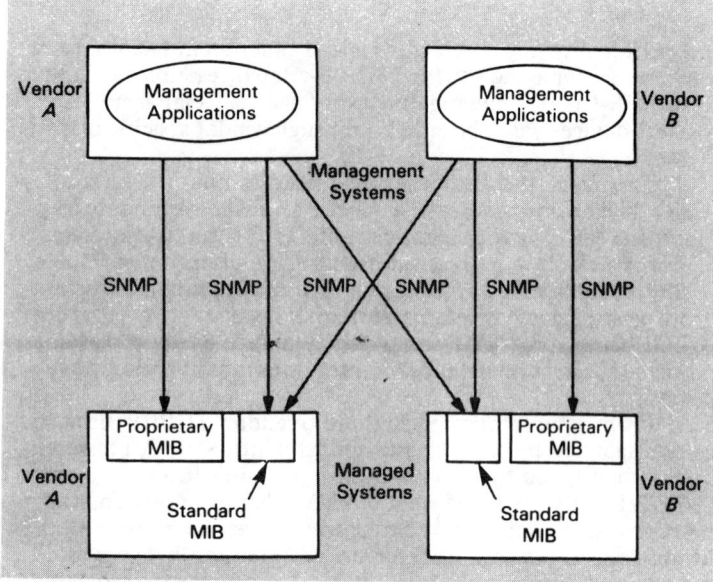

Fig. 5. Emerging SNMP network management systems.

## SNMP

Several IETF subgroups are currently working on SNMP-related standards. One group is working on implementation agreements for managing asynchronously generated SNMP events (traps) [12]. Another subgroup is writing a protocol specification that will provide authentication and privacy for SNMP network management [23].

The MIB working group that defined the SNMP MIB-I objects has also produced a MIB-II draft [24]. This document doubles the number of standardized SNMP objects to about 200 and includes support for the management of SNMP itself. SNMP managed object draft specifications have also been produced for the detailed management of IEEE 802.3 [25], IEEE 802.5 [26], Microsoft's LAN Manager, [27] and [28], the OSI Connectionless Network Protocol (CLNP) [29], and T1 circuits [30]. Berkeley UNIX 4.4 includes a SNMP agent that allows for the monitoring of MIB-I, CLNP, and UNIX memory buffer-related resources [18]. A new subgroup is working to produce a SNMP MIB specification for managing DECnet Phase IV resources.

As mentioned earlier, vendors have implemented SNMP over a variety of transport mechanisms. Draft standards have been produced that specify SNMP over Ethernet [31] and SNMP over OSI connectionless transport service [32] (see Figure 7).

## CMOT

The CMOT working group is now called the "OSI Internet Management" (OIM) working group. This group is focused on producing a set of implementors agreements that provide CMIP-based management of the IP and OSI LAN/WAN technologies present in the Internet. The group's specifications will be based on the new IS version of ISO CMIP and will specify protocol, SMI and MIB agreements. Wherever possible, the plan is to reference existing CMIP-based agreements rather than duplicate such work. Two such specifications that are likely to be referenced are the OSI Implementor's Workshop Network Management SIG (OIW NMSIG) Implementation Agreements and the OSI Network Management (OSI/NM) Forum Recommendations.

At least two different OIM protocol agreements will be produced: CMOT (CMIP over TCP, via a lightweight presentation protocol) and CMIP over a full seven-layer OSI stack. Depending on the migration strategies that are in place for TCP/IP to OSI migration, a third agreement may also be produced. If produced, this will specify CMIP over OSI presentation and session which would then be supported over TCP/IP [33]. (In all three cases, the OSI application layer-related agreements should be identical.)

The OIM SMI and MIB agreements will reference the Internet SMI [8] and MIB-II documents, respectively. The MIB agreements will contain the MIB-II object definitions translated into the appropriate ISO format for use with CMIP [34]. The OIM group will also produce documents specifying event management [35] and guidelines for the definition of Internet-managed objects. Several of the participating OIM vendor companies are working together to establish facilities for conformance and interoperability testing.

## Management Services Interface

A more recently chartered group called the "Management Services Interface" (MSI) group, is currently working to define a common set of services for managing systems in heterogenous multivendor environments. The group is defining a common Application Programming Interface (API) that will work over CMOT, SNMP, CMIP over OSI, and Remote Procedure Calls (RPCs) [36]. In the future, this will allow management applications to be written once to a common API. The API implementation will handle all required translations to the underlying management protocols.

# Future Directions

While SNMP has emerged as the current de facto standard for managing TCP/IP networks, CMOT remains the officially endorsed long-term solution for multivendor TCP/IP network management.

However, in the near future, SNMP is likely to spread beyond traditional TCP/IP environments. In addition to managing TCP/IP resources, it is also likely to be utilized to manage resources from operating systems (e.g., Berkeley UNIX), OSI networking protocols (e.g., CLNP), proprietary network protocols (e.g., DECNET), LAN media (e.g., IEEE 802.3), and LAN services (e.g., LAN Manager).

SNMP's current success lies in the fact that it is relatively easy to implement and does not require large amounts of processing and memory resources. This allows it to be squeezed into existing product architectures—an important issue for vendors since this implies that smaller products do not have to be redesigned in order to be managed. In addition, implementing SNMP today yields the benefit of multivendor interoperability for the monitoring of the MIB-I TCP/IP-related objects. Future interoperability with more objects is likely, assuming that a critical mass of vendors implement the MIB-related standards that are currently in progress. Also, since the SNMP specification is relatively straightforward and allows for few options, vendor implementations can usually interoperate at a basic level (without requiring the conformance testing prerequisite associated with OSI interoperability).

However, as SNMP starts to gain widespread deployment, vendors and network management personnel are finding themselves constrained by several of SNMP's limitations:

- The SNMP management paradigm (largely based on polling) is not well-suited to the monitoring of large networks. For large networks, polling results in volumes of routine SNMP messages and yields problem detection response times that are often unacceptable [12].
- SNMP is inefficient and slow for retrieving large amounts of data from managed devices (e.g., retrieving portions of a routing table from a router).

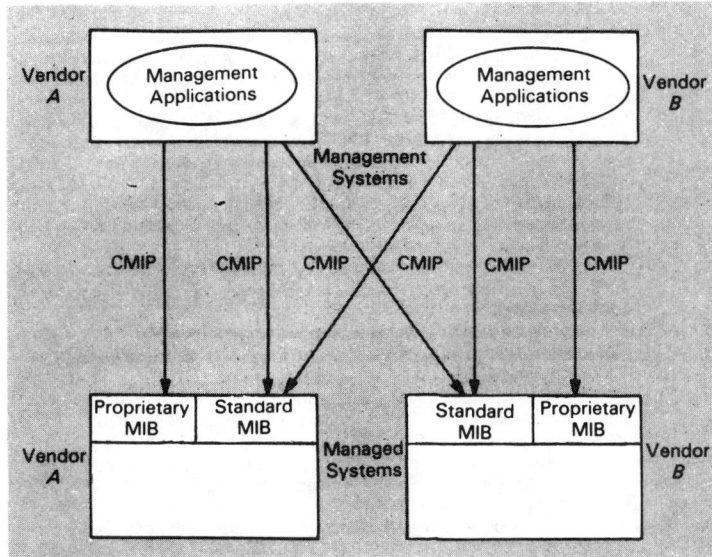

*Fig. 6. Future ISO network management systems.*

- SNMP traps (event messages) are unacknowledged and when sent over UDP/IP are not guaranteed to be delivered; a managed device that sends a "link down" trap can never be sure that the message actually reached the destination management system.
- Current SNMP implementations only provide trivial authentication; as a result, today SNMP is more useful for monitoring than control.
- SNMP does not provide for the definition and execution of product specific imperative commands (e.g., "perform self test").
- The SNMP management information model is limited and most current implementations do not provide applications that would allow network administrators to make sophisticated management queries based on object values and types.
- SNMP does not provide a solution for the problem of manager to manager communications; for example, there is no mechanism that allows a management system to learn about the network managed by another management system.

OSI network management specifications address the above SNMP limitations. Implementing OSI network management also offers the potential to provide a broader set of integrated management services that leverage other existing OSI applications such as directory service (X.500), file transfer (FTAM), and Virtual Terminal (VT). Also, current SNMP- and CMOT-based management transactions can only take place between two systems (a single manager communicating with a single agent). Implementing CMOT will allow one to utilize future OSI applications, such as Commitment, Concurrency, and Recovery (CCR), Transaction Processing (TP), and Remote Database Access (RDA), that offer a framework for the management of multicasting and distributed environments.

Despite these potential benefits, so far CMOT has only been implemented by a handful of vendors. There are several reasons for this:

- The CMIP and CMIS draft specifications have been the subject of many detailed changes during the last few years and only recently progressed to the IS stage.
- Related documents that comprise the OSI network management framework are still not complete. For example, the SMI-related documents are currently undergoing change. As a result, it is difficult for vendors to implement OSI-managed object definitions in their products.
- CMOT implementations require significant memory and processing resources. For many products (especially those that only contain partial stacks), implementing CMOT often involves the redesign of existing product architectures.
- The complexity associated with CMOT conformance and interoperability testing poses a barrier for potential implementors.
- Towards the end of 1989, initial vendor support for SNMP passed a critical mass. Vendors that follow realize that they need to implement SNMP in order to interoperate in today's marketplace.

Given the above facts, what does the future hold? An early 1989 Infonetics survey of 150 information managers from Fortune 500 companies reported that at least through 1991, SNMP will be more important than CMOT for managing TCP/IP networks [37]. Even by end 1991, there appeared to be little interest in CMOT; the respondents indicated that they were interested in integrated TCP/IP network management rather than in migration to CMOT. A follow-up survey conducted earlier this year shows that the above opinions continue to hold true today [38].

Is the critical mass achieved by SNMP enough to create a reality in which the market will compromise on limitations and settle on SNMP as the only standard for managing TCP/IP networks? The future of CMOT depends on several other factors, whose outcomes still remain to be seen:

- The success of other CMIP-based implementors agreements, such as the OIW NMSIG and the OSI/NM Forum. If the OSI/NM Forum demonstrations (scheduled for late-1990 and 1991) are successful, then this is likely to send vendors and users the green light for CMIP-based network management.
- Future U.S. government GOSIP network management procurement requirements will have a large impact on the protocols utilized by vendor implementations. It is likely that the government will issue a CMIP-based network management FIPS by mid-1991.
- Several international bodies are working on standardizing detailed managed object definitions for use with CMIP [39]. The availability and proliferation of OSI-managed object definitions are likely to have a positive impact for CMOT.
- The functionality delivered by the installed base of SNMP network management applications and agents. If SNMP is able to meet user needs for integrated TCP/IP network management, then migration to CMOT is likely to be delayed.
- The CMIP-based management offered by CMOT is likely to be the natural target for TCP/IP networks that migrate to OSI.

Nevertheless, it seems clear that future TCP/IP enterprise networks will contain products that implement a mix of SNMP and CMIP-based network management solutions [40]. Based on its simplicity and current market position, SNMP has the potential to remain the leading choice for managing smaller and partial stack devices. On the other hand, CMOT is best positioned for communications between enterprise management systems. CMOT agents will probably be deployed first on systems with larger resources such as workgroup servers. CMOT is also likely to be implemented first on devices that require a richer set of management services (e.g., the management of computer systems.)

The IEEE 802.1 working group recently reissued a new "CMIP-like" IEEE 802.1B draft LAN/MAN network management protocol specification [41], along with a companion guidelines recommendation [42]. This management protocol works directly over the LLC sublayer at the data link level. If this IEEE work gains vendor support, then future TCP/IP LANs will also be managed with the IEEE 802.1B network management protocol.

At the workgroup level, SNMP is likely to continue to be implemented directly over LAN media (SNMP/LLC and SNMP/

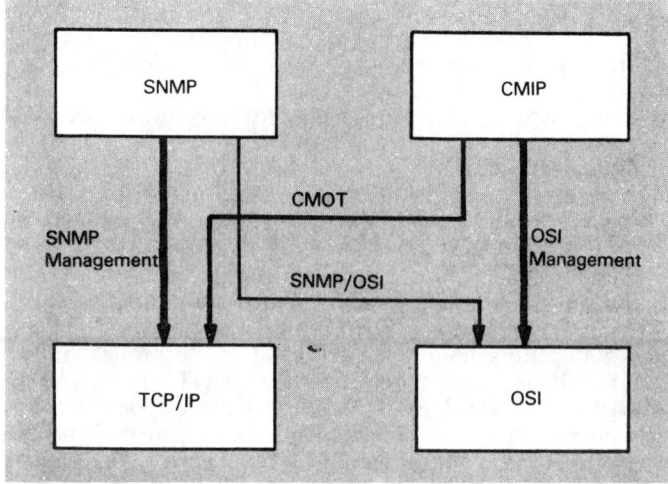

Fig. 7. SNMP and CMIP over ISO and TCP/IP stacks.

Ethernet). In the future, one is also likely to see SNMP, CMOT, and IEEE 802.1B-based network management integrated with technologies such as IEEE 802.1E download servers, X.500 directory servers, and LAN Manager type services. For example, directory server implementations may provide applications utilizing SNMP implementations with object descriptions for SNMP product-related object identifiers.

The mix of CMOT and SNMP implementations will lead to the emergence of management proxy and communications gateway systems. The management proxy systems will translate between SNMP and CMOT management messages and managed object views. The communications gateway systems will carry the management messages over the different ISO and IP WAN and LAN technologies embedded in TCP/IP enterprise networks. These proxy and gateway systems will provide the threads required for end-to-end network management of the TCP/IP enterprise networks of tomorrow.

Looking ahead, management of tomorrow's TCP/IP enterprise networks is really nothing more than the management of constant change, involving a diversity of vendors, technologies, interfaces, and versions. Network management protocols, such as SNMP and CMOT, represent only a small (but critical) piece of the "plumbing" required for integrated TCP/IP network management. Plumbing mechanisms for remote login, software download and distribution, and user and workgroup administration also need to be standardized and implemented. Other technologies related to user interfaces, expert systems, and object-oriented databases are also key to laying the foundation for future TCP/IP network management applications.

## Acknowledgments

Several of our network management colleagues provided us with valuable input for this article. We thank Jon Biggar and Anne Lam for providing us with implementation-related information. We also thank Beverly Bernoske, Alice Chen, Skip Jonas, Dian Keng, Ravi Kumar, George Mouradian, Rich Nici, John Paggi, Suresh Reddy, David Reed, and Robert Tymchyshyn, for their valuable comments on this work.

## References

[1] V. G. Cerf, "Information Infrastructure," *IEEE Net. Mag.*, vol. 4, no. 2, pp. 6–11, Mar. 1990.
[2] V. G. Cerf, "IAB Recommendations for the Development of Internet Network Management Standards," Corp. for National Research Initiatives, RFC 1052, Apr. 1988.
[3] J. D. Case, M. S. Fedor, M. L. Schoffstall, and J. R. Davin, "A Simple Network Management Protocol (SNMP)," Univ. of Tennessee at Knoxville, NYSERNet, Rensselaer Polytechnic Inst., and MIT Lab. for Computer Science, RFC 1098, Apr. 1989.
[4] C. Davin, J. Case, M. S. Fedor, and M. Schoffstall, "A Simple Gateway Monitoring Protocol (SGMP)," RFC 1028, Proteon, Univ. of Tennessee at Knoxville, Cornell Univ., and Rensselaer Polytechnic Inst., Nov. 1987.
[5] U. Warrier and L. Besaw, "Common Management Information Services and Protocol over TCP/IP (CMOT)," RFC 1095, Unisys and Hewlett-Packard, Apr. 1989.
[6] ISO 9696, "Common Management Information Protocol Specification (CMIP), Information Processing Systems—Open Systems Interconnection."
[7] A. Ben-Artzi, "CMOT Architecture and Implementation," *Proc. of the Sys. Design and Networks Conf.*, Santa Clara, CA, IEEE Comp. Soc., pp. 77–80, May 1989.
[8] M. Rose and K. McCloghrie, "Structure and Identification of Management Information for TCP/IP-based Internets," RFC 1065, The Wollongong Group, Aug. 1988.
[9] K. McCloghrie and M. Rose, "Management Information Base for Network Management of TCP/IP-based Internets," RFC 1066, The Wollongong Group, Aug. 1988.
[10] ISO 9595, "Common Management Information Services Definition (CMIS), Information Processing Systems—Open Systems Interconnection."
[11] M. T. Rose, "ISO Presentation Services on Top of TCP/IP-based Internets," RFC 1085, The Wollongong Group, Dec. 1988.
[12] L. Steinberg, "Draft Memorandum for Managing Asynchronously Generated Alerts," RFC Draft, IBM, Feb. 1989.
[13] H. Takagi, *Analysis of Polling Systems*, MIT Press, 1986.
[14] U. Warrier, A. Relan, O. Berry, and J. Bannister, "A Network Management Language for OSI Networks," *Proc. of ACM SIGCOMM '88*, Dec. 1988.
[15] U. Warrier, "Large-Grained Management of Heterogenous Networks," *Proc. of the 1988 Symp. on Parallel Processing Sys. and their Applications*, Dec. 1988.
[16] U. Warrier and C. Sunshine, "A Platform for Heterogenous Interconnection Network Management, *IEEE J. on Sel. Areas in Commun.*, Jan. 1990.
[17] "Cisco MIB," Cisco Systems, Nov. 1989.
[18] "Berkeley UNIX 4.4 MIB," Performance Systems Int'l, Mar. 1990.
[19] "ACC MIB," Advanced Computer Communications, Apr. 1990.
[20] "Novell MIB," Novell, Apr. 1990.
[21] "SynOptics MIB," SynOptics Communications, Apr. 1990.
[22] A. Ben-Artzi, "Interoperable Network Management System," *Proc. of the Internat'l Symp. on Interoperable Information Systems*, Tokyo, Japan, pp. 185–191, Nov. 1988.
[23] J. M. Galvin, K. McCloghrie, and J. R. Davin, "Authentication and Privacy in the SNMP," RFC Draft, Trusted Information Systems, Hughes LAN Systems, and MIT Lab. for Computer Science, Jan. 1990.
[24] M. T. Rose, "Management Information Base for Network Management of TCP/IP-based Internets," RFC Draft, NYSERNet, Sept. 1989.
[25] "IEEE 802.3 Layer Management Draft M Compatible Management Information Base for TCP/IP Networks," RFC Draft Proposal, 1989.
[26] "IEEE 802.5 Layer Management Compatible Management Information Base for TCP/IP Networks," RFC Draft Proposal, 1989.
[27] J. Greuel and A. Ben-Artzi, "Management Information Base for LAN Manager Management," RFC Draft Proposal, Hewlett-Packard and 3Com, June 1989.
[28] J. Greuel and A. Ben-Artzi, "Management Information Base for LAN Manager Alert Management," RFC Draft Proposal, Hewlett-Packard and 3Com, June 1989.
[29] G. Satz, "Experimental MIB Objects for the CLNP," RFC Draft Proposal, Cisco Systems, 1989.
[30] M. T. Rose and F. Baker, "Experimental Definitions of Managed Objects for the T1-Carrier Interface Type," RFC Draft, Apr. 1990.
[31] M. L. Schoffstall, J. R. Davin, M. S. Fedor, and J. D. Case, "SNMP over Ethernet, Rensselaer Polytechnic Inst., MIT Lab. for Computer Science, NYSERNet, and Univ. of Tennessee at Knoxville, RFC 1089, Feb. 1989.
[32] "SNMP over CLTP," RFC Draft, 1990.
[33] M. T. Rose and D. E. Case, "ISO Transport Service on Top of the TCP Version: 3," RFC 1006, Northrop Research and Tech. Center, May 1987.
[34] L. LaBarre, "OSI Internet Management: Management Information Base," RFC Draft, OIM Working Group, Dec. 1989.
[35] L. LaBarre, "Tutorial on OSI Event Management, Alarm Reporting, and Log Control for TCP/IP Networks," RFC Draft, OIM Working Group, Feb. 1990.
[36] O. Newkerk, "Management Services Application Programming Interface," RFC Draft, Digital Equipment Corp., April 1990.
[37] "Network Management: User Requirements and Buying Plans," Infonetics, Apr. 1989.
[38] "TCP/IP: User Requirements and Buying Plans," Infonetics, Jan. 1990.

[39] A. Chandna and D. J. Sidor, "Managed Object Definitions: Directory of References and Index," Draft, NIST OSI Implementors Workshop, Network Management SIG, Sept. 1989.

[40] A. Ben-Artzi, "Architecture for a Multi-Vendor Network Management System," *Integrated Network Management I*, B. Neandzija and J. Westcott, eds., *Proc. of the First IFIP Symp. on Integrated Network Management*, Elsevier Science Publishers, 1989.

[41] "IEEE 802.1B Draft Standard: LAN/MAN Management," Network Management Task Group, IEEE 802.1 Working Group, Mar. 1990.

[42] "IEEE 802.1F Draft Recommended Practice: Guidelines for the Development of Layer Management Standards," Network Management Task Group, IEEE 802.1 Working Group, Mar. 1990.

# Biography

**Amatzia Ben-Artzi** received his B.Sc. degree in mathematics from Tel-Aviv University, Israel and his M.Sc. degree in computer science from San Jose State University. He is Vice-President, Technology Development, with SynOptics Communications in Mountain View, California. Prior to joining SynOptics, Mr. Ben-Artzi was Director of Systems Architecture with 3Com Corporation and was responsible for the company's overall network management architecture. Mr. Ben-Artzi has over fifteen years of experience in data communications and network management.

**Asheem Chandna** received his B.S. and M.S. degrees in electrical and computer engineering from Case Western Reserve University. While in graduate school, he developed an Ada-based MAP token-bus protocol simulation system for General Motors Corporation. He is a Network Management Consultant at AT&T Bell Laboratories in Middletown, New Jersey. His background includes experience in data communications, software engineering, and network management. His network management responsibilities have included systems engineering, architecture, standards participation, and competitive analysis, for both TCP/IP and OSI environments. He is a member of the ACM, the IEEE, and the SME.

**Unni Warrier** received his Masters' degrees in physics and computer science and will be receiving his Ph.D. from UCLA. He is President of Netlabs, a network management company based in Los Angeles. He has worked in the areas of network modeling and management for the past ten years, both as a scientist and as a consultant with various companies. He is a member of the ACM and the IEEE.

# Glossary

**Accounting Management:** One of the five OSI systems management functional areas (SMFAs). Consists of facilities that enable the detection, isolation, and correction of abnormal operation of the OSI environment.

**Application Layer:** Layer 7 of the OSI model. This layer determines the interface of the system with the user and provides useful application-oriented services.

**Availability:** The percentage of time that a particular function or application is available for users.

**Bridge:** An internetworking device that connects two similar local area networks that use the same LAN protocols. The bridge operates at layer 2 of the OSI model.

**Bus:** A LAN topology in which stations are attached to a shared transmission medium. The medium is a linear cable; transmissions propagate the length of the medium and are received by all stations.

**Byte:** A group of bits, usually eight, used to represent a character of other data.

**Communications Architecture:** The hardware and software structure that implements the communications function.

**Configuration Management:** One of the five OSI systems management functional areas (SMFAs). Consists of facilities that exercise control over, identify, collect data from, and provide data to managed objects for the purpose of assisting in providing for continuous operation of interconnection services.

**Cyclic Redundancy Check (CRC):** An error-detecting code in which the code is the remainder resulting from dividing the bits to be checked by a predetermined binary number.

**Datagram:** In packet switching, a self-contained packet, independent of other packets, that carries information sufficient for routing from the originating data terminal equipment (DTE) to the destination DTE without relying on earlier exchanges between the DTEs and the network. Generally, the delivery of datagrams is unreliable.

**Data Link Layer:** Layer 2 of the OSI model. Converts an unreliable transmission channel into a reliable one.

**End System (ES):** A device other than an intermediate system attached to a subnetwork in an internet. End systems on different subnetworks exchange data by transmitting the data through one or more intermediate systems.

**Encapsulation:** The addition of control information by a protocol entity to data obtained form a protocol user.

**Encrypt:** To convert plain text or data into unintelligible form by means of a reversible mathematical computation.

**Error Detecting Code:** A code in which each data signal conforms to specific rules of construction, so that departures from this construction in the received signal can be automatically detected.

**Error Rate:** The ratio of the number of data units in error to the total number of data units.

**Fault Management:** One of the five OSI systems management functional areas (SMFAs). Consists of facilities that enable the detection, isolation, and correction of abnormal operation of the OSI environment.

**Flow Control:** A function performed by a receiving entity to limit the amount or rate of data sent by a transmitting entity.

**Frame:** A group of bits that includes data plus one or more addresses and other protocol control information. Generally refers to a link layer (OSI layer 2) protocol data unit.

**Frame Check Sequence:** An error-detecting code inserted as a field in a block of data to be transmitted. The code serves to check for errors upon reception of the data.

**Gateway:** An internetworking device that connects two computer networks that use different communications architectures.

**Header.** System-defined control information that precedes user data.

**Intermediate System (IS):** A device attached to two or more subnetworks in an internet and that performs routing and relaying of data between end systems. Examples of intermediate systems are bridges and routers.

**Internet:** A collection of communication networks interconnected by bridges, routers, and/or gateways.

**Internet Protocol:** An internetworking protocol that executes in hosts and routers to interconnect a number of packet networks.

**Internetworking:** Communication among devices across multiple networks.

**Layer:** In a network architecture, a group of services, functions, and protocols that is complete from a conceptual point of view, that is one out of a set of hierarchically arranged groups, and that extends across all systems that conform to the network architecture.

**Network Layer:** Layer 3 of the OSI model. Responsible for routing data through a communication network.

**Network Monitoring System:** An integrated set of hardware and software that measures and analyzes communications-related parameters in a network.

**Network Technical Control System:** A system, consisting of hardware probes and supporting software, that deals with fault detection, fault isolation, and fault recovery.

**Octet:** A group of eight bits, usually operated upon as an entity.

**Open Systems Interconnection (OSI) Reference Model:** A model of communications between cooperating devices. It defines a seven-layer architecture of communication functions.

**Packet:** A group of bits that includes data plus control information. Generally refers to a network layer (OSI layer 3) protocol data unit.

**Packet Switching:** A method of transmitting messages through a communications network, in which long messages are subdivided into short packets. Each packet is passed from source to destination through intermediate nodes. At each node, the entire message is received, stored briefly, and then passed on to the next node.

**Performance Management:** One of the five OSI systems management functional areas (SMFAs). Consists of facilities needed to evaluate the behavior of managed objects and the effectiveness of communication activities.

**Physical Layer:** Layer 1 of the OSI model. Concerned with the electrical, mechanical, and timing aspects of signal transmission over a medium.

**Presentation Layer:** Layer 6 of the OSI model. Concerned with data format and display.

**Propagation Delay:** The delay between the time a signal enters a channel and the time it is received.

**Protocol:** A set of semantic and syntactic rules that determines the behavior of functional units in achieving communication.

**Protocol Data Unit (PDU):** Information that is delivered as a unit between peer entities of a network and may contain control information, address information, or data.

**Response Time:** In a data system, the elapsed time between the end of transmission of an enquiry message and the beginning of the receipt of a response message, measured at the enquiry terminal.

**Router:** An internetworking device that connects two computer networks. It makes use of an internet protocol and assumes that all of the attached devices on the networks use the same communications architecture and protocols. A router operates at OSI layer 3.

**Routing:** The determination of a path that a data unit (frame, packet, message) will traverse from source to destination.

**Security Management:** One of the five OSI systems management functional areas (SMFAs). Addresses those aspects of OSI security essential to operate OSI network management correctly and to protect managed objects.

**Service Access Point (SAP):** A means of identifying a user of the services of a protocol entity. A protocol entity provides one or more SAPs, for use by higher-level entities.

**Session Layer:** Layer 5 of the OSI model. Manages a logical connection (session) between two communicating processes or applications.

**Software Monitor:** A software module resident in main memory on a host or communications processor that can gather and report statistics on configuration and communications and software activity.

**Subnetwork:** Refers to a constituent network of an internet. This avoids ambiguity since the entire internet, from a user's point of view, is a single network.

**Systems Management Function (SMF):** A part of OSI systems management activities which satisfy a set of logically related user requirements.

**Systems Management Functional Area (SMFA):** A category of OSI systems management user requirements.

**Transport Layer:** Layer 4 of the OSI model. Provides reliable, sequenced transfer of data between endpoints.

**Virtual Circuit:** A packet-switching mechanism in which a logical connection (virtual circuit) is established between two stations at the start of transmission. All packets follow the same route, need not carry a complete address, and arrive in sequence.

# List of Acronyms

| | |
|---|---|
| ACSE | Association Control Service Element |
| ANSI | American National Standards Institute |
| ASN.1 | Abstract Syntax Notation One |
| CCITT | International Consultative Committee on Telegraphy and Telephony |
| CLNP | Connectionless Network Protocol |
| CMIP | Common Management Information Protocol |
| CMIS | Common Management Information Service |
| CMISE | Common Management Information Service Element |
| CMOL | CMIP Over LLC |
| CMOT | CMIP Over TCP/IP |
| CRC | Cyclic Redundancy Check |
| DBMS | Database Management System |
| FTAM | File Transfer, Access, and Management |
| IAB | Internet Activities Board |
| IETF | Internet Engineering Task Force |
| IP | Internet Protocol |
| ISO | International Organization for Standardization |
| LAN | Local Area Network |
| LLC | Logical Link Control |
| MIB | Management Information Base |
| NM | Network Management |
| NMS | Network Management System |
| OSI | Open Systems Interconnection |
| PDU | Protocol Data Unit |
| RMON | Remote Network Monitoring |
| ROSE | Remote Operations Service Element |
| RTSE | Reliable Transfer Service Element |
| SDU | Service Data Unit |
| SMF | Systems Management Function |
| SMFA | Systems Management Funcitonal Area |
| SMI | Structure of Management Information |
| SMP | Simple Management Protocol |
| SNMP | Simple Network Management Protocol |
| TCP | Transmission Control Protocol |
| UDP | User Datagram Protocol |

# Annotated Bibliography

## Books

AIDAROUS, S. and T. PLEVYAK, eds., *Network Management into the 21st Century*, IEEE Press, New York, N.Y., 1993. A collection of original papers that provides a detailed technical treatment of network management technology and standards for telecommunications.

BALL, L., *Cost-Efficient Network Management*, McGraw-Hill, New York, N.Y., 1992. A relatively nontechnical treatment of the issues confronting the network user and/or system manager who must deal with the specific problems of managing and using networks.

BLACK, U., *Network Management Standards*, McGraw-Hill, New York, N.Y., 1992. An overview of SNMP and OSI systems management. Although the treatment is technical, a number of aspects of both schemes receive rather modest treatment.

CHIU, D. and R. SUDAMA, *Network Monitoring Explained: Design and Application*, Ellis Horwood, New York, N.Y., 1992. A detailed look at the network monitoring aspects of network management.

HELD, G., *Network Management: Techniques, Tools, and Systems*, Wiley, New York, N.Y., 1992. Covers the basic low-level tools for monitoring and, in some cases, controlling analog and digital lines and communications equipment such as modems. The book does not provide an overall look at network management systems.

IEEE COMM. SOC., *IEEE Network Operations and Management Symp.*, IEEE Service Center, Piscataway, N.J., 1992. The three-volume proceedings contains papers on a wide range of topics related to network management.

KAUFFELS, F., *Network Management: Problems, Standards, and Strategies*, Addison-Wesley, Reading, Mass., 1992. A discussion of network management oriented towards products rather than basic principles and standards. SNA and DEC network management are covered, as well as SNMP and OSI systems management, although the standards are treated superficially.

KERSHENBAUM, A., M. MALEK, and M. WALL, eds., *Network Management and Control*, Plenum Press, New York, N.Y., 1990. Contains the proceedings of Network Management and Control Workshop held in Sept. 1989.

KRISHNAN, I. and W. ZIMMER, eds., *Integrated Network Management, II*, North-Holland, New York, N.Y., 1991. Contains the proceedings of the IFIP TC 6/WG 6.6 Second Int'l Symp. on Integrated Network Management, held in 1991.

LEINWAND, A. and K. FANG, *Network Management: A Practical Perspective*, Addison-Wesley, Reading, Mass., 1993. A practical discussion of the key functional areas of network management, plus an overview of the major standards. The book also includes a detailed discussion of MIB-II.

MEANDZIJA, B. and J. WESTCOTT, eds., *Integrated Network Management, I*. North-Holland, New York, N.Y., 1989. Contains the proceedings of the IFIP TC 6/WG 6.6 Symp. on Integrated Network Management, held in 1989.

ROSE, M., *The Simple Book: An Introduction to Management of TCP/IP-based Internets*, Prentice-Hall, Englewood Cliffs, N.J., 1991. A detailed description of SNMP. Does not include RMON, secure SNMP, or SMP.

SCHATT, S., *Understanding Network Management: Strategies and Solutions*, Windcrest/McGraw-Hill, New York, N.Y., 1993. Provides an overview of networking components and technology that need to be managed, a discussion of general network management strategies, and a description of major commercial network management systems.

STALLINGS, W., *SNMP, SNMPv2, and CMIP: The Practical Guide to Network Management Standards*, Addison-Wesley, Reading, Mass., 1993. A comprehensive and detailed treatment of the two families of standards.

TERPLAN, K., *Communication Networks Management*, Prentice-Hall, Englewood Cliffs, N.J., 1992. A comprehensive discussion of network management technology. Covers all key areas of network management and network management system design.

## Periodicals

*Int'l J. of Network Management*, John Wiley & Sons Ltd., Baffins Lane, Chichester, West Sussex PO191UD, UK. Practical, relatively nontechnical articles on network management, generally from the user's point of view.

*Networking Management*. Address: Circulation Dept, P.O. Box 2417, Tulsa, Oklahoma 74101. Trade magazine oriented toward users and customers. Available free to "qualified" subscribers.

*The Simple Times*. Available free of charge via electronic mail in PostScript or MIME (multi-media 822 format); send request to st-subscriptions@simple-times.org. Also available free in hard-copy form from most SNMP vendors. Each issue includes a refereed technical article, an industry comment, and several featured columns.

## Electronic Mailing Lists

A useful way to track developments in a particular area and a forum for getting answers to questions is to join a mailing list. A mailing list is really nothing more than an alias that has multiple destinations. Mailing lists are usually created to discuss specific topics. Anyone interested in that topic may join that list. The general convention for being added to or deleted from a mailing list is to send a message to list-request@host. Once you have been added to a list, you will receive a copy of every message posted to the list. If you wish to ask a question or respond to someone else's question, send a message to list@host. Your message will be posted to the list. As a member of the list, you will yourself receive a copy of the message, which serves as a check that the message was posted.

SNMP mailing list. Discussion of topics related to SNMP. Currently, this is a very active list, covering details of existing SNMP implementations as well as future versions of the protocol, such as SMP. Address: snmp@psi.net

RMON mailing list. A recent mailing list devoted to the RMON MIB portion of SNMP. Address: rmonmib@jarthur.claremont.edu

Network management mailing list. Discussion of general topics related to network management and network operations. Currently, not very active. Address: net-ops@decwrl.dec.com

## Papers and Reports

### Chapter 1: Network Management Technology

ADAMS, E. "Global Commonality in User Requirements," *Proc. Second Int'l Symp. Integrated Network Management*, Elsevier Science Publishers B.V., Amsterdam, The Netherlands, 1991. Presents results of a survey by the Network Management Forum of network management users' requirements.

AGUILAR, L. "Using RPC for Distributed Systems Management," *Proc. Second Int'l Symp. Integrated Network Management*, Elsevier Science Publishers B.V., Amsterdam, The Netherlands, 1991. Discusses the use of remote procedure calls to implement the proxy concept for managing devices that do not support the network management protocol in use.

AMER, P. and L. CASSEL, "Management of Sampled Real-Time Network Measurements," *Proc. 14th Conf. Local Computer Networks,* IEEE CS Press, Los Alamitos, Calif., 1989, pp. 62-68. Discusses the design issues related to the use of sampling for gathering network management information. Appropriate statistical tools for sampling and analyzing traffic in real time are presented.

BASSETT, B. et al., "Customer Network Management: A Service Provider's View," *IEEE Comm. Magazine,* Mar. 1990, pp. 31-34. Discusses the types and organization of network management tools that may be provided by a carrier for customer management of their private networks.

BOULOUTAS, A., G. HART, and M. SCHWARTZ, "On the Design of Observers for Fault Detection in Communications Networks," *Proc. Network Management and Control Workshop.* Describes a framework for implementing the fault detection function, and gives an example of its use on LLC.

CASSEL, L. and P. AMER, "Management of Distributed Measurement Over Interconnected Networks," *IEEE Network*, Mar. 1988, pp. 50-56. Describes a model for managing stand-alone network measurement devices distributed over an interconnected internet.

CASSEL, L., C. PARTRIDGE, and J. WESTCOTT, "Network Management Architectures and Protocols: Problems and Approaches," *IEEE J. Selected Areas in Comm.*, Sept. 1989, pp. 1104-1114. Using the OSI system management functional areas as a framework, examines requirements and techniques in each area for network management.

CERCHIO, L. and A. PELAGGI, "Software Management: An Important Side Issue of Network Management," *1992 IEEE Network Operations and Management Symp.*, IEEE Service Center, Piscataway, N.J., 1992. Looks at problems and design solutions for managing the software portion of a network configuration.

CRONK, R., P. CALLAHAN, and L. BERNSTEIN, "Rule-Based Expert Systems for Network Management and Operations: An Introduction," *IEEE Network,* Sept. 1988, pp. 7-21. A survey article covering a variety of approaches to applying expert system techniques to network management.

DOLL, D., "The Future of Customer Control," *IEEE Comm. Magazine,* Mar. 1990, pp. 76-80. Surveys the state of the art in the various segments of the customer control network management business and examines future requirements.

DUPUY, A. et al., "Network Fault Management: A User's View," *Proc. First Symp. Integrated Network Management,* Elsevier Science Publishers B.V., Amsterdam, The Netherlands, 1989. Describes typical fault management problems in large-scale, heterogeneous, real-time transaction processing networks, and presents a design approach for providing fault management.

EDELMAN, M., "How to Win the Battle of Network Management," *Connexions,* July 1992. Presents a set of requirements with which to evaluate various network management products.

FEHSKENS, L., "An Architectural Strategy for Enterprise Management," *Proc. First Symp. Integrated Network Management,* Elsevier Science Publishers B.V., Amsterdam, The Netherlands, 1989. Discussion of key practical issues in the design of a network management system for large enterprise internets.

FRIED, S. and J. TJONG, "Implementing Integrated Monitoring Systems for Heterogeneous Networks," *Proc. Network Management and Control Workshop,* 1989. Describes the requirements of, and a software architecture for, network monitoring.

GOLDSMITH, S. and U. VIZCAINO, "Enterprise Network Management," *Proc. First Symp. Integrated Network Management,* Elsevier Science Publishers B.V., Amsterdam, The Netherlands, 1989. Proposes a framework for managing an enterprise network that supports voice, data, and video. Basic functional requirements and architectural approaches are examined.

GOYAL, S., "Knowledge Technologies for Evolving Networks," *Proc. Second Int'l Symp. Integrated Network Management,* Elsevier Science Publishers B.V., Amsterdam, The Netherlands, 1991. Presents examples of laboratory technologies in each of three key areas of AI from the standpoint of telecommunication network management: distributed AI, knowledge representation, and machine learning.

HAVERLOCK, P., "The Formula for Network Immortality," *Data Comm.*, Aug. 1988. A detailed examination of the concept of availability and its application to network design and management.

HUNTER, B. et al., "Surveying Far-Flung Networks," *Byte*, Aug. 1992. Describes general principles of remote monitors and then discusses various products on the market.

JACOBSON, D. et al., "A Master/Slave Monitor Measurement Technique for an Operating Ethernet Network," *IEEE Network*, July 1987. Describes performance measures and a performance measurement technique for LANs.

JOSEPH, C. and K. MURALIDHAR, "Integrated Network Management in an Enterprise Environment," *IEEE Network*, July 1990, pp. 7-13. Discusses various aspects of integrated network management for enterprises, including the network management environment, available network management elements, and an outline of architectures and strategies.

KHERADPIR, S. et al., "Managing the Network Manager," *IEEE Comm. Magazine*, July 1992, pp. 12-21. Describes a software testbed for developing, testing, and integrating different network management techniques for multiservice circuit-switched networks. The system supports modeling of different network traffic and behavior characteristics so as to be able to evaluate various network management techniques in a simulated environment.

KIMMINS, J., "Network Security Management and Administration: Concepts and Issues," *Proc. 1992 IEEE Network Operations and Management Symp*, IEEE Service Center, Piscataway, N.J., 1992. A detailed examination of functional requirements for network security management.

MAKIK, A., "Network Management and Control Systems and Strategic Issues," *IEEE Comm. Magazine*, Mar. 1990, pp. 26-29. An overview of the integrated telecommunications network (ITN) of American Express. The article discusses general principles and strategies for managing a large worldwide computer and telecommunications complex.

MANSON, C. and S. HAUGDAHL, "Dynamic and Distributed," *Byte*, Mar. 1991. Describes some of the most common tools and techniques used to manage distributed systems and relates these to underlying requirements.

MOGUL, J., "Efficient Use of Workstations for Passive Monitoring of Local Area Networks," *Proc. SIGCOMM '90 Symp.*, Assoc. Computing Machinery, New York, N.Y., 1990. Describes performance measures and a performance measurement technique for LANs.

PATEL, A., G. MCDERMOTT, and C. MULVIHILL, "Integrating Network Management and Artificial Intelligence," *Proc. Symp. Integrated Network Management*, Elsevier Science Publishers B.V., Amsterdam, The Netherlands, 1989. Discusses the application of AI techniques to network management, providing a survey of various AI capabilities and their applicability to network management.

RABIE, S., "Integrated Network Management: Technologies and Implementation Experience," *Proc. IEEE INFOCOM*, Vol. 2, IEEE CS Press, Los Alamitos, Calif., 1992, pp. 1020-1027. Presents an analysis of the requirements and key enabling technologies for network management of enterprise networks.

SALLUSTIO, P., "Implementing Network Management in a Multi-Vendor Environment: A User Perspective," *Proc. Network Management and Control Workshop*, 1989. Describes a technique and set of measures which utilize a trouble reporting database to provide the statistics to manage networks. The approach is applicable to multivendor networks and emphasizes quality of service.

SHIM, Y. and C. RAMAMOORTHY, "Management of Distributed Systems," *Proc., 9th Ann. Int'l Phoenix Conf. Computers and Comm.*, IEEE CS Press, Los Alamitos, Calif., 1990, pp. 689-696. Discusses issues involved in the design of network management system.

STEPHENSON, P., "Mixing and Matching LANs," *Byte*, Mar. 1991. Describes the various functions required for configuration management of a LAN or internet of LANS.

STEVENSON, J., "Management of Multivendor Networks," *IBM Systems J.*, No. 2, 1992. Describes the multivendor environment, customer network management requirements, and IBM's approach.

STINE, R. et al., "A Practical Introduction to Network Management," *Connexions*, Aug. 1990. Provides practical guidance for managing TCP/IP-based networks, using basic protocol facilities. No special-purpose management protocol, such as SNMP is used. The paper gives a good feel for what can be accomplished with minimal tools.

TERPLAN, K., "Integrated Network Management," *Proc. Network Management and Control Workshop*, 1989. A detailed overview of network management functions, organized using the OSI systems management functional areas.

TJADEN, G. et al., "Integrated Network Management for Real-Time Operations," *IEEE Network*, Mar. 1991, pp. 10-15. Describes an approach to integrated network management that does not require management protocol conformance and provides applications that isolate and resolve faults. The approach uses off-the shelf artificial intelligence tools and client/server workstation technology.

VALOVIC, T., "Network Management: A Progress Report," *Telecommunications*, Aug. 1992. Examines the types of distributed organizations of network management that are becoming popular and surveys available standards.

WANG, Z., "Model of Network Faults," *Proc. First Symp. Integrated Network Management*, Elsevier Science Publishers B.V., Amsterdam, The Netherlands, 1989. Examines the environment in which network faults occur and presents a model of network faults. Various aspects of network faults are discussed and fault propagation is investigated in detail.

WARRIER, U. and C. SUNSHINE, "A Platform for Heterogeneous Interconnection Network Management," *IEEE J. Selected Areas in Comm.,* Jan. 1990, pp. 119-126. Proposes an architecture for managing a configuration in which multiple protocol stacks are present.

YEMINI, Y., G. GOLDSZMIDT, and S. YEMINI, "Network Management by Delegation," *Proc. Second Int'l Symp. Integrated Network Management,* Elsevier Science Publishers B.V., Amsterdam, The Netherlands, 1991. Discusses strategies for employing a hierarchy of network managers to manage a large distributed system.

YOSHIDA, M., M. KOBAYASHI, and H. YAMAGUCHI, "Customer Control of Network Management from the Services Provider's Perspective," *IEEE Comm. Magazine,* Mar. 1990, pp. 35-40. Discusses approaches for providing network management tools by a carrier for customer management of their private networks

### Chapter 2: Management Information

ANDERSON, D. et al., "Application of Object-Oriented Techniques to the OAM&P of Telecommunications Networks," *Proc., ICC '91,* June 1991. Examines recent efforts of the ANSI T1M1.5 committee to apply object-oriented data modeling techniques to the development of standards for the operations, administration, maintenance, and provisioning of telecommunications networks.

CASE, J. and C. PARTRIDGE, "Case Diagrams: A Tool for Diagraming Management Information Bases," *Computer Comm. Rev.,* Jan. 1989; reprinted in *Connexions,* Mar. 1989. Introduces a diagram methodology for indicating the relationship among managed objects that represent traffic flows. This technique is extensively used in developing and documenting MIBs for SNMP.

MAYMON, G., "An Information Model for Configuration Management of Switching Network Elements, Using OSI Tools," *Proc. ICC '91,* June 1991. Discusses an object-oriented information model for configuration management.

MCCLOGHRIE, K., M. ROSE, and C. PARTRIDGE, "Defining a Protocol-Independent Management Information Base," *Proc. First Symp. Integrated Network Management,* Elsevier Science Publishers B.V., Amsterdam, The Netherlands, 1989. Describes the philosophy behind the SNMP SMI.

OSBERG, B. and T. RICE, "Status Calculation, An RDBMS Solution," *IEEE Network,* July 1990, pp. 29-34. Examines the use of a relational database management system to implement a management information base. The article examines limitations of the relational approach and proposes solutions.

SCHWAB, B. et al., "Data Base Management for an Integrated Network Management System," *Proc. Network Management and Control Workshop,* 1989. Presents requirements for the database management support of a network management system. The paper describes performance tests conducted on seven commercially-available relational database management systems.

TUCKER, J., "A Common Approach to Managed Objects," *Proc. First Symp. Integrated Network Management,* Elsevier Science Publishers B.V., Amsterdam, The Netherlands, 1989. Considers the definition of managed objects and suggest that the "core" capability developed for OSI could also be adopted in other network management contexts.

### Chapter 3: The SNMP Family of Network Management Standards

BORSOOK, P., "Meditations on TCP/IP Management," *Network World,* May 21, 1990. A discussion of the relative merits of SNMP and CMOT.

CASE, J. et al., "Introduction to the Simple Gateway Monitoring Protocol," *IEEE Network,* Mar. 1988, pp. 43-49. A detailed examination of the protocol from which SNMP evolved.

CASE, J. et al., "Network Management and the Design of SNMP," *Connexions,* Mar. 1989. A rationale for the design decisions embodied in SNMP.

CASE, J. et al., "Internet Network Management Using the Simple Network Management Protocol," *Proc., 14th Conf. Local Computer Networks,* IEEE CS Press, Los Alamitos, Calif., 1989, pp. 156-159. Provides a brief introduction to SNMP and describes its architectural principles.

CASE, J., "Management of High Speed Networks with the Simple Network Management Protocol," *Proc., 15th Conf. Local Computer Networks,* IEEE CS Press, Los Alamitos, Calif., 1990, pp. 195-199. Describes the application of SNMP to high-speed networks such as FDDI, SMDS, T1, and T3. This paper illustrates the way in which the SNMP MIB may be extended.

CASTALDO, A. and S. FLYNN, "Managing the Hubs, Managing the Net," *LAN Technology,* Dec. 1992. A survey of LAN hubs that support SNMP, with a detailed comparison of capabilities.

DUATE, E. and B. LEMERCIER, "SNMP for non-TCP/IP Sub-networks: An Implementation," *Proc. Second Int'l Symp. Integrated Network Management,* Elsevier Science Publishers B.V., Amsterdam, The Netherlands, 1991. Discusses experience in implementing SNMP for a heterogeneous internet.

FEDOR, M., "Case Study: Using SNMP to Manage a Large Network," *Connexions,* Aug. 1990. Relates the experience gained and lessons learned from using SNMP to manage a corporate internet.

GALVIN, J., K. MCCLOGHRIE, and J. DAVIN, "Secure Management of SNMP Networks," *Proc. Second Int'l Symp. Integrated Network Management,* Elsevier Science Publishers B.V., Amsterdam, The Netherlands, 1991. Describes the security enhancements that have been added to SNMP.

Heywood, P., "Bringing SNMP to End-Node Management," *Data Comm.*, July 1992. Describes one of the first workstation management packages to be based on SNMP.

Jander, M., "Extending SNMP to the Desktop," *Data Comm.*, Nov. 21, 1992. An overview of the work of the Desktop Management Task Force, an industry consortium that is developing a set of application program interfaces (APIs) that will allow different vendors' desktop management applications to share common memory space on a PC and to communicate with any type of management system, including those based on SNMP and CMIP.

Jander, M., "Beyond RMON: Making Sense of Remote Data," *Data Comm.*, June 1992. Describes a product that integrates the RMON capability into a user-friendly network management station.

Jander, M., "Coming Soon to a Network Near You," *Data Comm.*, Nov. 1992. An overview of SMP, with an emphasis on its impact on the industry.

Jones, K., "Network Management in the World of Standards: The Role of the SNMP Protocol in Managing Networks," *Int'l J. Network Management*, Sept. 1991. A nontechnical overview of SNMP.

Koren, D., "So Many MIBs!" *Int'l J. Network Management*, Sept. 1992. A brief discussion of the many MIBs defined for SNMP, including a discussion of the advantages and pitfalls of this proliferation of management information.

Krall, G., "SNMP Opens New Lines of Sight," *Data Comm.*, Mar. 21, 1990. An overview of SNMP.

Lew, H. and J. Roberston, "TCP/IP Network Management with an Eye Toward OSI," *Data Comm.*, Aug. 1989. An overview of SNMP and CMOT.

Mansfield, G. et al., "An SNMP-Based Expert Network Management System for a Large-Scale OSI-Based Campus Network," *Proc. 11th Ann. Int'l Phoenix Conf. Computers and Comm.*, IEEE Service Center, Piscataway, N.J., 1992, pp. 695-700. Describes a system in which SNMP-generated information is used by an expert system, in conjunction with a network knowledge base, to reconstruct the overall network-traffic characteristics, evaluate the status of the network, and to take/suggest some actions.

McCloghrie, K. and M. Rose, "Network Management of TCP/IP-based Internets," *Connexions*, Mar. 1989. A brief overview of SNMP.

Mier, E., "Network World, Bell Labs Evaluate SNMP on Bridges," *Network World*, Apr. 22, 1991. A detailed comparative analysis of SNMP bridge agent products from seven different vendors.

Mier, E., "Buyer's Guide: SNMP Management Tools," *Network World*, June 24, 1991. A comprehensive survey of SNMP products on the market at the time of the article.

Mier, E., "Network World, Bell Labs Test Routers' SNMP Agents," *Network World*, Apr. 22, 1991. A detailed comparative analysis of SNMP router agent products from nine different vendors.

Morgenthal, S. and F. Henderson, "Router Management — The SNMP Way," *Int'l J. Network Management*, Sept. 1992. A case history illustrating the principles involved in applying SNMP to manager routers.

Partain, D., "An Implementation of SNMP Security," *The Simple Times*, July/Aug. 1992. Reports on an implementation of the recent SNMP security specification. The paper discusses modifications to an SNMP implementation to incorporate security features.

Rose, M., "Network Management is Simple: You Just Need the Right Framework!" *Proc. Second Int'l Symp. Integrated Network Management*, Elsevier Science Publishers B.V., Amsterdam, The Netherlands, 1991. Primarily an overview of SNMP, with some comment on its superiority to OSI management.

Sanghi, S. et al., "How Well Do SNMP and CMOT Meet IP Router Management Needs?" *Proc. Second Int'l Symp. Integrated Network Management*, Elsevier Science Publishers B.V., Amsterdam, The Netherlands, 1991. Compares SNMP and CMOT in the management of routers.

Scott, K., "Bringing Order to Chaos," *Data Comm.*, Mar. 21, 1990. A history of the development of SNMP.

Scott, K., "Taking Care of Business with SNMP," *Data Comm.*, Mar. 21, 1990. A survey of SNMP vendors.

Vandenberg, C., "MIB-II Extends SNMP Interoperability," *Data Comm.*, Oct. 1990. Describes MIB-II, the standard MIB for SNMP.

Waldbusser, S., M. Nair, and M. Hoerth, "SNMP Management Goes Down to the Wire," *Data Comm.*, May 1992. An overview of RMON.

Wilkinson, S. and T. Capen, "Remote Control," *Corporate Computing*, Oct. 1992. A discussion of the practical issues that a network management system should address, followed by a comparative analysis of three SNMP network management station products.

## Chapter 4: OSI Systems Management

Antonelline, M. and L. Sebastiani, "Error Rates: A Convenient Technique for Triggering Fault Management Procedures," *First Symp. Integrated Network Management*, Elsevier Science Publishers B.V., Amsterdam, The Netherlands, 1989. Discusses how local error rate monitoring may be used to trigger the execution of OSI event notifications.

Aronoff, R., K. Mills, and M. Wheatley, "Transport Layer Performance Tools and Measurement," *IEEE Network*, July 1987. Describes transport-layer measurements appropriate for network management and presents software tools for the purpose.

Aronoff, R. et al., "Management of Networks Based on Open Systems Interconnection (OSI) Standards: Functional Requirements and Analysis," *Nat'l Inst. Standards and Technology, Special Publication 500-175*, Nov. 1989. A detailed examination of functional requirements for each of the OSI systems management functional areas.

CARUSO, R., "Network Management: A Tutorial Overview," *IEEE Comm. Magazine,* Mar. 1990, pp. 20-25. Provides background on the evolution of network management, and then presents an overview of OSI network management in that context.

COLLINS, W., "OSI Management Service Elements, Protocols, and Application Layer Structure (ALS)," *First Symp. Integrated Network Management,* Elsevier Science Publishers B.V., Amsterdam, The Netherlands, 1989. Discusses the application service elements required for OSI systems management, including CMISE, ROSE, and ACSE.

COLLINS, W. and K. KOROSTOFF, "OSI Management: What It Is and What It Isn't," *Network World,* Oct. 9, 1989 and Oct. 16, 1989 (two parts). An overview and tutorial on OSI systems management.

EMBRY, J., P. MANSON, and D. MILHAM, "An Open Network Management Architecture: OSI/NM Forum Architecture and Concepts," *IEEE Network,* July 1990, pp. 14-22. Summarizes the architecture and key concepts that have been adopted by the OSI/Network Management Forum for interoperable network management. This work aligns with the OSI network management standards.

FELDKHUN, L. and J. ERICKSON, "Event Management as a Common Functional Area of Open Systems Management," *Proc. First Symp. Integrated Network Management,* Elsevier Science Publishers B.V., Amsterdam, The Netherlands, 1989. Provides a model for event management and explores the related concepts and functions.

FISHER, S., "Dueling Protocols," *Byte,* Mar. 1991. A comparison of SNMP and CMIP.

FORD, W., "Security Techniques for Network Management," *Proc. 1992 IEEE Network Operations and Management Symp.,* IEEE Service Center, Piscataway, N.J., 1992. A discussion of techniques that are useful for the security management portion of OSI systems management.

JANDER, M., "Can CMOL Challenge SNMP?" *Data Comm.,* May 21, 1992. An overview of the IEEE 802 specification for running CMIP directly over LLC for LAN management.

JOHNSON, P., "Security and Security Management — Overview of Concepts, Standards Status, and Some Current Issues," *Proc. 1992 IEEE Network Operations and Management Symp.,* IEEE Service Center, Piscataway, N.J., 1992. A presentation of the requirements for security management as part of network management, and the role of the OSI systems management standards.

KLERER, S., "The OSI Management Architecture: An Overview," *IEEE Network,* Mar. 1988, pp. 20-29. Despite its age, a good introduction to the OSI management framework.

KNIGHT, G., G. PAVLOU, and S. WALTON, "Experience of Implementing OSI Management Facilities," *Proc. Second Int'l Symp. Integrated Network Management,* Elsevier Science Publishers B.V., Amsterdam, The Netherlands, 1991. Describes experiences with a pilot project to implement OSI management and plans for a more elaborate follow-on.

MODIRI, N., "An Implementation of the Common Network Management Information Service Element Interfaces," *IEEE Comm. Magazine,* July 1991, pp. 29-38. Reports on an implementation of CMISE and how it interacts with other protocol layers.

MURRILL, B., "The OSI/Network Management Forum: Achievements and Objectives," *Connexions,* Oct. 1990. An overview of the Network Management Forum and its intended output.

PARTRIDGE, C. "Integrating Network Measurement Agents Into the OSI Management Architecture," *Proc. First Symp. Integrated Network Management,* Elsevier Science Publishers B.V., Amsterdam, The Netherlands, 1989. Presents a general definition of measurement agents, or monitors, and describes an approach to integrating these into the OSI management architecture.

PRESUHN, R., "Considering CMIP," *Data Comm.,* Mar. 21, 1990. Compares CMIP and SNMP.

RAMAN, L., "OSI Upper Layer Protocol Requirements for TMN Operations," *Proc., INFOCOM '88,* IEEE Service Center, Piscataway, N.J., 1988, pp. 181-185. Discusses the OSI upper layer protocols and services required for telecommunications network management.

ROMAN, L. and C. PITTMAN, "Telecommunications Network Management Standards — An Overview," *Proc. 1992 IEEE Network Operations and Management Symp.,* IEEE Service Center, Piscataway, N.J., 1992. Discussion of the use of OSI systems management to develop standards specific to telecommunications management.

SUGARBROAD, I., "An OSI-Based Interoperability Architecture for Managing Hybrid Networks," *IEEE Comm. Magazine,* Mar. 1990, pp. 61-69. Describes network management requirements for customer management of a telecommunications network that includes both private and switched network components.

TANAKA, A., N. MATSUMOTO, and K. MORINO, "An Application of OSI Systems Management to Intelligent Network Services," *Proc. Second Int'l Symp. Integrated Network Management,* Elsevier Science Publishers B.V., Amsterdam, The Netherlands, 1991. Describes approaches to using OSI systems management to support the provision of intelligent services by public telecommunications providers, including private networks and software-defined networks.

TERPLAN, K., "Standardized Multivendor Network Management," *Proc. 1992 IEEE Network Operations and Management Symp.,* IEEE Service Center, Piscataway, N.J., 1992. Lists user requirements for network management and compares SNMP and CMIP based on those requirements.

ZAKREWSKI, E., *Management Procedures and Algorithms for Control of Integrated Comm. Networks,* D.Sc. Thesis, George Washington Univ., Washington, DC, May 1991. Examines implementation issues associated with OSI systems management. The focus is on performance problems and architectural approaches to minimizing performance overhead.

# About the Author

William Stallings is an independent consultant with nearly twenty years of experience in data and computer communications. His clients have included major corporations and government agencies in the United States and Europe. Prior to forming his own consulting firm, Comp-Comm Consulting of Brewster, Massachusetts, he has been vice president of CSM Corp., a firm specializing in data processing and data communications for the health care industry. He has also been Director of systems analysis and design for CTEC, Inc., a firm specializing in command, control, and communications systems.

The author holds a PhD from M.I.T. in computer science and a BS from Notre Dame in electrical engineering. He is a frequent lecturer and the author of numerous papers and a dozen books on networking and computers, including *Data and Computer Communications* (Macmillan, 1991), which has become the standard in the field. The popularity of his books is demonstrated by the fact that all but the most recent of these books are in a second, third, or fourth edition.

**Textbooks:**

- *Data and Computer Communications,* Fourth Edition, Macmillan, 1994
- *Business Data Communications,* Second Edition, Macmillan, 1994
- *Local and Metropolitan Area Networks,* Fourth Edition, Macmillan, 1993
- *Computer Organization and Architecture,* Third Edition Macmillan, 1993
- *ISDN and Broadband ISDN,* Second Edition, Macmillan, 1992
- *Operating Systems,* Macmillan, 1992

**Professional/Reference Books:**

- *SNMP, SNMPv2, and CMIP: The Practical Guide to Network Management Standards,* Addison-Wesley, 1993
- *Networking Standards: A Guide to OSI, ISDN, LAN, and MAN Standards,* Addison-Wesley, 1993
- *Handbook of Computer-Communications Standards, Volume I: The Open Systems Interconnection (OSI) Reference Model and OSI-Related Standards,* Second Edition, Howard W. Sams, 1990
- *Handbook of Computer-Communications Standards, Volume II: Local Area Network Standards,* Second Edition, Howard W. Sams, 1990
- *Handbook of Computer-Communications Standards, Volume III: The TCP/IP Protocol Suite,* Second Edition, Howard W. Sams, 1990
- *The Business Guide to Local Area Networks,* Howard W. Sams, 1990
- *A Manager's Guide to Local Networks,* Prentice-Hall, 1983

**Edited Collections of Papers:**

- *Advances in Local and Metropolitan Area Networks,* IEEE Computer Society Press, 1993
- *Network Management,* IEEE Computer Society Press, 1993
- *Computer Communications: Architectures, Protocols, and Standards,* Third Edition, IEEE Computer Society Press, 1992
- *Advances in ISDN and Broadband ISDN,* IEEE Computer Society Press, 1992
- *Integrated Services Digital Networks and Broadband ISDN,* IEEE Computer Society Press, 1990
- *Reduced Instruction Set Computers,* Second Edition, IEEE Computer Society Press, 1989

# ADVANCES IN ISDN AND BROADBAND ISDN

edited by William Stallings

This new tutorial is a sequel to the author's previous tutorial published in 1988, *Integrated Services Digital Networks*, second edition. All the material and every single one of the reprinted papers are new and the new title reflects the broadened scope of the text.

The book provides a comprehensive introduction to ISDN and B-ISDN and explores key topics related to their architecture and standards. It details the architecture that exploits the emerging application of digital technology to integrate voice and data transmission and to provide structured interfaces and transmission services. Also, it discusses the development of standards covering the broad range of protocols, architecture, and services for ISDN and B-ISDN.

A number of new developments reflected in this new tutorial are:

- Products and services based on the standards of the 1988 CCITT Recommendations on ISDN and Signaling System Number 7
- Frame Relay, a major innovation in ISDN work
- 1990 set of interim Recommendations for ISDN, which expand some areas of ISDN and provide more detail on frame relay
- 1990 set of interim Recommendations for broadband ISDN (B-ISDN), providing specifications of its services and protocols

The tutorial examines the architecture and protocols that relate to the user-network interface, provides a detailed look at frame relay, introduces the latest developments in ISDN technology and standards, and examines the services and architecture of broadband ISDN. The book also provides an overview and introduction to ATM and SONET in its investigation of B-ISDN transmission and switching.

**Sections: ISDN Overview, ISDN Protocols and Network Architecture, Frame Relay, Broadband ISDN, ATM and SONET/SDH, Glossary, List of Acronyms, Annotated Bibliography.**

*272 pages. July 1992. Hardcover. ISBN 0-8186-2797-2.*
*Catalog #2797-01 — $45.00 - Members $35.00*

# Systems Network Architecture
## SNA Networks

edited by Edwin R. Coover

This tutorial introduces the reader to the design, operation, and management of IBM's Systems Network Architecture. Each chapter begins with an overview of the principal issues, a discussion of the terminology, and a summary of each paper included in that chapter.

The papers in *Systems Network Architecture Networks* examine the:

- Principal components of an SNA network and their functions
- Role SNA plays in providing future computer-based services
- Operation and maintenance aspects of SNA
- Extent of SNA's network options
- Development of SNA and its current capabilities
- Technologies employed in managing SNA networks

The first chapter focuses on the initial SNA offering and the market economics that influenced its design and distribution. Chapter 2 details how changes in the user environment forced IBM to extend SNA capabilities. The third concentrates on such operational aspects as user/application declarations, session types, global flow control, constructing routing tables, device control specifications, and other aspects of SNA network creation, operation, and maintenance. The next chapter examines SNA hardware and software support of office systems and environments. The final two chapters deal with the development of effective management support structures for SNA networks and how they are affected, and examine challenges to SNA.

**Sections: Introduction; The Beginnings: The Early "Star" Network and SNA Terms; Extending the Network; SNA Operations and Maintenance; SNA and the Office; SNA Network Management; The Future of SNA; Glossary; Annotated Bibliography.**

*464 pages. September 1992. Hardcover. ISBN 0-8186-9131-X.*
*Catalog #2131-01 — $58.00 - Members $45.00*

## INTEGRATED SERVICES DIGITAL NETWORKS
(ISDN), 2nd Edition

edited by William Stallings

The key concepts of ISDN are explored in the following four general categories reflecting the continued evolution and expansion that has necessitated this second edition.

- **Underlying Technology:** digital transmission and switching technologies and their use in integrated networks.
- **Architecture:** applications of digital technology to integrate voice and data transmission, and to provide structured interfaces and transmission service.
- **Standards:** standards for a wide range of ISDN services.
- **Services:** a wide variety of current and new digital services.

This edition contains 23 new articles, and an entire section devoted to ISDN protocols, the specific protocols used to access ISDN for users and vendors.

**Sections:** Overview, Standards and Regulations, Transmission Structures, User Access, ISDN Protocols, Integrated Digital Networks, Glossary.

*408 pages. 1988. Softcover. ISBN 0-8186-0823-4.*
*Catalog #823-01 — $49.00 - Members $30.00*

## X.25 AND RELATED PROTOCOLS

by Uyless Black

This monograph presents a tutorial view of X.25, discusses other protocols with which it operates, and provides a convenient reference guide to these protocols. The text contains all original material, six appendices, over 100 illustrations, and more than 50 tables.

*X.25 and Related Protocols* explains X.25 operations, the advantages and disadvantages of X.25's use, the concepts and terms of packet networks, and the role other standards play in the operation of X.25. It presents a considerable amount of detailed information about X.25 and its role in various systems such as LANs, PBSs, and ISDNs. The book covers a wide variety of subjects such as:

- Switching and Routing in Networks
- High-Level Data-Link Control (HDLC)
- The OSI Model
- X.25 Packet Structures and Types
- Physical-Layer Protocols and Interfaces
- Internetworking with SNA, DECnet, X.75, LANs and ISDN

**Sections:** The X.25 Network; Layered Protocols, OSI, and X.25; X.25 and the Physical Layer; X.25 and the Data-Link Layer; The X.25 Network Layer; X.25 Facilities; X.25 Companion Standards; Internetworking X.25 with Other Systems; The PAD Standards; X.25's Future; Examples of Packet Networks; Link Protocols; Diagnostic Codes.

*304 pages. July 1991. Hardcover. Illustrations and Tables.*
*ISBN 0-8186-8976-5.*
*Catalog #1976-04 — $60.00 - Members $45.00*

## BROADBAND SWITCHING:
Architectures, Protocols, Design, and Analysis

edited by Chris Dhas, V.K. Konangi, and M. Sreetharan

This tutorial investigates the latest information and research on broadband switching and provides supporting material and insight into the correlated areas of networking, performance analysis, and alternate technologies. The text describes:

- Performance Modeling Techniques
- Multistage Interconnection Networks
- Architectural Options Available for Switches
- Experimental Architectures for ISDN and ATM Techniques

*Broadband Switching* also examines numerous trends in network architectures designed to meet the user's high bandwidth requirements, packet replication and switching in broadcast switching systems, important issues of bandwidth allocation and flow and congestion control, and photonic switching techniques and technology.

The book details broadband switching and networking issues, and present s solid information on network architectures, network requirements, protocols, and performance modeling.

**Sections:** Network Architecture; Interconnection Networks; Experimental Architectures; Switch Fabric Design and Analysis; Switch Architectures; Broadcast Switching Networks; Bandwidth Allocation, Flow, and Congestion Control; Performance Modeling; Photonic Switching Systems; Bibliography.

*528 pages. August 1991. Hardcover.*
*ISBN 0-8186-8926-9.*
*Catalog #1926-01 — $65.00 - Members $50.00*

# Other titles from IEEE Computer Society Press

**Current Research in Decision Support Technology**
*edited by Robert W. Blanning and David R. King*

This tutorial presents recent studies on DSS and identifies research issues of current interest that offer significant promise for further development. The areas covered explore the use of expert systems in DSS construction, recent research on logic modeling and integration, and group DSS and the determination of the organizational impact of DSS on understanding organizational information processing and decision-making.

Sections: Introduction, Advanced Decision Modeling and Model Management, Knowledge-Based Decision Support, Organizational Issues in DSS Development.

*256 pages. 1993. Hardcover. ISBN 0-8186-2807-3. Catalog # 2807-01 — $45.00   Members $35.00*

**Groupware:**
**Software for Computer-Supported Cooperative Work**
*edited by David Marca and Geoffrey Bock*

Investigates the task of designing software to fit the way groups interact in specific work situations and emphasizes the technical aspects involved in the development of software within the bounds of strong social and organizational factors. The book provides a guide to the computer-supported cooperative work field, highlights key trends and ideas, and covers the perspective of work as a cooperative and social endeavor being done by groups, not just individuals.

Sections: Introduction, Groups and Groupware, Conceptual Frameworks, Design Methods, Enabling Technologies — System-Related, Enabling Technologies — UI-Related, Computer Supported Meetings, Bridging Time and Space, Coordinators, What Makes for Effective Systems.

*592 pages. 1992. Hardcover. ISBN 0-8186-2637. Catalog # 2637-01 — $75.00  Members $45.00*

**Information Systems and Decision Processes**
*edited by Edward A. Stohr and Benn R. Konsynski*

This book focuses on DSS and vital issues in the application of information technology to decision making, and introduces some promising new directions for research. It contains the collaborative studies of DSS researchers and explains the potential opportunities and problems in the application of information systems to the decision process in organizations.

Sections: Review and Critique of DSS, Decision Processes, Behavioral Decision Theory and DSS, Group Decision Support Systems, Organizational Decision Support Systems, Technology Environments to Support Decision Processes, Model Management Systems, Research Challenges, Research Approaches in ISDP.

*368 pages. 1992. Hardcover. ISBN 0-8186-2802-2. Catalog # 2802-04 — $45.00   Members $35.00*

**Fault-Tolerant Software Systems:**
**Techniques and Applications**
*edited by Hoang Pham*

A collection of 12 papers investigating the rapidly growing field of software fault-tolerant computing. It provides a concise overview of the latest theories and techniques to reveal the recent directions of research, and to stimulate more research in this field.

Papers: Definition and Analysis of Hardware and Software Fault-Tolerant Architectures, An Environment for Developing Fault-Tolerant Software, Assuring Design Diversity of N-Version Software, Modeling Execution Time of Multi-Stage N-Version Software, Performance Analysis of Real-Time Software Supporting Fault-Tolerant Operation, Reliability Analysis Fault-Tolerant Systems.

*128 pages. 1992. Softcover. ISBN 0-8186-3210-0. Catalog # 3210-05 — $35.00  Members $25.00*

 **IEEE COMPUTER SOCIETY**

▼   To order call toll-free: 1-800-CS-BOOKS   ▼

▼   Fax: (714) 821-4641   ▼

10662 Los Vaqueros Circle     Los Alamitos, CA  90720-1264     Phone: (714) 821-8380

# IEEE Computer Society Press

## Press Activities Board

Vice President: Ronald G. Hoelzeman, University of Pittsburgh
Mario R. Barbacci, Carnegie Mellon University
Jon T. Butler, Naval Postgraduate School
J.T. Cain, University of Pittsburgh
Bill D. Carroll, University of Texas
Doris L. Carver, Louisiana State University
James J. Farrell III, VLSI Technology Inc.
Lansing Hatfield, Lawrence Livermore National Laboratory
Gene F. Hoffnagle, IBM Corporation
Barry W. Johnson, University of Virginia
Duncan H. Lawrie, University of Illinois
Michael C. Mulder, University of S.W. Louisiana
Yale N. Patt, University of Michigan
Murali R. Varanasi, University of South Florida
Ben Wah, University of Illinois
Ronald Waxman, University of Virginia

## Editorial Board

Editor-in-Chief: Jon T. Butler, Naval Postgraduate School
Assoc. EIC/Acquisitions: Pradip K. Srimani, Colorado State University
Dharma P. Agrawal, North Carolina State University
Oscar N. Garcia, The George Washington University
Uma G. Gupta, University of Central Florida
A.R. Hurson, Pennsylvania State University
Yutaka Kanayama, Naval Postgraduate School
Frederick E. Petry, Tulane University
Dhiraj K. Pradhan, University of Massachusetts
Sudha Ram, University of Arizona
David Rine, George Mason University
A.R.K. Sastry, Rockwell International Science Center
Ajit Singh, Siemens Corporate Research
Mukesh Singhal, Ohio State University
Murali R. Varanasi, University of South Florida
Ronald D. Williams, University of Virginia

## Press Staff

T. Michael Elliott, Executive Director
True Seaborn, Publisher
Catherine Harris, Managing Editor
Mary E. Kavanaugh, Production Editor
Lisa O'Conner, Production Editor
Regina Spencer Sipple, Production Editor
Penny Storms, Production Editor
Edna Straub, Production Editor
Robert Werner, Production Editor
Perri Cline, Electronic Publishing Manager
Frieda Koester, Marketing/Sales Manager
Thomas Fink, Advertising/Promotions Manager

## Offices of the IEEE Computer Society

**Headquarters Office**
1730 Massachusetts Avenue, N.W.
Washington, DC 20036-1903
Phone: (202) 371-0101 — Fax: (202) 728-9614

**Publications Office**
P.O. Box 3014
10662 Los Vaqueros Circle
Los Alamitos, CA 90720-1264
Membership and General Information: (714) 821-8380
Publication Orders: (800) 272-6657 — Fax: (714) 821-4010

**European Office**
13, avenue de l'Aquilon
B-1200 Brussels, BELGIUM
Phone: 32-2-770-21-98 — Fax: 32-3-770-85-05

**Asian Office**
Ooshima Building
2-19-1 Minami-Aoyama, Minato-ku
Tokyo 107, JAPAN
Phone: 81-3-408-3118 — Fax: 81-3-408-3553

# IEEE Computer Society

## IEEE Computer Society Press Publications

**Monographs:** A monograph is an authored book consisting of 100-percent original material.

**Tutorials:** A tutorial is a collection of original materials prepared by the editors, and reprints of the best articles published in a subject area. Tutorials must contain at least five percent of original material (although we recommend 15 to 20 percent of original material).

**Reprint collections:** A reprint collection contains reprints (divided into sections) with a preface, table of contents, and section introductions discussing the reprints and why they were selected. Collections contain less than five percent of original material.

**Technology series:** Each technology series is a brief reprint collection — approximately 126-136 pages and containing 12 to 13 papers, each paper focusing on a subset of a specific discipline, such as networks, architecture, software, or robotics.

**Submission of proposals:** For guidelines on preparing CS Press books, write the Managing Editor, IEEE Computer Society Press, PO Box 3014, 10662 Los Vaqueros Circle, Los Alamitos, CA 90720-1264, or telephone (714) 821-8380.

## Purpose

The IEEE Computer Society advances the theory and practice of computer science and engineering, promotes the exchange of technical information among 100,000 members worldwide, and provides a wide range of services to members and nonmembers.

## Membership

All members receive the acclaimed monthly magazine *Computer*, discounts, and opportunities to serve (all activities are led by volunteer members). Membership is open to all IEEE members, affiliate society members, and others seriously interested in the computer field.

## Publications and Activities

*Computer* **magazine:** An authoritative, easy-to-read magazine containing tutorials and in-depth articles on topics across the computer field, plus news, conference reports, book reviews, calendars, calls for papers, interviews, and new products.

**Periodicals:** The society publishes six magazines and five research transactions. For more details, refer to our membership application or request information as noted above.

**Conference proceedings, tutorial texts, and standards documents:** The IEEE Computer Society Press publishes more than 100 titles every year.

**Standards working groups:** Over 100 of these groups produce IEEE standards used throughout the industrial world.

**Technical committees:** Over 30 TCs publish newsletters, provide interaction with peers in specialty areas, and directly influence standards, conferences, and education.

**Conferences/Education:** The society holds about 100 conferences each year and sponsors many educational activities, including computing science accreditation.

**Chapters:** Regular and student chapters worldwide provide the opportunity to interact with colleagues, hear technical experts, and serve the local professional community.